WHY THE WEST WAS WILD

WHY THE WEST WAS WILD

A Contemporary Look at the Antics of Some Highly Publicized Kansas Cowtown Personalities

by
NYLE H. MILLER
and
JOSEPH W. SNELL

Foreword by Joseph G. Rosa

UNIVERSITY OF OKLAHOMA PRESS
NORMAN

Library of Congress Cataloging-in-Publication Data

Miller, Nyle H.
Why the West was wild : a contemporary look at the antics of
some highly publicized Kansas cowtown personalities / by
Nyle H. Miller and Joseph W. Snell, foreword by Joseph G. Rosa.
p. cm.
Originally published: 1st ed. Topeka : Kansas State
Historical Society, 1963.
Includes bibliographical references and index.
ISBN 0-8061-3526-3 (alk. paper)—ISBN 0-8061-3530-1 (pb : alk. paper)
1. Kansas—Biography. 2. Outlaws—Kansas—Biography. 3. Peace
officers—Kansas—Biography. 4. Frontier and pioneer life—Kansas.
5. Kansas—History, Local. I. Snell, Joseph W. II. Title.

F680 .M5 2003
978.1'031'0922—dc21
[B]
2002035029

The paper in this book meets the guidelines for permanence and
durability of the Committee on Production Guidelines for Book
Longevity of the Council on Library Resources, Inc.

1   2   3   4   5   6   7   8   9   10

In Order of Appearance

Additional Illustrations

The fading Wild West portion of Kansas as depicted by
Rand, McNally & Co., in 1886. This map graphically illus-
trates how expanding settlements put an end to the open
range and trail drives to Kansas railheads.

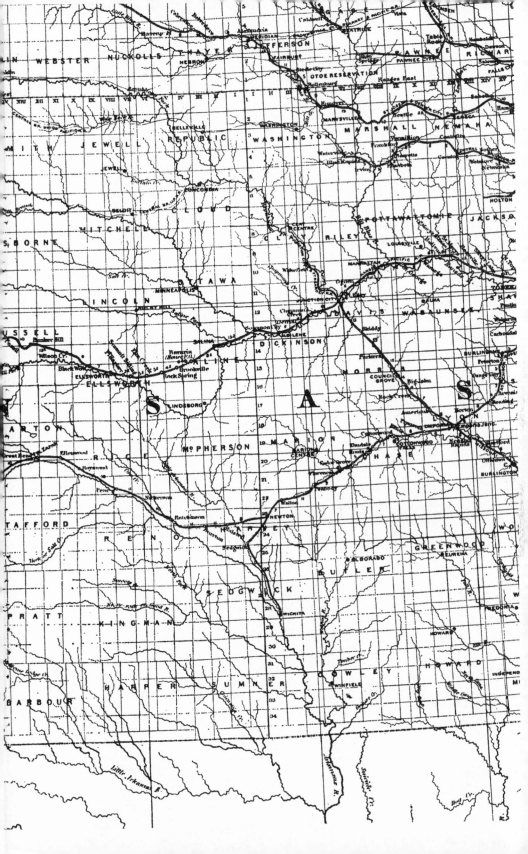

Foreword

In the mid-1950s I wrote to the Kansas State Historical Society from my home in England to ask for information on Wild Bill Hickok. Lela Barnes, the Society's late curator of manuscripts, answered my letter and offered further assistance, which prompted me to write again. Soon, I was addressing as many as four letters a month to the Society to inquire about Hickok.

Years later, Kansas Historical Society Director Nyle Miller told me my first letter aroused little interest because the Society received many such requests. Most people wrote only once or twice, but my letters kept coming, and when my questions grew more complicated Lela asked Miller what she should do. Nyle decided I was serious and should be encouraged. Fortunately for me, Lela Barnes's assistant curator was a young man named Joseph W. Snell who, unknown to me, shared my interest in James Butler Hickok and understood my problems.

Joe Snell's skill as a researcher and ability to interpret my questions brought unexpected results. He found material on Hickok that no one then alive or interested was aware of, and he did not stop there. He soon discovered that the Society held an invaluable cache of information on "Wild West" characters. Recognizing both his ability and his enthusiasm, Miller told Snell to peruse all the available Kansas cowtown newspapers for information. Snell was overjoyed, but his research was no picnic because his normal work continued as well. Nonetheless, his output was prolific. Besides material on Hickok, those old Kansas newspapers divulged much information on various Kansas figures, together with background on events long forgotten or ignored.

Snell copied entire newspaper articles onto half sheets with the usual scientific citation to source. Even where sheets were made for police court docket entries, he typed the information exactly as he found it and again cited it to source. One item per sheet was the system. He then filed the sheets by town, by date.

By 1959, Snell had found so much material that he and Miller talked of publication, but they did not think quotations from newspapers alone would be sufficient. Snell then checked all available contemporary documents, including local city council minutes, police court dockets, state and federal records, diaries, letters, and other similar sources. They ruled out secondary material, however; everything was to be primary. Snell's archival digging aroused a lot of interest, and he recalls making many new friends. One of them, the late Mrs. Merritt Beeson (whom I had the pleasure of meeting and who once presented me with an ivory poker chip from the Long Branch Saloon), donated some wonderful material and photographs.

By 1960, it was agreed that some of the material should be published in the *Kansas Historical Quarterly*, the Society's quarterly history journal. Under the title "Some Notes on Kansas Cowtown Peace Officers and Gunfighters," the articles appeared in eleven segments between spring 1960 and autumn 1962. The "Notes" could not have come at a better time. The "Western" was a staple in television programming worldwide. (British television, for example, featured *Gunsmoke*, *Maverick*, *Wagon Train*, *Rawhide*, *Bonanza*, and other Western programs each week in 1959 along with occasional feature-length Western movies.) Many of these programs drew from Kansas history, and the Society frequently received letters from people who claimed kinship with such characters as Matt Dillon, the U.S. Marshal played by James Arness in *Gunsmoke*.

Still, response to the Society's gunfighter series was astonishing, and as requests poured in for copies of the articles Miller and Snell came to believe the material should be made available more widely. As director, Miller approached the Kansas State Legislature for an appropriation to publish the series in book form. He received $8,000, which enabled the Society to print 1,355 hardcover copies. Titled *Why The West Was Wild*, the book was published late in 1963. Snell recalls that shortly before the book appeared, Miller sent out notices of its forthcoming publication, and almost the entire edition sold out before it was off the press.

The book nonetheless caused a sensation. Western history buffs, historians, and general readers alike were fascinated by the information it contained on western heroes and villains. In some instances, the book exposed myths about the people it discussed; in others cases, it enhanced their reputations. Reaction from reviewers was unanimously favorable. Western author Helena Huntington Smith wrote

Foreword

that the Society's imprint guaranteed a sound book, adding that the authors had "not let academic trimmings interfere with the robust sense of humor and drama which is a must for dealing with the rowdy West." Smith thought the authors' formula was striking. "Their material is all drawn from contemporary police and city hall records and other documents, but above all from newspapers." Western historian Ramon Adams considered *Why the West Was Wild* "one of the most important books on this period." As requests for copies accumulated from all over the country, Canada, and even Europe, the book soon sold out, but the Kansas legislature made no provision for a reprint.

Stirred by the reaction from his peers and the public, Miller determined to keep the book in print. Snell remembered Miller's trying to find a publisher and, in 1966, he turned to the University of Nebraska Press, which issued an abridged version in 1967. Offered both in hardcover and paperback under the title, *Great Gunfighters of the Kansas Cowtowns, 1867-1886*, the University of Nebraska Press edition has sold well since, especially in paperback, but it retained only twenty-one of the original fifty-seven sketches of Kansas gunfighters, and it omitted the original appendix. Happily, the University of Oklahoma Press has restored these deletions in this new, fortieth anniversary edition.

The original hardcover edition published by the Kansas State Historical Society has become highly prized by collectors, and it has served as the model for a number of other volumes devoted to western gunfighters and other western figures. But few of these have enjoyed the success of *Why the West Was Wild*. The book was an innovator, for it made for better writing and research on western history and especially western gunfighters. No longer could historians and gunfighter buffs write on such topics simply from other books. Instead, they would have to consult and cite court documents, census returns, and other local records when assessing contemporary newspaper reports. *Why the West Was Wild* re-educated writers of western history and prompted a cycle of research that continues to the present day. My hope has always been that other state historical societies would produce similar volumes, but so far none has.

If Nyle Miller were still alive, he would be delighted that his book is again available in complete form. It is an essential source for research, and younger readers who wish to get beyond the mythical West of movies and television will find it rewarding and exciting.

JOSEPH G. ROSA

Ruislip, Middlesex, England

Bat Masterson uncovers "Doctor" Meredith, visiting lecturer on private diseases, after defending him from a mock assault by a Dodge City "southside exhorter with one eye in a sling. . . ." (See pp. 406, 407.)

A Note on Bat Masterson

The purpose of this reprint of *Why the West Was Wild* is not to update its content but rather to make the original limited edition volume available to more people. Consequently, no changes have been made to any of the sections with one exception: this update to try to settle what had been a long disputed question affecting the value of the book.

When *Why the West Was Wild* was published originally, I had concerns about how W. B. Masterson earned his nickname, "Bat." I was skeptical of the proffered reasons (that he batted opponents over the head with his walking stick or that he reminded old timers of a frontiersman named Baptiste Pourrier, or Brown), because a few contemporary records indicated his middle name was really Bartholomew, and I knew "Bat" was an accepted diminutive form of that name.

Being well taught by Nyle Miller, who not only was executive director of the Kansas State Historical Society but also its chief editor, I knew we did not have sufficient evidence to say definitely that Bartholomew was truly Bat's real middle name, but I did explore the issue publicly in footnote 13 to "Diary of a Dodge City Buffalo Hunter, 1872-1873," which I edited for the *Kansas Historical Quarterly*, volume 31, number four (Winter, 1965).

In June, 1967, however, a Masterson devotee in London named Chris Penn wrote to me and to Waldo Koop, an outstanding amateur historian of Wichita, Kansas, to say that he had obtained a copy of the record of Masterson's baptism. "It was traced in the 1853 Register of the Parish of St. George, County Rouville, Province of Quebec," he wrote, "and the official translation reads:

November 27th 1853, we undersigned Priest, have baptized Bertho-
lomiew born yesterday of Thomas Masterson and Catherine McGurk
of this parish. Godfather Charles McGurk and godmother Mary Anne
Oshea who except the godfather have signed.

[signed]   THO. MASTERSON
Mary Anne Oshea
F. St. Aubin, Priest."

That discovery cinched our belief that Masterson was really named
William Bartholomew Masterson soon after his birth. The question of
why he later changed his name to William Barclay Masterson remains
obscure as does the period of his life when he did so. We do know that
by August 3, 1907, the day he attested to his will, Masterson had made
the alteration.

JOSEPH W. SNELL
Executive Director Emeritus

Kansas State Historical Society

WHY THE WEST WAS WILD

Prologue

Kansas cowtowns were the principal shipping centers for Texas trail herds from 1867 until 1885. The world remembers these places chiefly for their extreme violence and for the men who supposedly cleaned them up. Much of what is known of this facet of the West's history has been decidedly slanted, knocked askew by a host of writers who have failed to look into first-hand accounts of the actions they were recreating. The following pages are presented in the hope that some of the misconceptions about cowtowns, and especially about the men who were the law there, can be corrected and knowledge of the Wild West brought into a proper focus.

Seven Kansas cowtowns have been studied to provide material for this book, though several others qualified as cattle shipping centers during this same era. For each town chosen an attempt has been made to unearth all contemporary police references available in the files of the Kansas State Historical Society, in the various city and county archives, in private collections, and elsewhere.

Much of this material was originally published in *The Kansas Historical Quarterly* (1960-1962), in serial form. As the series progressed, Western buffs and other friends helped to locate new information in sources not before known to exist. Consequently this present version is more nearly complete and offers compiled data on all the major peace officers who trod the streets of Kansas cowtowns. In addition to lawmen, certain other persons who were either astraddle or outside the law are covered. This latter category includes such well-known Western characters as Luke Short, Clay Allison, and John H. "Doc" Holliday, as well as some lesser known but equally "deserving" persons such as Rowdy Joe Lowe.

It was thought best to introduce each character separately, giving material relating to him in his own section. This method was chosen to overcome the confusion which would result from over-lapping activities, varying bases of operation, and spasmodic appearances. In this manner each individual can easily be traced from his first service (or appearance) in a cowtown to his last.

All the material is from primary sources, that is, if contemporary newspaper reports can be considered primary. At any rate, nothing has been included which reflects the reminiscences of a participant, for it is painfully noticeable that most individuals have a tendency to overdraw their own roles as the span of time widens between the doing and the telling. No material relating to a particular individual or incident—whether favorable or not—has been excluded unless repetition would result. Attention has been drawn in the footnotes to the location of any items omitted (usually newspaper notices in cases where a town had more than one paper at a time). Only the major cowtown years were studied, though some of the actors have been carried over into other periods when it seemed their careers justified such coverage.

Abilene was chosen because it was the first of the major Kansas shipping centers, serving as such from 1867 through 1871. There is little material to reflect Abilene's history before 1870, however, for the town did not incorporate until its cowtown era was nearly over and hence did not possess a police force of its own. Abilene's newspaper, likewise, was not established until 1870.

Newton, Ellsworth, Solomon, Salina, and Brookville all vied for the cattle trade beginning in 1871. No study was made of the last three towns, for they (and Newton) soon lost out to Ellsworth, Wichita, Dodge City, and Caldwell. Newton was included among the seven cowtowns primarily because of its "General Massacre." Little is reported from that town later than 1871 for after its one big season the trade shifted south, down a newly completed Santa Fe branch line to Wichita.

Ellsworth, on the other hand, was studied at length. Several well-known episodes are linked with her history and much material is available for research. Also, the place remained a major cattle shipping center for five years—1871 through 1875. The town was established in 1867 when the Union Pacific, Eastern Division (later known as the Kansas Pacific), built through the area. By 1872

Ellsworth had a well organized city administration, an effective county police force and a newspaper, the *Reporter*. Such inhabitants as James Butler "Wild Bill" Hickok, Chauncey B. Whitney, and Ben Thompson would serve to place Ellsworth on any list of cowtowns to be studied.

In 1872 Wichita became a prominent cattle shipping center after rails connected it with the Santa Fe main line at Newton. Texas cattle, which had been bypassing the town since 1868, could now be sent from Wichita to Eastern markets. Considerable material is available covering Wichita's adolescence, including four contemporary newspapers; city, county, and township records; and district court proceedings. Research on Wichita was concluded with the year 1876, though cattle still played a part in her history through 1877. By 1875, however, shipments lessened because of Dodge City's rise to prominence.

Dodge had been enjoying a boom since its establishment in the summer of 1872, just before the Santa Fe railroad arrived. Some cattle were shipped out during 1874, but in the early years (1872-1874) buffalo hunting and the sale of hides were the chief activities. Soon great numbers of cattle arrived, and until 1885 the city was indeed the "Queen of the Cowtowns." Dodge's cattle era lasted longer than most and the town was inhabited by more top-notch lawmen and gun fighters than any other cowtown ever had. Wyatt Earp, Bat, Ed, and Jim Masterson, Doc Holliday, William Tilghman, Clay Allison, Ben and Billy Thompson, Luke Short, and many others spent time in Dodge City. Truly Dodge was the "beautiful, bibulous, Babylon of the frontier," an epithet conferred on her in 1878 by the editor of the neighboring Kinsley *Graphic*.

Above all, Dodge City editors had a peculiar knack for setting things down so that the files of their newspapers still make fascinating reading. Dodge had at least five newspapers in its cattle trail period, six if one counts the single number of Bat Masterson's *Vox Populi*, a four-page political sheet issued November 1, 1884. For a time the city's police court dockets were available, but now they seem to have disappeared and newspapers are almost the sole contemporary material remaining for research. Fortunately the Dodge City journalists reported police matters faithfully, and few gaps remain in the general story of law enforcement after 1876.

Sharing the spotlight from 1880 through 1885 was Caldwell, the self-styled "Border Queen." Like Wichita, Caldwell had been on the Chisholm trail since the town was established in 1871, but lack of railroad facilities prevented her from achieving status as a trail-end resort. Finally, in 1880, this deficiency was eliminated by the coming of the Cowley, Sumner & Fort Smith railroad (operated by the Santa Fe) and for the next six years Caldwell challenged Dodge City for the cattle trade.

An almost complete set of Caldwell police court dockets is still in existence. They offer a great deal of valuable and interesting information. In addition, the files of three Caldwell newspapers published during the trail era describe in detail much of the police activity in the town.

One may wonder why the seventh place, Hays, was chosen inasmuch as it achieved little status as a cowtown. Hays was primarily an army town and a freighting center supplying much of the West and Southwest, and attracted the rougher element in droves. She could not be ignored, especially since Wild Bill Hickok achieved considerable prominence there. Hickok has long been a favorite Western character, though there is little documented writing about him. Consequently the sources of information on the so-called "Prince of Pistoleers" have been closely checked in the hope that more facts could be sorted from legend. As a result some Hickok material presented here has never before been generally available.

In short, the plan of this book allows contemporaneous accounts to tell the story with as little second-hand interpretation as possible. The quoted material is presented with the punctuation and spelling errors of the original. Necessary inserts connecting the various incidents and accounts have been kept brief. Data have been summarized only when too bulky for verbatim presentation. The quotations offered in this work, then, are from individuals who knew, and were living in, the era under scrutiny and their words were set down *at the time*—not many years later.

The Stage and Plot

For about 51 weeks a year the average old-time cowboy could be classified as a hard working, fairly sober, and usually conscientious individual. During the 52nd week, however, he might erupt into a rip-snorting, free-spending hell raiser bent on divesting himself of his earnings in the quickest and most enjoyable manner possible.

What caused this usually mild and law-abiding creature to undergo such a metamorphosis? He was celebrating—making up for the long and lonely weeks he had just spent on the trail drive from Texas. He was delighted with the thought that no more, for a few weeks at least, would he spend his nights trying to nurse edgy cattle into tranquility. No more would he suffer through a thunderstorm which might at any moment precipitate a stampede. No more would an improper diet and alkali water give him bad blood and running sores. No more would he eat dust while riding drag. No more would long hours in the saddle gall his hide. No more would he sweat in the heat of a Great Plains sun. He was free now—unemployed, uninhibited, and rich—until tomorrow or next week!

And waiting for the trail cowboy and his cash, almost rubbing its hands in anticipation, was the cowtown.

As seen through the eyes of the fun-starved trail herder the cowtown was a circus of pleasure, an oasis in the desert of labor. There was no limit to the kind and amount of divertissement his money could buy. Businessmen went all out to make things ready for his annual coming. For example, the Wichita *Eagle*, May 28, 1874, described a period of preseason activity:

. . . there are a good many people moving around, and a good deal of business going on. It is a motly crowd you see. Broad-brimmed and spurred Texans, farmers, keen business men, real estate agents, land seekers, greasers, hungry lawyers, gamblers, women with white sun bonnets and shoes of a certain pattern, express wagons going pell mell, prairie schooners, farm wagons, and all rushing after the almighty dollar. The cattle season has not yet fully set in, but there is a rush of gamblers and harlots who are "lying in wait" for the game which will soon begin to come up from the south. There was a struggle for awhile which should run the city, the hard cases or the better people. The latter got the mastery, and have only kept it by holding a "tight grip." Pistols are as thick as blackberries. The taxes are paid by the money received from whiskey sellers, gambling hells, and the *demi monde,* and thousands of dollars are obtained besides to further the interests of the town. Wichita flourishes off the cattle business, and these evils have to be put up with; at least that is the way a large majority of the people see it. But notwithstanding this a man is as safe in Wichita as anywhere else if he keeps out of bad company. The purlieus of crime there are no worse than in many eastern cities of boasted refinement and good order. But woe to the "greeny" who falls into the hands of the dwellers therein, especially if he carries money. From these must come most of the stories of outrage at Wichita. They are entitled to little sympathy because they can find plenty of good company if they desire it.

Four years later, the Dodge City *Times,* May 4, 1878, almost resorted to poetry in discussing that city's prospects:

In this delectable city of the plains the winter of discontent is made glorious by the return of the cattle trade. With the countless herds come the hordes of bipeds. Weeks and months before, through the blasts of winter and the gentle zephyrs of spring, has impecuniosity longed for the opening of the cattle trade, in which Dodge City outshines all envity and rivalry.

This "cattle village" and far-famed "wicked city" is decked in gorgeous attire in preparation for the long horn. Like the sweet harbinger of spring, the boot black came, he of white and he of black. Next the barber "with his lather and shave." Too, with all that go to make up the busy throng of life's fitful fever, come the Mary Magdalenes, "selling their souls to whoever'll buy." There is "high, low, jack and the game," all adding to the great expectation so important an event brings about.

The merchant and the "hardware" dealer has filled his store and renovated his "palace." There are goods in profusion in warehouse and on shelves; the best markets were sought, and goods are in store and to arrive. Necessarily, there is great ado, for soon the vast plains will be covered with the long horn—and the "wicked city" is the source from which the great army of herder and driver is fed. . . .

The towns to which the herds came were not made up of row upon row of ivy-covered cottages. Dodge City, as described by an outsider in this article from the *Times* of September 1, 1877, was typical of most cowtowns:

6

. . . Dodge has many characteristics which prevent its being classed as a town of strictly moral ideas and principles, notwithstanding it is supplied with a church, a court-house, and a jail. Other institutions counterbalance the good works supposed to emanate from the first mentioned. Like all frontier towns of this modern day, fast men and fast women are around by the score, seeking whom they may devour, hunting for a soft snap, taking him in for cash, and many is the Texas cowboy who can testify as to their ability to follow up successfully the callings they have embraced in quest of money.

Gambling ranges from a game of five-cent chuck-a-luck to a thousand dollar poker-pot. Nothing is secret, but with open doors upon the main street the ball rolls on uninterruptedly. More than occasionally some dark-eyed virago or some brazen-faced blond, with a modern sun-down, will saunter in among the roughs of the gambling houses and saloons, entering with inexplicable zest into the disgusting sport, breathing the immoral atmosphere with a gusto which I defy modern writers to explain. Dance houses are ranged along at convenient distances and supplied abundantly with all the trappings and paraphernalia which go to complete institutions of that character. Here you see the greatest abandon. Men of every grade assemble to join in the dance. Nice men with white neck-ties, the cattle dealer with his good clothes, the sport with his well-turned fingers, smooth tongue and artistically twisted moustache, and last but not least, the cowboy, booted and spurred as he comes from the trail, his hard earnings in his pocket, all join in the wild revel; and yet with all this mixture of strange human nature a remarkable degree of order is preserved. Arms are not allowed to be worn, and any noisy whisky demonstrations are promptly checked by incarceration in the lock-up. Even the Mayor of the city indulges in the giddy dance with the girls and with his cigar in one corner of his mouth and his hat tilted to one side, he makes a charming looking officer.

Some things occur in Dodge that the world never knows of. Probably it is best so. Other things occur which leak out by degrees, notwithstanding the use of hush-money. That too is perhaps the best. Men learn by such means.

Most places are satisfied with one abode for the dead. In the grave there is no distinction. The rich are known from the poor only by their tombstones, so the sods upon the grave fail to reflect the characters buried beneath them; and yet Dodge boasts two burying spots, one for the tainted, whose very souls were steeped by immorality, and who have generally died with their boots on. "Boot-Hill" is the somewhat singular title applied to the burial place of the class just mentioned. The other is not designated by any particular title, but is supposed to contain the bodies of those who died with a clean sheet on their bed—the soul in this case is a secondary consideration.

That same month the *Times*, September 15, quoted the Hays City *Sentinel* as saying, "Dodge City is dull at the present time, and the town is relapsing into morality. At this writing there are only seventeen saloons and dance houses, sixty prostitutes, thirty gamblers and eighty cowboys in the entire town." Hays itself, toward

7

the end of its frontier heyday, had been described by the Junction City *Union,* July 8, 1871, as "a row of saloons on the Kansas Pacific railway. . . . Having visited the place, we should call it the Sodom of the plains. . . ."

What was the appearance of these cowboys—the catalysts who made the cowtowns what they were? One 1882 description published in D. W. Wilder's *Annals of Kansas,* p. 964, said that

The typical cowboy wears a white hat, with a gilt cord and tassel, high-top boots, leather pants, a woolen shirt, a coat, and no vest. On his heels he wears a pair of jingling Mexican spurs, as large around as a tea-cup. When he feels well (and he always does when full of what he calls "Kansas sheep-dip"), the average cowboy is a bad man to handle. Armed to the teeth, well mounted, and full of their favorite beverage, the cowboys will dash through the principal streets of a town, yelling like Comanches. This they call "cleaning out a town."

Nearly all the cowtowns intentionally or unintentionally separated the rowdy portion of their population from the genteel. The *Kansas State Record,* Topeka, August 5, 1871, clearly pointed this out:

. . . Before dark you will have an opportunity to notice that Abilene is divided by the railroad into two sections, very different in appearance. The north side is literary, religious and commercial, and possesses . . . [V. P.] Wilson's *Chronicle,* the churches, the banks, and several large stores of various description; the south side of the road is the Abilene of "story and song," and possesses the large hotels, the saloons, and the places where the "dealers in card board, bone and ivory" most do congregate. When you are on the north side of the track you are in Kansas, and hear sober and profitable conversation on the subject of the weather, the price of land and the crops; when you cross to the south side you are in Texas, and talk about cattle, varied by occasional remarks on "beeves" and "stock." Nine out of ten men you meet are directly or indirectly interested in the cattle trade; five at least out of every ten, are Texans. As at Newton, Texas names are prominent on the fronts of saloons and other "business houses," mingled with sign board allusions to the cattle business. A clothing dealer implores you to buy your "outfit" at the sign of the "Long Horns"; the leading gambling house is of course the "Alamo," and "Lone Stars" shine in every direction.

At night everything is "full up." The "Alamo" especially being a center of attraction. Here, in a well lighted room opening on the street, the "boys" gather in crowds round the tables, to play or to watch others; a bartender, with a countenance like a youthful divinity student, fabricates wonderful drinks, while the music of a piano and a violin from a raised recess, enlivens the scene, and "soothes the savage breasts" of those who retire torn and lacerated from an unfortunate combat with the "tiger." The games most affected are faro and monte, the latter being greatly patronized by the Mexicans of Abilene,

8

who sit with perfectly unmoved countenances and play for hours at a stretch, for your Mexican loses with entire indifference two things somewhat valued by other men, viz: his money and his life. . . .

It may be inferred from the foregoing that the Texan cattle driver is somewhat prone to "run free" as far as morals are concerned, but on the contrary, vice in one of its forms, is sternly driven forth from the city limits for the space of at least a quarter of a mile, where its "local habitation" is courteously and modestly, but rather indefinitely designated as the "Beer Garden." Here all that class of females who "went through" the Prodigal Son, and eventually drove that young gentleman into the hog business, are compelled to reside. In the amusements we have referred to does the "jolly drover" while the night away in Abilene.

Day in Abilene is very different. The town seems quite deserted, the "herders" go out to their herd or disappear in some direction, and thus the town relapses into the ordinary appearance of towns in general. It is during the day, that, seated on the piazzas of the hotels, may be seen a class of men peculiar to Texas and possessing many marked traits of character. We allude to the stock raisers and owners, who count their acres by thousands and their cattle by tens of thousands. . . .

An obvious inference from many available descriptions is that cowtown saloons outnumbered other businesses two to one. They were not, as might be popularly supposed, fabulous palaces of pleasure with block long bars, gambling devices of every description, plush furnishings, and regular floor shows consisting of beautiful bare legged can-can girls who later roamed the hall as early counterparts of B-girls. Quite the opposite.

In the very early days the saloon might be a tent or dugout, bare inside except for a plank laid across two beer kegs. Even in their more elegant periods the towns could boast nothing fancier than a long and narrow room decorated by a bar and some tables. The bar itself might be ornately carved and made of fine mahogany or walnut replete with polished glass mirrors and even a gaudy painting of a nude female. But the remainder of the room remained drab. Few gambling devices were available. Chuck-a-luck tumblers, faro boxes, and now and then a roulette wheel made up the fixtures. Often the walls were not plastered. They might have been unfinished planks nailed up vertically. There was no stage. There were no beautiful can-can girls, though some saloons were frequented by prostitutes who were given soliciting privileges. In some cases the saloon even provided small rooms in the rear for their use, naturally withholding a cut of the profits.

9

In spite of what some people now assume, these frontier saloons offered more than a straight line of rot gut and snake head whiskies. Fine liqueurs, brandies, and the latest mixed drinks could be had in many. Ice was usually available so that beer could be served cold. To say the least, cowtown drinking was not primitive.

Many saloons offered some type of musical entertainment, a piano player, a singer, or even, like Chalk Beeson's Saratoga (and later his Long Branch), a full orchestra. Mr. Beeson was one of the early residents of Dodge, a gentleman and music lover who exercised taste in providing entertainment. The Dodge City *Times,* September 29, 1877, commented on his place of business:

> It is a rare treat to drop in at the Saratoga upon Mr. Beeson, and listen to his last and best musical combination. Mr. Beeson is a thorough lover of good music, and by his skilful selection of good performers, has always kept that part of the city in the best condition of good nature. Mr. Lawson's well known face is now to be seen nightly upon his music stand, and as often as evening comes around "The Lakes of Killarney" and others of his well rendered specialties draw crowds of attentive listeners.

Other saloons, said the *Times,* June 2, 1877, offered an escape from din:

> The Alamo swung its doors open to the public yesterday. As a model in its line it takes the lead. It is new and bright and quiet. It will have no music, and those who resort to its well kept parlor can hear themselves talk as well as think. A partition separates the bar from the large room, making the latter a quiet, pleasant resort, where the cigar and refreshments can be enjoyed at leisure. The best brands of cigars are kept here. It is the intention of the proprietors, Messrs. Hoover and Cook, to make the Alamo the most suitable place of its kind for stock men to patronize.

Some offered food as well as drink. The *Times,* July 27, 1878, mentioned one:

> A good story is told of a well known citizen of this city, whose name we suppress. The story runs in this wise. He went into _____'s saloon, took a seat, threw his feet on the table, and called for a glass of beer, a sandwich and some Limberger cheese, which was promptly placed upon the table beside his feet. He called to _____ and told him that the cheese was of no accounts, as he could not smell it, where upon the proprietor replied: "Damn it, take your feet down and give the cheese a chance."

After a man's thirst was slaked he turned to the cards and chips. Not all of the innocents were cowboys, however, as this article from the *Times,* March 24, 1877, testifies:

10

The Stage and Plot

EX-GOV. CARNEY GOES BROKE ON A POKER GAME IN DODGE CITY.

Last Thursday morning our political magnates were agreeably surprised by the intelligence that the once famous political boss of the State, ex-Gov. Thos. Carney, of Leavenworth [governor from 1863 to 1865], had arrived on the 6 o'clock train. It was at first whispered among the knowing ones that the Gov. was about to open up a canvass for his election to J. J. Ingalls' place to the U. S. Senate a year from next winter, and this theory was strengthened by the fact that he was observed in close communion with R. W. Evans. Gov. Carney, however, soon dispelled this illusion by informing some of our business men that his operations in Dodge City were to be of an exclusively commercial nature; in fact, that he was buying hides and bones for a St. Louis firm. It seems from later developments that the Governor's real business in Dodge City was to entice our unsophisticated denizens into the national game of draw poker, and fleece them of their loose cash, as Schenck used to do the beef eaters over in England, the talk he made about the hide and bone business being merely a blind to cover up his real design.

The Governor's reputation and dignified bearing soon enabled him to decoy three of our business men into a social game of poker, 'just to kill time, you know.' Gov. Carney's intended victims were Col. Norton, wholesale dealer and general financial operator; Hon. Robert Gilmore [more widely known as Bobby Gill], and Chas. Ronan, Esquire. The game proceeded merrily and festively for a time, until, under the bracing influence of exhilerating refreshments, the stakes were increased, and the players soon became excitedly interested.

At last the Governor held what he supposed to be an invincible hand. It consisted of four kings and the cuter, or 'imperial trump,' which the Governor very reasonably supposed to be the ace of spades. The old man tried to repress his delight and appear unconcerned when Col. Norton tossed a $100 bill into the pot; but he saw the bet and went a hundred better. Norton didn't weaken, as the Governor feared he would, but nonchalantly raised the old gent with what he supposed was a fabulous bluff. Governor Carney's eyes glistened with joy as he saw the pile of treasure which would soon be all his own, loom up before his vision, and he hastened to see the Colonel and add the remainder of his funds, his elegant gold watch and chain. Norton was still with the game, and the Governor finally stripped himself of all remaining valuables, when it became necessary for him to 'show up' his hand.

A breathless silence pervaded the room as Gov. Carney spread his four kings on the table with his left hand, and affectionately encircled the glittering heap of gold, silver, greenbacks and precious stones, with his right arm, preparatory to raking in the spoils. But at that moment a sight met the old Governor's gaze which caused his eyes to dilate with terror, a fearful tremor to seize his frame, and his vitals to almost freeze with horror. Right in front of Col. Norton were spread four genuine and perfectly formed aces, and the hideous reality that four aces laid over four kings and a 'cuter' gradually forced itself upon the mind of our illustrious hide and bone merchant. Slowly and re-

11

luctantly he uncoiled his arm from around the sparkling treasure; the bright, joyous look faded from his eyes, leaving them gloomy and cadeverous; with a weary, almost painful effort he arose from the table, and, dragging his feet over the floor like balls of lead, he left the room, sadly, tearfully, and tremulously muttering, 'I forgot about the cuter.'

The next eastward bound freight train carried an old man, without shirt studs or other ornament, apparently bowed down by overwhelming grief, and the conductor hadn't the heart to throw him overboard. Gov. Carney is not buying bones and hides in this city any more.

Confidence games were another hazard. The *Times* of July 13, 1878, reported on that and other matters:

AN EVENTFUL DAY.

Friday is said to be an unlucky day. It is hangman's day. Some star having special gravity struck with sporadic force yesterday, and illuminated some of the social phases in the zodiac of Dodge City.

There was a gambling sport who was chaired by a pugilistic concubine.

A drunken prostitute led to the 'tannery' by her stocking-leg protector. But it was no go; she broke loose and was again on the street.

A gambler was spittoned on the head by a show-case capper. Some blood.

Another event. The morning air echoed with the cries of 'police'—a stranger had come to town and was taken in, verifying the adage that a fool and his money is soon parted. He was from near St. Joe and on his way to the San Juan country. He had a pony he wished to sell, and was lured into an 'insurance office' by a seemingly rural youth, who informed him that the 'insurance' agent wished to purchase a hoss. It was the lottery agent who engaged the pretended rural youth in a game of chance, which induced the dubious Missourian to stake $81, which suddenly disappeared before two flying coat tails; but which was robbed from him, says the innocent Missourian; as he had no intention of betting on any game or engaging in any lottery scheme. After this, of course the pretended rural youth and 'insurance' hoss dealer were not visible to the Missourian's optics—they had taken the back door, and old St. Joe, squealing like a stucked pig, rushed frantically into the street and vociferously yelled, police.

He represents that it was a clear case of robbery, and he was endeavoring yesterday to have the parties arrested; but did not meet with encouragement, as General ALIBI would step in with his forces and vanquish the solitary wanderer, who being a stranger was kindly taken in and done for. This damnable and nefarious, robbing business cannot long with sweet forbearance be a virtue. It will meet with its deserts—it will find that there is a h--- hereafter. The day draws nigh. . . .

Another major business, prostitution, was a flourishing enterprise in all the towns. Special areas seem to have been set aside for this trade. Abilene called her tenderloin district "McCoy's addition" after the then Mayor Joseph G. McCoy who was also father of the Kansas cattle trade. The "Beer Garden" was another name given this place. Newton labeled her district "Hide Park" while Ellsworth's was known as "Scragtown" and "Nauchville." Wichita had "Delano," an area which was more often called West Wichita. Caldwell actually had a Red Light dance hall but the prostitute section apparently had no name of its own. Dodge City merely referred to the main rowdy district as the area below the "dead line," the line being the Santa Fe tracks.

During the summer months prostitutes constituted a significant portion of the cowtown population. In Wichita's last big trail year (1874), for instance, the number of prostitutes ran between 45 and 50, according to official fee collection records of the city. By September the number began to drop and remained low during the winter.

Several prostitutes achieved some little fame—or notoriety, if you please. Ida May, Rowdy Kate Lowe, Josephine DeMerritt, Big Nose Kate Elder, and many others are favorites of Western buffs. One particular soiled dove of Ellsworth, though famous in legend for her walking portrayal of Lady Godiva down the main street of the town, must remain anonymous, for her performance has yet to be authenticated in contemporary sources.

The newspapers of the cowtowns seemed to assume a patronizing attitude toward the girls, probably since they provided so much first rate news. Take for example this little item from the Dodge City *Times*, March 24, 1877:

On Wednesday a gust of wind removed seven dollars out of the stocking of Alice Chambers as she was walking up Front street. After a six hours search, participated in by all the tramps in town, one dollar was recovered. We had supposed that the Kansas wind was of a higher order, and did not stoop to such larceny. The thing is now settled, that under some circumstances even the wind can be found feeling around in by and forbidden paths.

Poor Alice died the next year and was buried on Dodge City's Boot Hill, the only woman, supposedly, ever to be accorded that honor.

Frankie Bell was another Dodge City personality who gave the editor of the *Times* some help in filling his columns. "Miss Frankie Bell and one of her associates were deposited in the dog house this afternoon," he mentioned on August 18, 1877. The next week he said: "Frankie Bell made an oath before Judge [D. M.] Frost not to indulge in spirits fermenti until next Christmas. Then wont she make Rome howl." It was Frankie Bell, too, who had been struck by citizen Wyatt Earp in July for using words which offended Mr. Earp's ears. (*See* the section on Earp.)

Less well known girls also provided newspaper fodder. The *Times*, March 24, 1877, told of one episode involving a "girl of the period":

The office of City Attorney [Harry E. Gryden] was thrown into extatic convulsions at precisely 4:30 P. M., Monday, by the appearance of Fannie. (Fannie is a beauty, and the color of a Colorado Claro, as found at Beatty & Kelly's.) She complained of one James Cowan (Maduro color) and on the case being tried Mr. Gryden developed the following facts: That Fanny was peacefully ironing at the residence of Mrs. Curly, when James entered (three-sheets-in-the-wind drunk) called Fannie a soldier b----, throwed her on the floor, elevated her paraphanalia, spanked her, and finally busted her a left hander in the right eye, accompanying the same with a kick in the stomache. The City Attorney went to the court and for the defendant, touched up the Louisiana and South Carolina questions, and closed by flinging the star spangled banner over the contraband female, sending the defendant to the regions of the unjust—$5 and costs.

About two years later, the *Ford County Globe*, January 21, 1879, reported on an occasion when two doves behaved in a manner that was neither peaceful nor ladylike:

"SCARLET SLUGGERS."

A desperate fight occurred at the boarding house of Mrs. W., on "Tin Pot Alley," last Tuesday evening, between two of the most fascinating doves of the roost. When we heard the noise and looked out the front window, which commanded a view of the situation, it was a magnificent sight to see. Tufts of hair, calico, snuff and gravel flew like fir in a cat fight, and before we could distinguish how the battle waned a chunk of dislocated leg grazed our ear and a cheer from the small boys announced that a battle was lost and won. The crowd separated as the vanquished virgin was carried to her parlors by two "soups." A disjointed nose, two or three internal bruises, a chawed ear and a missing eye were the only scars we could see.

An interesting side study connected with this profession involves the names by which frontiersmen referred to the ladies in question. For the benefit of any future historian inclined to pursue research down these avenues (or alleys) here are a few samples: nymphs du prairie, nymphs du pave, fairs, fair Dolcinas (Dulcineas?), girls of the night, girls of the period, soiled doves, fancies, calico queens, painted cats, scarlet ladies, demi mondes. And of course there were the more mundane appellations such as laundress, dancehall girl, and waitress by which many were shown on census records. Attention, too, should be called to the existence of portable brothels or "cat wagons" which seem to have given the military authorities particular trouble.

One reason the cowtowns were loath to expel the girls was that they were the source of considerable revenue through the imposition of fines which were actually nothing more than licenses to operate. W. E. Stanley, county attorney of Sedgwick county and later governor of Kansas (1899-1903), made the point clear in a letter to the city administration of Wichita near the end of that town's cowtown era. His letter, which now reposes in the city clerk's office, says:

. . . Houses of prostitution are advertising themselves, by open doors on some of the most public streets of our city, prostitutes in half nude forms take their morning airings under the eyes of many of our most respectable citizens and flaunt the indicia of their "trade" in all public places and gatherings without hindrance from the authorities.

I am of the opinion that the time has come when these places of vice must be at least regulated if not entirely suppressed, and I am also of the opinion that as they are "city institutions" and as the city has received large financial benefits ? from this source, that they should be regulated through the city courts and by the city officials. . . .

In Caldwell prostitutes contributed more than one half of the city's total income during the cattle season (*see* the section on James Johnson). Wichita fined the ladies $8 per month plus $2 court costs. Keepers of brothels were fined $18 plus $2 costs per month. If they sold whisky they also paid a flat $25 monthly license fee. Occasionally inmates and keepers were fined for other reasons, such as disorderly conduct or drunkenness, which swelled the receipts even more. Prostitution paid Wichita at least $390 in August, 1873, an average "in season" month. Liquor licenses amounted to $625; total revenue was $1,796.26. The police force earned $450.60 from the city during that same period.

The Caldwell *Post*, July 28, 1881, in a typical item noticed the money angle but preserved its principles by deprecating the immorality of prostitution:

Our city treasury was increased to the amount of $50 last Tuesday morning [July 26], by the City Marshal [possibly Mike Meagher] taking two soiled

15

doves in and pulling the Dive in the flat for being a disorderly house. The aforesaid Dive is a holy terror, and should be obliterated from the face of this fair country. The comet must have had some effect on this planet, judging from the cussedness of things in general.

Often shootings took place in the brothels and dance halls. The Junction City *Union,* January 15, 1870, told of one:

Thursday night last a terrible shooting affair occurred at a dance house in Ellsworth. Two men named Reed and Gardner and a female named Fanny Collins were killed, and another female named Nettie Baldwin, was shot through the stomach and breast, and the latest account was that she could not live. The affair originated in an attempt of one man to rob another.

Not all the townspeople were gamblers and keepers of bawdy houses. There were the growing elements representing the "decent" way of life who in the beginning were too busy trying to get a toe hold in the community in which they lived to do much toward cleaning up the Front and Texas streets. Inevitably their influence was brought to bear and sooner or later varying degrees of law and order were established.

Actually, the people who really milked the cowboy were the transients. An article in the Pueblo (Colo.) *Chieftain,* in 1878, put it this way:

The cowboy is apt to spend his money liberally when he gets paid off after his long drive from Texas, and the pimps, gamblers and prostitutes who spend the winter in Kansas City and other large towns, generally manage to get to the point where the boys are paid off so as to give them a good chance to invest their money in fun.

The people who own Dodge City and live there do not look with favor on the advent of these classes, and only tolerate them because they cannot well help themselves. They follow the annual cattle drive like vultures follow an army, and disappear at the end of the cattle driving and shipping season. It is this feature of the business that makes people averse to the Texas cattle business coming to their towns, and Dodge has already a strong element opposed to cattle coming there to be shipped. . . .

Among early indications that there was another way of life in Dodge City was this item tucked away in the columns of the Dodge City *Times,* June 8, 1878:

The "wicked city of Dodge" can at last boast of a Christian organization— a Presbyterian church. It was organized last Sunday week. We would have mentioned the matter last week but we thought it best to break the news gently to the outside world. The tender bud of Christianity is only just beginning to sprout, but as "tall oaks from little acorns grow," so this infant, under the guide and care of Brother Wright, may grow and spread its foliage

16

like the manly oak of the forest. Years ago John the Baptist preached in the wilderness of Judea, and his meat was locusts and wild honey, but he baptised many converts in the river of Jordan. Who can tell but that years hence another Luke may write a book about our minister preaching in the wilderness of Dodge City and baptising in the river Arkansas?

As might be expected the courts of the cowtowns were scenes of ribald humor perpetrated by those appearing before the bar of justice and those who made up the court. This article from the *Times*, September 29, 1877, will illustrate both:

HE SUED IN VAIN.

Judge R. W. Evans held court last Saturday evening [September 22]. The case was one of great interest, and about two hundred people were present. It was Mr. Brown of Garfield vs. somebody—Mr. Brown could not find out exactly who. But these are the particulars: While Mr. Brown was inoffensively taking a drink at Beatty & Kelly's some one ingeniously set fire to the lower extremities of his coat from behind. Mr. Brown exhibited great presence of mind by shedding his coat as soon as he felt the flames. Suit was brought to find out the guilty party and punish him. Owing to the great crowd the case was tried in Mayor Kelley's hall. But no decision was reached, owing to the fact that eggs were too freely used to suit his Honor, the Judge. The Judge took his seat with his usual gravity, and was beginning to investigate the case, when an egg struck him somewhere near the back of the head, and as eggs usually do when they strike, it scattered considerably. The Judge immediately adjourned court and proceeded to hunt soap and water. Mr. Brown says he has no faith in Dodge City courts, and will appeal his case to the Governor.

Some of the proceedings which took place in pioneer courts of law can hardly be believed in this day of respect for His Honor. The *Ellis County Star*, June 22, 1876, reprinted from the Dodge City *Times* to preserve this tidbit:

. . . State vs. Charley Beeson, shooting with intent to kill—N. R. Gilbert, prosecuting witness; W. N. Morphy and E. F. Colborn, attorneys for defendant. Prosecuting witness failed to appear, and defendant was released, on payment of costs. In discussing the case Mr. Colborn made a remark reflecting upon the dignity of the Court, which His Honor [Justice of the Peace W. Y. McIntosh] rebuked by leaning over the bench and remarking with great severity of manner: "I will permit no puppy to run this Court!" The attorney retorted by vaguely alluding to His Honor as being himself a relative of a certain variety of canine. The Judge, with his characteristic dignity, ruled that his position as Justice of the Peace in Ford county entitled him to the common courtesy due from one gentleman to another. Mr. Colborn inquired if common courtesy permitted a Judge on the bench to call an attorney a pup. His Honor explained that he did not refer to him in particular, but to all puppies in general. Mr. C then stated that he was an authorized attorney, and appeared before the Court in behalf of his client. The Court suggested that he would do well to go back to his old business. The lawyer inquired what his old business was. His Honor commenced to state that he had grave suspicions that he was an ex-bullwhacker, when Mrs. McIntosh, the Squire's estimable lady, who did not seem to take a proper pride in the able and masterly manner in which the Judge was getting away with the young attorney, peremptorily ordered him to "shut up!" In the temporary lull that followed Mr. C. fervently thanked God that there was another Justice of the Peace in the county, who would give a lawyer the same rights accorded a "yaller dog" in Court. The Court very appropriately remarked: "You and your d----d Justice may go to h--l for all I care. I don't want the d----d office!"

At this juncture County Attorney Sell and W. N. Morphy interfered, and the argument closed.

Some cowtown justice could be grisly business when Judge Lynch presided. Kansas newspapers recorded occasional so-called "necktie parties" celebrating conviction of—or supposed association with—criminals charged with everything from horse thievery to murder. This hanging in Pond City (a now extinct town once having 40 inhabitants, located in what became Wallace county), while not of cowtown origin, may serve to illustrate this type of enterprise:

. . . At Pond City this morning [August 25, 1869], about two o'clock, John Langford was taken out by the Vigilance Committee to be hung for his crimes. On ascertaining his certain fate, he told them he did not want them to hang him, and that he would hang himself; so he pulled off his boots, put the rope around his neck, climbed the tree and jumped off. Before doing this he acknowledged to killing six men, and said if he had had his fate postponed a few days he would have killed as many more. On being requested to make his peace with his Maker, he replied that if he had a Maker it was a damned poor one, as he had experienced considerable trouble in the last few years. He also said he would meet them all in hell, but none of them should gain admission except with hemp ropes ornamenting their necks. Langford was about twenty-two years old and was half Indian. He had led a desperate life all over the border.—*Times and Conservative*, Leavenworth, August 26, 1869.

The Junction City *Union*, May 15, 1869, described a more typical lynching which occurred in Ellsworth:

MURDER AND LYNCHING AT ELLSWORTH.

Ellsworth, May 12, 1869.

ED. UNION: I presume you will have heard of another murder in our town, and of course it will be exaggerated. I will tell you just exactly what it was. During the evening of the 11th, a man by the name of Fitzpatrick kept shoot-

18

ing on the street, endangering the lives of people who were passing, he also stopped several persons on the street putting his pistol against them and threatening to shoot. At 3 a. m. when the cars from the west came in he fired a shot through them and then went to the saloon at which for about one week past he has been employed. He there found a man sleeping by the name of William Brison; he shook him and waked him up and asked him how he came there. The man had been in the habit of sleeping there, and replied that he came in through the window. Fitzpatrick then struck him over the head with his revolver and on his getting up and endeavoring to escape fired at him, striking him in the groin. Bryson lived until about 8 a. m. and died. The coroner's inquest found a verdict *of murder in the first degree!* and the citizens turned out *en masse*, and at 1 p. m. took Fitzpatrick from the jail and proceeded to the river bank and hung him to the old historic cottonwood. Previous to being hung, he gave his name, age and place of residence, said that he was ready to die; that he had stabbed a great many men. He never paled or showed the least fear but braved it through to the last. He came here about one week since from Sheridan [end of track in present Logan county], having been warned to leave there. His people live in St. Louis. . . .

I. W. PHELPS.

More "normal" kinds of entertainment were offered from time to time by the settled element of the cowtowns, though some reports of these affairs make one wonder how normal they really were. The Dodge City *Times*, August 4, 1877, reported one soiree which was held in the ballroom of the Dodge House:

THE SOCIAL HOP.

Another of the social hops for which the Dodge House has become famous, was on yesterday evening indulged in by quite a number of our citizens who worship Terpsichore. The names of Ike Johnson, John Newton and G. E. Hadder as managers were sufficient to insure a success, notwithstanding the inclemency of the weather. Our special reporter who was detailed to write up the costumes of the ladies, and who was in our usual liberal way furnished an excessive amount of pocket money to make himself agreeable with, has in some way got the boot on the wrong leg, and submits the following varied description of the paraphanalia of the Lords of Creation:

Mr. J. F. L. appeared in a gorgeous suit of linsey wolsey, cut bias on the gourd with red cotton handkerchief attachment imported by Messrs. H[adder]. & D[raper]. [general outfitters] from Lawrence.

Mr. H. was modestly attired in a blue larubs wool undershirt, firilled. He is a graceful dancer, but paws too much with his fore legs. His strong point is "the schottisch, my dear."

Mr. I. G. J. was the envy of all; he wore his elegant blond moustache a la gin sling, and was tastefully arrayed in arctic over shoes with collar buttons and studs.

19

Mr. J. N.—The appearance of this gentleman caused a flutter among the fair ones; as he trimmed his nails, picked his nose and sailed majestically around the room, the burr of admiration sounded like the distant approach of the No. 3 freight train. His costume was all that the most fastidious could desire. His train cut "en regale," his mouth set "pour en milkpunch," it was evident that he sails on Love's golden pinions far into the blue etherial.

Mr. H. H.—The Duke! the Duke! was whispered as the nose and eye glasses of this gentleman commenced to appear in the doorway. This stranger is some distinguished foreigner traveling incog. It is darkly hinted that he is the Prince Imperial in disguise. He was beautifully ornamented with two pair of eye-glasses; his hair was trimmed by Mr. Sam. Samuels at an enormous expense; his beard cut a la pompadore, he was the loveliest flower of them all.

Mr. G. E. H.—"Oh! the charming creature," said a beautiful angel on our left, as Mr. H. appeared fantastically arrayed in a sad, sweet smile, which occasionally exploded into a laugh of the most unearthly sweetness. He wore full Georgia costume, lacking the collar and spurs.

Mr. A. H. J.—There was a split in the air, a streak of white whirling through space, and Sam was performing a highland fling with grape-vine accompaniments, as only Sam can do it. He was costumed as an angel playing on a harp of a thousand strings. Were it not for a slight gangsaw movement of his hind legs, which occasionally shook the foundation and jarred loose the bridge on the base viol, his dancing would indeed have been the essence of a car-load of long horns.

Notice.—It is evident that at this point something happened to our reporter. There is a maudling description of P., but it is so mixed with gin slings, straits, and cigars and lemons, as to be unintelligible.

The cowtowns appreciated another type of entertainment, illustrated by this write up in the *Times,* June 16, 1877:

A BLOODY PRIZE FIGHT IN DODGE CITY.

On last Tuesday morning the champion prize fight of Dodge City was indulged in by Messrs. Nelson Whitman and the noted Red Hanley, familiarly known as 'the red bird from the South.' An indefinite rumor had been circulated in sporting circles that a fight was to take place, but the time and place was known only to a select few. The sport took place in front of the Saratoga, at the silent hour of 4:30 a. m., when the city police were retiring after the dance hall revelry had subsided, and the belles who reign there were off duty. Promptly at the appointed time the two candidates for championship were at the joint. Col. Norton acted as rounder up and whipper-in for both fighters, while Bobby Gill ably performed the arduous task of healing and handling and sponging off. Norton called 'time,' and the ball opened with some fine hits from the shoulder. Whitman was the favorite in the pools, but Red made a brilliant effort to win the champion belt. During the forty-second round Red Hanley implored Norton to take Nelson off for a little while till he could have time to put his right eye back where it belonged, set his jaw bone and have the ragged edge trimmed off his ears where they had been

20

The Stage and Plot

chewed the worst. This was against the rules of the ring, so Norton declined, encouraging him to bear it as well as he could and squeal when he got enough. About the sixty-first round Red squealed unmistakably, and Whitman was declared winner. The only injuries sustained by the loser in this fight were two ears chewed off, one eye bursted and the other disabled, right cheek bone caved in, bridge of the nose broken, seven teeth knocked out, one jaw bone mashed, one side of the tongue chewed off, and several other unimportant fractures and bruises. Red retires from the ring in disgust.

Of course the cowtowns liked just plain fun too. The reader of this book probably will notice that Dodge City had a special character who could be made to appear at any time as functionary of a practical joke. The name given to this mythical figure was Luke McGlue and he appears in the annals of Dodge City with some frequency. A typical McGlue escapade was printed in the *Times*, March 24, 1877:

J. B. McManahan, a St. Joe cigar runner, was here this week, and while his cigars were spread out for the 'boys' to inspect, several boxes vanished. J. P. M.'s suspicions were excited against Luke McGlue, and, taking Constable [James H.] McGoodwin, he went through every saloon and business house in the city. Everybody was smoking and praising the cigars Luke McGlue had given them, but Luke could not be found.

The "Indian Act" was another favorite joke played by the boys of Dodge City. The *Times*, April 21, 1877, reported its successful operation on an Eastern tenderfoot:

ANOTHER INDIAN SCARE.

A Kansas City Drummer Chased
By Fiendish Red Men.

An incident occurred yesterday which agitated our city from center to circumference. It was a reproduction of the notorious Indian act, as a benefit to and in honor of Mr. Elias Cahn, of the House of Cahn & Co., clothiers of Kansas City, who was here trying to sell clothing.

All the morning the intrepid young Mr. Cahn had been relating to gaping crowds of our astonished denizens miraculous accounts of his own heroic exploits among the Indians, and expressing a blood-thirsty yearning for more Indians to conquer. Finally our boys resolved that he should be accommodated, and a hunting expedition was proposed, to which he eagerly assented. Mayor Kelley, Sam Sneider, of the firm of Somshine & Sneider, of Cincinnati; John Mueller, and our young Indian fighter made up the party. As soon as the hunters had started Messrs. Ed. Garland, J. M. Manion, S. E. Isaacson, C. H. Schultz, Mr. Wolf, C. M. Beeson, and Jas. Langton donned Indian costumes which were captured at the Doby Walls fight, and with faces hideously painted—superbly mounted, they started in a round-about way, to intercept Mr. Cahn and his party.

By the time the latter party had started the populace began to turn out. Roofs of houses, old freight wagons and telegraph poles were quickly covered with anxious spectators; mothers with young babies on their backs and older ones following behind might be seen frantically rushing up Boot Hill; the silvery locks of aged and decrepit men could soon be seen fluttering over the highest and most inaccessible pinnacles of the hills adjacent to our city.

When our party of Indian hunters had traveled about four miles they were suddenly startled by a fiendish Indian war whoop, and on looking up the hill on one side, they saw the blood thirsty devils riding furiously toward them in regular Indian file. Mr. Cahn, although armed with a murderous revolver carefully loaded with blank cartridges by Mr. Samuels, decided very promptly that discretion was the better part of valor, and, turning his fiery steed toward Dodge City, applied whip and spur without restraint. When the first shot was fired by the pursuers, Mr. Cahn exhibited his skill at Indian fighting by dodging the bullet so dexterously that his elegant cap flew off his head and was seen no more. The firing was rapid, but Mr. Cahn's head dodged faster, and he arrived safely within a mile of the city, when firing ceased, and he began to think he was saved. However it soon occurred to his mind that the city must be besieged, as the hill-tops were crowded with people, and an excited populace filled the streets. But his friend Sneider assured him, and both hunters and Indians made a triumphal entry into the city together, warmly saluted by the gang with eggs, Sitting Bull the Banta having one burst against the side of his head, to his infinite disgust.

Once the "Indian Act" boomeranged and thereafter the Dodge City gang seems to have abandoned this form of entertainment. The occasion, which almost ended in tragedy, was described as follows in the *Times* of August 18, 1877:

THE INDIAN ACT AGAIN.

This time an attempt was made to perpetrate the renowned Indian scare on the new jeweler, Mr. H. Harris. So far as we are able to learn Mr. Harris was not so badly scared as to be unable for business next day. Mr. Beatty and two or three others rode out with Mr. Harris last evening to take a look at the numerous herds and breathe the country air. Before they started some one informed Mr. H. that there were Indians in the vicinity of the city, which information tended to arouse suspicion within the breast of the intended victim, and he quietly primed his pistol and placed it in his boot. After the riders had rode a few miles west of the city, the Indians made their appearance in fantastic array. Mr. Harris' friends advised him to run for his life. Mr. Harris's horse became unmanageable and started to run towards town, the rider's hat blowing off in the meantime, and the Indians, yelling hideously, were pressing close in the rear. Now was the time for Mr. Harris to make a fight. The idea of riding into town bare-headed, pursued by Indians, was

22

more humility than he could bear. He turned his horse to the foe and rode back after his hat. As the Indians came near he drew from its hiding place a gun of dangerous proportions, and leveling it at the head of the foremost chief with unerring aim, was about to pull the fatal trigger, when the Indians scattered like chaff before the morning breeze.

Some amusement was provided from unexpected sources. The Dodge City *Globe Live Stock Journal,* February 23, 1886, told of one such happening:

The buffalo that runs about town is accustomed to the music of the Cowboy band; it's Western in appearance and does not interfere with the peace and happiness of the buffalo, but there are some things that the buffalo won't stand, and among them is a strange lot of men blowing horns marching through the streets, headed by a drum major dressed in red trimmings and a woolly hat. Yesterday the buffalo observed the Simon Comedy Company's Hussar band parading the streets and took exceptions, and with head down and tail up charged that band. The music ceased with the first bellow of that wild animal, and the band done some excellent running. It was the worst broke up parade you ever saw. The buffalo took possession of the street, while the band roosted on fences, porches and small shanties.

These, then, were the Kansas trail towns—wild, reckless, and to some extent irresponsible. There is little wonder that they still are remembered for the violence that marked their early histories. Here gathered the assorted people who catered to the cowmen, "taking" them or each other, as they could. It was done according to the rules in most cases, crookedly in others, and by gunplay on occasions. Reputations of several of those who resorted to violence were boosted out of all proportion by journalists and authors who enjoyed good stories, even to the extent of spinning the yarns themselves if their subjects didn't. And the practice continues even unto today. Thus a few of the so-called good or bad guys have become much more fearsome on the printed page, according to their developing legends, than they were in the flesh.

On the pages which follow some major Kansas cowtown police officers and gun fighters appear in an alphabetical parade, introduced and described by their contemporaries. Most of their activities—though interesting, and often humorously reported in the newspapers—are in no way extraordinary. In a few cases it will be the readers' pleasure to be present when incidents of molehill proportions are deftly magnified into mountains. For an example, read the interview with Wild Bill Hickok by the famed English journalist, Henry M. Stanley (in the section on Hickok). Considering Stanley's credulous and fanciful mind it's no wonder that he was reported to have uttered the classic words, "Dr. Livingstone, I presume?" when he found the "lost" Livingstone in Africa a few years later. Some journalists obviously are unable to avoid dramatics, even in straight reporting.

Be that as it may, the Kansas men and women discussed in this book, even without the exaggerations heaped upon some of them, are largely responsible for the notoriety they brought to the cowtowns. Without their antics the West might not so easily have achieved its Wild image.

The Characters

ALLISON, CLAY (——1887)

Much has been written in various books about Clay Allison's reputed colorful adventures in Dodge City but actually little mention of him was found in the town's newspapers. On August 6, 1878, the *Ford County Globe* noted that "Clay Allison, one of the Allison Bros., from the Cimarron, south of Las Animas, Colorado, stopped off at Dodge last week on his way home from St. Louis. We are glad to say that Clay has about recovered from the effects of the East St. Louis scrimmage."

The affair referred to might have been this one which was reported in the St. Louis *Missouri Republican*, July 25, 1878:

FOUND HIS MAN.

A lively encounter occurred at the Green Tree house yesterday afternoon between Alexander Kessinger and a Texas drover from the St. Louis National stock yards. It appears that the Texan, who gives his name as Allison, had made some inquiries concerning Kessinger and stated that if he found him he intended to kick him. He did not know Kessinger by sight, but by reputation, and desired to meet him. The latter was informed of this by his friends, and the Texan was pointed out to him. They met in the bar-room, Kessinger had the advantage of being posted. He approached the Texan and engaged him in conversation, and finally asked him if he was looking for a man named Kessinger. The latter replied that he was.

"I understand that you have some difficulty to settle with him."

"Yes, I want to meet him; he is said to pride himself on being brave and a good fighter, and I want to see for myself, and when I meet him he will hear and feel me."

"I know Kessinger and he is not going to allow anyone to get the drop on him."

"O, I understand that he is handy with weapons, I am a shootist also."

With this last remark the Texan made a motion towards his pistol pocket, as if to draw a weapon, and Kessinger, who thought that the Texan who pre-

25

tended not to know him actually did know him, and that he was about to commence shooting, hauled off and struck the Texan, who measured about 6 feet 2 inches in his stocking feet, knocking him down and afterwards pounded him fearfully until he cried for quarter.

Allison visited Dodge again on September 5, according to the *Ford County Globe,* September 10, 1878, and then on Febuary 26, 1880, prepared a statement for the *Globe,* which it published on March 2, explaining his version of the St. Louis difficulty. Whether Allison was referring to a similar and more recent fight or had merely waited for a year and a half to state his position is not known. At any rate he gave some interesting biographical information in his statement:

A CARD FROM CLAY ALLISON.

To the Editor of the Globe:

About the 26th of July there appeared in one of the St. Louis papers an account of an altercation between myself and one Tisinger, in East St. Louis, in which account there appeared several gross misrepresentations which I desire to contradict.

1st It was alleged that I was a murderer of fifteen men. In answer to this assertion I will say that it is entirely false, and that I stand ready at all times and places for an open inspection, and any one who wishes to learn of my past record can make inquiries of any of the leading citizens of Wayne county, Tennessee, where I was born and raised, or of officers of the late rebellion, on either side. I served in the 9th Tennessee regiment, Co. F, and the last two years of the service was a scout for Ben McCulloch and Gen. Forrest. Since the war I have resided in Mexico, Texas and Kansas, principally on the frontier, and will refer to any of the tax payers and prominent men in either of the localities where I have resided. I have at all times tried to use my influence toward protecting the property holders and substantial men of the country from thieves, outlaws and murderers, among whom I do not care to be classed.

2nd, It was also charged that I endeavored to use a gun on the occasion of the St. Louis difficulty, which is untrue, and can be proven by either Col. Hunter, of St. Louis, or the clerk of Irwin, Allen & Co. It was also stated that I got the worst of the fight. In regard to this I also refer to Col. Hunter. I do not claim to be a prize fighter, but as an evidence of the correct result of this fight I will only say that I was somewhat hurt but did not squeal, as did my three opponents.

My present residence is on the Washita in Hemphill county, Texas, where I am open for inspection and can be seen at any time.

CLAY ALLISON.

Dodge City, Feb. 26, 1880.

St. Louis and other papers please copy.

26

Clay Allison

Clay Allison made another appearance on the streets of Dodge City August 15, 1880, for the *Globe* of August 17, said: "Clay Allison came up from the Pan Handle Sunday." Dodge City newspapers apparently carried no mention of further visits.

Seven years later Allison was dead, according to the Santa Fe *Daily New Mexican* of July 19, 1887:

CLAY ALLISON DEAD.

Poor old Clay Allison! The Lookout, Lincoln County, correspondent of the Independent writes:

"On July 1 Clay Allison fell off of Geo. Larrimore's wagon and was killed. The accident happened about forty miles from Pecos City. Allison was coming to his ranch at Pope's crossing. He lived about forty-five minutes. He leaves a wife and one child. His remains were taken to Pecos City."

The *Globe Live Stock Journal* of Dodge City, July 26, 1887, copied Clay's death notice from a Trinidad, Colo., paper which in turn had copied from the Las Vegas (N. M.) *Optic*. The editor of the *Globe* added some personal comments of his own:

CLAY ALLISON'S DEATH.

TRINIDAD DAILY CITIZEN.

Clay Allison, a brave, true-hearted and oft-times dangerously reckless man, when in his cups, has at last died with his boots on, but not by the pistol route. He fell from his wagon in Texas, some days ago, the wheels of the same running over his neck and breaking it. The career of Clay Allison is perhaps unparalleled in the western country and should be written up by some one conversant with it.—Las Vegas *Optic*.

All of our old timers knew Clay Allison. He knew no fear, was a good looking man. To incur his enmity was about equivalent to a death sentence. He contended always that he had never killed a man willingly; but that the necessity in every instance had been thrust upon him. He was expert with his revolver, and never failed to come out first best in a deadly encounter. Whether this brave, genteel border man was in truth a villian or a gentleman is a question that many who knew him never settled to their own satisfaction. Certain it is that many of his stern deeds were for the right as he understood the right to be.[1]

1. Additional information on Clay Allison can be found in F. Stanley, *Clay Allison* (World Press, Inc., Denver, 1956), and Harry E. Kelsey, Jr., "Clay Allison: Western Gunman," *1957 Brand Book of the Denver Westerners* (Johnson Publishing Co., Boulder, 1958), pp. 383-404.

BASSETT, CHARLES E. (1847?-1896)

The first sheriff of Ford county was Charles E. Bassett. Chosen at a special election June 5, 1873, he was re-elected twice and served a total of about four and one-half years.[1] For nearly three years after his first election, Bassett's history remains blank. Then, in 1876, he appears in connection with a lynching.

In early April, 1876, young John Callaham and a stranger named Cole, who was sharing Callaham's camp on Saw Log creek some 15 miles from Dodge City, were hanged by a posse from Sumner county. The posse, pursuing horse thieves, believed that both Callaham and Cole were guilty but later events seem to indicate that John Callaham was the innocent victim of lynch law.[2]

R. C. Callaham, a Topeka sewing machine salesman and father of John Callaham, conferred with Gov. Thomas A. Osborn and then journeyed to Dodge. He carried with him this letter from the governor to Sheriff Bassett and the county attorney of Ford county:

April 24[, 187]6

To THE COUNTY ATTORNEY &
SHERIFF OF FORD COUNTY.

GENTLEMEN:—

This will be handed to you by Mr. R. C. Callaham, whose son, John F. Callaham, was executed by mob violence in your county, on the 8th inst. He visits Ford County for the purpose of making a thorough investigation of all the facts and circumstances attending the death of his son. He claims that there is no doubt of his son's innocence, and if this claim is correct the [word illegible] atrocity of the crime—an utterly law-defying one at the best— certainly demands the attention of all law-abiding people, and more especially of the officers to whom is entrusted the execution of the law and the preservation of the public peace.

I trust that you will extend to Mr. Callaham all the assistance, counsel and encouragement which it may be in your power to extend. There must be an end to mob violence in this state, and local officers exercising vigilance and energy in its suppression and punishment may rely upon the Executive for support and assistance. Let me know in what manner I can be of service in bringing to justice the perpetrators of this recent outrage, and I shall not be slow in responding to any practical suggestion. In the meantime I trust that you will do everything in your power to facilitate the inquiry which Mr. Callaham proposes to institute.

Very Respectfully,
Your Obed't Servant,
THOS. A. OSBORN.[3]

Charles Bassett

Shortly after Callaham's arrival in Dodge City, Sheriff Charles
E. Bassett wrote to Governor Osborn and reported Callaham's
findings as well as his own feelings in the matter:

SHERIFF'S OFFICE,
FORD COUNTY, KAS.,
DODGE CITY, April 28, 1876

THOS. A OSBORN
Gov. State Kans
DEAR SIR

Mr. R. C. Calleham presented to me your letter of the 24 inst.

I gave the Gentleman all the encouragement I could but as I was ignorant
of the facts in the Case, My suggestions as council could be of little benifit
to him.

Through what little information I gave him and his own exertions he has
ascertained the fact that his son, John Calleham, was at Dodge City, on the
3rd day of April 1876 the day on which we held our municipal election. It
appears from the statements made by the Sumner County and other papers
that the horses were stolen on the 30th inst., and that the parties in persuit
followed the thieves a distance of 300 miles. The theory is that if the deceased John Calleham was here on the 3rd day of April that it would be
physically impossible for him to have stolen those horses. Several Citizens of good standing are willing to qualify [sic] that they spoke with him on
the 3rd of April, at Dodge City. If he was one of the thieves the time given
him to travel over 300 miles of ground was 3 days from the night of the
30th of March to the morning of the 3rd of April. I do not hesitate to say that
this fete could not be performed by any one horse or horseman in the time
given, especially as the ground was so soft, as to leave an impression, so plain
that it could be followed at a very rapid gait.

To be brief I am now of the opinion that the man was innocent of the
crime alledged, and for which he has suffered death. Mr. Calleham wishes
me to go to Sumner County and arrest the parties interested in the hanging,
but without the assistance of the executive department I am totally unable to
do anything, as I am in a poor fix financially to undertake so lengthy a Journy.
And as I have to deal with men who have themselfs disregarded the law, I
will nessarily have to take with me three men to assist in making those arrests.
This of course will be some slight expense to the State, without which I am
unable to opperate.

I hardly think it safe to entrust my business to the Sumner Co Sheriff as
I think that possibly he might convey the intilegence to them and thereby
give the offenders an oppertunity to escape

Yours Very
Respectfully
CHAS E. BASSETT [4]

29

The financial aid which Bassett requested was not forthcoming. On May 1 Governor Osborn's secretary replied:

CHAS. E. BASSETT, ESQ.
Dodge City, Kansas.
DEAR SIR:—
The Governor directs me to acknowledge the receipt of your favor of the 28th ult. Though he is decidedly anxious that the parties who illegally executed young Callaham should be brought to justice, there is no public fund from which the expense of their re-capture can be defrayed. It is the duty of the local authorities to execute the law, and the Governor hopes that the County Board will provide the necessary means.

Yours Truly,
WARD BURLINGAME,
Private Sec'y.[5]

Further research has not disclosed the outcome of the Callaham case.

Little is known of Bassett's service as sheriff of Ford county from May, 1876, until the spring of 1877, when issues of Dodge City newspapers begin to appear regularly in the Kansas State Historical Society's files. The first known newspaper item which credited Bassett with having performed an official duty was in the Dodge City *Times*, March 31, 1877:

A slight horse-thief scare prevaded this morning. From what we learn it appears that twelve horses were missed from Mr. J. W. Miller's cattle camp on Crooked yesterday. Supposing they had been stolen, the authorities were informed, and Sheriff Bassett and Marshal [Lawrence E.] Deger started out this morning to see what they could find. About three miles west of town they discovered the horses, but no thieves were in sight.

Short items telling of Bassett going after a jewel thief, visiting Harvey county on official business, etc., appeared from time to time but apparently nothing of major importance happened which involved the sheriff of Ford county until September, 1877. On September 18 Sam Bass and five other men robbed a Union Pacific train of $60,000 at Big Springs, Neb. It was reported that the bandits were headed south and Sheriff Bassett set out to catch them. Here is the story from the *Times*, September 29, 1877:

IN PURSUIT.

A dispatch was received by Sheriff Bassett last Wednesday from Superintendent Morse, stating that the train robbers had started south and would probably cross the A. T. & S. F. near Lakin. Accordingly Bassett, under-sheriff [William B. "Bat"] Masterson and John Webb went west on the Thursday

30

morning train: but they heard nothing of the robbers and returned Friday morning, thinking it more likely that the robbers would cross near Dodge. A few hours before they arrived news was brought into town that five men had crossed the railroad going south about thirty miles west of here. As soon as preparations could be made, Bassett, Bat Masterson and Webb started southwest on horseback, intending to try to intercept the robbers if possible. Assistant Marshal Ed. Masterson and Deputy Sheriff [Miles] Mix went west the same day to find out what they could about the men who crossed the road. They could learn nothing of any importance except that the men had been seen on Thursday morning, but no one had taken particular notice of them. Masterson and Mix returned the same evening.

Nothing has been heard from Sheriff Bassett and his men since they started from here yesterday morning.

Probably the Bassett posse did not catch up with the bandits, for no further word of the chase was printed.

Later, Sheriff Bassett was embarrassed by a jail break, as the Dodge City *Times* reported October 27:

OUR BIRD HAS FLOWN.

FORD COUNTY'S ONLY JAIL BIRD PLUMES HIS PINIONS AND TAKES HIS FLIGHT.

. . . When Sheriff Bassett heard that his bird had flown he looked as sorrow-stricken as if he had lost his dearest friend, and immediately sought to find his prodigal and return him to his keeper, but George was still on the wing at last accounts. The following card shows that the sheriff means business:

FIFTY DOLLARS REWARD—BROKE JAIL,

The above reward will be paid for the apprehension of Geo. W. Wilson, who broke jail at this place on the night of October 22d. Wilson is 5 feet 11 inches tall, dark hair, blue eyes, good looking, straight built, 22 years old, small moustache and gotee, has a scar from a pistol shot in his back, wore dark clothes and a wide-rimmed white hat.

CHAS. E. BASSETT,
Sheriff Ford county, Kansas.

In December, while still sheriff, Bassett received an additional law enforcement duty. "Sheriff Bassett has been appointed by Mayor [James H.] Kelley to assist Marshal [Edward J.] Masterson in preserving order and decorum in the city. Mr. Bassett has had thorough training, and is a good man for the place," said the *Times*, December 15, 1877. Bassett's salary in this position was the same as the marshal's, $75 per month.[6]

Limited by the state constitution, Bassett could not run for a successive third regular term as sheriff. On January 14, 1878, he was replaced by William B. Masterson who had been elected on November 6. One of Bat's first acts as sheriff of Ford county was to appoint Bassett his under sheriff.[7]

In February and March, 1878, Bassett spent much of his time pursuing the men who had attempted to hold up a Santa Fe train at Kinsley on January 27. Since he was, in this episode, the subordinate of Bat Masterson the full account of the pursuit will be given in the section on W. B. Masterson.

In April, City Marshal Edward J. Masterson was killed by drunken cowboys. The city council of Dodge lost little time in appointing Assistant Marshal Bassett to the higher position and shortly thereafter he was given a salary increase to $100 per month.[8]

That summer Deputy United States Marshal H. T. McCarty was shot and killed in the Long Branch saloon, Cowboy George Hoy was shot by the Dodge City police and in September Dull Knife's band of Cheyenne Indians raided and pillaged across the state. These events threw the town into a frenzy of excitement. Toward the end of the cattle season Fannie Keenan, alias Dora Hand, was shot and killed. City Marshal-Under Sheriff Bassett participated in the pursuit and capture of Miss Keenan's alleged murderer, James Kennedy, but this tale, again, properly belongs to the sheriff of Ford county and details may be found under W. B. Masterson.

In reporting the January term of the Ford county district court the Dodge City *Times,* January 11, 1879, had this to say concerning the efficiency of the county peace officers:

The large criminal calendar suggests the "probability" of an "endeavor" on the part of the officers to do their duty. To an unprejudiced person, somebody has been making things lively. Sheriff Bat Masterson, Under Sheriff Bassett, and Deputies [William] Duffy and [James] Masterson, have evidently earned the high praise accorded to them for their vigilance and prompt action in the arrest of offenders of the law.

On February 15 Bassett, Sheriff Masterson and others were at Fort Leavenworth to pick up seven Cheyenne prisoners from the military authorities. The Indians, members of Dull Knife's band, were accused of committing atrocities during their September, 1878, flight across Kansas and were to be taken to Dodge City for trial. Further details may be found under W. B. Masterson.

April 5, 1879, saw one of Dodge's more famous killings and City Marshal Bassett played a role in the story as reported by the *Ford County Globe* on April 8:

Charles Bassett

ANOTHER TRAGEDY.

Frank Loving and Levi Richardson Fight With Pistols.
Loving Comes Out With a Scratch and Richardson Goes to His Grave.

There is seldom witnessed in any civilized town or country such a scene as transpired at the Long Branch saloon, in this city, last Saturday evening, resulting in the killing of Levi Richardson, a well known freighter, of this city, by a gambler named Frank Loving.

For several months Loving has been living with a woman toward whom Richardson seems to have cherished tender feelings, and on one or two occasions previous to this which resulted so fatally, they have quarrelled and even come to blows. Richardson was a man who had lived for several years on the frontier, and though well liked in many respects, he had cultivated habits of bold and daring, which are always likely to get a man into trouble. Such a disposition as he posessed might be termed bravery by many, and indeed we believe he was the reverse of a coward. He was a hard working, industrious man, but young and strong and reckless.

Loving is a man of whom we know but very little. He is a gambler by profession; not much of a roudy, but more of the cool and desperate order, when he has a killing on hand. He is about 25 years old. Both, or either of these men, we believe, might have avoided this shooting if either had posessed a desire to do so. But both being willing to risk their lives, each with confidence in himself, they fought because they wanted to fight. As stated in the evidence below, they met, one said "I don't believe you will fight." The other answered "try me and see," and immediately both drew murderous revolvers and at it they went, in a room filled with people, the leaden missives flying in all directions. Neither exhibited any sign of a desire to escape the other, and there is no telling how long the fight might have lasted had not Richardson been pierced with bullets and Loving's pistol left without a cartridge. Richardson was shot in the breast, through the side and through the right arm. It seems strange that Loving was not hit, except a slight scratch on the hand, as the two men were so close together that their pistols almost touched each other. Eleven shots were fired, six by Loving and five by Richardson. Richardson only lived a few moments after the shooting. Loving was placed in jail to await the verdict of the coroner's jury, which was "self defense," and he was released. Richardson has no relatives in this vicinity. He was from Wisconsin. About twenty-eight years old.

Together with all the better class of our community we greatly regret this terrible affair. We do not believe it is a proper way to settle difficulties, and we are positive it is not according to any law, human or divine. But if men must continue to persist in settling their disputes with fire arms we would be in favor of the duelling system, which would not necessarily endanger the lives of those who might be passing up or down the street attending to their own business.

We do not know that there is cause to censure the police, unless it be to urge upon them the necessity of strictly enforcing the ordinance preventing the carrying of concealed weapons. Neither of these men had a right to carry such weapons. Gamblers, as a class, are desperate men. They consider it necessary in their business that they keep up their fighting reputation, and never take a bluff. On no account should they be allowed to carry deadly weapons. . . .

The newspaper then gave the testimonies of individuals who had knowledge of the shooting. Those of Adam Jackson, bartender at the Long Branch, City Marshal Bassett, and Deputy Sheriff William Duffey are reproduced here, the others being similar.

Adam Jackson, bar-tender at the Long Branch, testified as follows:

"I was in the Long Branch saloon about 8 or 9 o'clock Saturday evening. I know Levi Richardson. He was in the saloon just before the fuss, standing by the stove. He started to go out and went as far as the door when Loving came in at the door. Richardson turned and followed back into the house. Loving sat down on the hazard table. Richardson came and sat near him on the same table. Then Loving immediately got úp, making some remark to Richardson, could not understand what it was. Richardson was sitting on the table at the time, and Loving standing up. Loving says to Richardson: 'If you have anything to say about me why don't you come and say it to my face like a gentleman, and not to my back, you dam son of a bitch.' Richardson then stood up and said: 'You wouldn't fight anything, you dam—' could not hear the rest. Loving said 'you try me and see.' Richardson pulled his pistol first, and Loving also drew a pistol. Three or four shots were fired when Richardson fell by the billiard table. Richardson did not fire after he fell. He fell on his hands and knees. No shots were fired after Richardson fell. No persons were shooting except the two mentioned. Loving's pistol snapped twice and I think Richardson shot twice before Loving's pistol was discharged.
A. A. JACKSON. . . .

Chas. E. Bassett testified: "When I first heard the firing I was at Beatty & Kelley's saloon. Ran up to the Long Branch as fast as I could. Saw Frank Loving, Levi Richardson and Duffey. Richardson was dodging and running around the billiard table. Loving was also running and dodging around the table. I got as far as the stove when the shooting had about ended. I caught Loving's pistol. Think there was two shots fired after I got into the room, am positive there was one. Loving fired that shot, to the best of my knowledge. Did not see Richardson fire any shot, and did not see him have a pistol. I examined the pistol which was shown me as the one Richardson had. It contained five empty shells. Richardson fell while I was there. Whether he was shot before or after I came in am unable to say. I think the shots fired after I came in were fired by Loving at Richardson. Richardson fell immediately after the shot I heard. Did not see any other person shoot at Richardson. Did not see Duffey take Richardson's pistol. Do not know whether Loving knew that Richardson's pistol had been taken away from him. There was considerable smoke in the room. Loving's pistol was a Remington, No. 44 and was empty after the shooting.
CHAS. E. BASSETT.

Charles Bassett

Wm. Duffey testified: "I was at the Long Branch saloon. I know Levi Richardson, who is now dead. I know 'cock-eyed Frank' (Loving) Both were there at the time. I heard no words pass between them. They had fired several shots when Frank fell by the table by the stove. I supposed that he was shot. I then had a scuffle with Richardson, to get his pistle, and threw him back on some chairs. Succeeded in getting his pistol. There might have been a shot fired by one or the other while we were scuffling. Cannot say whether Richardson had been shot previous to that time, but think he had, as he was weak and I handled him easily. Richardson then got up and went toward the billiard table and fell. I can't swear whether any shots were fired at Richardson by Loving after Richardson was disarmed. Don't think Loving knew I had taken the pistol from Richardson. It was but a few seconds after I took Richardson's pistol that he fell.   WILLIAM DUFFEY. . . ."

Five months later City Marshal Bassett again disarmed the victor of a fatal quarrel. The Ford County Globe carried the story on September 9, 1879:

A COWARDLY MURDER.
B. MARTIN BRAINED WITH A WINCHESTER
BY A. H. WEBB.

Dodge City has added another item to her history of blood, and rum has found another victim.

Yesterday afternoon B. Martin and A. H. Webb became involved in a dispute in a saloon on Main street. Many complimentary allusions to the parentage, habits and previous history of the parties, usually passed during such scenes in Dodge circles, were freely bandied between the two, ending by Webb knocking Martin down. Martin, who was a remarkably small man, generally inoffensive and timid, made an apology to Webb for some of his strongest epithets, and then went out and sat upon a bench in front of his little tailor shop adjoining Henry Sturm's saloon. Webb seemed to be very little placated by the submission of his little antagonist. He walked up Main street, threatening more vengeance at every step. He went into Zimmerman's hardware store and asked Mr. Connor to loan him a pistol, but he was refused. He then went to his house on the hill, saddled his horse, got his Winchester rifle and returned to Main street. He hitched his horse at Straeter's corner, walked to where Martin was seated, raised the rifle with both hands and brought the barrel of it down on Martin's head with terrific force. Martin fell like a log and never was conscious afterward.

Webb then jumped for his horse to make off. The murderous blow, however, had been seen by several persons, who ran to prevent the escape. Marshal Bassett seized him and took away his rifle, which was found to be loaded and cocked. He was first taken to the calaboose, but a crowd gathering quickly, among whom were some who favored lynching, the sheriff deemed it prudent to remove the prisoner to the county jail. . . .

On October 21, 1879, the Ford County Globe told of another railway robbery:

THE TRAIN ROBBERY.

At 1:45 Wednesday morning, Mr. J. M. Thatcher, Gen'l Ag't Express Co., received a telegram informing him of the express train at Las Vegas having been taken in by masked robbers. With Messrs. [Harry E.] Gryden, Bassett and [Chalkley M.] Beeson he immediately left for Las Vegas. From Judge Gryden, who returned this morning, we learn the following particulars.

The night being rainy five men entered the Express car immediately on leaving Las Vegas. Covering the conductor Mr. Turner, the messenger Mr. Monroe, and the baggage master, and compelling the messenger to open the safe "dam quick." The booty consisted of two $1,000 bills, $85.50 in C. O. D. packages and $1,000 in time checks of the A. T. & S. F. R. R., a package of $245 was overlooked. The three revolvers of the conductor, messenger and baggage master was also taken from them and all the lanterns, the parties then left the train without stopping it. Two of them have through the efficiency of Mr. Thatcher been arrested at Las Vegas, the others are known and will be caught. It was a neat and prompt job; but between Messrs. Thatcher and Judge Gryden they will, we have no doubt, be all landed in the penitentiary.

On November 4, 1879, the *Globe* reported that "Ex-Sheriff Charles E. Bassett returned last week from New Mexico, where he has been for the past ten days in the interest of the Adams express company." The day the *Globe* came out the city council met and appointed James Masterson city marshal to replace Bassett who had by then resigned.[9]

On December 23 Bassett was reported to be in St. Louis, Mo., but by January 6, 1880, when the January term of the Ford county district court convened, he was back in Dodge for duty as deputy sheriff.[10] His name appeared in the newspapers a few times in minor items which stated that he took prisoners to the penitentiary, but apparently he was involved in nothing of note for the remainder of his stay in Dodge City. On April 27, 1880, the *Ford County Globe* noted his exit from town: "Ex-Sheriff Chas. E. Bassett, accompanied by Mysterious Dave [Mather] and two other prospectors, started out last week in search of 'greener fields and pastures new.' They went in a two-horse wagon, after the style in the days of '49." The *Times*, May 1, stated that he was headed for the Gunnison country.

The newspapers of Dodge City did not mention Bassett again for more than 16 months. On September 13, 1881, the *Globe* noticed his return in this article: "Charles E. Bassett, ex-sheriff of Ford county, and formerly city marshal of Dodge City—one of the old timers— arrived the city last Tuesday after an absence of a year and a half.

Charley looks as natural as life, wears good clothes, and says Texas is suffering from dry weather." On September 8, two days after his return, he was mentioned as a possible candidate for sheriff,[11] but two weeks later he was in Kansas City and apparently planning to stay, judging from this item in the *Times*, September 22, 1881: "Hon. C. E. Bassett, a well known cattle man of Kansas and Texas, returned to the city yesterday after a brief stay at Dodge City. He will remain here for some time.—Kansas City Journal. Jim Kelley has charge of Mr. Bassett's herds during his absence."

Another 18 months passed before the name of Charles E. Bassett again appeared in the Dodge City newspapers. The *Ford County Globe* of March 20, 1883, reported that he had been in Dodge City from Kansas City "the first of last week and spent a day or two in our city visiting old-time friends."

Bassett was again in Dodge City in June, 1883, with several other prominent Western gun fighters, to aid Luke Short in his quarrel with the city authorities. (For further information *see* the section on Short.)

Twice more, on January 1, 1884,[12] and April 7, 1885,[13] Bassett was mentioned as being in Dodge City. No further contemporary information has been found on the Dodge City career of Charles E. Bassett.

1. "Ford County, Briefing of Commissioners' Journals" (transcribed by the Historical Records Survey of the Work Projects Administration, in archives division, Kansas State Historical Society), pp. 2, 4, 18. 2. Topeka *Daily Commonwealth*, April 21, 1876. 3. "Governors' Correspondence," archives division, Kansas State Historical Society. 4. *Ibid.* 5. *Ibid.* 6. Dodge City *Times*, January 5, 1878. 7. *Ibid.*, January 12, 19, 1878. 8. *Ibid.*, April 6-20, May 4, 11, 1878; *Ford County Globe*, April 16, 1878. 9. Dodge City *Times*, November 15, 1879. 10. *Ford County Globe*, December 23, 1879; Dodge City *Times*, January 10, 1880. 11. Dodge City *Times*, September 8, 1881. 12. *Ford County Globe.* 13. The *Globe Live Stock Journal.*

BEHRENS, JOHN (1840?-_____)

John Behrens' appointment as policeman on the Wichita force was confirmed by the city council on May 6, 1874.[1]

On July 24, 1874, he assisted in jailing a prisoner who had overcome his guard while on a street gang. After his recapture another officer began to beat the prisoner but was stopped by Behrens. (For the complete story *see* the section on William Dibbs.)

37

In October, 1874, Behrens and Wyatt Earp, at the instance of a Wichita merchant, collected an unpaid bill at gunpoint some 75 miles from the city. (The article reporting this incident is included in the section on Earp.)

Behrens was promoted to assistant city marshal on April 21, 1875, at a salary of $75 per month.[2]

In May "Behrens and Earp picked up a horse thief by the name of Compton from Coffey County . . . with the property in his possession," and on July 23 "John Behrens picked up a deserter from the 4th U. S. Cavalry." . . .[3]

Marshal Mike Meagher and Assistant Marshal Behrens were credited with the arrest of three thieves on November 5, 1875. The Wichita City *Eagle*, November 11, reported that "Wm. Potts and two colored men were arrested here last Friday by city Marshal, Mike Meagher and Assistant John Behrens, charged with stealing eight yoke of cattle and two wagons at Fort Sill, which property was found in their possession. The parties were lodged in jail." The Wichita *Beacon* gave Wyatt Earp and Meagher credit for this arrest.[4]

Also in its issue of November 11, 1875, the *Eagle* reported that "Ed. Hays was arrested and confined in jail Monday evening [November 8] by Assistant Marshal Behrens, on information received by letter from Great Bend. Hays is charged with passing counterfeit money." The *Beacon*, omitting mention of Behrens, gave Marshal Meagher credit for the Hays arrest.[5]

The Wichita *Weekly Beacon*, on November 17, 1875, reversed itself on who arrested Potts and Hays while complimenting Behrens for his efficiency:

While we are not aware that Deputy Marshal Behrens cares a fig for official honors, yet when he is justly entitled to credit it is due him to have the same. Far be it from us to withhold from so efficient an officer what belongs to him, much less give the praise to others. We say this much without the knowledge of Mr. Behrens, in order to set ourselves right in the matter of several arrests made last week; one of them Ed Hays, the other Bill Potts and his two associates. Deputy Marshal Behrens spotted all these parties, arrested Hays, himself; and traced the others to their lair, assisting Mike Meagher in the arrests.

The *Eagle,* on January 27, 1876, reported that:

Mr. John Behrens, deputy marshal, arrested two men on Tuesday afternoon [January 25], charged with stealing 136 skunk skins, one cow hide and one coon skin, from Messrs, Hale & Co. of Hutchinson. They started from Hutchinson with an ox team, but left it with a farmer on the road whom they hired to bring them with their plunder to this city. They gave their names as Smith and Kirkpatrick.

In the list of salaries paid for the month of April, 1876, John Behrens' name does not appear although he had received a full month's salary for March. At a meeting of the city council on May 22, 1876, that body heard a recommendation of the police committee that "Script of W. Earp & John Behrens be with held, until all moneys collected by them for the City, be turned over to the City Treasurer. . . ."[6] How this was settled is not known since this was the last contemporary item found concerning John Behrens.

1. "Proceedings of the Governing Body," Records of the City of Wichita, Journal A, p. 376. 2. *Ibid.*, Journal B, pp. 44, 55, 62, 66, 71, 75, 78, 85, 90, 96, 100; Wichita *Weekly Beacon*, April 28, 1875. 3. Wichita City *Eagle*, May 6, 1875; Wichita *Weekly Beacon*, July 28, 1875; *see, also,* section on Wyatt Earp. 4. November 10, 1875; *see* a reprint of this article in the section on Wyatt Earp. 5. November 10, 1875; *see* a reprint of this article in the section on Mike Meagher. 6. "Proceedings of the Governing Body," Records of the City of Wichita, Journal B, pp. 100, 112, 115.

BELL, HAMILTON B. (1853-1947)

"Ham" Bell was appointed deputy United States marshal for Ford county about May 22, 1880, succeeding W. B. Masterson.[1] There are contemporary records of his reappointment about May 30, 1882, and again about November 5, 1885.[2] At least one person, however, held the position between these latter dates.[3]

Few references were found concerning his performance of the duties of the federal office. One appeared in the *Ford County Globe* on April 11, 1882:

ON THE TRAIL.

April 1st, 1882.

. . . We are sorry to learn that a controversy has arose between Mr. Teasing and Mr. Shrader with regard to a tree-claim near "The Trail." It seems that Mr. Teasing filed on aforesaid claim about four years ago, and not complying with the requirements of the law (having skipped the country in advance of Bat Masterson's six-shooter), Mr. Shrader jumped said claim and did plow and sow to wheat ten acres. Then comes Mr. Teasing, and refusing to compromise, plowed under the ten acres of wheat and planted the same to trees. The latest reports are that Mr. Teasing skipped the country again, between two days, in fear of U. S. Marshal Bell. How this will terminate we do not know. Teasing, what is the matter with you; can't you behave yourself any more?

Another was in the *Globe* of October 23, 1883:

—Deputy U. S. Marshal H. B. Bell, of this city, returned Friday morning from Buffalo Park, Kansas, where he arrested Charles Ellsworth, better known as "Arkansaw," who it is supposed murdered Ellsworth Schuttleman in the latter part of August, who at the time was employed by Mr. Johns. "Arkansaw" was at the time employed at the V— ranch. It is also supposed that he was the party that stole a horse from J. W. Carter on the Saw Log, as the horse was found and had been sold by "Arkansaw," and the bill of sale is now in the hands of H. B. Bell.

Ham Bell's greatest service as a peace officer came after the trail-driving era was over. He was sheriff of Ford county from 1888 to 1892.

1. Dodge City *Times*, May 22, 1880. 2. *Ibid.*, June 1, 1882; *Ford County Globe*, May 30, 1882; Dodge City *Times*, November 5, 1885. 3. Fred Singer was appointed October 1, 1885. *See* the section on Singer.

BOTTS, SAMUEL (1829-____)

The Wichita City *Eagle*, June 11, 1874, reported that "Mr. Botts has been added to the police force, which business he understands, having been deputy marshal of Jacksonville, Illinois."

In July, while attempting to arrest a man for carrying a gun in the city, Botts was set upon by a dozen or more armed men and his would-be prisoner released. However, a secret citizens' police came to the rescue and all the gun toters were arrested. The Wichita City *Eagle* reported the event on July 9, 1874:

A little episode occurred upon our streets on Monday evening [July 6] which we hope will serve to teach certain roughs and would be bullies who infest this town, a lesson. Sam. Botts, one of our policemen, in attempting to enforce the law which says "that no firearms shall be carried within the city," was braved by some twelve or fourteen fellows who pulled their weapons upon him and prevented him from arresting a man whom he just disarmed. The police alarm was sounded and in a shorter time than it takes to write this, forty or fifty citizens armed with well loaded shot guns and Henry rifles, rushed to the aid of the officers. In the mean time the roughs had taken refuge in hotel. Of course they were arrested, and of course they were taken before the police judge and fined, just as they would have been had there been a hundred of them. We have a secret police force, all sworn and armed, numbering, we shall not say how many, which was organized in view of an outrage committed by the above class this spring in broad day light upon a principal street, and had it not been just at supper time these defiers of law would have been surprised at the array of armed and determined men that would have confronted them. As it was, but forty or fifty appeared, but they were from among our best and most substantial citizens, many of whom were officers of rank in the late war and who consequently know how and dare to use arms when it comes to sustaining the majesty of the law. There is no use talking or caviling about the matter, the laws of this city will and must be enforced and they shall be respected, whether our authorities feel able to so enforce or not. The past two years Texas dealers, cow boys, roughs and gamblers have obeyed our laws and regulations and respected our citizens; and, if they would advoid trouble, it would be well for them to continue to do so. There are no better class of people in the world than our permanent citizens— quiet, orderly, law abiding and moral, but they will not be run over and have their laws and rights trampled under foot, though it become necessary to clear the town of every vestage of the cattle trade upon half a day's notice.

On July 24, while taking a prisoner, who had attempted to escape, back to jail, Botts beat him over the head until he was stopped by Policeman John Behrens. (The article reporting this is reprinted in the section on William Dibbs.)

Apparently Botts made some remonstrance against what Milton Gabel, the editor of the *Beacon,* had said of his conduct in this matter, for in the August 5, 1874, issue of the *Beacon* Gabel printed this:

. . . With regard to the conduct of Samuel Botts . . . it is claimed by him that he did not strike McGrath, yet he admits that he "chucked him about roughly," and says that under the excitement—coming up as he did after the shooting had begun, and while McGrath was shooting at Dibbs the second time—thinking that Dibbs was fatally wounded, &c., and, in his over-zealous efforts to save him, etc. etc., he treated McGrath more roughly than he intended to, and, under the excitement, and what he considers aggravating circumstances, more so than he otherwise would have done, and thinks that should at least partially excuse the rough treatment, which we characterized brutality, and of which we made mention in Wednesday's article. This may in a measure palliate the offense, but it shows inefficiency, and even this I think will not justify the mistreatment of a prisoner disarmed, and on the way to the calaboose, and I will not alter my judgment on this matter as heretofore expressed. I gave the facts as they came under my own observation, together with the evidence of others, the truth of which can be substantiated by sworn statements of at least seven witnesses. . . .[1]

The last contemporary mention found concerning Samuel Botts was the payment of $42 for his services as policeman for "part of April," 1875.[2] At the rate which other policemen were being paid

($60 per month) this would indicate that Botts was on the force for about 21 days in April, 1875.

1. A full report on this incident will be found in the section on William Dibbs. 2. "Proceedings of the Governing Body," Records of the City of Wichita, Journal B, p. 55.

BRATTON, CHARLES G. (1849?-1874)

Wichita policeman Charles G. Bratton was appointed on October 24, 1871. The next day he, Marshal Mike Meagher and Assistant Marshal Simon K. Ohmert supposedly roughhoused and illegally arrested saloonkeeper Emil Werner. On November 15 Werner protested to the mayor and the city council but his protest was never acted upon. Werner's letter is included in the section on Meagher.

Bratton was off the force by February 19, 1872, for on that day he was reappointed, this time as a special policeman. He served four days and was paid $8.00 on February 21.[1] No further trace was found of Charles Bratton until December 22, 1874, when he was stabbed and killed while assisting the city marshal of Burlingame to take a drunken butcher to jail. The Wichita *Eagle*, January 7, 1875, reported:

Charley Bratton, a former policeman of Wichita, under Mayor Allen, was brutally murdered at Burlingame last week, by a butcher named Dan Wortz. Wortz was drunk and abusing his wife. Bratton, who was a city officer, interfered, when he was stabbed twice, both wounds being severe enough to produce death. The weapon used was a butcher knife. One stab severed a rib and sank deep into the kidney. Young Bratton was a quiet boy. He came to Burlingame with his parents, when quite a small boy. The murderer is in custody and will go up for life.[2]

1. "Miscellaneous Papers"; "Proceedings of the Governing Body," Records of the City of Wichita, Journal A, p. 148. 2. See, also, the Topeka *Daily Commonwealth*, December 27, 1874.

BRIDGES, JACK L. (1839?-___)

The earliest mention yet found of Jack Bridges as an officer of the law was in a letter from Maj. George Gibson of Fort Hays to Gov. James M. Harvey, dated October 3, 1869. Gibson stated that

Jack Bridges

Deputy United States Marshal Bridges and his assistant [Deputy U. S. Marshal C. J. Cox] had arrested one Bob Connors for the murder of a drover near Pond City and had lodged their prisoner in the fort's guard house to protect him from mob violence in Hays City. (A copy of the letter is reprinted in the section on James Butler Hickok.)

The 1870 United States census listed Bridges as a deputy United States marshal in Hays. Reporting as of June 25, the census showed Bridges as 31 years old, holding real estate valued at $1,800. He was born "at sea."

Bridges next turned up in Wichita in February, 1871. He arrived there well reinforced to arrest J. E. Ledford. Resistance was offered and Ledford was killed. Here is the story from the El Dorado *Walnut Valley Times*, March 3, 1871:

HORRIBLE AFFAIR AT WICHITA.

We have just learned the particulars of an unfortunate affair that occurred at Wichita on Tuesday afternoon the 26th [28th?] of February, at about four o'clock. It seems that Deputy U. S. Marshal Jack Bridges, and Lee Stewart, a scout, with a party of 25 soldiers under command of Capt. Randall of the 5th U. S. Cavalry [probably Lt. (Bvt. Capt.) Edward L. Randall, 5th U. S. infantry], from Fort Harker, came to Wichita to arrest J. E. Ledford, the proprietor of the Harris House at that place, on the charge of resisting a U. S. officer.

The troops came into town with a rush and immediately surrounded the hotel. Ledford seems to have had an idea that they were there to arrest him and secreted himself in an out building. Bridges, Lee Stewart and a Lieutenant, discovered Ledford in the out building and advanced to the door with their pistols in hand; Ledford seeing them advancing immediately threw open the door and came out; both parties immediately commenced firing, after emptying their revolvers at Ledford the three persons, Bridges, Lee Stewart, and the Lieutenant, turned and ran; Bridges, being badly wounded fell fainting; Ledford walked across the street into Dagner's store, mortally wounded. Dr. [E. D.] Hilliard immediately examined Ledford's wounds and pronounced them mortal, he being shot twice through the body and twice through the right arm. He was carried into the hotel parlor and lived about a half hour. In a difficulty last summer between Ledford and Bridges on the line of the Kansas Pacific railroad, Ledford gave Bridges a sound threshing, and Bridges is said to have threatened to shoot him on sight. The fatal wound received by Ledford was given him by Lee Stewart, who being behind him shot him in the back.

Ledford has had the reputation heretofore of being a wild and reckless man but had recently married a fine young lady at Wichita, and seemed to have settled down and was gaining the good will of all at that place. Deputy

U. S. Marshal Walker, who is also Sheriff of Sedgwick County, had recently arrested Ledford on the same charge for which these men proposed to arrest him, and Ledford had given bail for his appearance at the next term of the U. S. Court at Topeka. Our informant was an eye witness of the affair and we are satisfied that the statements are as near substantially correct as one can give them witnessing so sudden and exciting an affair, the whole of which transpired in a few moments time. This is the first instance of bloodshed by violence in the streets of Wichita since its organization all reports to the contrary notwithstanding.

Unfortunately the issue of the Wichita *Vidette* (then the town's only newspaper) which reported the shooting is missing from the files of the Kansas State Historical Society. However, the *Vidette* of March 11, 1871, stated that:

The Walnut Valley *Times* and the Emporia *News* both publish accounts of the "Wichita Murder," in which they give substantially the same statement of the affair as published by us. . . . The *News* says: "The impression prevails that there was no occasion for the arrest of Ledford, and that the pretext of arresting him was only a cloak for the premeditated intention of killing him.

Bridges was taken to the hospital at Fort Harker and from there four days later he wrote a letter to the Topeka *Daily Commonwealth* protesting its account of the shooting (which was much like the story printed by the *Walnut Valley Times*). The *Commonwealth*, March 9, 1871, carried the protest:

THE LEDFORD AFFAIR.

STATEMENT OF BRIDGES.

POST HOSPITAL, FORT HARKER,
Kansas, March 4, 1871.

To the Editor of the Commonwealth.

In your issue of March 4th, 1871, there is an item of news that contains some inaccuracies; it is the article relative to the arrest of one Ledford at Wichita, Kansas. Ledford was arrested on more serious charges than that of resisting the U. S. Marshal on the former occasion, though warrants were out against him for that offence; he was charged with horse stealing and obstructing the administration of justice. It was well known in Wichita, that proper legal warrants for the arrest of this man were in the hands of U. S. Marshals Bridges and Stewart. Ledford was discovered in a privy, and upon the appearance of Marshals Bridges and Stewart, who were accompanied by Lieut. [Bvt. Capt. Charles E.] Hargous, 5th infantry U. S. A., immediately opened the door and shot Bridges, and then fired upon Stewart and Hargous. Neither Bridges, Stewart or Hargous had their pistols in their hands, as your article states, at the time Ledford fired at them.

Respectfully,
J. T. BRIDGES.

44

On the day of Ledford's shooting a warrant was issued for the arrest of Bridges, Stuart and "another whose name is unknown." The Wichita township justice of the peace docket carried the charge as criminal action number 35:

Before H. E. VanTrees, J. P. . . .

N. A. English being duly Sworn Says that One Lee Stuart and two Other persons whose names are unknown being at and in the County of Sedgwick and State aforesaid, on the 28th of Feby 1871, Committed the Crime of Murder in the 1st degree by feloniously, Maliciously, premeditatedly, deliberately and with Malice aforethought by Killing John E. Ledford then and there being Contrary to the Statute in Such Cases made and provided.

February 28th 1871 a Warrant was issued returnable forthwith.

So far as can be ascertained none of the three ever answered the charge.

About three months after the shooting Bridges went east to recuperate from his wounds. The *Commonwealth*, May 20, 1871, said:

United States Deputy Marshal Jack Bridges, left yesterday for the Atlantic seaboard for the benefit of his wounds received in an encounter last winter at Wichita with Ledford. Jack was an excellent officer, a terror to evil-doers, brave as a lion, and we hope he may rapidly recover his usual health and strength.

Jack did recover and resumed his law-enforcement career. Two years later he was back in Topeka with 14 prisoners. The *Commonwealth*, March 4, 1873, described his catch:

THE INDIAN AND THE PALEFACE.

Deputy U. S. Marshal Bridges arrived yesterday with fourteen persons whom he had arrested on warrants sworn out by Indian Agent John D. Miles, for violating the intercourse laws of the Cheyenne and Arapahoe agency. the trials will commence on Wednesday, before U. S. Commissioner Hanback, of this city. On the same train were about forty individuals, whom Pope describes—

Lo the poor Indian, whose untutored mug
Sees liquor in a bottle, and smells it in a jug,

and who are to be used as witnesses in the case.

In the 1875 Kansas state census J. L. Bridges was listed as a "U. S. Marshal." Undoubtedly he was still a deputy, since a complete list of U. S. marshals for Kansas does not include his name. He was 36 years old at this time and his wife, Ada, was 21. His birthplace was given as Maine and that of his wife as Iowa.

The *Ellis County Star* of Hays, April 6, 1876, reported that Jack had captured a deserter in Lawrence:

John Tobin was a private in "A" Company, Fifth Cavalry. Becoming tired of answering to roll-call in a time of peace, John determined upon a trip East last month, and as the boys say: "he skipped out." When he arrived at Lawrence he found Marshal Bridges in waiting for him. To make a long story short, Tobin was brought back to the Fort [probably Fort Hays] and put in irons. On Wednesday evening he managed to release himself, since which time there has been a surplus ration.

On February 16, 1877, the Hays *Sentinel* reported that "Jack Bridges was in town yesterday."

Five years later Dodge City offered Bridges the marshal's badge. The Dodge City *Times*, June 29, 1882, announced that "Jack Bridges, well-known by old timers, will receive the appointment of City Marshal of this city. He is now in Colorado, and has telegraphed Mayor Webster that he will accept the appointment, and will be in Dodge City about July 10th." Bridges was sworn in on July 8, 1882. The *Times* commented on his appointment in its issue of July 13, 1882:

Jack Bridges was installed as City Marshal on Saturday last. Marshal Bridges was for a number of years Deputy U. S. Marshal in Western Kansas. He is a cool, brave and determined officer, and will make an excellent city marshal. Jack's friends speak highly of him and of his integrity and bravery. He has done some fine service for the government, and upon every occasion acquitted himself with honor. He is a pleasant man socially, and has courage for any occasion.

At about the same time Bridges assumed the office of city marshal the police force of Dodge City doffed its frontier clothing and donned newly acquired blue uniforms. "There is a metropolitan air in their manner," said the *Times*, July 13, 1882.

Bridges' appointment caused many to reminisce about the Ledford shooting. On July 20, 1882, the *Times* brought the subject up in this article:

LEDFORD'S LEAGUE.

Early settlers remember Ledford, the chief of a gang of horse thieves, counterfeiters and desperadoes that traversed the wild regions of Kansas, the Indian Territory and the Panhandle. Jack Bridges, City Marshal of Dodge City, at that time was Deputy U. S. Marshal. He caused the breaking up and arrest of the gang, and in the capture of Ledford a desperate encounter took place. . . .

There were some, however, who felt that Dodge had made a poor choice for city marshal. One of these was the editor of the Caldwell *Commercial* who published this attack, which the *Ford County Globe* reprinted on July 25, 1882:

The Times Dodge City says that Jack Bridges has been appointed City Marshal of that town. Jack, like Wild Bill and Bat. Masterson, belongs to the killer-class and it is only a question of time when he will lay down with his boots on. Jack might have made a respectable citizen at one time, but he got to running with a psalm-singing U. S. Marshal Jim Lane and Sid Clarke, shoved off upon Kansas at one time, and learned some of the said Marshal's pious tricks. He has never been worth a straw since. Still, if the Dodge folks think they have found a treasure in Jack, it isn't for us to find fault.— Caldwell Kansas Commercial.

Yes we need him in our business [the *Globe* added].

Then the Dodge City *Times,* on July 27, joined in with a vigorous counterattack:

Caldwell, through her newspapers, is jealous of Dodge City. The latest exhibition of jealousy appears in the Caldwell Commercial, edited by W. B. Hutchison. It is a scurrilous attack on Jack Bridges, City Marshal of Dodge City. Caldwell is incapable of self-government. Three city marshals have been cowardly slain in that city. Yet Hutchison animadverts on Dodge City. A friend comes to the rescue of Bridges, and furnishes us with the following:

FOR THE TIMES:

That the venom of the reptile, the sliminess of the toad and the odoriferous qualities of the skunk cling to them till death, was never more clearly illustrated than in the case of W. B. Hutchison and his article on the City Marshal of Dodge City. We happen to know the why and wherefore of this attack on Jack Bridges; we can now look back to the year 1867-8, when the said Hutchison, a Justice of the Peace, was the recognized backer, go-between and supporter of the infamous horse thieves of Ellis county. We remember to[o], how Jack Bridges, almost single handed, drove them from the country; how Ledford, Black and Strapp, attempted to assassinate him and almost succeeded; how at last they fled from the country accompanied by their companion Mr. Hutchison. How Bridges exterminated the gang, except Mr. H., whose Uriah Heap nature and tactics shielded him from Bridges and the law, and then we do not wonder after all that Hutchison's natural traits of character assert themselves and that he makes this scurrilous attack upon him. Jack is here and should Mr. H., mourning his friends and companions, wish to interview him, he can readily find him. The old citizens of Ellis county, many of whom are here, well remember the gang, their dressing as Indians while making a dash on a herd of horses, and the fact that Hutchison was one of the boys.

LEX.

Apparently all the editors concerned felt it was time to let well-enough alone, for the matter disappeared from the pages of the press.

No matter who the marshal was, he and his officers were to operate under a new and strict set of rules adopted by Mayor A. B. Webster. The regulations would be "an additional incentive to have officers perform their duties," reported the *Globe*, June 13, 1882. "He [the mayor] insists that these rules must be observed or he will speedily remove any officer that violates them."

The Dodge City *Times* published them on June 22, 1882:

POLICE REGULATIONS

1. Each and every member of the Police force shall devote his whole time and attention to the business of the department, and is hereby prohibited from following any other calling. They must at all times be prepared to act immediately on notice that their services are required.

2. Punctual attendance and conformity to the rules of the department will be strictly enforced.

3. Each and every member must be civil, quiet and orderly; he must maintain decorum, command of temper and discretion.

4. They must not compound any offense committed or withdraw any complaint unless authorized by the Mayor.

5. All officers on duty must wear the star or shield on the outside garment on the left breast.

6. No member of the police force while on duty shall drink any intoxicating liquor or allow any to be introduced into the city jail.

7. No member shall leave the city or be absent from duty without permission from the Mayor.

8. They must not render assistance in civil cases except to prevent an immediate breach of the peace, or quell a disturbance.

9. Every member will be furnished with a copy of these regulations and is expected to familiarize himself with the same and also with the city ordinances.

10. The members of the police force will as soon as practicable after making an arrest report the same to the City Attorney and execute, under his directions, the proper papers, and promptly attend the police court at the hour set for trial of causes.

11. Every officer will be held responsible for the proper discharge of his duties; following the advice of others will be no excuse, unless he be a superior officer.

12. The City Attorney will furnish information on legal matters on any officer's request, and will be responsible to the Mayor and Council for their correctness.

13. The presence of any infectious disease must be promptly reported to the Mayor.

48

14. A memorandum of all property taken from prisoners by the marshal or police, must be handed to the City Attorney, to be by him filed with a note of final disposition in the police court.

A. B. WEBSTER, Mayor.

In September, 1882, Bridges was involved in this interesting case on which the *Globe* reported, September 12:

AN ELOPEMENT.

On last Thursday [September 7] a gentleman presented himself at the Wright House and asked for board and lodging for himself and wife; a room was assigned to him, and he left for a few minutes to bring in the woman he claimed as his wife. While he was gone Mr. [W. H.] Lybrand selected the room and noted on the register, Mr. and Mrs. _____ and noting the number of the room. When the person returned he registered after the Mr. and Mrs., 'H. G. Petty,' the couple were shown to their room and remained there until Sunday, after the arrival of the three o'clock train, which brought with it a person by the name of F. Ruble, who at once made his mission known, saying he was in search of a recreant wife who he had reason to believe had come to this city in company with some other person. He closely scrutinized the hotel registers and failed to find anyone registered in the name he was looking for, but finally on making inquiries at the Wright House concerning certain individuals he was assured by some of the employees that a couple were occupying rooms there that answered the description he gave. This afforded enough clue for him and at once ascended the stairs and proceeded to said room and knock[ed] for admission. It appears that his approach had been noticed by the occupants and the door was barred against him. The loud talk brought Mr. Lybrand to the scene, who demanded to know the cause of all this disturbance. Mr. Ruble explained and told the landlord that his wife was in the room and that he wished to see her. Mr. Lybrand informed him that he would send for the city marshal and have the whole outfit arrested. At the same time preparations were going on inside for a hasty exit through the window. Sheets and quilts were tied together and the fellow made his descent and landed safe and sound, after which he made hasty steps across the hill, hotly pursued by the city marshal [Bridges] who brought him back to the city and took him before his honor Judge Burns, before whom a complaint was made against the individual for disturbing the peace and quiet of the city.'

Court was convened (although Sunday) and all the parties were brought face to face, all being charged alike. The court was promptly opened and the charge made, and the court prefaced his remarks by saying "that on account of its being Sunday he could enter no plea from either of said parties except the plea of guilty." Mr. Petty's case being the first called he plead guilty as charged, and the court before passing sentence insisted on knowing some few facts and proceeded to examine witnesses, and finally assessed a fine of twenty-five dollars and cost against number one. This he said he would not pay, but rather than to be further annoyed paid the fine. The other two

Mr. Ruple and his supposed wife were called on to plead, both of whom answered not guilty, and their cases were continued to Monday, both being required to give bond in the sum of one hundred dollars each, which bonds we learn were readily given.

Monday morning when court opened the lone and deserted woman was the only one of the trio to make their appearance in court, who was fined fifteen dollars and cost. What became of Ruple and his case we cannot say. Petty took the first train out of town, and the only one remaining is the woman, who is still here and disclaims being the wife of either.

In the spring of 1883 Bridges was caught in the middle of the Dodge City "war." As city marshal he was directly responsible to Mayor L. E. Deger, who was one of the protagonists in the affair. Finally Bridges declared that he was "as much the marshal for one party as the other"[1] and seemingly was content to remain astride the fence. The full story of that "war," including the role of Jack Bridges, may be found in the section on Luke Short.

On July 6, 1883, the city council of Dodge City increased the marshal's salary. The *Globe*, on July 17, 1883, reported the change in this article:

The City Council on the 6th inst. passed an ordinance which gives the City Marshal a salary of $150 per month and the assistant marshal $125 per month, and on the following day they considered it a retr[o]active ordinance and instead of allowing the salaries as prescribed by the old ordinance $100 per month for marshal and $75 for the assistant marshall, they allow them each two months' increase salary as prescribed by the new ordinance.

The Nickerson *Argosy* noticed the salary hike and mentioned some fringe benefits in this item which the *Globe* copied on July 24, 1883: "Dodge City pays her marshal $150 per month and the assistant marshal $125 per month. Besides this each of them is entitled to kill a cow boy or two each season."

The Dodge City *Times*, October 4, 1883, reported that "On Monday [October 1] a lot of drunken cowboys had another hurrah at Coolidge [115 miles west, on the Colorado line], shooting through doors, windows, etc., and making things lively generally. [Under Sheriff] Fred Singer and Jack Bridges arrested one of the leaders and placed him in jail Tuesday morning."

Frontier judges could also huff and puff as this article from the *Ford County Globe*, October 23, 1883, clearly shows:

The case of the State of Kansas vs. Charley Heinz was continued on account of the absence of Jack Bridges, witness for the State, who left for Pueblo the day before the day of trial was set. The court was very indignant and ordered Marshal Bridges to be arrested and brought before His Honor if he returned before court adjourned; and if he made his appearance after court adjourned he was to be arrested and incarcerated in the jail of Ford county and held there until next term of court, and further stated that no writ of habeas corpus would let him out. He wanted it distinctly understood that there was one court in Ford county that could not be trifled with.—Bridges is back, but as yet not under arrest.—Ed.

Later.—We learn that the court revoked the order before leaving.

Apparently Marshal Bridges' salary was reduced to its former level in the fall of 1883. In reporting the November 9 meeting of the city council, the Dodge City *Times*, November 15, 1883, listed his salary as $100 per month.

No further mention of Jack Bridges was found.

1. Topeka *Daily Capital*, May 17, 1883.

BROOKS, WILLIAM L. (1849?-1874?)

Bill Brooks, recently a stage coach driver operating out of El Dorado, Butler county,[1] but marshal of Newton in 1872, was wounded by cowboys in a June melee. On June 14, 1872, the Wichita City *Eagle* reported the fracas:

Bill Brooks, marshal of Newton, formerly a stage driver between that point and Wichita, was shot three times, on Sunday night last [June 9], in an attempt to arrest a couple of Texas men. As near as we can get at the facts, the Texas men were on a spree, and, as a consequence, making it hot for pedestrians. Brooks had run them out of the town, when they turned and fired three shots into him, with what effect may be judged, from the fact that he continued his pursuit for ten miles before he returned to have his wounds dressed. One shot passed through his right breast, and the other two were in his limbs. We learn from a driver here that he will recover. Bill has sand enough to beat the hour-glass that tries to run him out.

The *Kansas Daily Commonwealth* of Topeka, June 15, 1872, said that a "party of Texans, fresh from the trail, had corralled the proprietor of a dance-house with their six-shooters, and were carrying things on a high hand, when Marshall Brooks, being sent for, endeavored to preserve the peace. While thus employed, one of the party by the name of Joe Miller, fired at him, the ball striking the collar bone, but inflicting merely a trifling wound. . . ."

Marshal Brooks' official complaint was less descriptive. Sworn to before Justice of the Peace George Halliday, the document is part of the records of the Harvey county district court:

THE STATE OF KANSAS)
Harvey County   ss   ) Before George Halliday J. P. of said County and State.

W L Brooks being first duly sworn deposes and saiz that one John Doe and one Richard Roe, whose real names to this affiant is unknown on the 10″ day of June A D 1872 at the County of Harvey and State of Kansas in and upon the body of the said W L Brook then and there being did unlawfully make an assault with a loaded pistol, and did then and there, shoot at and towards the said W. L. Brooks with intent then and there to kill the said W L Brooks.

Contrary to the form of the statute in such case made and provided, and against the peace and dignity of the State of Kansas.

W L BROOKS

In addition to Brooks' statement, E. T. "Red" Beard, later an operator of a Wichita bawdy house, complained that he too had been the intended victim of John Doe who turned out to be James Hunt. A preliminary examination was called for June 10 but the state declared itself not ready for trial so the case was postponed until 10 o'clock on the morning of June 11. Brooks asked for a change of venue, stating that he believed "that he, on behalf of the State as complainant cannot have a fair and impartial trial before the aforesaid Justice on the account of the bias and prejudice of the said Justice against said complainant." The motion was not granted, however, and the examination proceeded, with the result that Hunt was bound over to the next term of the district court. Unfortunately the outcome of that trial is not known.

From Newton, Brooks may have gone to Ellsworth. On August 7, 1872, the Ellsworth city council authorized the payment of $17.50 salary to a W. L. Brooks for services as policeman. Since no other mention was made in the city council minute book it is difficult to say whether this is the same man who had so recently been wounded in Newton.

That winter Brooks was in Dodge City where, on December 23, he shot and killed a Santa Fe railroad man. The Wichita *Eagle*, January 2, 1873, reported:

We are indebted to T. E. Clark for the particulars of a shooting affray that occurred at Dodge City on Monday night of last week, between "Bully" Brooks, ex-marshal of Newton, and Mr. Brown, yardmaster at the former place, which resulted in the death of Brown. Three shots were fired by each party. Brown's first shot wounded Brooks, whose third shot killed Brown and wounded one of his assistants. Brooks is a desperate character, and has before, in desperate encounters, killed his man.

Five days later a Dodge City saloonkeeper was shot and killed by an unknown person but the blame was placed on Brooks. The Topeka *Kansas Daily Commonwealth,* December 31, 1872, repeated the accusation:

SHOT DEAD.
ANOTHER TRAGEDY AT DODGE CITY.

Passengers who came in from "the front" yesterday, on the A. T. &. S. F. railroad, brought intelligence of another shooting affray at Dodge City.

On Saturday evening last [December 28], as Matt. Sullivan, a saloon keeper, was standing in his place of business, a gun was pointed through the window and discharged, the ball striking Sullivan and killing him almost instantly.

It is supposed that the unknown assassin was a character in those parts called Bully Brooks, but nothing definite is known concerning the affair, or what led to it.

Henry H. Raymond, a buffalo hunter out of Dodge in 1873, mentioned in his diary (a copy of which is on file in the manuscript division of the Kansas State Historical Society) that on March 4 Brooks had been shot at but escaped unwounded. He wrote:

[Tuesday, March 4th, 1873.] beautiful day. down in town. Bill brooks got shot at with needle gun, the ball passing through two barrels of watter, lodging in outside Iron hoop. Jerdon shot at him.

The next day Raymond wrote that he "Saw Brooks and Jerden [*sic*] compromise today. . . ."

News of the affair must have drifted east to Wichita, for this note appeared in the *Eagle,* March 20, 1873: "Billy Brooks, the whilom Wichita stage driver, is not dead, as was reported, but is on duty in Dodge City."

In late July, 1874, a W. L. Brooks was captured as one of a gang of mule thieves in Sumner county. Possibly this was the Brooks of Newton, Ellsworth and Dodge history. Although no contemporary newspapers thus far located connected the Sumner county horse thief with the ex-marshal of Newton, the story of the capture and of Brooks' death at the hands of vigilantes, from the *Sumner County Press,* Wellington, July 30, 1874, is included here nevertheless:

53

ARREST OF SUSPECTED HORSE THIEVES.

Scarcely had Sheriff [John G.] Davis time to refresh himself after the arduous campaign from which he returned last Sunday [July 26, in pursuit of other horse thieves], before he was ordered to proceed to Caldwell, and take into custody several parties who were charged in an information on file in Justice Dillar's court, with being connected with an organized gang of horse thieves, and also with being principals and accessories, in the wholesale theft of Vail & Co.'s mules. Some of the parties for whom warrants had been issued were known to be desperate characters, who were constantly on the look out, and who were always well armed. Understanding this fact, the Sheriff summoned to his assistance several of the citizens of Wellington with whom he left for Caldwell last Monday afternoon. Arriving in the vicinity of Caldwell, in the evening a scout who had been sent out in advance reported that the parties named in the warrant were armed and evidently preparing for a desperate resistance.— Concealing his presence the Sheriff waited for reinforcements, which soon began to arrive from all quarters until at two o'clock A. M., he entered the village with one hundred and fifty men. Disposing this force so as to prevent the escape of any of the parties, he began the search that ended in the arrest of L. B. Hasbrouck, A. C. McLean, William Brooks, Dave Terrill and Judd Calkins, all citizens and residents of Caldwell and vicinity. McLean was taken at his residence one mile south of Caldwell, Hasbrouck was captured in a corn field, Terrill was tracked to a dug-out three miles away, Calkins surrendered quietly and Bill Brooks, after several hours siege, came out of his fortification and delivered his arms to the sheriff. Two other men who were in company with Brooks, and who threatened resistance, were captured and disarmed, but afterward released. Charley Smith had lit out for the Territory before the arrival of the sheriff; but a party of fifteen men rode twenty-five miles into the Nation, picked him up and brought him into this city Tuesday evening. The sheriff returned with his prisoners about 3 o'clock Tuesday afternoon.

After a preliminary examination before J[ames]. A. Dillar, the same afternoon, Dave Terrill was discharged, there being no charge against him; and Judd Calkins was admitted to bail in the sum of five hundred dollars for his appearance yesterday morning. The other prisoners, Hasbrouck and Brooks, were placed in the calaboose, where Smith was also confined on his arrival. McLean was kept under guard during the night. Considerable excitement prevailed, and grave fears that an attempt would be made to lynch the prisoners, was entertained by not a few. These fears were shared by the prisoners, to their evident discomfort. The night however passed away quietly, and citizens, and country people retired to their homes, apparently satisfied that the law would be vindicated and justice meted out. Yesterday morning County Attorney [Charles] Willsie arrived, and having associated Judge John G. Woods with himself as prosecutor, the preliminary examination of all the prisoners was deferred till to-morrow at 10 o'clock, A. M. In the mean time, warrants had been issued for the reapprehension of Terrill and Calkins, who were yet supposed to be in town. Inquiry however developed the fact that they had flitted. Supposing they had left on the stage, Deputy Sheriff Riley and Doc. Culbertson started in pursuit, only to ascertain that they had chosen other means of locomotion. It afterward transpired that they had hired a livery team and left in the direction of Wichita, and two separate parties were dispatched to overhaul and bring them back. At this writing they have not reported. The other prisoners are still confined in the calaboose, which is securely guarded by armed men. Attorneys Willsie and Woods are actively engaged in preparing for the preliminary examination on the part of the State. What the testimony will be we are not prepared nor at liberty to state; but our readers may be prepared for startling disclosures, and the presentation of an array of evidence that will prove the existence of an organized band of horse thieves extending all along the border. *The end is not yet.*

This last sentence was prophetic, for after the type for the article had been set an angry mob raided the jail, dragged off the prisoners and hanged them. The same issue, July 30, 1874, carried this report of the lynching:

DEAD! DEAD!! DEAD!!!

THE VIGILANTS AT WORK.

THREE MEN HANGED BY THE NECK UNTIL THEY ARE DEAD.

A FEARFUL RETRIBUTION.

THE BEGINNING OF THE END.

Last night about 12 o'clock the calaboose in this city, in which the prisoners elsewhere spoken of were confined, was surrounded by a large party of armed and mounted men, who, after they had overpowered and disarmed the guards, took therefrom L. B. Hasbrouck, W. L. Brooks and Charley Smith, with whom they at once proceeded in the direction of Slate creek bridge. This morning the lifeless bodies of the three ill-fated men are dangling from the same tree. With others of our citizens we, early this morning, visited the spot and looked for a moment upon the ghastly spectacle. The bodies were hanging facing the south. Hasbrouck was on the left, Brooks in the center and Smith to the right and nearest to the tree. The distorted features of Brooks gave evidence of a horrible struggle with death. The other men looked naturally, and evidently died easily. A coroner's jury has been empanneled, and, as we go to press, an inquest is being held. Brooks' wife is in town, having arrived from Caldwell yesterday. Hasbrouck was a member of the Sumner county bar, and unmarried. Smith (an alias) has but one arm, and is believed to be a son of Ex-Governor Edwards, of Illinois.

At the Caldwell examination of A. C. McLean, August 5, the testimony of Burr Mosier depicted the part played by Bill Brooks.

The *Sumner County Press,* August 6, 1874, gave the testimony:

TRUTH STRANGER THAN FICTION.

STARTLING DISCLOSURES.

A BROTHERHOOD OF THIEVES.

THE SOUTH WESTERN STAGE COMPANY IMPLICATED.

A BAND OF ROBBERS HIRED TO SUPPRESS THE TRANSMISSION OF THE U. S. MAIL.

THE EXAMINATION OF A. C. McLEAN.

The examination of A. C. McLean, charged with being implicated in the theft of Vail & Co.'s mules, at Caldwell, on the night of the 29th of June, was commenced in Justice Dillar's court, at 10 o'clock A. M. yesterday. There being no lawyers present to badger witnesses, a mass of testimony in regard to the recent operations of horse thieves on the border was elicited, throwing a flood of light upon events that heretofore have appeared dark and mysterious. . . .

Burr Mosier sworn: I reside at Buffalo Springs in the Indian Territory. Have resided there since October, 1873. Kept a ranche. I have known the defendant A. C. McLean about thirteen years. He has resided during the past year one mile below Caldwell near Bluff creek. He has been engaged in keeping a ranche during that time, and farming on a small scale. About the first of July, Jasper Marion, alias Granger, came to my ranche for grub. While there he told me he had eight mules belonging to Vail & Co.; besides these he had a horse of his own and a mare that he said they had stolen through mistake. The mare belonged to A. E. Fletcher. He also told me the number and names of the men engaged in the theft of the mules at Caldwell on the night of the 29th of June. He said there were nine men engaged in it. The names of the parties as far as I recollect are, Hasbrouck, Charley Smith, Henry Hall, "Red," "Bob," "Jim," Jerry Williams, Jasper Marion alias Granger, and Bill Brooks. "Red," "Bob," and "Jim" were aliases; I do not know their real names. Granger told me that the mules were stolen at Caldwell and Skeleton Creek and that they were concealed about five miles from my ranche on Turkey creek. Five or six days afterward I saw the mules and horses, ten in number.

When I first saw the stock it was in charge of Brooks and Granger. Granger told me that he was assisted in bringing the mules down by all the rest of the party. Granger also told me that they were going down to Kingfisher, to clean out the station (steal the mules) belonging to Vail and Co.; and that Charley Smith had been sent to Stinking creek to steal the stock there. The party that went to Kingfisher, failed to get the mules there, because they were too well guarded by Al. Needham and two men who were armed with needle guns. As they were returning from Kingfisher, they were attacked by Indians, and Bill Watkins, who had gone down to help steal the mules, was killed and scalped, and Granger's horse was shot. Bradbury, who kept the station for the Southwestern Stage Company at Stinking Creek, was to help Smith steal Vail & Co.'s stock at that place. Bradbury formerly lived near Caldwell.

About the day before the Indians attacked and killed Pat Hennessey, two of Vail & Co.'s drivers came to my ranche with the U. S. mail. They had a sulky and one horse. After they had passed a few hours the S. W. Stage came in. William Brandon was driving. Bill Brooks was on the stage. He (Brooks) told me that he intended to overtake and steal the horse belonging to Vail & Co., that had passed down the road. Brandon and Brooks were both afraid of an attack by the Indians; so I armed myself and drove the stage down to Baker's, twelve miles below. Brooks told me that they, (the horse thieves) had taken the contract to run [ruin?] that mail line and that they intended to do it.

He said that they were employed by the South Western Stage Company to prevent Vail & Co. from fulfilling their mail contract, at all hazards; that they were to steal their stock and prevent, by any means, the transmission of the mails on the route from Caldwell to Fort Sill. That they (Brooks & Co.) were paid six hundred dollars by the South Western Stage Company for clearing the road, *i. e.* stealing the stock and stopping the mails, the first time. I was also told by Brooks and others to charge up their board to the S. W. Stage Co., as that company was to pay all expenses of the raid. . . .

The alleged fight for supremacy between the two stage companies deserves further research, but since this Bill Brooks was hanged and his connection with the affair terminated, this story must also swing to a close.

1. United States census, 1870, El Dorado township, Butler county, Kansas, p. 9, line 34.

BROWN, GEORGE S. (1854?-1882)

The Caldwell *Commercial* of November 3, 1881, reported that George Brown, as well as Mike Meagher and Dan Jones, had been offered the position of Caldwell city marshal. Each declined so John Wilson was finally appointed.

Mike Meagher was killed on December 17, 1881. At the coroner's inquest George Brown was one of the witnesses. The proceedings of this inquest, which the Caldwell *Post* reported on December 22, will be found in the section on Meagher.

By March, 1882, Brown apparently had accepted the marshalship of Caldwell. The *Commercial* on March 9, 1882, stated that "Since Geo. Brown has been acting as City Marshall, $216 in cash have been collected for fines by the Police Court."

According to the Caldwell police docket, which for 1882 begins with April, Marshal Brown performed his duties chiefly in connection with drunks, gamblers, madams, and prostitutes. In his brief tour of duty no record was found that he encountered more serious criminals until he was shot and killed by cowboys on June 22. The Caldwell *Commercial* of June 29 carried the details:

ANOTHER MURDER IN CALDWELL.
THE CITY MARSHAL SHOT DOWN IN COLD BLOOD.
ESCAPE OF THE ASSASSIN.

About half past nine o'clock on Thursday morning of last week, the city was alarmed by the report that Geo. Brown, our city Marshal had been shot dead at the Red Light. Proceeding up street, we learned that the killing had occurred but a few moments before and that the parties engaged in it had barely rode past the COMMERCIAL office which is located on the lower part of Main street, on their way to the Territory, the refuge for every fiend who perpetrates a crime upon the southern border of Kansas.

On going to the Red Light, we found the body of George Brown at the head of the stairs, his face covered with a clot of blood and his brains spattered on the wall and floor of the building, while the gore dripped through the floor to the rooms below. Dr. Hume had been called in and was engaged in washing off the blood in order to ascertain the nature of the wound which had caused Brown's death.

It is useless to give the various stories told as to how the murder occurred, and we shall only state the facts as made up from the statements of different parties.

Shortly after 8 o'clock in the morning, three men, two of them brothers going by the name of Steve and Jess. Green, and another whose name has not been ascertained so far, went to the Red Light. Brown at the time was on Main street, engaged in obtaining signatures to a couple of petitions in reference to voting bonds. Some one informed him (as near as can be ascertained) that a man had gone down there armed, and Brown requested Constable [Willis] Metcalf to go down with him, as he (Brown) did not want to go alone. Arriving at the Red Light Brown and Metcalf proceeded up stairs, the former in the lead. On reaching the top of the stairs they found three men, one of whom had a pistol in his hand. Brown laid his hand on the man with the pistol and told him to give it up. The latter replied "let go of me," when Brown grasped hold of the fellow's arm and pressed it against the wall. Meantime another man grasped Metcalf by the throat and backed him up into the corner, at the same time telling him to hold up his hands, the order being enforced by another who held a pistol at his head.

Just then another man jumped out of a room across the stairway and to the right of where Brown and the man he was holding stood, and called out "Turn him loose." This seems to have attracted Brown's attention momentarily, but that moment was most fatal to him, for the man whom he held turned his wrist and fired, the ball from the weapon crashing through the Marshal's head, and he fell to the floor dead, without a struggle or a groan.

The man who shot Brown and the other who held Metcalf then ran down stairs, while the fellow who had drawn on Metcalf guarded the retreat. The two former proceeded on up Fifth street to the alley in the rear of the Opera House, followed the alley to a passage between the buildings fronting on Main street, went through the passage, down Main street to the front of the Hardesty corner, where they mounted their horses and rode on down the street toward the Territory.

Fully ten minutes transpired before it was known that Brown had been shot, but as soon as the fact was ascertained and that his murderer had escaped, several citizens mounted their horses and started in pursuit.

It is needless to detail the operations of the pursuing parties. Suffice it to say that J. W. Dobson, who was among them ascertained that on reaching Bluff creek the murderers turned down the stream, crossed over Wm. Morris' farm, thence north across the creek and through E. H. Beal's place thence down the line to a point east of Cozad's place, where they turned into the bottoms of Bluff creek and probably remained there until towards evening.

When the pursuing party started out nothing was known or could be ascertained as to who the two men were, or whose herd they belonged to, although, as subsequent investigation showed, one or more persons knew all about them, but refused to give any information, fearing, perhaps, they might loose six bits worth of trade if they "gave away" a cowboy, no matter what crime he might commit. But it was learned before noon that the men belonged to Ellison's outfit, camped on Deer creek, and that of the others who were with them at the time of the murder, one was McGee, the boss of the herd, and the other two were herders. No effort seems to have been made to take in the Greens in case they went to camp, which they did about 6 o'clock, obtained fresh horses and ammunition, and then started off in a southeasterly direction. Up to the present writing the men have not been captured, and if any efforts have been put forth in that direction, the fact is kept a profound secret.

Geo. Brown, the murdered officer, was a young man about 28 years of age. He has resided in this city about two years, and has borne a good character. There was nothing of the bully or the braggart about him, but in the discharge of his duties he was quiet and courageous. It is not known that he had an enemy, therefore his murder would seem to be an act of pure fiendishness, perpetrated solely from a desire to take human life.

Of the Greens, Steve and Jess., we are informed that they are brothers, French Canadians by birth, and came originally from the vicinity of Collingwood, Ontario. They have been employed as herders for several years, and have visited Caldwell every season for the last three years. McGee, Ellison's foreman, says they came to the herd, and were employed by him, on the trail south of Red River; that they were desperate men, who did not seem to care for danger, but rather coveted it, but that they were good hands, doing their work faithfully and well. It is probable that they are outlaws, all the time fearing arrest, and constantly on the alert to prevent being taken alive. If not taken or killed for their last crime, it is only a question of time when they will yield up their lives in much the same manner in which they have taken the lives of others besides George Brown.

George Brown was a single man, resided on Fifth street, east of Main, his sister, Miss Fannie Brown, keeping house for him. When the terrible news was brought to her that her brother, her supporter and protector, had been cruelly shot down within a stone throw of his own door, the poor girl could not realize it at first, but when the truth forced itself upon her mind, she gave way to the most heart rending screams. Kind and sympathetic friends did everything in their power to solace her, but notwithstanding all their efforts it was feared at one time that she would not be able to survive the terrible blow. But nature, ever kind, came to her relief, and by Friday the intensity of her grief had given way to a calm resignation. Word was telegraphed to their father at Junction City, but owing to railroad connections he did not arrive until Saturday. George was buried on Friday afternoon, the funeral being largely attended by our citizens. All the business houses in the city closing out of respect for the deceased during the funeral.

A coroner's jury was summoned by J. D. Kelly, Esq., and an inquest began on Thursday afternoon. The inquest was not concluded until Monday afternoon, when a verdict was rendered that the deceased came to his death from a gun shot wound at the hands of J. D. Green.

DESCRIPTION OF THE GREENS.

J. D. or Jess Green as he is called, is a man about five feet ten inches in height, strong built, weighed about 180 pounds; full, broad face, dark complexion; hair black, coarse and straight, mustache and imperial colored black, but naturally of a sunburnt color. Had on dark clothes, leggings, and new white felt hat with a leather band around the crown.

Steve Green is about five feet six or eight inches high, heavy built, coarse black hair, mustache and imperial dyed, broad face, very dark; dressed about the same as his brother, save that his hat was not new. As stated above, the men are brothers, and from their appearance would be taken for Mexicans. When last heard from they were traveling west, evidently intending to make for New Mexico.

Shortly after Brown's death the sheriff of Sumner county, in which Caldwell is situated, wrote the governor of Kansas and asked that he offer a reward for the capture of the Greens.

Office of
J. M. Thralls
Sheriff Sumner County.

WELLINGTON, KAN., June 1882

GOVERNOR J. P. ST. JOHN
DEAR SIR—

On the 22" day of March [June] 1882 the City Marshal at Caldwell George Brown was killed— by one of two men giving their names as Jeff and Steve Green "Cow boys" The circumstances are about these— Brown went up to one

60

of them & asked him for his revolver he said he did not have any— When Brown and an assistant took hold of him he jerked loose and shot Brown through the head killing him instantly— Now are you not authorized to offer a reward of $500 apiece for their arrest and delivery to the Sheriff of Sumner Co We are having so much of this kind of work it does seem as tho the State should offer a good reward for some of these "Texas killers" and outlaws— This is the fourth murder within the last year at Caldwell and Hunnewell and no reward offered by State for any of them—

Yours truly J M THRALLS
Sheriff
Please answer [1]

Within days Gov. John P. St. John responded with this proclamation:

GOVERNOR'S PROCLAMATION.
$1000 REWARD!

STATE OF KANSAS,
EXECUTIVE DEPARTMENT, TOPEKA, July 6, 1882

WHEREAS, "JEFF. GREEN AND STEVE. GREEN" stand charged with the murder of George Brown, City Marshal of the City of Caldwell, in Sumner County, Kansas, on or about the 22nd day of March [June], 1882, and are now at large and fugitives from justice:

Now THEREFORE, I, JOHN P. ST. JOHN, Governor of the State of Kansas, by virtue of the authority vested in me by law, do hereby offer a reward of FIVE HUNDRED DOLLARS each, for the arrest and conviction of the said Jeff. Green and Steve. Green of the crime above stated.

In Testimony Whereof, I have hereunto subscribed my name, and [L. S.] affixed the Great Seal of the State, at Topeka, the day and year first above written.

JOHN P. ST. JOHN.

By the Governor:
JAMES SMITH,
   Secretary of State.[2]

The shooting of George Brown prompted at least one out of town newspaper to censure Caldwell's city officers. Wellington's *Sumner County Press*, June 29, 1882, claimed that all of Caldwell's troubles were caused by men who had been "fired to evil by bad whiskey and prostitute women, both of which were placed within their reach only by means of flagrant violations of the laws of the state, through and by the sanction of the city governments of Caldwell and Hunnewell. . . ."

These charges were not taken lightly by the Caldwell *Post* which answered in its issue of July 6, 1882:

WHISKY, PROSTITUTES, MURDER.

Under the above caption the Sumner County *Press*, of last week, proceeds to read the citizens of Sumner county, and officers of Caldwell and Hunnewell a lecture on morality and immorality. The editor states what he is pleased to call facts, what in reality is a string of falsehoods or mistakes. In the first place, he says there has been forty murders committed in Sumner county in the last ten years, all traceable to whisky and lewd women, and that only three of the murderers have been brought to justice, namely, Jackson, Chastain and Carter.

In the three cases above, the city of Caldwell had nothing whatever, to do. Jackson killed his man for money—was tried, convicted and allowed by his guards to escape them while they were playing cards. The guards were leading citizens of Wellington, and were not drinking whisky at the time.

If we remember right, the citizens of Wellington murdered three or four men in an early day, that was not decidedly traceable to mean whisky. A murder was committed in London township, and the murderer was tried and not convicted. The murder was not committed while either of the men was under the influence of whisky nor prostitutes.

The murder of two men in the early days of Caldwell was not traceable to either whisky or prostitution. One was hanged by the citizens for his cursedness, and the other was committed by an outlaw just for the fun of the thing, who was chased by the citizens and killed.

George Flat was killed to satisfy a grudge. Frank Hunt was killed for the same reason and not on account of either women or whisky.

George Spear was shot by citizens or officers while assisting the Talbot gang to escape.

Talbot shot Mike Meagher in a riot, not caused by whisky or women, but from a supposed insult. He was an outlaw, and the officers nor citizens were not responsible for his actions no more than the city of Wellington. He was killed in Texas about two weeks ago.

George Brown was shot in the discharge of his duties. The men who did the killing were not under the influence of whisky or lewd women. One of them had taken two drinks and the other had not taken any. They were outlaws and would have made the same play had they been anywhere else in the State. They would give up their arms only after they were past using them.

The *Press'* fine-spun theory in the above named cases is decidedly at variation with the truth.

George Woods was killed by a man who had not touched whisky in two years, and was the outgrowth of a feud and supposed insult, but was, we are willing to admit, brought about through prostitutes.

Rare cussedness has been the cause of nine-tenths of the murders committed in the county, and not whisky and public sentiment, as the *Press* would have one believe. The city authorities are no more responsible for the murders that are committed in Caldwell, than is the President of the United States, and it is a base slander for any one to make such a statement.

Sheriff Joseph Thralls, who was instrumental in having a state reward offered for Jesse and Steve Green, added $400 to the amount, according to the *Commercial* of July 13, 1882.

Out-of-town newspapers were still taking pot shots at Caldwell in November. Again the *Post* defended the town's honor in its issue of November 9, 1882:

GIVE THE DEVIL HIS DUES.

The cowboys have removed five city marshals of Caldwell in five years.— *Dodge City Times.*

We most emphatically deny the charge made by the *Times* that the cowboys removed five city marshals. The fact is, the cowboys have "removed" but one city marshal, and that one was George Brown. His murd[er]ers were escaped convicts from the Texas penitentiary, and were only making the profession of herding cattle a cover to their outlawry and cattle and horse-stealing operations. Jim Talbot killed Mike Meagher, assisted by cowboys, some of them being in a row of that class for the first time. Mr. Meagher was not a city marshal at the time of his death, nor was his murderer a cowboy at that time. The other marshals spoken of by the *Times* were not killed by cowboys, but by male prostitutes, to put it mildly.

It looks to us as though the charge contained in the item quoted from the *Times* comes with very bad grace from a man whose entire support—bread and butter, as it were—comes from men whose chief patrons are cowmen. The cowboys of our acquaintance are not the class of men that commit murders and raise riots simply because they can. They are, as a majority, well-educated, peaceable and gentlemanly fellows. The day of the wild and woolly cowboy is past, in this section, at least, if it is not in such ungodly towns as Dodge City. If the Dodge City editors would visit us once, and see what kind of people live here, we think they would not be so rash in their assertions.

The Caldwell *Post* meanwhile reported the capture of the Greens on October 19, 1882, and in the next issue, October 26, recounted the complete story:

MORE ABOUT THE GREENS.

Last week we gave a meagre account of the capture of the Green boys in Wise county, Texas, and as our information was entirely gained from telegrams, it was necessarily limited; but this week we are enabled to give the story as related to us by Mr. Frank Evans, who was sent to Texas to identify the boys and bring them to this county for trial. Mr. Evans' story is about as follows:

The parents of the Green boys moved from Smith county over into Wise county lately to a place the boys had purchased for them, and were living in a camp near the farm, until they could fix their place up. They were known in Wise county as Mr. and Mrs. Been, and the boys were known as

Ed and Jim Been. Previous to leaving Smith county the boys resisted and shot a deputy marshal, and there was a reward offered for them in that county.

A few days before the capture of the boys a Mr. Boon had his cow killed by some one, and the trail was followed to the camp of the Green boys, which had then been vacated by them. A constable and posse followed the trail made by them in leaving the camp, until they discovered the horses of the outlaws in a pasture, staked out, the fence being still down. The constable arranged his men on either side of the gap, and lay down in it himself. After waiting something over an hour, Jim was seen approaching the gap, walking along leisurely, with a six-shooter belt hanging over his shoulder. The constable allowed him to approach within ten steps of him, when he raised up with his shot gun, covered his man and commanded him to throw up his hands and surrender. Jim raised his hand, level with his shoulders, and quick as thought pulled his six-shooter and fired on the constable, the ball grazing his temples and knocking him out of time. Green then turned and started to run, but the constable soon came to, and was up and after him, but forgot his shot gun. The constable's posse rose and began firing at Jim, and after a chase of a hundred yards succeed[ed] in putting a ball into his back. The constable had emptied his six-shooter after Jim, and just as Jim fell his brother Ed came in sight carrying two shot guns and a Winchester. The constable skipped back to his friends. The Green boys got away, and the posse would not follow the constable.

This happened on Tuesday, and the outlaws traveled some eight or ten miles in short journeys, as Jim could stand, and got back near the camp of the elder Greens. A young chap who appeared to be acquainted with nearly all the business men of Caldwell, and who lives in that county, was put upon the trail of the boys, and for two days and nights he slid around among the brush and gullies, until his search was rewarded by discovering a camp fire along about one o'clock in the morning. He crawled up to within some 25 steps of it, and discovered the Green boys sitting near it. Jim, having become cold and chilly, and his wounds being so painful, was obliged to have a fire; and that fire gave them away.

The boy slid out and notified the constable who had been after the boys previously. He gathered up a party of men armed with shot guns and Winchesters, and surrounded the camp. The party crawled up to within thirty steps of the camp, and stationed themselves behind trees, etc., when the constable stepped out in plain view of the camp, covered the reclining forms of the Greens with his shot gun and called upon them to surrender, and told them they should not be hurt. There being no answer he called a second time. Still no answer; but he could see movements under the blankets. He called a third time, and just as the words were spoken, both the Greens bounded to their feet and turned loose a pair of shot guns toward the spot where they thought the constable was, but failed to hit any one. The constable at once said "Turn her loose, boys," and a perfect storm of bullets rained upon the outlaws.

Ed fell dead instantly, with two bullet holes through his head obliquely, one from his right cheek, coming out back of his left ear, and the other from his left cheek thro' behind his right ear. Jim fell and remained unconscious for several hours. His wounds consisted in fourteen bullet holes in his body, made by thirteen balls, one passing through his leg. A Winchester ball struck him in the back to the right of the spinal column, and lodged near the skin under his right arm. Another Winchester ball cut the extreme point of his chin, thence to his collar bone, and lodged under his left shoulder blade. One ball struck just to the left of the center of the forehead, entering the skin and flattening against the skull bone. This ball is supposed to have knocked him out of time. He has several bullet holes in his breast, scattered around promiscuously, and in various other parts of his body.

Mr. Evans left Decature on Wednesday morning of last week with Jim, and arrived in Wellington Saturday night with his man, who is reposing in the county jail. We called upon him Tuesday evening, and found him lying on a mattress on the floor of his cell, with his pillow under his shoulder to protect his wounds from coming in contact with the bed clothes. His wounds were ghastly things, but he would not have any of them bound up. Said they hurt him worse. He certainly has more nerve than any one we ever saw, and while talking with us his voice was strong, full and without a quaver, and if his wounds do not heal up too suddenly, he will probably live long enough to be hanged in good shape.

NOTES.

Ed and Jim Green were escaped convicts from the Texas penitentiary, they having been sent there for stealing cattle. A reward of $250 is offered for their return.

They shot a deputy U. S. Marshal in Smith county Texas, whereupon a reward of $250 was offered for them.

Jim says they got into a row in the Territory and killed three men before they got away. Ed had his six-shooter shot out of his hand while engaged in the row.

We felt three balls under Jim's skin that he said he got about 18 months ago in a fracas.

Jim told Capt. Smith, a prominent man in Wise county, Texas, when he became conscious, that there was a reward offered for both of the boys at Caldwell, Kansas, and for him to ship the bodies up here and get the money. He said it was for $400 each, but we presume he knew nothing of the State reward of $1,000.

Jim related the entire story of the killing of Brown, their escape and the reason they killed him.

Green died November 5. Sheriff J. M. Thralls notified the governor and asked how to obtain the reward for the correct persons:
Office of
J. M. Thralls
Sheriff Sumner County.

WELLINGTON, KAN., Nov 7" 1882

GOVERNOR J. P. ST. JOHN
DEAR SIR:

You doubtless remember having offered a reward about July 1st for the arrest and conviction of the murderers of City Marshal George Brown of Caldwell— I had issued cards describing them as minutely as possible and sent them to *every* P. O. in the I. T.— N. M.— Colorado— and the western half of Texas— besides getting them into the hands of all Officers possible— The result was the Officials of Wise County Texas— got after them had a fight with them— on Monday Oct 9"/82 when they whiped the constables' posse— and escaped with one of them carrying a Winchester ball in his right side— which disabled him from traveling much. They were again overtaken on the following Wednesday morning— When asked to surrender they replied with a Shot gun and Revolver— The posse replied killing one instantly— and hitting the other 12 times— 2 Winchester balls and 10 Buck Shot— entered his body— but did not disable him so badly but what we could bring him to this County. his right side was paralyzed so he could not handle himself— We have had him in our Jail since— until today— last Saturday he was taken suddenly ill and became unconscious all at once and died Sunday morning— The Post mortem examination showed that one Buck Shot, of small size, entered his forehead— and passed through the lower part of his brain— and stoped near the back part of head— Then had puss formed along the course of the ball— which caused his death. That ends the course of the two murderers of George Brown— Now what is necessary for us to do to get the State reward— which goes to their captors in Texas— We can give you several affidavits of his own admission to killing Brown The one that died in our Jail is the one who fired the fatal shot while the other, his bro— was present and assisted by keeping off Brown's Deputy— and came near shooting him— He told the boys in Jail (5 of them) the circumstance of their flight after the murder—

If you will indicate in what way we can get the State reward— I think we can fully satisfy you as to their identity and guilt— If you will appoint some attorney— in this section of the country we will furnish him the witnesses— as to Identity and guilt, or any attorney from any where so it is not too Expensive to us— We are asking this for the Texas Officers who have done good work in the case— And what was dangerous work, in good faith, and at some expense, now I would like to see them rewarded to make our part of the contract good

Hoping to hear from you soon I remain   Yours Respectfully,
J. M. THRALLS.[3]

1. "Governors' Correspondence," archives division, Kansas State Historical Society. 2. *Ibid.* 3. *Ibid.*

BROWN, HENRY NEWTON (1857-1884)

Shortly after the murder of Caldwell City Marshal George Brown, on June 22, 1882, the city council appointed B. P. "Bat" Carr as his replacement with Henry N. Brown as Carr's assistant. The Caldwell *Commercial* voiced its approval of the appointments in this article, July 6, 1882:

The City Council on Monday night appointed Henry Brown, formerly marshal of Tuscosa, Texas, Assistant City Marshal. Mr. Brown is a young man who bears an excellent reputation, and although he has acted in similar capacities for several years, has never acquired any of those habits which some seem to think are absolutely necessary to make an officer popular with the "boys." With Mr. Carr for Marshal, and Henry Brown for assistant, we think the city has at last secured the right kind of a police force. Carr is a quiet unassuming man, but there is that look about him which at once impresses a person with the idea that he will do his whole duty fearlessly and in the best manner possible. We have not the least doubt but he will give entire satisfaction, and it is now the duty of every citizen to see that he is promptly and efficiently sustained in his efforts to preserve the peace of the city and the safety of its inhabitants.

Henry Brown

The Caldwell *Post*, July 6, 1882, called upon the city to back its new officers for better law enforcement:

Messrs. B. P. Carr and Henry Brown are on the police force of our city now as Marshal and Assistant Marshal. These gentlemen will do their utmost to see that order is kept, and the peace of the city preserved, if a little bit of fine shooting has to be indulged in by them. If our citizens will back the officers, there will be a great deal less trouble with the lawless classes than there has been heretofore.

We have a new Assistant Marshal on the police force now—Mr. Henry Brown—and it is said that he is one of the quickest men on the trigger in the Southwest.

In August, 1882, Brown assisted Marshal Carr in preventing a fist fight which had certain religious connotations. The newspaper item reporting this may be found in the section on B. P. Carr.

About the middle of September, 1882, Henry Brown resigned as assistant marshal in order to accompany Sheriff J. M. Thralls' posse into the Indian territory after the killers of Mike Meagher.[1] The expedition, however, was a failure. The Caldwell *Commercial*, October 12, 1882, recorded the posse's adventures:

AFTER THE TALBOTT GANG
A HUNT OF TWO WEEKS AND NO CAPTURE.

About the 14th or 15th of last month information was received from below that the Talbott gang, or part of them, was located in the southwest part of the Indian Ter., and had with them a lot of stolen horses and cattle. The information came from a reliable source, and acting upon it, Sheriff Thralls organized a party to hunt up and if possible capture the gang.

The sheriff and his men left on the 19th of September, returned last Thursday the 5th inst., having been gone seventeen days. From Henry Brown, Assistant Marshal of this city, who accompanied the expedition, we learn that the party went from here to the Cheyenne and Arapahoe agency, and after consulting with Agent Miles a detachment of troops was secured to accompany Sheriff Thrall's party, and if need be assist in the capture of the outlaws.

It was also learned at the agency that Dug. Hill and Bob Munsing were among the outlaws, the former going by the name of Bob Johnson and the latter by the name of Slocum; also that Dug Hill had been connected with and employed in the camp of a man named Kooch, holding cattle on Quartermaster creek, ever since the 27th of last July.

Thrall's party traveled about one hundred miles southwest of Cantonment, to Seger's cattle camp, where they halted and Seger went over to Kooch's camp, about twenty miles distant, to ascertain the exact whereabouts of Hill and Munsing. Brown says it took Seger two days and one night to travel the forty miles, and when he returned he stated that from the description given of Dug Hill, the man at Kooch's camp going by the name of Bob Johnson, could not be Dug. However, the sheriff's party proceeded to Kooch's camp, and on arriving there found that "Bob Johnson" was gone, and that "Mr. Slocum" had cut his foot and gone to Cantonment to get some medicine for it.

The Thrall's party then followed Quartermaster creek to where it empties in the Washita and not obtaining any trace of the fugitives, came on home.

Mr. Brown also informs us that in addition to the camp of Seger and Kooch, the Standard Cattle Co., Ben Clark, Henry Street, and others are holding cattle in that section of the Territory. The country is supposed to be a part of the Kiowa and Comanche reservation, but whether that is the fact we are unable to say.

Having returned to Caldwell Brown was reappointed assistant marshal. The Caldwell *Post*, October 12, 1882, announced his re-employment.

Henry Brown is again on the police force, after a two-weeks' lay-off. Henry has been down in the Wichita mountains on the lookout for "rustlers," but the birds had been notified of his coming, and had flown. There must be an underground railway connected with these cattle thieves' camps and the border towns, or they could be taken in with less trouble.

Shortly after Brown's return, Marshal Carr took a leave of absence and the assistant marshal assumed the duties of acting city marshal. The Caldwell *Commercial*, October 19, 1882, reported:

Henry Brown is acting as City Marshal during the absence of Bat Carr, with Ben Wheeler as assistant. Henry is all business, yet withal quiet and obstrusive, and will do his full duty in preserving the peace of the city. Of this fact he has given ample evidence in his former position as assistant City Marshal.

On November 2, 1882, the *Commercial* reported that:

Henry Brown, acting city marshal, received a letter on Tuesday from Ben Franklin, Will Quinlin's foreman, notifying him that he had the horse and saddle stolen from Jim Sibbets on Sunday night, October 22. The horse was taken while Jim was in church. No particulars were given by Mr. Franklin as to how the horse came into his possession.

Bat Carr returned to his Caldwell position on November 2, 1882,[2] and Brown resumed his job as assistant.

On December 28, 1882, it was announced in both the *Post* and the *Commercial* that Henry Brown had been appointed city marshal. Said the *Post*:

The City Council appointed Henry Brown as city marshal Thursday evening last [December 21]. Henry has been assistant marshal for some time past, and is now promoted to the chiefship. Mr. B. is a good one, and will have the moral as well as physical support of our citizens in running the city as it should be.

The *Commercial* reported Brown's appointment as effective Friday rather than on Thursday as stated by the *Post*.

In the same issue of December 28, the *Commercial* noticed that "Henry Brown was the recipient of two very useful presents—that is they may be in the near future, if things turn out satisfactorily to all parties concerned—given him by some unknown friend on the Methodist Christmas tree, being a rattle box and a tin horn."

On New Year's Day the citizens of Caldwell presented Brown with a fine rifle. The Caldwell *Post* recorded the event on January 4, 1883:

A HANDSOME PRESENT.

A few of the citizens of this city, appreciating the valuable services of Mr. Henry Brown, city marshal, concluded to present him with a suitable token of their esteem, and so settled upon an elegant gold-mounted and handsomely-engraved Winchester rifle, as an article especially useful to him and expressive of services rendered in the lawful execution of his duties. The gun was presented to him Monday, Mr. Frank Johnes making the presentation speech, and a handsome one it was, too (we mean the speech this time). On the stock of the gun is a handsome silver plate bearing the inscription "Presented to City Marshal H. N. Brown for valuable services rendered the citizens of Caldwell, Kansas, A. M. Colson, Mayor, Dec., 1882." Henry is as proud of his gun as a boy of a new top. He appreciates the present very highly, but not half so much as he does the good will shown and approval of his services by the citizens of this city, as implied by the present.

The *Commercial*, in its edition of January 4, differed with the *Post's* version of the inscription:

A FINE NEW YEAR'S PRESENT.

On Monday afternoon our efficient City Marshal, Henry Brown, was quietly tolled into York-Parker-Draper M. Co.'s store, and in the presence of a few friends presented with a new Winchester rifle. The presentation speech was made by Frank Jones, to which Henry responded as well as he could under his astonishment and embarrassment at the unexpected demonstration. The rifle is of superior workmanship, the barrell being octagon, the butt end beautifully engraved and plated with gold. The stock is made of a fine piece of black walnut, with a pistol grip, and one side of it has a silver plate inscribed, "Presented to H. N. Brown by his many friends, as a reward for the efficient services rendered the citizens of Caldwell. A. M. Colson Mayor, Jan 1, A. D. 1883."

The present is one worthy of the donors and testifies in a substantial manner their appreciation of a most efficient officer and worthy gentleman.

At the end of January, 1883, Brown obtained leave to visit his home in Missouri. The *Commercial*, in announcing his absence, commended his performance of duty:

Henry Brown, our city marshal, having obtained a leave of absence from the mayor and council, left yesterday [January 31?] on a visit to his old home at Rolla, Missouri, after an absence of ten years. Mr. Brown during the past eight months has given his entire time and attention to his duties first as assistant marshal, and then as marshal, has proven himself a most efficient officer and fairly earned the holiday. It is no flattery to say that few men could have filled the position he has so acceptably occupied. Cool, courageous and gentlemanly, and free from the vices supposed to be proper adjuncts to a man occupying his position; he has earned the confidence of our best citizens and the respect of those disposed to consider themselves especially delegated to run border towns. One other thing may be said in his favor: he has never been the recipient of self-presented testimonials, nor hounded the newspaper offices of the surrounding villages for personal puffs, and it gives us supreme satisfaction to state these facts. For one the COMMERCIAL hopes Mr. Brown will heartily enjoy his trip, the visit to scenes of his childhood, and return with renewed energy for the duties of his position.[3]

Brown returned to Caldwell about a month later. The *Commercial* on March 8, 1883, reported that "H. N. Brown, city marshal, returned on Saturday [March 3] from a visit to his old home in Missouri, and has resumed the duties of his office. Since his return, the boys are not quite so numerous on the streets at night."

Apparently Brown entered into the social life of Caldwell for on March 22, 1883, the *Commercial* reported that "A party of young folks, headed by Prof. Sweet, guarded by City Marshal Brown . . . started last Sunday for the classic shades of Polecat in order to enjoy a picnic. . . ."

In April, after the annual city election, the new city council of Caldwell met and reappointed both Brown and his assistant Wheeler.[4] A few days later Brown and Wheeler accompanied Deputy United States Marshal Cassius M. Hollister to apprehend some horse thieves. In making the arrest the officers killed a man. The article reporting this battle may be found in the section on Hollister.

City Marshal Henry Brown killed an Indian in a Caldwell grocery store on May 14. Here is the story from the *Journal*, May 17, 1883:

KILLED BY THE MARSHAL.

Spotted Horse is no more. He departed this life last Monday morning, at the hands of the city marshal, H. N. Brown. The manner of his death and the circumstances leading thereto are as follows:

Spotted Horse was a Pawnee Indian, whose custom it was to make periodical visits to Caldwell with one or more of his squaws, bartering their persons to the lusts of two-legged white animals in whom the dog instinct prevailed. Last Friday or Saturday Spotted Horse drove into town in a two-horse wagon, with one of his squaws, and went into camp on a vacant lot between Main and Market streets. About half past six on Monday morning he walked into the Long Branch Restaurant with his squaw and wanted the proprietors to give them breakfast. This they refused to do, when he left and wandered around town, taking in the Moreland House, where he was given a sackful of cold meat and bread. From thence he and the squaw went over to E. H. Beals' house on Market street, north of Fifth. Mr. Beals and his family were just sitting down to breakfast when Spotted Horse and his squaw walked in without the least ceremony and demanded something to eat. Mr. B's. wife and daughter were considerably alarmed, and the former ordered the Indians to leave. They went out and then Spotted Horse handed to the squaw the bundle of grub he had obtained at the Moreland, and walked back into the house, up to the table and put his hand on Miss

71

Beals' head. Mr. B. immediately jumped to his feet and made signs for the Indian to go out, at the same time applying an opprobrious epithet to him. The Indian immediately pulled out his revolver, and Mr. Beals told him to go out and they would settle the trouble there. Spotted Horse put up his pistol and walked out, and Mr. B. after him. Once outside, the Indian pulled his revolver again, and Mr. Beals seized a spade that was at hand. Just about this time Grant Harris run up to the Indian and told him to go away, that he ought not to attack an old man. The Indian then opened out with a volley of abuse, directed to Mr. Beals, in good plain English. Young Harris finally induced him to put up his pistol and leave.

The next heard of S. H. and his squaw was that they had walked into the back door of the Long Branch kitchen and helped themselves to breakfast, Louis Heironymous being the only one connected with the restaurant present in the building at the time, made no objections, and the two reds had a good feast.

It appears that after breakfast the squaw went to the wagon, while Spotted Horse strolled into Morris' grocery, one door north of the Long Branch. Meantime a complaint had been made to city marshal Brown in reference to the Indian's conduct at Beals' house, and the marshal had started out to hunt him up, finally finding him in Morris' grocery. The marshal approached Spotted Horse and requested him to go with him to Mr. Covington, in order that the latter might act as an interpreter. The Indian refused, when the marshal took hold of him. Spotted Horse didn't like that, and commenced to feel for his revolver. The marshal pulled his out and told the Indian to stop. On the latter refusing to do so, the marshal fired at him. In all four shots were fired by the marshal, the last one striking the Indian about where the hair came down to his forehead, and came out at the back of his head. Parties who were present state that if the officer's last shot had failed, the Indian would have had the advantage, because he had just succeeded in drawing his revolver when the shot struck him.

The Indian was shortly after removed to the ware house two doors north, where every attention was given him, but he died in about two hours without uttering a word, although he seemed to be conscious up to within a few moments before breathing his last.

Coroner Stevenson was telegraphed for and came down late in the afternoon, viewed the body and held an inquest that night. On Tuesday morning the jury brought in a verdict that the deceased came to his death by a gun shot wound in the hands of H. N. Brown, and that the shooting was done in the discharge of his duty as an officer of the law, and the verdict of the entire community is the same.

The squaw, we are told, upon hearing the first shot fired, hitched the horses to the wagon and drove off as fast as she could toward the Territory.

Toward the end of May, 1883, Brown, Wheeler, and Hollister again teamed up to arrest a thief. The *Journal* reported the story on May 31, 1883:

72

On Tuesday morning [May 29] Constable McCulloch might have been seen wending his way to the office of Squire Ross. Preceding him was a lively young man of apparently twenty-five summers, or some'ers about, who bore upon his broad and stooping shoulders a heavy saddle, such as the festive cowboy is wont to sit upon while chasing the flying bovine, a saddle blanket and other paraphrenelia necessary to clothe a range horse. As the two took their solemn and stately walk up the stairs leading to the justice's office, with the bearer of burthens in the lead, our curiosity became excited, and, following the cavalcade into the sacred precincts of justice, we ascertained that the bearer of the saddle was one who gave his name as John Caypless; that, in company with two others, he had been loafing around the outskirts of the town for three or four days; that the attention of Brown, Hollister and Ben Wheeler had been called to the fact; that on Friday night Moores & Weller lost a saddle, which fact they reported to the police. On Monday night they ran across Mr. Caypless and interviewed him so successfully that he finally consented to show where his wicked partners—who had vamoosed the ranch— had hid the saddle. They accompanied him to the spot, which proved to be the ravine near I. N. Cooper's place, on Fall creek, where, hidden in a clump of bushes, the saddle was found. Mr. Capless' attendants, taking into consideration the fact that he had packed the saddle to its hiding place, concluded that he could carry it back to town, which he did. Caypless, on examination, was bound over, and, as the poor fellow had missed his breakfast, Mac took him to get a square meal, after which the train took him to Wellington, where he is now receiving the hospitalities of the hotel de Thralls. Had Caypless and his friends succeeded in their schemes, there is no doubt that other saddles would have been missing, like-wise three good horses.

The Caldwell police force, made up of Henry Brown and Ben Wheeler, was more than paying its own way. The Caldwell *Journal*, August 2, 1883, reported:

Marshal Brown and his assistant, Ben Wheeler, have certainly earned their salaries for the past five months. During that time they have run into the city treasury, for fines for violations of city ordinances, the sum of $1,296, being just $421 more than the salary they have received for that time. A very good showing for a quiet town like Caldwell.

Ordinarily the arrests which Marshal Brown was required to make during his day-to-day routine consisted of nothing more serious than apprehending persons gambling, operating "houses of ill fame," carrying weapons within the city limits, fighting, swearing, and disturbing the peace. A fine of from one to ten dollars was usually assessed and the offender released.[5] On December 20, 1883, however, the Caldwell *Journal* reported a more serious adventure of Marshal Brown's:

NEWT BOYCE KILLED.

Newt Boyce, a gambler, was shot last Saturday night [December 15] by City Marshal Henry Brown, and died about three o'clock the next morning. The coroner was telegraphed for, but word was sent back that he was out of town. Squire Ross, therefore, had a coroner's jury impanneled, and proceeded to hold an inquest.

The testimony went to show that on Friday night Boyce had some trouble in a saloon a few doors north of the post office, and had cut a soldier, and one of the proprietors of the saloon, with a knife. Ben Wheeler assistant city marshall, afterward took the knife away from Boyce and made him go home. Subsequently while Brown & Wheeler were in the Southwestern Hotel, some one informed them that Boyce was out again and liable to do some harm. The officers started out to hunt him up, and while passing Hulbert's store, saw Boyce in there. Brown stepped in, and seeing a knife and revolver lying on the counter, which B. was paying for, pushed the implements to one side, arrested Boyce, and put him in the cooler, where he stayed all night.

The next day he was brought before the police judge and fined, but at the time did not appear to be angry at the officers for what they had done. During the day, however, he got to drinking, and made threats against both Wheeler and Brown.

About an hour before he was killed, Wheeler saw Boyce in the saloon north of the post office, dealing monte. B. asked him where Brown was, at the same time applying epithets regarding Brown. Wheeler afterward met Brown and told him to look out, that Boyce was a dangerous man, and was liable to do him some harm. Brown then went to the saloon, and some words passed between the two men, Boyce remarking that as soon as he was through with that game he would settle with Brown.

Shortly after Wheeler met Boyce in front of Moore's saloon, and B asked him where Brown was, that he wanted to see that fighting S. B. etc. Wheeler told him that Brown was in the saloon, but advised Boyce to go home and behave himself. While they were talking, they heard footsteps, as if some one [were] approaching the door from the inside. Boyce immediately stepped to the alley way between the saloon and Moore's, and, as he did so, Wheeler noticed that he had his right hand under his coat, on the left side T. L. Crist came to the door, and Wheeler, seeing who it was, turned to go north. Boyce immediately jumped out of the alley way, pulled his pistol, cocked and pointed it directly at Wheeler's back, but seeing Crist at the same time, he put back the weapon and started down the alley.

Crist called to Wheeler and informed him regarding Boyce's actions, and while they were talking Brown came out of the saloon. Wheeler informed him what had occurred, and cautioned him to look out, that he believed Newt Boyce intended to do him some harm. Brown said if that was the case he would go and get his Winchester, because he didn't want to be murdered by any one.

After Brown got his gun, he and Wheeler walked north on the west side of Main street, and when opposite Unsell's store they saw Boyce standing on

74

the sidewalk in front of Phillip's saloon. Brown immediately started across the street, and when within about thirty feet of Boyce, called out to him to hold up. Boyce ran his right hand into his breast, as if feeling for a weapon, and stepped around so as to put one of the awning posts between himself and Brown. The latter fired two shots from his Winchester, and Boyce started toward the door of the saloon, at the same time telling Brown not to kill him. Brown followed him into the saloon, and shortly after entering it, Boyce fell. Dr. Noble was called in, and an examination showed that the ball had struck Boyce in the right arm, close to the shoulder, broken the bone and penetrated the right side. Every effort was made to save his life, but he expired the next morning from the loss of blood.

Boyce had a wife here, who had the remains encased and started with them, Tuesday, for Austin, Texas, where Boyce's father lives.

The verdict of the jury was that the deceased came to his death at the hands of an officer while in the discharge of his duties.

On January 24, 1884, the Caldwell *Journal* suggested that the city police should be elected constables:

The JOURNAL nominates for constables of Caldwell township, to be voted for on February 5, Messrs. Henry Brown and Ben Wheeler. The boys would make excellent constables, and the offices would be a great advantage to them when pursuing criminals outside of the corporations. When a city marshal makes an arrest outside of the corporation limits of the city in which he is serving, he does it as a private citizen, and if he kills a man while resisting arrest, he can be successfully prosecuted for murder, whereas were he a constable he could make the arrest legally and be protected by the statutes.

No record was found of their subsequent nomination or election. On March 27, 1884, the *Journal* announced Brown's marriage:

BROWN-LEVAGOOD.

But he did not Lev(a)good girl at all, but took her unto himself for better or for worse, in true orthodox style, at the residence of Mr. J. N. Miller, in this city, last evening. Rev. Akin officiated, and in a few quiet remarks joined Mr. Henry N. Brown and Miss Maude Levagood in the holy bonds of wedlock. A company of select friends witnessed the ceremony, and extended congratulations to the happy couple. The JOURNAL, metaphorically speaking, throws its old shoe after the young folks and wishes them a long and prosperous life.

Apparently Brown intended to settle permanently in Caldwell for on April 10, 1884, the *Journal* reported that "Henry Brown has bought the Robt. Eatock place, and has gone to house-keeping."

Also in April Brown was appointed city marshal for the third time.[6]

Less than a month later Caldwell was shocked to learn that its marshal and assistant marshal had attempted to rob a bank at

Medicine Lodge. The *Journal* May 8, 1884, elaborated on an earlier dispatch:

A TERRIBLE DAY!
MEDICINE LODGE WITNESSES AN ATTEMPTED BANK ROBBERY, TWO MURDERS AND FOUR LYNCHINGS IN ONE DAY.
CALDWELL'S FORMER MARSHAL AND ASSISTANT THE LEADERS OF THE BAND.
RETRIBUTION, SWIFT AND SURE OVERTAKES THE DESPERADOES.
THE BRAVERY OF THE MEDICINE LODGE MEN.

Last Thursday morning a dispatch came to this city stating that the Medicine Valley bank, at Medicine Lodge, had been attacked by robbers Wednesday morning, and that the president and cashier were both killed. This much last week's JOURNAL contained. This was considered startling news enough to justify a second edition of the paper, which contained all the particulars that could be obtained.

Not until late Thursday evening was the startling announcement flashed over the wire that Caldwell was directly interested in the affair, other than as a sister city mourning the loss of her neighbor's prominent citizens; but when the news came it fell like a thunderbolt at midday. People doubted, wondered, and when the stern facts were at last beyond question, accepted them reluctantly.

The evidence that has since come to light shows that the plan was of mature deliberation, and that it had been in consideration for weeks. Just who the originators were will, perhaps, never be known. It is surmised that it was originated in this city this spring; that it was a deep-laid scheme to perpetrate several robberies, the Lodge first, the banks at this place the next, and a train on the Santa Fe the next. This is, however, only rumor; but from remarks made by members of the band before they were captured, it can be accurately conjectured that they had an extensive campaign planned, which only the vigilance and bravery of Medicine Lodge men prevented being carried into execution. That the termination was as short as it was terrible is a matter of congratulation.

THE START.

One week ago Sunday afternoon, Henry N. Brown, marshal of this city, and Ben F. Wheeler, his deputy, having obtained permission from the mayor to be absent from the city for a few days, mounted their horses and rode out of town, going to the west. The excuse they made for leaving was, that there was a murderer a short distance down in the Territory, for whom there was a reward of twelve hundred dollars, and they thought they would be able to capture him. Previous to starting, they both had their horses shod for running, and supplied themselves with a large quantity of ammunition. Both carried 44-calibre revolvers and Winchester rifles. They were joined, it is supposed, on Monday by [William] Smith and [John] Wesley, cowboys. The former worked on the T5 range, and the latter for Tredwell & Clark. Both were hard men, and at the last Smith showed himself to be the bravest man of the party.

76

The first news that reached here was brought by telegraph Thursday evening. It was in few words, and caused more excitement than there has been in this city for years. People gathered on the streets, and business for the evening was stagnated. Every one discussed the matter, and not until a late hour were the streets deserted. The telegram was received about 6:30 Thursday evening, and in an hour was known all over the city.

The following is a copy:

MEDICINE LODGE, Ks., }
May 1, 1884. }

BEN S. MILLER, Caldwell, Kan.:

The bank robbers were Brown and Wheeler, marshal and deputy of Caldwell, and Smith and Wesley. All arrested. Tried to escape. Brown killed. Balance hung. Geppert dead. Payne will die.

CHAS. H. ELDRED.

Of the account of the tragedy at Medicine Lodge, we can give it no more accurately than it was published in the *Cresset*, of that city. We reproduce it entire. It will be remembered, however, that this was published last Thursday morning, and that there are facts that have since come to light:

Our little city was yesterday (Wednesday, April 30) thrown into a state of intense excitement and horror by the perpetration of a murder and attempted bank robbery, which, for cold-bloodedness and boldness of design, was never exceeded by the most famous exploits of the James gang.

The hour was a little after nine, a heavy rain was falling and comparatively few people were upon the streets, when four men rode in from the west and hitched their horses back of the bank coal shed. The bank had just opened up; Mr. Geppert, had taken his place and begun work on settling the monthly accounts; E. W. Payne, president, was sitting at his desk writing, when, as nearly as we can learn, three of the robbers entered. According to a preconcerted plan, we presume, one advanced to the cashier's window, one to the president's window, while one seems to have gone around into the back room to the iron lattice door. Almost immediately after the men were seen to enter the bank,

SEVERAL SHOTS WERE HEARD,

in rapid succession. Rev. Friedly who happened to be just across the street, immediately gave the alarm, and Marshal [Sam] Denn, who was standing near the livery stable, across the street from the bank, fired on the robber outside, who returned the fire, fortunately without effect. The robbers now saw that the game was up, and broke for their horses, mounted and rode out of town, going south. It was but a few minutes until a score or more men were in hot pursuit.

To those who remained, on going into the bank, a horrible sight was presented. George Geppert, the esteemed cashier, lay at the door of the vault

WELTERING IN HIS BLOOD,

and dead. A hole in his breast showing where the ball had entered and probably severed the carotid artery, told the tale. Mr. Payne, the president, lay near him

77

GROANING WITH PAIN.

An examination showed that a pistol ball had entered the back of the right shoulder blade, and ranging across had probably grazed his spine and lodged somewhere under the left shoulder blade.

[Mr. Payne died Thursday morning, May 1st, about 11 o'clock, having suffered for twenty-four hours, eighteen which he was conscious. We give his obituary in another place.—ED. JOURNAL.]

THE PURSUIT.

Going back to the pursuing party, we get the story of the exciting chase from a participant. The pursuing party first came in sight of the robbers beyond the crossing of the Medicine south of town. The party, seeing that they were about to be overtaken, turned and opened fire. Several volleys were exchanged. While the fight was going on, Charley Taliaferro and we believe one or two others rode around the robbers and headed them off on the south. Seeing that they were cut off in this direction they left the road and started almost west, toward the breaks of gypsum hills, but were so hotly pursued that they took refuge in a canyon some three or four miles southwest of town. The boys in pursuit surrounded the canyon to prevent the possibility of escape, and George Friedley and Charley Taliaferro came in for reinforcements. In a short time every gun and horse that could be brought into service was on the road to the canyon. Before the reinforcements arrived on the ground, however, the robbers had surrendered. The surprise of the captors can be better imagined than expressed when, on taking charge of the outfit, they found that they were all well known. The leaders of the gang were

HENRY BROWN, MARSHAL OF CALDWELL,

and Ben Wheeler, assistant marshal of the same city; the other two were well known cowboys, William Smith, who has been employed for some time on the T5 range, and another cowboy who is known by the name of Wesley, but having several aliases.

Of these men, Brown is the only one who has acquired any notoriety. His history on the frontier began with his connection with "Billie the Kid" in New Mexico. It is said that he was a companion of the noted desperado in some of his most exciting adventures. Of late years, however, he seemed to have sobered down. Some three years since he was elected assistant marshal of Caldwell, and for the past two years has occupied the position of marshal of our neighboring city. In appearance Brown does not show the criminal particularly. He is a man of about medium height; strong, wiry build; wears no beard except a mustache, and his face indicates firmness and lack of physical fear. During the time he has held his office he has killed several men, but was generally considered justifiable.

Ben Wheeler, the man who fired the shot that killed George Geppert, is a large and powerfully-built man, dark complected, with rather an open countenance. So far as we know he has never been noted as a desperado. He has occupied the position of assistant marshal of Caldwell for the past two years,

78

and has been considered, we believe, a good officer. His action yesterday, however, showed him to be the most cold-blooded murderer in the gang.

Wesley is rather under medium size, and has an evil, reckless expression of countenance, and is just such a boy as would aspire to be a desperado.

Smith is also an undersized man with dark complexion and rather a hardened expression of countenance.

When the party were brought in they were surrounded by a crowd of exasperated citizens, and cries of

HANG THEM! HANG THEM!

sounded on every side, and for a while it looked as though they would be torn from the hands of the officers and lynched on the spot. A somewhat calmer feeling came over the crowd, not that the feeling was any the less intense, but the desire to do the job up in a more business-like style was greater.

All afternoon little knots of quiet, determined men could be seen, and all over town was that peculiar hush which bodes the coming storm. Little was said, but the impression prevailed that before many hours the bodies of four murderers would swing in the soft night air.

So ended the most exciting and the most sorrowful day in the history of Medicine Lodge. No bank robbery ever chronicled in the annals of crime was ever bolder in its design or accompanied by more cold-blooded murder in its attempted execution. That the desperadoes failed in accomplishing their full purpose was not the fault of their plan, but was due to the courage and promptness of a number of our citizens and others—a promptness and courage, in fact, which has rarely been equaled on any similar occasion anywhere.

CLOSING SCENES.

About nine o'clock the stillness of the night was broken by three shots fired in rapid succession, and at the signal a crowd of armed men advanced toward the jail and demanded the prisoners. This was refused, but, notwithstanding their spirited resistance, the sheriff and his posse were overpowered and the doors of the jail opened, when the prisoners who were in the inner cell unshackled made a sudden

DASH FOR LIBERTY.

In an instant the moonlight was so mingled with bullets that it was a highly unsatisfactory locality for a promenade, and the fact that no one except the prisoners was injured is a matter of wonder. Of the robbers, Wheeler, Smith and Wesley were captured, Wheeler badly wounded. Brown ran a few rods from the jail and fell dead, riddled with a charge of buckshot, besides having a few stray Winchester balls in various parts of his body.

Wheeler, Smith and Wesley were taken by the crowd to an elm tree in the bottom east of town, and told if they had anything they wished to say, now was their time to say it, for their time of life was short. Wheeler at the last showed great weakness, and begged piteously for mercy. Wesley was also shaken, but managed to answer, in reply to inquiry, that he was born in Paris, Texas, in 1853, and requested that word of his fate be sent to friends in Vernon, Texas. Smith displayed great nerve, and gave directions coolly, to sell his horse and saddle and some few other trinkets, and send the money to his mother, in Vernon, Texas.

After the remarks the ready ropes were fastened on the necks of the robbers, the end tossed over a limb, and in a moment more their bodies swung in the wind. So ends the chapter. Mob law is to be deplored under almost any circumstance, but in this case the general sentiment of the community will uphold the summary execution of justice by the taking of these murderers' lives.

THE VICTIM.

Of the deceased, who was shot down in such cold blood, we have not space to speak in fitting eulogy. He has been a resident of our town for some four years past, and was widely known and universally respected by all his acquaintances. A man of excellent business capacity, he had already accumulated a handsome competence. In the prime of life and vigor of his manhood, with a most comfortable home and a pleasant family, the future seemed to have in store for him abundant years filled with golden fruitage of happiness. The respect of his fellow citizens was shown by the fact that the business houses of the town, we believe withou[t] an exception, were draped in mourning. His death has aroused the deepest and most general sympathy. We have lost a most excellent man, a kind husband and father, and one of our most enterprising citizens.

This ends all there was known Thursday morning. While in jail at the Lodge Brown wrote a letter to his wife. We reproduce it below, only leaving out such parts as are of a purely business character and of no interest to the public. They contained minute directions how to dispose of his property and as to the payment of some debts.

BROWN'S LAST LETTER.

MEDICINE LODGE, April 30, '84.

DARLING WIFE:—I am in jail here. Four of us tried to rob the bank here, and one man shot one of the men in the bank, and he is now in his home. I want you to come and see me as soon as you can. I will send you all of my things, and you can sell them, but keep the Winchester. This is hard for me to write this letter but, it was all for you, my sweet wife, and for the love I have for you. Do not go back on me; if you do it will kill me. Be true to me as long as you live, and come to see me if you think enough of me. My love is just the same as it always was. Oh, how I did hate to leave you on last Sunday eve, but I did not think this would happen. I thought we could take in the money and not have any trouble with it; but a man's fondest hopes are sometimes broken with trouble. We would not have been arrested, but one of our horses gave out, and we could not leave him alone. I do not know what to write. Do the best you can with everything. I want you to send me some clothes. Sell all the things that you do not need. Have your picture taken and send it to me. Now, my dear wife, go and see Mr. Witzleben and Mr. Nyce, and get the money. If a mob does not kill us we will come out all right after while. Maude, I did not shoot any one, and did not want the others to kill any one; but they did, and that is all there is about it. Now, good-bye, my darling wife.

H. N. BROWN.

This shows that he anticipated the doom which awaited him, and realized in his calmer moments the awful atrocity of his crime.

Mrs. Brown is also in receipt of a very kind letter from Sheriff Riggs of Barber county, of which the following is a verbatim copy.

THE SHERIFF'S LETTER.

MEDICINE LODGE, May 1st.

MRS. H. N. BROWN, Caldwell, Ks.

Madame:—It becomes my painful duty to inform you of the death of your husband, H. Newton Brown, at the hands of an infuriated mob. Your husband and three others attempted to rob the Medicine Valley Bank, and in so doing killed Mr. Geo. Geppert, the cashier, also wounding the president, Mr. Payne, from which wounds he will surely die. I wish to say that in my capacity as sheriff of this county I did my best to protect my prisoners; but by being overpowered I was forced to submit. Perhaps it will be some satisfaction to you to know that his death was instantaneous and quite painless, being shot two or three times, dying instantly, while his comrads in crime were taken some distance from town and hung. There are some effects in this town the property of your husband, and as soon as I can get them together I will forward them to you. I also send to you a letter written by your husband and handed to me to send to you. He wrote it a little before dark last evening.

C. F. RIGG,
Sheriff.

Friday morning last Messrs. Ben. S. Miller, John A. Blair, S. Harvey Horner and Lee S. Weller started over to the Lodge, Messrs. Miller and Blair to give their sympathy to the bereaved families, and Messrs. Weller and Horner to look after property that belonged to them. From them we learn the full details, and give them below as nearly as possible:

Mr. Payne and Mr. Geppert had been warned of the attack, and had agreed to surrender. When Brown and Wheeler entered the bank, the positive character of Mr. Payne asserted itself and to defend his property he reached for his revolver. This was his death warrant. Brown shot him, and Wheeler immediately shot Geppert while that gentleman had his hands up! Wesley, thinking to add to the terrible work already done, shot him again to make assurance doubly sure. After being shot twice, Mr. Geppert, true to his trust, staggered to the vault and threw the combination lock on, and then sat down in front of the vault a corpse, the contents it guarded safe from the profaning hands of his murderers.

The story of the capture is briefly told. Nine men were the principles in it. Barney O'Conner was the first man to mount his horse and start in pursuit, and in all of the short, final run guided the pursuing party to ultimate success. After the failure the robbers were completely demoralized. They had not taken failure into consideration in their plans. They were without an appointed leader, and all wanted to lead; hence the capture. One horse began weakening, and they left the main road and turned into a canyon in the gypsum hills. This led into a small pocket thirty or forty feet deep, with only one exit, that by which they entered. The bottom of the canyon was covered with water from a foot and a half to two feet deep, and it was raining hard and water running down the sides. Here resistance was kept up for two hours, many shots being exchanged but no one hit, all having to shoot at a disadvantage. The cold water was the greatest friend the pursuers had. It cooled the ardor of the pursued, and in two hours after they entered this place they surrendered. Brown was the first to lay down his arms and walk out, and was followed by the rest. When they rode into the city the people were wild, and loud threats of lynching them were made; but not until night were they put into execution. In the afternoon comparatively good pictures of the band were taken, and also of the captors. They ate two hearty meals while in the jail, and Brown wrote the above letter. Wheeler tried to write, but broke down.

BIOGRAPHICAL.

Henry Newton Brown is the only one of the band who has achieved any notoriety as a desperado. He was a native of Rolla, Phelps county, Missouri, but at an early age left his home for the West. He went first to Colorado, and from there drifted into a cow camp in Northern Texas, where he killed a man after firing three shots at him. He shortly went into the band of the celebrated "Billie the Kid," and participated in many of his most daring exploits. In the Lincoln county war he was with the Kid's party when they lay ambushed for Sheriff Brady's party and killed him and nearly all of his men. In the fall of 1878 he was at Tuscosa, Texas, with the Kid with between 75 and 100 stolen horses. In a short time he went to New Mexico and was employed as boss of a ranch, but owing to a shooting scrape there he left for Texas, having been among the number pardoned by the governor of that State for participation in the Lincoln county war. He was appointed deputy sheriff of Oldham county by Capt. Willingham in 1880, but only held the office a short time, when he started up the trail and came to Caldwell. Batt Carr was then marshal of this city, and having known Brown as deputy sheriff in Texas, had him appointed as his deputy marshal in the summer of 1882. In the fall of that year, Carr having resigned, he was appointed marshal, and has since held that position, being reappointed the third time only four weeks ago. Since in office he has killed two men. The only fault found with him as an officer was that he was too ready to use his revolver or Winchester. He had gained the entire confidence of the people however, and had conducted himself in such a manner that the doors of society were always open to him. He neither drank, smoked, chewed nor gambled. In size he was rather under the medium, but compactly built, and such a man as would be supposed capable of great physical endurance. He was very light complexioned, blue eyes and light mustache. He was twenty-six years old last fall. He leaves relatives in R[o]lla, Missouri, and a sister in Iowa.

Only six weeks ago he was married to a most estimable young lady in this city, Miss Alice M. Levagood.

Ben Robertson, alias Ben F. Burton, alias Ben F. Wheeler, was a native of Rockdale, Milam county, Texas, where he was born in 1854, and where he has a number of relatives who are most estimable people. One of his brothers was at one time general land agent of the State of Texas. Wheeler, as he was known here, left Texas about six years ago on account of a shooting scrape in which he severely wounded a man. He went to Cheyenne, Wyoming Territory, where he stayed for some time and then started south again with cattle. At Indianola, Nebraska, he met Miss Alice M. Wheeler. In November, 1881, they were married under the name of Burton, at her parents' residence in that place, where they lived happily together until the next spring. He then left and came to this place, where he was soon appointed deputy marshal. She came in a few months, but he refused to keep her here, and told her if she would go away he would support her. She stayed away most of the time, but last winter spent several weeks here. Her father died last December, and she is left alone to support her aged mother and one sister, and also her eighteen-months-old child. She is willing and anxious to work for their support, and in her brave resolution she will no doubt meet with ready help from the kind-hearted ladies of this city.

Of Smith and Wesley little is known other than that they were natives of Texas, one of Vernon and the other of Paris. Smith was employed on the T5 Range, and had just been given charge there. He was about 28 years of age. Wesley has been employed on Treadwell & Clark's ranch all winter, and when he left Sunday afternoon he stated he was going to meet Smith in Kansas. He was always considered a hard citizen, but a good hand about the ranch. He always carried his six-shooter, and never retired at night without his Winchester was within his reach. He was about thirty years old.

Wheeler is said to also have a wife and four children in Texas, under the name of Robertson.

FINALE.

There was another heavy sound,
    A hush and then a groan,
And darkness swept across the sky,
    The work of death was done.

The tragic death of the robbers has already been told. That it was just, all know; that it was a terrible penalty for their crime, visited on them by the iron hand of judge lynch, all admit. There have been cases before where it was surely justifiable and there will be others to come. The near relations which two of the principals bore to the citizens of this city made it doubly horrible. They had made many warm friends in this city, and while here had made two as good officers as the city has ever had. They had been given credit for honor and bravery, and while here no man can say, and say truthfully, that they had not been worthy this trust. That they have brought disgrace on the city, no one can help; and that they met their just deserts, all rejoice. But let the mantle of charity fall over their memory, and like the tear of the

83

repentant sinner which the peri brought to the gates of heaven, let it obliterate them as it did the sins of the penitent, blot them out from existence, and let them be judged by the Higher Court where we are taught to believe that all shall receive justice. Let them fall into the past as beings that are gone and forgotten; and while the dark cloud that obscures the final ending is rent by a few rays of golden light, let no rude hand be stretched passionately forth to close forever from sight those redeeming glimmerings.

1. Caldwell *Post*, September 28, 1882. 2. Caldwell *Commercial*, November 9, 1882. 3. February 1, 1883. 4. Caldwell *Commercial*, April 5, 1883. 5. "Police Docket," Records of the City of Caldwell, July, 1882-May, 1884. 6. Caldwell *Journal*, April 10, 1884.

BROWN, J. CHARLES

For several days following the August 15, 1873, shooting of Sheriff Chauncey B. Whitney, the city of Ellsworth had police problems. The men on duty at the time of Whitney's death were summarily dismissed by the mayor and new officers were appointed. Twelve days later they, too, were fired. Not until August 27 did the police force assume any semblance of permanency. On August 28, 1873, the Ellsworth *Reporter* gave the names of the new officers in this article: "The entire police force was changed at a special meeting of the City Council yesterday, Richard Freeborn was appointed City Marshall, with power delegated to select two policemen. He selected J. C. Brown and [John] DeLong."

In September Brown shot and killed John Morco, a former Ellsworth policeman, for wearing weapons within the city limits. "The coroner's inquest over the body of 'Happy Jack' decided that John Morco came to his death from the effects of two bullet wounds, discharged from a six-shooter in the hands of Chas. Brown, a police officer of the city of Ellsworth, in self defence, while in discharge of his duty, and was justified in the act," said the *Reporter*, September 11, 1873. The article which reported the shooting may be found in the section on Morco.

Policemen Brown and DeLong resigned on November 7, 1873, but eleven days later Brown was appointed marshal to fill the vacancy created by Freeborn's resignation that same day, November 18.[1]

Several months afterward Charles Brown assisted the Ellis county sheriff in arresting Dutch Henry Born, a widely known horse thief. The Ellsworth *Reporter* carried this article on June 18, 1874:

84

HENRY BORN ARRESTED.—AN EXCITING CHASE.

Last Monday afternoon [June 15] an arrest was made near this city that occasioned considerable stir among our population. Sheriff [Alexander] Ramsey came down from Ellis county, and armed with a United States warrant and revolver proceeded to obey orders, having called to his assistance under-sheriff Stephens of this city.—About five miles from town as they were riding horseback they discovered their man riding across the prairie. Riding after him Ramsey ordered him to surrender—in answer Born raised his revolver. Ramsey and Stephens dismounted from their horses and each fired at Born. Born galloped off to Oak creek where he secreted himself in the bushes. Ramsey ordered Stephens to ride to Ellsworth for more men and some guns. Stephens returned with City Marshal Brown and S. G. John, each being armed with guns. Arriving at the creek it was found that Born had hid himself in a cave and had afterwards crept up a ravine. He was soon found by the party, hid in the grass. Not answering the sheriff's orders to give himself up, a shot from that officer's revolver, which inflicted a slight wound on his face, and the presentation of three long guns in different directions, brought him to terms and he was disarmed, brought into the city and lodged in jail. The people here meanwhile knew what was going on and were out en masse watching the result. When the party rode in, a great crowd of men and boys gathered at the jail to see the prisoner. He was wounded in three places—but none of the shots were dangerous. He was cared for by our physicians. Sheriff Ramsey took his prisoner up to Hays City on the 10:35 train and will duly hand him to the U. S. authorities at Topeka. The prisoner was arrested for stealing mules from the Government. He was once before arrested by Sheriff Whitney, but there being some informality in the arrest he was released.— Born and his brother have had a claim on Oak creek for two years—though it is said that they have never entered their claim at the Land Office.

Nothing more was found concerning Marshal Brown until July 22, 1875, when the following appeared in the Ellsworth *Reporter:*

CITY COUNCIL MEETING.

At a regular meeting of the city council, held July 20th, Mr. Beebe introduced the following resolution:

WHEREAS, Our Marshal, J. C. Brown, having resigned his position to fill one of like character on the frontier. Be it

Resolved, That in severing the connection of the Marshal with this city. Mr. J. C. Brown, has for the past two years, performed his duty to the entire satisfaction of our citizens.

That we cheerfully recommend him as an officer who is fearless, prompt, honest, and always on hand to attend to his duty and equal to any emergency.

That a copy of these resolutions be signed by the mayor and, with the seal of the city attached, be presented to Mr. J. C. Brown.

On motion of Mr. Montgomery, the above resolution was adopted and

ordered spread upon the record, and the minutes of this meeting containing such, ordered published in the Ellsworth REPORTER.   M. NEWTON,
Attest: *Mayor*
   W. F. TOMPKINS, *City Clerk.*

1. "Minutes of the City Council," Records of the City of Ellsworth, pp. 107, 108.

BROWN, JOHN

The Dodge City *Times,* April 13, 1878, reported that "Joseph Mason and John Brown have been placed on the Police force to serve temporarily." On May 7 Brown was paid $52.50 for "salary as Ass't Marshal," according to proceedings of the city council published in the *Times* on May 11, 1878. Also it reported that on "motion of C. M. Beeson the appointment of John Brown as policeman was confirmed." The *Times,* from its issue of April 20 through the issue of May 11, 1878, listed Brown as assistant marshal in its "Official Directory."

Brown served as policeman under Marshal Charles E. Bassett and Assistant Marshal Wyatt Earp. "Dodge City is practically under an efficient guard," wrote the editor of the Dodge City *Times,* May 18, 1878. "The city fathers have wisely provided for the honor, safety and character of the city by the appointment of an excellent police force. We believe no better men for the positions can be found anywhere."

In May, June, and July Brown remained on the police force. At a city council meeting held August 6, 1878, it was decided that "the police force [should] be reduced; and the clerk be instructed to notify Policeman John Brown that his services would no longer be required." [1]

If the policeman mentioned in this article from the *Ford County Globe,* August 6, 1878, was John Brown then this may have been the cause of his dismissal:

The policeman who pounded the Mexican over the head with a six-shooter, last Thursday night [August 1], did not display either much manhood or bravery. When we consider the fact that the poor "greaser" was sitting on a bench almost helpless from the effects of a previous beating, we don't think that even a Dodge City policeman (who is nearly the greatest man in the world) has any right to walk deliberately up to him without any provocation, and knock out one or two of his eyes.

A few weeks later Brown was taught a lesson in etiquette, Western style. The *Ford County Globe* reported the affair on September 24, 1878:

THE FESTIVE REVOLVER.

A man named Brown, formerly one of our policemen, spat at Al Manning's face last Wednesday. Al very promptly responded to this insult by emptying a six-sho[o]ter at Brown, who being an expert runner and dodger, evaded the bullets. We are, however, sorry to say that a young man by the name of Wm. Morton caught one of the bullets in his foot. He is at present confined to bed nursing his wounded foot. While we regret very much to hear of the use of the revolver where innocent parties are liable to be hurt, we are glad to believe that Mr. Brown has learned a lesson he'll not forget soon.

The last mention found of Brown in Dodge City was in the proceedings of the city council meeting of December 3, 1878, as reported in the *Times*, December 7. At this meeting Brown was paid $12.50 for "balance of salary," perhaps for the six days he had served in August.

1. Dodge City *Times*, August 10, 1878.

BROWN, NEIL (NEAL) (1847?-1926)

James Masterson and Neil Brown were appointed marshal and assistant marshal of Dodge City on November 4, 1879. These "off season" appointments were occasioned by the recent resignations of Marshal Charles E. Bassett and Assistant Marshal Wyatt Earp. In reporting the appointments, the Dodge City *Times*, November 15, 1879, concluded with the statement that "these men make good officers." Brown and Masterson each received $100 per month for their police services.[1]

On March 30, 1880, the *Ford County Globe* reported that "Capt. Dan Gardiner officiated as police officer yesterday in the temporary absence of the marshal. He succeeded in steering another weakneed rooster over to the dog house, but his courage failed when policeman Brown arrived and proposed to put the two in together."

Both James Masterson and Neil Brown were reappointed by the city council on May 4, 1880.[2]

In June Brown arrested one of Dodge's first citizens and roughed him up somewhat in the process. The *Globe* reported the incident on June 8, 1880:

IN THE BASTILE.

Dr. [S.] Galland and Capt. Howard, proprietor and clerk, respectively, of the Great Western Hotel, were, after a short preliminary skirmish, in which the Doctor received a patronizing welt or two from the festive revolver of Policeman Brown, arrested and locked up in one of the dismal cells of the bastile, where they remained until the Policeman saw fit to kindly liberate them. The cause of the arrest was for a failure to pay hotel license. Yesterday the two culprits were brought before Judge [D. S.] Weaver who fined the Doctor one dollar and cost and dismissed the case against Howard. The Doctor and his friends claim that he was mistreated and abused by the policeman, and that the affair was caused by the Doctor's resignation last week as a member of the Council. Such cases of "unpleasantness" are not proper amusements for Christians to indulge in, and our voice is for peace.

Action was brought against Brown for his method and the trial was reported in the *Ford County Globe,* June 15, 1880:

The case of the State of Kansas vs. Policeman Brown, charged with a felonious assault upon Dr. S. Galland, late member of the City Council, was called last Saturday in Chief Justice [R. G.] Cook's court. Nelson Adams, of Larned, appeared for the defendant and [Thomas S.] Jones and [D. M.] Frost for the State. The court took the case under advisement until Monday, and when Monday came he took the case under advisement for another week. In the fullness of time we presume the judge will render an elaborate opinion.

The case was finally concluded in January, 1881. Brown was convicted and fined $10 and costs.[3]

In August, 1880, Brown wounded a man while making an arrest. The *Globe,* August 24, 1880, reported:

Policeman Brown undertook to disarm a stranger last Friday [August 20], who was carrying a pistol in his pocket. The stranger refused to disgorge and started to run, whereupon the policeman gave chase and fired two shots, one of them passing through the stranger's foot and bringing him to a stand-still. He was taken to the calaboose and fined eight dollars, which he paid and took his departure from this beautiful city on the first train, taking with him quite a severe wound.

The city council, at a meeting held October 5, 1880, decided to reduce the salaries of the marshal and his assistant. The Dodge City *Times* reported the action on October 9: "On motion of W. C. Shinn, seconded by T. J. Draper, that after the 31st of October 1880, the expense of Marshal and Assistant be reduced to one hundred dollars per month, which passed; the mayor will take notice to have such offices filled for amount named above."

The decision was reaffirmed at the December 7, 1880, meeting of the council:

88

The minutes of the previous meeting were read and approved, after they were corrected by motion of W. C. Shinn and seconded by M. W. Sutton, that the motion of W. C. Shinn in the previous minutes in regard to expense of city to read as follows: That after the 30th day of October, 1880, the total expense of the city marshal and assistant be reduced to one hundred dollars per month to keep the peace and quietude of said city, and the mayor take notice to have such offices filled for amount named above, passed the council Oct. 5, 1880.

The following bills were presented and allowed.

Jas. Masterson, salary for 1 month $100 00

Neil Brown,   100 00. . . .

The bills of James Masterson and Neil Brown, as marshal and assistant in the month of November, for one hundred dollars each, was presented, and on motion of W. C. Shinn, seconded by T. J. Draper, That fifty dollars be paid (the bills reduced that amount) and remainder laid over until the next meeting of the council for consideration, passed the council Dec. 7, 1880.[4]

On April 6, 1881, after the annual city elections, the newly elected city council met and declared the positions of marshal and assistant marshal to be vacant and new officers were appointed. Brown and Masterson were each paid $420 on April 12.[5]

When the trouble occurred between Luke Short and the city authorities in the spring of 1883, Brown was still a resident of Dodge. Though his part in the troubles is difficult to ascertain, he was prominent enough to be included in the famous photograph of the "Dodge City Peace Commission." The story of the "war," and what is known of Brown's role, will be found in the section on Luke Short.

The Dodge City *Times* of August 30, 1883, printed a list of members of Dodge's recently formed militia unit, the Glick Guards. Neil Brown appeared as a member along with Luke Short, Bill Tilghman, Clark Chipman, and others famous in Dodge City's early history.

In January, 1889, when Cimarron and Ingalls were fighting a "war" for the county seat of Gray county, Brown was involved in a sharp and bloody battle in the streets of Cimarron. Other former Dodge City policemen who also participated were: James Masterson, Fred Singer, Ben Daniels, and Bill Tilghman. The full story of the fight may be found in the section on Tilghman.

1. Dodge City *Times*, January 17, April 10, May 8, July 10, August 7, September 11, October 9, December 11, 1880. 2. *Ibid.*, May 8, 1880. 3. *Ford County Globe*, January 25, 1881. 4. Dodge City *Times*, December 11, 1880. 5. *Ibid.*, April 7, 14, 1881.

BUGG, THOMAS (____-1883)

Contemporary evidence of Tom Bugg's law enforcement career is sketchy at best. In July, 1881, Bugg testified at the coroner's inquest over the body of Joseph McDonald who had been killed by Dodge City Marshal Fred Singer. At that inquest Bugg is quoted by the *Ford County Globe*, July 26, 1881, as saying "I am deputy sheriff. . . ." (The testimony may be found in the section on Fred Singer.)

The sheriff at that time was George T. Hinkle; the under sheriff was Fred Singer. Just when Bugg was appointed deputy sheriff of Ford county is not known. On November 3, 1881, the Dodge City *Times* reported that "Thomas Bugg, Deputy Sheriff, has resigned his office. Sheriff Hinkel has not yet designated Mr. Bugg's successor."

Apparently Bugg was reappointed a deputy sheriff for on March 7, 1882, the *Globe* mentioned that "Sheriff Hinkle has relieved Thomas Bugg of his office as Deputy Sheriff. Sensible move."

Bugg later held another law enforcement position as this article from the *Times*, August 10, 1882, shows: "Thos. Bugg, acting constable, was yesterday accidentally shot. The ball passed through the left leg above the knee, and left arm above the elbow. He was scuffling with a man and the pistol fell out of the scabbard and was discharged. The wounds are not dangerous." [1]

In October, 1882, Bugg was a member of a posse, led by Ford county Under Sheriff Singer, which went to Lakin for several cowboys who had shot into a Santa Fe passenger train. (The account of the cowboys' capture may be found in the section on Singer.)

Tom Bugg died on February 10, 1883. The Dodge City *Times*, February 15, published the following obituary:

THE DEATH ROLL.

Like the plant that has stood the variable climate, wither and die the early citizens of the border. There is nothing remarkable about the death of the old-timer, but to the surviving old-timers there is a lurking spirit of sadness on the sudden demise of those who have borne the brunt of the battle on the plains. None here who have not enjoyed the full measure of life's pleasure, endured its hardships and for a period survived its vicissitudes. But there is a limit to physical endurance. Energy and work will sustain life, but poor whisky, the bane of the hail fellow, saps the foundation and soon destroys the manly physical body. Tom Bugg, who died Saturday night, after a brief illness, deserves no particular mention for either good or bad deeds. He was a hero withal. He struggled for an existence and bore the burden of his life's troubles. Whisky has done for Tom Bugg what it will do for all who tarry long at the social glass. It was heart disease, the doctor said; and how many more of the poor wanderers, sentinels on the border, are there in our midst, barring against that fate that awaits all of the human family! But these are of Tom Bugg's class. Their ebb of life is fast flowing and the receding stream is drawing them—

"Nearer, my God, to thee."

The preacher Sunday night delivered a doleful sermon on the grave. He preached the funeral service of the countless millions who pass to the other shore, unwept, unhonored and unsung. Appropos, the spark of life had no sooner left Al Updegraff, than came eternity's chariot and carried away Tom Bugg. Another, less known, but no less a man, though of a dark skin, also passed in his chips, and called the turn. Wm. Davis, the colored barber, died in Speareville, of pneumonia caused by exposure and over indulgence in strong drink. . . .

Tom Bugg was a carpenter by trade, and followed that business until about two or three years ago. He held the office of deputy constable at the time of his death. He resided in Dodge for several years. Of his antecedents we know nothing. His death was rather unexpected, he apparently being in the enjoyment of good health a few days previous to his death.[2]

1. *See, also, Ford County Globe,* August 15, 1882. 2. *See, also, ibid.,* February 13, 1883.

CARR, B. P.

The murder of George Brown, June 22, 1882, left Caldwell without a city marshal. Only one arrest was recorded in the Caldwell police court docket between the date of Brown's death and July 1, and that was on complaint of J. A. Neal, a policeman. On July 1, 1882, the name of Marshal B. P. Carr began to appear on the docket. Both the Caldwell papers, the *Post* and the *Commercial,* in issues of July 6, 1882, mentioned that B. P. Carr had been appointed but no exact date was given.

"Carr is a quiet unassuming man, but there is that look about him which at once impresses a person with the idea that he will do his whole duty fearlessly and in the best manner possible. We have not the least doubt that he will give entire satisfaction . . .," said the *Commercial's* article.[1]

Apparently Carr gave immediate satisfaction, for within two weeks the citizens of Caldwell took up a collection and presented him a gift of appreciation. The *Post*, July 13, 1882, reported the presentation:

ARMED.

The citizens of Caldwell, seeing the necessity of having an officer well armed, proceeded to raise seventy-five dollars yesterday morning by subscriptions from business men on Main St, Col. Jennison heading the list. He purchased a brace of fine six-shooters, and presented them to Mr B P Carr in behalf of the citizens. Col. Jennison said, in substance: Mr Carr:—In behalf of the citizens and business men of this city, I present you with these weapons, not that we would encourage the use of them, but that you may better protect the rights of property and life, and maintain the dignity and honor of the city and your office as Marshal. It is not for the intrinsic value of the present we offer you, but in it our appreciation of your services as an officer. I request you to accept these pistols from the citizens of this city as a slight token of their confidence in your ability to protect the same from being used for any purpose other than the defense of the city and maintaining peace and quiet in the same.

The presents were handsome ones, and Mr. Carr fully appreciates the sentiments that induced the citizens to present them to him.[2]

In the same issue the *Post* had occasion to mention Marshal Carr's dexterity with that type of weapon:

City Marshal Carr put it onto a wild and woolly negro that was promenading the street the other day. Carr concluded that the fellow had a six shooter on him and asked him for it. The negro instantly went down to get it, with the intention of standing the marshal off; but quicker than thought a "45" was shoved up under his nose, accompanied by a gentle request to throw up. He threw up both hands in short order, and was disarmed and taken to Judge Kelley's sanctuary and stuck for $12 50, and told that he had better leave his gun off, in the future.

Bat Carr put a new twist in the interpretation of law at Caldwell when he saved a cowboy from going home completely broke. The *Commercial*, July 20, 1882, carried the story:

City Marshal Carr had to bruise a fellow last Friday [July 14], and all about a cowboy. It seems the latter came in from camp a day or two previous, with a couple of horses, one of which he sold. A chap running one of the gambling games in the city got hold of the cowboy, filled him up with whisky and then played him out of his money. The next morning the cowboy, partially sobered up and dead broke, undertook to sell the other horse, when Marshal Carr was informed of the circumstances. The marshal hunted up the youth, put him on his horse, and started him off for camp. Supposing everything all right, the marshal went off to attend to some other matters, when his attention was called to the fact that the gambler was endeavoring to have the cowboy remain, and had offered the latter $40 on his horse in the game. The marshal went up and invited the gambler to move on and let the cowboy alone. The man of games couldn't see it, and not content with refusing to go off, gave the marshal some slack. The latter settled the question very promptly by flooring the gambler, and compelling the cowboy to go to camp. Of course there was some indignation at the course of the marshal, but the more considerate portion of the community think he did just right. It has, in the past, been too common a thing for some of the sporting fraternity to beat every cowboy they could get hold of out of his hard earned money, and apparently without any det [sic] or hinderance on the part of the police force. That a change in that state of affairs has been inaugurated, and for the better, gives cause for congratulation. Our present force seem to comprehend the fact that men coming into the town are not to be openly robbed without any interference on their part, and we are glad of it.

The editor of the Caldwell *Commercial* seemed pleased on August 24, 1882, to report the growing use of fists over six guns:

Civilization is advancing in the west, particularly in that portion of it covered by the town of Caldwell. And for why? Because the Winchester and self-cocker have given place to nature's arms, good "bunches of fives," and perhaps a stick. Two ructions of that kind occurred last week, one on Thursday and the other on Saturday. Uncle Bill Corzine says the first row arose from the circumstance of one of our well known citizens having attended church or prayer meeting (we have such things in Caldwell) the night previous, where he learned for the first time that the Jews had killed the Gentile Savior something over eighteen hundred years ago. It incensed him to such an extent that the next morning he pitched on the first Jew he met. Bat. Carr and Henry Brown, both of whom appear always to be in the way when any fun is going on, stepped up just in time to stop the citizen in his mad endeavor to avenge the wrongs of eighteen centuries standing, and quietly conducted him before his honor Judge Kelly. Uncle Bill says that his honor, putting on all his magisterial dignity, asked the prisoner in his most impressive tones: "What have you to do with Christ, anyhow?" Being unable to answer the conundrum his honor told him to contribute to the depleted city treasury the amount of five dollars, with an extra "In God we trust," to maintain the dignity of the court. The next imitation of a Democratic ward meeting, was brought about by a difference arising from a financial settlement. Both parties got the worst of the row, physically and financially. But while they may feel sore and somewhat distressed, we must congratulate them upon being pioneers in the new order of things that makes the six shooter in this community of no more account than a toy pistol.

Civilization was indeed advancing in Caldwell and in "the new order of things" a local saloon had discovered the value of sex appeal. "A new device to get the cow boy's money—and we are afraid it catches a good many others—a woman dealing hazzard in one of the saloons," the *Commercial* reported on August 31, 1882.

Carr could also clamp down on the cowboy when it became necessary. The *Commercial*, September 7, 1882, said:

Monday is rather an uninteresting day in Caldwell, either in police, or other circles, but last Monday [September 4] proved an exception. At least Bat Carr, our city marshal, thought so. A hilarious chap from the range came into town Monday morning, and enthused by the pure air and easy going surroundings of Caldwell, undertook to have a little fun all by his lone self, so he mounted his kyuse and gaily galloped about the village. In his wild career he run across Dr. Noble's place where some of the doctor's fine sheep were sauntering around, like tony men saunter in front of a popular place where beverages are sold, and he proceeded at once to practice throwing the lariat upon them. It was fun for the ranger, but the sheep did not appear to enjoy the matinee. While engaged in his pleasant pastime, Bat. rode up along side of the ranger's pony, relieved the chap of his shooting iron, and conducted him to the presence of Judge Kelly. He gave his name as William St. John, but the St. John part did not relieve him from contributing a goodly sum to the city treasury, and when the shades of evening hovered o'er the village, William took his departure, poorer in purse, but doubtless happy in the consciousness that he had a "good time."

It appeared that gamblers were the particular prey of Marshal Carr. "Bat. Carr, our city marshal, the other morning rounded up a lot of gamblers who had been in the habit of going around with pops stuck down in their clothes. They had to pay a fine and give assurance that hereafter they would obey the city ordinance against carrying concealed weapons," reported the *Commercial*, September 28, 1882. On October 5, 1882, the *Commercial* said:

Some of the gamblers in Caldwell are terribly worried because Bat. Carr thinks the low down thieving games, such as "nine dice," three card monte," etc. ought not to be allowed. The final result was, that Bat. had some of them interview Judge Kelly on Tuesday morning, and the city treasury is richer by several dollars. We admire Bat's pluck, and hope he will keep up the fight until he runs every thieving gambler out of the town. Gambling in its mildest and most correct form is an injury at the best, but where it descends into down-right robbery, with no show whatever for the victim, it ought to be suppressed.

Caldwell citizens indicated approval of their marshal's actions by presenting him with a solid gold badge. The Caldwell *Post*, October 12, 1882, reported:

A little the handsomest badge we ever saw is the one worn by Batt Carr, our City Marshal, and presented to him last week by the citizens of Caldwell. It is solid gold in the form of a shield suspended from a plate at the top by chains. The lettering is in black enamel, and bears the inscription, "Batt Carr, City Marshal, Caldwell, Kan." On the reverse is, "Presented by the Citizens of Caldwell." Take it all together, it is the handsomest thing in that line we ever saw. Batt is deserving of the best regards of the citizens of Caldwell by reason of his excellent management of the rougher element that is common in any new community, and they take this method of showing it. The cost of the jewel was over $75, and was bo't through Henry Auling, our jeweler, by a few of our businessmen and stockmen.[3]

"Bat Carr has obtained a leave of absence and leaves on a business visit to Colorado City, Texas, next Monday," reported the *Commercial*, October 12, 1882. "Bat expects to return in fifteen or twenty days. We request the Colorado folks to handle him with care and send him back on time and in good condition." Henry Brown served as marshal in Carr's absence with Ben Wheeler acting as assistant city marshal.

On November 9, 1882, the Caldwell *Commercial* announced Carr's return:

Bat. Carr, our city marshal, returned last Thursday [November 2] from his visit to Texas. The *Commercial Clipper*, of Colorado, Texas, makes mention of his visit in the following style:

Capt. Battie Carr, city marshal of Caldwell, Kansas, is in our city shaking hands with his numerous friends and looking after his interests here. He has located at Caldwell, and has this week put his property here on the market. He has six neat residences north of and near the public square, which he offers cheap for cash. Battie was one of the early settlers of Colorado City, and showed faith in its future by investing in town lots and improving them as soon as lots were exposed to sale, showing a spirit of enterprise that enthused others to invest, and so the city started and has been rapidly improving all the time until we now have a lovely city of 3,500 souls and still the rush goes on. Carr is a man of cool nerve, and anything he undertakes he goes at it with a determination to win. He can now dispose of his property at an advance of 100 per cent. on first cost, and will reinvest in the thriving young town of Caldwell. From the handsome gold badge that he supports on his breast we see that his worth as a brave and efficient officer is appreciated by the city of his adoption, it having be[en] presented to him by the good citizens.

Bat brought back with him a splendid gold-headed cane, which he presented to Mayor Colson.

Robert Gilmore, more commonly known in his time as Bobby Gill, was a tramp familiar to nearly all the cowtowns of Kansas. Caldwell was no exception. The *Commercial*, November 9, 1882, recorded a visit in this article:

EXIT "BOBBY GILL."

Nearly all the tramps, bunko steerers, bummers and dead beats who have traveled over the main lines and prominent branches in Kansas, know "Bobby Gill." Bobby is and has been an odorous citizen for several years, one of those unfortunate contrasts necessary to show, by comparison, the advance made in civilization by the mass of humanity. Well, Bobby projected his carcass into Caldwell a few weeks ago, fuller than a tick and with a crowded case of samples of his ordinary meannesses. After remaining in his abnormal state a short time, he pulled himself together and toned down to a clean shirt and sobriety—for a few days. But Bobby couldn't stand that course for any length of time. It was too rich for even his aristocratic blood, and he soon went back to his old lay. By persistent effort Sunday evening found him with his tank full and his shirt looking as if it had been worn by a Cheyenne Indian ever since the white man began to follow the aforesaid aboriginee's track.

To make a long story short, being in that condition, Mr. Gill concluded to go to church, for a change, and while Brother Foster was reading the usual Bible lesson at the beginning of services last Sunday night [November 5], Bobby walked into the door, up the isle, and planted himself right into the amen corner, in close proximity to Bros. Edwards, Ross and Lange. Bobby took in the entire services, and we must say in truth, conducted himself in a more reverential manner than many professed worshippers usually do. At the close of the services he retired quietly and unostentatiously, seemingly deeply impressed by the singing of the choir and the tender appeals of the pastor to erring humanity.

But alas, for good conduct. The next morning the gamblers insisted on Bobby leaving town. He had disgraced the profession by going to church, and they couldn't stand it; so they raised some money to pay his fare to the home of all such refugees, Dodge City, and at three o'clock, Bat Carr escorted him to the depot in style and saw him safely ensconsed in a reclining chair, and we hope, that by this time, he is under the protecting care of Mayor Webster.

Poor Bob! His career and condition, if we look at it philosophically—only serves to show what many of us, who hold our heads so high above him, might have been under like adverse circumstances.

There are vessels made to honor, and vessels made to dishonor, and no man can say, given the same conditions, that he is better than another.

The Caldwell *Post*, November 9, 1882, reported more of Carr's activities against the gambling element: "Bat Carr, Chief of Police, is making it lively for the slick-fingered gentry and gamblers. He fired half a dozen or so out yesterday and pulled several others." On November 23, 1882, the *Post* said that "Bat Carr gathered in five hurrah fellows one day last week between six and seven o'clock, and two more the next morning—and it was not a good time for the business, either."

In December a shoe thief was caught. The *Commercial*, December 7, 1882, had this article:

In going to the postoffice on Tuesday [December 5], we met Marshal Bat Carr with a pair of ladies' shoes, and wondered what was the meaning of such a freak. Upon inquiring, we found that the colored man working for Dr. Noble had stolen the shoes from F. W. Leonard, our young enterprising boot and shoe man, and had been trying to sell the stolen goods to different parties. Bat went to him and told him he would take his company down town. The n—— said "Does you want dem shoes, Mr. Carr?" whereupon Bat told him he did, and if they were not forthcoming, he would take him to the cooler. The gentleman in question replied: "I nebber stoled dem shoes, I jest borrowed 'em," and he went to a small house and after a time brought forth the property. Bat watches the pilferers closely and their way is a hard one to travel while he is around.

On December 21, 1882, the *Commercial* announced that "City Marshal Carr, left last week for Texas, and it is rumored around that he will bring back with him a frau. Wish you much joy, Bat." The same day Henry Brown was appointed city marshal of Caldwell.[4]

The next summer it was rumored that Bat Carr had been killed in Texas. The Caldwell *Journal*, August 30, 1883, said: "A report comes to us to the effect that Bat Carr, formerly marshal of this city, was recently killed in one of the border towns of Texas. The report lacks confirmation, still it is possibly correct."

But Bat Carr was very much alive:

BAT CARR HEARD FROM.

DALLAS, TEXAS, Sept 7, 1883.

ED. JOURNAL:—I notice in the local columns of the JOURNAL of the 30th, ult., a paragraph setting forth that Bat Carr, former city marshal of Caldwell, had been killed in one of the border towns of Texas. This short message from Bat himself will suffice to deny the report; and through the columns of your valuable paper let me extend to the citizens of Caldwell my kindest regards and well wishes for their future prosperity; through life will I cherish in memory the fond recollections of my sojourn in your little city. When the JOURNAL is returned, marked by the P. M., "Not taken," then you may suspect the correctness of a like report.

Respectfully, BAT CARR.[5]

1. *See* the section on Henry Brown for reprints of these two articles. 2. *See, also,* the Caldwell *Commercial*, July 13, 1882. 3. *See, also, ibid.,* October 12, 1882. 4. Caldwell *Post,* Caldwell *Commercial,* December 28, 1882. 5. Caldwell *Journal,* September 13, 1883.

CARSON, THOMAS

Tom Carson was temporarily appointed to the police force of Abilene during that town's last trail-driving season. The marshal of Abilene then was Wild Bill Hickok. On June 14, 1871, the city

clerk of Abilene recorded Carson's appointment in these words:
"Thomas Carson appointed as policeman pro tem with the understanding that he should be appointed regularly his pay dating from
the time he commenced work." [1]

Carson was appointed a regular member of the force on June 23,
1871.[2] In less than a week he was in trouble with the city authorities
over a difficulty he had with fellow policeman J. H. McDonald.
The official records of the city carry this entry dated June 28, 1871:

The Hon Mayor of the City of Abilene. You are hereby requested to call
[a council meeting] on the evening of the 28th day of June 1871. For the
purpose of investigating a certain affray occurring between Thomas Carson and
J. H. McDonald policeman of said City on the 28th day of June A. D. 1871.
"Signed"

> J. A Gauthie
> S. H[A.] Burroughs
> J. A Smith
> Dr Boudinot
> Samuel Carpenter [members of the city council].

Whereupon it is hereby ordered by J. A. Gauthie acting president that a
Meeting be held on said evening. On Motion the Council proceed to make an
investigation as aforesaid. J H McDonald Thomas Carson Jessee Moon.
Thomas & Craiman were duly sworn to make true statements in regard to said
controversy. The Council after having heard the testimony moved that the
said officers be sent forth again to their duty, after being first reprimanded by
the President (Carried) J. A. Gauthie then proceeded to advise the officers
& to admonish them that if brought up again they would be discharged. . . .[3]

While Abilene was having its last cattle driving season in 1871,
Newton, a new town sired by the Santa Fe railroad in Harvey
county, was having its first. And it was in Newton that Thomas
Carson next showed up as a police officer.

Born in March, the town of Newton was a lusty, brawling adolescent in August. By then it was reported that ten "dance" houses
were running full blast and three more were under construction.
One writer said:

. . . I have been in a good many towns but Newton is the fastest one I
have ever seen. Here you may see young girls not over sixteen drinking
whisky, smoking cigars, cursing and swearing until one almost looses the
respect they should have for the weaker sex, I heard one of their townsmen
say that he didn't believe there were a dozen virtuous women in town. This
speaks well for a town claiming 1,500 inhabitants. He further told me if I
had any money that I would not be safe with it here. It is a common expression that they have a man every morning for breakfast.[4]

Tom Carson

Early Sunday morning, August 20, 1871, a gun battle took place which left nine men dead or wounded. Referred to by many as "Newton's General Massacre," it was described in *The Kansas Daily Commonwealth* of Topeka, August 22, 1871:

NEWTON.

MORE WHOLESALE BUTCHERY.

THREE MEN KILLED.

SEVERAL WOUNDED.

While at Newton, a few days ago, we were informed that inasmuch as a man had been killed there on the morning of the day of our arrival, a week would probably elapse ere another killing scrape would occur; that usually after a killing in that town no events of any moment, saving an occasional head breaking or an unimportant stabbing affray, occurred for a week or so. That information was correct for just a week sped by before a season of bloodshed and slaughter was again inaugurated. On Sunday (which is the devil's favorite day for big operations in that town) last, the demon of discord was again let loose, and riot, blood and murder was rampart to an unusual degree. It seems as if the week of respite had sharpened the appetite of the devil and given him additional vigor and disposition to riot in a carnival of blood. The following particulars are furnished us by an eye witness:

Ever since the shooting affair between McCluskie and the Texas man, Bailey, which resulted in the death of the latter, a great dissatisfaction has been not only felt but expressed on the part of Texas men and "war" was declared to the bitter end against McCluskie should he ever again venture to put in his appearance in the town. But as the natural result of all such broils, McCluskie was to come and McCluskie did come and McCluskie saw but did not conquer. The affair started at one of the dance houses about 2 o'clock A. M. on Sunday morning. McCluskie was warned that his life was in peril, but thinking himself proof against powder and ball, scorned the warning and went into the dance to come out a dead man. A great many shots were exchanged before any serious damage was done.

John Martin, a Texan, was the first man killed and the only one that was killed instantly, and he received an accidental shot as he was trying to effect a reconciliation between the parties. Martin was a general favorite among all the boys and was called "good natured Martin." McCluskie received three wounds, any one of which would probably have proved fatal. He only live[d] a few hours. Since he died, another wounded Texan has died whose name we did not learn. Two railroad men were hit by chance shots, who were not in the muss at all but were hit by shots intended for others. One was a foreman on the track named Hickey. He was shot through the calf of the leg making only a flesh wound; the other was a brakeman on the freight train named Pat Lee; who was wounded quite seriously through the abdomen. Three men are now dead. Six others were wounded, and some of them quite seriously. One Billy Garrett, a Texas man, was shot in the arm, and it is thought, was internally injured by some blow. He lies in a very critical state, and is not expected to live. Many are inclined to blame the Texas men for all the trouble, but it is the opinion of our informant that others are just as much to blame as they are, and that in very many instances more so. How all this will end is a problem that must yet be solved. It seems to be a great mistake that a town can only be incorporated and get an organization in the three first months of the year, as something seems to be quite necessary in Newton—a good efficient police force and a set of officers that mean business and will take some measures to make it safe for people to walk the streets. It is worse than "Tim Finnegan's wake."

———

Since the foregoing was in type we received at 11 P. M. yesterday, by the night train on the A. T. & S. F. R. R., the following full and graphic account of the Newton tragedy, from the pen of a correspondent of the N. Y. World. We publish it to the exclusion of our usual variety of local matter, knowing that it will be read with interest by our readers:

NEWTON, Aug. 21, 1871.

To the Editor of the Commonwealth.

The air of Newton is tainted with the hot steam of human blood. Murder, "most foul and unnatural," has again stained the pages of her short history, and the brand of Cain has stamped its crimson characters on the foreheads of men with horrible frequency.

The cessation of travel on the railroad and the want of telegraphic communication from this town on the Sabbath, have prevented the data contained in this letter from reaching you until the present date; but with the exception of a single dispatch transmitted yesterday to the mother of McCluskie in St. Louis, announcing his death, no particulars have passed on the wires, and your readers will consequently have as prompt and complete a narrative of the tragedy of Sunday morning as is possible under the circumstances.

Your exhaustive and highly graphic article of a few days since, in which Newton, and particularly that part of it known as "Hide Park," appeared as the central figure, created a flutter of excitement in this community, and, notwithstanding the caustic, even stern criticisms on the general looseness of morals and disregard of both state and municipal laws, the almost unanimous verdict was that it was "true, temperate and unbiased." Nay, more than that: the wish has been loudly and earnestly expressed that the Editor of the COMMONWEALTH had been an eye witness of the tragedy in order that, with its horrible features ever fresh in his recollection, his indignant pen might be persuaded to cut still deeper into the rottenness which underlies and pervades the social and political system of Newton. I may be pardoned for the statement that the opportunity is yet a golden one, and for the hope that it will not be thrown away.

It will be remembered that about ten days since a Texas desperado by the name of [Wm.] Baylor, a man who is reputed to have killed at least two men in drunken brawls, met his death while murderously assaulting one McCluskie, lately in the employ of the Atchison, Topeka & Santa Fe railroad. The common belief is, and the probabilities are, that McCluskie fired the fatal shot; whether true or not, however, such was the impression that obtained among the Texas men, nearly all of whom in this vicinity, are cattle owners or drivers. These latter are a large and distinctive element of the population, and though generally of a rough and forbidding exterior, still show some sterling qualities of character; standing by one another with a dogged obstinacy that might be called chivalrous, were it not so often exercised in a bad cause. The deceased was popular among his fellows. Good natured, generous, dangerous only when maddened by liquor, his bad qualities were forgotten and Texas sympathy was oblivious to ought but what endeared him to them. Sympathy, strengthened by bad counsels, intensified itself into rage; rage feeding on itself, verged into revenge; revenge, muttered and whispered and finally outspoken, culminated in murder. Of murder we have now to deal. It was past midnight. The moon had sought her couch, and the stars alone were nature's watchers. Away out on the prairie from among a cluster of low-roofed houses, twinkled lights and issued sounds of revelry and mirth. The town was buried in repose and naught animate was visible save an occasional pedestrian, hurrying home or the ghostly outline of a distant horseman returning to his camp.

To the casual looker-on, the scene was bewitching; bewitching through its quietness and natural beauty; bewitching through its *promise* of quiet and rest. Of a sudden, however, the scene changes. Groups of men walking hastily and conversing in low, hurried tones, are seen approaching the town along the road leading to the place where the lights still twinkle and the sound of mirth flows on unbroken.

Of what are they talking?

"There will be a fracas to-night, boys, and Mac is a dead man," says one, a heavily bearded man, around whom his companions cluster in respectful attention. "Texas is on the rampage to-night in dead earnest, and before morning there will be lively music over yonder," pointing with his thumb to the place they had just left. "We haven't more than quit in time. I would have told Mac, but they were watching me, and I didn't get a chance."

Another group crosses the railroad track and pauses to look back. "I shouldn't wonder but what there will be shooting at Perry's before long," remarks one. "I know it," says another; "and I," "and I," so echo the rest. "The boys have sworn to kill McCluskie, and they are going to do it to-night; You see, if they don't," says a bushy-haired man, with two revolvers in his belt, and a huge bowie knife protruding from his shirt front. These were Texans, who knew what was on foot, but who by their criminal silence, have made themselves "accessories before the fact."

Still groups and stragglers came along the road, the majority talking in the same vein, and nearly all actuated by the one motive of self preservation. They wanted to take no risk of chance bullets, and they hurried away. But did any one try to avert the impending danger? No, not one. "It's no business of mine," was the common sentiment. "Every one for himself, and the devil for the hindmost." "I'm sorry, but it can't be helped."

A walk of a few moments brings us to the dance houses, one kept by Perry Tuttle, and another, the Alamo, by E. P. Crum. They are but thirty yards

101

apart, and around them are the other houses, built and used for purposes which the reader can divine without unnecessary explanation. Women are the attraction and—. The grass is stubbed and yellow hereabouts, and dim lanes, worn by the feet of customers, radiate in every direction. Men are continually crossing from one house to the other to seek occasionally a change of music, but oftener a fresh partner. The proprietors of these houses are all men who have many friends, and who by their personal qualities are universally popular. Quiet, never intoxicated, and generous to a fault, their constant aim has been to keep quiet and orderly establishments; and they or their employees have always suppressed any signs of tumult or disorder immediately on their inception. It must be said, to their credit, that no disturbance would ever occur could their efforts quell it. One of the houses, the Alamo, had closed shortly after midnight. The music had been discharged, and business for the night was over. In the other house the dance was prolonged until after 1 o'clock, when, the crowd thinning out, the proprietor gave the signal for closing.

Now begins the tragedy. The victim was ready and the sacrificial priests stood waiting to receive him. The victim was Mike McCluskie, or, as he afterwards on his deathbed stated his name to be, Arthur Delaney. The priests were all Texans, Hugh Anderson, Solado, Belle county, Texas; Jim Martin, Refugio, Texas; Wm. Garrett, Solado, Texas; Henry Kearnes, Texas, Jim Wilkerson, Kentucky, and J. C. U., Solado, Texas. One of the priests sat talking to the victim with the evident intention of distracting his attention in order to allow one of the order to give the death blow. The order stood back watching, and waiting for the entrance of the high priest, their eyes roving alternately from the victim to the door. The high priest enters, and striding along the room, confronts his victims and begins the death song. His weapon is in his hand, with death looking grimly from its muzzle. His words come hot and hissing, beginning low and rising with his passion until they are shrieked out with demoniacal force. "You are a cowardly s-n of a b—h! I will blow the top of your head off", are the words that fall from his lips, at the same time the hammer falls, and a ball goes crashing through the neck of the victim. The latter rises partially to his feet and presenting his weapon full at the breast of his adversary, presses the trigger. Malediction! The cap hangs fire, and the victim, bathed in his own blood, but still discharging his weapon, falls to the floor. The high priest now gives the death stroke and reaching over, again taps the fountain of life by sending another bullet through the back of the prostrate man. The work is done, that is partially.

As the leader rises to his feet, the attendant priests discharge their weapons. Whether they found another victim, no one can say. Murder has already accomplished its mission, and the days of McCluskie are numbered. But there is an avenging Nemesis on the track. A stalwart figure suddenly appears on the scene. For an instant he remains motionless, as if studying the situation. Then a sheet of flame vomits forth, apparently from his hand, and a Texan staggers from the room across the area and falls dead at the door of the "Alamo." Another and another and another shot follows, until six men, all priests, have bowed to his prowess.[5]

There were others injured, one, Patrick Lee, a brakesman on the railroad, who was a quiet and inoffensive looker on, shot through the bowels, and another, Hickey, a shoveler on the same road, wounded in the leg.

There was work enough for the doctors. The only two in town were immediately summoned. They were Drs. Gaston and Boyd,[6] and they were untiring in their professional efforts.

By the time they arrived, the dead man, Martin, had been taken into the Alamo, where he lay saturated with his own blood. McCluskie had been taken upstairs as soon as he was shot. Both dance houses were turned into hospitals. The dying and wounded have received every care and attention. The women nursed them with touching assiduity and tenderness. The floors and sides of both halls were everywhere sprinkled with blood, and the gory stains yet remain. The magistrate of Newton declares his intention to suppress all dance houses in the future. Many question his authority to do so, but the citizens will nearly all support him in case a demonstration is made to that effect. Coroner C. S. Bowman held an inquest over the remains of Martin and McCluskie yesterday morning, and a verdict was returned that Martin came to his death at the hands of some person unknown, and that McCluskie came to his death at 8 o'clock a. m., this 20th day of August, by a shot from a pistol in the hands of Hugh Anderson, and that the said shooting was done feloniously and with intent to kill McCluskie. A warrant was accordingly issued and served by Marshal Harry Nevill upon Anderson. It is ascertained what will be the fate of some of the wounded men. Two at least, it is thought, will die. The following is a list of the names of the sufferers in the fracas: Arthur Delaney, St. Louis, neck, back and leg, dead. Jim Martin, neck, dead. Hugh Anderson, high priest, thigh and leg, doing fairly. Patrick Lee, bowels, critical. Jim Wilkerson, nose, slight. —— leg, slight. —— Hickey, leg, slight. Henry Kearnes, right breast, fatal. William Garrett, shoulder and breast, fatal.

Last evening, some of the Texans having made threats that they would kill Tom Carson, a nephew of the late Kit Carson, if he were appointed on the police, a large number of the citizens went about thoroughly armed to preserve the peace. No disturbance arose, however, and never is likely to arise, as the number of law abiding citizens is fully equal to that of the desperadoes, and the latter unless they think they have an overwhelming majority, will never initiate a disturbance.

By to-morrow's mail I hope to be able to send you further particulars.

ALLEGRO.

In the Abilene *Chronicle's* report of the affair, August 24, 1871, it was stated that Mike McCluskie had been appointed to the Newton police force after the shooting of Bailey. The *Chronicle* also included this paragraph on Carson's appointment:

On Monday evening last threats were made, by many desperadoes, that in case Tom Carson, late a policeman in Abilene, was placed upon the police force, that they would kill him. He was, however, appointed a police officer, and that evening patroled his allotted beat as unmolested as if he were in Abilene, no disturbance whatever occurring.

Further news appeared in the *Commonwealth* on August 23, 1871:

THE NEWTON TRAGEDY.

DEATH OF THREE MORE VICTIMS.

SIX DEATHS IN ALL.

From passengers on the night train of the Santa Fe railroad, who arrived at Topeka last evening, we learn that three more persons who were wounded during the murderous affray at Newton on Sunday morning last, died yesterday. Lee, the brakeman on the Santa Fe railroad, was one of the unfortunate victims. His body arrived on the train last night and will be buried in Topeka to-day.

This is the most terrible tragedy that has ever occurred in Kansas during civil times. It is a burning shame and disgrace to Kansas, and measures should at once be adopted to prevent a repetition. It will be remembered that Newton has no municipal government, and then it is dependent upon its township authorities for protection. As they are inadequate to govern such a lawless and reckless class as predominates in that town, we believe it would be an act of humanity for the military branch of the government to take possession of it and control it until a civil organization can be formed, and in which there is strength enough to offer protection to its people. Let us have no more of such sickening and shocking tragedies.

On August 27, 1871, the *Commonwealth* reported some progress toward the enforcement of law in Newton:

NEWTON

"AFTER THE BATTLE"—A DODGE TO SECURE
ANDERSON'S ESCAPE—CONDITION OF THE
WOUNDED. . . . "QUIET REIGNS IN WARSAW"
—THE HATCHET BURIED BETWEEN THE "LONG HORNS"
AND "SHORT HORNS"—THE DESPERADOES
"VAMOOSED"—SAFETY OF LIFE IN NEWTON
—NO SOLDIERS WANTED—A CALABOOSE
ERECTED—ORGANIZATION OF A CITY GOVERN-
MENT—A TOWN HOUSE. CHURCH AND
SCHOOL HOUSE TO BE ERECTED.

CORRESPONDENCE OF THE COMMONWEALTH.

The wave of agitation set in motion by the late terrible tragedy at "Hide Park" has not yet spent its force, although the oil of peace has been freely poured forth, and the clouds of danger have dissipated and scattered, and left the horizon once more clear and bright. The "seven day's excitement," which the popular saying attaches to everything which runs out of the ordinary groove of every day experience, and which partakes of a morbidly interesting nature, has yet to run its course, and the dead and the wounded, and the incidents which led to their condition, are as freely, though more calmly discussed, as they were on the morning of the day of the tragedy.

104

Tom Carson

In my first letter I stated that a warrant had been served on Hugh Anderson for the murder of Delaney. This turns out to be partially incorrect. A warrant was filled out and handed to the marshal, but in the condition in which the wounded man then was it was not deemed advisable to serve it, as any unusual excitement (it was going out) would prove fatal. This proved to be simply a dodge to get Anderson out of the way, for three nights since he was secretly removed from town, and it has been impossible to ascertain his whereabouts. Some say he has been taken to Kansas City or St. Louis, while others are positive that he is now in the Indian territory. If the latter surmise be correct, he is far from being safe from arrest, as a United States marshal can serve the warrant at any moment, and cause him to be brought back to trial.[7] There have but four men died of those who were wounded. Lee and Garrett were buried on successive days. Anderson's wounds will no doubt prove fatal, and Kearnes is in a very critical situation. The others are doing well, and will shortly be about. . . .

All parties, and particularly the Texans, who own at least a third of the town, are keen and unyielding in the determination to preserve peace and the majesty of the law. A meeting was held a few days since, at which it was resolved to bury all past difficulties, and to appoint a police force composed of Texas men and Newtonians. It departed amid a burst of enthusiasm and good feeling, which showed how sincere was the common wish for, and the determination to, maintain a peaceable, law-abiding town. The few desperadoes who have been in the habit of making their neighbors uncomfortable by a bravo display of pistols and knives, have wisely taken to the prairie, and an ordinance is published and rigidly carried out which disarms any and all persons who may be found carrying dangerous weapons within the township of Newton. There has been considerable talk about the propriety of applying for a company of soldiers with which to keep order. The suggestion is by no means a necessary one. Ten days ago it might have been well timed, but with the increase of the police force by the appointment of five deputies, the town may be considered as able to protect itself. By to-morrow evening a calaboose will have been erected, capable of containing any reasonable number of prisoners. There has been nothing of the kind heretofore. Judge [R. W. P.] Muse, who seems to be the head and front of the peace movement, declares that the history of Newton is now to begin afresh. Who will not rejoice to hear of it?

Last evening a mass meeting of the citizens was held to take steps to form a city government. Another meeting will be held to-night to nominate candidates. The offices to be filled are those of mayor, police judge, marshal and five councilmen. All persons now living here, who intend to locate or remain for a reasonable length of time, will be permitted to vote. The election takes place to-morrow, when, undoubtedly, a heavy vote will be polled. Steps are also being taken to raise the necessary funds to build a town house, church and school house.   ALLEGRO.

Since writing the above, at an informal meeting of some of the principal citizens, the following ticket was put in nomination: For mayor, Mr. [R. M.] Spivey; for councilmen, Messrs. [L. E.] Steele, Cunningham, Gregory, Dow, Hurd; for police judge, J. J. Baker, the present justice of the peace; for sheriffs [probably deputy sheriffs or constables], Tom Carson and C. B. King.
NEWTON, August 25.

Both Carson and King were hired, but in exactly what capacity is not certain. The following article in *The Kansas Daily Commonwealth*, September 28, 1871, reported King a "deputy sheriff" and Carson as "acting constable":

NEWTON.

THE CARNIVAL OF BLOOD—THE ASSASSIN
STILL AT WORK—MURDER OF OFFICER
C. B. KING.

NEWTON, Sept. 27, 1871.
TO THE EDITOR OF THE COMMONWEALTH.

A several day's absence on a buffalo hunt, from which I have but just returned, has prevented me from mailing you the details of the murder of Deputy Sheriff King on Saturday last. Your readers are already acquainted with the fact of his death. A few particulars may, perhaps, be found sufficiently interesting to warrant a perusal, and I give them, apologizing in the outset for the *bous trophedon* style of description.

The coroner's jury rendered this verdict: That C. B. King came to his death by a pistol wound inflicted by one Thomas Edwards, and that the shooting was done feloniously and with intent to kill.

On Saturday evening last, about ten o'clock, Officer King, in accordance with the requirements of the law, discovered Edwards while the latter was in one of the dance houses. As he met with some resistance, Tom Carson, an acting constable, stepped to King's assistance, and leveling his revolver ordered him with an oath to "throw up his hands." The pistol was then given up and Edwards was released. Carson returned to Newton while King remained on the premises. Some two hours later, as King was standing outside of the door, in the same fated area which drank the blood of Martin and others of the victims of the Sunday morning horror of a month ago, Edwards approached him and placing a Derringer close to his breast, fired, the ball lodging near the heart. King staggered into the house, exclaiming "Who shot me?" and immediately fell over on his arm. His friends caught him and the blood gushed from his mouth in a thick, black stream, and a moment later he was dead. Edwards fled and has not since been seen.

Thus perished Officer King, than whom there was no better gentleman nor truer friend, and no more respected man in Newton. Thus does the red hand of the assassin continue to do its bloody work, for the taking of King's life is *known* to have been a premeditated act,—plotted by others and accomplished by Edwards.

106

Newton is tremendous with excitement and indignation over it. The officers of the law say they are on the lookout for the murderer and his accomplices, but no one as yet has been arrested, and, if the chances be properly weighed, no one in all probability will be arrested. Cannot Topeka send us a couple of detectives who will do their duty fearlessly and vigilantly? Brute force without sagacity is plenty enough here, but we want men who possess both.

The funeral of King took place on Monday, and was largely attended. Business houses generally closed during the funeral ceremonies.

The man who was accidentally shot by Edwards during his scuffle with King, is doing well, the ball having entered the fleshy part of the thigh.

ALLEGRO.

By November, 1871, Carson was back in Abilene and on the police force again. "On motion Tom Carson and 'Brocky Jack' [John W. Norton] were allowed fifty dollars each for police duty, and the same ordered paid," wrote the city clerk in the minute book of Abilene's city council, November 4, 1871 (p. 99).

The Junction City *Union*, November 25, 1871, reported that "A shooting affair occurred at Abilene, during the fore part of the week, which resulted in the wounding of John Man, a bar tender, at the hands of Tom. Carson, who was acting as policeman at the time. It is said the shot was fired without provocation. Man was struck somewhere about the hip, and is slowly recovering."

On November 27, 1871, the city clerk made this entry in the minute book (p. 105): "On Motion City Marshall be instructed to discharge Thomas Carson & Brocky Jack from off Police force from & after this 27th day of Nov 1871 (Carried)."

Both Tom Carson and Brocky Jack Norton remained in Abilene until, one day late in January, 1872, Carson shot Norton. The reason is unknown, the only information coming from this article printed in the Abilene *Chronicle*, February 1, 1872:

IN JAIL.—Tom Carson had a preliminary examination before 'Squire [E.] Barber, lasting three days, was bound over to the next term of District Court, and because Tom could not furnish the requisite $1,000 bail, he was committed to the tender mercies of Sheriff [C. L.] Murphy.—Brocky Jack, the man whom Tom shot, is recovering.

Carson never appeared before the court. The *Chronicle*, February 22, 1872, reported his last known activity in Kansas:

BROKE JAIL.

THE DICKINSON COUNTY JAIL EMPTY.

On last Sunday night [February 18], about nine o'clock, the prisoners in jail—four in number—escaped by making a hole through the stone wall under

107

one of the windows. The names of the "birds" are as follows: Tom Carson, awaiting trial for shooting with intent to kill; Thos. Keenan, charged with horse-stealing; and a Mexican and another prisoner. As usual much fuss was made about the escape, but without capturing the fleeing fugitives.

It is thought they they carry enough brass in their faces to return of their own accord, when it will be an easy thing to capture and fetter them so that they will "stay." The fact is, outside of the cells our jail is not worth a fig for the safe keeping of prisoners.

1. "City Council Minute Book," Records of the City of Abilene, p. 70. 2. *Ibid.*, p. 69. 3. *Ibid.*, p. 74. 4. Wichita *Tribune*, August 24, 1871. 5. Judge R. W. P. Muse, writing a "History of Harvey County, Kansas, for One Decade—from 1871 to 1881," in *Edwards' Historical Atlas of Harvey Co., Kansas, 1882*, gave the earliest known identification of the "avenging Nemesis." Muse, who was in the town that night, wrote: "Standing near the door, at the time the affray commenced, was a friend of McCloskey [*sic*], a boy named Riley, some 18 years of age, quiet and inoffensive in deportment, and evidently dying from consumption, . . . [who] coolly locked the door . . . and drawing his revolver, discharged every chamber. . . ." No known contemporary source, however, identified the stranger. 6. Allegro erred. Actually these names belonged to one physician, Dr. Gaston Boyd, one of the original settlers of Newton. It is not known who the other doctor might have been. 7. Hugh Anderson was spirited away to Kansas City, then Texas, where he recovered. He was killed at Medicine Lodge in June, 1873, in a fierce hand to hand duel with Mike McCluskie's brother. Strangely enough Allegro was again on hand and reported the fight, in which the avenging brother also died, to the New York *World.—*See Colin W. Rickards, "Vengeance: Kansas 1870's Style," *The English Westerners' Brand Book*, London, v. 4, no. 1 (October, 1961), pp. 2-9.

CHIPMAN, CLARK E. (1856?-____)

On June 10, 1882, the mayor and council of Dodge City appointed an entirely new police force. Peter W. Beamer was named marshal, C. E. Chipman, assistant, and Lee Harlan, policeman. "The appointment of the new police force will give general satisfaction. They are sober and honest men, and will no doubt discharge their duties faithfully and satisfactorily," wrote the editor of the Dodge City *Times*, June 15, 1882.[1]

The same day he was appointed assistant marshal, the 26-year-old Chipman, in his concurrent role as township constable, captured a wanted man after a grueling chase. The *Times*, June 15, 1882, reported:

C. E. Chipman, Constable, had quite an adventure after a prisoner on Saturday last. The man was charged with a State offense, but eluded the vigilance of the officers. Constable Chipman pursued his man over the prairie, never relaxing his speed until opposite Ryan's ranch, 18 miles down the river, having in the meantime changed horses. At this point the Constable "rounded

C. E. Chipman

up" the man in short order. The prisoner was brought to this city, and after paying a fine was released. On the route Constable Chipman lost some money and valuables from his pockets, together with the "using up," of the horses, did not compensate him; but he has the proud satisfaction of having done his duty, well and faithfully, but at the sacrifice of some loss and a few injured limbs of his own body, caused by the excessive ride. The distance traveled was about 55 miles. This should be a warning to evil doers in Dodge township. Constable Chipman is an officer who will follow his man until the last horse is run down.

In July, 1882, Jack Bridges replaced Beamer as city marshal but Chipman remained in the number two position. Harlan was relieved in September, leaving only the marshal and assistant on the force.

The Dodge City police did not make the local press again until the outbreak of the Dodge City "war" (see the section on Luke Short) in the spring of 1883. Chipman was involved since he was on the police force, and the Luke Short faction considered him one of the chief instigators of the plot to oust the little gambler. One newspaper believed the refusal of Mayor L. E. Deger to dismiss him, as W. H. Harris (Luke Short's partner in the Long Branch saloon) had requested, was a prime cause of the trouble.[2] The part played by Clark Chipman in the Dodge City "war" is described under Luke Short.

About the first of June, 1883, Chipman was replaced by Mysterious Dave Mather and reduced to the rank of policeman. His subsequent dismissal provoked an indignant letter published in the Ford County Globe, July 17, 1883:

DODGE CITY, KAS., July 12, 1813 [1883].

EDITOR GLOBE.—Why was C. E. Chipman put off of the police force. A man that was as good an officer as ever was on the force, and the only man that had any interest in the city, the only officer that pays a cent of taxes. Why is it that the Mayor and Council puts on Tom Dick and Harry, men that are imported in here from other countries. There are citizens here that would like to have it and would give just as good satisfaction as men from Colorado and New Mexico. There are men here that are citizens, have families and are property owners that would like to have it at a reasonable salary per month. It is a shame and a disgrace on the citizens at Ford County and at Dodge City to pay men one hundred and fifty dollars per month, when our own men would do it for the same. Now let their be a warning to tax payers at this city and at the next city election elect a man that is a property owner and a citizen, and a man that will work to the interest of our community. Look at the condition of our town. Has there been any reform about which Deger puffed and

109

blowed so much? An ignorant man is not competent to tell what to do. That is what is the matter with our mayor.

As we stated above the only tax payer on the force was put off and what was he put off for? No one knows. There is not any one that can say a harmful word of him and he is a man that has always done his duty, always could be found at any time and as good a lawabiding citizen as there is in our city.

He is the only officer that got out and worked for the Deger ticket, and the way he has been treated is a shame. If he has done anything to be discharged for, why don't the Mayor and Council investigate it.

CITIZEN AND TAXPAYER,

As well as a former Deger supporter.

The exact end date of Chipman's police services has not been determined. He was paid $40.00 for June service and $50.00 for "special services in July." [3] His name does not appear on subsequent salary lists.

On July 31, 1883, the *Globe* published this letter in answer to the questions put by the "citizen and tax payer":

DODGE CITY, July 26, 1883.

EDITOR GLOBE:

The "former Deger supporter's" able letter and pertinent questions as to the whys and wherefores of Clark Chipman's removal as assistant marshal are to the initiated easily understood. Here it is. In 1876, Deger being marshal, arrested a man named Blake and placed him in the same cell of the calaboose with Ferguson, Henderson and Boyle, three horse thieves since hung. This against the remonstrance of Blake, who begged him to place him somewhere else, telling him they (F., H. and B.) would surely kill him. The authocratic Deger "didn't care a d——," and in fifteen minutes Blake's yells brought aid, when Blake was found with one eye cut out by the use of a jack knife, and nearly dead from kicks and stabs. Blake sued the city, who employed four attorneys to aid Mr. Colburn, city attorney, whereupon Judge Peters held that the city was not liable, but that the marshal was the wrong doer. The great Deger being at that time totally worthless (financially) no suit was brought. [See the section on Deger.]

All this was known to Clark Chipman, and right here comes the gist of Clark's removal. A few days after the scepter of absolute power as Mayor had been clutched by his Greatness, and while he was preparing to remove to his castle OUTSIDE OF THE CITY OF DODGE CITY, (see Dass. Stat., chapter 19, article 1, Sec. 12, page 188,) and where he now resides contrary to said Statute, meeting Clark upon the street, Deger in manner and voice imitating our idea of the Czar of Russia, ordered Clark to "immediately throw that d—— [D. M.] Frost [editor of the *Ford County Globe*] into the calaboose." Chipman knew he must either be cognizant of an offense having been committed or have a warrant, and he so told his royal highness,—it was enough. Clark was dismissed and taught "not to contend with the Spirits of

110

Heaven," and learned that this was an absolute majorality, whose gratitude for favors closed with the closing of the polls, and whose election meant "pap for my supporters and persecution for those who differed with me and my clam." JUSTICE.

On August 30, 1883, Chipman was listed by the Dodge City *Times* as being a member of the Glick Guards, a militia unit of Dodge City. Many of the Luke Short faction in the recent troubles were also listed as members.

Chipman, as a special deputy sheriff, aided Sheriff Pat Sughrue in taking a prisoner to court in Larned in January, 1884. (*See* the section on Sughrue.) This was the last mention found of C. E. Chipman as a police officer.

1. *See, also,* the *Ford County Globe,* June 13, 1882. 2. *Topeka Daily Kansas State Journal,* May 17, 1883. 3. *Ford County Globe,* July 17, August 14, 1883.

CODY, WILLIAM FREDERICK (1846-1917)

The boy who became known the world over as Buffalo Bill was born in a log cabin about two miles west of LeClaire, Iowa, on February 26, 1846. His father, Isaac, already a pioneer several times over, moved his family into newly-opened Kansas territory on June 10, 1854, and once more established a wilderness home. Their house was located in Salt creek valley not far from the Fort Leavenworth military reservation.

Isaac Cody was an active man. Much of his time was spent in promoting the town of Grasshopper Falls, now Valley Falls, Jefferson county, which he had surveyed. Consequently he was gone from home a great deal and young Will felt the responsibility of an early manhood.

Shortly after the family came to Kansas father Cody was stabbed by pro-slave ruffians supposedly because of his abolitionist sentiments. He apparently recovered, but less than three years later, in 1857, he came down with a chill while working in the rain and died on March 10. The family believed his death was due to complications resulting from the stabbing.

With his father gone young Will sought to aid his mother by working wherever he could. While still an adolescent he hired out to the freighting firm of Majors and Russell and made three trips across the Plains. Later he was reported to have been a rider on the Pony Express which the expanded firm of Russell, Majors & Waddell operated from April, 1860, until October, 1861.

By late winter of 1864 Will apparently considered himself ready for military duty and enlisted in Co. H, Seventh Kansas Volunteer cavalry on February 19. He remained in the army until the regiment was mustered out on September 29, 1865.[1]

After the war Will tried several occupations, among them hotel keeping, stage driving and army scouting. Apparently the latter appealed to him most for the next several years were spent in this general line of work. He was stationed in western Kansas mostly, and was in Ellis county when a newspaper story regarding him appeared in the Leavenworth *Daily Conservative*, November 26, 1867.

A hunting excursion had taken several Ohio and eastern Kansas gentlemen to Fort Hays where on Friday, November 22, they embarked on a buffalo chase. "Much anxiety was created on Saturday night by the non-arrival of Judge Corwin, who had strayed from the party on Friday. On Sunday, Lieut. [Wm. B.] Kennedy, of Co. G, 5th [10th] cavalry, with a party of his men, and Buffalo Bill, with fifteen or twenty citizens volunteered to go out and look for him," reported the *Conservative*. "After a long ride the latter named party, found the lost man about five miles from the fort, nearly starved and almost exhausted."

On January 11, 1868, the *Conservative* printed this item from the Hays City *Advance:*

Buffalo and elk meat is as plenty as cranberries in Michigan or shad in Connecticut, and as cheap.

Bill Cody and "Brigham" [his horse] started on a hunt Saturday afternoon, and came in Tuesday. The result was nineteen buffalo. Bill brought in over four thousand pounds of meat, which he sold for seven cents per pound, making about $100 per day for his time out.

The Lawrence *Kansas Weekly Tribune*, February 20, 1868, reported:

At Hays City considerable anxiety exists in regard to the safety of a party of the citizens who were out buffalo hunting. There were ten in all in the company, among whom were George and Henry Field, brothers of Mr. Samuel Field, of this city, and Mr. Parks, the traveling correspondent of the Journal, all under the direction of Cody, the noted guide and hunter. They left Hays ten days since, and were to return on Friday last, but have not been heard of

112

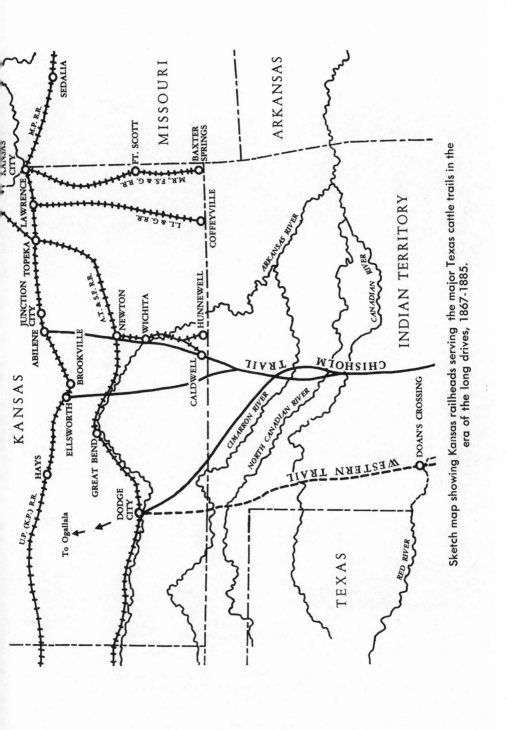

Sketch map showing Kansas railheads serving the major Texas cattle trails in the era of the long drives, 1867-1885.

Ellsworth's Main street in 1872, with the Drovers Cottage, moved
from Abilene, on the right.

Looking north up Broadway from North Second avenue in Abilene, 1875,
four years after the flow of Texas cattle had been shut off.

Newton's Main street, north of the Santa Fe tracks, in 1872.

Intersection of Main and Douglas, the heart of Wichita, 1873.

A Caldwell saloon in the 1880's.

W. H. HARRIS, rancher, gambler, rare coin collector, and vice-president of the Bank of Dodge City.

CHALKLEY M. BEESON was a partner with W. H. Harris in the COD ranch and the Long Branch saloon.

Dodge City's famous Long Branch saloon as it looked near the end of the cowtown era. Clark Chipman, policeman, stands at the end of the bar.

CLAY ALLISON, a self proclaimed "shootist," became one of the legendary figures
of the West.

BEN DANIELS, Dodge City assistant marshal in 1885 and 1886, killed Ed Julian
after leaving office.

LARRY DEGER (above), an early Dodge
City marshal, later was mayor and a key
figure in the famous "war" of 1883.

BILLY BROOKS (right), a policeman in
Newton and Ellsworth in 1872. Was he
the W. L. Brooks who was hanged in
Sumner county for mule stealing in 1874?

LUKE SHORT, gambler and epitome of frontier sartorial perfection, was chief protagonist in the celebrated "war" between Dodge City ins and outs.

GEORGE W. GLICK, the state's ninth governor (1883-1885), contended that due process of law—not mob rule—should prevail in the Dodge City "war."

The main block of Dodge City's Front street as it appeared in 1878. Taken from the Santa Fe tracks, the view looks northwest toward Boot Hill which lies out of sight behind the buildings. The Long Branch saloon is the second building from the left.

BIRD'S EYE VIEW OF

DODGE CITY, KANS.

COUNTY SEAT OF FORD COUNTY

1882

POPULATION 1200

1. Court House.
2. School House.
3. U. S. Signal Service Office.
4. Odd Fellows Hall.
5. A. T. & S. F. R. R. Depot.
6. Post Office, Lloyd Shinn, P. M.
7. Dodge City Grist Mill, H. P. May & Co., Prop's.
X—Methodist Episcopal Church.
A—Presbyterian

D—Dodge City Times, N. B. Klaine Ed'r and Prop.
E—Ford Co. Globe, Frost & Shinn, Ed's and Prop's.
F—Dodge House, Cox & Boyd, Prop's.
G—Iowa   "   W. C. Beebe, Prop.
H—South Side House, South end of Bridge,
     (Wm. Slates, Prop.
J—Great Western Hotel.
K—Wright House.

Beck & Pauli, Lithographers, M. [...]

[...], Madison, Wis.

since. Fears are expressed that they have been captured or killed by the Indians, who have shown decided symptoms of hostility of late. Some efforts are being made toward organizing a party to go in search of them.

The Leavenworth *Daily Conservative*, March 5, 1868, again borrowed from the *Advance:* "Bill Cody has made a match to run the Brigham pony ninety miles in twelve hours. Brigham is to 'tote' 175 pounds, and the race is to come off next month."

Cody and Wild Bill Hickok visited Topeka on official business in March, according to the Topeka *Weekly Leader*, April 2, 1868:

BAND OF ROAD MEN CAPTURED—W. F. Cody, government detective, and Wm. Haycock—Wild Bill—deputy U. S. Marshal, brought eleven prisoners and lodged them in our calaboose on Monday last. These prisoners belonged to a band of robbers having their headquarters on the Solomon and near Trinidad, and were headed by one Major Smith, once connected with the Kansas 7th. They are charged with stealing and secreting government property, and desertion from the army.

Seventeen men, belonging to this same band, were captured eleven miles from Trinidad, on the 13th March, and sent to Denver, Colorado Territory, for trial.

This scant material may be augmented by one more newspaper article which actually has nothing to do with Buffalo Bill in Kansas. It concerns a long disputed phase in Cody's career, however, and is worthy of being reprinted here. The *Ellis County Star*, Hays, August 3, 1876, carried the story in the form of a correspondent's letter:

THE BLACK HILLS.
NOTES FROM THE FIELD OF OPERATIONS.
FT. LARAMIE, July 22d, 1876.

EDITOR STAR:

Again I find time to send you a few lines regarding our trip. Since my last our time has been occupied by scouting over the country lying between this point and the Black Hills. . . . On the morning of the 17th two men of "C" company overtook us, bearing dispatches to Col. Merritt, who was down the creek about five miles. They pushed on, but had not gone more than a mile when we saw a large body of mounted men on a ridge east of us. At first we took them to be a portion of our command, but soon discovered that they were Indians. The two companies of Infantry that were with us tumbled out of the wagons remarkably lively and took their places beside them.

Three or four Indians started out on a run to cut off the dispatch bearers. They had not seen the command, and were not aware that we were in that vicinity; but Bill Cody and his scouts were watching them, and when he saw

121

what they [were] up to, he thought that several more might play at the same game. He then got around the Indians and when they felt sure of the couriers Cody raised up from behind a little hill and shot the pony of one of the redskins. Then starting after his victim he soon had him killed and his scalp off. As soon as he fired the command charged and after a run of three miles killed three more and wounded five. Taking two days rations we pushed on after the Indians and run them right into Red Cloud Agency. Private Seffers of "D" company was hurt by the falling of his horse down an embankment, being the only person injured during the entire trip.

The Indian killed by Buffalo Bill proved to be Yellow Hand, a sub-war chief of the Southern Cheyennes. He was leading a band of 75 warriors to Sitting Bull's army. . . .

This incident became one of Cody's show business standbys and the subject of a once famous picture labeled "The first scalp for Custer!"

From the West Buffalo Bill Cody ventured over much of the world and became a master showman, though not so successful in the business office. He was instrumental in developing the area around Cody, Wyo.; was a generous friend to any who required his aid; a hospitable host at North Platte, Neb., or Pahaska Teepee, Wyo.; and a symbol of the West of the wide open spaces. He was, and is, perhaps the best known product of the American frontier.

1. *Report of the Adjutant General of the State of Kansas, 1861-'65* (Topeka, 1896), p. 247.

For a complete and documented biography of Cody *see* Don Russell, *The Lives and Legends of Buffalo Bill* (University of Oklahoma Press, Norman, 1960), and also "Julia Cody Goodman's Memoirs of Buffalo Bill," edited by Russell, in *The Kansas Historical Quarterly,* Topeka, v. 28, pp. 442-496.

COUNCELL, JOHN L.

John L. Councell (or Council) was appointed marshal of Ellsworth on April 3, 1872, replacing C. B. Whitney who had resigned that day. Councell's appointment was for one month and on May 2 he was reappointed. The marshal's salary at this time was $75 a month and $2.50 for each conviction resulting from arrests made by him.[1]

Marshal Councell's first and apparently only newspaper notice in the Ellsworth *Reporter,* May 16, 1872, did not exactly portray the modern-day conception of a frontier officer's duties:

FEMALE POLITICIAN.—The other morning we witnessed the Marshall and assistant arguing a point with a woman. The point in dispute seemed to be the proper way to go to the cooler. The Marshall insisted on her walking and she insisted on being carried. As is always the way the women came out victorious. Drunk was no name for it.

Possibly the marshal and his staff were attending to some private business on the side for on June 8, 1872, the council instructed the city clerk to "notify the City Marshal and Policeman that their presence is required within the City limits at all times." [2]

A few weeks later Marshal Councell and his assistant, John Norton, were fired. The council, July 24, 1872, again gave instructions to the city clerk, this time to "notify John L. Council and J. W. Norton that they had this day been removed from office." On July 29, Mayor M. C. Davis re-appointed Councell as marshal but his action was not sustained by the city council. As a compromise Ed Hogue was named Chief of Police "until time of next regular meeting." [3] After this, John Councell never again played a part in Ellsworth's cowtown police history.

1. "Minutes of the City Council," Records of the City of Ellsworth, pp. 15, 23, 28, 38, 41, 42; "Ordinance Number Nine, Ordinance Book," Records of the City of Ellsworth. 2. "Minutes of the City Council," Records of the City of Ellsworth, p. 31. 3. *Ibid.*, pp. 39, 40, 41.

CRAWFORD, ED (____-1873)

The murder of Sheriff Chauncey B. Whitney, August 15, 1873, inaugurated a series of shootings and killings in Ellsworth which continued for nearly three months.

The first of these affairs occurred on August 20 and was recorded in the Ellsworth *Reporter*, August 21, 1873:

ANOTHER TRAGEDY.
CAD PIERCE KILLED BY A POLICEMAN.

Yesterday about four o'clock the citizens of Ellsworth were startled at the report of two pistol shots. In a moment there was a large crowd in front of J. Beebe's store, and it was ascertained that Cad Pierce was shot. The report was true. The excitement of course, was great. Pierce was a leader of the Thompson element and upheld and defended them in all the disturbances they have made. While the police were out searching for the murderer of Whitney, it was Cad Pierce who offered $1,000 reward for the capture [murder] of the whole police force. We have interviewed the city marshal, Mr. Hogue, who gives the following particulars:

123

"John Good, Neil Kane and Cad Pierce came up to me and said they heard by certain parties that I had given Happy Jack [Morco] papers, ordering them to leave the town. I told Cad Pierce that it was no such a thing, that he ought to know better. He then told me to come with him, that he wanted to give Happy Jack a talking to and he wanted me to go with him. I told him that I would not do it, for there had been too much talk already. Ed. Crawford [who had been appointed policeman on August 15, 1873] was standing in the crowd; he said yes, a d--m sight too much talk; and he said, bad talk on your side. Crawford asked what did you say yesterday when you had that shot gun in your hands? You said this gun had killed one short horn son of a bitch, and that it cost $100 and you would not take $200 better for it. I then spoke to Crawford, don't multiply words! Come away! Cad Pierce then made a reply, but I could not hear what it was; but I heard Crawford say, what is that you say?—If you want to fight here is the place for it—as good as any! He then stepped back, laid his hand on a six shooter, but did not draw it until Cad Pierce put his hand behind his back— apparently to draw his six shooter; when Crawford drew his and fired twice. At the first shot, Cad Pierce ran into Beebe's store, the second was fired just as he ran into the door."

Policeman Crawford says that Pierce wanted a fight and he reached for his revolver but "I was to quick for him."

Pierce lived but a few minutes. Neil Kane had a narrow escape. Happy Jack presented two revolvers at him.—Kane begged for mercy and at the intervention of the city Marshal he was saved. He took his horse and fled.

We cannot but deprecate such scenes of violence as were enacted yesterday—but the battle had to come off. Whitney has been partly avenged. There are threats of burning the town and policemen are also threatened—but it will be hardly safe to do either. If it is done, or the attempt made the crime will be fastened upon some of the leaders and they will have to suffer for it.

The police showed the greatest bravery yesterday, appearing separately among the excited crowd. They are resolved to stand by the city at the sacrifice of their lives, if necessary. Let the brave boys be upheld. Perfect quiet reigns now and it is to be hoped that our city has had its last shooting affair.

Policeman Crawford, along with the rest of the Ellsworth force, was relieved on August 27, 1873, according to the *Reporter*, August 28.

The death of Ed Crawford, on November 7, 1873, ended the long period of violence Ellsworth had suffered that year. The *Reporter*, November 13, 1873, carried the story:

ED. CRAWFORD SHOT.

Last Sunday Ed. Crawford came to Ellsworth. His presence here was a surprise, as it was understood that his life would not be safe here, on account of his shooting Cad Pierce. He was warned that his life was in danger, but he

124

"was not afraid." Thursday he was pretty full of whiskey, and Friday evening we noticed he was considerably under the influence of liquor. With some friends, or possibly decoying enemies, he went down to Nauch-ville and visited two houses; he was pretty drunk and rough; at the second house he visited there was a crowd of men, mostly Texans, and he had been there but a few moments, before, having stepped into the hall, he was shot twice, the first ball passing through his head, the second into his body. It is not known for certain who fired the fatal shot, but it is supposed to have been one, Putman, and that he did it to avenge the murder of Cad Pierce. It was reported that Crawford fired, but it was probably incorrect. He was shot down by some person secreted in the hall and he made no fight or scarcely a struggle. With this last murder we hope the chapter of crime in this city is complete for 1873, and for many years to come.

D'AMOUR, GEORGE (1846?-1875)

George D'Amour was appointed second assistant marshal of Wichita on October 4, 1871. His salary was $60.00 a month.[1]

In April, 1872, he was elected constable of Wichita township.[2]

D'Amour was made first assistant marshal on the city police force when first assistant Thomas Parks was relieved, June 5, 1872. The same day D'Amour was paid $416.00 for services as "asst Marshal and Special Policeman." [3]

It may have been that D'Amour's service on the force was not continuous from his appointment as second assistant marshal to the appointment as first assistant, for the Wichita City *Eagle*, June 7, 1872, reported that the "city council at their meeting on Wednesday night appointed two additional men on the police force of the city, viz: Geo. D'Amour and D. F. Parks. . . ."

In August, 1872, D'Amour assisted Marshal Mike Meagher in arresting one Teets. The article reporting the arrest may be found in the section on Meagher.

On December 4, 1872, the city council authorized the mayor "to order Geo D'Amour to settle Judgment against the City of Wichita as garnishee." On March 5, 1873, it resolved "that the salaries of all City officers be allowed for the month of February A D 1873 with the exception of Geo D'Amour," and that "the matter in regard to Geo D'Amour . . . [be] refered to Committee on Jail & Police." [4]

The Wichita City *Eagle,* March 27, 1873, reported: "Our city marshal, Mike Meagher, returned last week from a fruitless pursuit of the absconding and multifarious officer, George D'Amour." No information has been found which would indicate the cause of George D'Amour's leaving Wichita.

Two years later the *Eagle,* February 25, 1875, reported the end of the one-time Wichita peace officer:

Geo. DeAmour, sometimes called George Moore, here, formerly deputy marshal under Mike Meagher, and deputy sheriff under Johnny Meagher, was shot and killed in a saloon at Oro City, Colorado territory, on the 7th inst., by one John Murphy. It seems Murphy charged George with having stolen three hundred dollars from him while they were drunk together. After getting duly sober, Murphy walked into a saloon where DeAmour was engaged at a game of cards, drew a revolver and shot a ball through his right temple, which from the proximity and force of the discharge, went clear through, and out at the back of his head. DeAmour only lived a few moments. Murphy slid away on snow shoes.

Geo. DeAmour was a member of the masonic lodge of this city, to whom the following letter in confirmation of the killing has been sent, and which the secretary has permitted us to copy:

ORO CITY, COL., Feb. 14th, 1875.

SECRETARY, Masonic Lodge, Wichita, Kan.

DEAR SIR:—Mr. Geo. DeAmour, a member of your lodge, was shot and killed here on the 7th inst. Please inform me of his place of birth, as I want to inform his friends. If you wish I will send you particulars of his death. Yours Fraternally,

C. H. STONE.

1. "Proceedings of the Governing Body," Records of the City of Wichita, Journal A, p. 115. 2. Wichita City *Eagle,* April 12, 1872. 3. "Proceedings of the Governing Body," Records of the City of Wichita, Journal A, p. 182. 4. *Ibid.,* pp. 245, 272, 273.

DANIELS, BEN

Ben Daniels was appointed assistant marshal of Dodge City on July 24, 1884; he had previously served as a special policeman, being paid $25 for ten days' service on July 10, 1884.[1] Too, he had been a deputy sheriff and was one of the officers who arrested Dave St. Clair for the murder of cowman Bing Choate on July 6, 1884. The newspaper articles telling of the altercation between Choate and St. Clair are presented in the section on William Tilghman.

Daniels' salary as assistant marshal was $100 a month while that of his superior, Marshal Tilghman, was the same with $25 added each month for services as collector.[2]

One of Daniels' earliest exploits published in the Dodge City press appeared in the *Democrat*, August 9, 1884:

A BIG NOISE WITH SIX-SHOOTERS.

On last Monday night [August 4], a cowboy went into Nelson Cary's saloon and commenced playing at one of the "free-for-all" games. He had not played long, however, before him and the dealer got to quarlling, both using some very bad language. The cowboy then started out, but when within about three feet of the door he reached down and pulled a six-shooter from his boot and commenced firing at the gambler. After firing three shots he turned and run, with the assist. Marshal in close pursuit. He could not be captured, however, and the Marshal returned after giving him a long chase and firing five or six shots at him. The only blood that was drawn was when young Hart went through the back window. He was going at such a speed through that he received but slight injuries.

In December Daniels captured a man wanted in Newton. The *Democrat*, December 13, 1884, stated the case:

On last Wednesday evening [December 10] Ass't Marshal Daniels arrested a German by the name of Claussen, who had attempted to injure a young German girl at Newton, by throwing vitriol on her. Fortunately the vitriol only struck a heavy cloak that the lady had on and the only damage was the destruction of the cloak and her dress. Claussen had been keeping company with the young lady for some time and was cast off for some other fellow, therefore his attempt to disfigure her. He will be taken back to Newton and no doubt receive a sentence of some time behind the bars. LATER.—F. H. Curry, the Marshal of Newton, arrived on Thursday, and took the prisoner back. He stated that the girl was disfigured for life, and that it would go pretty hard with Claussen.

As had several other frontier police officers, Ben Daniels discovered that one of the most difficult arrests to make was that of a scratching, fighting female. The Dodge City *Kansas Cowboy*, May 16, 1885, reported Ben's success with one, however:

Miss Fannie Nash, a soiled dove of color, who has been in the habit of giving Ben Daniels a little chin music, was caught up by him last Monday [May 11] and put in the jug. Ben was a little afraid of getting his eyes scratched out, so encircled his arms around her and walked her off in a very pleasing manner.

The assistant marshal was also efficient at finding lost children. Apparently S. H. Barrett's New United Monster Railroad Show proved too much for the lad in this *Democrat* story of June 6, 1885:

Quite an excitement was created on the show grounds last Saturday night [May 30] by the disappearance of a little boy belonging to a German family of this city. The father and mother were almost crazed with grief, and accused the show people of stealing him. Assistant Marshal Daniels soon found the little fellow, who had started home and got into a neighbor's house and gone asleep.

"A little 'scrapping match' took place on Front street last Monday evening. The combatants were promptly given quarters in the 'cooler' by Marshal Daniels," said the *Democrat*, August 15, 1885.

Ben served as assistant marshal until April 10, 1886.[3] Five days later he shot and killed Ed Julian. The *Globe Live Stock Journal*, April 20, 1886, reported:

ANOTHER KILLING FOR DODGE.

On last Thursday evening [April 15] at about six o'clock, a shooting scrape took place on the south side of the railroad on the sidewalk in front of Utter-back's hardware store, two doors west of Ed. Julian's restaurant, the latter gentleman being the victim in the affray; and his antagonist, ex-assistant city marshal Ben Daniels. Four shots were fired, all by Daniels, all of which took effect on Julian. While Julian was found to be armed, he however, did not get to fire a shot; there is much diversity of opinion in the matter, some claiming it to have been a deliberate murder, while others assert it to have been justifiable. The evidence taken at the preliminary trial does not fully sustain either. It was a well known fact that these parties had been bitter enemies to each other for a long time, and both had made threats against each other, which fact was not only elicited at the preliminary, but was known to many of our people long before the shooting took place. Ben Daniels, at the preliminary before Justice Harvey McGarry, was placed under a $10,000 bond for his appearance at the next term of court.

The remains of Ed. Julian were taken in charge by the members of Lewis Post, G. A. R., of this place, who gave them a very respectable burial with appropriate ceremonies. This was a very unfortunate occurrence for this place, and that too at a time when everything appeared to be moving along so harmoniously and quietly. But it appears that no one could have prevented this tragedy, not even our officers, no matter how vigilant they might have been; the bitterness which existed between them was almost certain to bring them together sooner or later, and as many predicted, that one or the other, or perhaps both would be mortally wounded, if not killed outright.

In January, 1889, Daniels, Tilghman, Fred Singer, Neil Brown, James Masterson, and others were involved in the Gray county seat war. On January 12, while attempting to take the county records from Cimarron to Ingalls, they were fired upon by local citizens.

Larry Deger

In the resulting battle one man was killed and several wounded. For a full account *see* the section on Tilghman.

1. Dodge City *Democrat*, July 12, August 9, 1884. 2. *Ibid.*, September 6, October 11, November 8, December 6, 1884, January 10, March 7, 1885; *Globe Live Stock Journal*, June 9, July 21, August 11, September 15, October 13, November 10, December 15, 1885, January 12, February 9, March 9, April 13, 1886. 3. *Ibid.*, April 13, 1886.

DEGER, LAWRENCE E. (1845-____)

The earliest issue of the Dodge City *Times* in the files of the State Historical Society, October 14, 1876, lists L. E. Deger as city marshal. His deputy was Wyatt Earp (*see* section on Earp).

Deger had been marshal at least as early as the previous spring, when the *Ellis County Star*, April 6, 1876, carried this story:

EDITOR STAR: . . .

L. E. Deger is the big man of the town [Dodge City], weighing 307 lbs. He wears on the lappel of his coat a badge with the word "Marshal." Larry takes the same interest in church affairs here that he did in Hays City. The other evening he was master of ceremonies at the hop, and during the evening he commenced one of his long stories. While busily engaged with it, some one remarked: "Oh! Larry, wipe off your chin." Poor Larry had not heard of the late slang phrase and immediately drew forth his bandana and began to mop off his chin, much to the amusement of the audience. . . . .

In March, 1877, the Dodge City *Times* told of a chase Deger made with Sheriff C. E. Bassett to corral a horse thief. This short item may be found in the section on Bassett.

Deger was reappointed in April, 1877. The *Times,* April 7, reported:

L. E. Deger has been re-appointed City Marshal, to serve under the new administration. It was thought by many that a change would be made in this branch of the government, but the Mayor and Council wisely concluded that no better man for the place could be found.

Marshal Deger's salary was $75 per month.[1] In his spare time he was a partner in the saloon firm of McGinty & Deger.[2]

In June, 1877, while providing Bobby Gill with incentive, in the form of "paternal kicks in the rear," to move more rapidly toward the city jail, Deger was set upon by young Bat Masterson who objected to his methods. With the help of a policeman and six or so Texans, Deger subdued Bat and jailed both him and Bobby.

129

The Dodge City *Times* article describing this episode may be found in the section on Masterson.

Because it was a city of transients during the summer when trail hands swarmed over the plains, Dodge City suffered from countless fly-by-night operators, con men and petty thieves. In July, 1877, one such person called "Curley" set up shop on the streets of Dodge and began to offer chances on jewelry which he displayed in a portable showcase. Finally, as it began to dawn on the victims of his chicanery that they were being duped, they appealed to the authorities. The Dodge City *Times*, July 14, 1877, reported that the

City Marshal, speaking as a private citizen, said that he would squelch the institution if the vox populi would back him. The word was said. The Marshal hesitated not a moment, but repaired to the scene, and gathering the show-case in his brawny arms, pitched it into the street, contents and all. Smash! Silver watches, jewelry, silver cutlery, diamond pins and other valuables rolled in the dust.

There are no jewelry stores in Dodge City at the present writing. It is not considered a safe business.

Next, Marshal Deger and Dodge City Mayor James H. Kelley had a set-to which the *Times* described in its July 21, 1877, issue:

THE MAYOR AND CITY MARSHAL BOTH BEFORE HIS HONOR.

It is seldom we are compelled to give the particulars of an affair in which the public manifest a deeper interest than the difficulty which terminated yesterday morning in an open rupture between Mayor Kelley and City Marshal L. E. Deger. There may be some personal matters which had something to do with bringing about the result, but of these we will not make mention, briefly stating what happened at the time of the difficulty:

Yesterday morning about 2 o'clock the Marshal arrested and confined Mr. Chas. Ronan in the city jail. Immediately after the arrest Mayor Kelley ordered the Marshal to release the prisoner, and the Marshal positively refused to do so. Finding his orders not obeyed, the Mayor ordered the Marshal to cease performing the duties of City Marshal, deliver his badge to one of the other officers and consider himself suspended. The Marshal refused to recognize the order of the Mayor and continued to act as Marshal, whereupon the Mayor ordered the Assistant Marshal [Edward J. Masterson] and policeman [Joe Mason] to arrest him. The Marshal at first refused to be arrested, and drawing his revolver ordered the Mayor and officers not to approach him. Here the Assistant Marshal and policeman were placed in a doubtful position, not knowing their exact duty in the matter. In order to settle the difficulty in the easiest manner, Mr. Masterson, the Assistant Marshal, suggested to the Marshal that he submit to arrest in order to prevent further collision, until the disagreement between himself and the Mayor could

130

Larry Deger

be investigated. This the Marshal consented to and allowed himself to be confined in the city jail, where he remained only about ten minutes, being released on his own reconnaissance.

During the forenoon a complaint was filed against Mayor Kelley for interfering with an officer in the discharge of his duty and he was also placed under arrest. The Marshal's case was tried first. No complaint was filed against him, and the officers who made the arrest were the only witnesses. The decision of the Police Judge was that the Marshal had committed no offense against any of the city ordinances. He was therefore released. The Mayor's case was postponed until this afternoon at 4 o'clock. Before that hour a meeting of the City Council was held, and an order passed directing Mr. L. E. Deger to resume his duties as City Marshal. When the trial came up for hearing a petition was presented, signed by a majority of the Council, favoring the entry of a nolle prosequi in the case, and all parties consenting it was so entered and the Mayor discharged. The municipal machinery is now running smoothly.

Marshal Deger was instrumental in raising funds for Bobby Gill to leave Dodge City according to this article from the *Times*, July 21, 1877:

LEAVES FROM THE DOCKET.

A WEEK OF HISTORICAL INCIDENTS IN THE DODGE CITY POLICE COURT.

We are loth to believe that Dodge City is retrograding in its morals, or that its people are becoming more wicked and lawless, although it might seem so to those not understanding the causes leading to some of the difficulties which stained the records of our police court this week. . . .

The City of Dodge City against Robert Gilmore, charged with vagrancy and having no visible means of support. Robert's sensitive feelings were very greatly hurt upon hearing that charge, and his plea was not guilty. He said he knew he was a sinful man and pursued a calling which was not of the highest order. All he asked of this court was a chance for his life. He asked the mercy of the Police Judge unto him as a sinner, stating as a precedent that Christ died to save just such sinners. The witnesses for the city testified that they knew of no visible means whereby he gained a support. Also that he was the instigator of many quarrels and street fights—that he was not a law-abiding, peaceable citizen. In defense, several witnesses were sworn who testified that the prisoner had money to pay his bills, and that he had means of support. On this evidence the Judge was compelled to render a decision of not guilty. But public sentiment was so strongly antagonistic to Mr. Gilmore's remaining in the city, and he had cost the officers so much annoyance, that Robert consented to seek a livelihood elsewhere, if a donation could be secured to pay his fare to Emporia. Through the efforts of the City Marshal the money was soon raised, and Mr. Gilmore gathered about him his earthly treasures and departed. This is the second time Bobbey has shook the dust of the city from his feet by request, and we hope some day to see him conducting himself in a more exemplary manner than he has

131

heretofore. He is not a desperate character, and has good sound sense, which only needs a proper application to business. . . .

On August 4, 1877, the Dodge City *Times* noted that "Marshal Deger resigned his position of Deputy Sheriff this week, at the request of Under Sheriff [Bat] Masterson."

In spite of its wild reputation, Dodge City had docketed only 204 cases before the police court between the date of the city's incorporation, November 2, 1875, and August 16, 1877, reported the *Times*, August 18, 1877.

Deger's size hampered his efforts at law enforcement, as this article in the *Times*, September 8, 1877, disclosed:

FLEEING FROM THE WRATH TO COME.

To Mr. William Brady, a gentleman from Texas, belongs the credit of creating the most profound sensation of the week. Mr. Brady came to the city last Sunday [September 2], and during that hour when our citizens were assembled to worship at the church on Gospel Ridge, did carry strapped to his manly person a navy revolver of a deadly character. William says he did not intend to make a killing; he only carried the gun as an ornament; but a policeman took him under his wing all the same and steered him to the dog house. When Monday morning came, William, not being ready for trial, succeeded in getting Jim Anderson to go his bail until 4 o'clock, placing his horse in Anderson's stable for security. But while William was waiting for 4 o'clock to come, he went against the boose joint to such an extent as to make him feel like a giant among small men. He resolved and finally decided, that no court or no officers or no town could hold him. He secured his revolvers, went to Anderson's livery stable, and finding no one but old uncle Huggins around, presented his revolvers to the old man in a hostitle attitude and ordered him to saddle up the horse he had left there for security. Of course the old man obeyed, and William was seen soon after riding recklessly out of town. As soon as the police heard what had happened their wrath was up and they decided to give chase. Assistant Marshal Masterson was the first to get started, and Marshal Deger next, mounted on a horse about half as large as himself. On his shoulder he carried a shot-gun, and blood was in his eye. A few moments after the Marshal started, Jim Anderson learned what had been done, and feeling himself interested, took out his fastest horse, and said "we'll catch 'im."

The news had spread over town and the population could be counted by hundreds on the tops of freight cars, on the roofs of buildings and other high places. William crossed the river and started east on the run. He had a good horse, and a hot race was expected, and a fight when the officers came in contact with him. Anderson's horse soon passed Deger, whose pony grunted at every jump under its heavy load, and afterwards passed Masterson, and was gaining on the fugitive, whose courage seemed to have failed, inasmuch as he slackened his speed when he saw Anderson coming. Anderson

132

rode up to him and they both stopped. The lookers-on expected to see some shooting at this stage of the game, but Anderson made no move to shoot, and Brady only placed his hands on his revolver in a playful manner. Just then Masterson came up, and before Brady saw him ordered him to throw up his hands or be killed. Brady threw up his hands and Anderson took his revolvers. Deger soon arrived, but was too late to use the shot gun. Brady begged Anderson's pardon and said he would never have acted so had he been sober. He was confined in the calaboose until the next day, when he was brought before Judge Frost and fined $10 and costs, which he paid.

On October 2, 1877, the police force was reduced so that only Marshal Deger and Assistant Marshal Ed Masterson remained.[3]

Since Sheriff C. E. Bassett could not run for re-election in 1877, due to a constitutional limitation, the office was sought by Deger, George T. Hinkle, and Bat Masterson. Deger announced in the *Times* of October 13, 1877, that he would run: "At the solicitation of many of my friends I hereby announce myself as a candidate for the office of Sheriff of Ford county. If elected I shall spare no effort to fill the office honestly and faithfully." The newspaper added: "The most of the voters of Ford county know 'Larry' better than we do—at least have known him longer. He has been City Marshal of this city for a long time, and his ability to keep the peace has been often tested. Give him a fair consideration. He is a substantial, honest and upright man."

Toward the end of October Hinkle stepped out of the race and declared in the October 27, 1877, issue of the *Times* that he would support Deger.

The day Hinkle's announcement was made a "Peoples' Mass Convention" assembled in the Lady Gay saloon to nominate candidates for the November election. Both Deger and Bat Masterson were suggested to the convention as the candidate for sheriff. After seconding speeches by W. N. Morphy (who in two months would help found the *Ford County Globe*) in favor of Deger, and Attorney M. W. Sutton in favor of Masterson a ballot was taken in which Masterson received the majority of votes. Though he had not been chosen by the convention, Deger stated that "I am still in the field as a candidate for the office of Sheriff of Ford County."[4]

At the election held November 6, 1877, W. B. Masterson edged out Deger with a three-vote majority, he having received 166 votes to Deger's 163.[5]

On November 10, 1877, the *Times* noted:

Two worthy birds, "Stock Yards Shorty" and a cow boy, participated in a little slugology yesterday morning, in front of Jake Collar's store. After exchanging a few slugs, Shorty knocked the cow boy through one of Mr. Collar's large window lights. The cow boy in return drew a crimson stream from Shorty's proboscis. Our worthy Marshal interfered in their innocent amusement, and took them off to the lime kiln.

And on December 1, 1877, the *Times* reported:

DARING THEFT.

While the excitement caused by the burning of the Great Bend City Jail was attracting everybody to that part of the city, one day last week, a thief quietly unhitched a farmer's team from a post in front of one of the Great Bend stores, seated himself in the wagon and drove westward. He reached this city this week and camped out in the adjacent hills. The proprietor of the team got track of the thief and followed him to Dodge City. Learning that his thief was somewhere near around he informed Marshal Deger of his errand and straightway search was instituted. The Marshal soon succeeded in finding and recovering the team, but the thieves made a hasty flight. Great was the joy of the farmer when he recovered his stolen property, and he even went so far as to give his horses a fond embrace.

The city council of Dodge City, at its meeting of December 4, 1877, relieved Deger from the marshalship and the mayor appointed Ed Masterson in his place. The editor of the *Times* wrote on December 8, 1877:

City Marshal Edward Masterson receives the congratulations of his many friends without a show of exhultation. Notwithstanding the fact that considerable feeling was manifested against the removal of Mr. Deger, no one accuses Mr. Masterson of seeking the position. In fact he preferred to retain his old position as Assistant, which gave him the same salary and engendered less responsibilities. As an officer his reputation is made, and it is a good one.

In justice to Mr. Deger we will say that no charge of misconduct was brought against him. He has been an excellent officer, and retires with no stain upon his official character. The powers that be saw fit to make the change, and it was made. It was made on the principal that "there are just as good men in the party as out of it."

Deger had filed a contest of election suit against Bat Masterson which he withdrew in January, 1878. On January 15 the *Ford County Globe* printed his explanation:

COMMUNICATED.

DODGE CITY, Jan. 11, 1878.

EDITOR GLOBE. As considerable inquiry and comment has been made respecting the withdrawal of my contest for the Sheriff's office, to satisfy my

134

friends and the public generally, I submit the following: Not wishing to involve my friends in trouble or expense, politically or financially when nothing could be accomplished thereby, I concluded when the appointment of Judges had been made by the Probate Court that it would be folly to proceed when I was sure of getting the worst of it. When I filed my papers of contest I expected to get a square deal from the Probate Court. One of the judges selected to try the contest had previously voted in the city council for my removal from the office of City Marshal because I would not withdraw the contest. As I understand the position of both parties in the contest, and know that it was convenient for this councilman to vote as he did, I have nothing to say except that a much fairer selection of judges could have been made.

Aside from the glaring injustice done me in the appointment of judges I wish further to say to the City Council, that, as the contest was a county affair and could not interfere with the discharge of my duties as City Marshal. I cannot understand why they should have taken upon themselves to establish an arbitrary precedent which will work no good to them or the men who advised it. The sympathy of such men who degrade their official positions I scorn. I always endeavored to perform my duty as an officer, impartially, friends and foes I treated alike—my conduct, good, bad, and indifferent have approved. I ask no favors from anyone other than what common decency would dictate.   L. E. DEGER.

The Dodge City *Times,* January 12, 1878, said of the withdrawal:

THE CONTEST WITHDRAWN.

The contest suit of Larry E. Deger vs. W. B. Masterson, for the office of Sheriff of Ford county, has been withdrawn, and thus the agony is over. Contest suits are prolific endless sources of bad blood, and rarely end in success to the contestor.

It is true the election was a close one, but an opening of the ballots would only tend to make hostility more bitter and to open wounds that would be running sores in future election contests.

Mr. Deger's efficiency and popularity will secure him confidence for a future race before the people, which he cannot forego for the sake of a fruitless and prolonged contest suit, which could be carried to the end of the term for which he sought. Mr. Masterson will make a capable and energetic officer, and we trust will receive the support of every one in the execution of his official duties.

The attorneys in this matter were fully prepared for the tug of war, but their legal swords have been turned into tuning forks, and the Russian harp is made to discourse its sweet delightful strains a la Brokhisstiffnek.

On January 22, 1878, the *Globe* printed this exchange, which implied that Deger was incapable of composing the January 11 letter:

DODGE CITY, }
Jan. 21st, '78. }

The following inuendo appeared in the "Dodge City times," Jan. 19th.:

QUESTION.

"Will the wise man who wrote the communication for Deger, please inform an inquiring public, if a City Marshall degrades his official position, by standing in with (so called) show case game for ten per cent of the games."

SUBSCRIBER.

In reply I have but this to say: I wrote the communication refered to, myself. And although I don't pretend to much wisdom, I try to live honestly and tell the truth. I consider that the City Marshall, who would take any per cent. of any show case game, or other game of like character, not only degrades his official position, but becomes a scoundrel. Sign your name next time.   L. E. DEGER.

For a while it was believed by some that Deger had been a member of the gang which attempted to rob a Santa Fe train at Kinsley on January 27, 1878. The *Globe*, February 5, 1878, reported:

One of the most laughable things connected with the late train robbery, was, a detective shaddowed Lary Deger for two days, supposing him to be the big fellow who put the pistol to the engineers head. Another is that a stranger in Kinsley, while eating supper at the hotel, supposing our respected townsman, A. B. Webster, to be [William M.] Tilgman, one of the arrested parties, extended his sympathy to Web. assuring him that he didn't believe he was guilty. Web. promptly assured him that he was innocent, and didn't believe that the prosecution could convict him.

On June 2, 1880, Deger was listed by the United States census as being a resident of Dodge township, a laborer, and 35 years old.

In April, 1883, Deger defeated W. H. Harris for mayor of Dodge City by a vote of 214 to 143.[6] "The true city issue was whisky vs. whisky or Indian fight Indian, in which the GLOBE had no particular interest, but could quietly stand by and watch the result, which was sure to prove beneficial to the best interests of this city. The more fight among the Indians the less Indians," said the *Ford County Globe*, April 3, 1883.

Within a month of Deger's election the so-called Dodge City "war" erupted. Lawrence E. Deger, not A. B. Webster as so many sources state, was the Dodge City mayor who had Luke Short arrested and subsequently run out of town for having female "entertainers" in his saloon in violation of city ordinance. The story of the "war" will be presented in the section on Luke Short.

On July 26, 1883, a disgruntled *Globe* reader accused Deger of misconduct in 1876, when he was city marshal. The letter, which was printed in the *Ford County Globe*, July 31, may be found in

the section on C. E. Chipman. The matter to which the letter re-
ferred was tried as a civil case before the June, 1877, term of the
Ford county district court and was reported in the Dodge City
Times, June 30, 1877:

THE JUNE TERM OF COURT.

. . . By far the most important case, however, was the case of John
Blake vs. Dodge City. The allegations of the complaint were that Blake was
incarcerated by a judgment of the Police Court in a 10 x 12 cell, that against
his remonstrance there were confined with him three desperadoes (two of
whom were afterwards hung,) that these three men were allowed to have in
their possession a knife and pistol, that they assaulted Blake and shot out his
left eye, and otherwise injured him, for which he claimed damages in $5,000.
The suit was brought by Messrs. [M. W.] Sutton and [Harry E.] Gryden, and
came up on a demurrer to the reply. Mr. [E. F.] Colborn, for the city, cited a
number of authorities, making a strong case of non-liability for the city. Mr.
Gryden followed. He argued that where there is a wrong committed, there
must be a remedy, that the age of the Seal Chambers of Venice and the Black
Hole of Calcutta were past, that if the city could confine an old man in a den
of murderers, who had vowed to kill him, they could also incarcerate the
maiden with the raving maniac, or employ the thumbscrews and the iron
boots of the inquisition as their agents. Mr. Gryden's argument occupied
about one hour, and was spoken of by the bar with flattering encomiums.
Captain [J. G.] Waters closed the argument for the city, showing by a long
list of authorities that a city occupied the position of a State in the regulating
of her municipal affairs, that if a liability existed, it was against the agents
of the city. That she could be no more liable in this case than would the
Warden of the Penitentiary be responsible for the killing of one convict of
another. Strong and able arguments were, of course, expected from City
Attorney Colborn and Captain Waters, and they were in this case fully realized.
The court sustained the demurrer, and rendered judgment for costs against
Blake, to which plaintiff excepted, and gave notice of appeal to the Supreme
Court.

No record was found of a subsequent hearing before the supreme
court in the case of Blake vs. Dodge City.

As a postscript to the spring "war," the Dodge City council
passed an ordinance on August 31, 1883, making it illegal for music
of any type to be played publicly except for purposes "literary or
scientific." This, of course, was aimed at the female "entertainers"
of the local saloons and dance halls. Mayor Deger, having borne
the responsibility for most of the actions of and reactions to the
Dodge City "war," wrote to William A. Johnston, Kansas' attorney general, for legal opinion on the validity of the ordinance:

Office of the Mayor of .
DODGE CITY KANSAS Dec 18/83

ATTERNY GENERLL
STATE OF KANSAS
SIR

I enclose you a coppey of an Ordnece the Validity of wich I would most respectfile ask your Oppinion. I order the dance Halls closed under this Ordnece and have Stoped the Musick and free & Easeys in the Salons Some of our aterneys here claim that they can Beat the Ordnece in the Dis Court as the Ordnece is to sweaping in its nattur and the parties thretin to open and see if they could beat it. but I inform them if the[y] did I would have complint made in the Dis Court and try them under the Statute wich had the desierd affect. but I if I am Sertin that the Ordnece is good would rather have them brought in the City Courts I would Respectfully as these questions

1St. upon the face of this Ordnice is it within the Power of the Mayor & Council to Pas and Inforse it.

2nd—Can the Police Court take Judicl Knolage of the Vices & Evels this Ordnece atemts to Surpress

3rd If Vallid will the Intenton of the Mayor and Councel be the Gide for the Courts.

4th Will an Ordince Passed by the Mayor & Councl prohibiting the Sale of Liquor Eexcept on phormacy licence under the Licens Sistem Still remain Vallid and in force or must the M. & C. pass a new ordnece under the new order of things. Yours L E DEGER Mayor Dodge City

In answer, Attorney General Johnston informed Mayor Deger that the ordinance was too general to be valid, that the disturbances it was designed to suppress were already taken care of by powers granted to cities by state statute and that moreover there were "uses of music other than for literary and scientific purposes which would not be vicious, immoral or disorderly." [7]

After serving only one term as mayor of Dodge City, Lawrence E. Deger retired to private life. In September, 1885, he moved to Kiowa in Barber county.[8]

1. Dodge City *Times*, April 7, May 6, June 9. July 7, August 11, September 8, October 6, November 10, December 8, 1877. 2. *Ibid.*, May 6, 1877. 3. *Ibid.*, October 6, 1877. 4. *Ibid.*, November 3, 1877. 5. *Ibid.*, November 10, 1877. 6. *Ibid.*, April 5, 1883. 7. "Correspondence of the Attorneys General," archives division, Kansas State Historical Society. 8. *The Globe Live Stock Journal*, September 8, 1885.

DIBBS, WILLIAM (1850?-_____)

William Dibbs was appointed policeman on the Wichita force, April 15, 1873; Mike Meagher was renamed city marshal for the third consecutive year and Daniel Parks became assistant marshal.[1]

On April 15, 1874, Mike Meagher was replaced by William Smith. Dan Parks and William Dibbs were reappointed to their respective positions and James Cairns became the fourth member of the force.[2] Other policemen were added as the season progressed.

In July Dibbs' treatment of a prisoner caused the captive to disarm and tree the policeman. The Wichita *Weekly Beacon*, July 29, 1874, reported:

A SHOOTING AFFRAY.

THE PURSUED TURNED PURSUER.
A BRAVE "COPE" MAKES TIME.

Last Friday afternoon [July 24] a shooting affray occurred on Second street, between the BEACON office and the Occidental hotel, which happily resulted in nothing more than frightening a policeman, and arousing the indignation of all who witnessed the affair, at his brutality and cowardice. The particulars of the affair are as follows:

A young man, said to be a gambler, by the name of Thomas McGrath, had been arrested on a charge of vagrancy and fined. Unable to pay the amount, he and another were put at work on the streets, under charge of policeman Wm. Dibbs. While they were at work Dibbs, for some cause, threatened to put a ball and chain upon McGrath, when the latter started to run away. Dibbs pursued, pistol in hand, and overtaking the fleeing man on Main street, struck and pulled him around as if he was a dog. Coming back with his prisoner, Dibbs heaped upon him a volley of oaths and threats, which were replied to by McGrath in much the same style of language. Turning the corner of Main and second streets, Dibbs, in an angry and excited tone said he could put a ball and chain on McGrath if he wished, and could kill him if he wanted to. In reply to McGrath's denial of his assertions, Dibbs ordered him to shut up. This, McGrath said he would not do, when, without warning and to the astonishment of those who had been attracted to the scene, Dibbs with his left fist dealt the prisoner a blow in the face, and followed it up by another with his right. McGrath attempted to ward off the blows, when the parties clinched, and in the struggle McGrath managed to get possession of one of Dibbs' pistols, and at once prepared for defense and attack.

So soon as Dibbs saw the revolver in the hands of McGrath, a deadly pallor o'er spread his face and he turned and fled, his ashen lips crying, "Hold on, hold on! Don't shoot." In his flight Dibbs ran towards the rear of the BEACON office, but before he reached the sidewalk McGrath managed to fire one shot at him, which only served to increase his speed. McGrath in turn became the pursuer, and followed Dibbs, who ran, like a scared wolf, behind

139

the buildings. In the flight Dibbs managed to fire one shot from his remaining revolver, while his pursuer fired twice. None of the shots took effect. McGrath finally overhauled Dibbs as he reached the rear of Dr. Gray's house, where he attempted to wrest the other pistol from the city guardian. In the struggle Dibbs' pistol was discharged, the ball striking McGrath on the lower part of the left hand, inflicting a slight wound.

About this time Mr. Newman came up and separated the parties, and almost simultaneously policemen [Samuel] Botts and [John] Behrens came up and seized McGrath, while Dibbs limped off with the assistance of two gentlemen, fully impressed with the idea that he was fatally shot. He was taken to the office of the police judge for attention. Arriving there, an examination disclosed the fact that he was only frightened, not hurt. Then his courage returned, and seizing his revolvers he thrust them into his belt; then taking the triangle he rushed to the door and rang an alarm which brought together a large number of armed citizens.

McGrath, meantime, was being taken to the calaboose by Botts and Behrens. We are informed that while on the way, and after arriving at the calaboose, Botts showed his brutality by beating the prisoner over the head, and was only prevented from further fiendishness by the efforts of the other policeman.

The above is a plain statement of the affair, without attempt at coloring or giving the minute particulars. It requires no comment. We could not make it appear worse for Dibbs were we so disposed. If a full investigation and a thorough overhauling of the police force fails to result from it, then a total disregard of the people's wishes will be shown, and lack of a sense of justice exhibited we are loth to attribute to our Mayor and Councilmen.

The Wichita City *Eagle*, July 30, 1874, in reporting the affair said:

. . . We hope the incident will prove of value to incautious and over brave officers, if we have any more upon the force. No ordinary sized policeman with only two revolvers should attempt to handle one of these small red-whiskered fellows single handed. Seriously we think that whenever it comes to the pitch that vagrants or others defy our authorities and on the pretense of the disgrace resist and threaten officers it is well for the mayor to shut down most vigorously. As to the police force, it will be remembered that we asked for a re-organization this spring. All the people desire is such men upon that force as are respectable and as will command the respect of good citizens and be dreaded by rogues. We have some good men on the police, but there are others who, however brave, should never be officers of the law. . . .

Immediately after the *Beacon* reached the streets, Dibbs stormed into the office of Milton Gabel, the editor. Gabel described the resulting scene in the August 5, 1874, issue:

A CARD.

DIBBS—BURRIS—BOTTS.

TO THE CITIZENS OF WICHITA:—As many false rumors are afloat respecting a little difficulty which occurred in this office last Wednesday afternoon [July

William Dibbs

29], I desire to give the facts in the case, in order to correct the erroneous impressions concerning the affair. It grew out of an article, which appeared in Wednesday's Beacon, criticising the action of policeman Dibbs for mistreating a prisoner.

About three o'clock in the afternoon Mr. [Fred A.] Sowers and myself were sitting by a table in this office, when Wm. Dibbs entered the room accompanied by an armed ex-policeman. Dibbs came up to the table, and in a threatening, angry and excited manner demanded to know "who put that piece in the paper?" when I answered that I did. Dibbs then said, "The man that put that in is a liar," (this was emphasized by three loud and well-rounded oaths,) after which he received my undivided attention for a few moments; but seeing his confederate, [Sam] Burris, who stood in the background eyeing me closely, place his hand on his hip as if ready to draw his revolver, I quite naturally watched the latter while dealing with Dibbs. When Dibbs called me a liar, I hurried around the railing in front of the table towards him, and, just as I got outside the railing, he struck at me. I warded off the blow and struck him a very slight blow while looking at Burris. Dibbs then struck again when I dodged to one side, the blow merely grazing my hair on the left side of my head, and knocking off my hat. I then ordered him out of the office, when he and Burris both left the room. He then hurried to the police office anxious to plead guilty to fighting and having whipped me. Right here I wish it understood that he did not do this—in fact, neither of us were hurt in the least. But his cowardice may be known by the fact of his coming to my office, not alone like a man, but with an armed man to back him; and this action only confirms to me what he has previously shown himself to be, a villainous coward. Besides this, Wm. Dibbs, though a weak man generally, has proven himself an able-bodied liar. He stated in the police court that Burris had no revolver, and that Burris walked from the Beacon office down town on the east side of Main street with him, when in fact, Burris crossed Main street directly opposite this office, and went down the street on the west side. This we can prove by Mr. Kramer, and one other gentleman, whose reputation for truth and veracity will certainly have more weight in this community than that of Wm. Dibbs or Sam. Burris. Again, Sam. Burris has perjured himself. He swore positively in the police court that he had no revolver on his person, when two of the employes in this office saw it, and, it was also seen by Mr. James Davidson and a boy at Hills & Kramers store, just as he started up the stairway leading to this office.

Late Wednesday evening I remarked to Burris, "All your actions plainly indicated to me that you came there to aid Dibbs." "Yes," said he, "I intended to see him through." This needs no comment. As to Dibbs striking McGrath in the manner as given by me in Wednesday's article, I can only reiterate that, and, in fact, everything concerning Dibbs as to what occurred afterwards. This matter is narrowed down to a question of veracity between Wm. Dibbs on the one side, and myself and quite a number of our best citizens on the other, and if he undertakes to "clean out" everyone who asserts the facts as we gave them, he will certainly find it extremely laborious to entirely complete his work.

With regard to the conduct of Samuel Botts (who was in no way connected with Wednesday's affair), it is claimed by him that he did not strike McGrath, yet he admits that he "chucked him about roughly," and says that under the excitement—coming up as he did after the shooting had begun, and while McGrath was shooting at Dibbs the second time—thinking that Dibbs was fatally wounded, &c., and, in his over-zealous efforts to save him, etc. etc., he treated McGrath more roughly than he intended to, and, under the excitement, and what he considers aggravating circumstances, more so than he otherwise would have done, and thinks that should at least partially excuse the rough treatment, which we characterized brutality, and of which we made mention in Wednesday's article. This may in a measure palliate the offense, but it shows inefficiency, and even this I think will not justify the mistreatment of a prisoner disarmed, and on the way to the calaboose, and I will not alter my judgment on this matter as heretofore expressed. I gave the facts as they came under my own observation, together with the evidence of others, the truth of which can be substantiated by sworn statements of at least seven witnesses.

I do not seek difficulties; on the other hand try to avoid them. But the affair of Wednesday was thrust upon me. I regret exceedingly to have had any connection with the difficulty, and, if my friends will forgive me, I promise that such a thing shall not occur again, at least until another villainous fiend, hungry for trouble, presents himself in the same manner. I would not willfully wrong or injure any one, but I have a duty to perform as a public journalist, and that I purpose doing let come what may.

MILTON GABEL.

Dibbs apparently was relieved from the force because of the McGrath affair but on September 2, 1874, the city paid him $3 for "Disbursing Money Cleaning Calaboose," [3] and on January 5, 1876, he was paid $4 for two days' duty as special policeman at Wichita's December 17, 1875, fire.[4]

1. "Proceedings of the Governing Body," Records of the City of Wichita, Journal A, pp. 287, 288; Wichita City *Eagle*, April 17, 1873. 2. "Proceedings of the Governing Body," Records of the City of Wichita, Journal A, p. 371; Wichita City *Eagle*, April 23, 1874. 3. "Proceedings of the Governing Body," Records of the City of Wichita, Journal B, p. 15. 4. *Ibid.*, p. 85.

DUFFEY, WILLIAM

The name of William Duffey first appeared in the Dodge City newspapers as a law officer on August 17, 1878, when the Dodge City *Times* reported:

Sheriff W. B. Masterson and Deputy Sheriff Wm. Duffy, are indefatigable in their efforts to ferret out and arrest persons charged with crimes. Scarcely

142

a night or day passes without a reward for their vigilance and promptness. We do not record all these happenings, because evil doing is of such common occurrence. There is a pleasant contemplation in the fact that we have officers who are determined to rid the community of a horde that is a blight upon the well being of this over ridden section.

On the next page the *Times* noted that "Sheriff W. B. Masterson and Deputy Duffey Monday night [August 12], arrested one James Smith, three and a half miles from town, on a charge of horse stealing. The prisoner is bound over for ten days to await trial and identification by parties in Ellis county."

In September, 1878, Duffey was responsible for the escape of two county prisoners. The articles reporting this may be found in the section on Bat Masterson.

Duffey, in October, 1878, was a member of the posse which captured James Kennedy, the supposed murderer of Dora Hand. The report of this, too, may be found in the section on Masterson.

The *Ford County Globe*, October 29, 1878, reported that "Deputy Sheriff Duffy had an unruly prisoner last week who undertook to purloin the six-shooter worn by his keeper, who was giving him a promenade in the hallway, but was unsuccessful."

On December 6, 1878, four prisoners escaped from the county jail. The *Globe*, December 17, reported the unsuccessful pursuit of one of the escapees:

Deputy Sheriff Duffey, in company with Archie Keach left here a week ago yesterday, in search of the missing prisoner Brown, who, it is supposed, stole [C. S.] Hungerford's fine grey mare and made good his escape. After a fruitless search for nearly a week they return to Dodge, Keach arriving here Saturday and Duffey Sunday. They report a very rough trip.[1]

Duffey shared in the praise given the Ford county officers (mentioned earlier in the section on C. E. Bassett) by the Dodge City *Times*, January 11, 1879. These men, the paper said, had "earned the high praise accorded to them for their vigilance and prompt action in the arrest of offenders of the law."

In March, 1879, Duffey and Bat Masterson participated in the struggle between the Atchison, Topeka and Santa Fe and the Denver and Rio Grande Western railroads for the right of way through the Grand Canyon of the Arkansas—the Royal Gorge. The Dodge City phase of this fight may be found in the section on Masterson.

Deputy Sheriff Duffey, on April 5, 1879, disarmed Levi Richardson, the loser of a duel fought with Frank Loving in the Long Branch saloon. This was reported in the section on Charles E. Bassett.

Later in April Duffey accompanied Mike Sutton to Garden City to make an arrest. Sequoyah (Finney) county, in which Garden City was located, was one of 13 unorganized counties attached to Ford county for judicial purposes. The *Times*, April 26, 1879, reported:

County Attorney Sutton and officer Wm. Duffy went up to Garden City Thursday [April 24]. They caused the arrest of L. T. Walker, who stabbed D. R. Menke. Both are citizens of Garden City. The cause of the stabbing grew out of some words over a business transaction. Mr. Menke was stabbed in the abdomen, and is in a dangerous condition. Walker was brought to this city and placed in jail.

On August 30, 1879, the *Times* noticed that "Officer Duffey arrested a man Thursday [August 28] on a telegram from Colorado," and on September 9, 1879, the *Globe* recorded the episode:

ANOTHER LUNATIC.

For some time past the Bohemian named Szinek, confined in the county jail awaiting his trial in the district court on the charge of attempting to steal Mr. Cotton's horses, has been acting queer. In fact he has been acting very queer, cutting various kinds of pranks, and even going so far as to try to but[t] his brains out against the sides of the prison wall. He said he wanted to die, and when Mr. Duffey kindly offered to shoot him he was perfectly willing and even anxious for the shooting to commense, but Mr. Duffey was compelled by a feeling of delicacy to politely decline the honor. On Saturday [September 6] he was taken before Probate Judge [Nicholas B.] Klaine, who impaneled a jury and gave him an examination. He was adjudged insane and will be sent to the asylum. The cause of his lunacy is undoubtedly an abominable crime against nature which he has practiced.

The *Ford County Globe*, November 18, 1879, again mentioned an adventure of Duffey's:

FIRE GUARDS.

Our tenacious Deputy Sheriff Mr. William Duffey, had a novel experience last week with a gentleman of color whom he wished to "see" in regard to bad intentions. It was night, and as Mr. Duffey rapped at the front door of his victim's pallatial residence and announced his errand, there was a slight rustle of bed clothing and then all was still. Mr. Duffey effected a forcible entrance and was shocked to find that his bird had flown through the back window.

Duffey apparently left his public office at the end of the Bat

Masterson administration. On October 13, 1881, the Dodge City *Times,* quoting a colorful story in the Las Vegas (N. M.) *Optic,* reported that he was fighting Apaches with Col. Ranald Mackenzie's 4th cavalry:

"Duffey," the veteran scout, is with MacKensey's outfit and will prove a valuable acquisition to his forces. Duff is an old-timer and will be remembered by all the boys of Dodge City and other western Kansas towns. It is said of him that once upon the frontier of Texas a company of buffalo soldiers was sent to arrest him for some trivial offense, and before they were aware of what was ahead of them he had sent the entire outfit to the happy hunting grounds. He was for a long time the deputy and trusted henchman of the somewhat famous Bat Masterson, in Ford county, Kansas, and shared with him the dangers of holding down the hardest town on the continent. He is an experienced Indian fighter, and will, if given a chance, adorn his wigwam with many an Apache's scalp before winter. If the Government would employ a number of such men and leave the cadets at home to court their girls, the Indian war would progress more satisfactorily.—[Las Vegas Optic.

1. *See, also,* Dodge City *Times,* December 21, 1878.

EARP, WYATT BERRY STAPP (1848-1929)

In spite of Wyatt Earp's own statement, recorded by a biographer over 50 years after the event, that he had been the one who disarmed Ben Thompson after the fatal shooting of Sheriff Chauncey B. Whitney in Ellsworth that August day in 1873, no contemporary record is known to exist which places Earp in the town at that time.

Similarly, though Earp, through his biographer, stated that he arrived in Wichita in May, 1874, and was soon hired as deputy marshal, no evidence of his official police employment could be found in the Wichita city records or in either of the town's newspapers until April, 1875.

In May, 1874, the police force consisted of Marshal William Smith, Assistant Marshal Daniel Parks, and Policemen James Cairns, Joe Hooker, John Behrens, and William Dibbs. In June Sam Botts was added as policeman. During the summer several others, but apparently not Earp, served as special policemen for short periods.

There were Earps in Wichita as early as May, 1874, however, and Wyatt may have been among them. Bessie Earp, wife of James, Wyatt's brother, was fined in Wichita police court in May, 1874, for being a prostitute. So was Sallie Earp, who apparently shared the same dwelling, but for whom no other identification has thus far been found. Bessie and Sallie were each fined eight dollars and two dollars court costs. Their names appeared regularly in the city's prostitute fine list through February, 1875, and Bessie's through March, 1875.

On June 3, 1874, Sallie and Bessie were arrested upon the complaint of Samuel A. Martin who swore that they did

Set up and Keep a bawdy house or brothel and did appear and act as Mistresses and have the care and management of a certain one story frame building Situated and located north of Douglas Avenue near the Bridge leading across the Arkansas River used and Kept by Said parties as a house of prostitution in the City of Wichita, County and State Aforesaid Contrary to the Statutes of Kansas made and provided.

Sallie and Bessie (or Betsy as she was named in the information) were arrested that same day by Constable J. W. McCartney, pleaded guilty and were remanded to the next term of the district court. Unable to put up their bail of $250 each they were assigned places in the county jail. Apparently they eventually found the requisite sums for the monthly city prostitute fine lists testify to their continued "business" activity.

The Earp girls came up before the district court on September 15, 1874, but upon motion of their attorney, William Baldwin, their case was dismissed.[1]

In July, 1874, one Eva Earp was fined for prostitution and in August, 1874, J. Earp [James?] was fined five dollars and two dollars costs for an undetermined infraction of the law. August, 1874, saw two other Earps (or Earbs as they were sometimes listed) fined for prostitution—Kate and Minnie. The latter was similarly fined in September and October. Morgan Earp was arrested and fined one dollar and costs in Wichita during the month of September, 1875, but again the reason is unknown.[2]

While some of the Earps listed above may not have been related to Wyatt's family, the surname is distinctive enough to warrant their inclusion in this sketch. Only Bessie Earp has been definitely established as Wyatt's sister-in-law. The authoritative contemporary source is the 1880 United States census for Tombstone, Pima county, Arizona territory, which lists Bessie, then 36 years old, as James' wife.

The first known Wichita mention of Wyatt Earp appeared in the

146

Wichita *City Eagle,* October 29, 1874. Though the article referred to him as an "officer," it did not state whether he was a city, county, federal, or private officer. It is not likely that as a city police officer he would have made the collection described so far from the limits of the town, yet his partner, John Behrens, was probably still on the city force at the time. It would seem more likely that Behrens and Earp were hired as private officers to collect an unpaid private debt. The article is presented here for the reader's own interpretation:

The Higgenbottom outfit, who attempted to jump the country at an expense of twenty or thirty thousand dollars to Wichita, it appears had, among other games, stuck M. R. Moser for a new wagon, who instead of putting himself in communication, by telegraph, with the outside world just got two officers, John Behrens and Wiatt Erp, to light out upon the trail. These boys fear nothing and fear nobody. They made about seventy-five miles from sun to sun, across trackless prairies, striking the property and the thieves near the Indian line. To make a long and exciting story short, they just levelled a shotgun and six-shooter upon the scalawags as they lay concealed in some brush, and told them to "dough over," which they did, to the amount of $146, one of them remarking that he was not going to die for the price of a wagon. It is amusing to hear Moser tell how slick the boys did the work.

The official Kansas state census, 1875, purportedly showing the occupation and ages of all individuals, reported as follows on three Earps who were living in Wichita:

The name of every person whose place of abode on the first day of March, 1875, was in this family.	Age	Sex	Color	Occupation	Place of birth	Where from to Kansas
Bessie Earp	32	F	W	Sporting	New York	Iowa
					[page 23, line 4.]	
Jas. Earp	34	M	W		Kentucky	Iowa
W. S. Earp	26	M	W		Illinois	Illinois
					[page 32, lines 24 and 25.]	

Though the census was supposed to have been taken as of March 1, 1875, there is strong evidence to indicate that the Wichita portion, at least, was prepared between April 6 and April 21. Since all the known policemen of Wichita were so indicated in the occupation columns of the census, had Earp been on the force prior to April 21, 1875, he presumably would have been listed similarly.

On April 21, 1875, Wyatt Earp was appointed policeman on the Wichita force, and the appointment entered on the records of the city. This was the first time that Earp's name appeared in the city's official records. Wichita's police force now consisted of Marshal Mike Meagher, Assistant Marshal John Behrens, and Policemen James Cairns and Earp.[3] The marshal's salary was $91.66, Behrens earned $75.00, and Cairns and Earp each were paid $60.00 a month.[4]

Wyatt's first recorded Wichita arrest was reported in the *Weekly Beacon*, May 12, 1875:

AN ARISTOCRATIC HORSE THIEF.

On Tuesday evening of last week [May 4], policeman Erp, in his rounds ran across a chap whose general appearance and get up answered to a description given of one W. W. Compton, who was said to have stolen two horses and a mule from the vicinity of Le Roy, in Coffey county. Erp took him in tow, and inquired his name. He gave it as "Jones." This didn't satisfy the officer, who took Mr. Jones into the Gold Room, on Douglass avenue, in order that he might fully examine him by lamp light. Mr. Jones not liking the looks of things, lit out, running to the rear of Denison's stables. Erp fired one shot across his poop deck to bring him to, to use a naughty-cal phrase, and just as he did so, the man cast anchor near a clothes line, hauled down his colors and surrendered without firing a gun. The officer laid hold of him before he could recover his feet for another run, and taking him to the jail placed him in the keeping of the sheriff. On the way "Jones" acknowledged that he was the man wanted. The fact of the arrest was telegraphed to the sheriff of Coffey county, who came down on Thursday night and removed Compton to the jail of that county. A black horse and a buggy was found at one of the feed stables, where Compton had left them. After stealing the stock from Coffey county, he went to Independence, where he traded them for a buggy, stole the black horse and came to this place. He will probably have an opportunity to do the state some service for a number of years, only to come out and go to horse stealing again, until a piece of twisted hemp or a stray bullet puts an end to his hankering after horse flesh.

The Wichita *City Eagle*, May 6, 1875, merely stated: "Behrens and Earp picked up a horse thief by the name of Compton from Coffey County, yesterday, with the property in his possession."

A ruckus loving young cowboy successfully eluded the Wichita police on May 23. The *Eagle*, May 27, 1875, reported:

The three shots that were fired on Main street between the Occidental and Empire last Sunday night, were showered into the innocent air by a hilarious party of the name of Higinbotham, who was a horse back, and heavily armed for the sport. The police chased him to the corporate limits, but could go no further.[5]

About August 4, 1875, Cairns and John Martin, who had been

appointed in April, were dropped from the force, leaving only the marshal, Assistant Behrens, and Policeman Earp.[6]

On November 10, 1875, the *Beacon* reported an arrest by Marshal Meagher and Earp:

THE TERRORS AND TEMPTATIONS OF BULL WHACKING.

Last Friday [November 5], being hangman's day and generally regarded by the superstitious as the twenty-four hours in all the week, for all time, which the devil has reserved for himself against the holy Sabbath, appropriated by his enemies, it befell three turbulent twirlers of the long lash, stimulators of the patient ox, to be wooed into ways that are dark and tricks that proved vain, and on the devil's own day. A bull train, consisting of two large waggons and eight yoke of oxen, had arrived at West Wichita, corralled and went into camp early that morning. There was nothing very remarkable in this fact, being of daily, almost hourly occurrence, but in the sequel, in the reproof of chance lay the proof of crime, with an apology, if it so please you, for spoiling one of Williams best and most quoted. Marshal Meagher, as the wires and mails would so have it, had a description of this identical outfit in his pocket, with the names of the parties to it. The intelligence conveyed to him was that one Bill Potts, assisted by two gentlemen of color, had actually stolen these oxen and wagons, and stranger yet, under the very nose of their owner, and as slow as oxen travel, had most miraculously succeeded in eluding pursuit, evading highways and coming through the long prairie grass, reached Wichita, from Fort Sill, where this wholesale theft was committed. If nothing of reputation is left this little crowd of depredators, one thing will ever remain tenaciously with their names, that they made the best bull time on record and are therefore entitled to the name of being the champion bull whackers of the Sill. We expect to see a dime edition out soon, with some such title and the usual daredevil wood cut, emblazoning in red, yellow and magenta this identical trio, whipping, goading and spurring amain the frantic longhorns.

Be that as it may, Mike Meagher soon spotted good M. Potts, the only white man in the crowd, who was threading his way through the busy throng on lower Main street making with all possible speed and with a business-like air, towards the individual whom he had put up to be the innocent purchaser. He sought out several buyers. In the meantime, Marshal Meagher, having business always near by. At last Mr. Potts betook himself to Davidson's stables and securing a horse for himself, had old Mr. Davidson to mount another and together they crossed the long bridge, Mr. Davidson going to look at the cattle and make up his mind whether to buy or not. Mike Meagher with Policeman Erp, also took an airing on horseback about the same time clattering the bridge with the music of their horses' hoofs in beautiful quartette with those that bore Mr. Potts and his victim, and so, until all the parties halted in the marauders' camp, when good Mr. Potts and his too sable assistants were compelled to surrender at the point of the six shooter and were, when we saw them, marching up the center of Main street, three abreast, with the two

149

mounted officers in the rear, herding them to jail. There they now are, waiting the certainty of that hour that will bring them to face offended law, and to go hence and be forgot, at least for a term of years. That is to say, and it is written with this express understanding, if they do not break jail.

The *Eagle*, November 11, 1875, said the arrest was made by Meagher and Behrens:

Wm. Potts and two colored men were arrested here last Friday by city Marshal Mike Meagher and Assistant John Behrens, charged with stealing eight yoke of cattle and two wagons at Fort Sill, which property was found in their possession. The parties were lodged in jail.

Realizing it had erred, the *Beacon* corrected itself on November 17, 1875:

While we are not aware that Deputy Marshal Behrens cares a fig for official honors, yet when he is justly entitled to credit it is due him to have the same. Far be it from us to, withhold from so efficient an officer what belongs to him, much less give the praise to others. We say this much without the knowledge of Mr. Behrens, in order to set ourselves right in the matter of several arrests made last week; one of them Ed Hays, the other Bill Potts and his two associates. Deputy Marshal Behrens spotted all these parties, arrested Hays, himself; and traced the others to their lair, assisting Mike Meagher in the arrests.

On December 15, 1875, the *Beacon* again mentioned Wyatt Earp:

On last Wednesday [December 8], Policeman Erp found a stranger lying near the bridge in a drunken stupor. He took him to the "cooler" and on searching him found in the neighborhood of $500 on his person. He was taken next morning before his honor, the police judge, paid his fine for his fun like a little man and went on his way rejoicing. He may congratulate himself that his lines, while he was drunk, were cast in such a pleasant place as Wichita as there are but few other places where that $500 roll would ever been heard from. The integrity of our police force has never been seriously questioned.

One night early in 1876 Wyatt nearly lost his life as a result of a freak accident. Disobeying one of the first laws of gun toters he had left the hammer of his pistol resting on a loaded chamber. The weapon fell from his belt and—but let the Wichita *Beacon*, January 12, 1876, tell the story:

Last Sunday night [January 9], while policeman Erp was sitting with two or three others in the back room of the Custom House saloon, his revolver slipped from its holster and in falling to the floor the hammer which was resting on the cap, is supposed to have struck the chair, causing a discharge of one of the barrels. The ball passed through his coat, struck the north wall then glanced off and passed out through the ceiling. It

150

was a narrow escape and the occurrence got up a lively stampede from
the room. One of the demoralized was under the impression that some
one had fired through the window from the outside.

The affair is particularly interesting in light of a statement
Wyatt reportedly made to his biographer, Stuart Lake, 50-some
years later:

I have often been asked why five shots without reloading were all a
topnotch gun-fighter ever fired, when his guns were chambered for six
cartridges. The answer is, merely, safety. To ensure against accidental
discharge of the gun while in the holster, due to hair-trigger adjustment,
the hammer rested upon an empty chamber. As widely as this was known
and practiced, the number of cartridges a man carried in his six-gun may
be taken as one indication of a man's rank with the gun-fighters of the
old school. Practiced gun-wielders had too much respect for their weapons
to take unnecessary chances with them; it was only with tyros and would-bes
that you heard of accidental discharges or didn't-know-it-was-loaded
injuries in the country where carrying a Colt's was a man's prerogative.[7]

Was Wyatt, tongue in cheek, remembering that day so long ago
which temporarily branded him a "tyro and would-be"?

In April, 1876, Policeman Earp found himself on the receiving
end of law enforcement. The trouble was recorded in the Wichita
Weekly Beacon, April 5, as follows:

On last Sunday night [April 2] a difficulty occurred between Policeman Erp
and Wm. Smith, candidate for city marshal. Erp was arrested for violation of
the peace and order of the city and was fined on Monday afternoon by his
honor Judge Atwood, $30 and cost, and was relieved from the police force.
Occurring on the eve of the city election, and having its origin in the canvass,
it aroused general partisan interest throughout the city. The rumors, freely
circulated Monday morning, reflected very severely upon our city marshal.
It was stated and quite get [*sic*] generally credited that it was a put up job
on the part of the city marshal and his assistant, to put the rival candidate for
marshal *hors de combat* and thus remove an obstacle in the way of the re-
election of the city marshal. These rumors, we say, were quitely largely
credited, notwithstanding their essential improbability and their inconsistency
with the well known character of Mike Meagher, who is noted for his manly
bearing and personal courage. The evidence before the court fully exhonorated
Meagher from the charge of a cowardly conspiracy to mutilate and disable a
rival candidate, but showed that he repeatedly ordered his subordinate to
avoid any personal collision with Smith, and when the encounter took place,
Mike used his utmost endeavor to separate the combatants. If there is any
room to reflect on the marshal, it is that he did not order his subordinate out
of Smith's room as soon as he entered, knowing as he did, that Erp had
fight on the brain. It is well known that in periods of excitement people do
not always act as they would when perfectly collected and unexcited. The

151

remarks that Smith was said to have made in regard to the marshal sending for Erp's brothers to put them on the police force furnished no just grounds for an attack, and upon ordinary occasions we doubt if Erp would have given them a second thought. The good order of the city was properly vindicated in the fining and dismissal of Erp. It is but justice to Erp to say he has made an excellent officer, and hitherto his conduct has been unexceptionable.

At the city election held the day before the *Beacon* was printed Meagher had defeated Smith for the marshalship.[8] The new city council, which had also been elected on April 4, met on the 19th and included among other business the nomination of police officers. The city clerk recorded the nominations and appointments in the minute book:

Numerous nominations were made for policeman the vote on Mr. Wyatt Earp stood 2 for and 6 against.

Mr. R. C. Richey was elected policeman vote standing 6 for and 2 against. Mr. Dan Parks was also duly elected policeman. vote standing—5 for and 3 against. On motion the vote taken on Mr. Earp was reconsidered the result of the ballots showing— 4 for and 4 against.

On motion of Mr. Walker to defer the appointment of more policemen until next regular meeting— was carried.[9]

When the city council met on May 8 it allowed Wyatt Earp $40 for 20 days' work on the force in April. The councilmen also ordered the committee on jail and police to investigate "the matter relating to the collection of moneys due the City by persons not authorized. . . ."[10]

On May 10, 1876, the police committee wrote this report:

We the police Com. Respectfully submit the following report. That Policeman L. [R. C.?] Richey be relieved from further duty & that the marshall enforce the vagrant act in the case of the 2 Erps, the long haired man, the man whose trial has been postponed, Sol Woodmancey & "Red." That the scrip of W. Erp & John Behrns be with-held from payment until all moneys collected by them for the city be turned over to the city treasurer.[11]

The identity of the "2 Erps" against whom the vagrancy act was to be enforced is not known. Only Wyatt's presence has been definitely established in Wichita in May, 1876. The police report concerning him came before the city council on May 22:

Report of the Police Committee relating to the discharging of policeman Richey and also to the enforcement of the vagrant act and further recommending that Scrip of W. Earp & John Behrens be with held until all moneys collected by them for the City be turned over to the City Treasurer was sanctioned and accepted.[12]

152

With that, Wyatt Earp bowed out of Wichita. On May 24, 1876, the Wichita *Weekly Beacon* reported: "Wyatt Earp has been put on the police force at Dodge City."

Little is known about him in Dodge during 1876 and 1877. The only 1876 Dodge City newspaper in the files of the Kansas State Historical Society is a single issue of the *Times* dated October 14. On the first page, in a box labeled "Official Directory," Earp's name appeared as deputy city marshal. The next issue of this paper in the Society's files is that of March 24, 1877. Earp was similarly listed in the directory of this issue as well as in that of March 31. However, the *Times* of April 7, 1877, in reporting the proceedings of the city council meeting of April 4, said the salary of Marshal Lawrence E. Deger was allowed for March, but no mention was made of Wyatt Earp.

On July 7, 1877, the Dodge City *Times* noted:

Wyatt Earp, who was on our city police force last summer, is in town again. We hope he will accept a position on the force once more. He had a quiet way of taking the most desperate characters into custody which invariably gave one the impression that the city was able to enforce her mandates and preserve her dignity. It wasn't considered policy to draw a gun on Wyatt unless you got the drop and meant to burn powder without any preliminary talk.

Earp was still in Dodge City two weeks later according to this article from the *Times* of July 21, 1877:

. . . Miss Frankie Bell, who wears the belt for superiority in point of muscular ability, heaped epithets upon the unoffending head of Mr. Earp to such an extent as to provoke a slap from the ex-officer, besides creating a disturbance of the quiet and dignity of the city, for which she received a night's lodging in the dog house and a reception at the police court next morning, the expense of which was about $20.00. Wyatt Earp was assessed the lowest limit of the law, one dollar.

The Dodge City papers did not mention Earp again until January 22, 1878, when the *Ford County Globe* noted that "Wyatt Earp, our old assistant Marshal, is at Ft. Clark, Texas."

The ex-officer returned to Dodge on May 8, 1878. Said the *Times*, May 11: "MR. WYATT EARP, who has during the past served with credit on the police arrived in this city from Texas last Wednesday. We predict that his services as an officer will again be required this Summer."

By May 14 the *Ford County Globe* was able to report that "Wyatt Earp, one of the most efficient officers Dodge ever had, has just returned from Fort Worth, Texas. He was immediately appointed Asst. Marshal, by our City dads, much to their credit."

This time Earp served under City Marshal Charles E. Bassett, appointed to replace Edward J. Masterson who had been killed on April 9, 1878. Ed's brother, Bat, was sheriff of Ford county and James H. Kelley served as mayor of Dodge City. Earp's salary now was $75.00 per month.[13]

For the first two months of Wyatt Earp's second tour of duty on the Dodge City police force the newspapers had little to report in the way of excitement. On June 11, 1878, the *Ford County Globe* felt that "Marshal Earp deserves credit for his endeavors to stop that 'bean business' at the Theatre the other night." On June 18 it stated that "Wyatt Earp is doing his duty as Ass't Marshal in a very creditable manner.—Adding new laurels to his splendid record every day."

On July 26 Dodge's second fatal shooting within two weeks occurred. The *Times* reported the affair in these words:

BULLETS IN THE AIR.

MUSIC FROM THE FESTIVE REVOLVER.

TWENTY SHOTS FIRED AND ONLY ONE MAN WOUNDED.

Yesterday morning about 3 o'clock this peaceful suburban city was thrown into unusual excitement, and the turmoil was all caused by a rantankerous cow boy who started the mischief by a too free use of his little revolver.

In Dodge City, after dark, the report of a revolver generally means business and is an indication that somebody is on the war path, therefore when the noise of this shooting and the yells of excited voices rang out on the midnight breeze, the sleeping community awoke from their slumbers, listened a while to the click of the revolver, wondered who was shot this time, and then went to sleep again. But in the morning many dreaded to hear the result of the war lest it should be a story of bloodshed and carnage, or of death to some familiar friend. But in this instance there was an abundance of noise and smoke, with no very terrible results.

It seems that three or four herders were paying their respects to the city and its institutions, and as is usually their custom, remained until about 3 o'clock in the morning, when they prepared to return to their camps. They buckled on their revolvers, which they were not allowed to wear around town, and mounted their horses, when all at once one of them conceived the idea that to finish the night's revelry and give the natives due warning of his departure, he must do some shooting, and forthwith he commenced to bang away, one of the bullets whizzing into a dance hall near by, causing no little commotion among the participants in the "dreamy waltz" and quadrille. Policemen Earp and [James] Masterson made a raid on the shootist who gave

154

them two or three volleys, but fortunately without effect. The policemen returned the fire and followed the herders with the intention of arresting them. The firing then became general, and some rooster who did not exactly understand the situation, perched himself in the window of the dance hall and indulged in a promiscuous shoot all by himself. The herders rode across the bridge followed by the officers. A few yards from the bridge one of the herders fell from his horse from weakness caused by a wound in the arm which he had received during the fracas. The other herder made good his escape. The wounded man was properly cared for and his wound, which proved to be a bad one, was dressed by Dr. [T. L.] McCarty. His name is George Hoy, and he is rather an intelligent looking young man.[14]

Hoy died on August 21, 1878. The *Ford County Globe*, August 27, said of him:

DIED.—On Wednesday last, George Hoy, the young Texan who was wounded some weeks since in the midnight scrimmage, died from the effects of his wound. George was apparently rather a good young man, having those chivalrous qualities, so common to frontiersmen, well developed. He was, at the time of his death, under a bond of $1,500 for his appearance in Texas on account of some cattle scrape, wherein he was charged with aiding and assisting some other men in "rounding up" about 1,000 head of cattle which were claimed by other parties. He had many friends and no enemies among Texas men who knew him. George was nothing but a poor cow boy, but his brother cow-boys permitted him to want for nothing during his illness, and buried him in grand style when dead, which was very creditable to them. We have been informed by those who pretend to know, that the deceased, although under bond for a misdemeanor in Texas, was in no wise a criminal, and would have been released at the next setting of the court if he had not been removed by death from its jurisdiction. "Let his faults, if he had any, be hidden in the grave."[15]

Earp may have been one of the policemen who "interfered" in this melee reported by the *Globe*, August 20, 1878:

Another shooting affair occurred on the "south side" Saturday night [August 17]. It appears that one of the cow boys, becoming intoxicated and quarrelsome, undertook to take possession of the bar in the Comique. To this the bar keeper objected and a row ensued. Our policemen interfered and had some difficulty in handling their man. Several cattle men then engaged in the broil and in the excitement some of them were bruised on the head with six shooters. Several shots were accidentally fired which created general confusion among the crowd of persons present. We are glad to chronicle the fact that none were seriously hurt and nobody shot. We however cannot help but regret the too ready use of pistols in all rows of such character and would like to see a greater spirit of harmony exist between our officers and cattle men so that snarling cayotes and killers could make their own fights without interesting or draging good men into them.

Early in the morning of October 4, 1878, one James Kennedy fired two shots into the small frame house occupied by Fannie Keenan, a vocalist whom the Dodge City *Times* once described as a "general favorite" of the town. Miss Keenan, alias Dora Hand, was killed and within half a day a Dodge City posse was on Kennedy's trail. Earp was a part of that posse but since its direction properly came under the duties of the sheriff of Ford county, the full story may be found under W. B. Masterson.

The shooting of Dora Hand and the capture of James Kennedy was the last excitement in which Earp participated for some time judging from the Dodge City newspapers.

In December, 1878, the city council cut the salaries of the assistant marshal and the single policeman,[16] but on April 9, 1879, about the time the season's trail herds began to arrive, it more than restored the cut. The *Ford County Globe*, April 15, 1879, carried the following story:

CITY FINANCES.

The City Council did a wise thing in endeavoring to wipe out the city indebtedness by raising the dram shop license from one hundred to three hundred dollars. The city has a debt of nearly $3,000 hanging over it. But while the Council had their eyes on a depleted treasury they also had their attention called to the large pockets of our police force and City Attorney, to whom they have allowed an additional amount for their invaluable services. While they have left the City Marshal's salary at $100, they have raised the salary of Assistant Marshal and Policeman from $50 to $100 per month, making the expense of police force $300 per month. . . . When an officer makes an arrest he is allowed a fee of $2.

The Dodge City *Times*, in its article on the same subject, April 12, 1879, added: "The revenue derived from fines on gambling and prostitution, which will be revived next month, will pay the police force."

The local papers carried no items about arrests made by Earp until May 24, 1879, when the Dodge City *Times* reported:

Officers Earp and Jas. Masterson served a writ on a horse drover, out on Duck Creek, Wednesday [May 21], in order to obtain the claim of a darkey against the drover, for services rendered by the aforesaid colored individual. Seven brave horse herders stood against the two officers, who, showing no signs of "weakening," soon obtained satisfaction of the claim, the drover promptly paying the debt when resistance was no longer available.

On September 5, 1879, some of Dodge's characters engaged in

what the editor of the *Globe* headlined "A Day of Carnival." This is the story:

It was casually observed several times by several old timers last Friday that Dodge City was redeeming herself. By this remark they intended to convey the idea that we were extricating ourselves from that stupid lethargy which had fallen upon us of late, and were giving vent to our uncurbed hilarity— "getting to the booze joint," as it were, in good shape, and "making a ranikaboo play for ourselves." We speak in the plural number because a large portion of our community were "to the joint" and we cannot mention the pranks of each without overlooking some and causing them to feel slighted. The signal for the tournament to begin was given by a slender young man of handsome external appearance who regaled his friends with a pail of water. The water racket was kept up until it merged into the slop racket, then the potatoe and cucumber racket, and finally the rotten egg racket, with all its magnificent odors. This was continued until the faces, eyes, noses, mouths and shirt bosoms of several of the boys were comfortably filled with the juicy substance of the choicest rotten eggs, compelling them to retire from the field, which they did in a very warlike manner. As the evening shades began to appear the skirmishers were soon actively engaged, and at a little before the usual hour slugging commenced all along the line. One or two "gun plays" were made, but by reason of a lack of execution, were not effective. We cannot indulge our readers with a lengthy description of the scenes of this glorious occasion. It is described by many eye witnesses as being equal to the famous "Mystery of Gil-Gal," where the inspired poet says:

"They piled the 'stiffs' outside the door,
I reckon there was a cord or more,
And that winter, as a rule,
The girls went alone to spelling-school."

Upon the sidewalks ran streams of the blood of brave men, and the dead and wounded wrestled with each other like butchered whales on harpooning day. The "finest work" and neatest polishes were said to have been executed by Mr. Wyatt Earp, who has been our efficient assistant marshal for the past year.

The finest specimen of a polished head and ornamented eyes was bestowed upon "Crazy Horse." It is said that his head presented the appearance of a clothes basket, and his eyes, like ripe apples, could have been knocked off with a stick. He was last seen walking up the railroad track, on his way to Las Vegas. It was not until towards morning that the smoke cleared away, the din of battle subsided and the bibulous city found a little repose. And such is life in the far, far west.[17]

In the same issue, September 9, the *Globe* reported that "Mr. Wyatt Earp, who has been on our police force for several months, resigned his position last week and took his departure for Las Vegas, New Mexico." Wyatt was paid $13.32, for four days' service in September, by the city council on October 7, 1879. On September

30 the *Globe* mentioned that he was still in Las Vegas but by March 30, 1880, he was in Tombstone and said to be a rich man:

We understand that our fellow townsman Mr. Harry Finaty is contemplating a trip to the Tombstone district of Arizona to look after his interest in a mine which was recently sold by his partner Mr. Wyatt Earp for thirty thousand dollars. The mine is called the "Cooper Lode" and is not worked at present owing to the quantity of foul air that has accumulated in the shaft. . . .18

Late in November it was reported that Earp had been killed. The *Times* reprinted the story and added its own thoughts on the matter in its issue of November 27, 1880:

It is reported that Wyatt Earp, at one time a policeman in Wichita, but more recently of Dodge City, was shot and killed on Sand Creek, Colorado, by Jas. Kennedy, of Texas, a week or two ago. Earp had shot and wounded Kennedy in the shoulder a year or two since, and meeting at Sand Creek both pulled their revolvers, but Kennedy got his work in first, killing Earp instantly.— Caldwell Commercial.

The above statement is not believed in Dodge City. Earp is engaged as a special messenger by Wells, Fargo & Co., on a division of the railroad in New Mexico. The story looks like a fabrication. Earp was never engaged in a difficulty with Kennedy. The latter was shot in the shoulder by a posse of officers at one time in pursuit of him. Earp was not of that party.

By January 18, 1881, Earp was back in Tombstone. The *Ford County Globe* wrote: "Wyatt Earp, ex-City Marshal of Dodge City, and W. H. Harris, C. M. Beeson's partner, are at Tombstone, Arizona, one of the promising young cities of that Territory."

Within a few months Earp's supposed wealth was mentioned again. The *Globe* on October 11, 1881, said that "Wyat Carp [*sic*], formerly a policeman in this city, is now one of the wealthy men of Tombstone. He owns a large portion of the land on which the town is built, and some valuable mining property."

Two weeks later, October 26, the famous gunfight at the OK Corral occurred. The *Globe* reported the shootout in these words:

A Tombstone, Arizona, dispatch says: Four cow boys, Ike and Billy Clanton and Frank and Tom McLowery, have been parading the town for several days, drinking heavily and making themselves obnoxious. On Wednesday last the city marshal [Virgil Earp] arrested Ike Clanton. Soon after his release the four met the marshal, his brother Morgan and Wyatt Earp, and a citizen named [John H. "Doc"] Holliday. The marshal ordered them to give up their weapons, when a fight commenced. About thirty shots were fired rapidly. Both the McLowery boys were killed. Bill Clanton was mortally wounded, dying soon after. Ike was slightly wounded in the shoulder. Wyatt Earp was slightly wounded, and the others were unhurt.19

158

On November 8, 1881, the *Globe* added:

The Earp boys, who had the fight with the cow boys, at Tombstone, Arizona, which resulted in the killing of three cow boys, have been arrested by the friends of the men who were killed. The Earp boys were acting as peace officers, and from all reports were justified in doing what they did. Wyat Earp was formerly city marshal of Dodge City, and a paper setting forth his good qualities was circulated last week and signed by all the prominent citizens.

Trouble is likely to arise from the recent shooting of cowboys by Marshal Earp and posse, at Tombstone. Earp to-day telegraphed Gen. Wilcox to send a company of cavalry to protect him from the cowboys. Wilcox referred the matter to Acting Governor Gosper and ordered a company of cavalry at Huachua to be ready to march if required. Sheriff Bedau [probably Johnny Behan], of Tombstone, telegraphs that everything is quiet there. The examination of the Marshal's posse is going on with closed doors. A large amount of money has been raised to assist the prosecution by the friends of the cowboys.

The *Times* of December 8, 1881, reported Earp's acquittal:

Wyatt Earp, formerly a city marshal in this city, was recently under trial before a magistrate in Tombstone, Arizona, charged with homicide. Great interest was taken in trial which lasted four weeks. From the voluminous testimony taken the Justice makes a long review of the case and discharges the defendant. The following is an extract from his decision: "In view of all the facts and circumstances of the case; considering the threats made, the character and position of the parties, and the tragical results accomplished, in manner and form as they were, with all surrounding influences bearing upon the res gestae of the affair, I cannot resist the conclusion that the defendants were fully justified in committing these homicides; that it was a necessary act, done in the discharge of an official duty."

An Earp was shot on December 28, 1881, and the incident was reported in the Dodge City *Times*, January 5, 1882:

ATTEMPTED ASSASSINATION.

A Tombstone, Arizona, dispatch of Dec. 29, to the St. Louis Globe-Democrat says when the Clanton and McClary gang were shot by the Earps and Doc Holliday, about six weeks ago, the friends of the cow boys vowed they would have revenge for what they called the cold-blooded murder of their friends. Only a fortnight ago, Mayor [John P.] Clum, of Tombstone, was shot at in a stage near the city and one bullet grazed his head. Clum was a warm sympathizer with the Earps, and did much to secure their acquittal at the preliminary examination. Wednesday night, just before midnight, an attempt was made on the life of United States Deputy Marshal Earp, as he was crossing the street, between the Oriental Saloon and the Eagle Brewery. When in the middle of the street he was fired upon with double-barreled shotguns, loaded

159

with buckshot, by three men concealed in an unfinished building diagonally across on Allen street. Five shots were fired in rapid succession. Earp was wounded in the left arm just above the elbow, producing a longitudinal fracture of the bone. One shot struck him above the groin, coming out near the spine. The wounds are very dangerous, and possibly fatal. The men ran through the rear of the building and escaped in the darkness.

Nineteen shots struck the side of the Eagle Brewery, three going through the window and one passing about a foot over the heads of some men standing by a faro-table. The shooting caused the wildest excitement in the town, where the feeling between the two factions runs high.[20]

On an inside page of the same issue, the *Times* said: "Virgil Earp, and not Wyatt Earp, was shot at Tombstone. At last accounts he was resting easy with chances of recovery. The wounded arm will probably have to be amputated."

In May, 1882, Ed Colborn, a Dodge City attorney visiting in Gunnison, Colo., wrote the *Ford County Globe* of an "absorbing" conversation with Wyatt Earp about the Tombstone business and Wyatt's somewhat grandiose plans for the future. The *Globe* printed Colborn's letter on May 23, 1882:

LETTER FROM E. F. COLBORN.

GUNNISON, COL., May 20.

EDITOR GLOBE:

. . . Wyatt and Warren Earp arrived here some days ago and will remain awhile. Wyatt is more robust than when a resident of Dodge, but in other respects is unchanged. His story of the long contest with the cow boys of Arizona is of absorbing interest. Of the five brothers four yet live, and in return for the assassination of Morgan Earp they have handed seven cow boys "over to the majority."

Of the six who actually participated in the assassination they have killed three—among them, Curly Bill, whom Wyatt believes killed Mike Mayer [Meagher], at Caldwell, last summer. [Frank] Stillwell, Curly Bill and party ambuscaded the Earp party and poured a deadly fire into them, Wyatt receiving a charge of buckshot through his overcoat on each side of his body and having the horn of his saddle shot off. Wyatt says after the first shock he could distinguish David Rudebaugh and Curly Bill, the latter's body showing well among the bushes. Wyatt lost no time in taking him in, and will receive the reward of $1,000 offered. From what I could learn, the Earps have killed all, or nearly all of the leaders of the element of cow boys, who number in all about 150, and the troubles in Arizona will, so far as they are concerned, be over.

Wyatt expects to become a candidate for sheriff of Cochise county this fall, and as he stands very near to the Governor and all the good citizens of Tombstone and other camps in Cochise county he will without doubt be elected. The office is said to be worth $25,000 per annum and will not be bad to take. . . .

160

Late in April, 1883, trouble broke out in Dodge City. Luke Short, part owner of the Long Branch saloon, and several other gamblers were run out of town by city authorities. At his request, some of Short's old friends came back to Dodge to help him regain his property and position. Wyatt Earp was one of these. He arrived in Dodge City on May 31, 1883, and the *Ford County Globe*, in reporting his coming, said nothing about the purpose of the visit: "Wyatt Earp, a former city marshal of Dodge City arrived in the city from the west, last Thursday. Wyatt is looking well and glad to get back to his old haunts, where he is well and favorably known." [21]

For the next ten days Earp was in and out of Dodge City. Finally the trouble was settled; seven friends of Short gathered for a group photograph and Dodge fell back into its normal ways. (A full account of the Dodge City "war" is included in the section on Luke Short.)

Earp visited Dodge City again during its cowtown days. In November, 1883, it was recorded:

W. B. Masterson, formerly sheriff and ex-city marshal, and Wyat Earp, ex-city marshal of this city quietly and unostentatiously dropped in onto our inhabitants early last Tuesday morning, and their presence about the polls on that day had a moral effect on our would-be moral element, that was truly surprising. It is needless to say every thing passed off quietly at the city precinct on election day.[22]

Three months after Wyatt Earp's last Dodge City visit of record, he turned up in the gold fields of Shoshone county, Idaho. Known as the Coeur d'Alene rush, it developed during the winter of 1883-1884. Wyatt was there early, at least by February 1, 1884, in time for spring and consequent accessibility to the mountains.

Through the research of Attorney Richard G. Magnuson, Wallace, Idaho, it has been determined that Wyatt belonged to a sort of combine consisting of, besides himself, his brother James, John Hardy, J. E. Enright, Alfred Holman, and Daniel Ferguson. Magnuson also learned, through the records of the Shoshone county district court, that this group on at least three occasions was sued for claim jumping or possession of land by force. Twice the group received unfavorable judgments.

Another time it seems that Wyatt Earp purchased the tent saloon of Sanford and Owens but did not obtain or renew the lease for

161

the land on which it was situated in Eagle City (now Eagle). The land owner, W. Payne, sued Earp and won, judgment being release of the land and $33.61. Mr. Payne instituted the suit on May 14, 1884.

In addition to these operations Magnuson discovered that Wyatt Earp located at least four lode mining claims: the "Consolidated Grizzly Bear" on May 10, 1884; the "Dividend" on May 11; the "Dead Scratch" on May 18; and the "Golden Gate" on June 1. Wyatt located two placer claims also: the "Enola" on March 15, 1884, and an un-named claim, April 3. Jim Earp located the "Jesse Jay" lode claim on May 29, 1884.

Saloon operation seemed to offer remuneration comparable to mining, for issues of the Eagle City *Coeur d'Alene Weekly Eagle* (in Magnuson's possession) carry advertisements which indicate that Wyatt and Jim re-entered that business about July, 1884. They called their place the White Elephant.

Other records detail Wyatt's business activities in Idaho until at least September 26, 1884, when he disappeared from the scene. The records do not indicate that either of the Earp brothers performed any kind of police duty while there.

From Idaho, Wyatt Earp roamed the West. It has been said that he prospected in California, served as a private detective on the Mexican border, refereed national prize fights and operated for awhile in the Yukon during that gold rush. He died quietly in his early 80's, at Los Angeles, in 1929.

    1. "State of Kansas vs. Bessie Earp and Sallie Earp," Case Records of the Sedgwick County District Court; "State of Kansas vs. Bessie Earp and Sallie Earp," Proceedings of the Sedgwick County District Court, September, 1874, term, case no. 814.   2. "Miscellaneous Papers," Records of the City of Wichita.   3. "Proceedings of the Governing Body," Records of the City of Wichita, Journal B, pp. 44, 53; Wichita *Weekly Beacon,* April 28, 1875.   4. "Proceedings of the Governing Body," Records of the City of Wichita, Journal B, pp. 55, 62, 66, 71, 75, 77, 78, 81, 85, 90, 96, 100.   5. *See, also,* the Wichita *Weekly Beacon,* May 26, 1875.   6. "Proceedings of the Governing Body," Records of the City of Wichita, Journal B, pp. 66, 67, 71.   7. Stuart N. Lake, *Wyatt Earp, Frontier Marshal* (Boston, 1931), pp. 42, 43, used by permission of the author.   8. "Proceedings of the Governing Body," Records of the City of Wichita, Journal B, p. 103.   9. *Ibid.,* p. 107.   10. *Ibid.,* p. 112.   11. "Miscellaneous Papers," Records of the City of Wichita.   12. "Proceedings of the Governing Body," Records of the City of Wichita, Journal B, p. 115.   13. Dodge City *Times,* June 8, July 6, August 10, September 7, October 5, December 7, 1878.   14. July 27, 1878; *see, also,* the *Ford County Globe,* July 30, 1878.   15. *See, also,* the Dodge City *Times,* August 24, 1878.   16. Dodge City *Times,* December 7, 1878.   17. September 9, 1879.   18. *Ford County Globe,* March 30, 1880.   19. November 1, 1881.   20. *See, also,* the *Ford County Globe,* January 3, 1882.   21. June 5, 1883.   22. *Ford County Globe,* November 13, 1883.

FLATT, GEORGE W. (1853?-1880)

Though "old" by frontier standards, Caldwell was not yet incorporated and consequently had no police force of its own when the Caldwell *Post* printed this news story on July 10, 1879:

A TERRIBLE TRAGEDY!

A LAWLESS MOB MAKES AN ATTACK UPON THE OFFICERS—
TWO OF THE MOB KILLED OUTRIGHT!
ONE OFFICER TWICE WOUNDED AND STILL VICTORIOUS—
INQUEST AND BURIAL.

Last Monday evening [July 7] our usual quiet little city was thrown into intense excitement by an attack upon our officers of the law by a couple of desperadoes from the Chickasaw Nation, who came into town during the afternoon of the day above mentioned, and commenced spreading themselves over a sufficient quantity of "rot-gut" whiskey to become very troublesome. Agged on by one H. F. Harris, a sneak-thief ruffian, who has been a terrible bore to the citizens of the town for the past few weeks, they concluded to "take the town," and began to fire their six-shooters promiscuously on the streets, endangering the lives of our citizens. They finally went back into the Occidental Saloon where they had been, threatening and bragging about the poor victims who had heretofore fallen before the muzzles of their pistols. Dave Spear, who was in the saloon at the time started out, when one of the men cocked his pistol and sprang at him exclaiming at the same time, "that boy is going to give me away," James Moreland caught him and prevented his shooting. About this time Constable W. C. Kelly, and Deputy Constable John Wilson who had summoned a posse, among whom was the brave and daring George Flatt, to go and suppress them in their lawlessness, came up; Wilson entered the front door and past to the back part of the room near the middle door, Flatt followed stopping at the bar, in front of the room where the men were standing. They dropped on the object of Wilson and Flatt, and cocking their pistols, which was distinctly heard by the officers and holding them down by their sides at the same time making for the door, but Flatt seeing their object was to get between him and the door backed out right in front of them, on reaching the door they both leveled their six-shooters on him demanding his arms; Flatt replied: "I'll die first;" and at that instant one of the fellows fired; the ball passing close by Flatt's head and grazed the temple of W. H. Kiser, who stood a little in the rear. Flatt then drew both of his pistols which he had kept concealed behind him, and fired with the one in his right hand at the man who had got farthest out the door, the ball taking effect on the right hand, taking off the end of the fore-finger, and also the trigger the finger was on and penetrating the body in the upper part of the right breast ranging downward passing through both lungs and coming out a little below the left shoulder blade, which caused him to drop heavily to the sidewalk and rolling off in the street died almost instantly.

The man who stood in the door and shot first, received a ball in the right side, which passed straight through his body, from the pistol held in Flatt's left hand; the man returned the fire at Flatt, and then turned and fired at Wilson, who was closing in the rear, the ball glazed Wilson's wrist, making a slight flesh wound, Wilson returned the fire so rapidly that the man failed to get his work in, although he is said to have been an expert with a six-shooter. Wilson's first shot took effect in the right hand of the fellow, and the second in the abdomen just below the short-ribs, from which he fell, shooting Wilson in the thigh as he went down. After the excitement subsided somewhat, Esq. [James M.] Thomas acting as coroner summoned a jury of six men and held an inquest over the dead bodies of the two men. From what testimony could be gathered their names were supposed to be George Wood and Jack Adams. They had just arrived from the Chickasaw Nation with Johny Nicholson with a herd of cattle, had been discharged and came in for a spree. The jury, after a partial examination adjourned until nine o'clock the next day, at which time quite a number of witnesses were examined. The jury returned the following verdict: "That said men came to their death by pistol shots fired from the hands of the officers of the law and their deputies, while in the act of performing their duties." Their bodies were properly interred.

LATER.—Coroner J. H. Folks arrived about forty-eight hours after the fatal shooting; summoned a jury; raised the bodies, which had been buried, and held another inquest, with about the same result—that the killing was done by officers in the discharge of their duties, and in self-defense.

Rumor and legend being at least half of a gun fighter's reputation, little time was lost in adding to Flatt's prowess with a six shooter. The *Post*, July 24, 1879, squelched the attempt with this paragraph, ending in a commercial:

The rumor of "George Flatt killing another man," as was reported in the *Vidette* of last week is a false report. A more peaceable and quiet citizen cannot be scared up in Caldwell or any other place than George. But when it comes down to the work and our citizens lives are in danger he is always there, ready to uphold law and order. And we will take occasion to state right here that Flatt & Horseman have just opened an elegant saloon south of the City Hotel one door, where they would be pleased to see their friends at any time, and where you can always find that "that's good for shore."

On July 22, 1879, Caldwell was incorporated under order of W. P. Campbell, judge of the Sumner county district court, and an election for city officers was ordered held on August 7. The first mayor and the first city council, who were elected at that time, adopted, on August 14, an ordinance which created the office of city marshal. The *Post*, August 21, 1879, printed the ordinance which also defined the duties of the officer and established his rate of remuneration:

164

George Flatt

ORDINANCE No. 3.

An Ordinance providing for the appointment of City Marshal, and relating to his duties and compensation.

Be it ordained by the Mayor and Councilmen of the city of Caldwell:

Sec. 1. The Mayor shall, by and with the consent of the Council, appoint some suitable person to the office of City Marshal.

Sec. 2. The Marshal shall, in addition to the powers, duties, privileges and liabilities prescribed by the laws of the State, file complaints for any and all violations of the city ordinances; provided, however, that he shall not be liable for costs in any action so instituted by him.

Sec. 3. He shall have charge of the city prison, and any person arrested for the violation of state or city laws may be given into his custody for safe keeping.

Sec. 4. He may appoint any number of assistants, or deputies, for whose official acts he shall be liable, but they shall have no claim against the city for services.

Sec. 5. The Marshal, or any assistant, or deputy, or other officer of the city empowered to make arrests, is hereby authorized to call upon any male inhabitant of the city to assist him in making an arrest, or in quelling a disturbance of the public peace. Whoever neglects or refuses in said case, when called upon to assist said officer, shall be liable to a fine of not less than five dollars and not exceeding ten dollars.

Sec. 6. Whoever commits an assault upon, or resists, an officer in the discharge of his duty, or attempts to rescue a person lawfully arrested, shall be liable to a fine of not less than twenty-five dollars and not exceeding one hundred dollars.

Sec. 7. The Marshal shall receive for his services, $33⅓ dollars per month, and in addition thereto, the following fees, viz: For making an arrest authorized by law, two dollars; for serving legal process, the same fee as Sheriffs in like cases; provided, however, that in no case shall the city be liable for said fees.

Sec. 8. Before entering upon the duties of his office, the Marshal shall execute, to the city of Caldwell, a bond, with sufficient surety to be approved by the Mayor, in the penal sum of two hundred dollars, conditioned to faithfully discharge the duties of his office, and file the same with the City Clerk.

Sec. 9. This ordinance shall take effect from and after the date of its first publication in The Caldwell Post.

Approved August 14th, 1879,

Attest: N. J. Dixon, Mayor.

J. D. Kelly, Jr.,
City Clerk.

[L. S.]
Published August 21st.

The man named to the position created by this ordinance was George W. Flatt.

The first arrest recorded in the Caldwell police court docket, September 6, 1879, was made by Marshal Flatt. "J. H. Wendels was arraigned and plead guilty to the charge of fast driving . . .," wrote the police judge, James D. Kelly. Wendels was fined $3 and cost but the fine was remitted on October 13.

On October 30, 1879, the Caldwell *Post* printed this story of a successful getaway:

John Dean came into town yesterday afternoon and after getting a little full concluded that he was a second Henion, swore he would not be arrested in Caldwell. Some one discovering fire-arms on his person, informed the marshal of the fact, he at once, accompanied by his deputy Wm. Jones, better known as "Red Bill" proceeded to hunt him up and inform him of the fact that it was against the city ordinance to carry fire-arms in the city limits. Mr. Dean getting wind of their intentions and determined not to be disarmed, mounted his horse and started out of town firing his revolver promisquously. The marshal started in pursuit and commanded him under arrest, he answered their summons with a shot from his six-shooter. At the crack of his pistol the marshal and deputy turned loose with their six-shooters. Dean being mounted and moving pretty lively, the distance between the parties became so great, the marshal and deputy being pretty well out of wind, they did no very accurate shooting, although they emptied their revolvers at him before he got out of the corporation. The papers are in the constable's hands for his arrest, for assaulting the officers with a deadly weapon.

On October 29, 1879, the police court docket recorded Dean's arrest on complaint of Deputy City Marshal Dan Jones. Dean, on advice of his attorney, pleaded guilty and was fined $3 and costs of $10.90, not for assault but for the unlawful discharge of a weapon.

Flatt served as marshal probably until the city election of April 5, 1880. The last arrest credited to him in the police court docket was dated March 23. On April 5, Mike Meagher, ex-city marshal of Wichita, was elected mayor and he, with the city council, named William Horseman to Flatt's post.[1]

The United States census of 1880, enumerated in Caldwell on June 5, listed both George Flatt and his wife, Fanny. Flatt, then 27, was born in Tennessee and was a detective, according to the record. Fanny was just 18 and had married Flatt within the 1879-1880 census year.

On June 19, 1880, George Flatt was gunned down on a Caldwell street. The *Post,* June 24, reported:

THE BULLET DOES ITS WORK.

GEORGE W. FLATT ASSASSINATED—
A DELIBERATELY PLANNED AND EXECUTED MURDER.

This city has for months been exceedingly free from any serious disturbances—and the citizens of Caldwell began to flatter themselves with the idea that the day of the shot-gun and the revolver had forever departed from its limits, but last Saturday morning between twelve and one o'clock this notion was suddenly and forcibly dispelled. The saloons were all closed and the quiet of the night was unbroken, when all of a sudden there rang out upon the air the reports of several firearms fired in quick succession. The people rushed out of their houses towards the place from which the shooting seemed to come, and found George W. Flatt weltering in his blood. The police force was immediately upon the ground and shortly after Justice Kelly and Dr. [Wm. A.] Noble arrived upon the scene. Upon the examination of the body by Dr. Noble, it was found that life was entirely extinguished, and the remains were, upon the direction of Justice Kelly, removed to Mr. [Peter B.] Hohler's new barber shop adjoining the Caldwell Post building. The coroner, Mr. Folks, came down on the construction train Saturday morning and an inquest was commenced shortly after his arrival. An extract of the inquest up to Monday evening will give our readers some information of the assassination of George Flatt. From Tuesday morning the examination was held in secret. The following gentlemen were summoned as a coroner's jury:

John Hinchcliffe, T. A. Mills, C. T. Avery, C. B. Dixon, James Roberts and T. A. Cooksey.

The jury after being sworn proceeded to view the body, and Drs. Noble and [D.] MacMillan exhibited and explained the wounds. The coroner and jury then adjourned to the room in the rear of Meagher & Shea's saloon where the examination of witnesses took place. Doctor Noble testified that he was called to examine the body of George W. Flatt about half past one that morning. When he arrived the body was lying on the sidewalk in front of [Lawrence G.] Bailey's harness shop on Main street. Flatt was lying on his back with his head lying to the southwest, but he had evidently fallen forward. On examination he found that one ball entered at the base of the skull almost in the center; he also found a wound just under the right shoulder and that morning he found two more wounds which he did not detect when he examined the body on the sidewalk. He did not find any ball or leaden missel of any kind. He did probe the wound and struck either a bone or bullet of some kind but could not tell which. The ball which entered the base of the skull proved fatal, that which entered the neck might also prove fatal but not necessarily so. He could not say what killed Flatt, whether it was buckshot or pistol balls. He could of course give closer and more correct opinion by more minute examination. The coroner then issued an order to Drs. Noble and MacMillan to make a post mortem examination of the body of George W. Flatt.

Samuel H. Rogers was the next witness who was called. He testified in substance—that he is a member of the city police force, was acquainted with Flatt in his lifetime. The last time he saw him alive, was when he was walking with him about one o'clock that morning—Saturday—in front of Bailey's harness shop, on south side of Main street. He was walking south in company with Flatt and C. L. Spear. Spear was nearest the buildings and a little ahead of Flatt, then came Flatt, and he, the witness, was on the outside and about a step behind Flatt. When about one hundred feet from the northwest corner of Main and Fifth streets, heard a report of a firearm, and Flatt fell forward and a little in front of the witness, several shots were then fired in rapid succession, the balls striking the buildings all around him. The witness immediately backed out. He thought about a dozen shots were fired. The first shot was fired so close to his left ear that it deafened him, should say it was fired a little above, as if coming from the awning. The other shots came from across the street, from about the scales or well. He backed off about thirty feet and hallooed, "Let up, you have killed that man." At the first report he saw sparks fall off Flatt's head, the blaze of the fire arms seemed to be all around them. He, the witness, had no knowledge that shots would be fired. Had seen Flatt off and on during the preceding evening, he went to the dance hall to get him away. The witness had heard that Flatt had had trouble with Frank Hunt and others and he went to get him to go home, fearing that he might cause trouble, went with Flatt and others from the dance hall to the Kentucky Saloon, and then went over to the I. X. L. Saloon. Flatt was accustomed to sleep in rear of that saloon, tried to get Flatt to bed, he said, "I want to go and take a lunch first," or words to that effect. Flatt, Spear and the witness then started for Louis Segerman's restaurant to get some lunch, did not see any one on the street, nor heard any noise as if persons were walking, the first witness, saw after the shots were fired and Flatt fell, were the city marshal, the mayor, Dan Rogers, Dan Jones and Spear, who came back. The first man he spoke to was Dan Jones. The marshal, mayor and Spear came from the south. This was the last witness examined before the noon hour.

Upon the reassembling of the jury after dinner, the coroner informed the jury that his business and sickness in his family did not permit him to remain any longer that day, and would therefore adjourn the inquest till Monday, the 21st inst., at one o'clock p. m.

The first witness examined on Monday afternoon was C. L. Spear, one of the persons who were with Flatt at the time he was shot.

Mr. Spear testified substantially that he had been acquainted with Geo. W. Flatt for about one year and a half, saw Flatt last alive in front of the barber shop on Main street about seventy-five feet from the corner of Fifth street, between twelve and one o'clock last Saturday morning. Flatt was walking south on Main street between Sam Rogers and witness, witness was on the inside on the sidewalk, Flatt was on his right and a little behind, and Rogers to the right of Flatt and about a step behind him. They were all coming from the I. X. L. Saloon and were going to Louis Segerman's for a lunch. The first that happened was the firing, and he, Flatt, fell, and the shot was so close that the light shone on him. The shot came from the rear of us. Flatt fell forward on his face and right side. Witness stopped at once, but somebody commenced firing from the opposite side of the street and he ran around

168

Meagher & Shea's saloon building. Didn't see Flatt move after he fell, believe he died at once. The witness testified further: There might have been two shots fired from a double barreled shot gun, both barrels going off at the same time; then came a moment's lull and then commenced the other firing, which seemed to come from near some salt barrels by Smith & Ross' grocery store. There were between six and a dozen shots fired. When the bullets commenced to strike the building, he ran away to escape being hit, saw flashes around the hay scales and stairway between Smith & Ross' and [Levi] Thrail-kill's stores, met Mike Meagher and the city marshal and some third person, whom the witness believed was Frank Hunt. When the witness turned the corner of Meagher & Shea's saloon, those persons were coming from the other side of the building. They asked "what shooting that was," and he replied that some one had shot Flatt. Mike was the first he saw, the others came after him, then all walked to where Flatt lay. It was not more than a minute from the time he left Flatt till he returned. Dan W. Jones, Sam Rogers and some other persons were at the body, when they came up, Flatt had two pistols on his body, and witness had one, don't know whether Rogers had any pistol or not. The witness then testified regarding his habit of carrying a weapon at night when he went from his saloon to his home.

Question by Mr. Cooksey—Did you see any persons with shot guns in their hands?

Answer—Those parties I met when I came around the corner had guns, also Dan Jones had a gun, I don't know whether they were shot guns or rifles.

Doctors Nobles and MacMillen testified similarly in regard to the post mortem examination of the body of George Flatt. They found that the bullet which entered at the base of the brain had severed the spinal cord, and striking the spheroid bone, glanced off, passing either out of the neck or down the spinal column. The wounds were not made by anything larger than No. 1 buckshot. The tendency of the balls were very slightly upwards, and were evidently made by the same sized balls. The wounds might have been made by No. 2 buckshots. The course of the balls for the four wounds were the same. Flatt was killed instantly by the shot which severed the spinal cord, and was the only shot which brought him down. Both doctors were of the opinion that he received the four wounds at one fire.

James Johnson testified that he was on duty as policeman at the time of the firing, and was then sitting at a front window in Reily's new building, saw and heard the firing on the street down by [C. T.] Canida's barber shop, there were between six and a dozen shots fired, heard Flatt talking down the street immediately before the shooting. He started at once for the place where the firing was. Came across Sam Rogers, then the crowd seemed to come from every direction. Johnson further testified to the actions of Flatt during the evening previous to the murder, that he pulled his revolver on the witness and threatened to shoot his feet off, and also that he drew his revolver to shoot Policeman Hunt. Witness said he saw no one on the street immediately preceding the firing.

The next witness was H. A. Ross, the jeweler, who testified substantially as follows: I was acquainted with Flatt during his life time, my place of business is at Horner's drug store, saw Flatt Saturday morning about forty rods from where he was killed, he was coming down the street, saw him when he was killed in front of the saddler shop, two gentlemen were with him, one of whom I recognized as Sam Rogers, as they walked past the bank building, Flatt said, he was the "cock of the walk of Caldwell," and just then he was killed. The shots came from the north of him, and he, Flatt, dropped. I think the shot which brought him down came from the alley-way north of the bank building; can't tell how many shots was fired, I was scared so bad that I couldn't tell, some shots came from my side of the street, I was sitting in front of my shop, didn't see any person on my side of the street, there is an opening between the buildings near the stairway on my side of the street, heard Sam Rogers say, "Let up, the man is dead or killed," or words to that effect, then I saw Rogers fall back and the other man ran ahead. I sat quite still while the shooting was going on, was rather scared, saw Dan Jones after the firing, he was standing south from where I was, on the sidewalk on the same side of the street I was, I followed Dan Jones across the street. Rogers came from the north. Dan Jones had a gun when he crossed the street, can't tell whether it was a shot gun or rifle.

Mr. Ross' testimony closed the examination on Monday evening, at which time the inquest was adjourned till the following day at the school house. The coroner at the beginning of the examination on that day, announced that the inquest would be secret after that time. Nothing is therefore known of the proceedings from that time except that an adjournment was ordered on Wednesday, until Friday afternoon at 2 o'clock.[2]

The death of Flatt had several political ramifications which will be presented in the section on Mike Meagher.

Flatt was buried the afternoon of the same day he was killed. The *Post*, June 24, 1880, said:

The funeral of Geo W. Flatt took place Saturday afternoon. At the Sunday morning services, at the school house, Rev. S. Wood, made some appropriate remarks upon the death of Mr. Flatt, and expressing feelingly the sympathy he felt, with many others, for the young widow left to mourn such a fearful death of one who to her, at least, was very dear.

A tragic part of Flatt's death was an event which occurred only four days after he was shot: "Mrs. Flatt, the widow of George Flatt, gave birth yesterday to a fine boy. Mother and child are doing well," reported the Caldwell *Commercial*, June 24, 1880.

The decision of the coroner's jury, if ever made available, was not disclosed in the newspapers of Caldwell. However, in the spring of 1881 William Horseman, city marshal at the time of Flatt's death, was tried for the murder but was acquitted.[3]

1. Caldwell *Post*, April 15, 1880. 2. *See, also,* Caldwell *Commercial*, June 24, 1880.
3. *Ibid.*, April 28, 1881.

GAINSFORD, JAMES (1840?-____)

On November 5, 1870, James Gainsford and C. C. Kuney captured Moses Miles and Andrew McConnell, the men who had killed and nearly beheaded Abilene Chief of Police Thomas J. Smith on November 2. The Abilene *Chronicle*, November 10, 1870, reported:

CAPTURE OF THE MURDERERS.—Miles and McConnell, the murderers of U. S. Marshal and Chief of Police, Thos. J. Smith, were captured on last Saturday morning by Police Magistrate C. C. Kuney, and James Gainsford, of this place. These gentlemen with a large number of others repaired to the scene of the murder on last Wednesday afternoon. Kuney and Gainsford were the only persons who started in pursuit and continued on the trail until the murderers were captured. They traveled almost day and night; they lost track of the murderers on the Republican river, some ten miles from Junction City and traveled nearly one hundred miles out of the way, going nearly to Waterville and back before they got on the trail again, which they found at Milford, ten miles north of Junction, from whence they traveled to Clay Center, where they were joined by Sheriff Rodman [P. Rothman?], M'Laughlin and Mr. Lindsey. Knowing that they were now close upon the fleeing criminals the party renewed the pursuit at 3 o'clock on Saturday morning, and about sunrise reached a farm house fifteen miles northwest of Clay Center. Before reaching the house they learned upon inquiry that two men had stopped there the previous evening. On reaching the house, Mr. Gainsford made for the rear door, while Squire Kuney entered the house at the front door. Gainsford met Miles outside of and in the rear of the house, while Kuney encountered M'Connell immediately upon entering. Both criminals surrendered without offering resistance, although M'Connell could have used his gun had he been so disposed—but it is probable that he considered it useless to do so with any prospect of escape.

The murderers were brought to Abilene, reaching town on the Sunday morning train. From a telegraphic dispatch, sent from Junction City, news got out that they were captured, and a large crowd gathered at the depot on the arrival of the train, and deep threats were made of lynching the prisoners—but the officers were on the alert and hurried them into a room in the second story of the court house, where they were securely guarded until Monday when they were brought before Esquire [E.] Barber. They waived an examination, and were remanded to the custody of the sheriff. Court is in session and we presume their trial will take place during the present week. Too much praise cannot be awarded to Messrs. Kuney and Gainsford, for the persistent and unflaging pursuit which resulted in the capture of the fugitives, who were making their way for the mountains in Colorado, where it seems that one or both once resided for a period of ten or twelve years. It is said that both have been desperadoes, and it is probable that they have more than once imbrued their hands in the blood of their fellow men. In all human probability their stay in this world is short. God have mercy upon their souls.

For their work, Kuney and Gainsford were each rewarded with $100 by the Abilene board of trustees on March 11, 1871.[1]

In April Gainsford was elected constable of Grant township, in which Abilene is located.[2]

The city clerk of Abilene made this entry in the city council minute book on June 16, 1871: "James Gainesford and J. H. McDonald were appointed as policemen by the mayor at the unanimous request of the Council. The mayor protesting against the appointment of McDonald." [3]

The only mention found of a duty performed by Gainsford as a member of the Abilene police force was the gathering of "names of lewd women, Gaming tables &c." [4]

Gainsford was also a deputy United States marshal. The Abilene *Chronicle*, July 13, 1871, told how he arrived, one time, too late to exercise his official prerogative:

BLOODY AFFRAY.

"CURLEY" WALKER, A NOTORIOUS DESPERADO, HORSE AND CATTLE THIEF KILLED—IS SHOT THROUGH THE HEART BY CAPT. WEMPLE OF SAND SPRING.

From Deputy U. S. Marshal Gainsford, who returned a few days ago from Fort Dodge, we learn the following particulars of the death of the notorious Curly Walker, who was a pest to all stock owners in this section of country. Several weeks ago Capt. Wemple, of Sand Spring, this county, had a small herd of cattle stolen and driven off. He tracked them to Fort Dodge, in Southern Kansas, and there learned that his cattle had been brought in by Curly Walker and sold. The Captain immediately dispatched word to Deputy Marshal Gainsford of this place to come down and arrest Walker, who was loitering around Fort Dodge, unsuspicious of anything wrong. Before Gainsford arrived, Walker "smelled a mice," and commenced making preparations to leave, but Capt. Wemple could not see that, and determined to detain Walker until the arrival of Gainsford. Capt. Wemple accordingly rode up to Walker and asked him where he had obtained those cattle he had sold to parties at the fort. Walker replied that it was none of Wemple's business, whereupon Wemple told Walker to "throw up his hands, that he wanted him." Instead of complying, Walker "went for" his revolver. Capt. Wemple immediately pulled his revolver, and they commenced shooting at one another, Walker firing five shots, and Wemple seven. Wemple's fifth shot passed through Walker's heart, killing him instantly. Wemple escaped uninjured but his horse was killed. It is said that Walker was a member of the band, a portion of whom "passed in their checks" at the hands of Vigilance Committee, near Wichita, last fall. He was a great villain and "his loss is our gain." Let the work continue until the country is cleared of such thieves and cut throats as Curly Walker.

The Topeka *Kansas Daily Commonwealth*, July 7, 1871, said

172

that John "Curley" Walker was an old plainsman and scout and that he had been killed on June 22.

Gainsford was relieved from the Abilene force on September 2, 1871. The minute book of the ?˙ ⁄ council, pp. 86 and 87, carried this entry:

The propriety of reducing police force was discussed by Mayor and Council and after due deliberation and consideration the following resolution was adopted and ordered recorded.

Be it resolved by the Mayor and Council of the City of Abilene

That J. H. McDonald and James Gainsford be discharged from off the Police Force of said City from and after this 2d day of Sept. A. D. 1871, and that a copy of this resolution be given by City Clerk to City Marshall [James B. Hickok] and to be served upon said J. H. McDonald and James Gainesford by the said City Marshall

2d Be it further resolved that the said J. H. McDonald and James Gainsford are discharged by reason that their services are no longer needed.

Passed the Council
September 2d A D 1871
E. H. KILPATRICK
City Clerk

1. "City Council Minute Book," Records of the City of Abilene, p. 49. 2. "Dickinson County Commissioners Journal," v. 1, p. 157. 3. Page 71. 4. "City Council Minute Book," Records of the City of Abilene, p. 69.

HICKOK, JAMES BUTLER (1837-1876)

Wild Bill Hickok began his career as a Kansas peace officer in 1858. On March 22, though only 20 years of age, he was elected constable of Monticello township, Johnson county. On April 21, 1858, Gov. James W. Denver issued Hickok's commission and the act was recorded in the "Executive Minutes, Kansas Territory," now a part of the archives of the Kansas State Historical Society. According to the territorial census for 1859, which is also in the Kansas archives, Hickok had come to Kansas in 1855.

Records of the United States War Department, Office of the Quartermaster General, show that on October 30, 1861, J. B. Hickok was hired as wagon master at Sedalia, Mo. His pay was $100 a month.

Similar records from the Office of the Provost Marshal General show that a William Hickok (Wild Bill?) served as a special policeman in the corps during March, 1864. In the section on "Scouts, Guides and Spies, 1861-1866" this item was found:

The United States, to William Hickok Dr.

March 10" 1864   For

> Services rendered as Special Police under the direction of Lt. N. H. Burns A Pro Mar Dist S. W. Mo at Springfield Mo from March 1" to March 10" 1864 inclusion being 10 days at $60.00 per month.

$20.00

I certify that the above account is correct and just; that the services were rendered as stated, and that they were necessary for the Public Service, as per my Report of "Persons and Articles," Abstract of Expenditures for March 1864.

N. H. Burns

1 Lieut   1 Ark Inf. Actg. Pro. Mar.

Approved

John B. Sanborn

Brig. Genl. Comd.

On the reverse this terse sentence was written:

Disapproved and ordered filed by Col Sanderson, for the reason that no authority was issued by the Pro Mar Genl of Dept of the Mo, for the employment of this man.

Wm K Patrick

July 20 '64   Auditor

A like reference to service from March 11 to March 31 was also recorded:

The United States, to Wm Hickok Dr.

March 31" 1864   For

> Services rendered as Special Police under the direction of Lt W. H. McAdams Pro Mar Dist S. W. Mo. at Springfield Mo from March 11" to March 31" 1864, inclusion being 20 days at $60.00 per month

$40.00

I certify that the above account is correct and just; that the services were rendered as stated, and that they were necessary for the Public Service, as per my Report of "Persons and Articles," Abstract of Expenditures for March 1864.

W. H. McAdams

Lt. 24" Mo. Vol. Pro. Mar. Dist. S. W. Mo.

Approved

John B. Sanborn

Brig. Genl. Comd

And on the reverse the same terse sentence:

Disapproved and ordered filed by Col Sanderson, for the reason that no authority was issued by the Pro Mar Genl of Dept of the Mo, for the employment of this man.

Wm K Patrick

July 20 '64   Auditor

Wild Bill Hickok

Near the end of the Civil War, Hickok wrote this letter:

CASSVILLE, Mo., *February 10, 1865.*

Brigadier-General SANBORN:

I have been at Camp Walker and Spavinaw. There are not more than ten or twelve rebels in any squad in the southwest that I can hear of. If you want me to go to Neosho and west of there, notify me here. It was cold; I returned back.

J. B. HICKOCK.

General Sanborn replied:

HEADQUARTERS DISTRICT OF SOUTHWEST MISSOURI,
Springfield, Mo., February 11, 1865.

J. B. HICKOCK,
Cassville, Mo.:

You may go to Yellville or the White River in the vicinity of Yellville and learn what Dobbin intends to do with his command now on Crowley's Ridge, and from there come to this place.

JOHN B. SANBORN,
Brigadier-General, Commanding.[1]

It was in Springfield five months later that Hickok shot and killed Dave Tutt. The Springfield *Missouri Weekly Patriot,* July 27, 1865, gave the killing only scant notice in its "locals" column:

David Tutt, of Yellville, Ark., was shot on the public square, at 6 o'clock P. M., on Friday last [July 21], by James B. Hickok, better known in Southwest Missouri as "Wild Bill." The difficulty occurred from a game of cards. Hickok is a native of Homer, Lasalle county, Ills., and is about twenty-six years of age. He has been engaged since his sixteenth year, with the exception of about two years, with Russell, Majors & Waddill, in Government service, as scout, guide, or with exploring parties, and has rendered most efficient and signal service to the Union cause, as numerous acknowledgements from the different commanding officers with whom he has served will testify.

Wild Bill was tried and on August 5, 1865, was acquitted. The *Patriot* reported on August 10:

The trial of Wm. Haycock for the killing of Davis Tutt, in the streets in this city week before last, was concluded on Saturday last, by a verdict of *not guilty*, rendered by the jury in about ten minutes after they retired to the jury room.

The general dissatisfaction felt by the citizens of this place with the verdict in no way attaches to our able and efficient Circuit Attorney, nor to the Court. It is universally conceded that the prosecution was conducted in an able, efficient and vigorous manner, and that Col. Fyan [*sic*] is entitled to much credit for the ability, earnestness and candor exhibited by him during the whole trial. He appeared to be a full match for the very able Counsel who conducted the defense.—Neither can any fault be found with the Judge, who conducted himself impartially throughout the trial, and whose rulings, we

175

believe, gave general satisfaction. As an evidence of the impartiality of his Honor, we copy the instructions given to the jury, as follows:

1st. If they believe from the evidence that the defendant intentionally shot at the deceased, Davis Tutt, and the death of said Tutt was caused thereby, they will find defendant guilty, unless they are satisfied from the evidence that he acted in self-defense.

2d. That defendant is presumed to have intended the natural and probable consequences of his own acts.

3d. The defendant cannot set up in justification that he acted in self-defense if he was willing to engage in a fight with deceased.

4th. To be entitled to acquital on the ground of self-defense, he must have been anxious to avoid a conflict, and must have used all reasonable means to avoid it.

5th. If the deceased and defendant engaged in a fight or conflict willingly on the part of each, and the defendant killed the deceased, he is guilty of the offense charged, although the deceased may have fired the first shot.

6th. If it appear[s] that the conflict was in any way premeditated by the defendant, he is not justifiable.

7th. The crime charged in the indictment is complete, whether there was malice or not.

8th. If the jury have any reasonable doubt as to the defendant's guilt, they will give him the benefit of such doubt, and acquit him.

9th. But such doubt must be a reasonable doubt, not a mere possibility. It must be such a doubt as leaves the mind disatisfied with a conclusion of guilt.

10th. This rule, as to a reasonable doubt, does not apply as to matters set up in justification.

11th. If the defendant claims to have acted in self-defense it is his duty to satisfy you that he so acted, and it is not sufficient to create a doubt in your minds whether he so acted or not.

12th. The jury will disregard evidence as to the moral character of deceased, and as to his character for loyalty, as the character of the deceased could afford no excuse for killing him.

13th. Every murder includes in it the crime of man-slaughter, and if the jury believe that the defendant has committed the crime of murder in the first or second degree, they will find him guilty under this indictment of man-slaughter, the crime charged in this indictment.

14th. The Court instructs the jury that they may disregard all that part of the evidence of Tutt's declaration to Lieut. Warner.

15th. The Court instructs to disregard all Werner's testimony.

16th. That the jury will disregard any threats made by Tutt against Haycock prior to the meeting at the Lyon House in Haycock's room.

Those who so severely censure the jury for what they regard as a disregard of their obligations to the public interest, and a proper respect for their oaths, should remember that they are partly to blame themselves. The citizens of this city were shocked and terrified at the idea that a man could arm himself and take a position at a corner of the public square, in the centre of the city, and await the approach of his victim for an hour or two, and then willingly

176

engage in a conflict with him which resulted in his instant death; and this, too, with the knowledge of several persons who seem to have posted themselves in safe places where they could see the tragedy enacted. But they failed to express the horror and disgust they felt, not from indifference, but from fear and timidity.

Public opinion has much to do with the administration of justice, and when those whose sense of justice and respect for law should prompt them to speak out and control public sentiment, fail to do so, whether from fear or from indifference, we think they should not complain of others. That the defendant engaged in the fight willingly it seems is not disputed, and lawyers say—and the Court instructed the jury to the same effect—that he was not entitled to an acquital on the ground of self-defense unless he was anxious to avoid the fight, and used all reasonable means to do so; but the jury seems to have thought differently.

Hickok was still in Springfield on January 25, 1866, and witnessed the killing of James Coleman by Policeman John Orr. Coleman and his brother, Sam, had objected to the manner in which the Springfield police were arresting a man named Bingham. A scuffle ensued and James was killed. Hickok gave his testimony before a coroner's jury, published in the *Missouri Weekly Patriot*, February 1, 1866:

J. B. Hickok, being duly sworn, says: When I got where the fuss was, the police took a man [Bingham] off a horse; after they had got him off the horse, Charles Moss [city marshal] came and took hold of him; he did not appear to want to come with the police; kept talking, and when they got opposite Jacob's store, he commenced scrambling, and they threw him down the second time; then they took him along to where Ladd keeps grocery, and by that time one of his comrads came up; those they stopped; Samuel Coleman commenced talking, and the one who was killed had tied the horses at the blacksmith shop and came up and joined them at Ladd's, or near Ladd's grocery; the two Colemans wanted to stop the police and have a talk with the police; from that they got to jarring worse and worse until the[y] commenced shooting; the first I saw of the shooting I saw John Orr jerk his pistol and put it up against the man and shot; did not see whether James Coleman had a pistol in his hand or not; his back was to me; and Samuel Coleman grabbed a stick and struck, but did not know whether he struck John Orr or Charles Moss, and as soon as the first shooting was done, Orr turned and shot Samuel Coleman; the crowd scattered around, and some person or persons grabbed the first man arrested [Bingham] and ran off down town this way; we pulled the man [James Coleman] upon the platform and intended taking him into Ladd's but he was locked up, and he was then carried to the drug store of N. P. Murphy & Co.; affray commenced first opposite the Lyon House and closed opposite Ladd's grocery, on South street, Springfield, Missouri.

About the end of January, 1867, the February issue of *Harper's New Monthly Magazine* arrived in Kansas. The lead article, authored by Col. George Ward Nichols, was destined to make James Butler Hickok nationally famous. Then, as now, printed versions of Hickok's career became the subject of controversy. The Leavenworth *Daily Conservative,* January 30, 1867, said:

QUEER.—The story of "Wild Bill," as told in Harper's for February is not easily credited hereabouts. To those of us who were engaged in the campaign it sounds mythical; and whether Harry York, Buckskin Joe or Ben Nugget is meant in the *life* sketches of Harper we are not prepared to say. The scout services were so mixed that we are unable to give precedence to any. "Wild Bill's" exploits at Springfield have not as yet been heard of here, and if under that cognomen such brave deeds occurred we have not been given the relation.

There are many of the rough riders of the rebellion now in this city whose record would compare very favorably with that of "Wild Bill," and if another account is wanted we might refer to Walt Sinclair and also to the Park Stables.

One of the most spirited criticisms appeared in the Springfield *Patriot* on January 31, 1867. The editor of that paper, having known Hickok during the war years, apparently felt especially qualified to criticize the article. He wrote:

"WILD BILL," HARPER'S MONTHLY AND "COLONEL" G. W. NICHOLS.

Springfield is excited. It has been so ever since the mail of the 25th brought *Harper's Monthly* to its numerous subscribers here.—The excitement, curiously enough, manifests itself in very opposite effects upon our citizens. Some are excessively indignant, but the great majority are in convulsions of laughter, which seem interminable as yet. The cause of both abnormal moods, in our usually placid and quiet city, is the first article in *Harper* for February, which all agree, if published at all, should have had its place in the "Editor's Drawer," with the other fabricated more or less funnyisms; and not where it is, in the leading "illustrated" place. But, upon reflection, as Harper has given the same prominence to "Heroic Deeds of Heroic Men," by Rev. J. T. Headley, which, generally, are of about the same character as its article "Wild Bill," we will not question the good taste of its "make up."

We are importuned by the angry ones to review it. "For," say they, "it slanders our city and citizens so outrageously by its caricatures, that it will deter some from immigrating here, who believe its representations of our people."

"Are there any so ignorant?" we asked.

"Plenty of them in New England; and especially about the Hub, just as ready to swallow it all as Gospel truth, as a Johnny Chinaman or Japanese would be to believe that England, France and America are inhabited by cannibals."

"Don't touch it," cries the hilarious party, "don't spoil a richer *morceaux* than

178

ever was printed in Gulliver's Travels, or Baron Munchausen! If it prevents any consummate fools from coming to Southwest Missouri, that's no loss."

So we compromise between the two demands, and give the article but brief and inadequate criticism. Indeed, we do not imagine that we could do it justice, if we made ever so serious and studied an attempt to do so.

A good many of our people—those especially who frequent the bar rooms and lager-beer saloons, will remember the author of the article, when we mention one "Colonel" G. W. NICHOLS, who was here for a few days in the summer of 1865, splurging around among our "strange, half-civilized people," seriously endangering the supply of lager and corn whisky, and putting on more airs than a spotted stud-horse in the ring of a county fair. *He's the author!* And if the illustrious holder of one of the "Brevet" commissions which *Fremont* issued to his wagon-masters, will come back to Springfield, two-thirds of all the people he meets will invite him "to pis'n hisself with suth'n" for the fun he unwittingly furnished them in his article—the remaining one-third will kick him wherever met, for lying like a dog upon the city and people of Springfield.

JAMES B. HICKOK, (not "William Hitchcock," as the "Colonel" mis-names his hero,) *is* a remarkable man, and is as well known here as Horace Greely in New York, or Henry Wilson in "the Hub." The portrait of him on the first page of *Harper* for February, is a most faithful and striking likeness—features, shape, posture and dress—in all it is a faithful reproduction of one of Charley SCHOLTEN's photographs of "Wild Bill," as he is generally called. No finer *physique*, no greater strength, no more personal courage, no steadier nerves, no superior skill with the pistol, no better horsemanship than his, could any man of the million Federal soldiers of the war, boast of; and few did better or more loyal service as a soldier throughout the war. But Nichols "cuts it very fat" when he describes Bill's feats in arms. We think his hero only claims to have sent a few dozen rebs to the farther side of Jordan; and we never, before reading the "Colonel's" article, suspected he had dispatched "*several hundreds* with his own hands." But it must be so, for the "Colonel" asserts it with a parenthesis of genuine flavorous Bostonian piety, to assure us of his incapacity to utter an untruth.

We dare say that Captain Kelso, our present member of Congress, did double the execution "with his own hands," on the Johnnies, during the war, that Bill did. This is no disparagement to Bill. Except his "mate" TOM MARTIN, (who swore yesterday that Nichols' pathetic description of his untimely murder in 1863, in that article, was not true,) Bill was the best scout, by far, in the Southwest.

The equestrian scenes given are purely imaginary. The extraordinary black mare, Nell, (which was in fact a black stallion, blind in the right eye, and "a goer,") wouldn't "fall as if struck by a cannon ball" when Hickok "slowly waved his hand over her head with a circular motion," worth a cent. And none of our citizens ever saw her (or him) "wink affirmatively" to Bill's mention of her (or his) great sagacity. Nor did she (or he) ever jump upon the billiard table of the Lyon House at "William's low whistle;" and if Bill had, (as the "Colonel" describes it on his own veracity,) mounted her in Ike Hoff's saloon and "with one bound, lit in the middle of the street," he would have got a severe fall in the doorway of the bar room, *sure*, to make no mention of clearing at "one bound" a porch twelve feet wide, and five feet high, a pavement twelve feet, and half the width of the roadway, (twenty-five feet by actual measurement) making a total of forty-nine feet, without computing any margin inside the room from which she (or he) "bounded."

We are sorry to say also that the graphic account of the terrible fight at Mrs. Waltman's, in which Bill killed, solitary and alone, "the guerrilla Mc-Kandlas and ten of his men"—the whole bilen of 'em—is not reliable. The fact upon which this account is *founded*, being, that before the war, and while yet out in the mountains, Wild Bill did fight and kill one McKandlas and two other men, who attacked him simultaneously. These little rivulets in the monthlies, weeklies and dailies, all run into and make up the great river of *history* afterwhile; and if many of them are as salty as this one, the main stream will be very brackish at least. We must, therefore tell the truth to "vindicate history."

Bill never was in the tight place narrated, and exhibited in the illustrating wood cut, where half down on the edge of Mrs. Waltman's bed, with his bowie-knife up to the hilt in one bushwhacker's heart, with half a dozen dead men upon the floor in picturesque attitudes; two of the three remaining desperadoes have their knives puncturing his westcoat, and the final one of the ten is leveling terrific blows at his head with a clubbed musket. We congratulate Bill on the fact that that picture and narrative was rather *not* true. It would have been too risky even for Bill, the "Scout of the Plains." 2

We have not time or space to follow the article further. We protest, however, that our people *do not* dress in "greasy skins," and bask in the sunshine prone upon our pavements. We will die in the belief that we have people here as smart, and even as well dressed as "Colonel" G. W. NICHOLS. Mrs. E. M. BOWEN advertises in our columns the latest styles of "postage stamp" bonnets, and Mde. Demorest's fashions, for our ladies; and we know that SHIPLEY has not been in fault, if our gentlemen are not presentable in costume, even in the "salons" of the Hub.

We must add the remark that so far as we are capable of judging, "Captain Honesty" (who can forget more than Nichols ever knew, and scarcely miss it,) speaks very intelligible, good English. He was at least considered so capable and reliable an A. Q. M. as to be retained by the War Department for more than a year after the war had closed, and his regiment mustered out, to administer and settle the government affairs in one of the most important posts in the country.

In reading the romantic and pathetic parts of the article, "the undercurrent about a woman" in his quarrel and fatal fight with Dave Tutts; and his remarks with "quivering lips and tearful eyes" about his old mother in Illinois, we tried to fancy Bill's familiar face while listening to the passage being read. We could almost hear his certain remark, "O! hell! what a d--n fool that Nichols is." We agree with "Wild Bill" on that point.

The editor of the Leavenworth *Conservative* remembered that he had known Wild Bill in 1864, and on February 1, 1867, told of his acquaintance:

"WILD BILL."—Since the publication of the paper in Harper's, setting forth the exploits of "Wild Bill," there has been a determined research in memory by those who participated in the closing scenes of the war in Northern Arkansas. Since the subject of the sketch in Harper has been prominently given to the country we have furbished our recollection, and the result is that we knew Bill Hitchcock in 1864 and recognize his portrait in the magazine for February. It is a fair representation for a wood cut. "Wild Bill," as he is called, rode in company with the writer, and with Adjutant Mackle and Lt. Col. Hoyt from Newtonia, subsequent to the battle in October, to the Arkansas river, we think, but perhaps he remained at Fayetteville. The general description of the man, as given by Harper, is tolerably correct, but in the language used the narrator is much at fault. In appearance throughout Bill Hitchcock is gentlemanly, and grammatically accurate in conversation, and in all belies the character given him as a desperado. He came into Gen. Blunt's camp on the morning after the battle of Newtonia, having previously been with Price, and having spent several months in the camps in Arkansas, as stated in the article in question. As to his pet mare we are skeptical, and the river adventure would hardly be credited among those on the staff in the fall of 1864. "Wild Bill" is a fit subject for romance, but not more so than a dozen now in this town, who throughout the war, were in the fore front of danger. A special to the Democrat says he is now a gambler at Junction City, which statement we have no reason to doubt. "Wild Bill" has made a mark in the war for the Union, and we accord him full credit for his risks and reward for results attained.

The Atchison *Daily Champion,* February 5, 1867, also felt that some criticism and correction was due. The *Champion's* article was reprinted by the Leavenworth *Conservative* on February 7:

"WILD BILL."—Since the publication in Harper concerning "Wild Bill" the origin, existence and actions of that personage have been very thoroughly canvassed. Elsewhere, we give the Springfield, Mo., version, which is not at all creditable to Geo. Ward Nichols. Speaking of Bill the Atchison Champion says:

"The real name of 'Wild Bill,' the scout described in Harper's Magazine for this month, is William Haycock, and not Hitchcock, as given in the last paragraph of the article referred to. He kept, up to the time of the McKandles difficulty, the Overland Stage Co.'s ranche at Rock Creek, beyond Marysville. The McKandles gang consisted of only the leader and three others, and not of fourteen as stated in the magazine. Of these 'Wild Bill,' in the fight referred to, shot McKandles through the heart with a rifle, and then stepping out of doors, revolver in hand, shot another of the gang dead; severely wounded a third, who ran off to a ravine near by, and was found there dead, and slightly wounded the fourth, who ran away and was not heard of afterwards. There was no grudge existing between the McKandles gang and 'Wild Bill,' but the former had a quarrel with the Stage Company, and had come to burn the sta-

WHY THE WEST WAS WILD

tion 'Bill' was in charge of. The other men, hearing of their coming, ran off, leaving 'Bill' to defend the property alone. He did it with the greatest coolness and courage, and the Company rewarded him very handsomely for his action afterwards.

"'Wild Bill' is, as stated in the Magazine, a splendid specimen of physical manhood, and is a dead shot with a pistol. He is a very quiet man, rarely talking to any one, and not of a quarrelsome disposition, although reckless and desperate when once involved in a fight. There are a number of citizens of this city who know him well.

"Nichols' sketch of 'Wild Bill' is a very readable paper, but the fine descriptive powers of the writer have been drawn upon as largely as facts, in producing it. There are dozens of men on the Overland Line who are probably more desperate characters than Haycock, and are the heroes of quite as many and as desperate adventures. The wild West is fertile in 'Wild Bills.' Charley Slade, formerly one of the division Superintendents on the O. S. Line, was probably a more desperate, as well as a cooler man than the hero of Harper's, and his fight at his own ranche was a much more terrible encounter than that of 'Wild Bill' with the McKandles gang. Slade, however, unlike Haycock, was naturally quarrelsome, and could hardly feel comfortable unless he had shot a man within two or three days."

The identity of the scout will probably be settled within the next three months. However, the remarks of the Champion as to other scouts may be taken as correct. There are many in Kansas whose adventures, illustrated, would read as well as those of Wild Bill.

By February 19, 1867, when this item appeared in the *Conservative*, Hickok was something of a celebrity in Leavenworth:

"WILD BILL."—This somewhat noted individual was in the city yesterday, having recently arrived from Riley with a lot of furs and skins. He was the observed of a good many observers.

Wild Bill had been in government service, as a scout, since the first of the year. In April he was ordered to accompany the Indian expedition of Maj. Gen. Winfield Scott Hancock west of Fort Larned. Lt. Col. (Bvt. Maj. Gen.) George Armstrong Custer, executive officer and acting commander of the Seventh U. S. cavalry, and Henry M. Stanley, a newspaper reporter later famous for finding Dr. David Livingstone in Africa, were also members of the expedition. The Topeka *Weekly Leader,* April 25, 1867, reported:

GENERAL HANCOCK'S INDIAN EXPEDITION.

Phillip D. Fisher, of Topeka, now engaged in surveying the route for the Union Pacific Railway, eastern division, west of Salina, writes, as follows to Harper's Weekly. Mr. Fisher also sketched Fort Harker, which appears in "Harpers" for April 27th:

"The Government, aroused at last to the necessity of doing something to prevent a repetition of the massacre at Fort Phillip Kearney, has sent an expedition to the Plains under Major-General Winfield S. Hancock. The command reached Fort Harker on the first of April, and went into camp on the "Smoky Bottom," just west of the post; from which camp it moved on the third of April, going to Fort Larned on the Arkansas River, distant from Harker about eighty miles.—The troops are under command of Gen. A. J. Smith [colonel of the Seventh U. S. cavalry]. They number about two thousand men.

"Wild Bill," who, since the publication of his exploits in the February number of Harper's Magazine, has had greatness thrust upon him, is attached as a scout, and quite a number of Delaware Indians accompany the command in the capacity of scouts, guides, hunters, and interpreters. . . .

Before the expedition left Fort Harker, Stanley, reporting for the St. Louis *Missouri Democrat*, had written this description and almost unbelievable interview with Hickok under dateline of April 4:

James Butler Hickok, commonly called "Wild Bill," is one of the finest examples of that peculiar class known as frontiersman, ranger, hunter, and Indian scout. He is now thirty-eight [29] years old, and since he was thirteen the prairie has been his home. He stands six feet one inch in his moccasins, and is as handsome a specimen of a man as could be found. We were prepared, on hearing of "Wild Bill's" presence in the camp, to see a person who might prove to be a coarse and illiterate bully. We were agreeably disappointed however. He was dressed in fancy shirt and leathern leggings. He held himself straight, and had broad, compact shoulders, was large chested, with small waist, and well-formed muscular limbs. A fine, handsome face, free from blemish, a light moustache, a thin pointed nose, bluish-grey eyes, with a calm look, a magnificent forehead, hair parted from the centre of the forehead, and hanging down behind the ears in wavy, silken curls, made up the most picturesque figure. He is more inclined to be sociable than otherwise; is enthusiastic in his love for his country and Illinois, his native State; and is endowed with extraordinary power and agility, whose match in these respects it would be difficult to find. Having left his home and native State when young, he is a thorough child of the prairie, and inured to fatigue. He has none of the swaggering gait, or the barbaric jargon ascribed to the pioneer by the *Beadle* penny-liners. On the contrary, his language is as good as many a one that boasts "college larning." He seems naturally fitted to perform daring actions. He regards with the greatest contempt a man that could stoop low enough to perform "a mean action." He is generous, even to extravagance. He formerly belonged to the 8th Missouri Cavalry.

The following dialogue took place between us: "I say, Mr. Hickok, how many white men have you killed to your certain knowledge?" After a little deliberation, he replied, "I suppose I have killed considerably over a hundred." "What made you kill all those men? Did you kill them without cause or provocation?" "No, by heaven! I never killed one man without good cause." "How old were you when you killed the first white man, and for what cause?" "I was twenty-eight years old when I killed the first white man, and if ever a man deserved killing he did. He was a gambler and counterfeiter, and I was then in an hotel in Leavenworth City, and seeing some loose characters around, I ordered a room, and as I had some money about me, I thought I would retire to it. I had lain some thirty minutes on the bed when I heard men at my door. I pulled out my revolver and bowie knife, and held them ready, but half concealed, and pretended to be asleep. The door was opened, and five men entered the room. They whispered together, and one said, 'Let us kill the son of a _____; I'll bet he has got money.' Gentlemen," said he, "that was a time—an awful time. I kept perfectly still until just as the knife touched my breast; I sprang aside and buried mine in his heart, and then used my revolver on the others right and left. One was killed, and another was wounded; and then, gentlemen, I dashed through the room and rushed to the fort, where I procured a lot of soldiers, and returning to the hotel, captured the whole gang of them, fifteen in all. We searched the cellar, and found eleven bodies buried in it—the remains of those who had been murdered by those villains." Turning to us, he asked: "Would you not have done the same? That was the first man I killed, and I never was sorry for that yet." 3

The records of the Quartermaster General, "Reports of Persons and Articles Hired, 1861-1868," show that Hickok had entered government service on January 1, 1867. Engaged as a scout, he was paid $100 per month. By July 31, 1867, the last month of his recorded employment, the government owed him $300 in back pay. In May and June he was listed as "scouting with 7th Cavly in the field."

Hickok and Jack Harvey, another of Hancock's scouts, visited Junction City in May. The Junction City *Weekly Union*, May 11, 1867, reported: "Wild Bill came in from the west the other day. He reports all qui[e]t at the front. Jack Harvey has also returned. Hancock will be in in a day or so. Custar will be the only notable left behind."

Henry Stanley was in Junction City, too, and that same day, May 11, sent another of his dispatches. Hickok still had him captivated, for he wrote:

"Wild Bill," who is an inveterate hater of the Indians, was . . . chased by six Indians lately, and had quite a little adventure with them. It is his custom to be always armed with a brace of ivory-handled revolvers, with which weapons he is remarkably dexterous; but when bound on a long and lonely ride across the plains, he goes armed to the teeth. He was on one of these lonely missions, due to his profession as scout, when he was seen by a group of the red men, who immediately gave chase. They soon discovered that they were pursuing one of the most famous men of the prairie, and commenced to retrace their steps, but two of them were shot, after which Wild Bill was left to ride on his way. The little adventure is verified by a scout

184

named [Thomas] Kincaid, who, while bearing despatches for General Custer, was also obliged to use his weapons freely. The lives of these Indian scouts are made up of these little experiences." [4]

Since Hancock's expedition had failed in its primary mission, which was to persuade the Indians by show of force not to follow the war path that year, military operations against the red man were active throughout the summer. The Leavenworth *Daily Conservative*, July 10, 1867, reported on a rumored skirmish with the Indians:

> FROM THE PLAINS. . . .
> [From Our Special Correspondent.]
>
> FORT HARKER, July 8, 1867.
> . . . I noticed in the Commercial of Saturday morning the following interesting paragraphs relative to Fort Harker and Indian matters:
> "A gentleman, just from Fort Harker, says the town is full of vague and indefinite rumors of Indian depredations, outrages, etc.
> On the 2d inst. it was reported that four men had been killed and scalped some eight miles west of Fort Harker. Troops were immediately put in readiness, and, under the direction or guidance of Wild Bill, started in pursuit of the bloody depredators. The next day Wild Bill and his party returned, bringing five red skins with them, and having killed some eight or ten Indians on the trip.
> As the train left Fort Harker on the morning of the Fourth, picket firing was heard in various directions around the Fort, indicating the presence of skulking Indians."
> If there is such a town as Fort Harker "your own" has failed to discover it. If it has an existence, it is in the imagination of the author of the paragraphs above quoted.[5]
> As to the second paragraph it is true in part. Four men were reported killed on the 2d inst., and a scouting party was sent out to investigate. The party returned on Friday, but with nary a dead Indian; neither had they seen a live one.

On October 26, 1867, the editor of the Manhattan *Independent* described Hickok as follows:

> On Monday [October 21] we took the cars of the U. P. R. W. E. D. for Leavenworth. We make no mention of this because there is any peculiar significance in our visiting the metropolis of Kansas. Like almost everybody in Kansas we do so occasionally. But upon this occasion it was our fortune to fall in with quite a number of persons of whom it might interest our readers to learn something.
>
> WILD BILL
>
> the celebrated scout, with Jack Harvey and some dozen of their companions were upon the train, having just come in from a scouting expedition under

185

Gen. Sherman. All the party were more or less affected by frequent potations from their bottles, and Wild Bill himself was tipsy enough to be quite belligerent.

He is naturally a fine looking fellow, not much over 30 years of age, over 6 feet in height, muscular & athletic, possessing a fine figure, as lithe and agile as the Borneo Boys. His complexion is very clear, cheek bones high, and his fine auburn hair, which he parts in the middle hangs in ringlets down upon his shoulders, giving him a girlish look in spite of his great stature. He wore a richly embroydered sash with a pair of ivory hilted and silver mounted pistol stuck in it. Doubtless this man and his companions have killed more men than any other persons who took part in the late war. What a pity that young men so brave and daring should lack the discretion to sheath their daggers forever when the war terminated! But such is the demoralizing effect of war upon those who engage in it and certainly upon all who love the vocation.

We learn from a gentleman who has frequently met these wild and reckless young men, that they live in a constant state of excitement, one continual round of gambling drinking and swearing, interspersed at brief intervals with pistol practice upon each other.

At a word any of the gang draws his pistol and blazes away as freely as if all mankind were Arkansas Rebels, and had a bounty offered for their scalpes.

How long these Athletes will be able to stand such a mode of life; eating, drinking, sleeping (if they can be said to sleep) and playing cards with their pistols at half cock, remains to be seen. For ourself, we are willing to risk them in an Indian campaign for which their cruelty and utter recklessness of life particularly fit them.

Wild Bill ran for sheriff of Ellsworth county on November 5, 1867. The Ellsworth county commissioners' journal records five aspirants for the office, one of them being "J. Hacock." He received 156 votes, all but one of which were cast in the city of Ellsworth. Rural county votes defeated Bill however, and E. W. Kingsbury won.

Shortly thereafter the Hays City *Railway Advance*, November 9, 1867, said:

We find the following in the Democrat's special from Springfield, Ill. It is erroneous. The Wild Bill of Harper's Monthly was, at the time mentioned, in Ellsworth. He is Deputy U. S. Marshal and was a candidate for the office of sheriff of that county, at the recent election, but was defeated. We set the Democrat right in justice to Mr. Haycock, the original Wild Bill.

["]Quite an interesting and somewhat exciting habeas corpus case was argued in our Circuit Court this morning. The prisoner, Henry O'Connor, was charged with the robbery of the bank of Pettis & Inglas, in Tremont, Tazewell

186

county, of some one hundred thousand dollars in bonds, but was brought before Judge Rice on a writ, which was quashed by the Judge, and the prisoner remanded to Tazewell to be tried. It may be interesting to the curious to know that O'Connor was a distinguished Union scout during the rebellion, and is no other than the Wild Bill of Harper's Monthly.["]

In December Wild Bill was mentioned as being in Hays. The *Conservative*, December 14, 1867, gave this article taken from the Hays City *Advance*: "U. S. Marshal [Charles C.] Whiting, Wild Bill, Jack Harvey, Surcey and others called in at our quarters Tuesday. They were all welcome. William is still around, probably engaged in preparing his LIFE for DeWitt."

Frank A. Root, editor of the Atchison *Daily Free Press*, wrote in that paper on January 6, 1868:

In Hays I formed the acquaintance of Wm. Haycock, better known as "Wild Bill." He is a man about thirty years of age, over six feet high, straight as an arrow, with long black hair hanging over his shoulders. He is in the employ of Government as a detective and is probably better acquainted with the plains than any other man living, of his age.

Hickok was a deputy United States marshal when he wrote this letter:

HAYS CITY KANSAS
March 28" 1868

CAPT SAML OVENSHINE
Comdg Post of Fort Hays Kans
Capt:
I have the honor to request that a guard of a Corpl and five men be detailed to assist me in conveying the prisoners of the U. S. Marshal now in the Post Guard House to Topeka Kans I should respectfully call your attention to the number and character of these prisoners and the feeling in their behalf in this community which renders a guard of U. S. Soldiers absolutely necessary.
I am Captain, very respectly
Your obd't servt
J B HICKOK
Dept U. S. Marshal.[6]

Capt. Ovenshine complied with Hickok's request and issued this order for an escort:

SPECIAL ORDER   HEADQUARTERS FORT HAYS KANS
No. 51.   March 28th 1868
III. Sergt William Alloways Co. "H" 5th Inft and five (5) Privates of Co. "G" & "H" 5th Inft. will proceed to Topeka Ks as guard to a number of citizen prisoners, accused of stealing Government property, who are about to be taken to that place for trial. Having turned over the prisoners Sergt

187

Alloways with his party will return at once to this post. The A. A. Qr. Mr will furnish transportation for the guard.

By Order of
CAPT SAM'L OVENSHINE

Copies
Forwarded to
Dept & Dist HdQrs
April 3" 1868 [7]

[J. A. SOUDERS]
2nd Lieut 38th Inft & Brvt Capt USA
Post Adjt.

William F. "Buffalo Bill" Cody also accompanied Hickok. The Topeka *Weekly Leader*, April 2, 1868, reported their safe arrival:

BAND OF ROAD MEN CAPTURED—

W. F. Cody, government detective, and Wm. Haycock—Wild Bill—deputy U. S. Marshal, brought eleven prisoners and lodged them in our calaboose on Monday last [March 30]. These prisoners belonged to a band of robbers having their headquarters on the Solomon and near Trinidad, and were headed by one Major Smith, once connected with the Kansas 7th. They are charged with stealing and secreting government property, and desertion from the army.

Seventeen men, belonging to this same band, were captured eleven miles from Trinidad, on the 13th of March, and sent to Denver, Colorado Territory, for trial.

Hickok was still in Hays, or again in Hays, in August, 1868. Reporting the adventures of a western excursion, a writer in the *Leader*, August 13, 1868, related:

EXCURSION TO MONUMENT.

. . . Hays city, three hundred miles west of State line, is the present live town of the plains. The first man we saw was "Wild Bill." He was ready, waiting to give welcome to the excursionists. Gentle William said he had brought two hundred of the nastiest, meanest, Cheyennes to Hays that we might get a sight at the red men who did most of the murdering and scalping during the troubles of the past two years.

Hickok was once more employed by the army on September 1, 1868. This time he was carried on the rolls as a guide and was paid $100 per month. He was hired by the 10th U. S. cavalry "near Skimmerhorne Ranche [probably on Elkhorn creek in present Elkhorn township, Lincoln county], Kansas." Available records show Hickok employed in this capacity through the remainder of 1868.[8]

Wild Bill's service took him to Colorado territory where he was instrumental in saving several cattlemen who were surrounded by Indians. His part was described in a letter from M. M. DeLano to Acting Governor and Territorial Secretary Frank Hall, September

188

4, 1868. The communication was reprinted in the Central City (Colo.) *Daily Register,* September 8. It said in part:

Our boys . . . selecting a daring man called "Wild Bill," put him on their fleetest horse and started him for the [Bijou] Basin [near the line between present Elbert and El Paso counties and the headwaters of Bijou creek] for relief. He ran the gantlet through the enemy's line, receiving only a slight wound in the foot, and reached the Basin at 8 o'clock.

In October the 10th cavalry and Wild Bill were at Fort Lyon, Colo. The Denver *Rocky Mountain News,* October 30, 1868, reported:

The *Chieftain* states that five companies of the tenth (colored) cavalry arrived at Fort Lyon last week. There are now about nine companies at that Post. Gen. Penrose [Brevet Brig. Gen. William H. Penrose, captain, Third infantry] is organizing an expedition against the Indians. It is his purpose to move southward next week with about seven companies. He has reason to believe that the villages of the Cheyennes, Arapahoes and Kiowas are located on the Cimmaron, and his first object will be to find them. The expedition will be accompanied by some of the best scouts in the country, among them Tom Tobens, Mariana Autubees and Wild Bill.

In July, 1869, the St. Joseph *Union* reported that Hickok had been shot but no details of the shooting were given. The Leavenworth *Times and Conservative* reprinted the article on July 17:

The St. Joseph Union is responsible for the following:

WILD BILL, of Harper notoriety, was shot three times in Colorado the other day. Wounds not mortal. If the enthusiastic admirers of this old plainsman could see him on one of his periodical drunks, they would have considerable romance knocked out of them.

Within a couple of weeks Hickok was seen in Hays. The Junction City *Weekly Union,* July 31, 1869, in an article reporting an excursion to "end of track," mentioned him:

EXCURSION TO SHERIDAN.

On Monday last [July 26], a party, consisting of Richard Bowne, Esq., a prominent member of the New York bar; Mrs. Bowne; Misses Eliza and Annie Bowne; Mr. T. C. Bowne; Mr. E. W. Parsons, of New York city; Mr. Charles E. Alioth of Lausaune, Switzerland; and Mr. and Mrs. Boller of this place, started on a trip to Sheridan, the present terminus of the Kansas Pacific railway. . . .

At Hays City, the excursionists had the pleasure of meeting "Wild Bill," of Harper's Magazine notoriety; and were besides greatly impressed with the air of respectability which characterized all the inhabitants of that wealthy and flourishing metropolis. . . .

In August, 1869, Wild Bill was elected sheriff of Ellis county.

189

Although the county was organized in 1867, it had difficulty in retaining its peace officers. It is known that Thomas Gannon was elected sheriff on December 5, 1867,[9] but it is possible that at least two other persons held the office within the next 18 months. By the summer of 1869, Ellis county was in need of still another sheriff. On July 7, 1869, several citizens of Hays petitioned Gov. James M. Harvey to appoint R. A. Eccles to the post.[10] Though no record of the governor's reply has been preserved, he apparently did not appoint Eccles since a special election was called and Hickok was chosen. The Leavenworth *Times and Conservative,* September 2, 1869, reported:

HAYS CITY ITEMS.

HAYS CITY, Aug. 31, 1869.
EDITOR TIMES AND CONSERVATIVE:
At the election held here a few days ago . . . J. B. Hickok, familiarly known as "Wild Bill," [was] elected Sheriff of the county.

Possibly Hickok was sheriff of Ellis county before August 18. On August 22, 1869, the *Times and Conservative* had carried a correspondent's letter dated Hays City, August 18, which said in part that the greatest need of Sheridan is a magistrate. If Wild Bill arrests an offender [the area in which Sheridan was located was attached to Ellis county for judicial purposes] there is a log jail to receive him, but no justice to try the case. Justices of the Peace have before been appointed, but they resign so fast that the Governor has become disgusted and gone off to New York. . . .

On August 21 Wild Bill turned two deserters over to the post commander of Fort Hays who wrote:

HEAD QRS FORT HAYS KAS
August 26th 1869

To THE ASST ADJT GENL
    Department of the Mo
        Fort Leavenworth, Kas
SIR
    I have the honor to report that J. B. Hickok delivered at this Post on the 21st inst. a Mulatto and a negro whom he claims to be deserters from the 10th U. S. Cav. Troop "C." I have ascertained since the men have been confined at this Post, that they came from Sheridan, Ks. where they have been living for some time past, that they there acknowledged that they were deserters, and left precipitately, when Capt Circy U. S. Marshall, attempted to arrest them the name of the Mulatto is given as Ed. Fry and of the Negro as George _____[Allen] his last name being unknown.
    They are reported to have deserted at some time during the last winter, in Indian Territory, Fry being Sergeant of the Guard at the time and to have

190

taken a number of horses with them   I have the honor, to request to be informed whether information of any such deserters has been received at Dept
Head'qrs.   also what disposition be made of these prisoners.

> I am Sir Very Respectfully
> Your Obdt. Servt.
> GEO. GIBSON
> Maj. 5" Infantry
> Brvt. Lt. Col. U. S. A.
> Commanding [11]

Wild Bill was certainly sheriff by August 24, 1869, for this item
from the *Times and Conservative*, of Leavenworth, August 26, stated
that he had shot and killed a man:

J. B. Hickok (Wild Bill) shot one Mulrey at Hays Tuesday [August 24].
Mulrey died yesterday morning.   Bill has been elected sheriff of Ellis county.

On September 27, 1869, Sheriff Hickok shot and killed Sam
Strawhim, a Hays city ruffian.   Previously the Junction City
Union, July 31, 1869, had reported a shooting involving Strawhim,
Joe Weiss, and A. B. Webster:

A special from Hays City to the Leavenworth Commercial states that Joe
Weiss, formerly of the Leavenworth penitentiary, and lately of the plains, was
shot through the bowels Friday afternoon [July 23?], by A. D. [B]. Webster.
The affair occurred in the post office, in which Webster was a clerk, and was
a most justifiable act.—Weiss, together with another ruffian named Strawhan,
threatened Webster's life because he served upon them a notice to leave town,
by order of the vigilance committee. They entered the post office about 3 p. m.,
abused, slapped, and finally drew a revolver upon Webster, who was too quick
for them, with the above result.   Webster has been acquitted.

Weiss, whom the Leavenworth *Times and Conservative*, May 4,
1869, had called a deputy U. S. marshal, either died from this wound
or else within a year received another one which proved fatal.
(*See* the U. S. census extract p. 197.)   Now, in September, it was
Strawhim's turn to die.   The *Times and Conservative*, September 28,
1869, carried this telegraphic report:

FROM HAYS CITY
[Special to THE TIMES AND CONSERVATIVE]
HAYS CITY, Sept. 27.

A man named Sam'l Stranghan was shot and instantly killed by "Wild Bill,"
(J. B. Hickok) Sheriff, at one o'clock this morning.   It appears that Stranghan
and a number of his companions being "wolfing" all night, wished to conclude
by cleaning out a beer saloon and breaking things generally.   "Wild Bill"
was called upon to quiet them.   In the melee that followed Stranghan was
killed.   The Coroner's verdict this morning was justifiable homicide.   Stranghan
was buried this afternoon.

191

The Lawrence *Kansas Daily Tribune*, September 30, 1869, re-printed the news from the Leavenworth *Commercial*:

WILD BILL PRESERVES ORDER.—

The Leavenworth *Commercial* of Tuesday has a special dispatch from Hays City, dated September 27th, which says:

"About twelve o'clock last night a difficulty occurred in this place at the house of John Bittles, between a party of roughs and the proprietor. Policemen Hickok and Ranahan [probably Peter Lanihan, deputy sheriff] interfered to keep order, when remarks were made against Hickok—Wild Bill. In his efforts to preserve order, Samuel Stringham was shot through the head by him, and instantly killed. Justice Joyce held an inquest on the body to-day, six well-known citizens being selected for the jurymen. The evidence in one or two instances was very contradictory. The jury returned a verdict to the effect that Samuel Stringham came to his death from a pistol wound at the hands of J. B. Hickok, and that the shooting of said Stringham was justifiable.[12]

Sometime shortly before Wild Bill killed Strawhim in Hays, a murder, which eventually involved Hickok, had been committed near Fort Wallace. The *Times and Conservative*, September 16, 1869, reported:

FROM SHERIDAN.
SHOOTING AFFRAY.

[Special to THE TIMES AND CONSERVATIVE.] SHERIDAN, Sept. 15.

A telegram was received here this morning from Fort Wallace to arrest a man named Bob Conners for the murder of a drover named Hammy. Before there had been time to deliver the telegram Conners passed through town, and Marshal Ferguson, accompanied by California Bill, half an hour later gave chase and came in sight of him at Gopher Switch, talking with section men. As soon as Conners saw he was pursued he put spurs to his horse, and soon left Mr. Ferguson, who was too poorly mounted to pursue him further.

Conners had been in the employ of Mr. Hammy. Last night Hammy was awakened and caught Conners with his hand under his pillow. This morning Hammy discharged Conners, and when paying him, Conners said "I will show you how to accuse me of stealing!" at the same time shooting him and killing him instantly.

There were several in the employ of Mr. Hammy, and it is believed it was their intention to kill him and take his stock. He had 1,300 head of sheep and some horses.

Conners is following the track east. His description has been sent to all the telegraph stations along the road, and he will probably be taken before he gets off the plains.

On September 18, Jack Bridges captured Connors in Hays. The *Times and Conservative*, September 21, 1869, reported:

FROM HAYS CITY.

CAPTURE OF ROBT. CONNORS. . . .

[Special to THE TIMES AND CONSERVATIVE.]

HAYS CITY, Sept. 20

Robert Connors, the man who shot the sheep drover at Fort Wallace a few days ago, was captured here Saturday, on an extra train, on his way east. He got on the train at Buffalo Station, eighty miles west of here. He attempted to get on an A. Anderson extra train, which came down same day, but they would not let him on. He was delivered over to the commanding officer at the Fort for safe keeping, and it is thought that he will be sent to-morrow to Sheridan or Topeka for trial. He took a horse belonging to the murdered man, which he sold at Buffalo for eighty dollars.

Within a few days the commandant telegraphed the governor of Kansas for instructions regarding the prisoner and on October 3 reported his actions in accordance with those instructions:

FT HAYS, KAS.

October 3rd—69

To HIS EXCELLENCY

The Governor of Kansas

JAS. M. HARVEY

DEAR SIR:

If you will be pleased to recollect I telegraphed you on the 24th day of Sept last asking you whether I should deliver a certain Bob Connors to any one but the parties who had placed him in my Guard House for safe keeping.

Bob Connors is charged with being the murderer of a Drover near Pond City several weeks since, and was arrested by Deputy U S Marshal Bridges & Asst of Hays City. They claiming the use of my Guard House in order to protect him as they alledged from threatened violence at the hands of some of the citizens of Hays.

It having been represented to me that in all probability Connors would be Lynched, were he taken back to Sheridan I deemed it to be my duty to urge upon his Captors (by letter, a copy of which I have carefully preserved on file) that justice demanded that they should take him to Topeka and confer with your Excellency in regard to the proper disposition to be made of him under the circumstances.

Up to the present moment they have made no formal demand for him.

In reply to my telegram you directed that Connors should only be given up to the proper legal authorities.

This morning about 10 o'clock Mr. J. B. Hickok (commonly known as Wild Bill) presented himself at my office accompanied by an Asst whom he called Pete [Deputy Sheriff Peter Lanihan?], and made a formal demand for Connors, handing me what he claimed to be a Warrant for the arrest of said Connors signed by John Whitteford claiming to be a Justice of the Peace for the County of Wallace, Kansas. The document in question did not bear upon its face any seal.

193

Inasmuch as the Warrant directed Mr. Hickok as *Sheriff* of Ellis County to make the arrest I demanded to see his Commission which was not produced, he acknowledging that he had never been Commissioned by you. Under the circumstances I deemed it to be my duty to decline turning him over. Further I had no evidence that there was any regularly constituted Justice of the Peace for Wallace County.

Acting then purely agreeable to your instructions I have the honor to request that should any State Official endeavor to interfere with me in regard to my non Compliance in this case that you will at once interpose your strong arms in my behalf.

> With Sincere respect
> Yr Excellency's Obedt Servant
> GEO GIBSON
> Major 5th Inf
> Bt Lt Col USA
> Comdg Post [13]

On October 5 Connors was placed in charge of Deputy United States Marshal C. J. Cox, who had accompanied Bridges the day the prisoner was placed in the guardhouse.[14] Connors was taken to Sheridan for examination and acquitted. The following letter from Major Gibson mentions this and also adds another minor laurel to the crown of Wild Bill:

COL W. G. MITCHELL   HEAD QRS FORT HAYES KAS
A A A Genl. Dept of Mo.   Oct 27" 1869
Saint Louis Mo.
Colonel

I have the honor to represent that on the first Tuesday of the Coming month (November) an Election will take place at Hayes City for various County Officers. Among others that of Representative to the Kansas Legislature. During a brief visit to the town to day one of the Candidates a Dr McIntosh, asked me if in the Event of any disturbance Occuring at the Poles leading to riot and possibly bloodshed, would I feel myself warranted in promptly putting the Same down by Military force.—I of Course Committed myself to no policy. As far as my Knowledge goes I believe both Candidates (namely Messrs. McIntosh and Wright) to be really Excellent and law abiding Citizens and would faithfully represent this Section at Topeka. Whilst I have not the right personally, and would not desire to do so Even if I had, to Exercise the right of Suffrage on the Occasion, yet I presume the Various Civilian Employes Engaged here in the Several departments will claim an opportunity of Voting. Up to the present moment my intercourse with all classes Composing the population of Hayes has been, I may say, of an Exceedingly gratifying nature. In the absence of Legally Constituted Authorities in the town (see the Enclosed letter of Gov Harveys) I have been Exceedingly Careful in my dealings with the Citizens, when law and Order were Called in question. It will be perceived that the Communication of the Governors was

Called forth by a letter addressed by me to him under date of Oct 3" 1869 a copy of which is Enclosed. That my Course was proper is Evidenced by the fact that after all the excitement had blown over at Sheridan, Connors was Surrendered by me to the U. S. Marshal who had put him in my guard House, which resulted in his being taken to Sheridan, where after a hearing in his Case before the proper tribunal, he was Acquitted.

Several Saturdays Since, during the Evening, a discharged Qr. Mr. Employe from Camp Supply, Shot a German Employed by Messrs. Caplice and Ryan (Traders in Hayes) through the liver injuring an intestine. The would be murderer (named Cole) was placed in charge of a Vigilant Committee man in a drinking Saloon and it is alledged attempted to draw his pistol a Second time, when the party having him in charge fired at him, Shooting him through the lung. It being reported to me the next morning (Sunday) that some of the people in the town had gone So far as to put a rope around Coles neck for the purpose of dragging him out and hanging him (which I must say was prevented by Wild Bill) I drove over unattended and demanded That he be Surrendered to me which was done promptly. With a desire to Conciliate all parties, I brought him over and put him in my Hospital under Guard together with the man whom he had shot through the liver. Strange to say (through the admirable Skill of our Post Surgeon who I believe introduced a new Combination of remedies in their treatment, namely Carbolic Acid & Morphia) The German is This day walking about the Streets of Hayes nearly well, and has requested me to withdraw the guard over Cole (also rapidly recovering) it being his intention not to prosecute him. They having became reconciled to Each other in Hospital Through the intervention of a Catholic Priest. It will be perceived by the Major General Commanding That my policy has been to avoid making unnecessary display of military force in what I Conceived to be a proper discharge of my duty as a Conservator of the Peace.

In the Case of the approaching Election I beg leave to be instructed in regard to his wishes by telegraph so as to be in time.

I am
Very Respectfully
Your Obdt Svt
GEO GIBSON
Maj 5" Inf
Bvt Lieut Col U. S. A.
Comdg Post [15]

The election on November 2, 1869, passed off very quietly, probably much to the relief of Major Gibson. Wild Bill was defeated for re-election by his own deputy Peter Lanihan. A correspondent of the Leavenworth *Times and Conservative* reported the result of the balloting in the issue of November 5, 1869:

ELLIS COUNTY.

EDITOR TIMES AND CONSERVATIVE:
The vote in Ellis county stands as follows:
Sheriff, J. B. Hickok, independent 89; Peter Lannihan, Democratic, 114.

. . .

In the Leavenworth *Times and Conservative* of November 21, another correspondent described the young town and mentioned that "Wild Bill is sheriff and makes a good officer." The correspondence was dated November 16.

Wild Bill visited Topeka on November 17. The *Kansas Daily Commonwealth* mentioned him twice in its November 18, 1869, issue:

"Wild Bill," whom they have attempted to kill, but who has the inexorable will to perambulate the earth still, and who is always ready for a "mill," save when he may chance to be ill, yesterday came up the Topeka hill to get a stomach fill.

Sheriff Hickok, of Ellis county—yclept, in many a well-known story of border-life, "Wild Bill," is in town, registered at the Topeka House. Long may he at Hays,
"Shake his ambrosial locks and give the nod,
The stamp of fate, the sanction of a god!"

At the same election in which Hickok was defeated, the chosen candidate for Ellis county representative was accused by his defeated opponent of irregularities of conduct. Acting in his capacity as sheriff of the county, Hickok served certain legal papers on J. V. Macintosh, the accused. Hickok certified, through his deputy, the deliverance of the papers with this statement which was included in the evidence gathered by the house of representatives and published in the *House Journal* for 1870:

Served the within notice at Hays City, Kansas, on the 9th day of December, A. D. 1869, by delivering a certified copy of the same, at the usual place of residence of the within named J. V. Macintosh.

J. B. HICKOK,
Sheriff.
By PETER LANIHAN,
Deputy Sheriff.[16]

The same day the papers were served, December 9, 1869, the Topeka *Commonwealth* mentioned that "Hays city under the guardian care of 'Wild Bill' is quiet and doing well."

On December 20 Hickok sent a buffalo to the proprietor of the Topeka House. The *Commonwealth,* December 21, 1869, reported: "Jas. B. Hickok, *alias* Wild Bill sent a whole buffalo to McMeekin yesterday, from Hays city. Mac serves up buffalo roasts and steak to-day with the usual etcetras."

Sometime during Hickok's stay in Hays he wrote this letter or bill for services rendered:

ELLIS COUNTY—
To J B Hickok Dr
To Services as policeman 1 month & 19 days at $75.00 per Month $122.50
   I certify that the above account is correct and remains due and unpaid.
                              J. B. HICKOK.[17]

The mortality schedule of the 1870 United States census listed four deaths in Hays between June 1, 1869, and June 1, 1870. Of the three caused by gunshots, two may have been through the pistols of Wild Bill Hickok. Admittedly one must stretch his imagination to believe that Straughn was Strawhim and that Murphy was Mulrey.

SCHEDULE 2.—Persons who Died during the Year ending 1st June, 1870, in Hays City, in the County of Ellis, State of Kansas, enumerated by me, M. E. Joyce, Ass't Marshal.

Name of every person who died during the year ending June 1, 1870. . . .	Age	Sex	Color	Place of Pirth	The Month in which the person died	Occupation	Cause of Death
Ryan, Michael......	48	M	W	Ireland	January	Laborer	Whiskey
Weis, Joseph........	32	M	W	Ill.	March [July?]	Teamster	Shot
Straughn, Samuel.... [Strawhim?]	28	M	W	Ill.	April [September?]	Teamster	Shot
Murphy, John....... [Mulrey?]	25	M	W	N. Y.	August	Soldier	Shot

   I certify that the above return was taken according to law and instruction.
                     M. E. JOYCE
                     Asst. Marshal

Total number of deaths, 4. . . .

REMARKS: The above embrace all the names of persons who died in my district during the year ending June 1st 1870. The three persons reported shot were killed in fights on the street. The one reported "from Whiskey" died while drunk and supposed to died from the Effects of liquor.

By February, 1870, Wild Bill was in Topeka. The *Common-wealth,* February 8, reported: "Wild Bill was up before Judge

[G. B.] Holmes yesterday, and fined five dollars for striking straight out from the shoulder and consequently hitting a man." On April 29, 1870, the paper mentioned that " 'Wild Bill' is in the city again."

One of the most popular stories told of Wild Bill concerned the time, on New Year's Eve while he was still sheriff of Ellis county, that Tom Custer (the colonel's brother) and some soldiers of the Seventh cavalry drove the lawman out of his own bailiwick. In the scuffle which preceded the flight Hickok was supposed to have killed three troopers and sent Custer scurrying to Fort Hays for reinforcements.

Sometimes legends are indeed based on a bit of fact. The fight occurred, but long after Hickok had shed his star. Variations in contemporary reporting might have been the cause for some of the discrepancies of the legend. Three stories are given here, the first from the Topeka *Kansas Daily Commonwealth*, July 22, 1870:

On Monday last [July 18] "Wild Bill" killed a soldier and seriously wounded another, at Hays City. Five soldiers attacked Bill, and two got used up as mentioned above. The sentiment of the community is with "Bill," as it is claimed he but acted in self-defense.

The Junction City *Union*, July 23, 1870, said:

Two soldiers of the Seventh cavalry were shot at Hays City last Tuesday night [July 19] by Wild Bill. The names of the men were Langan and Kelly. The greatest excitement prevails in the town owing to the outrage. After the shooting was over Wild Bill made for the prairie and has not been heard of since. The citizens were out *en masse* looking for Bill, so that he might be summarily dealt with. The parties were all under the influence of liquor at the time.

And the Clyde *Republican Valley Empire*, August 2, 1870, reported:

Wild Bill, of Harper and plains notoriety, got into a friendly scuffle with a soldier at Hays City on the 20th, which ended in a row. Bill shot and mortally wounded another soldier who had a hand in the muss and left for parts unknown.

The actual date of the row was Sunday, July 17, 1870. That day Privates Jeremiah Lanigan and John Kelly, Co. M, Seventh U. S. cavalry, were admitted to the post hospital at Fort Hays for treatment of gunshot wounds according to the "Register of Sick and Wounded at Fort Hays, Kansas, During the Month of July, 1870" (Records of the War Department, Office of the Adjutant General,

National Archives, records group 94). Lanigan was returned to duty on August 25, 1870, but Kelly died July 18.

In a letter to Joseph G. Rosa, Ruislip, Middlesex, England, the National Archives stated April 15, 1963, that on a muster roll of the Seventh cavalry for July and August, 1870, the man killed was listed as John Kile of Co. I. He died of a "pistol shot wound received July 17th, 1870, at Hays City, Kansas, in a drunken row and not in the line of duty."

Although Fort Hays post returns, also from the National Archives, supposedly record the name of every commissioned officer stationed at or attached to the fort, no officer named Custer appeared for July, 1870.

The only remaining unanswered question concerning this famous Hickok fight is whether Wild Bill left Hays voluntarily or was driven out by public sentiment. Available information offers no solution.

Since the November 2, 1870, death of Chief of Police Tom Smith, Abilene had been without an effective chief law enforcement officer. In April, 1871, the newly elected city government, spurred by the approaching cattle season and its attendant increase in lawlessness, appointed a city marshal within days of its election. The man chosen was Wild Bill Hickok, and on April 15 he was sworn into office.[18] Hickok's pay in this capacity was to be $150 a month plus one-fourth of all fines assessed as a result of arrests made by him.[19]

The first recorded excitement of Hickok's Abilene career occurred on May 8, 1871. The city clerk noted the episode in his minute book:

At an adjourned meeting of the Mayor & Councilmen of the City of Abilene all members were present. On motion of G. L. Brinkman the order of business was suspended and the resignations of members considered. Moved by G. L. Brinkman that both resignations of councilmen be considered at once motion unanimously carried. Moved by G. L. Brinkman that the resignations of Messrs. L. Boudinot and [Samuel] Carpenter be accepted, carried. S. A. Burroughs voting against. S. A. Burroughs left the Council without permission and on motion of Mr. Brinkman the Marshal was instructed to compel his attendance. Mr. Burroughs brought in by the marshal and immediately left the council. On motion of G. L. Brinkman the marshal was instructed to again bring Mr. Burroughs back which order was executed.[20]

V. P. Wilson, editor of Abilene's only newspaper, the *Chronicle*, was a leading critic of Mayor Joseph G. McCoy. The council episode made McCoy an apt target for Wilson's editorial cannon. On May 18, 1871, Wilson ran this article in the *Chronicle:*

THE PICTURE MAN.—A short time since our Mayor, J. G. McCoy, ordered the Marshal to arrest and bring into the meeting of the council, only two members being present, one of the members who did not wish to be present. The councilman was arrested and carried into the room by the Marshal. There was not the least shadow of law for such a proceeding, there being no ordinance to compel the attendance of councilmen. Of course the Marshal simply obeyed orders—whether legal or not—and is not to blame. But our silly mayor goes down to Topeka, publishes his exploit in the papers, gets up a picture which pretends to represent the transaction, carves upon it in big letters, "Who's Mayor now," and sends them all over the country to be hawked about and laughed at as a standing disgrace to his own town. If boyish silliness can beat such a small trick we'll acknowledge that Abilene is blessed with a mayor of prudent sense. If you wish to see such nonsense continued vote McCoy's ticket for councilmen on next Tuesday [21]; but if you prefer a council that will oppose the eccentricities and extravagances of our picture mayor, be sure to vote for Boudinot and Carpenter. They are men of good sense, and will do what they think is right.

In June Wild Bill posted notices that the carrying of weapons in the city would be forbidden. The *Chronicle*, June 8, 1871, said:

FIRE ARMS.—The Chief of Police has posted up printed notices, informing all persons that the ordinance against carrying fire arms or other weapons in Abilene, will be enforced. That's right. There's no bravery in carrying revolvers in a civilized community. Such a practice is well enough and perhaps necessary when among Indians or other barbarians, but among white people it ought to be discountenanced.

But the ordinance was disregarded by some and on June 22, 1871, the *Chronicle* reported a shooting:

A shooting affray occurred this morning on First Street, between two men. It seems that hard words passed between them, when one drew his revolver, and No. 2 remarked "you know you have got the advantage of me." No. 1 then put back his weapon, whereupon No. 2 drew a Derringer and fired at No. 1 who also managed to draw his six-shooter. Each fired two shots; one was hit in the wrist and the other in the shoulder. The police were promptly on hand and arrested the parties in time to prevent one or both from being killed. The men are, at this writing, having a hearing before Judge [E.] Barber. Each party violated the law by carrying weapons while in town. As to which one is to blame for the shooting we are not advised—but the slight value that some men place upon human life is a sad commentary upon the custom of carrying firearms among people who claim to be civilized. And the cowardly custom of shooting at a man when he is not prepared to defend himself is far from being in accordance with the "code of honor" observed by all men who lay claim to bravery or chivalry. To stand up and shoot at a man, who has an equal chance with you, indicates that you are not a coward, but to fire at a man when you know that he is defenceless and can't return the compliment, is next to the lowest species of cowardice known among men.

Wild Bill Hickok

If a man is doing any good in the world, his life is worth preserving—but if he is of no use to himself or anybody else, then it don't make much difference how soon his body is put under the ground. And yet, life is sweet to all—and ought to be held sacred by people who are not completely buried in moral darkness.

By now Hickok's staff included Tom Carson, a nephew of Kit Carson; James Gainsford; and J. H. McDonald.

On June 28, 1871, another source of income was added to Wild Bill's salary when the city council authorized the city treasurer to pay him 50 cents for each unlicensed dog that he killed.

"A committee was appointed," on July 8, 1871, "to confer with the City Marshall defining him certain duties to be performed;" on July 15 he was "instructed to stop dance houses and the vending of Whiskeys Brandies &c in McCoys addition to the town of Abilene;" and on July 22 he was "instructed to close up all dead & Brace Gambling Games and to arrest all Cappers for the aforesaid Games." [22]

Mrs. Agnes Lake's "Hippo-Olympiad and Mammoth Circus" showed in Abilene on July 31, 1871, and it was probably on this occasion that Wild Bill met the widow who was to become his wife five years later. "The attendance was large at each performance," said the *Chronicle*, August 3.

Further instructions were issued the marshal by the city council in late summer. On September 2 Hickok was ordered "to suppress all Dance Houses and to arrest the Proprietors if they persist after the notification," on September 6 he was "instructed to inform the proprietor of the Abilene House to expell the prostitutes from his premises under the pain and penalties of prosecution," and on September 23 he was told to "notify all prostitutes and gamblers to come forward and pay fines." [23]

The only recorded Abilene shooting scrape in which Hickok was involved occurred on October 5, 1871. One of the victims was Phil Coe, who until August had been part owner of an Abilene saloon. It has been said that his partner in that business was Ben Thompson. At the time of the shooting Coe was a gambler. On October 12, 1871, the Abilene *Chronicle* reported the incident:

SHOOTING AFFRAY.

Two Men Killed.

On last Thursday evening a number of men got on a "spree," and compelled several citizens and others to "stand treat," catching them on the street and

201

carrying them upon their shoulders into the saloons. The crowd served the Marshal, commonly called "Wild Bill," in this manner. He treated, but told them that they must keep within the bounds of order or he would stop them. They kept on, until finally one of the crowd, named Phil. Coe, fired a revolver. The Marshal heard the report and knew at once the leading spirits in the crowd, numbering probably fifty men, intended to get up a "fight." He immediately started to quell the affair and when he reached the Alamo saloon, in front of which the crowd had gathered, he was confronted by Coe, who said that he had fired the shot at a dog. Coe had his revolver in his hand, as had also other parties in the crowd. As quick as thought the Marshal drew two revolvers and both men fired almost simultaneously. Several shots were fired, during which Mike Williams, a policeman, came around the corner for the purpose of assisting the Marshal, and rushing between him and Coe received two of the shots intended for Coe. The whole affair was the work of an instant. The Marshal, surrounded by the crowd, and standing in the light, did not recognize Williams whose death he deeply regrets. Coe was shot through the stomach, the ball coming out through his back; he lived in great agony until Sunday evening; he was a gambler, but a man of natural good impulses in his better moments. It is said that he had a spite at Wild Bill and had threatened to kill him—which Bill believed he would do if he gave him the opportunity. One of Coe's shots went through Bill's coat and another passed between his legs striking the floor behind him. The fact is Wild Bill's escape was truly marvelous. The two men were not over eight feet apart, and both of them large, stout men. One or two others in the crowd were hit, but none seriously.

We had hoped that the season would pass without any row. The Marshal has, with his assistants, maintained quietness and good order—and this in face of the fact that at one time during the season there was a larger number of cut-throats and desperadoes in Abilene than in any other town of its size on the continent. Most of them were from Kansas City, St. Louis, New Orleans, Chicago, and from the Mountains.

We hope no further disturbances will take place. There is no use in trying to override Wild Bill, the Marshal. His arrangements for policing the city are complete, and attempts to kill police officers or in any way create disturbance, must result in loss of life on the part of violators of the law. We hope that all, strangers as well as citizens, will aid by word and deed in maintaining peace and quietness.

The Junction City *Union* reported on October 7, 1871:

Two men were shot at Abilene, Thursday evening. The circumstances were about as follows, so our informant says: Early in the evening a party of men began a spree, going from one bar to another, forcing their acquaintances to treat, and making things howl generally. About 8 o'clock, shots were heard in the "Alamo," a gambling hell; whereupon the City Marshal, Haycock, better known as "Wild Bill," made his appearance. It is said that the leader of the party had threatened to kill Bill, "before frost." As a reply to the Marshal's demand that order should be preserved, some of the party fired upon him, when, drawing his pistols "he fired with marvelous rapidity and characteristic accuracy," as our informant expressed it, shooting a Texan, named Coe, the keeper of the saloon, we believe, through the abdomen, and grazing one or two more. In the midst of the firing, a policeman rushed in to assist Bill, but unfortunately got in the line of his fire. It being dark, Bill did not recognize him, and supposed him to be one of the party. He was instantly killed. Bill greatly regrets the shooting of his friend. Coe will die. The verdict of the citizens seemed to be unanimously in support of the Marshal, who bravely did his duty.

The Saline County Journal, Salina, October 12, 1871, concluded its report of the shooting with the statement that Coe had "resided in Salina a short time during the past summer, and was regarded by those who knew him as a quiet and inoffensive man."

On October 28, 1871, the *Union* reported that "one of Wild Bill's recent victims gets a handsome eulogy in a Texas paper; Wild Bill never hurts any one who behaves himself."

Another attempt to kill Marshal Hickok was reported in the *Chronicle,* November 30:

ATTEMPT TO KILL MARSHAL HICKOK
He Circumvents the Parties.

Previous to the inauguration of the present municipal authorities of Abilene, every principle of right and justice was at a discount. No man's life or property was safe from the murderous intent and lawless invasions of Texans. The state of affairs was very similar to that of Newton during the last season. The law-abiding citizens decided upon a change, and it was thought best to fight the devil with his own weapons. Accordingly Marshal Hickok, popularly known as "Wild Bill," was elected marshal. He appointed his men, tried and true, as his assistants. Without tracing the history of the great cattle market, it will suffice to say that during the past season there has been order in Abilene. The Texans have kept remarkably quiet, and, as we learn from several citizens of the place, simply for fear of Marshal Hickok and his *posse.* The Texans, however, viewed him with a jealous eye. Several attempts have been made to kill him, but all in vain. He has from time to time during the last summer received letters from Austin, Texas, warning him of a combination of rangers who had sworn to kill him. Lately, a letter came saying that a purse of $11,000 had been made up and five men were on their way to Abilene to take his life. They arrived in Abilene, but for five days they kept hid, and the marshal, although knowing their presence, was unable to find them. At last wearied with watching and sleepless nights and having some business in Topeka, he concluded to come here and take a rest. As he stood on the platform of the depot at Abilene he noticed four desperate looking fellows headed by a desperado about six feet four inches high. They made no special demonstrations, but when the marshal was about to get on the train, a friend who was with him overheard the big Texan say, "Wild Bill is going on the train." He was informed of this remark and kept a watch upon the party. They got on the same train and took seats immediately behind the marshal. In a short time, he got up and took his seat behind them. One of the party glanced around and saw the situation, whereupon they left the car and went into the forward car. The marshal and his friend, then, to be sure that they were after him, went to the rear end of the rear car. The marshal being very tired, sought rest in sleep, while his friend kept watch. Soon the Texans came into the car, and while four of them stood in the aisle, the leader took a position behind the marshal, and a lady who was sitting near, and knew the marshal, saw the Texan grasping a revolver between his overcoat and dress coat. The marshal's friend, who had been a close observer of the party, went to him and told him not to go to sleep. This occurred about ten miles west of Topeka. When the train arrived at Topeka, the marshal saw his friend safely on the bus and re-entered the car. The party of Texans were just coming out of the door, when the marshal asked them where they were going. They replied, "We propose to stop in Topeka." The marshal then said, "I am satisfied that you are hounding me, and as I intend to stop in Topeka, you can't stop here." They began to object to his restrictions, but a pair of 'em convinced the murderous Texans that they had better go on, which they did. While we cannot justify lawlessness or recklessness of any kind, yet we think the marshal wholly justifiable in his conduct toward such a party. Furthermore, we think he is entitled to the thanks of law-abiding citizens throughout the State for the safety of life and property at Abilene, which has been secured, more through his daring, than any other agency.

With the end of the cattle season, Abilene no longer needed the expensive services of Wild Bill Hickok. In December the city clerk noted the council's action in the minute book:

Be it resolved by Mayor & Council of City of Abilene That J. B. Hickok be discharged from his official position as City Marshall for the reason that the City is no longer in need of his services and that the date of his discharge take place from and after this 13th day of December A D 1871. Also that all of his Deputies be stopped from doing duty. On motion . . . that Jas. A. Gauthie be appointed City Marshall of the City of Abilene, for the period of one month commencing this 13th day of December A D 1871, at a salary of $50.00.[24]

From Abilene Bill reportedly traveled east. The *Saline County Journal,* January 18, 1872, said he was in Boston:

It is said that Hacock, the scout, known in this country as "Wild Bill," is exhibiting himself to the inhabitants of Boston. Ever since his achievements were narrated in Harpers' Magazine, three or four years ago, Wild Bill's star has been ascending, and now the credulous New Englanders have an opportunity to interview in person the man who has shot men down in cold blood by the scores and is as big a criminal as walks the earth. If it is pleasure for those down-easters to welcome a gambler, a libertine and a rowdy, we can furnish those of the same ilk, just as deserving, by the hundreds, from our "wicked plains." Bill is making money showing himself, so they say. "A prophet is not without honor save in his own country."

In the fall Bill played a part in a minor bloodless re-enactment of the Civil War. The stage for the show was the Kansas City, Mo., Exposition. The Topeka *Kansas Daily Commonwealth*, September 28, 1872, reported:

TELEGRAPHIC

DOMESTIC.

THE KANSAS CITY FAIR. . . .

WILD BILL AND THE TEXANS.

PLUCK SUPERIOR TO PISTOLS. . . .

SPECIAL DISPATCH TO THE COMMONWEALTH. . . .
There were 30,000 people on the fair grounds yesterday, and to-day the crowd was not lessened. Wild Bill made a big point at the fair grounds. A number of Texans prevailed upon the band to play Dixie, and then the Texans made demonstrations with the flourishing of pistols. Wild Bill stepped forward and stopped the music, and more than fifty pistols were presented at William's head, but he came away unscathed.

Five months later it was reported in Abilene that Wild Bill was dead, killed in Galveston, Tex., by someone avenging Phil Coe's death. The *Dickinson County Chronicle*, February 20, 1873, said:

WILD BILL.—It is stated that Wild Bill was murdered in Galveston, Texas, about two weeks ago, by some of Phil Cole's friends, who it will be remembered by our citizens, Bill shot in a fracas, while he was marshal of Abilene. Cole's friends vowed vengeance and finally accomplished it. So they go.

The rumor of Bill's death was false, of course, as were several others which were floating around at the same time. The *Kansas Daily Commonwealth*, March 1, 1873, reprinted some of them from an article in the Kansas City *News:*

WILD BILL.

LIONIZING IN NEW YORK,

VISITING FRIENDS IN SPRINGFIELD, MO.,

KILLING INDIANS IN THE WEST,

KILLED IN GALVESTON,

AND RIDDLED WITH BULLETS AT FORT DODGE.

FROM THE KANSAS CITY NEWS.
A few days ago we published a short item stating, on the authority of an Abilene paper, that Wild Bill, or William Hickox, who gained so much notoriety as scout during the war, a frontiersman afterwards, and subsequently marshal of Abilene, and who made this city his headquarters the past year and a half, until within the past few months, had been killed recently in Galveston,

Texas by a brother of the man Cole, who was shot by him while acting as marshal of Abilene. This report started many others in regard to the whereabouts of Hickox. Mr. Dan Pixley a few days ago, saw a letter of a recent date, stating that he was visiting some relatives or friends near Springfield, Mo., others produce letters and papers to prove that within three weeks he has been in New York airing his long hair and exciting the wonder of the timid by perambulating the streets of that city; others again declare upon the authority of Omaha papers that he is far out on the Union Pacific railroad, where, the other morning, in a fit of pleasantry, and because they objected to drinking cold coffee with him, insisting that it should be hot, he shot and killed three Indians—these same parties stating, also, that they read a letter from him received only a few days ago, by McDaniels [J. H. McDonald?], his old deputy at Abilene, and which was dated at some point on the Union Pacific.

Last evening, however, a man arrived from Fort Dodge with an entirely different report. He says Wild Bill is dead, that he was murdered in a saloon in Fort Dodge last Saturday night week, and that he, the informant, was present when the affair occurred. He says Bill had been there for some time, but was very careful of his person, and guarded himself as well as possible from danger, knowing he had enemies. Finally, two men whom he had thought were his friends, proved treacherous, and murdered him in the following manner.

The three were going about the small town on the night of the murder, and the assassins being very friendly, and finally they entered a saloon where at a signal the lights were all extinguished. Simultaneous with the going out of the lights, firing commenced, with the first report, the tall form of the man who had proven such a terror on the plains fell at the feet of his enemies, vanquished by death, a bullet having pierced his brain, entering his skull in the center of his forehead. The firing was kept up in the dark by the assassins, one shot entering Bill's heel another his shoulder, and four others perforating his body in different places. Then all ran out, and when the lights were again turned on all that was left of Wild Bill was a dead and bleeding body, fulfilling the prophecy in connection with him and all his class that he would "die with his boots on." It is almost certain that the two false friends at least were concerned in the murder, although others may have joined in the firing. It was dark; no one could see another do the deed, and in that country they consider that they have no evidence sufficient to warrant the arrest of any one for the crime.

The informant says he is positive the man killed was Wild Bill, ex-marshal of Abilene, as he knew him well at that place. Notwithstanding this last report, many of the friends of Bill in this city refuse to believe that he is dead, or that he was in the section where his murder is reported to have been committed.

Two weeks later the *Commonwealth* reprinted an article from the Kansas City *Journal of Commerce* refuting most of the earlier statements. The *Commonwealth* carried the item on March 14, 1873:

"WILD BILL."
The Fiery, Untamed Individual Still Survives.

From the Kansas City Journal.

If anybody in this city has shed tears or rejoiced because of the late announcements of the death of Mr. William Hickox, better known as Wild Bill, these presents will inform them that they have had their trouble for nothing. William isn't dead; the public placed some reliance in the report of his demise, when the scene thereof was located in Galveston; it was the first report; but when it came to killing him in Ft. Dodge also, the thing began to look fishy; nobody believed he had been killed twice. Now, here comes a communication from Springfield, to say that he has not been killed at all. Those papers that have been wringing their hearts for a suitable obituary of Wild William, had better adopt the plan of a certain Kansas paper in reference to another individual whom it had killed and buried several times, and wait with their obituaries until he notifies them of its necessity.

SPRINGFIELD, Mo., March 6, 1873.

JOURNAL OF COMMERCE:

The paraded accounts of Wild Bill, or Wm. Hickox's death, are simply farces. I have seen the gentleman "in flesh and blood" in this city to-day, and from his appearance should judge that he was not accustomed to "laying in his gore" in saloons at Fort Dodge.

His friends in Kansas City may be pleased to hear an authentic report concerning him.

Yours,
C.

Wild Bill himself put an end to the excitement with a letter to the editor of the St. Louis *Daily Missouri Democrat* which was reprinted by that paper on March 15, 1873:

NOT "CORRALLED" YET.

In last Wednesday's DEMOCRAT the following item of news appeared, and though the source of our information was supposed to be reliable, the following letter received yesterday, proves that it was not:

"It begins to look as if 'Wild Bill' was really dead. The latest report is that the Texan who corraled the untamed William did so because he lost a brother by Bill's quickness on the trigger. When the Texan shot Wild Bill, he asked the crowd in the bar-room if any gentleman had any desire to 'mix in;' if so, he would wait until he was 'heeled', and take great pleasure in killing him. No gentleman expressing a desire to be killed, the Texan got on his horse, and remarking that he had business in Texas, slowly started for the Lone Star State."

SPRINGFIELD, Mo., March 13, '73.

To the Editor of the Democrat:

Wishing to correct an error in your paper of the 12th, I will state that no Texan has, nor ever will "corral William." I wish you to correct your statement, on account of my people. Yours as ever.

J. B. Hickok.

P. S. I have bought your paper in preference to all others, since 1857.

J. B. Hickok
or "Wild Bill."

We take much pleasure in laying Mr. Hickok's statement before the readers of the Democrat, most of whom will be glad to learn from his own pen that he is still "on deck." But, in case you *should* go off suddenly, William, by writing us the particulars we will give you just as fine an obituary notice as we can get up, though we trust that sad pleasure may be deferred for many years. "Wild Bill," or any other man killed by mistake in our columns, will be promptly resuscitated upon application by mail. It is not necessary for the deceased to call in person. He will receive just as much—in fact, more—attention by simply writing.

The postscript to the 1873 flurry of Wild Bill articles had some uncomplimentary things to say about the gentleman. It appeared in the *Kansas Daily Commonwealth*, May 11, 1873:

Col. Norton, of the Arkansas *Traveler*, pricks a bubble which the oriental romantic ignorance of the social status of western notables hath monstrously inflated. Hear him:

It is disgusting to see the eastern papers crowding in everything they can get hold of about "Wild Bill." If they only knew the real character of the men they so want to worship, we doubt if their names would ever appear again. "Wild Bill," or Bill Hickok, is nothing more than a drunken, reckless, murderous coward, who is treated with contempt by true border men, and who should have been hung years ago for the murder of innocent men. The shooting of the "old teamster" in the back, for a small provocation, while crossing the plains in 1859, is one fact that Harper's correspondent failed to mention, and being booted out of a Leavenworth saloon by a boy bar tender is another; and we might name many other similar examples of his bravery. In one or two instances he did the U. S. government good service, but his shameful and cowardly conduct more than overbalances the good.

"Buffalo Bill" is a *fac simile* of the former. We have men on the border to-day, whose names have never been glorified in print, who would not disgrace themselves by associating with this hero of Harper—"Wild Bill."

Despite the opinion of Hickok and Cody held by some Westerners, the two were in demand by certain Easterners and Englishmen who were willing to pay good prices to obtain their services as guides over the Great Plains. The Denver *Rocky Mountain News*, July 31, 1874, mentioned one such safari:

Those English millionaire hunters, with "Buffalo Bill" and "Wild Bill" for guides, who came out here to out-do the sporting achievements of the Grand Duke Alexis, took the saddle last Monday [July 27], and by this time have fairly commenced the extermination of all the wild game in the Platte valley. Major Moore, with a company of cavalry, has gone out with the party, merely to keep the Englishmen from destroying the redskins, while exterminating the buffaloes.

In 1876, Hickok, married now to Mrs. Lake, was in Cheyenne. A correspondent of the *Ellis County Star*, Hays, reported seeing him there in June:

THE BLACK HILLS EXPEDITION.

Ft. LARAMIE, June 18th, 1876.

ED. STAR:

We loaded up and left Denver for Cheyenne about 6 p. m., of the 7th, and after considerable tugging and pulling arrived at the latter place, on the morning of the 8th about 7 o'clock. I took a good look at the town and was indeed astonished to see the substantial improvements made in it since I was there last. The town is at least four times as large as in 1870. The notorious Wild Bill is stopping here, and I have been told from a pretty reliable source that he was arrested on several occasions as a vagrant, having no visible means of support. . . .[25]

On August 2, 1876, Wild Bill was dead—shot from behind by Jack McCall. The report of his death in the *Star*, August 17, erroneously named his assassin Bill Sutherland:

"WILD BILL"

. We learn from recent dispatches that Mr. J. B. Hickok, (Wild Bill), well known to the older citizens of Hays City, was shot in the head and instantly killed, by a man named Bill Sutherland, while playing cards in a saloon in Deadwood Gulch, Wyoming [Dakota territory]. From the report it seems that Bill had killed a brother of Sutherland's in this city, several years ago, and in revenge the latter shot Bill, taking him unawares.

This is the long-looked for ending of the career of one who deserved a better fate. For nearly his whole life time Bill was on the frontier, a portion of the time acting as scout, and then as an officer of the law in some frontier town. He was elected Sheriff of this county in 1868 [1869], and did good service in keeping order. While here he killed several men; but all their acquaintances agreed that he was justified in so doing. He never provoked a quarrel, and was a generous, gentlemanly fellow. In person he was over six feet tall, broad-shouldered, and a specimen of perfect manhood throughout. He was a dead shot, wonderfully quick in drawing and shooting, the latter faculty filling his enemies with a very wholesome respect, when in his presence. Living as he did in constant fear of his life, he always kept his revolvers with him, and had the fellow that shot him given him a fair fight, and not taken the cowardly advantage that he did, Wild Bill would not have been killed.

1. *The War of the Rebellion*: *A Compilation of the Official Records of the Union and Confederate Armies* (Washington, Government Printing Office, 1880-1901), Series I, v. 48, pt. 1, pp. 810, 819.   2. Some contemporary information concerning the Hickok-McCandles fight has been reprinted in *Nebraska History Magazine*, Lincoln, April-June, 1927 (v. 10, No. 2).   The original "Wild Bill" article by G. W. Nichols has also been reprinted in this volume.   3. Henry M. Stanley, *My Early Travels and Adventures in America and Asia* (London, 1895), pp. 5-8.   4. *Ibid.*, p. 97. 5. Fort Harker was a military post, first called Fort Ellsworth, established in 1864. A new location was selected in January, 1867, four miles east of the city of Ellsworth.   The town of Kanopolis now occupies the site and includes the few remaining buildings within its bounds.   6. "Records of the War Department, United States Army Commands, Fort Hays, Kansas, 1866-1889; Letters Received at Post Headquarters," National Archives.   7. *Ibid.*, "Special Order Book, October 15, 1866- May 26, 1868."   8. "Records of the War Department, Office of the Quartermaster General; Reports of Persons and Articles Hired, 1861-1868," National Archives. 9. Leavenworth *Daily Conservative*, December 11, 1867.   10. "Governors' Correspondence," archives division, Kansas State Historical Society.   The petition was signed by many persons including Jack L. Bridges; A. J. Peacock, later a prominent Dodge City resident; A. B. Webster, several times mayor of Dodge City in the cowtown days; and Samuel Strawhim, a victim of Wild Bill's marksmanship.   It was from the petition signature that the correct spelling of Strawhim's name was determined. 11. "Records of the War Department, United States Army Commands, Fort Hays, Kansas, 1866-1889; Letters Sent by the Post Commander," National Archives.   12. *See, also*, the Junction City *Weekly Union*, October 2, 1869, and the preceding footnote. The *Union* spelled the name "Strangham."   13. "Governors' Correspondence," archives division, Kansas State Historical Society.   14. "Records of the War Department, United States Army Commands, Fort Hays, Kansas, 1866-1889; Letters Received at Post Headquarters," National Archives.   15. *Ibid.*, "Letters Sent by the Post Commander." 16. Pages 256, 257.   17. Manuscript division, Kansas State Historical Society.   18. "City Council Minute Book," Records of the City of Abilene, p. 55; Junction City *Weekly Union*, April 22, 1871.   19. Abilene *Chronicle*, May 18, 1871.   20. Page 64.   21. A special election to replace resigned Councilmen Boudinot and Carpenter.   22. "City Council Minute Book," Records of the City of Abilene, pp. 73, 77, 79, 81.   23. *Ibid.*, pp. 87, 88, 94.   24. Pages 107, 108.   25. June 29, 1876.

HINKLE, GEORGE T. (1845?-1922?)

George T. Hinkle was the third man to serve as sheriff of Ford county, Kansas.   In 1877 he had been a candidate for the office against Bat Masterson and L. E. Deger, but shortly before the election he withdrew and threw his support to Deger.   Despite this, Masterson won and became Ford county's second sheriff, following C. E. Bassett.

In 1879 Hinkle again ran for sheriff.   He received early mention in the *Ford County Globe*, September 16, 1879:

CANDIDATES FOR SHERIFF.

SPEAREVILLE, KAN., Sept. 14.

EDITOR GLOBE:—Will you be kind enough to let the farmers of the east end of Ford county know through the columns of your paper who the candidates

210

are that are seeking the office of Sheriff this fall, besides Masterson? We have
enough of the Masterson rule. SUBSCRIBER.

For the information of our subscriber we will say that as yet we have heard
the name of but one man mentioned, aside from the present sheriff, and that is
George T. Hinkel, of this city, who would make an excellent officer. He is not
seeking the office, but would certainly make a strong candidate.

Apparently Hinkle did not campaign actively. The *Globe*, October 28, 1879, said:

Geo. T. Hinkel hasn't made much of a boom during his canvass; but in his
quiet way he has made many a strong vote.

No person will regret casting a vote for Hinkel for Sheriff. Let all his friends
come out on election day and give him their united support. He is worthy and
competent.

At the election on November 4, 1879, Hinkle defeated Bat Masterson in all of the Ford county precincts and racked up a majority of
136 votes, beating the incumbent 404 to 268.[1]

Sheriff Hinkle assumed the duties of his office on January 12, 1880.
The Dodge City *Times*, January 17, 1880, reported the new sheriff's
appointments:

THE NEW OFFICERS.

The county officers elected in November last, assumed their duties on Monday last. George T. Hinkle as Sheriff, G. W. Potter as County Clerk, and
W. F. Petillon as Register of Deeds. F. C. Zimmerman does not take hold of
the office of Treasurer until October next. Chas. Van Tromp was re-elected to
the office of Surveyor, and John W. Straughn was re-elected to the office of
Coronor.

Sheriff Hinkle has appointed Fred Singer under Sheriff, and John W.
Straughn Deputy Sheriff, and Jailor. Mr. Hinkle is to be congratulated upon
these appointments. Both gentlemen make excellent officers.

One of Hinkle's first official acts was to deliver Arista H. Webb to
the state penitentiary. The *Ford County Globe*, January 27, 1880,
reported:

Sheriff Hinkle and Chas. E. Bassett on last Friday evening departed for the
State Penitentiary with A. W. [H.] Webb, who received his death sentence at
the last term of court in this county. Mr. Webb was charged with the murder
of Barney Martin, and found guilty on said charge.

The newspaper article which described Webb's crime was reprinted in the section on Charles E. Bassett.

On January 31, 1880, the *Times* reported that "Sheriff Geo. T.
Hinkle, and Chas. E. Bassett returned from Leavenworth Tuesday
morning, where they safely lodged A. H. Webb, convicted of murder."

211

In June, 1880, Hinkle was enumerated in the 10th United States census, his occupation being listed as "saloon liquor dealer" and his age as 35 years. He had been married to Miss A. C. Robinson, of Chillicothe, Mo., on May 7, 1879.[2]

More prisoners were taken to the penitentiary in July. The *Globe*. July 6, 1880, reported:

Sheriff George T. Hinkel and under-sheriff Fred Singer returned yesterday from their trip to Leavenworth, to which place they took Pat York and Frank Wilcox, who were sentenced to the penitentiary at the last term of court.

The same type of activity was recorded by the *Globe* again on January 25, 1881:

THE PUNISHMENT OF THE UNGODLY.

Sheriff Hinkel and Under-Sheriff Fred Singer started for the State Penitentiary last Saturday evening [January 22] with two prisoners in their charge, to-wit: John Gill, alias "Concho," convicted of the murder of Henry Heck, and sentenced to 15 years; William Chapman, convicted of Grand Larceny, sentenced to 15 months. We trust the boys will have ample time for serious reflection during their stay in the penitentiary.

On March 3 the Dodge City *Times* reported:

Sheriff Hinkle is slowly recovering. Under Sheriff Singer has been on the sick list also. We trust they will be all right soon. A. B. Webster has been acting sheriff for some weeks past, during the sickness of the above named officers.

Whatever the nature of his illness, Hinkle was still not fully recovered in May. The *Times*, May 12, 1881, said that "Sheriff Hinkle and wife have gone to the Arkansas Hot Springs for the benefit of Mr. Hinkle's health."

In June he was back though still not fully recovered. The *Ford County Globe*, June 14, 1881, stated:

Sheriff Geo. T. Hinkle and wife returned from Hot Springs, Arkansas, last week, to which place Mr. Hinkel was advised to go for his health. He thinks he has been somewhat benefitted, but is still far from enjoying his former robust health. Mrs. Hinkel is now absent visiting her relatives in Missouri.

The *Ford County Globe*, September 27, 1881, reported a Hinkle arrest:

A MIDNIGHT ROBBER.

Last Sunday night [September 25] a party gained admittance to the Grand Central Hotel and interviewed the various sleeping apartments, relieving the occupants of sundry articles of clothing, pocket change, watches, etc., and escaped as quietly as he had gained admittance, without detection or hindrance.

212

J. Bambridge, an occupant of one of the rooms, was interviewed by the petty thief and relieved of a $97 check and $15 in cash. Frank Smith was the next victim, being relieved of his coat and vest. The proprietor, T. J. Draper, was hunted up and had his pants pockets turned inside out and the contents taken charge of, which consisted of articles of no particular value, and relieving him of his vest and suspenders. From the proprietor's room, he took in nearly every room in the house, and it is reported that in the grand round-up the party had secured about $300 in money and checks, several good watches, pocket knives, and numerous articles of clothing. Sheriff Hinkel was at once informed of the robbery and was soon on the track of a party by the name of J. H. Gould, who was arrested on suspicion.

In November, 1881, Sheriff Hinkle, running on the "Peoples'" ticket against independent Michael Sughrue and three other minor party candidates, was re-elected by a majority of 35 votes.[3]

On December 19 the sheriff received a telegram which stated that Edward F. Hardesty, formerly a prominent Dodge City attorney, had killed a man. The *Globe*, December 20, 1881, reported:

FATAL AFFRAY AT COOLIDGE.

The following dispatch, fully explanatory of itself, came over the wire:

COOLIDGE, Dec. 19.

GEORGE HINKEL, sheriff of Ford county,
Dodge City, Kansas:

Edward Hardesty killed a man named Barney Elliott at six o'clock this morning. Bring the coroner and come on the first train.

Sheriff Hinkel and Attorney Gryden started on the afternoon train for Coolidge, in response to the above telegram.

The Dodge City *Times*, December 22, described the crime in more detail:

THE KILLING AT COOLIDGE.—A man by the name of Barney Elliott, who was in the employ of Ed. F. Hardesty, at Coolidge, on the State Line, 125 miles west, was killed by the latter early on Tuesday morning last. Hardesty was absent from home Monday night, and returned at daylight. About four o'clock in the morning Elliott, who in physical appearance resembles Hardesty, entered Mrs. Hardesty's room and crept into her bed, leaving the room before daylight. Upon the arrival of the husband the outraged wife realized the terrible mistake that had been made and was thrown into hysterics. The husband smarting under this outrage, procured two revolvers and sought the man who inflicted this shame and disgrace upon him. When charged with the outrage, Elliott neither denied nor affirmed it, making no reply. Hardesty avenged the honor of his wife by firing eleven shots at Elliott, killing him almost instantly. Mrs. Hardesty is within a few weeks of confinement, and is now in poor condition. Sheriff Hinkle and Attorney Gryden were summoned to Coolidge. An inquest was held. From them we gathered the above narrative of circumstances. Hardesty was brought to this city. Owing to the feeble condition of Mrs. Hardesty

213

the trial has been postponed. E. F. Hardesty and wife formerly resided in this city. This sad affair is much regretted.

Elliott was a temperate man and was highly regarded by his acquaintances. He had been in Hardesty's employ about five or six days. There was some indignation in Coolidge over the killing, and mob violence was reported threatened, but Sheriff Hinkel experienced no trouble in bringing the prisoner here. H. E. Gryden is employed as attorney for Hardesty.

Hardesty was acquitted at the June, 1882, term of the Ford county district court.[4]

Giving no names, the *Ford County Globe* came out with this article on January 3, 1882:

TENDERFOOT VS. OLD TIMER.

Although of common occurrence with the verdant tenderfoot, it is seldom that an old timer—that glorious relic of the halcyon days of yore—is unwary enough to be caught betting on what he considers a sure thing, as was the case during the late political contest in this county. Unlike the t. f., who, when he drops his bullion on the above idea, seeks some sequestered nook on the boundless prairie in which to weep unseen at his innocence and folly, the o. t. proceeds to replevin the ingots of gold thus placed in jeopardy and tries to compel the stakeholder to fork over the rhino under due process of law. Like a cat with its fur stroked contrarywise, it goes against the old timer's grain to part with his ducats even when gambling on chance; but when a sure thing is played open and comes up coppered, the true character of the man floats to the surface, and he comes to the front with a remarkable display of adamantine cheek seeking to recover by a process advocated by none and despised by all. Pass him the cookie.

To which Sheriff Hinkle replied through the columns of the Dodge City *Times*, January 5:

To THE EDITOR OF THE TIMES.

Nearly every one supposed that any unpleasant feelings engendered by the late election were past, and that the "kicking" had been done. It seems, however, that the editor of the Globe has a tender spot yet, and gives vent to his pent up feelings in an article entitled "Tenderfoot vs. Old Timer." As I am one of the parties alluded to in said article, I will say in reply, that a bet was made between W. J. Howard and myself, and the stakes were placed in the hands of Dr. S. Galland, who was to hold the amount until the result of the contest was known; and an agreement was made by the parties betting, both of whom were to be present when the stakes were to be delivered. Dr. Galland gave up the stakes on Howard's representing to him that I had declared myself satisfied and was willing to give up the bet. I never made any such agreement, and I shall collect the amount staked by me, by due process of law, unless Dr. Galland or Mr. Howard returns the amount to me. I can bring good witnesses who will swear, that by the terms of the bet, I was the winner; and while the law does not recognize betting, I have good grounds for recovery from the stake-holder, as I shall demonstrate very soon.

In regard to the allusion to my character, I have no hesitancy in asserting that my record will compare favorably with that of the editor of the Globe. While I may not be, strictly speaking, a white dove, what little property I possess has not been whitened with contraband paint, nor were the window sashes procured from the Government. In conclusion I will add, that if the gentleman wants any more of this, I shall be ready and willing to go into further details.   GEO. T. HINKEL.

The poke taken by Hinkle at the editor of the *Globe*, D. M. Frost, had reference to Frost's arrest in 1879 for having received stolen military paint, window sashes, etc. At the time of Hinkle's letter, the case had not been settled. The section on Bat Masterson contains more information on Frost's arrest.

In January Hinkle arrested a jewel thief. The *Globe*, January 17, 1882, reported:

A JEWELRY DEALER NABBED.

Sheriff Hinkel took in a passenger on the east bound train from Pueblo yesterday morning who answered the description of a party that was wanted by the Pueblo authorities, charged with robbing a jewelry establishment in that city. The party was taken in by our sheriff and a large amount of jewelry found in his possession. He will be held here until the proper papers arrive, when he will be taken back to the city which he so eagerly left.

The *Times*, March 9, 1882, said: "Geo. T. Hinkle, Sheriff, having retired from business will devote his entire attention to the duties of the office of Sheriff. Sheriff Hinkel is an excellent officer."

Sheriff Hinkle took more prisoners to the penitentiary in June. The *Times*, June 15, 1882, reported:

Three men sentenced at the term of the District Court last week, were taken to the penitentiary at Leavenworth, on Sunday evening [June 11], by Sheriff Hinkel, Under Sheriff Singer and H. P. Myton, County Clerk. These men were charged with robbery at Pierceville last fall.

In July some of Sheriff Hinkle's prisoners escaped from the county jail. The *Ford County Globe*, July 18, 1882, recorded their flight:

PRISONERS BREAK JAIL.

On last Friday afternoon [July 14] seven out of the eight prisoners incarcerated in the county jail, made good their escape at a moment when the jail was left unguarded. The manner in which they made their exit was by digging a trench underneath the walls of the jail, which was done with a case knife and cold chisel, making a hole large enough for them to squeeze through and thus gain their freedom. To accomplish this they were obliged to dig down on the inside of the prison to get to the level of the foundation from which they took two good sized rock which gave them sufficient room to pop through and dig up on the other side of the wall which required the removal of from four and one-half to five feet of earth over them before they could expect to get a glimpse of the rays of a July sun. The remaining prisoner who at the time of the break was down in the city in charge of a deputy to purchase some clothing, informs us that the work of excavation had been going on for nearly three weeks, that the earth taken out was carried to different parts of the jail and packed down so as not to leave any loose dirt exposed about the premises, taking the precaution to smoothly cover up the entrance of their cave whenever an officer made his appearance. In this manner they kept their work concealed until the final break-out was made and their freedom gained.

Under Sheriff Keith, who had charge of the county jail, as a matter of fact will have to bear the blame and responsibility in the escape of the seven prisoners from the county jail last Friday, and that too when he was performing the major portion of the duties of the office of sheriff. At the time the prisoners escaped, he was absent from the city on official business, leaving the jail and prisoners in charge of a deputy, of course. When he returned he found that his birds had flown, as they had prepared for this break for weeks before hand and were only waiting for an opportunity when they could find the principal officer absent, to make the break. Of course Keith will have to bear all the blame and mortification for trying to do too much, and possibly loose his commission for his over zealousness in performing all the duties of the office of the sheriff of the county.

Sheriff Hinkle's spiritual advisor, incarcerated in the county jail for stealing a cow, left with the balance of the boys.

The county officers made a minor arrest in October which the *Times* recorded on October 26, 1882:

Three men, supposed to be sneak thieves were arrested Tuesday [October 24] by Sheriff Hinkel and Under Sheriff Singer. In their possession were found some skeleton keys, a lady's gold watch, big brass watch, one American silver watch, open face, and a British bull-dog pistol. The men were put in jail to await identification.

On December 5, 1882, the *Ford County Globe* mentioned that "Sheriff Hinkle is contemplating resigning his office as sheriff of the county," but he stayed on and apparently served out his term which had only a little more than a year to go. A few days later, December 14, the *Times* reported that another jail break had been tried:

An attempt was made Sunday [December 10] by the prisoners to break out of the county jail. There are eleven prisoners confined there and they nearly

216

succeeded in making an escape thro' a hole in the wall near the northeast corner of the jail, having punched the stone out of the wall with a broom handle. The prisoners were placed in the cells and the desperate cases shackled. The jail officers and sheriff's officers promptly secured the prisoners as soon as the attempted break was discovered. A massive stone doorway has lately been put up at the main jail entrance, and the present defect will necessitate additional strength to the jail walls.

The most exciting event during Hinkle's two terms as sheriff of Ford county was the Dodge City "war" of 1883. Hinkle was a chief correspondent and agent of Gov. G. W. Glick during this matter and was at times on the verge of despair over the see-saw motion of public and official opinion. The story is told in the section on Luke Short.

On July 24, 1883, the *Globe* reported Hinkle's impending removal from Dodge: "Sheriff Hinkel on last Friday sold his city residence together with all the household furniture to Charley Heing [Heinz?], for 1,800 cash. Mr. Hinkel will engage in the Saloon business at Garden City, Kansas." Hinkle, however, remained sheriff of Ford county until January, 1884, when Patrick F. Sughrue was sworn into office.

1. Dodge City *Times,* November 8, 1879. 2. *Ibid.,* May 17, 1879. 3. *Ibid.,* September 15, November 10, 1881. 4. *Ford County Globe,* June 13, 1882.

HOGUE, EDWARD O. (1847?-1877)

Ed Hogue held a unique office in the Ellsworth city police department. City Marshal John L. Councell had been relieved by the city council on July 24, 1872, and instead of promoting Assistant Marshal John W. "Brocky Jack" Norton the council fired him also. Apparently the mayor and council were not yet ready to appoint a regular marshal so they named Ed Hogue Chief of Police "until time of next regular meeting. . . ."[1] So far as can be determined Hogue was the only officer to hold this title in Ellsworth's cowtown era.

Hogue had served on the police force a few days previous to this appointment—having been paid five dollars on July 22, 1872.[2]

At succeeding council sessions Hogue's appointment was renewed each time until the "next" meeting. On August 12 he was "appointed Chief of Police until such time as the office of City

217

Marshall is filled." Finally, none other having been acceptable to both mayor and council, Hogue was appointed city marshal on August 26, 1872.[3]

Ellsworth's first shooting of the 1872 cattle season occurred while Hogue was chief of police. The *Reporter*, August 1, 1872, published the story:

THE FIRST SHOT!
Two Men Wounded, No One Killed.

Ellsworth, which has been remarkably quiet this season, had its first shooting affair this season last Saturday [July 27] at about six o'clock, at the Ellsworth Billiard saloon. The room was full of "money changers" at the time, busily at work, and lookers on intently watching the games. Among others I. P. Olive was seated at a table playing cards. All of a sudden a shot was heard and sooner than we can write it, four more shots were fired. Kennedy came into the room, went behind the bar and taking a revolver walked up in front of Olive and fired at him—telling him "to pass in his checks." Olive threw up his hands exclaiming "don't shoot."—The second, third and fourth shot took effect, one entering the groin and making a bad wound, one in the thigh and the other in the hand.

Olive could not fire, though he was armed; but some one, it seems a little uncertain who, fired at Kennedy, hitting him in the hip, making only a flesh wound. The difficulty arose from a game of cards in the forenoon, Kennedy accusing Olive of unfair dealing. Olive replying in language that professionals cannot bear. The affair made considerable excitement. The wounded were taken in custody and cared for. Drs. [W. M.] Duck & Fox extracted the bullet from Olive and a piece of his gold chain which was shot into the wound. It was feared that Olive would not survive, but the skill of the doctors save[d] him. Kennedy was removed to South Main street and put under the charge of three policemen, but by the aid of friends he escaped during the night from the window and has not since been heard of.

All has been quiet since the affair and is likely to remain so.

As long as he was on the force, Hogue was one of the most active officers of the town judging from entries in the Ellsworth police court docket. Then, for an unknown reason, he was relieved as marshal on October 8, 1872, and replaced by Brocky Jack Norton.[4] Hogue apparently reverted to policeman for he continued to make arrests well into November, 1872.[5]

At a meeting of the Ellsworth city council held March 21, 1873, Hogue was again appointed policeman at a salary of $65 a month, "to continue in office until the new Council should have qualified and taken their seats." At this same meeting the policeman was ordered "to notify all owners and occupants of houses and premises

within the limits of Ellsworth City to clear up their premises streets
and alleys in rear thereof of all filth and garbage." [6]

Hogue was paid salaries on April 17 and May 13, 1873,[7] but
it is not clear whether he was a regular member of the force after
the city election of April 8, 1873. In any case he was re-appointed
policeman on June 11. Other members of the force were Happy
Jack Morco, Long Jack DeLong and High Low Jack Branham, all
serving under Brocky Jack Norton, city marshal.[8]

The same day Ed Hogue, who may have been called Short
Jack, was placed on the police force, June 11, 1873, he arrested
Billy Thompson for being "unlawfully disorderly" and for "carrying on his person a certain deadly weapon commonly called a
revolver" and who "did unlawfully shoot of[f] and discharge said
pistol on a public street within the limits of the City of Ellsworth
contrary to and in violation of the ordinances of said city. . . ."

Police Judge V. B. Osborne found Billy guilty and fined him five
dollars plus ten dollars costs.[9]

On June 21, 1873, Ellsworth held a special election to choose
a man to replace Mayor W. H. Brinkman who had resigned.
James Miller won the office with 96 votes. J. W. Gore, of the
Drovers Cottage, collected 83 votes and one vote was cast for
policeman Ed Hogue.[10]

The Ellsworth *Reporter,* July 10, 1873, commended Ed by saying
"We never shall forget the display of bravery in the discharge of
his duty, that Ed. Hogue performed last Saturday [July 5] in
making an arrest." The arrest might have been of "McVey" who
was charged with being "unlawfully drunk and was unlawfully
disorderly and was unlawfully disturbing the peace and did unlawfully resist him the said Ed O Hogue a police officer of said
city while in the line of his duty."

McVey pleaded guilty on July 9, 1873, and was fined one
dollar and costs of $14.50.[11]

Ed Hogue had also served as deputy sheriff for almost two
years.[12] It was as a deputy that he took Ben Thompson's weapons
after Bill Thompson had shot and killed Ellsworth county sheriff,
Chauncey B. Whitney. The *Reporter,* August 21, 1873, said that
after Mayor James Miller had summarily dismissed the Ellsworth
police force for not disarming the Thompsons, "the city was left
without a police, with no one but Deputy Sheriff Hogue to make

arrests. He received the arms of Ben Thompson on the agreement of Happy Jack [Morco] to give up his arms!" The complete story of the murder of Sheriff Whitney is included in the section on Whitney.

The same day that Hogue and the other officers were fired the city council met in special session to appoint a new force. Mayor Miller preferred John DeLong for marshal but the council did not agree. The mayor then suggested Ed Hogue and the council concurred. For policemen Marshal Hogue was given Morco, DeLong and Ed Crawford.[13]

The new police force remained in office only twelve days. On August 27 they were dismissed and a new group appointed.[14] Ed Hogue never again served in the Ellsworth police department.

In September, 1873, Hogue announced as a candidate for sheriff but no record was found of the number of votes he received.[15] He was not elected.

The *Reporter*, November 27, 1873, mentioned that "Ed. Hogue is employed by the business men of town as a night watchman. He is just the man to catch any incendiary or thief who wants to get into the penitentiary." That was the last mention of Ed Hogue in the Ellsworth newspaper.

After leaving Ellsworth, Hogue went to Dodge City and was there at least as early as 1875 when he was listed by the Kansas state census as a French born 28-year-old deputy sheriff. Two years later Ed Hogue was dead. The Dodge City *Times*, June 9, 1877, reported his death:

AN OLD TIMER GONE.

News has been received through the Denver papers that Ed. O. Hougue, former Deputy Sheriff of this county, died in Wyoming Territory not long since. Fever was the cause.

A few weeks after Hogue's death the case of M. Hoffman and J. C. Bronicke versus Ed. O. Hogue, Louisa J. Hogue, A. J. Peacock and Emma L. Peacock came before the Ford county district court. Judgment of the court decreed that Sheriff Charles E. Bassett offer for sale lot number four in block number one of Locust street, sale to be conducted on August 17, 1877.[16] Next day the *Times* reported that "the Ed. Hougue residence was sold yesterday at sheriff's sale for $325." This was the last time Ed Hogue's name appeared in cowtown Dodge City newspapers.

1. "Minutes of the City Council," Records of the City of Ellsworth, p. 39. 2. *Ibid.*, p. 38. 3. *Ibid.*, pp. 41, 43-45, 47. 4. *Ibid.*, p. 56. 5. *Ibid.*, p. 58. 6. *Ibid.*, p. 66. 7. *Ibid.*, pp. 70, 78. 8. *Ibid.*, p. 87. 9. "Police Court Docket," Records of the City of Ellsworth, June 11, 1873. 10. "Minutes of the City Council," *ibid.*, p. 88. 11. "Police Court Docket," *ibid.*, July 9, 1873. 12. Ellsworth *Reporter*, September 25, 1873. 13. "Minutes of the City Council," Records of the City of Ellsworth, pp. 98, 99. 14. *Ibid.*, p. 103; Ellsworth *Reporter*, August 28, 1873. 15. *Ibid.*, September 25, 1873. 16. Dodge City *Times*, July 14, 1877.

HOLLIDAY, JOHN HENRY (1852-1887)

John H. "Doc" Holliday had this advertisement placed in the Dodge City *Times*, June 8, 1878:

DENTISTRY.

J. H. Holliday, Dentist, very respectfully offers his professional services to the citizens of Dodge City and surrounding country during the summer. Office at room No. 24, Dodge House. Where satisfaction is not given money will be refunded.

If Holliday remained in Dodge "during the summer" he was not involved in any sort of trouble that made the pages of either of the local newspapers for his name did not appear there again until October, 1881.

When the Earp-Clanton difficulties broke out in late 1881 and early 1882 at Tombstone, Ariz., Holliday's name was mentioned by the Dodge City papers as a participant in that now famous feud. These articles are included in the section on Wyatt Earp.

Doc Holliday

In the spring of 1883, when the Dodge City "war" erupted, Doc was among those mentioned by Eastern newspapers as coming to the aid of Luke Short. No proof has been established that he really did come to Dodge at that time but the news items are reprinted in the section on Short.

HOLLISTER, CASSIUS M. (1845-1884)

Caldwell's first mayor, Noah J. Dixon, died suddenly on September 23, 1879. A special election was called for Tuesday, October 28, to fill the vacancy. Cash Hollister resigned as clerk of the St.

James Hotel and ran for the office against W. N. Hubbell. The Caldwell *Post*, October 30, 1879, reported the result:

C. M. Hollister was elected Mayor by a majority of eleven, on Tuesday last, over his opponent W. N. Hubbell. The contest was close and everything went off smoothly, with a general good feeling among the candidates and people in general.

Hollister did not run for re-election at the regular city election and was replaced on April 6, 1880, by Mike Meagher, the successful candidate.

While Cash was mayor of Caldwell he was arrested by George Flatt, the city marshal and the mayor's subordinate, for assaulting Frank Hunt who was later appointed a Caldwell policeman during the Meagher administration. Cash was fined one dollar and costs on his plea of guilty. Two days later, on November 24, 1879, Hunt was fined a similar sum on a similar charge of assaulting Mayor Hollister. Cash had squared accounts.

As the years rolled on, Cash Hollister's name appeared in the Caldwell police court docket several times for minor offenses. For instance, on May 12, 1882, George Brown arrested him for "fiting in the city of Caldwell contrary to the ordinance of the city of Caldwell and was fined in the sum of one dollar and cost of suit."

Perhaps Cash's proclivity for fighting earned him the appointment of deputy U. S. marshal which he received early in 1883. In this position he captured a horse thief in March, 1883. The story was told in the Caldwell *Commercial*, March 22:

HORSE THIEF ARRESTED.

Last Sunday [March 18], Capt. Nipp and Mr. McIntire came over from Arkansas City, and during the remainder of the day were engaged in very close conversation with Mayor Colson and others. On Monday the party suddenly disappeared, and early the next morning returned to town with Deputy U. S. Marshal Cash Hollister, who had in charge a young fellow going by the name of Frank Hostetter. The circumstances which led to Hostetter's arrest are about as follows:

For some time stockmen on the range have been missing their horses, but all efforts to trace the stock were unavailing until one day last week, when Hostetter appeared in Arkansas City and sold a horse which he claimed he had bought from an Indian. After which he left town, and on his way stole a horse from Mr. Warren and put out.

Capt. Nipp and Mr. McIntire immediately started for Caldwell, and securing the services of Mr. Hollister, started to find the thief. They came upon him near Johnson's ranch, finding him in company with Jay Wilkinson, another party who has for some time been suspected of being engaged in stealing stock. The latter, however, getting away, taking one of Johnson's horses to aid him in his escape.

Hostetter was taken to Arkansas City, where he will be examined before the U. S. Commissioner.

As for Mr. Wilkinson, he will yet be taken in. The stock owners on the Strip are determined to break up the system of cattle and horse stealing which has been carried on for some time, and if the thieves don't have a care, some of them may find themselves at the end of a rope one of these fine spring mornings.

Next month Hollister teamed up with Caldwell City Marshal Henry N. Brown and his assistant, Ben Wheeler, in arresting more horse thieves. The *Commercial*, April 12, 1883, described the adventure:

A FIGHT WITH HORSE THIEVES.
ONE KILLED AND ONE DANGEROUSLY WOUNDED.

Last Sunday [April 8] J. H. Herron, of Clay county, Texas, came into town and hunted up Deputy U. S. Marshal Hollister, to whom he stated that he wanted some assistance in capturing a band of horse thieves he had followed from Texas. The thieves had stolen two mules and two horses from Mr. Herron, besides a lot of other stock from other parties.

Hollister started out with Herron, and run foul of the party a few miles southeast of Hunnewell. The party consisted of a man named Ross, his wife, daughter, two sons, daughter-in-law and her child. There was another party camped close by. The latter, while not apparently connected with the Ross outfit, had been their traveling companions.

Hollister, finding he could do nothing alone, returned on Tuesday, and securing the services of Henry Brown and his assistant, Ben. Wheeler, the party left about 11 o'clock p. m. At Hunnewell the party picked up Jackson, the marshal of that place, and Wes. Thralls [deputy sheriff of Sumner county].

From Hunnewell the party struck out for the camp of the thieves, and just at the gray dawn surrounded the outfit.

The Ross party, in reply to a demand to surrender, opened fire with their Winchesters. The shooting lasted for about half an hour, when it was found that the oldest Ross boy was killed and the younger one dangerously wounded in two or three places. The latter, after the capture, made a statement regarding the stealing of the stock they had with them, and also stated that two of the original party had left for Wichita on Sunday with some of the stock. From the wounded boy's statement, it is supposed that the party left Texas with about forty head of horses and mules, among the number a fine stallion, for which a reward of $500 is offered.

The dead Ross was taken to Hunnewell, and the other members of the party to Wellington.

Messers. Brown and Wheeler returned to Caldwell about 11 o'clock yes-

223

terday morning, and from them we gathered the above particulars. They also gave us some minute details of the fight, which time and space will not permit publishing at this time.

In May the three peace officers again joined forces to arrest John Caypless, a thief. The Caldwell *Journal* article reporting this has been reprinted in the section on H. N. Brown.

Hollister arrested a mule thief in August. The *Journal*, August 9, 1883, reported:

Deputy U. S. Marshal Hollister, on Sunday night [August 5] arrested John A. Moore on the charge of stealing a span of mules from the Cheyenne and Arapaho agency last spring. Moore has been hanging around among the Indians for the past three years, and if all reports are true, has been up to all kinds of tricks. The agency ordered him out of the Territory over a year ago, but he managed to keep out of the way, in the meantime appropriating the mules charged to his account. Word had been sent to Mr. Hollister to keep a lookout for him, and Moore, coming up with the Indian train last week, dropped into Hollister's hands like a ripe apple. Moore was taken to Wichita, where he will have an examination before the U. S. Commissioner.

In October Hollister learned of the murder of Clement Bothamley in the Indian territory. The deputy marshal journeyed to the area and arrested Nellie Bailey. The Caldwell *Journal*, October 18, 1883, told of the initial scenes:

PROBABLE MURDER.
A MAN AND WOMAN ARRESTED.

Deputy U. S. Marshal Hollister received word that a man had been shot on Sunday night, Oct. 7th, on Hackberry, near Skeleton Ranche, in the Territory. Inquiring into the matter, Mr. Hollister ascertained the report to be true, and that the man killed was C. Bothamley, who formerly resided at Newton, and was, at the time of his death, on his way to Texas with 2000 head of sheep.

It was also ascertained that he had some friends at Newton, and a telegram was sent notifying them of the affair. In answer to the telegram, A. W. Carr, representing the British Association of Kansas, of which Bothamley was a member, came down, and at his solicitation, Hollister went down to Skeleton, exhumed the body, brought it up to this city, from whence it was forwarded to Newton.

Hollister also arrested a man and woman, whose names were ascertained to be Wm. Dodson and Nellie C. Bailey. A boy, who was along with them, was also taken in charge. The woman claimed that she and the deceased were brother and sister and that Dodson was working for the deceased. That on the night of the 7th, the boy went out to where the man was taking care of the sheep, and while he was gone Bothamley shot himself. Afterwards Dodson claimed that the Bailey woman was his wife. We

224

did not learn the name of the boy, but understand that his parents live at Newton. The boy's story is to the effect, that Dodson was out with the sheep, while the woman, the deceased and himself were at the camp. The woman told him to go out and help Dodson with the sheep, and he started to do so. He had only gone a short distance when he heard a pistol shot, and on returning found Bothamley lying dead. The three were taken to Wichita where the man and woman were locked up. The boy was taken charge of by Mr. Carr, who took him to Newton.

We presume an examination of the persons will be held before the U. S. Commissioner at Wichita, when all the facts in regard to the parties will be brought out.

The next week (October 25, 1883) the *Journal* related more of the Bothamley story:

THE BOTHAMLEY AFFAIR.

Deputy U. S. Marshal Hollister returned yesterday from Skeleton, bringing with him the personal property of Bothamley. In one trunk was found a lot of diamond jewelry, a fine dress and other wearing apparel, which evidently formerly belonged to his deceased wife. In another trunk was found about 300 pounds of silverware. All the property, including the sheep, was turned over to Mr. Carr, the agent of the administrator of Mr. Bothamley's estate.

Mr. Hollister also brought up several witnesses who were cognizant of the burial of the body of Bothamley, and will go to Wichita with them to-day. The examination of the woman Bailey and the man Dodson will likely take place to-morrow.

While Bothamley was at Wichita, on his way down, a deed was made out to Bothamley's farm near Sedgwick City, in favor of Sarah E. Laws. Afterward, a deed was made out by Sarah E. Laws to Nellie C. Bothamley for the same property. After Bothamley was buried, the Bailey woman sent the first deed to Newton to be recorded, but Hollister, getting hold of the facts, telegraphed in time and had the recording stopped. Afterward the woman told Hollister about the second deed, and made a deed of the property to the heirs of Bothamley.

A preliminary examination was held at Wichita within a week and Nellie was bound over for trial before the U. S. district court. There, on January 19, 1885, she was acquitted of the murder of Clement Bothamley.

At various times, from October 1, 1883, to August 6, 1884, Hollister's name showed up on the Caldwell police docket as the arresting officer. He was noted as "ast. marshal," "special policeman," "city marshal," or just "C. M. Hollister."

In November, 1883, Hollister and Ben Wheeler killed Chet Van Meter. The Caldwell *Journal*, November 22, 1883, reported:

A MAN FOR SUPPER.

KILLED BECAUSE HE WOULD NOT SURRENDER.

On Wednesday [November 21], about supper time, C. M. Hollister and Ben. Wheeler drove up to the Leland Hotel in a spring wagon and lifting out the body of a man deposited it on one of the tables in the front basement of that house. When the body was laid out, we found it to be that of a young man apparently about 23 or 24 years of age, about five feet seven inches in height; dark complexion, smooth face, except a brown mustache, black hair, high forhead, narrow between the temples, a long straight nose, something after the Grecian style, with large nostrils; mouth fair size, with thin compressed lips. It was the body of Chet. Van Meter, son of S. H. Van Meter living near Fall Creek, in this township, about seven miles northwest of this city.

T. H. B. Ross, Justice of the Peace, immediately telegraphed for Coroner [R. W.] Stevenson and County Attorney [J. T.] Herrick. The former was out of town, but the latter came down on the night train, and this morning a coroner's jury was summoned, consisting of D. [Dave] Leahy, Wm. Morris, S. Swayer, Wm. Corzine, John Phillips, E. H. Beals, and an inquest was held before Squire Ross.

We cannot give the testimony in detail, but the substance of it was to the effect that Chet. Van Meter had married the daughter of Gerard Banks, a widower living on a farm in Chikaskia township, about nine miles from town; that he was living with his father-in-law, and that on the night of the 20th he beat his wife. That he also, on that same night, fired at J. W. Loverton and Miss Doty, threatening to kill them, and on the following morning had beaten his brother-in-law, Albert Banks, a boy about fifteen or sixteen years of age, and made threats that he would kill half a dozen of them in that neighborhood before he got through. Young Banks and Loverton came in on Wednesday and swore out a warrant for the arrest of Van Meter, before Squire Ross, stating the above facts, and the Justice deputized C. M. Hollister to serve it, at the same time telling him to get some one to go with him, and to go well armed, as, from the statement of the complainants, Van Meter was a dangerous man, and would likely resist a peaceable arrest.

With this understanding, Mr. Hollister requested Ben Wheeler to accompany him, and about four o'clock in the afternoon the party started for the home of Mr. Banks. Arriving there it was ascertained that Chet had gone to his father's, about five miles south. Driving over to Van Meter's, they found Chet standing near the southeast corner of the house, with a Winchester in his hands. Wheeler and Hollister jumped out of the wagon, and the former ordered Chet to throw up his hands, and he did so, but he brought up his gun at the same time, and fired, apparently at Hollister, as near as the evidence went to show. Wheeler and Hollister fired almost simultaneously, but as Chet did not fall and attempted to fire again, they both shot the second time, and he fell, dead. They then, with the assistance of Loverton and young Banks, loaded the body into the wagon, and brought it to town.

An examination of the body this morning by Dr. Noble disclosed the fact that it had seven bullet holes in it, one evidently made by a large ball, entering

226

the right side between the second and third ribs, passing through the lungs and liver and coming out between the ninth and tenth ribs. The other shots entered his chest, and one penetrated the abdomen just above the navel. There were also two gun shot wounds on each hand. The Winchester he held also showed marks where the buckshot from Hollister's gun had struck it.

The examination of witnesses closed at 3 o'clock, when the jury retired, and after a short absence returned a verdict to the effect that the deceased came to his death from gunshot wounds at the hands of C. M. Hollister and Ben. Wheeler, while in the discharge of their duties as officers of the law, and that the killing was not felonious.

After the verdict was rendered the body was turned over to S. M. Van Meter, father of the deceased, who had it encased in a coffin and took it home for burial.

And thus the latest, and we trust the last, sensation incident to border life in Southern Kansas has ended.

Deputy U. S. Marshal Hollister was also a deputy sheriff of Sumner county. The Caldwell *Journal*, September 4, 1884, told of his arresting the owner of an outlying dance hall:

Cash Hollister, deputy sheriff, went out to the dance hall some twelve miles west of this place Monday evening [September 1], and arrested Frank Swartz, proprietor of the same. The hall has been run as an every-day-in-the-week concern, and Sunday nights especially. Beer and other prohibited articles have been sold without stint, and a general hurrah of a time has ruled. The officers came to the conclusion that if a stop was not put to it, some one would be killed in a drunken brawl, and Caldwell be blamed for it, so they quietly laid their plans and took Mr. S. in under the prohibitory law. He will be tried in the district court at Wellington this week, and probably get the full benefit of all the fines, etc., attached. It is not likely this move would have been made if Mr. Swartz had confined himself to the legitimate business of a dance hall in the wild, free west.

A week later Hollister resigned his federal commission. The *Journal*, September 11, 1884, said:

Cash Hollister tendered his resignation as deputy U. S. marshal while at Wichita, Tuesday [September 9]. The marshal [Benjamin F. Simpson] and others connected with the office, appear to want Cash to do the work, and then not have any of the pay for the same, which, of course, he kicks about. There ought to be a deputy marshal here, and also a U. S. Commissioner, but there seems to be a feeling extant that the thing must not be allowed.

On October 18, while attempting to make an arrest, Hollister was shot and killed. The Caldwell *Journal*, October 23, 1884, carried a long story about the affair:

ANOTHER MURDER.

BOB CROSS SPEEDS THE BULLET THAT SENDS
DEPUTY SHERIFF C. M. HOLLISTER TO HIS GRAVE.

Cass M. Hollister, the brave officer and warm friend, is no more. On Saturday morning last the murderers bullet cut the cord of life and let this noble soul take its flight to the great unknown. Bob Cross, a desperado and villain of the deepest dye, sped the fatal ball, and now awaits in jail the slow but sure course of the courts of justice, to answer for this awful crime. His own home and that of his victim made desolate by the same small leaden messenger, and himself doomed to linger out his miserable existence in the dark cells of the penitentiary, and all for what? Simply the innate deviltry of a desperate and vicious mind, coupled with an overpowering passion for notoriety.

Bob Cross was the son of a highly respected Christian minister and gentleman, but he went astray and is now waiting his doom for breaking the highest and most sacred law of God and man. "Thou shalt not kill." While his victim, a man whose bravery and devotion to his duty, his friends and family, was proverbial, sleeps the sleep of eternity beneath the sod of Kansas sacred soil, whose laws he was upholding and supporting at the time of his death.

A short biography of the deceased would not be out of place here and hence we give it, together with that of his murderer.

C. M. HOLLISTER

was born December 7th, 1845, near Cleveland, Ohio, and resided there until in 1877, when he came to Kansas and Caldwell. On July 19, 1878, was married in this city to Miss Sadia [Sarah] Rhodes, daughter of Mr. and Mrs. Abram Rhodes, removed to Wichita soon after his marriage and remained there until Dec. 2, '78. In the fall of 1879 he was elected mayor of the city of Caldwell to fill a vacancy caused by the death of N. J. Dixon; served faithfully and well until the spring of 1880. He served several terms as city marshal, deputy marshal, and was always one of the first called upon to make arrests of "bad men," and was very successful in this line of business. In 1883, he was appointed Deputy United States Marshal by Hon. B. S. Simpson, and in February last was appointed Deputy Sheriff of Sumner county by Frank Henderson, and on Saturday last met his death at the hands of a man whom he had three states warrants for, in attempting to serve them and secure his arrest. He leaves a heart broken wife and five-year-old son [Wildie] to mourn his untimely death.

BOB CROSS,

the murderer, is a native of Texas, the son of a prominent and pious Baptist minister, whose grey head will be bowed to the earth with sorrow when he hears the extent of his son's crimes and the consequence of their commission. Cross came up the trail with Real Hamlet in the spring of 1883, and after the herd was sold out that he came up with, borrowed a horse from Peyton Montgomery to ride to this city. After arriving here he sold the horse for $15.00 and skipped out on the money. This was his first bad break here and since that time he has been constantly without the pale of the law, for numerous and repeated examples of his deviltry. Quite recently, he, in connection with his brother-in-law, Fin Warrensburg, went through the Jew store out west on the county line breaking up the show cases, pounding up the owner, and committing other depredations too numerous to mention. He escaped arrest at the time and had kept out of the way of the officers. On Sunday before last he abducted a young daughter of Mr. Joshua Hannum, a well-to-do farmer of Bluff township, and carried her off with him to Cedar Vale in Chautauqua county. On Thursday he returned with her to Wellington, put her on the train that night and sent her to this city, agreeing to meet her here on Friday morning. She found that she had been deserted and went home to her father. Cross met his wife somewhere in Bluff township on Friday and together they rode to their brother-in-law's farm one mile north and two miles east of Hunnewell, arriving there some time Friday morning. Cross was married to a Miss McGuire, a resident of this county, a little over a year ago, and has one child by this union. In resisting arrest for these crimes he murdered a brave and generous hearted man and officer.

THE CIRCUMSTANCES,

as near as we are enabled to gather them from all sources are substantially as follows:

Warrants were sworn out for the arrest of Bob Cross by Mr. Hannum for abducting his daughter, and placed in the hands of Deputy Sheriff Hollister to serve on Friday night last; two other warrants, but for different offences, were also placed in his hands for Cross' arrest. George Davis and Mr. Hannum were sworn is [as] a posse to assist in making the arrest. It was heard that Cross was at T. M. Warrensburg's place near Hunnewell and the party at about 11 o'clock Friday night left here for Hunnewell. There they found the marshal of Hunnewell, Mr. Reilly, and got him to accompany them to assist them. The party then drove to Warrensburg's house, arriving there about three o'clock Saturday morning.

The officers at once surrounded the house, leaving Mr. Hannum to hold the team, and demanded the surrender of Cross. The woman said that Cross was not in the house. The door was then kicked open, and the women came out and swore by all they held sacred that Cross was not in the house at that time and that the officers might search the house if they did not believe it. The officers were not satisfied with this answer and demanded that a lamp should be lighted so they could see. This was refused. When the women again closed the door, it was kicked open, whereupon Cross fired two shots at the officers, who were standing directly in front of it. Fortunately, neither shot took effect. The officers then became more cautious and informed the occupants of the house that they would burn it down if they did not come out. The women came out, but Cross failed to show up. Davis brought some hay, placed it under the house and was just finishing all preparations for starting the fire when a shot was fired. Hollister fell and Davis took refuge behind a wood pile a few feet away. Marshal Riley was stationed at the northeast corner of the house to guard two windows and

229

Mr. Hollister was at the southwest corner and not quite out of the range of the door, through which Cross fired when Hollister was killed.

Davis at first thought Hollister had dropped down to avoid shots from the house, and as he lay so quiet he went to him and found that he was dead. Davis at once informed Reilly, who told him to guard the door, but Davis' only thought then was to get Hollister away. So he carried him to the wagon and in attempting to put him in the team became frightened and ran away. They were finally caught and returned and Hollister's body placed in the wagon.

In the meantime, Mrs. Cross entered the house and when she again came out, Cross followed her and kept her between himself and Officer Reilly. As he passed the corner of the house Reilly pulled down on him with his gun. Instantly Mrs. Cross sprang between the men, grasped the gun, placed the muzzle to her breast and held it there. Reilly extricated it and again leveled it at the fleeing man and again Mrs. Cross caught it and prevented his firing. Cross escaped from the house with nothing but his shirt and guns on his person.

The officers arrested the women, loaded them into the same wagon with the body of Mr. Hollister and drove to Hunnewell, where another team was secured and the remains and prisoners were brought to this city, arriving about 10:30 A. M.

As soon as the party arrived in Hunnewell, Mayor Morris was telephoned to and a party from here went out to meet the remains.

About 11 o'clock word was received that Cross had been seen near Hunnewell; a party was at once organized and started in pursuit of him, as was a party from Hunnewell.

To return to Cross. He secured a pair of overalls, and about 10 o'clock had made his way out of the settlement into the Indian Territory some two or three miles southwest of Hunnewell. He found an old man herding sheep and by the persuasive power of a Winchester rifle caused him to give up his horse, which Cross at once mounted and rode off to the river. Soon coming to a wire fence he abandoned the horse and took to the bed of Chikaskia river, following this upstream some two miles. Being bare footed he could walk in the sand with but little inconvenience. He finally left the river and crossed over to Bluff creek, which at this place is but a few hundred yards from the river, hid in a small ravine, where he was finally found by the pursuing party about four o'clock.

The pursuing party, headed by Bedford Wood of this city and Marshal Reilly of Hunnewell, struck Cross' trail where he left his horse at the fence, and followed it until he reached Bluff creek, where it was lost. They searched every bunch of grass, ravine, brush pile, or hollow, and after several of the party had passed Cross, they finally discovered him lying flat on the ground in a little draw. Two shots were fired in close proximity to his person to intimidate him, and his capture was at once and easily effected. He reached for his gun once or twice, but the ugly muzzle of a double-barreled shot gun leveled at his head made him throw up and surrender.

Cross, being informed that he had killed Hollister and left his wife and

230

child with no one to protect them, said that he had a wife and child to support and would have been killed. He was taken at once to Hunnewell and there kept closely guarded until about ten o'clock, when several officers took him across the country to Wellington. It is well they started when they did, or his body would have been found hanging to a telegraph pole the next morning. On the road to Wellington he said that he had killed Hollister and that he thought if he could get him out of the way he could get away from the other fellows. That he killed him with a Winchester rifle—the same one that he gave up to Reilly when captured.

Mr. Hollister's remains were interred in the cemetery north of town at ten o'clock Sunday morning, and were followed to their last resting place by almost the entire population of the city. The moans of his widow at the last parting at the grave were enough to chill the heart of a stone and many were the vows there registered that the murderer of that husband should pay the penalty of his crime if the laws of the country failed to reward him with iron bars or the hangman's noose.

Coroner Stevenson came down Saturday and began the inquest, which was continued on Monday until late in the evening. Many witnesses were examined and all the evidence, except that of Mrs. Cross, was to the same effect—that he came to his death at the hands of Robert Cross.

Mrs. Cross swore that Robert Cross was not at the house during the entire night on which Hollister was killed; that he had left the evening before; that she was positive there was no fire arms in the house, nor were there any men in the house. Her evidence was taken with a large grain of allowance, on account of the relationship she bore to the prisoner.

After the evidence was all in the jury rendered the following

STATE OF KANSAS,   VERDICT:
Sumner County.

An inquisition holden at the city of Caldwell, Sumner county, Kansas, on the 18th and 20th days of October; A. D. 1884, before R. W. Stevenson, coroner in and for said county of Sumner, on the body of C. M. Hollister, here lying dead, by the jurors whose names are hereunto subscribed. The said jurors, upon their oaths, do say that C. M. Hollister came to his death at about 3 o'clock in the morning of the 18th day of October, A. D. 1884, from a gunshot wound at the hands of Robert Cross. Said gunshot wound being inflicted with what is commonly known as a Winchester rifle loaded with gunpowder and leaden bullets, and that said killing was felonious.

In testimony whereof, the said jurors have hereunto set their hands the day and year above written.   (Signed,)   JAMES D. KELLY,
Foreman,

CLARK BLACK,
J. W. HOCKADAY,
H. C. UNSELL,
GEO. W. EYESTON,
N. M. LEMON,
Jurors.

Attest, R. W. STEVENSON, Coroner of Sumner County, State of Kansas.

HORSEMAN, WILLIAM N. (1857?-____)

William Horseman was appointed city marshal of Caldwell on April 12, 1880, the second man to serve in that office. D. W. Jones was made assistant marshal and James Johnson, policeman. The Caldwell *Post*, April 15, 1880, commented facetiously: "Boys you had better behave yourselves now, or the 'police' will catch you. With Horseman as marshal, Dan Jones as assistant and James Johnson as policeman, there will be no fooling. The weather is getting too hot, for a sojourn in the cooler."

Apparently it was a good police force. The *Post*, May 6, 1880, said of it: "Our city police are as vigilant as hawks, and we cannot enough praise them for their efficiency."

A few days later the marshal and his assistant had a row with some soldiers. The *Post* told the story on May 13, 1880:

A row took place in the Keno room last Tuesday evening [May 11], caused by a drunken soldier and a gambler getting into a dispute about the game. The lie was passed and the matinee commenced. All the soldiers took a hand, and then the police waltzed in to add the finishing touches to the performance.

The Chief of Police got a whack along the side of the head. Dan Jones had his off foot stepped on, judging from the way he tripped around. For a while it was lively, as the number of cut heads and bloody noses bear witness. The cooler received its portion of the spoils of the row. There is a rumor to the effect, that several of the soldiers intended to go in and have a row, and during the jubilee some of them should cabbage all the money. Anyway, it was a disgraceful affair. The officers in command, ought to learn the tendencies of their men, when they have money in their pockets and whiskey is handy, and if necessary, put every mother's son of them on guard.

In June Horseman and two companions captured a pair of horse thieves. The *Post*, June 10, 1880, reported:

On last Sunday morning [June 6] Wm. Horseman, city marshal; Frank Hunt, deputy policeman, and John Meagher [Mayor Mike Meagher's brother], receiving information that a couple of suspicious characters were hiding in the brush on Fall creek, went down to the creek as if on a fishing excursion, and on finding their men, succeeded in arresting them. They were incarcerated in the cooler, and confessed to stealing the two horses they had with them, at Wichita. On Monday, Sheriff [Joseph] Thrall came down to the city on business and finding the prisoners here took them to Wellington where they are now in jail.

The same issue of the *Post* mentioned that Marshal Horseman had developed a new method of collecting fines:

232

Sprawled on the boardwalk in front of a Hays saloon, two dead soldiers, perhaps the victims of a drunken brawl, await transportation to the Fort Hays cemetery.

DOC HOLLIDAY (left) practiced dentistry in Dodge City in the summer of 1878. His fame as a gunslinger developed from his participation with the Earps in the OK corral fight in Tombstone, Ariz., in October, 1881.

WYATT EARP, policeman at Wichita, 1875-1876, was assistant marshal at Dodge City, 1876-1877, and 1878-1879. Wyatt is reported to have said that only "tyros and wouldbes" rested a revolver hammer on a loaded chamber. Apparently he forgot that once as a Wichita policeman, his own gun, with all chambers loaded, slipped from its holster and blasted a .45-calibre hole in his coat, sending everyone scurrying to cover.

LUMBER AND BUILDING MATERIAL,

DRESSED OR UNDRESSED.

Framing Timbers, Sash, Doors, Blinds, Moldings, etc.

YARDS SOUTH OF RAILROAD TRACK.

DODGE CITY, KANSAS.

Newspaper correspondents are apt to give the worst phase of social life in Dodge City, but Bona in the Pueblo Chieftain, does not make an overdrawn picture. We make a few extracts on things generally:

Dodge City contains about one thousand regular inhabitants, but during the cattle season it swells to several times that number of people, which of course makes it good for hotels, restaurants, saloons and other caterers to the wants of the cow boys and cow owners.

The average Texas cow man gambles, and to supply this want almost, if not every saloon in the city, has one or more gambling tables. Faro, monte, and the other usual games are dealt openly, and most of the saloons have a private room for the votaries of draw poker.

Three dance houses are in full blast and appear to be making money. The cow boy is apt to spend his money liberally when he gets paid off after his long drive from Texas, and the pimps, gamblers and prostitutes who spend the winter in Kansas City and other large towns, generally manage to get to the point where the boys are paid off so as to give them a good chance to invest their money in fun. The people who own Dodge City and live there do not look with favor on the advent of these classes, and only tolerate them because they cannot well help themselves. They follow the annual cattle drive like vultures follow an army, and disappear at the end of the cattle driving and shipping season. It is this feature of the business that make people average so the Texas cattle business coming to their towns, and Dodge has already a strong element opposed to cattle coming there to be shipped.

Dodge City is the county seat of Ford county, and has an excellent two story brick court house, a first rate graded school, a Union church, two newspapers, and all the appliances of religion and civilization found in other towns of its size in Kansas Extremes meet here, and Dodge can show some of the best as well as some of the worst elements of frontier life.

There are but few eastern cattle buyers here, as yet, but several of the owner of

DENTISTRY.

J. H. Holliday, Dentist, very respectfully offers his professional services to the citizens of Dodge City and surrounding country during the summer. Office at room No. 24, Dodge House. Where satisfaction is not given money will be refunded.

Mr. R. P. Edwards, boss header for Henry Sevens, came up from the Canadian this week, where he has been holding cattle during the winter. He started for Paladuro, on Wednesday to bring up about 800 calves that have been sold by Mr. Stevens.

Bona, in his Dodge City account to the Pueblo Chieftain pays us this compliment: The Dodge City Times is one of the old stand by institutions that has helped build up the town, and its proprietors Messrs. Shinn & Klaine deserve well of the people of Kansas. They have a good job office and their paper is a credit to the town and Ford county.

Last Saturday the Pueblo Chieftain celebrated its tin wedding. It says: Ten years ago to-day the first number of the Chieftain, the pioneer newspaper of Southern Colorado, made its appearance. At that time no newspaper existed in Colorado south of Denver, and the whole of the rich grazing, mining and agricultural region lying south of the divide was an unknown country inhabited, according to

COMMODORE FURLING.

In common with other great "stuffs," Commodore Furlong is sensitive of his proper title. Last week we styled him 'Colonel' Furlong. It should have read Commodore Furlong. He served in the navy and was with Farragut's flotilla at New Orleans, and was general rooster during the siege. The Commodore is not in love with Kansas. Life is hard to sustain here. There are too many hard knocks required to meet whisky and bread bills. He proposes to go to the Sandwich Islands and invest himself with King 'Calico's' authority, that potentate being a particular friend of Furlong's. It not furnished transportation he will beat his way to the Cannibals. In that sunny, lazy atmosphere, under a bread tree, and in the lascivious embraces of the voluptuous cannibal maiden, Furlong can revel in the delight of his passion.

CITY COUNCIL.

Regular meeting of the council of the city of Dodge City, held Tuesday, June 4th, 1878.

Present—James H. Kelley, Mayor; D. D. Colley, James Anderson, Walter Straeder, John Newton, Councilmen.

Absent—C. M. Beeson.

Minutes of previous meeting read and approved.

The following bills were allowed.

Chas. E. Bassett salary as Marshal	100 00
Wyatt Earp, salary as assis't Marshal	75 00
John Brown salary as Policeman	75 00
Chas Trask salary as Policeman	72 50

Portion of a page from the Dodge City Times, June 8, 1878, showing the "Dentistry" advertisement of Doc Holliday, and a salary item for Assistant Marshal Wyatt Earp.

Report of a Wichita police committee in 1876 (see p. 152) which voted to withhold from payment the scrip of Wyatt Earp until he had turned over to the city all the moneys he had collected. Although it was stated that the vagrancy act was to be enforced against "the 2 Erps," it is not clear which two were meant. The 1875 federal census listed three Earps in Wichita: Wyatt, his brother Jim, and the latter's wife, Bessie, whose occupation was "Sporting."

James Butler "Wild Bill" Hickok bringing in the reticent Abilene city councilman (see p. 199). This is the picture for which Mayor Joseph G. McCoy was censured by the Abilene *Chronicle*, May 18, 1871.

Wild Bill Hickok as depicted by *Harper's New Monthly Magazine*, February, 1867. Several who knew him said the sketch was a good likeness, but they voted the accompanying story "not easily credited hereabouts."

Right, a portion of the Lake circus advertisement in the Junction City *Union*, July 29, 1871. The circus also played at Abilene, where Agnes Lake met Wild Bill. Later they married.

ED MASTERSON, Bat's older brother, who, as a Dodge City marshal, was shot and killed by drunken cowboys April 9, 1878.

JIM MASTERSON, a younger brother, was marshal of Dodge, 1879-1881, and involved in the Front street battle of April, 1881.

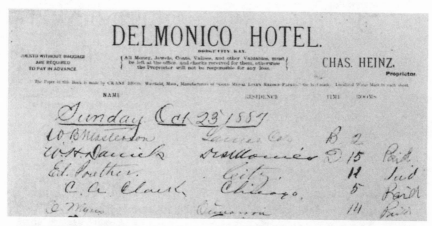

Portion of a page from the Delmonico Hotel register, Dodge City, bearing the signature of Bat Masterson. Note also the signature of Ed. Prather, a victim of Bill Tilghman's six-gun accuracy on July 4, 1888.

BAT MASTERSON, buffalo hunter, Indian fighter, scout, gambler, sheriff, practical joker and newspaperman, as he appeared in his Dodge City days.

FANNIE GARRETTSON, Dora Hand's roommate, wrote a first hand account of her friend's murder in Dodge City. (A Beeson restricted photo.)

Survivors of the last Indian raid in Kansas (September, 1878), these seven Cheyennes were photographed April 30, 1879, on the steps of the Ford county courthouse at Dodge City where they had been taken to stand trial for murder.

Various authorities have identified them as: top row—Tangled Hair (or Frizzle Hair or Wakabish), Left Hand (or Manitou or Rain in the Face), Crow (or Old Crow), Porcupine (or Left Hand or White Antelope); bottom row—Wild Hog, George Reynolds (interpreter), Old Man (or Noisy Walker), Blacksmith (or Muskekon). The bearded man at the top is Franklin G. Adams, first long-time secretary of the Kansas State Historical Society.

ROWDY JOE LOWE, the notorious Wichita dance hall proprietor who shot down his feuding business rival, Red Beard.

TOM NIXON, assistant marshal of Dodge, who was killed by Mysterious Dave, his predecessor. (A Beeson restricted photo.)

MYSTERIOUS DAVE MATHER, all decked out, about 1883, in his Dodge City policeman's "uniform."

William Horseman

Our city marshal has an original method to compel delinquents to work out their fines on the streets. He proposes, if they refuse to work, to put a ball and chain on them, get a good heavy anvil, chain them to it, and leave them in the middle of the street while he goes and takes a—seat in the shade.

George W. Flatt, who had been Caldwell's first city marshal, was killed on June 19, 1880, by unknown assassins. Marshal Horseman and Mayor Mike Meagher were among the first to arrive at the scene.[1] Within a few days, not only Mayor Meagher but also the entire police force and three other citizens were arrested for suspected complicity in the crime. The two Caldwell newspapers seemed vague as to why the men were charged, neither of them sure that the coroner's inquest had pointed the finger of guilt at the officers.[2] One, the Caldwell *Commercial*, felt that the whole business was a put up job on the part of Wellington (the county seat) authorities.

On June 30, while the hassle was in progress, the city council of Caldwell relieved Horseman and his deputies.[3] By July 3 the preliminary examinations were concluded and Horseman, Frank Hunt, Dan Jones, and James Johnson were bound over for the approaching term of the district court. Bail was set at $500 each. Again the *Commercial* claimed ineptness and downright graft as the reasons for accusing the Caldwellites.[4]

On July 8, 1880, the whole police force was reinstated.[5] A week later Marshal Horseman was arrested again. The *Sumner County Democrat*, of Wellington, July 21, 1880, reported:

On Thursday last [July 15] Marshal Horseman, of Caldwell, and policeman Hunt, were arrested by Sheriff Thralls and brought to this city on a charge of assault and battery on the person of Abram Rhodes. The case was first brought before 'Squire King, but a change of venue was then taken and the case brought before 'Squire Cox, [who] after hearing the evidence, discharged the prisoners.

Horseman was once more relieved from the police on August 10 though the remainder of the force was retained. The Caldwell *Commercial*, August 12, 1880, stated:

The City Council had one of its interesting seances on Tuesday night. It labored and wrestled with the police question, throwing the light of its gigantic intellect upon the subject with all the force and nerve at its command, and finally wound up by removing Horseman from the position of City Marshal and appointing Jas. Johnson in his place. Frank Hunt was reappointed policeman, and Newt Miller added to the force. Newt is an old hand at the business, having had considerable experience at Wichita.

241

The Caldwell *Post,* however, reported on the same date that "William N. Horseman has resigned the office of city marshal."

A continuance was granted the ex-officers in November. The Caldwell *Commercial,* November 11, 1880, was still of the opinion that no case really existed against the men:

> The trial of "our boys" who are under bonds to appear at court for the killing of George Flatt, has been put off till the spring term. It would probably have been as well if the Judge had dismissed the case entirely as in our opinion nothing but additional expense to the county will come of it.[6]

Horseman's case was finally tried in April, 1881. The *Commercial,* April 28, reported his acquittal:

> The jury in the case of Wm. Horseman, charged with the killing of Geo. Flatt, last summer, returned a verdict of "not guilty" last Friday morning [April 22], and Horseman was discharged. The verdict gives general satisfaction.

1. Caldwell *Post,* June 24, 1880. 2. *Ibid.,* July 1, 1880; Caldwell *Commercial,* July 1, 1880. 3. Caldwell *Post,* July 1, 1880. 4. Caldwell *Commercial,* July 8, 1880. 5. Caldwell *Post,* July 8, 1880. 6. *See, also,* Caldwell *Post,* November 11, 1880.

HUNT, J. FRANK (1853?-1880)

Frank Hunt was appointed a Caldwell deputy policeman during the first week of May, 1880.[1] On May 4 the police court docket first carried his name as an arresting officer.

Hunt's first press notice appeared in the Caldwell *Post,* May 27, 1880: "A number of the cavalry boys couldn't forego the pleasure of indulging too much last Monday night [May 24]. Result, three of the noisiest troopers were trotted off to the calaboose, under the kind guidance of Johnson and Hunt, our vigilant peelers." The three, James E. Whipple, Dan Sulivan, and John Kelly, were found guilty of drunkenness and disorderly conduct and were fined $1 and costs each, according to the police court docket.

In June Hunt assisted City Marshal William Horseman in arresting two horse thieves. This *Post* article was reprinted in the section on Horseman.

When Former City Marshal George Flatt was killed, June 19, and the city authorities subsequently arrested for suspected complicity, Hunt was included among that number. This has been more fully covered in the sections on Horseman and Flatt.

Toward the end of summer Policeman Frank Hunt inadvertently

killed a cowboy's horse when he fired at the herder in self defense. The Caldwell *Post*, September 9, 1880, reported:

Last Thursday afternoon [September 2] the city had a light shooting scrape. It seems that one W. F. Smith, a herder—had liquored up pretty freely, so that the ordinances of the quiet city of Caldwell became a myth—and the police even entirely forgotten. He rode around the town now and then flourishing his revolver, believing no doubt he was lord of all he surveyed. Of course he struck the "red-light"—they all do it. Then he commenced firing a salute; but that was sufficient signal for the police to appear on the stage and take a hand in the matinee. When they came, our valiant cow-boy went off, but his arrest being determined upon, the police scattered out to effect the same. They were told that Smith was a "bad" one and quite on the shoot. He was the same who made things lively over in Hunnewell some weeks ago. Policeman Hunt met him about George's stable, and ordered him to halt. In reply he drew his revolver, when Frank elevated his shot gun and lodged a buck shot in Mr. Smith's knee, and killing his horse. A great deal of sympathy was expressed for the horse. Smith was taken to the police court, where he pleaded guilty to disorderly conduct, and paid his fine, after which he was taken in hand by Dr. Noble. We are very sorry that some of the cow-boys who come in here allow whisky to get the better of them; because when sober, they are as are the majority of them, as nice fellows as ever lived. We expect them to have all the fun they can get, but they must acknowledge that the citizens of our town have a right to insist upon a strict compliance with the city's laws. Visitors had better bear that in mind, and also the fact that we have a police force determined to do their duty. This state of affairs is as profitable for people visiting our city as for ourselves.

Hunt was himself killed a month later, just a few days after he had been relieved from the police force. The Caldwell *Commercial*, October 14, 1880, said:

ASSASSINATION OF FRANK HUNT.

Last Friday night [October 8], between the hours of ten and eleven o'clock, Frank Hunt was shot while sitting by a window in the Red Light dance hall, on the corner of Fifth and Chisholm streets. The particulars, so far as developed, are about as follows: During the evening Hunt had some difficulty with one of the cyprians belonging to the house, and considerable bad blood was engendered between Hunt, the woman and her "man." Shortly before the shooting Hunt had taken part in a dance, and after it was over sat down by a window on the north side of the room. A few moments after a shot was fired, and Hunt jumped from his seat exclaiming, "I'm killed! He did it out there!" at the same time pointing to the window.

City Marshal J. W. Johnson and D. W. Jones, who was assisting Johnson that night as special policeman, being present, immediately ran to the east door of the hall, but finding it fastened Jones made his way out in front. Meantime Johnson forced open the east door, got out and ran around to the north side of the house. As he did so he heard some one running near the stage barn,

243

and followed after, but it being dark he could see no one, and whoever the fleeing party was he escaped.

Hunt was taken care of as soon as possible, placed on a table in the center of the room and Dr. MacMillan sent for. On his arrival an examination was made, and it was found that Hunt was shot in the left side, near the back, the ball entering between the ninth and tenth rib. Hunt was removed to a building on Main street, and on Saturday morning a dispatch was sent for his brother, D. M. Hunt, who lives in Ray county, Missouri. Subsequently Hunt was removed to the Leland Hotel, where he died about noon on Monday. His brother reached Caldwell sometime during Sunday night, and was with him up to the time of his death.

Immediately upon the death of Hunt a coroner's jury was summoned, by Squire Kelly, and an inquest began. A post mortem examination of the body was made by Drs. Noble & MacMillan, when it was found that the ball had passed through the upper portion of the tenth rib, through the liver and the lower part of the stomach, and lodged to the right of the stomach.

On Tuesday D. M. Hunt returned to Missouri, taking the body of his brother with him, and it will be buried at Lathrop, Clinton county, where his parents reside.

J. Frank Hunt was a young man, aged 29 years [the 1880 U. S. census listed Hunt as 27 years old]; was born in Ray county, Missouri, where he was raised. His parents afterward removed to Lathrop, Clinton county, where they now reside.

Frank came to Caldwell about a year ago. Last year he was appointed on the police force, which position he occupied until the last meeting of the Council, when the force was reduced and Hunt was discharged. During all the time he was on the force Hunt was strictly temperate, quiet and unobtrusive, prompt and strict in the discharge of his duties. While he made some enemies, as such a man always will, he made more friends, and was generally regarded as one of the best men on the police force.

As to who fired the fatal shot there are many conjectures, but pending the investigation of the coroner's jury it is not worth while to give them. Every effort is being made to ferret out the assassin, and if found it will go hard with him.

The jury is composed of the following citizens: B. M. Odom, L. G. Bailey, S. Donaldson, R. Bates, E. C. Henning and W. B. Hutchison. When it shall have finished its work and made a report we will endeavor to give the main points of the evidence brought out in the examination.

The Caldwell *Post*, October, 14, 1880, reported that 17-year-old Dave Spear was the suspected murderer:

ANOTHER MURDER.

Last Friday evening this city was again thrown into an excitement over another murder. About ten o'clock some cowardly assassin shot Frank Hunt and inflicted, what afterwards proved a fatal wound. Hunt was down at that den of iniquity, the Red Light dance house, and while sitting at the north window in the dance hall, some one shot him, the ball entering his body on the left side, passing over and fracturing the tenth rib and lodging in the ninth costal cartilage on the right side. The shot was fired through the open window, by some person standing outside. Who that person was is only a matter of rumor and suspicion. Doctors Noble & MacMillan attended to the wounded man until his death, which happened last Monday. A jury was at once summoned by Judge Kelly, who, in the absence of a Coroner, acted in his place. The jury consisted of W. B. Hutchison, B. M. Odom, S. Donaldson, R. Bates, L. G. Baily, and C. H. Henning. The State is represented by L. M. Lange, Esq. The session of the Coroner's jury being held in secret the testimony is not accessible; but enough is known of their proceedings to assert that a thorough examination is being made to feret out the guilty party.

Shortly after the death of Frank Hunt, David Spear, of this town, was arrested under a warrant from Justice Kelly, and is still held in custody.

Hon. Thomas George, of Wellington, is engaged to represent Spear, and is admitted to the coroner's jury.

We understand that Hunt made statements before his death; but of course they are as yet denied us for publication.

We cannot refrain from saying that it is our opinion that if the Council had listened to our protestations against the running of the "dance house," this murder would not have happened in our place. The Post again and again lifted up its voice against it, and calling to mind what like dens have done for other cities. Our words have proved true, and we charge the Council with being blameable for these shameful, horrid happenings in our midst. Both the murder of Flatt and of Hunt goes straight back to the Red Light dance house.

The *post mortem* examination of the remains was performed Monday afternoon, by Drs. Noble & MacMillan, and revealed a wound which must have been of itself necessarily fatal. After passing through the abdominal wall the bullet pierced both the pyloric end of the stomach and left lobe of the liver, and was found embedded in the 9th costal cartilage. The arteries were then injected with a preserving liquid and the body turned over to the brother of the disease [*sic*] who took it back to Missouri for interment.

The city looses in the death of Frank Hunt an able and efficient officer and valuable citizen, and his friends have our sincerest sympathy, both on our own account and from the fact that one so promising should have come to his death under such painful circumstances.

LATER.—The Coroner's inquest concluded its work this noon, and found the following verdict: "That said J. Frank Hunt came to his death from a pistol ball fired from a pistol held in the hand of David Spear, on the night of October 8th, between the hours of 10 and eleven o'clock, and that this was done feloniously and with malice aforethought, and they further find that one Lumis or Loomis, at that time engaged as night-watch at the Red Light saloon in said city of Caldwell, was an accessory before the fact.

Spear is under arrest and closely guarded, and we understand that Loomis was caught at Wellington by Sheriff Thralls.

Spear was tried on October 22, 1880, but was released.[2] No further mention was found of Loomis.

1. Caldwell *Post*, May 6, 1880.   2. *Ibid.*, October 28, 1880.

JOHNSON, JAMES W.

James Johnson was appointed policeman on the Caldwell force, April 12, 1880. The marshal and assistant, appointed the same day, were William Horseman and D. W. Jones.[1]

The first record of an arrest by Johnson appeared in the Caldwell *Post*, April 29, 1880:

On Saturday evening [April 24], one of Uncle Sam's boys, was indulging in the, to him, pleasing enterprise of breaking window panes. He carried a six-shooter, and hinted that no officer could take him, but as soon as Dan Jones and James Johnson heard of the matter "they gathered him in" and gave him quarters in the cooler. Afterwards a sergeant came and paid his fine and took him to camp where he was drilled in the old fashioned, but very disagreeable, manual of "right shoulder and left shoulder log."

In May Frank Hunt arrested Lum O'Connell for "fast riding on the streets." [2] The *Post*, May 6, 1880, reported that Johnson had made the arrest:

A young man from the country, came to town last Monday, riding on a mule. He got loaded up with "tanglefoot" and on starting for home was very joyful. He manifested his happiness by running his mule up Main street and informing the public that "by G— he was going home." Policeman Johnson interfered with his arrangements, and informed him that he couldn't "go home till morning," and that for that night he had to remain in the cooler. The morning found a more sober, sadder and we hope a wiser young man.

The Caldwell police court docket recorded O'Connell's fine as $3 and costs.

Johnson and Frank Hunt, who by then was also a Caldwell policeman, arrested three drunken soldiers on May 24, 1880. The short article reporting this has been included in the section on Hunt.

On May 15, 1880, Thomas J. Ingram had charged Policeman Johnson with assault. After a trial before the Caldwell police judge, James D. Kelly, Sr., the case was dismissed and Johnson released.[3] On June 3 Ingram tried to kill Johnson. The Caldwell *Post*, June 10, 1880, reported:

246

On last Thursday night about twelve o'clock, Mr. J. W. Johnson, our efficient policeman, was informed that one T. J. Ingraham had a pistol contrary to the ordinances of the city. Mr. Johnson stepped up to Ingraham and asked him if he had a revolver, to which he replied, "Yes, you son-of-a-b—h," and, pulling the revolver from his coat pocket snapped it three times in Johnson's face. Fortunately the cartridges did not explode, and Johnson, grasping the revolver, after a severe tussle succeeded in arresting the cuss. He was fined the next morning by the police Judge for carrying concealed weapons, ten dollars and costs, and he is now working out his fine on the streets. We believe he should be arrested under a state warrant for assault with intent to kill.

The police court docket, June 3, 1880, merely carried this terse statement of Ingram's sentence: "Sent to Prison."

James Johnson was among those of the Caldwell city government arrested for suspected complicity in the murder of George Flatt, June 19, 1880. This has been more fully covered in the sections on Flatt and William Horseman.

About a month after the Caldwell police force had been reinstated, Johnson was promoted city marshal in place of Horseman. The Caldwell *Commercial* article, August 12, 1880, reporting this, was reprinted in the section on Horseman.

The majority of arrests made by the Caldwell police force in the summer of 1880 were for minor crimes. Drunkenness, fighting, carrying weapons, gambling, and prostitution constituted the general run of arrests recorded in the police court docket.

A typical week was that of August 17 to 23, 1880. The Caldwell *Post*, August 26, stated that "police court fines for the week ending August 23d, 1880, amounted to $52.75, of which $29.00 was paid and $23.75 was worked out on the streets." The docket, however, recorded fines totaling $44 plus costs. Three arrests for drunkenness were made—a man named Cole was fined $1 and costs on August 18, L. C. Porter was fined $3 and costs on August 21, and the case of "John" was dismissed on August 22.

Charles Reinhart and A. C. Jones were arrested on August 18 for "loud and boisterous and profane language." Reinhart was fined $5 and costs of $18.75. Jones' case was granted a continuance. On August 20, 1880, H. Kinney was fined $5 and costs for "running a gaming table."

All the other arrests that week, five in number, were for being inmates of "houses of ill fame" or for operating such places. Lucy Breno, August 17; Ida Wickham, August 19; and Maggie Deming and Jennie Burk, both August 23, were all fined $5 and costs each for being "inmates." L. E. Brown was fined $10 and costs on August 19 for operating a house.

Caldwell, like all cowtowns, relied on sinners to support its city government. Liquor (dramshop) licenses, and gambling and prostitution fines were the primary sources of city revenue. Since Caldwell police court records were available, a study of the various fines has been made. This concentration on Caldwell, however, does not imply that the town was any more or less immoral than any of the other cowtowns.

During the cattle season of 1880, which ran from about April 15 to October 15, 207 arrests were recorded in the Caldwell police court docket. Fines assessed on the 188 convictions resulting from these arrests totaled $833. If court costs could be accurately computed and added to this figure it would then total at least three times that amount.

The leading cause for arrest that summer was prostitution and the keeping of houses of prostitution. Sixty-two such arrests were made netting the city $390 exclusive of costs. In addition prostitutes were arrested 15 times for drunkenness and creating a disturbance, which added $44, again exclusive of costs, to the treasury. Besides this, five arrests, though not explicitly stated, were probably of prostitutes and an operator and added another $30 to the till. Thus prostitutes accounted for 82, or 40% of all the arrests made in Caldwell those six months, and for $464, or 56%, of the total amount of fines assessed.

The second leading cause for arrest was drunkenness and creating a disturbance. Fifty-three such arrests were made (including the 15 mentioned above) which accounted for $101 in fines. This constituted 26% of the total arrests made and 12% of the total assessed fines.

Gambling was third in number of arrests with 31 or 15% of the total, but second in amount of fines assessed with $149 or about 18% of the total.

Twenty-six arrests and $82 in fines were assessed for carrying or shooting weapons in the city. Swearing, fighting, reckless riding, assault, resisting arrest, keeping a dog, lack of a saloon license, stealing, and causes not stated made up the remainder of reasons for arrests.

248

The tinkling of tainted coins as they dropped into the police court coffer undoubtedly inspired this purchase, mentioned in the Caldwell *Commercial*, August 26, 1880: "The police force of our city now sport neat silver badges—a donation from the city council."

Seven times during the season arrests were made for the unlawful discharge of firearms within the city limits. Fines ran from one to five dollars and costs, the costs generally being several times higher than the smaller fines. The Caldwell *Post*, September 9, 1880, mentioned the low number of such arrests:

This city has been comparatively free from the infernally reckless firing off of revolvers inside the limits—and offenders have generally been "gobbled." Only once or twice the guilty parties have escaped. Last Monday night [September 6] there was quite a brisk firing around town, presumably by some chaps so full of fire within that it made their revolvers go off accidentally (?). The accident plea is too thin, and ought to be very strongly corroborated if it should be taken for "good fish" in the future. The Police Justice has determined to give every person who shoots within the city limits, without authority to do so, the full benefit of the law. He is determined, so far as in him lies, to put a stop to that nuisance, which endangers the life of our citizens.

The whole town must have been law abiding, according to this statement made in the *Post* on September 16, 1880: "The police court is terribly quiet. No arrests, no drunks, no nothing. If the police keeps up this kind of racket, the calaboose will lose all its interest and only be fit for a chicken coop."

To the Caldwell *Commercial* the quiet did not justify the discharging of all but Marshal Johnson from the police force, an act which was accomplished on October 4. On October 7, the *Commercial* said:

Some of these odd days—or nights—the City Council will awake to the realizing sense that one policeman is too small a force for the preservation of order in a town the size of Caldwell. Economy is a good thing for communities, as well as individuals, but it don't lie in the direction of an inadequate police force.

The *Commercial* was right. The next day, on October 8, Frank Hunt, a recently discharged policeman, was shot and killed. Though Marshal Johnson and a special policeman were in the same building in which Hunt was killed, they failed to catch his murderer. The article reporting Hunt's death was included in the section on Hunt.

The admonitions of the *Commercial* and the murder of Hunt apparently did not immediately impress the city council with the need for a larger force. When these items appeared in the *Post*, October 21, 1880, Johnson was still the only policeman in Caldwell:

Several violators of the city ordinances have been arrested within the last week. Experience, it seems, should convince the disorderly element that they cannot, with impunity, violate the laws. Our policeman is watchful, and stickles for the right. Those who feel that they can not exist without indulging in a spree or making hurrah plays are recommended to betake themselves to the quiet woods or boundless prairies, where the mule-eared rabits and viscious mosquitoes roam, and where Jim Johnson goeth not.

Manipulators of six-shooters in the dark hours of night should feel satisfied by this time that they are too much for a police force of one. In a city the size of Caldwell, with a police force of one man, they can easily fire their pistols and escape without detection. It is believed that the prime object is to tantalize the force, who, we know, has did his utmost to discover the perpetrators. As their sport is an annoyance to good citizens they will accept a discontinuance of the same as an individual favor.

On November 1, 1880, a second man was placed on the force and the owner of the Red Light dance hall and saloon, George Wood, hired his own policeman and placed him under the direction of City Marshal Johnson. The *Post*, November 4, 1880, said:

Joe Dolan was appointed Assistant Marshal, at the late meeting of the Council, and one Reed was appointed special Policeman at the Red-Light. Mr. Reed is under full control of the city and Marshal, but is paid by Mr. Wood, at whose request he was appointed. Reed also furnished a good and sufficient bond for the faithful execution of his duties.

Maggie Wood, wife of the Red Light's owner, was, by the way, one of the chief contributors to the Caldwell city treasury through the intermediate office of the police judge. The United States census of 1880 listed four girls (three of them under 21) living under Mag's roof whose occupations were given as "dancing." The names of all, including Mag's, appeared regularly on the pages of the Caldwell police court docket as inmates and owner of a house of ill fame—the Red Light.

In November the case of Johnson, Horseman, and Jones, regarding the Flatt murder was continued. In April, 1881, Horseman was acquitted. Dan Jones, his name having been omitted from the information, was released. The county attorney entered a *nolle prosequi* in Johnson's case, thus freeing him.[4]

City Marshal James W. Johnson's last mention in the Caldwell press occurred on December 30, 1880, when the *Commercial* reported: "The boys say our police behaved themselves remarkably well on Christmas day, because they did not make a single arrest. Jim Johnson says 'they didn't have to.'"

The last arrest credited to Johnson in the police court docket was made on February 6, 1881. No dockets for March exist.

1. Caldwell *Post*, April 15, 1880. 2. "Police Court Docket," Records of the City of Caldwell, May 4, 1880. 3. *Ibid.*, May 15, 1880. 4. Caldwell *Post*, November 11, 1880; Caldwell *Commercial*, November 11, 1880; *Sumner County Press*, Wellington, April 28, 1881.

JONES, DANIEL WILLIAM (1846?-____)

Caldwell was incorporated on July 22, 1879, and the city government was formed following the election of August 7. One week later city ordinance No. 3, providing for a marshal and policeman, was passed. Appointed under this ordinance were George W. Flatt, marshal, and Dan W. Jones, deputy.

That Deputy Marshal Jones was a courageous man there can be little doubt, for he had exhibited considerable fortitude after being thrown from a horse, December 31, 1878. The Caldwell *Post* of January 2, 1879, described the misfortune:

PAINFUL ACCIDENT.
THROWN FROM HIS HORSE—OUT ON THE PRAIRIES
ALMOST THIRTY-SIX HOURS WITHOUT FOOD—
RESCUED AT LAST.

Dan Jones, who is well known to the people in these parts, met with a very painful accident last Tuesday, the particulars of which are as follows: In the morning of the day named, he started on horseback from the Red Fork ranch, I. T., intending to look at a herd of cattle some distance below. After part of the distance had been accomplished, and when Dan was little thinking of danger, his horse fell and threw him, breaking his leg. Unable to remount, and too far away from any human being to make himself heard by shouting, he began to think of some means whereby assistance might be obtained. Although suffering terribly with the broken limb, the brave man strapped it to the other and commenced *crawling* toward a high ridge overlooking Red Fork ranch. All Tuesday night the plucky fellow was out, without any covering save the clothing he wore. How many of our readers, under similar circumstances suffering to the intensest degree the agony of a broken leg, and almost freezing to death from the severity of the cold, would have displayed the grit that he did. Nor has all been told.

Daylight came at last, and with it the hopes of the brave man rose, for the worst, he thought, had been passed. Slowly creeping on his painful journey,

Dan at length saw the much-wished-for ridge. At last it was reached, and taking his hat he waved it feebly—for his strength was fast leaving him. Geo. Haines, the keeper of the ranch, saw it, and thinking it was a hunter who had killed a deer, and that he was signaling for help, went to his assistance. Imagine his surprise when, instead of finding the hunter and the slain deer, he saw the man who had the day before started from his house, in such a pitiable condition. Mr. Jones was taken to the ranch, and word sent to Dr. Hodge, at Fort Reno, who came up and attended to the needs of the sufferer.

It was Tuesday morning when the accident happened, and three o'clock P. M., Wednesday, when the man was found. It shows the stuff of which the man is made, when he crawled three miles with a broken leg, while almost freezing, and being without food for nearly thirty-six hours. At last accounts the wounded man was improving, and we hope it may not be long before he will be able to "go it alone" again.

Caldwell's police court docket, the initial entry being dated September 6, 1879, recorded Jones' first arrest on September 22. On that same day this embarrassing incident occurred, and was recorded in the *Post*, September 25:

That "mistakes occur in the best of regulated families" was only verrified by the singular and unexpected incarceration and disarming of Deputy City Marshal Dan Jones last Monday night, the circumstances of which are very difficult to detail so that a modest public might clearly and unmistakably comprehend the situation, but the trials and tribulations of the news-monger can only be surmised by those who were so unfortunate as to read of Mr. Beecher in his balmy days, however, we will proceed by saying that Dan is a very efficient officer, and where Dan can't be found, you can't find any one, as the sequel will show.

It happened at one of Caldwell's fashionable hotels, and, like all other fashionable hotels, has two small rooms—over each door is an inscription by which a person may know whether he is to be admitted or not, but it being dark, and Dan's "business" qualifications not allowing him to stop and read everything that is hung up entered. About this time a lady attempted to enter but was foiled by Dan turning an inside latch—the lady hastened away, but soon returned with the key—(this is not a romance)—locked, unlocked and relocked and finally left to return no more.

Now as Dan's occupation calls him on the street he concluded that he might depart with safety, but imagine his feelings when he discovered that he had been locked in, but, as will be seen, Dan is equal to all emergencies, and began trying to extricate himself from his odorous prison. There is a seat in the room just opposite the door upon which Dan sat himself down, put his feet against the door, and with Heenan like strength pushed the door asunder, and at the same instant back went Dan's revolver down, down to the bottomless— after which a light was brought into requisition— it was fished up, a tub of water, barrel of soft soap and scrubbing-brush were readily used up and the pistol looks as natural as ever, and if the street gossip don't mention this we will never a say a word about it to Dan.

On October 29, 1879, Marshal Flatt and Deputy Jones failed to catch John Dean, who was firing his pistol within the city limits. Dean's escape and later arrest is reported in the section on Flatt.

Under his first appointment, Jones' final arrests, recorded in the police court docket, were made November 3, 1879, when he brought in four alleged violators of the law.

On April 12, 1880, Dan Jones was nominated assistant city marshal by the newly elected mayor of Caldwell, Mike Meagher. The city council confirmed his appointment as well as those of William Horseman, marshal, and James Johnson, policeman, reported the *Post*, April 15, 1880.

Jones' first arrest under this new appointment was made April 19. The Caldwell police court docket stated:

One Jersey Defendant arrested on the complaint of D. W. Jones, Assist Marshall charging that on the 19 day of April A. D. 1880, at the said City of Caldwell the said Defendant Riding his horse at Full Speed Through the streets of Caldwell.

Deft Pleads Guilty.
Fine $3.00 + cost.

J. M. THOMAS
Police Judge

Fine and cost paid.
J. M. THOMAS
Acting Police Judge
Paid to treasure[r] by J. M. Thomas

Jersey's arrest was recorded in the Caldwell *Post*, April 22, 1880:

One day in the early part of the week one of our noble defenders, holding the exalted rank of corporal in Uncle Sam's army, was vainly attempting to get up a race with some one. At last he made up his mind he would try to beat his own shadow, so putting spurs to his horse, he went down Main street like a thousand of brick. Dan Jones, our assistant marshal considered himself capable of being referee in the matter and declared "a foul." The corporal goodnaturedly paid the city $7 for the use of the race course.

Jones and Policeman Johnson arrested another soldier on April 24. The article reporting this arrest appears in the section on James Johnson.

Soldiers were also the cause of a fight which took place in the "Keno room" on May 11, 1880. This story is told in the section on William Horseman.

There is some confusion as to the terminal date of Jones' second appointment. The Caldwell police court docket did not list him as a complaining officer after May 8, 1880, but the United States census, enumerated as of June 5, recorded him as assistant marshal. Apparently he was not on the city force when George Flatt was killed, June 19. He was at that time, however, a township constable and the first man to whom Flatt spoke after he had been shot.

Jones was among those arrested for suspected complicity in the crime. The Caldwell *Commercial*, July 1, 1880, labeled him "constable" in its report of the arrests while the *Post* of the same date merely identified him as "Mister" Jones. When the Flatt murder case was tried at the April, 1881, term of the district court, Jones was released because his name had been omitted from the information. The sections on Flatt, Horseman, Johnson, and Meagher contain more material on the arrest and trial of the city authorities.

Constable Jones arrested a horse thief on July 21, 1880. The Caldwell *Commercial* of July 22, reported:

There was quite a little flurry of excitement at the Eldorado stables yesterday morning, caused by the arrest of a horse thief. The thief's name is D. Waterman, and the horse was stolen on Monday night from a man named J. C. Brain, living between Winfield and Arkansas City. Brain discovered the loss of the animal some time during the night, and at once sent parties out to catch the thief and recover the property. Among those who started out were C. McKerlie and D. W. Ramage. They struck Waterman's trail at Arkansas City, followed him from there to Caldwell, reaching here about dark, some three or four hours after Waterman had arrived and put up his horse at the Eldorado stables. Finding the man and horse both here, and not likely to get away, they waited until yesterday morning before taking in the outfit.

At daylight Waterman concluded it was about time for him to start out, and mounting his horse, put out for the north. Ramage and McKerlie immediately went in search of a policeman, and finding Dan Jones, pursuit was given and the thief overhauled before he had time to get any distance from town. Waterman owns up to the theft and says he stole the horse because he was broke and wanted to raise a stake. And he succeeded beyond his most sanguine expectations. He will be staked to a few years grub and hard work under the fostering care of the State institution near Leavenworth.

Jones was reappointed several times for short periods of service as a special policeman. Arrests made by him were docketed on September 13 and October 14, 1880. On October 9 he aided Marshal Johnson in the fruitless pursuit of Frank Hunt's killer. The article reporting Hunt's death and the actions of the marshal and his special assistant are printed in the section on Hunt.

Red Bill Jones, a name given Dan Jones by the Caldwell *Post*, October 30, 1879, reappeared in the *Post* and the Caldwell *Commercial*, October 27, 1881. Said the *Commercial:*

Bill Jones, better known as "Red Bill," turned himself loose for a little racket on Tuesday night [October 25]. Bill was taken in and locked up in the cooler, but upon going to that institution yesterday morning, Marshal [John] Rowen found the door broken open and the bird gone. A states warrant has been issued against William and the next time he puts in an appearance he will be arrested again and trotted through on high pressure.

It seems unlikely that Policeman Dan "Red Bill" Jones and this "Red Bill" Jones were one and the same. Only a few days after the above event Dan Jones was offered the marshalship of Caldwell, a proposition hardly to be tendered an escapee with a state warrant on his head. Dan Jones, as well as Mike Meagher and George Brown, refused the position and with that Jones disappeared from the annals of the Caldwell police force.

LOWE, JOSEPH (1845?-1899?)

Joseph "Rowdy Joe" Lowe, and his wife Rowdy Kate, were two colorful characters in Wichita's tough district, Delano. The couple operated what was ostensibly a dance hall and saloon but which was actually a house of prostitution. Delano, more often called West Wichita, was not a part of the city of Wichita but was a separate community across the Arkansas river. City authority did not extend beyond the river and West Wichita had no law of its own. When things would get too "hot" for trouble makers in Wichita they merely had to cross the bridge at the foot of Douglas avenue to find refuge in West Wichita. From the earliest days there were some persons who felt that West Wichita should be annexed and law extended over its bounds but others saw the place as a safety valve, a necessary adjunct to house the lively element attendant on any cowtown.

In June, 1872, after a visit to Wichita, the editor of the Emporia *Ledger* had this to say about West Wichita:

THE IMMORALITY

of Wichita is not of such a terrible nature after all. The city is governed by an excellent body of officers, due strictness and enforcement being paid to law. We saw nothing while there to induce us to encourage the report for crime and

wickedness which has already gone forth. "Over the river" may be called the red-hot place of Wichita, where everything originates and culminates to give a hard name to this youthful city. Some are agitating the addition of West Wichita to the city, but we believe that in doing so the city proper will be injured more than benefitted, because authority will be required to cover too much ground, and in leaving it out the city has now some point for a vent to everything bordering upon crime. If West Wichita should become a part of the city there would be just as much freedom to transcend the decencies of civilization in one portion of the city as any, but leaving it out, all such parties will go over the bridge to be

Rowdy Joe Lowe and Red Beard

buried. With the present condition of things we ask no better protection than Wichita now offers.[1]

Rowdy Joe was his own policeman. When a customer became too rambunctious after a night of swilling and gaiety, Joe would calm him down with a pistol whipping. Such an incident took place July 19, 1872, and was reported in the Wichita *Eagle* on July 26:

A fracas occurred at the dance house of Joseph Lowe, in West Wichita, on last Friday evening, in which a man by the name of Joseph Walters, who was at the time drunk, was badly bruised and cut about the face and head, by a revolver in the hands of the keeper of the house. Dr. [W. T.] Hendrickson dressed the man's wounds. From what we can learn Walters invited the attack by very disorderly conduct. At this writing the wounded man lies in a very critical condition.

A correspondent (perhaps S. S. Prouty, general manager) of the Topeka *Daily Kansas Commonwealth* described Rowdy Joe's on October 15, 1872:

Rowdy Joe Lowe

A description of Wichita would be incomplete without a notice of the notorious dance house on the west side of the river, kept by that singular personage

ROWDY JOE,

or Joseph Lowe, his real name. Joe has been a frontiersman for many years, and has experienced about as much roughness as any other man. His dance house is patronized mainly by cattle herders, though all classes visit it; the respectable mostly from curiosity. I understand that the receipts over his bar average over one hundred dollars per night for months. The receipts are for drinks. No tax is levied for dancing, but it is expected that the males will purchase drinks for themselves and female partners at the conclusion of each dance. Joe is his own policeman, and maintains the best of order. No one is disposed to pick a quarrel with him, or infringe upon the rules of his house. A dancing party at this place is unique, as well as interesting. The Texan, with mammoth spurs on his boots, which are all exposed, and a broad brimmed *sombrero* on his head, is seen dancing by the side of a well-dressed, gentlemanly-appearing stranger from some eastern city; both having painted and jeweled courtezans for partners. In the corner of the hall are seen gamblers playing at their favorite game of poker. Jests and conversation suitable to the place and oc[ca]sion are heard. I would not recommend the establishment as one adapted for the schooling of the rising generation, but to those of mature years, who should become acquainted with all phases of society, Rowdy Joe's is a good place to get familiarized with one peculiar phase. While I would not recommend Rowdy Joe as a model for Sunday school scholars, yet I am constrained to say that there are many men passing in society as gentlemen whose hearts are black in comparison with his.

Possibly the correspondent did not know that the person whose heart he so charitably described had been involved in several early day escapades. For instance, on July 16, 1869, Joe and a companion drugged and robbed a man in Ellsworth. The Junction City *Weekly Union,* July 24, 1869, reported the act:

Friday night of last week a man was found drugged and robbed in Ellsworth by fellows known as Jim Bush and Rowdy Joe, the people got after them and in a few days secured the robbers and about seven hundred and fifty dollars of the money. They turned the money over to a pal named Howe who was also secured. The parties were permitted to leave the country. . . .

In November, 1870, Lowe was accused of stealing a mule. The case was recorded in the docket of the Wichita township justice of the peace:

THE STATE OF KANSAS
AGAINST — Criminal Action 35
JOSEPH LOW

Comes now T. I. McAdams this   day of November 1870, and after being sworn according to Law deposes and Says that one Joseph Low on or about the 12th day of October A. D.   1870 at and in Said County of Sedgwick and State of Kansas, then and there being, did feloniously Steal take and carry away One Slate Colored Mule of the Value of One Hundred and Seventy five Dollars   the personal property of Thos J. McAdams

November   1870   State Warrant issued returnable forthwith

Served this warrant by arresting Joseph Low alias Rody [sic] Joe at Ellsworth City   Ellsworth County Kans and bringing him to Wichita Sedgwick County Kansas before Justice Van Trees Wichita J. P. Kans This 17th day of March 1871.

Fees Serving Warrant	75
Milage 200 miles	20.00
Board	5 00
Jailor	10 00
Expenses	5 00

$40.75

W. N. WALKER Sheriff
J. C. SEIBER Deputy

And now towit on this 17th day of March 1871 this Cause Comes on for hearing, the Prosecuting Witness not appearing, the County Atty Dismissed this action at the Costs of the Prosecuting Witness T. I. McAdams.

Costs taxed at $49.40.   VAN TREES J. P.

In Ellsworth, too, Rowdy Joe and Kate kept a saloon but the United States census enumerator for the county forever branded their real occupation on his tally sheet when in scarlet letters he wrote before their names—"house of ill fame." Kate, by the way, was only 19 years old when the census was taken on July 1, 1870, while Joe was 24.   Both were born in Illinois.

From Ellsworth Rowdy Joe and Kate moved their operations to Newton and were there in the riotous summer of 1871.   The records of the Harvey county district court, sitting in Newton, show that Joe was indicted for operating a house of prostitution there, too:

THE STATE OF KANSAS }
    HARVEY COUNTY } ss. In the District Court of the 9" Judicial District of the State of Kansas at the July term thereof 1872 holden in said Harvey County.

THE STATE OF KANSAS }
    AGAINST } Indictment
    JOSEPH LOWE }

The Grand jurors for the State of Kansas in and of the County of Harvey, duly impannelled and sworn and charged to inquire of offences committed within said County, in the name and by the authority of the State of Kansas upon their solemn oaths do find and present that Joseph Lowe at the county of Harvey and State of Kansas on the 15" day of August A. D. 1871 and other days and times between that day and the day of the finding of this Bill of Indictment at the County of Harvey aforesaid unlawfully did set up, keep and maintain a certain Common Bawdy house and Brothel and in the said house for the Sucre and gain of him the said Joseph Lowe certain persons as well men as women of Evil name and fame, and of dishonest conversation, then and on the said other days and times, there unlawfully and willingly, did cause and procure to frequent and come together: And the said men and women in the said house of him the said Joseph Lowe at unlawful times as well in the night as in the day then and on the said other days and times, there to be and remain drinking, tippling, dancing, whoring and misbehaving themselves, unlawfully and wilfully did permit, and yet do permit and that to the corruption of good morals and the common nuisance of all the citizens of the State residing in the neighborhood.

Contrary to the form of the statute in such case made and provided and against the peace and dignity of the State of Kansas.

C. S. BOWMAN
County Attorney

No record has been found indicating the eventual disposition of Joe's case.

While in Newton Rowdy Joe shot and killed a man named Sweet. The Topeka *Kansas Daily Commonwealth*, February 21, 1872, gave the details:

HOMICIDE AT NEWTON.
PARTICULARS OF THE AFFAIR.

From private parties and correspondence we learn the following particulars of a shooting affair at Newton on Monday last [February 19]:

On Sunday evening there was a dance at Rowdy Joe's house, at which there were several strangers. During the festivities, one of the strangers made overtures to Rowdy Kate which she resented. The stranger complained to Joe of his treatment, and Joe slapped Kate for the alleged insult. Seizing the opportune moment, a man by the name of A. M. Sweet, formerly of Topeka, "made up" to Kate, got her drunk and took her to the house of Fanny Grey, formerly of Leavenworth.

On Monday, Rowdy Joe heard that Sweet had threatened to kill him, and went to Fanny's house to see about the matter. As soon as he presented himself, Sweet pulled his revolver; but before he fired, Joe fired two shots, both taking effect in Sweet's body, from the effects of which he died in three hours. Rowdy Joe immediately went to the sheriff and gave himself up.

Back in Wichita, on May 17, 1873, sportsman Lowe was injured in an accident on his way home from the races. The *Eagle*, May 22, 1873, said:

On returning from the races last Saturday, Joseph Lowe's—familiarly known as Rowdy Joe—horse fell, throwing Mr. L. under him. He was picked up insensible and carried into the house of Ida May and a doctor sent for. At this writing (Monday) we have not heard further, but several who saw the accident thought him badly hurt.

Next door to Rowdy Joe's place in West Wichita a similar house was operated by E. T. "Red" Beard, another ex-Newtonian. On June 3 a shooting occurred there which eventually caused the destruction of Red's building and threatened the existence of Rowdy Joe's. The *Eagle,* June 5, 1873, reported:

A shooting affray occurred on the west bank of the river, opposite Wichita, on Tuesday morning, between a party of rowdies and some soldiers, in which a "girl of the period" named Emma Stanley received a severe wound, two soldiers also being seriously injured. Doley, a private, was shot through the neck, the ball being extracted from the throat. Another soldier, named Boyle, had his right shin bone splintered by another ball. Neither of the parties were implicated in the origin of the affray. The balls were extracted by Dr. [C. C.] Furley, and the parties are all doing well.

The Topeka *Commonwealth,* June 4, 1873, went into more detail:

A TERRIBLE SHOOTING AFFRAY AT WICHITA.
ONE WOMAN AND TWO SOLDIERS BADLY WOUNDED.
THE SOLDIERS' COMRADES HIGHLY INDIGNANT.
LIVELY TIMES EXPECTED. . . .

SPECIAL DISPATCH TO THE COMMONWEALTH.

Wichita, Kansas, June 3.—A shooting scrape occurred at Red's dance house in West Wichita, in which two soldiers of company A 6th cavalry, and Emma Stanley, an inmate of the house, were badly wounded. The shooting originated in a quarrel which one of the soldiers had with the woman. He claims that she was attempting to beat him out of five dollars, and that he threatened to shoot her unless she complied with his demands, which she treated with contempt. He then drew his revolver and shot her through the fleshy part of the thigh, six inches below the hip joint. As soon as the shot was fired Red instantly drew his self-cocking revolver and commenced an indiscriminate fusilade, shooting two soldiers. One soldier was shot an inch below the angle of the lower jaw, in the neck, the ball lodging in the throat at the base of the tongue, and nearly severing it in its passage. It was extracted by Dr. Finley [C. C. Furley], of this city, His comrade received a ball through the middle of the calf of the leg, severely splintering the shin bone. The soldiers who were shot were not engaged in the quarrel, and are spoken of by their comrades as being very quiet and gentlemanly. The soldier who commenced the affray escaped unhurt and deserted last night. The dance house was closed this morning when your reporter called, and no admittance could be obtained. Rumor has it that Red has disappeared and will not be seen until the soldiers leave, who are en route for Ft. Hays. They are terribly indignant and threaten to raze the house to the ground.

Lively times are expected to-night. . . .

Rowdy Joe Lowe

Not long after, the indignant soldiers returned. The *Eagle*, June 5, 1873, reported:

The soldiers have carried out their threat. This morning about 2 o'clock we were aroused from sleep by the rapid discharge of firearms across the river. Hurrying on our clothes we ran down to the bridge, by which time the lurid flames were bursting forth from "Red's" dance house, accompanied by a yell from a squad of some thirty soldiers, whom we met on the bridge, marching by fours. They appeared to be perfectly possessed, and after the order to "shoulder arms," asked us "how is that for high?" pointing to the burning building. Being the first upon the ground, we found a man lying some fifty yards in front of the burning building, who gave his name as Chas. Leshhart, wounded through the body. We saw no one else that was hurt, but we heard that one of the girls was wounded, and that the girl wounded in the melee on Monday night had received a fresh shot. In a few minutes hundreds of citizens were upon the ground, and by prompt action and considerable exertion the house of Joseph Lowe was saved. The soldiers went off up Water street. We have no room for comments, but upon the whole the affairs of Monday and last night are no credit to our neighbor town.

The avenging troopers had been well organized. The *Eagle*, June 12, 1873, mentioned their precautions: "Before the soldiers made their raid upon Red's dance house, on last Wednesday night, they stationed a guard around the sheriff's [John Meagher's] house, another at the end of the bridge, and another with the horses on a back street."

Rowdy Joe and his neighbor, Red, were fighting again the night of October 27, 1873, but this time they chose each other. The aftermath of the combat included Red's death and Rowdy Joe's hasty departure from Sedgwick county. The *Eagle*, October 30, 1873, reported:

The dance houses on the west side of the river were again the scene of a terrible and fearful onset, on Monday night last. We have heard the versions of the principal actors, as also that of outsiders and the officers, with little satisfaction. Suffice it to say that the proprietors of the two dance houses in West Wichita, which stand in close proximity, "Rowdy Joe" and "Red," both being mad from the effects of distilled poison, and armed with revolvers and shot guns, waltzed into a deadly melee. Rowdy Joe was shot in the back of the neck with a pistol ball. The wound is not dangerous. Red was wounded in the arm and hip by buck shot from a shot gun. The chances are that he will lose the lower part of his arm. A poor dance girl, Annie Franklin, sick at the time, received a shot in the abdomen, which the doctors think must prove fatal. Bill Anderson, who through mistake killed a man last spring, was shot in the head, the ball passing just back of the eyes. Was alive at last accounts. Rowdy Joe gave himself up, and is now out on $2,000 bail. No other arrests have been made, we believe. Comment is unnecessary, and a further dilation worse than foolish.

Red died on November 11. The Wichita *Eagle*, November 13, 1873, said:

E. T. Beard, better known as "Red," the proprietor of one of the dance houses across the river, paid the penalty of his misdeeds with his life, on Tuesday morning at 3 o'clock a. m. It will be remembered that he was shot in a row at his dance house some two weeks since. A post mortem examination was made upon the body day before yesterday by Dr. [H.] Owens, the coroner. In company with Mr. [Fred A.] Sowers, of the *Beacon*, we proceeded to the Eagle Hotel, where we found seven doctors and a coroner's jury. The examination disclosed that his right arm at the elbow had been shattered fearfully and was in a state of decay. The wound in the hip was also in the same state. In the latter wound a bullet was found imbedded in the bone. Traces of pus were discovered, we believe, about the wound and in the lungs. The examination was very thorough, but we withdrew before the entire process was gone through with. At the hotel were several frail women, who had been inmates of his house, who seemed much affected. We noticed also Rowdy Joe, who is charged with shooting Red, who wore a solemn countenance.

The post mortem examination, technically and properly stated, revealed the fact of death by infiltration of pus in the blood, the result of gun shot wounds.

E. T. Beard was formerly from Beardstown, Ill., which place was laid out and named after his father, who was wealthy. He was well educated, and had christian training. He has three children, two daughters and a son, nearly grown, who are now attending school somewhere in the east, and know nothing of their father's wild life in the west. He was about forty-five years of age, straight as an arrow, red hair, which fell in a profusion of curls upon his shoulders, and from which he took his name of "Red," an enormous moustache and large nose. He knew no such thing as fear and was counted one of the best shots on the border. At the time of the burning of his house last summer by U. S. soldiers, and at which time, in a desperate encounter against great odds, he shot and wounded several, he remarked to some of our citizens that he would not live the summer through. He told Dr. Furley last week that he followed the disreputable business only in the hopes of getting a start in the world again, but if he got over his wounds he would never go inside of a dance house again.

> "Oh, what a sign it is of evil life
> When death's approach is seen so terrible."

Beard left some property and money in the hands of parties here for the use and benefit of his children, in the shape of a regular bequest.

A Winfield editor, who had known Red in days before, gave some additional information:

"Red."—James Kelley, the editor of the Winfield *Courier*, who was in Wichita the day "Red" was burried, was acquainted with the desperado in his early life, and in his paper makes the following interesting note:

"Red was none other than Ed. Beard, whose father gave to Beardstown, Cass county, Illinois, his name. We remember Ed. Beard as a jolly, rollicking young man, without a single bad trait in his make up. He married an estimable young lady near Virginia, Cass county. The writer of this article met "Red" last July, at Wichita, for the first time since he left Illinois, ten or twelve years ago. He then gave us his solemn promise that so soon as the Texas "season" was over he would abandon forever his wild, infamous life. The next time we saw him was in his coffin, and while we stood and gazed on that lifeless clay, going back in thought to his wild reckless life for the last twelve years, in California, Oregon and Arizona, where his name was a terror to everybody, we could hardly convince ourselves that this was the handsome, jovial gifted Ed. Beard. Verily, the way of the transgressor is hard. Peace to his ashes." [2]

On November 20, 1873, the *Eagle* reported:

Joseph Lowe, charged with killing Beard, had his examination before Esquire [E. B.] Jewett this week, [H. C.] Sluss upon the part of the state, [S. M.] Tucker for the defendant, the result of which was, bound over in the sum of $2,000 for his appearance at the December term of court. The evidence is very voluminous, and, although we procured much of it, we cannot spare the space for its insertion.

Rowdy Joe's case came up before the Sedgwick county district court on December 9, 1873. The *Eagle*, December 11, reported:

The district court opened Monday noon, with Judge W. P. Campbell on the bench. . . .

Tuesday morning the case, state of Kansas vs. Joseph Lowe, alias, Rowdy Joe, was called. The court room filled with curious and interested people. In securing a jury the usual number of preemptory challenges were exhausted by the defense, but an unobjectionable jury was empannelled within an hour or two. H. C. Sluss for the state, [B. H.] Fisher, Tucker and [J. Smith] Deveny for the defense. Much interest has been evinced by court, bar and jury in the evidence given by the witnesses for the state, who, at this writing, Wednesday morning, we give in their testimony, and the prosecuting attorney will, in a few moments, rest his case. We understand that a large number of witnesses will be examined for the defense, and when the case will be given to the jury it is impossible to say, although a verdict may be reached before tomorrow morning. To give an opinion, or even to hazard a guess, as to what the verdict will be, would be impossible, of course, in this connection, but should one be rendered before going to press to-night we shall append it to this article.

A considerable amount of testimony was given at Joe's trial and for the most part the stories were the same. Beard's bartender, Walter Beebe, gave the most lucid and complete account:

I reside in Wichita. I resided on or about the 27 Oct in West Wichita. I was acquainted with E. T. Beard in his lifetime. I was residing at his house at that time. I saw Mr. Beard on the evening of the 27th Oct. 1873. It was right in the house, there in the dance room when I first saw him, it was just about dark, about 6 o'clock. He had just come home—came up to the bar to get a drink. He walked home at that time. Jim Goodwin, the one legged man that was examined yesterday, came with him.

When I next saw him he was drunk. He took a drink at the bar. I was tending the bar at that time & was tending the bar all that evening. The next thing that occurred then was I saw Mr. Beard go to his room and bring out his shotgun and pistol and he came to the bar again and set his shot gun at the end of the bar right next to the door & took a drink, then he took his gun & pistol with him & left the house.

I think no one left the house with him. I did not see him again there any more for probably an hour or an hour & a half. He came in to the house & he had his pistol in his hand. The first thing he done he shot at the white door knob on the hall door. There was another man there at the time by the name of Tom Pope. He drew his pistol & was going to shoot at the door knob too, & Mr. Beard put his pistol at his head & told him to put up his pistol or he would shoot him. There was dancing after the shot occurred & Mr. Beard danced himself. I suppose they danced probably an hour & Mr. Beard was out & in the house two or three times & I sent this Billie Anderson & Ohmert to watch him. I was afraid he was so drunk that he would get into some trouble & they would prevent it. The last time he came into the house he had been out of the house then I suppose 5 or 10 minutes.

Then when he came in he went up to the east window of the dance hall. He stood there probably 5 minutes looking through the window & I saw him raise his pistol up which he had in his hand all the time & he raised it up & took aim just so (with both hands a hold of the pistol) aiming right out of the east window & before I could say anything at all he fired. I went out from behind the bar & went to the window to see what he had shot at or where the ball had went to—I saw that the ball had went through the window & through Mr. Lows window too, I then returned behind the bar & I was talking to Billie Anderson about Mr. Beards shooting & I made some remark that I expected that he had shot at Mr. Low & then I saw Mr. Low come in at the front door & he made a remark he asked who had shot at him. I heard Mr. Beard say something, that I (Beard) done it, that was the substance of the remarks he made in answer to the remark that Mr. Low made. At the same time Mr. Beard raised his pistol & shot it off & Mr. Low shot his gun off at the same time. I could hardly distinguish the two different reports. At this time Mr. Beard was standing between the East end of the music stand & the east window & Mr. Low was standing in front of the front door about 2 feet in the room & Mr. Billie Anderson was standing at the north end of the bar & I was standing behind the bar near the north end watching the parties, and at the time these shots were fired I saw two men run going out at the east door. They were Texas men. Mr. Lows gun was pointed more at the direction of these men going out at the east door. He had his gun with the stock at his hips & the muzzle elevated. The shot would not have hit these men.

Mr. Beard was then going toward the south door.

At the time these shots were fired there was Ohmert in the room, Billie Anderson was there, I think Miss Kate Low was there, think she came in with Low. There was 4, 5 or 6 Texas men there I do not know the names of them.

Billie Anderson was shot. He was standing right at the end of the bar when he was shot. I did not know he was shot until I saw the blood dripping off the bar. I passed out behind him & did not notice that he was shot at the time. I did not distinguish more than two shots at that time. There was no other shot fired after Mr. Low got to the east door. After we let Mr. Beard up he stood at the hall door & shot the girl, before he shot the girl I asked him if he was shot & he said he was not shot—was not hurt at all. Up to the time he stood in the door & left the house he was not hurt at all. He had his pistol in his right hand all the time from the time he came into the house until he left the house. I saw Mr. Beard the next morning & I did not see him any more that night. I did not see Mr. Low after the shooting until the next Wednesday.

When I saw Beard again after the shooting he was shot in the right arm & had one shot in the hip.

There is an ell to this house (describing it) describing other parts of the house.

It was I suppose two to fifteen minutes after I last saw Beard when he left the house when a person came & told me he was shot.

I think there were two or three men came together. I think one of the men they called Shorty.

These are the men who informed me that Beard was shot on the bridge.

Mrs. Low started out at the side door at that time & Mr. Beard started & run out at the front door, but before he left Mr. Beard snapped his pistol twice at Mr. Low & Mr. Low snapped his shot gun at him, Mr. Beard, and the cap snapped, then Mr. Beard had been out of the house I suppose probably a minute & I saw him look in at the west window at the south end of the house, then he came in at the front door. He asked for his shot gun as soon as he came in. I told him he had left it over in Lowes. He made some remark that he did not & went to look for it in his room & he could not find it. Then he came out & stood at the hall door of the dance room, then he came out in the dance room & looked around there. He had his pistol in his hand all the time & he saw this Joe DeMerritt [a local madam who had seen service in Ellsworth and Newton in 1870 and 1871] in the room & he accused her of putting up a job on him. She said she had not & he asked her where the shot gun was. I believe she told him he had left it over in town. I think that is what she told him. He caught hold of her & threw her down on the floor & was going to shoot her I think, he had his pistol cocked right at her, then myself, Ohmert and this Texas man caught hold of him & held him until Miss Joe got away. Then we let him up & he got up & he went to the middle hall door. He stood there probably a minute or so. He raised up his pistol & shot it off back in the hall. I heard a woman scream & he, Beard, run out at the front door & I went back to see who he had shot.

Mr. Beard was standing up at the time he, Beard, was snapping his pistol and when Mr. Low snapped his gun Mr. Beard was running.

At the time Mr. Low snapped his gun he was standing in front of the east door or near the door & I noticed that he was bleeding at the neck. . . .

Cross Ex

Beards house and Lows are about 50 ft apart. There is only one window in the dance hall next to Lows house and there are two in Lows house on the side next to Beards. There was no glass out of the window of Beards window at that time the shot fired from Beards house broke the glass in Beards window. I saw the hole in Lows window made by Beards shot. It was in the south window of Lows house. It was in the lower pane of the upper sash and in the south side in the lower right hand corner as a person stands facing it on the outside.

The second time Beard came in the door after he came from town he said that he was going to have blood tonight. . . .

WALTER A. BEEBE

Carrie Beebe, the bartender's wife, described Red's dance hall in her testimony:

The dance hall has a bar in it. It is in the front part of the house on the right hand side as you go in.

The end of the bar comes clear up to the front part of the house & [word illegible] is just about three feet from the front door. There is a door at the same side of the house that the bar is at and four or five feet from the end of the bar and there is a window between the side door and the petition [partition].

There is a music stand in the northwest corner of the ballroom. There were seven bed rooms in the house at that time. There were four on the west side of the house and three on the east side of the house. There is a hall running through the house from the dancehall to the north end of the house.

The kitchen is near the front of the house & a shed room attached.

Carrie's testimony substantiated Beebe's. She, too, thought that Beard had shot Annie Franklin thinking her to be Josephine De-Merritt. Perhaps Josephine had indeed been up to something, for in December she was convicted of forging the deed to a parcel of Red Beard's property.

Apparently no one saw the fatal shooting of Beard later that night. According to Joe Lowe not even he was sure that he had shot Beard, so drunk was Lowe at the time. Rowdy Joe acted wisely, however, in surrendering to local authorities. City Marshal Mike Meagher told of this in his testimony:

I reside in the city of Wichita Kan—am City Marshall of City of Wichita. An acquainted with Joseph Low, was acquainted E. T. Beard in his lifetime.

I heard of the circumstances of Reds being shot. I saw Mr. Low on the night that Beard was shot. I saw him at the corner of the Progressive [Billiard] Hall standing outside of the door. He told me there had been some shooting

266

cross the river & he wanted to give himself up to witnessses & I told him I could not take care of him that he had better go & see Bill Smith [sheriff of Sedgwick county]. I went with him & found Bill & he Low gave himself up to Bill Smith. He said he did not know but what he had shot Red, that he did not know whether he had or not. Low looked to me as though he had been shot. He was bleeding at the neck. He, Low, said that Red had shot through the window.

MICHAEL MEAGHER.[3]

The trial went to the jury on December 10 and the next morning Rowdy Joe was pronounced not guilty. New warrants were then issued against him for wounding Anderson and for destruction of property, but Lowe had skipped out. The Wichita *Eagle*, December 18, 1873, said:

In the culmination of the trial of Rowdy Joe on last Wednesday evening, for the killing of Red, more than ordinary interest was evinced by the people of the city. The court room was crowded, the stage in the rear of the hall even being filled. The judge charged the jury at great length on what constituted murder in the second degree, including five lesser crimes, either of which the prisoner might be found guilty under the charge. There were four speeches made by counsel, of the average duration of an hour each. H. C. Sluss, for the state, opened with a review of the entire testimony, giving his constructions and conclusions. After supper he was followed by S. M. Tucker for the defense, who not only in a clever but able manner reviewed the case in all its legal bearings. He in turn was followed by Smith Deveny, of Olathe, in an appeal to the jury, in which was recited the redeeming traits of Rowdy Joe, and in which was pictured in not very enviable colors the vagabond and desperado, Red. By this time the interest of the spectators was visible to court and jury.

Mr. Sluss rose to close. His earnest manner told that he appreciated his surroundings. Embarrassed by his own witnesses, who were composed of men and women in full sympathy with the accused, whose sense of modesty and appreciation of right had long since been sacrificed with their virtue, and who cared little for the obligations of an oath, and less for the penalty that is attached to its violation, he had been conducting the case through almost hopeless surroundings. But unawed by menaces and undismayed in the absence of sympathy, with all the earnestness of his nature, he stood up to defend the sacred right to life, and the majesty of the law.

Despite the fact of being in a court of justice, upon closing his speech the spectators gave way to an uproarous applauding. It was a spontaneous acknowledgment by the better class of citizens of the able and conscientious manner in which the attorney for the people had discharged his duty. The jury retired at about 10 o'clock. A verdict of "not guilty" was rendered next morning.

Immediately another writ was issued for his arrest for shooting Anderson, also an action was commenced against him for damages. The pressure was too great, and Rowdy Joe came up missing last Sunday morning. He had eluded the vigilance of the officer, Mr. [John] Nugent, who had him in charge, and at this writing nothing has been heard of him. Sheriff [William] Smith with a posse followed all Saturday night, but returned disappointed. On Monday Smith had several parties arrested for participating or criminality in his escape, among them Rowdie Kate, the result of which we will inform our readers all in good season.

Sedgwick County Sheriff William Smith offered $100 for Rowdy Joe's return. The *Eagle*, December 18, 1873, published a description of the wanted man:

I will give $100.00 reward for the apprehension of one Joseph Lowe, alias Rowdy Joe, a fugitive from justice from Sedgwick county, Kansas. He is about 28 years old, 5 feet 9 inches tall, heavy set, dark complexion, black hair, and heavy black moustache, gruff manners,—formerly proprietor of a dance house. Had a scar on right side of neck from a pistol ball. Had on, when last seen, black pants, brown frock coat, and a brown overcoat, trimmed with fur; rode a bay horse with California saddle.—The foregoing is the matter of a notice sent to all sheriffs in the western states by Wm. Smith.

A few days after the trial, Rowdy Joe showed up in Osage Mission, a Neosho county town now known as St. Paul. William D. Walker, editor of the Osage Mission *Transcript*, did not know another warrant was hanging over Joe's head when, on December 19, 1873, he wrote: "ROWDY JOE the famous Wichitan is in town, and not much rowdy about him after all."

The same day, however, Editor Walker learned of the second charge against Lowe, but the culprit had flown—"GTT" (gone to Texas) as the frontiersmen called it. The editor immediately notified the Wichita *Eagle*, which reported:

Rowdy Joe, it seems from the following card, went direct east instead of south or southwest, as nearly every one supposed he had. Mr. Walker, who writes us, is the editor of the *Transcript* and knows Rowdy Joe, so there is no mistake:

OSAGE MISSION, Dec. 19th, 1873.

BROS MURDOCK:—Had your EAGLE reached here one day sooner, Rowdy Joe would have been taken. He has been here for several days, but left here yesterday morning for Texas. The horse is still in a stable. He watched the papers regularly in my office. Yours, WALKER.[4]

In spite of the fact that Lowe could not be caught, the Wichita *Eagle* seemed satisfied with the results of the trial:

Wichita is fast getting rid of that element which has proved such a curse to her prosperity, thanks to the county attorney and the improved sentiment of the place which is backing him up. Rowdy Joe made a telling shot that night. It shot "Red" into eternity; himself out of the country; Anderson through the head;

[Walter] Beebe, Red's bar tender, into the penitentiary [for assisting Joe to escape]; Joe De Merritt, Red's mistress, into the penitentiary; Rowdy Kate to parts unknown; and Smith, Omet and another into jail for perjury. "The mills of the gods grind slowly but they grind exceedingly small." Patten was sentenced for a year, Beebe for three years, and Josephine De Merritt for ten years.[5]

Rowdy Joe was finally arrested in St. Louis, Mo., on January 3, 1874. A dispatch from St. Louis, reprinted in the Wichita *Eagle,* January 8, notified the town of his capture and subsequent release:

ROWDY JOE.

St. Louis, Mo., Jan. 5.—Joseph Lowe, alias A. A. Becker, was arrested here on Saturday by orders received from Kansas, and was released to-day on a writ of habeas corpus, and after it was known that Sheriff Smith, of Sedgwick county, would arrive here on the first train to take him back to Kansas. Over $8,000 were found on Lowe.

Ex-Sheriff Smith arrived home yesterday. The facts above given, he says, are correct. After he was notified that Joe was under arrest he telegraphed to the officers of St. Louis three times to hold him, as he would procure a requisition and be down on the next train. Just as he got ready to start he was notified by telegraph that Joe had escaped upon a writ of habeas corpus. It is evident that somebody in St. Louis was bought up.

The St. Louis *Democrat* evidently felt the same way but in addition to the charge of bribery the *Democrat* included internal bickering within the St. Louis police department as a factor in Lowe's release:

RELEASE OF ROWDY JOE.

A Noted Character Allowed to Evade a Kansas Sheriff,

A Rather Strange Proceeding.

For some time past the chief of police and the detectives have not been on the most friendly terms. There were various causes for this, but the matter was kept very quiet, and few knew of it, save those whose daily duty brings them in contact with the police department. Yesterday this trouble rose to the surface, and there is a prospect that in a few days it will result in something serious. The cause of yesterday's rupture is as follows:

On Saturday last a noted character from Nevada named Joseph Low, familiarly known by the elegant cognomen of "Rowdy Joe," was arrested at the Laclede hotel by Detective Duckworth, one of the shrewdest men on the force. Low had been in the city some time and was under the surveillance of the detectives, who knew his reputation and suspected that his visit was not for any good. They were not aware that he was needed anywhere else until the receipt of the following telegram:

Leavenworth, January 2nd.

Arrest and hold A. A. Becker for breaking jail; about five feet ten inches; thirty years old; square shoulders; heavy built; very full face; black moustache,

eyes and hair; fresh scar across the back of his neck. He is to meet Kate Low to-morrow morning on arrival of one of the trains from Kansas City. Kate left here at 3 p. m. Kate is slender built; light brown hair; waterproof suit lined with red; has with her one large bull-dog in express car; also one small yellow lap dog; she will probably arrive by Missouri Pacific. A. A. Becker is an assumed name; is stopping at the Laclede hotel.   C. H. HALLETT,
Deputy United States Marshal.

Two days afterward another dispatch was received from Wm. Smith, sheriff of Sedgwick county, Kansas [Smith had been defeated for sheriff on November 4, 1873, and on January 1, 1874, turned the office over to the successful candidate, Pleasant H. Massey], asking if Low had been arrested, and on January 5th, still another came, as follows:

LEAVENWORTH, January 5th.
Is Low still in your custody? Answer quick. If so, I will be down on the next train.   WM. SMITH, Sheriff.

And yesterday morning, in answer to the telegram announcing the arrest of Lowe, a dispatch was received from Smith, stating that he would be down on the next train, and asking the Chief to hold the prisoner until his arrival.

When Low was arrested, the snug sum of $8,295 was found on him. He passed under the assumed name of A. A. Becker, and was having a gay time with the boys.

Yesterday morning Mr. R. S. MacDonald and Kate Low, the prisoner's wife, called on Chief McDonough and had a conference, which resulted in the chief sending a note to Mr. A. W. Mead, the attorney of the board, asking whether the money found in Low's possession could be turned over to his wife. Mr. Mead answered that if he was not arrested on a charge which involved the money, such as larceny, it could be turned over on an order from Low. The money was accordingly given to Mrs. Low. The next step was to secure Low's release before the arrival of the sheriff, and MacDonald proceeded at once to the court of criminal correction and took advantage of the "great writ of habeas corpus."

In the petition it was claimed that Low "is now unlawfully and illegally restrained of his liberty by one Capt. James McDonough, chief of police; that no warrant or criminal process has been issued against him; that he is [not] guilty of the violation of any law of the state; that he was arrested by order of said McDonough, illegally, and is in the custody and control of said McDonough, and is held by said McDonough in confinement against his will and consent; that there are no papers or process against him, and that his imprisonment was unlawful and unjust.

Judge Colvin ordered the writ issued, and it was immediately delivered to the Chief, who made the following return thereon:

"Executed the within writ, by delivering the within mentioned Joseph Low to the St. Louis court of criminal correction, this 5th day of January, 1874.
JAMES McDONOUGH,
"Chief of Police."

Low was then taken before Judge Colvin by Detective Duckworth and Tracy. The Judge asked Duckworth if that was all the return there was to

270

be made, and was answered that there were some telegrams. The chief however, was willing to have the man released, but the detectives wanted him held until the sheriff arrived. Judge Colvin said he would recognize only the Chief, and told Duckworth to go and ascertain if that was all the returns to be made. "Duck" soon returned with a note to the judge, saying that the only authority he had for holding the man was the above telegrams, which he forwarded for the judge's inspection and enlightenment. Judge Colvin was in a quandery after reading them, and in a very hasty manner told the detective that he might have kept the writ back twenty-four hours if he wanted to, and knew the sheriff was coming for his prisoner. "Duck" replied that he did not answer the writ.

Mr. McDonald moved that the prisoner be discharged, which was accordingly done, and Low, with several friends, rapidly disappeared from the court, entered a carriage and drove swiftly away.

There were many comments on the case made, and several parties were so rash as to hint that some one in authority received a portion of the small change that Mrs. Low received—a most preposterous idea!

Low is said to have escaped from jail, where he was confined on a charge of murder.[6]

By October, 1874, Joe was in Denison, Tex. A correspondent of the Wichita *Beacon* reported in that paper October 14, 1874:

FROM TEXAS.

"ROWDY JOE."

CORRESPONDENCE OF THE BEACON. MARSHALL, TEX., Oct. 1, 1874.

ED. BEACON.—I left the beautiful little city of Wichita a few weeks ago, and my inclinations and business led me towards the "Lone Star State." A trip down over the M. K. & T. R. R. from Emporia to Denison, Texas, is not an unpleasant one. . . .

Denison is purely a frontier town and one need only to walk up one street to be convinced of the fact. . . . Farmers coming in with cotton, and the usual number of loafers and gamblers standing on the corner, among whom might be seen "Rowdy Joe" of West Wichita fame. . . .

Later in the year Rowdy Joe supposedly was one of the early gold hunters in the Black Hills region of Dakota territory, and it was reported that he had been killed by Indians. The *Eagle* published the story October 29, 1874:

ROWDY JOE MURDERED.

Mayor [James G.] Hope received a letter from J. W. Brockett, now at Yankton, containing the information that Rowdy Joe, alias Joseph Lowe, so well known at Wichita, was with the party which was enroute for the Black Hills, and which was attacked by Indians and a portion of its number killed. The notorious Rowdy Joe fell first mortally wounded. We last week published an account of the attack, but the dispatches had his name John Lowe, instead of Joe. Thus this violent man met a violent death. Several of his victims are taking their last long sleep beneath the prairie sod of this border. Anderson, another, is here in Wichita, totally blind; Walter Beebe, who helped Lowe to escape the officers of the law at this place, is in the penitentiary, and Josephine Demerit keeps Beebe company. What a list of crimes Joe has gone to answer for.

Mayor Hope handed us an account of the attack clipped from a Yankton paper, from which we make the following extract:

"Of the Yankton company, Lowe was instantly killed three bullets piercing his body from a volley fired at the tent; Chas. Allen was wounded in the leg by an arrow; Baden was shot through the chest, probably fatally, while Orton received a flesh wound in the arm. The Indians then retreated from the field, when the Yanktonians put the body of Lowe, together with wounded man, Baden, into their wagon, and turning their faces homeward, traveled all night, leaving Mr. Baden at the Bohemian settlement and burying Mr. Lowe a few miles further east near a soldier camp, occupied by a detachment sent out from Randall to guard the settlers. The survivors arrived at Yankton on Thursday night. Their wagon bears unmistakable evidences of the bloody fight the party had with the Indians, being completely riddled with bullets and covered with the gore of their wounded and dead comrades, for it acted the part of a fortification behind which the boys concealed themselves as best they could during the time they were besieged. The survivors of this expedition will most likely give up opening a stock farm in that portion of Nebraska lately visited by them."

Regardless of his "death," mentions of Joe in San Antonio, Tex., appeared occasionally during the next few months. On March 31, 1875, the Wichita *Beacon* carried a correspondent's letter which said: "Col. Mrs. [Leo?] Sage is keeping a cigar store at San Antonio. Col. Rowdy Joe and Rowdy Kate are also there." Two months later, May 26, 1875, the *Beacon* reported a rift in the marital relations of the Rowdies:

The following, which we clip from the San Antonio (Tex.) daily *Herald*, may be of interest to the numerous friends of "Rowdy Joe:"

Mr. Joseph Lowe was found guilty of assaulting Kate Lowe yesterday afternoon and fined $100. A motion for a new trial was over-ruled, and notice of appeal given. The alleged cause for the offense was inconstancy.

In 1899 the Wichita *Eagle* again reported that Rowdy Joe Lowe had been killed, this time in a Denver saloon. Lowe, then 72 according to the paper, insulted the Denver police department and was shot by a former policeman.[7]

Thus the reader has a choice of endings for the character known as Rowdy Joe.

1. Wichita City *Eagle*, June 28, 1872. 2. *Ibid.*, November 27, 1873. 3. "State of Kansas vs. Joseph Lowe," Case Records of the Sedgwick County District Court. 4. Wichita City *Eagle*, December 25, 1873. 5. *Ibid.*, January 8, 1874. 6. *Ibid.*, January 15, 1874. 7. *Ibid.*, February 15, 1899.

McCARTY, HARRY T. (____-1878)

Harry T. McCarty, surveyor and draftsman, was appointed deputy United States marshal for Ford county (Dodge City) in April, 1878. The *Ford County Globe*, April 30, reported his commission:

DEPUTY U. S. MARSHALSHIP.

Our active, energetic fellow-citizen, H. T. McCarty, who is known to every man, woman and child in Ford County, has received his commission as Deputy U. S. Marshal, under U. S. Marshal [Benjamin F.] Simpson.

When we say that the appointment gives good satisfaction to our farmers and a large majority of our business men, we simply tell the truth. There are, of course, some who may not like his appointment, but by inquiry they will be found to be, either violaters of the U. S. laws themselves, or personal enemies of Mr. McCarty.

We know that no other man in the County is so well fitted and qualified for the position as he is; because of his unlimited information concerning the violations of laws which take place in this county, and his desire to stop them.

We are greatly pleased that such a judicious choice has been made by Mr. Simpson, and predict a faithful performance of duty, "according to Hoyle," by Deputy Marshal McCarty.

Harry McCarty served less than three months. On July 13, 1878, he was shot and killed. His tragic murder was first described in the Dodge City *Times*, July 13:

ANOTHER MURDER.
H. T. McCARTY COWARDLY ASSASSINATED.
THE MURDERED MAN'S OWN PISTOL THE DEADLY WEAPON.

H. T. McCarty, a well-known citizen of Dodge City, was shot this morning about 4 o'clock, at the Long Branch saloon. The shot took effect in the right groin, severing the femoral artery; and the unfortunate man, after profusely bleeding for about an hour, expired.

The circumstances of the shooting are about as follows: A party of men were ridiculing one of their number, one Thomas Roach, a half-witted, rattle-brained and quarrelsome wretch, who, becoming incensed at the jibes and jeers of the crowd, rushed to where McCarty stood at the bar, and drawing McCarty's pistol from the latter's side, flourished it once or twice and fired one shot, which took effect as we have stated. McCarty was quietly standing at the bar drinking, and was in no manner connected with the hilarious crowd. A pistol shot was fired at the murderer, Tom Roach, which grazed him, though he fell to the floor, pretending to be dead, which prevented a bystander from repeating the shot upon being informed that the murderer of McCarty was already dead.

McCarty was removed to the house of Chas. Ronan, where in about an hour he died, having bled to death. The murderer was arrested and placed in jail.

A coroner's inquest was held this morning and the facts were elicited about as we have stated.

There is a good deal of indignation manifested over this brutal, unwarranted murder; and while it may appear in the present temper of a large class of people that law's delays and uncertainties are dangerous to the peace, life and protection of the community, we hope the sober, second thought will prevail and justice take its course.

Limping Tom, the prisoner, as he is familiarly known, was a cook in the camp of Shiner Bros. He was once led out of town last night and bid his way to camp, the party knowing Tom's querulous nature when under the influence of liquor. He has been living in this section of Kansas since last fall, and is generally unknown.

The deceased, H. T. McCarty, was an old resident of the border and for several years a resident of Dodge City. He was well-known in this section of Kansas.

He held the office of Surveyor of Ford county for two years, and followed the occupation of surveying and painting. The deceased was a man of warm, genial nature, and though he made strong friends he had bitter enemies. He was a man of excellent attainments, though of rude culture; a forcible writer, and an artist and painter of no mean merit. While possessing virtues he had faults; but the kindlier nature takes hold of these people as the soul of the deceased is wafted to another sphere. His faults are buried with the body, and the virtues only hold in the affections and sympathy of the kind and generous people of Dodge City.

The funeral of the deceased McCarty takes place this afternoon at 4 o'clock under the auspices of the Dodge City Fire Company, of which company the deceased was a member.

The *Ford County Globe* reported the shooting in its issue of July 16:

ASSASSINATION.
A DEPUTY U. S. MARSHAL FOULLY MURDERED.
THE ASSASSIN UNDER ARREST.

Saturday at 3:30 A. M., two pistol shots fired in quick succession were heard issuing from the "Long Branch" saloon, the first of which it was soon found had summoned the genial, warm-hearted Harry T. McCarty, ex-county surveyor and Deputy U. S. Marshal for Ford county, from this world to another. The circumstances seem as follows: "Mack" had just came up the street and stepped into the "Long Branch;" while leaning on the counter talking to Mr. Jackson, a half drunken desperado named Thomas Roach snatched "Mack's" pistol (a 45 caliber Colt) from the scabbard, and as "Mack" turned to see who had so nimbly disarmed him, the assassin, giving the weapon a flourish or two, fired the fatal shot. The ball penetrated the right groin severing the femoral artery, thence passing through the thigh lodged in the floor. The deceased staggered toward the door where he fell—another shot was almost instantaneously fired at Roach by a bystander, the ball grazing his right side. Roach falling called

274

out "I am shot," and dropped to the floor, thus saving himself from the immediate penalty of his crime from the leveled revolvers about him. In the meantime medical assistance had been promptly summoned to the aid of his unfortunate victim, but it was soon found that he had passed that point when human aid however skilled could be of assistance. He was removed to the rooms of Charles Ronan to breath his last in a few minutes, recovering consciousness but for a brief period of time.

Even a stranger, unfamiliar with the circumstances, would have known as he passed up the streets an hour later that some sad tragedy had been enacted, by the air of gloom that pervaded every countenance, and the groups gathered upon the corners, some with minds too much occupied with the calamity to indulge in conversation, others in whispers that portended mischief, discussing the propriety of obviating the delays attendant upon legal process, and giving immediate illustration to the saying of our Savior, "Whoever sheds man's blood by man shall his blood be shed." But to the credit of Dodge City be it spoken, that the better counsel prevailed and even in the moment of excitement she determined to put herself on record as willing to submit to the law.

An inquest was held in the forenoon and a verdict rendered in accordance with the facts, and in the afternoon as quietly as possible (it being the desire of the officers to prevent anything that could tend to excite the already agitated crowd) an examination was held before R. G. Cook, Esq., at which time the prisoner was charged with murder in the first degree. Upon being brought up the charge was read to him, and he was fully instructed as to his rights, etc., by M. W. Sutton, County Attorney, and upon expressing it as his wish to waive an examination, he was recommitted to await trial at the next term of court.

Early in the forenoon the Dodge City fire company, of which deceased had been an active member since its organization, began to take the necessary steps to show their respect for the deceased. The hall was tastefully draped in mourning and the flag hung suspended at half mast. After services by Rev. O. W. Wright, at 4 P. M., the procession left the hall headed by the band, with Judge H. E. Gryden, M. W. Sutton, Dr. S. Galland, J. J. Webb, G. F. Jones and Marshal C. E. Bassett as pall bearers, followed by the entire company in uniform and a large concourse of citizens in carriages. The procession moved through the principal streets, the pavements being thronged with spectators gazing at the solemn cortege.

At the grave a short address was delivered by the Rev. Mr. Wright, and all that was mortal of Harry T. McCarty was mingled with the dust.

Immediately on the return of the fire company they assembled at their hall when a short address was delivered by Marshal [P. L.] Beatty followed by Judge H. E. Gryden who spoke in eulogistic terms of the deceased and offered the following resolutions which were passed and ordered to be printed in the "GLOBE" and "Times" and the secretary ordered to furnish copies of proceedings to relatives of deceased.

WHEREAS, In His mercy it has pleased the Father of all to, by the hands of an assassin, take from us our fellow citizen and brother fireman, HARRY T. McCARTY,

Resolved, That we deeply feel the loss, not only of an efficient fireman and true brother, but of one whose superior qualities of head and heart have ever commanded our love and esteem.

Resolved, That we tender our heartfelt sympathies to the relatives of the deceased, and especially to his aged mother, assuring her and them that the sudden and unjustifiable assassination of the deceased has cast a shadow and gloom over our entire community, and that, though many winters' snow may spread its cold covering over the place where his ashes lie mingled with the dust, and though the green grass of his prairie grave be as often sered by the frosts of autumn, while life lasts the memory of HARRY T. McCARTY will be ever fresh and green in our hearts of affection.

Resolved, That in honor of our dead brother the members of the Dodge City Fire Company will wear the usual badge of mourning for thirty days.

Thus all that was mortal of the third of the gallant little band of Dodge City Firemen, killed by the hand of the assassin, was consigned to Mother Earth. Let us hope that it will be the last. In the years to come when the silvery hairs of the few remaining charter members will be warning them of the grave, they will ever remember with love and respect their early companions, Masterson [City Marshal Edward J. Masterson, killed by drunken cowboys on April 9, 1878] and McCarty, and as the blossoms of spring peep from the prairies they will, we doubt not, long to strew garlands, bedecked with tears, upon their untimely graves.

Thomas O'Haran, alias Thomas Roach, was tried at the January, 1879, term of the Ford county district court, Judge S. R. Peters presiding. O'Haran plead guilty to manslaughter in the first degree and was sentenced to 12 years and three months in the state penitentiary, the Dodge City *Times* reported, February 1, 1879.

MASON, JOSEPH W. (1842?-____)

Joe Mason, a former scout and one of the "old timers" of Dodge City, was appointed policeman on the Dodge force May 9, 1877. Lawrence E. Deger was marshal and in June Ed Masterson became assistant. All three officers earned $75 a month salary.[1]

The Dodge City *Times*, May 12, 1877, said of the new officer: "Joe Mason was appointed policeman by Mayor [James H.] Kelley and confirmed by the Council this week. Joe is a quiet young man who attends strictly to his own business, but will not fail to 'go to the joint' in case of a row. He will make a good officer."

Two days after he was appointed Joe Mason stopped a cruel and bloody game of "lap jacket." The *Times*, May 12, 1877, reported:

We yesterday witnessed an exhibition of the African national game of "lap jacket," in front of Shulz' harness shop. The game is played by two colored men, who each toe a mark and whip each other with bullwhips. In the contest yesterday Henry Rodgers, called Eph for short, contended with another darkey for the championship and fifty cents prize money. They took heavy new whips from the harness shop and poured in the strokes pretty lively. Blood flowed and dust flew and the crowd cheered until Policeman Joe Mason came along and suspended the cheerful exercise.

In Africa, where this pleasant pastime is indulged in to perfection, the contestants strip to the skin, and frequently cut each other's flesh open to the bone.

On June 6, 1877, Policeman Mason helped subdue Bat Masterson who had "wound his arm affectionately around the Marshal's [Deger's] neck and let . . . [his] prisoner escape." Bat had objected to Deger's manner of taking Bobby Gill to jail. The article reporting this incident appears in the section on W. B. Masterson.

"The new policemen, Ed Masterson and Joe Mason, are covering themselves with glory, and their prompt and efficient action cannot be too highly commended," said the Dodge City *Times*, June 16, 1877.

Joe Mason stopped another fight a few days later, this time between "ladies," according to the *Times* of June 23, 1877:

THE JOINT.

A BATTLE OF THE BEAUTIES.

Presto Change! Josie Armstrong wears the belt. Now you wouldn't think to look at Miss Josie—a very pink of feminine symetry and grace—that she would buckle on her armor and go into the shoulder hitting business. But there are times when occasion demands great effort, and such a time always arrives with a woman when she falls in with the evidences of an intruding rival.

Last monday [June 18] Josie happened upon evidence of this kind. She didn't seize the weapon of her sex—broomstick—but she rolled up her delicate sleeves, and hand in hand with the green eyed monster, marched on to victory. (Here, were it not for the clamours of a curious public, we would gladly drop the curtain, for there is something about human carnage and the flow of human blood that harrows up our soul.)

In the fight that ensued there was a display of the most remarkable activity. The combatants unanimously waived the established rules of the London P. R. and fell to pulling hair and kicking shins in a way that will live in the minds of the bystanders long after the noble piles of architecture that surrounded the battle field have fallen into decay.

Just as the combat deepened and the prospect for two bald-headed maidens was bright, the irrepressible Joe Mason, regardless of the fact that

"Those who in quarrels interpose
Must often wipe a bloody nose,"

sallied in and restored the peace and dignity of the city. A similar display of muscular activity has never before been known in this community.

Such is the brief story of the combat, and thus is added to immortality two more Maids of Orleans.

On September 8, 1877, the *Times* stated that "Policeman Mason made six arrests this week." And on September 15: "Policeman Mason was this week presented with a magnificent air gun which opens with a padlock. Mr. Mix has it on exhibition at the Long Branch."

Also on September 15, 1877, the *Times* facetiously told of Joe's not too tranquil love life:

SHE LOVED NOT WISELY BUT TOO WELL
—TOTAL COST, $39.50.

"There are some hearts that like the tender vine
Cling to unkindly rocks and ruined towers,
Spirits that suffer, but do not repine,
Loving and sweet; like lowly trodden flowers
That 'neath the passer's heel arise,
And give back oderous breath instead of sighs."

But Mattie was not that kind of flower; her heart it is true had twined its fragile tendrils 'round the Apollo of Dodge, had bowed before the lavishness of his raven-winged moustache, his glittering police star and his immaculate top-boots, and, though he frequently would thin out her hair and adorn her eyes in the shadows of mourning, she still doted on the idol of her young love; her daring Joe.

But, there came a woman in the case, another woman, that is—a lovely, buxom grass widow from a little hamlet called Wichita. She was the latest arrival, and though not the youngest, she was "the loveliest of them all." It is the old, old story, fickle and perfidious man, cruel and heartless Joseph.

"He saw the widow's face more fair,
He liked the color of her hair,
Forgot his vows, his faith forswore,
And red-head Mat was loved no more."

They did not jump over a broomstick and thus become bone of one bone in the manner of the Highland lad and lassie of "auld lang syne," but they took unto themselves seven straights and a gin sling, which is according to the Dodge City creed, a sufficient abundancy for practical purposes.

All this transpired a week ago, and Mattie has of course dangled on the ragged edge of despair since that eventful night. Last Tuesday was her birthday; it was sweet sixteen (since she became 21) and she celebrated it by language implicating the moral conduct of the ancestors of our police force, particularly our Joe. She also used epithets both frequent and painful and free to and of "the widow," and was finally landed in the dog house by the

278

self same Joe, on whose manly bosom her head was wont to rest in innocent slumbers.

When Mat found herself in this unhallowed place, she

> "At once set up so wild a yell,
> Within that dark and narrow cell,
> As all the fiends from Heaven that fell
> Had peal'd the banner cry of Hell."

—And all for Joe!

The patrol at the Fort "turned out the guard," thinking the Indians were scalping the innocents. And the terrible Judge, who was basking in her smiles, a mile or more away, was cut short in his recitation of "Maid of Athens 'ere we part," and fled for the scene of carnage.

Wednesday morning brought Mattie before his Honor, Mr. Morphy appearing for the defendant and the City Attorney contrara. The case was hotly contested by the legal gladiators, but the steel had entered the Judge's soul and he made it $25 and costs—no moral lecture. The requisite $39.50 was "russeled" by friends and at 10 P. M. Mattie was again

> "A free and foolish Irish girl
> Just turned of sweet sixteen."

Policeman Mason tried to arrest the sheriff of Edwards county, not recognizing that gentleman when he arrived in Dodge on September 17 and mistaking him for a member of a gang of swindlers who had been operating in Dodge. The *Times* article reporting this is presented in the section on W. B. Masterson.

The city council of Dodge City discharged Mason from the police force on October 2, giving as the reason "that his services would no longer be required." [2] By October 13 Joe had become bartender of the Long Branch saloon. He left the Long Branch before November 24 and started working for one Russell; by December 1 he was again a police officer, this time a deputy sheriff under Charles E. Bassett. A week later, however, Mason was on his way to Sweetwater, Tex., with several other Dodgeites intending to open a saloon there. [3]

It was in Sweetwater that Mason shot and killed Ed Ryan. The Dodge City *Times*, January 12, 1878, reported:

A FATAL SHOT.

AN EX-DODGE CITY POLICEMAN KILLS HIS MAN.

ED. RYAN, A WELL KNOWN SPORTING MAN, THE VICTIM.

Last evening about dusk the overland stage from the south brought a letter from Sweetwater, Texas, in which the following paragraph appeared:

"Jo. Mason shot Ed. Ryan yesterday. He will be buried to-day. Jo. is willing to give himself up. Ed. was here three days before he was killed."

Mr. Reynolds, the mail contractor, confirms the news.

Jo. Mason is well known here, having served on the police force nearly all last summer. He never bore the reputation of being a "killer," and we believe this is the first time the click of his revolver has been the signal for a fatal shot.

Ed. Ryan was in Dodge City nearly all last Summer, and like many others in the wild frontier, followed that artistic and exciting profession, of which four aces is the highest accomplishment. Ed. Ryan was a very large, stout man, not over thirty years of age, and seemed to be of a good natured disposition when sober.

At one time last summer, while Mason was on the police force, the two men had a very bitter quarrel, which would have probably resulted seriously had not third parties interfered.

In the next edition, January 19, the *Times* gave some additional information:

CAMP SUPPLY.

CAMP SUPPLY, I. T., Jan. 13, 1878.

To THE EDITORS OF THE TIMES.

. . . News reached us this evening from Fort Elliott that Joe Mason formerly of Dodge City shot and killed a man at that post a week ago. Joe it seems is connected with a free-and-easy kind of a house at Sweetwater City, and at the time one of his old friends, a hunter, who it seems Joe had arrested while an official at Dodge, came up to him and commenced abusing him, and threatened that he would some day square accounts with him. Joe stood it for awhile and then gave the fellow the alternative of lighting out or a ball through his skull. It seems the fellow chose the latter for Joe fired and the bold hunter fell. Joe went out dug a hole six by two and placed his victim therein. Joe with his girl is on his way to Dodge City.

THE MASON-RYAN SHOOTING.

Joe Mason arrived in Dodge City yesterday. The following is a copy of the proceedings of a court of inquiry, which exonerates Mason, held at Sweetwater:

Proceedings of a Board of Officers convened at Fort Elliott, Texas, by virtue of the following order.

HEADQUARTERS FORT ELLIOTT, TEXAS,
January 5, 1878.

SPECIAL ORDERS, No. 4.

A Board of Officers to consist of Capt C Mauck 4th Cav, Capt E H Liscum, 19th Inf, and 2d Lt G K Hunter, 4th Cav, will convene at once to inquire into and report upon the killing of one Ed Ryan by Jos Mason, in the town of Sweetwater, last evening the 4th inst. The Board will make a report in writing on the merits of the case.

By order of Lt Col J P Hatch.

(Signed) THEO H ECKERSON
2d Lt   19th Inf, Post Adjutant.

FORT ELLIOTT, TEXAS, Jan 5, 1878.

The Board met pursuant to the foregoing order at 2.30 o'clock P M. Present, Capt C Mauck, 4th Cav, Capt E H Liscum, 19th Inf, and 2d Lt G K Hunter, 4th Cav.

The Board then proceeded to the examination of the following named witnesses. Tim Leavy, Harry Fleming, Granger Dyer, W H Weed, David Remington, Arrington, Norton and Dr. LaGarde. The Board after mature deliberation arrived at the following conclusion. That Ed Ryan came to his death from a gun shot wound at the hands of Jos Mason, and that the said Jos Mason was justifiable in the premises. There being no further business before it the board then adjourned sine die.

C MAUCK, Capt 4th Cav,
E H LISCUM, Capt 19th Inf.
GEO K HUNTEY, 2d Lt 4th Cav, Recorder.

HD QTS, FORT ELLIOTT, Jan 10, 1878.

The foregoing proceedings are approved.

JNO P HATCH,
Lt Col 4th Cav, Commanding.

Apparently feeling that his Dodge City friends would not think well of him, Mason wrote this note to the *Times* which was published on January 26:

TO THE EDITORS OF THE TIMES.

In your issue of January 19th I find among the items from your correspondent at Camp Supply, a description of the unfortunate shooting at Ft. Elliott some days ago. I only wish to say that your correspondent has misrepresented me. I was in no way connected with a "free-and-easy" at Sweetwater, nor did I "dig a hole and place the victim therein."

J. W. MASON.

The *Ford County Globe*, January 22, 1878, merely stated: "Joe Mason has returned from Elliott, he looks well and says he intends remaining in the city."

This epilogue appeared in the *Globe*, February 12, 1878: "Joe Mason received a letter yesterday morning, from Sioux city, Nebraska, containing a photograph of Ed Ryan, telling him that if the photo represented the man he killed he is entitled to the thanks of Sioux city."

Mason was temporarily reappointed to the Dodge City police force in April, 1878,[4] but no record was found of the length or effectiveness of his service.

In June he assisted Sheriff Bat Masterson in guarding some prisoners and on July 1 the board of county commissioners allowed him $18 for his services.[5]

The last mention found of Joe Mason in the Dodge City papers appeared in the *Ford County Globe,* May 17, 1881: "Joseph Mason, an old frontiersman and former police officer of Dodge City, after an absence from this place for over a year returned to the city Saturday last with a view of making this his permanent home."

1. "Kansas State Census," 1875, Ford county, p. 11; Dodge City *Times,* May 12, June 9, July 7, August 11, September 8, October 6, 1877. 2. Dodge City *Times,* October 6, 1877. 3. *Ibid.,* October 13, November 24, December 1, 8, 1877. 4. *Ibid.,* April 13, 1878. 5. *Ibid.,* June 15, July 6, 1878.

MASSEY, PLEASANT H. (1823-1919)

The Republicans of Sedgwick county, at a convention held in Wichita October 4, 1873, nominated P. H. Massey for sheriff. Massey, then a 50-year-old farmer, received the support of Wichita *Eagle* editor Marsh Murdock, who said of him:

PLEASANT H. MASSEY,

the nominee for sheriff, is an old resident of South Bend, Indiana, a Colfax Republican of many years standing. He has never voted any other ticket since the organization of the party. He served three years as deputy sheriff in that populous county. He is a farmer living in Ninesha township   was brought up a Whig. Mr. Massey is a pleasant gentleman, full of earnestness and life. From letters that we have been permitted to read we know that he must have stood well at his old home. He has been a resident of this county for three years and commands the respect of all who know him—and will be elected without a doubt.[1]

Massey's chief opponent was incumbent William Smith, a former Wichita city marshal and deputy sheriff who had been appointed in September, 1873, to fill the vacancy created by the resignation of Sheriff John Meagher.[2]

At the November 4 election Massey won handily over Smith and D. L. Green, a third candidate. The sheriff-elect received 665 votes, Smith 599, and Green 167.[3]

When the district court was scheduled to open in December, 1873, Massey, being the sheriff-elect, felt it was his duty rather than the duty of appointee Smith to announce the opening of the session. The *Eagle,* December 11, 1873, reported this controversy:

The district court opened Monday noon [December 8], with Judge W. P. Campbell on the bench. Preceeding the formal command for the sheriff to announce the opening, Mr. Stanley submitted the matter of difference between

Sheriff Smith, the appointee, and Sheriff Massey, elect. Mr. Balderston appeared on behalf of Sheriff Smith. It appeared that Mr. Massey had duly qualified, and his bonds having been approved by the commissioners, he claimed that under the law he was entitled to and that it became incumbent upon to assume the active duties of the office. The judge said that in chambers he had no power to adjudicate any such matter; that he should recognize as the officer of his court the individual who had the possession of the books and papers pertaining to said office of sheriff, and that after the court had regularly opened he would be ready to hear any matter brought before him in proper form in the regular practice. Mr. Smith opened the court, and so the matter stands at present.

The office was officially turned over to Massey on January 1, 1874. Said the *Eagle*, January 8: "Sheriff Smith delivered, on New Year's day, to Sheriff P. H. Massey the books and papers pertaining to the office of sheriff, and now friend Pleasant may be heard crying from an upper window, 'hear ye! hear ye!' etc."

Shortly before Massey was sworn into office, Wichita was shocked by an incendiary murder which the *Eagle* termed the "Christmas Cremation." Since Massey was only indirectly involved the complete story of the murder and the subsequent activity in capturing and trying the perpetrators is presented in the section on Mike Meagher, who was city marshal at the time.

Massey's primary concern with the case was in holding the prisoners before the trial and in acting as an officer of the court during the hearing. On March 5, 1874, the *Eagle* reported that "Sheriff Massey took McNutt and his wife [two of the accused murderers] to Topeka for safe keeping." Arthur Winner, the third accused killer, was being kept in Cottonwood Falls.

By May 17, 1874, the McNutts and Winner were brought back to Wichita for their trial. The two male defendants were placed in the sheriff's office, next door to the *Eagle* printing plant, and were not only chained to each other but also at night were chained to iron rings bolted to the sheriff's floor.[4] In spite of this security, Winner was able to give the sheriff some anxious moments. The Wichita *Eagle*, May 21, 1874, reported one incident:

Winner, who is chained to McNutt, both of whom have been for some days confined in the sheriff's office, adjoining that of our own, is as nochalant, gay and independent as he was during the preliminary examination last Christmas. Nothing appears to depress his spirits. On Sunday he constructed a key out of a pen point with which he unlocked his shackles, and laughingly exhibited the result of his feat to the sheriff, which officer then riveted his shackles.

On Monday one of the guards discovered him trying to part the rivets with a pocket knife. The fact being reported to Sheriff Massey, that officer attempted to search him and take away the knife, whereupon the wiry little fellow took it into his head to kick up a resistance. The noise and confusion made by the sheriff in taking the young man down startled us, and we rushed around to the door to find it locked. Treasurer Johnson came rushing up the hall with a cocked revolver in his hand, and Kellogg, Little and Phillips came puffing out of their offices, and for a moment the tableau was at least interesting, if not exciting.

A call from us, asking if help was desired, elicited no answer, but Nessley opened the door, when we found the sheriff holding in his iron grip the prostrate prisoner; who was wagging his tongue at a lively rate, declaring that it would take three such men to handle him if he had a show. He was mancled still more closely, when he cooled down and all was again serene. The rest of the prisoners sat around, appearing to enjoy the excitement. Winner asked us before we left to give the facts, and we guess we have. He is rather an odd boy, aggressive and fearless, and withal of a light and cheerful disposition.

Sheriff Massey opened the district court, May 18, and the trial of the murderers commenced May 21.[5] Apparently such a crowd was expected that certain alterations had to be made in the court room. The *Eagle*, May 21, 1874, reported: "Sheriff Massey has had a temporary railing put up in the court room, the court, its officers, jurymen and witnesses occupying one side and the spectators the other. Good idea."

Finding unprejudiced jurors was a difficult task for the sheriff. Editor Murdock felt it was a tribute to the *Eagle's* popularity in Sedgwick county:

Sheriff Massey and deputies, are out hunting fifty more men, qualified to sit on the trial of McNutt. The sheriff says when he finds a man in a lonely out of the way place, he asks the question, "do you read the EAGLE?" when if the answer is in the negative, he draws his papers on him, in the full assurance that another juryman has been found. He says he found one such man within four miles of the city—the fellow couldn't read at all.[6]

A jury was finally assembled with the result that both Winner and McNutt were sentenced to hang. Later their sentences were commuted to life.

While the Christmas cremation trial was in progress, a Texas cowboy named Ramsey shot and killed a Negro hod carrier, Charley Sanders. The article reporting this, May 28, 1874, is included in the section on William Smith. Ramsey had not been captured by July 23, 1874, when the *Eagle* reported a false lead:

Sheriff Massey is bound to catch the desperado that shot the colored man last spring. He heard that the outlaw was at Coffeyville last week and the next train of cars found him *en route* to trap the bird, which he successfully did, and in spite of a partial issued *habeas corpus*, brought him in irons to Wichita, but it proved to be a different rooster and he was released. We hope our officers will leave no stone unturned to bring the murderer to trial.

In August a man by the name of James Long stole a horse from a Wichita stable and headed east. Massey, learning that he had been in Fort Scott, left for that place. The *Eagle*, August 13, 1874, said: "Sheriff Massey has gone to Ft. Scott to accompany a man by the name of Long back to this place, Long having borrowed a horse at the diamond front stable which he forgot to return."

Long hoodwinked the citizens of Fort Scott and journeyed on into Missouri where he was finally caught. The Fort Scott *Daily Monitor*, August 18, 1874, reported Long's abilities as a confidence man:

HORSE THIEF CAUGHT.

About three weeks ago a man giving his name as Long, from Sumner county, arrived in our city and asked Mr. Tannehill to lend him some money, stating that he was after a horse thief, had run out of money and wished to proceed. Mr. T., having heard of the horses being stolen, took it for granted that it was all right and advanced the amount desired. It turned out, however, that Long was the horse thief and took this method of avoiding suspicion. Mr. Tannehill and Constable Avery started in pursuit and overtook him at Springfield, Mo., with three horses, and they are now awaiting a requisition from the Governor to bring him here.

Horse stealing is getting to be a dangerous business. In most every instance the thief is caught, and in many cases the punishment is swift and terrible.

While Massey chased Long over two states, his son acted as sheriff in his father's absence: "Sheriff Massey is still absent, and Tence, his son and deputy sheriff, has his hands full. He was detained in Jefferson City by a telegram from the Governor." [7]

On August 27, 1874, the *Eagle* reported that Sheriff Massey had returned with a prisoner. It is apparent that the captive was not the horse thief so eagerly sought but was rather someone who unfortunately remains unknown: "Sheriff Massey returned Saturday night with one prisoner, but he took the next eastern bound train for Springfield, Missouri, after Long, the man who hired a horse at the livery stable and forgot to come back."

The Fort Scott *Monitor*, August 28, 1874, reported that "Constable Avery has returned from Springfield, Mo., bringing with him the horse thieves which he arrested at that place a week or more ago.

They are in durance vile to await their trial at the next term of court."

Perhaps the Sedgwick county charge of horse stealing carried more weight than the Bourbon county charge of monetary theft for the sheriff soon showed up in Wichita with the two horse thieves: "Sheriff Massey came home from Springfield, Mo., last week with two prisoners charged with horse stealing," said the Wichita *Weekly Beacon,* September 2, 1874. The identity of the second thief is not definitely known but he may have been young Bill Wright who was convicted for pony stealing in October, 1874.

The next day, September 3, 1874, the *Eagle* complimented the sheriff and his son:

Sheriff Massey seldom if ever fails to get his man when he goes for him. He returned a few days since with Long, who will have justice meeted out to him we trust.

Sheriff Massey, who for the past three weeks has been continuously on the track of criminals in this and other states is again at home. Our boy, Tence, as deputy makes a splendid officer. He is prompt, affective and makes no mistakes.

The travels of Pleasant H. Massey were not yet over. On September 4, 1874, the sheriff headed back for Missouri:

Sheriff Massey, George Fessenden, D. M. V. Stewart and Jackson Bolend, will start to Jefferson City, Mo., on Friday to testify in the case of Dr. W. F. Bowie, before the United States District Court. Bowie was merchandising at Sedalia, Mo., went into bankruptcy, forfeited a bond of $15,000, and is now charged with perjury. His trial is set for the 7th of this month.[8]

Later in the month he visited the state penitentiary:

Sheriff Massey returned yesterday [September 30] from the state penitentiary, where he had delivered three prisoners convicted at the last term of court, viz: J. H. Hill, for two years for shooting Stewart, on the Ninnescah, last spring; James Long, for three years, for stealing a horse; Wm. Wright, a boy, for one year, for stealing a pony. The criminal docket was not entirely cleared up for want of time. Two prisoners yet remain in the sheriff's custody.[9]

About the beginning of Massey's second year as sheriff, the new Sedgwick county jail was finished. The jail was designed to house not only county prisoners but also the sheriff. The living section of the building was one of the most modern in town for it boasted a furnace *and* running water. Massey moved into his new quarters about the end of January, 1875. The *Eagle,* January 28, reported:

286

Sheriff Massey has moved his family into the city. His new home, the resident portion of the new jail, is one of the most complete and comfortable establishments, heated, as it is, by a furnace and supplied with soft water from an up-stairs tank.

A month later the sheriff celebrated his 52d birthday in his new home. The *Eagle*, February 25, 1875, reported the success of the surprise party:

Sheriff Massey's fifty-second birthday, the 22d, was the occasion of a feast and old fashioned frolic tendered him by his good wife, who made all the arrangements and done the inviting. In the evening the house of sheriff Massey was invaded by a hilarious surprise party consisting of young folks, who kept things lively until well nigh unto morning, with feasting dancing and merry-making. By a coincidence, Geo. Washington, the father of his country, was born on the same day that sheriff Massey was. But the sheriff gets away with George in the item of birthday celebrations.

Things were quiet in the sheriff's office the first few months of 1875. On March 31 the *Beacon* reported: "Sheriff Massey returned from Leavenworth last week having delivered his 'fresh fish' Becker and Hoss, sent up for horse-stealing, at the penitentiary. He says that McNutt is cutting leather in the shoe shop, while Winner works in the paint shop." On June 16 the paper stated: "Al Thomas was put in jail Sunday [June 13], by Sheriff Massey, but was allowed to go out on parole after a short imprisonment," and on June 23 it mentioned another trip east:

Sheriff Massey left yesterday morning for Topeka in charge of county commissioners York, Carpenter and Hobbs, who will invoke the aid of the supreme court through the instrumentality of a writ of *habeas corpus* to wrest them from the clutches of Judge Campbell who now holds them in contempt, with a fine of $100 each and "conditional" imprisonment in the county jail staring them in the face.

Sheriff Massey lost three prisoners from his jail on July 10. The *Beacon*, July 14, 1875, reported the escape:

THREE PRISONERS BREAK JAIL.

On Saturday afternoon the prisoners were allowed to promenade along the corridor of the jail which incloses the narrow space in front of the cells. This was only being partly restored to liberty, and the three prisoners took advantage of their position by cutting through an eighteen-inch thick brick wall with a knife and hatchet, while Sheriff Massey and family were at supper. How they obtained their instruments to work with, is not known. The work was done in a short time, and as the brick were taken out, they were placed in a blanket and carried to a cell, by which means a hole eighteen inches in diameter was soon made under one of the outer windows, through which the three men escaped.

When Mr. Massey returned from supper and called the prisoners to their cells no response was made and their absence was soon made conspicuous. Now in the first place these men were allowed too wide latitude, and in the second place it is a piece of stupidity to construct the outer walls of a jail with strong wrought-iron windows (through which it would be extremely difficult to effect an escape with a crow bar) in walls of brick, which can be dug through with a jack knife in twenty minutes. The heat in the cells is terribly oppressive, and, under the circumstances, Mr. Massey can hardly be censured for permitting the prisoners to breathe half-pure air for so short a time.

Wallace Bennett, the notorious thief and desperado who was recently captured in the territory, was one of the party. The other two, Geo. Houstin and W. W. Chamberlain, were awaiting trial for stealing in this city. No clue has yet been heard of them.

The *Eagle*, July 15, 1875, suggested that outside aid had been given:

"Last Saturday evening, just before being locked up for the night, three prisoners dug their way out of the jail. They had been assisted by outside confederates. Sheriff Massey has taken steps for their recovery."

The *Beacon*, July 28, 1875, published a description of two of the escapees and reported a $50 reward offered for their return:

Sheriff Massey has offered a reward of fifty dollars for Geo. Houston and W. W. Chamberlain who escaped from the jail on the 10th of July. They are described as follows:

Houston is about twenty-eight or thirty years old, dark complexion, dark hair, dark chin whiskers and moustaches; hight, about five feet eight inches; weighs about 145 pounds; had coarse shoes on, nearly new, and dark colored pants. Chamberlain is about twenty-seven years old, light complexion, light hair, short chin whiskers and moustaches; had on light colored pants, badly worn.

In July Massey failed to flush a horse thief from a corn field but a private citizen, coming upon the man later, put the outlaw permanently out of business. The *Eagle*, August 5, 1875, reported the incidents:

A week or two ago a telegram was received from Garnett giving the description of a man named Waterman who had stolen a horse. Sheriff Massey found the horse in the course of a few days near Eldorado. The thief was afterwards discovered near the depot where he ran into a corn field. The field was surrounded by the Sheriff, police and a posse but the bird had flown. The same night of his escape he stole a horse from a Mr. Allen, living between here and Douglas. Mr. Allen gave pursuit, and some time during the day came upon both man and horse, the former lying on the bank of a creek asleep, with a revolver in each hand. Mr. Allen aroused him up and told him to surrender or he would kill him. The thief said he would never surrender when Mr. Allen carried out his threat leaving the miscreant lying upon the prairie and he returning with his property home. This is as we got it and comment is unnecessary.

Pleasant H. Massey did not run for re-election in November, 1875. His successor was H. W. Dunning, who had been elected over two other candidates.[10] In December Dunning was deputized by Sheriff Massey in order that he might become acquainted with the duties and routine of the office. The Wichita *Eagle*, December 9, 1875, reported:

Maj. Dunning becomes Sheriff sooner than the law or the people contemplated. Sheriff Massey was compelled to leave on Monday for Topeka, where he had been summoned as a witness before the United States District Court, so to get the Major well started in, he just deputized the newly elected Sheriff. Yank Owens and Major Dunning appear to hold everything level, even the heels and heads of the lawyers, which are generally on a level with the tables.

The last official act performed by Sheriff Massey which was mentioned in the Wichita press was reported in the *Eagle*, December 23, 1875: "Sheriff Massey left yesterday morning for the State Penitentiary in charge of Henry Lee, whom Judge Campbell had sentenced to two years for pleading guilty to a charge of stealing a horse from a colored man by the name of Stevens."

From that point Pleasant H. Massey returned to the obscurity of private life.

1. Wichita City *Eagle*, October 9, 1873.   2. *Ibid.*, September 18, 1873.   3. *Ibid.*, November 6, 1873.   4. *Ibid.*, May 14, 1874.   5. *Ibid.*, May 21, 1874.   6. *Ibid.*, June 18, 1874.   7. *Ibid.*, August 20, 1874.   8. Wichita *Weekly Beacon*, September 2, 1874.   9. Wichita City *Eagle*, October 1, 1874.   10. *Ibid.*, November 4, 1875.

MASTERSON, EDWARD J. (1852-1878)

Thomas and Catherine Masterson raised a family of seven children of whom Edward J., born in 1852, was the oldest. William B. "Bat" was next, in 1853; James P. followed in 1855; Nelly was born in 1857; Thomas in 1858; George in 1860 and Emma, or Minnie as she was called, in 1862. The family had moved to Kansas from Illinois sometime between 1870 and the fall of 1872. Their Kansas home was an 80-acre farm in the southwest quarter of section 24, township 25 south, range 1 east or about 14 miles northeast of Wichita.

An Illinois friend of the Masterson family followed them to Kansas in November, 1872, and for the next 13 months kept a day-by-day record of his activities as a blacksmith, buffalo hunter and early Dodge City resident. This man, Henry H. Raymond, made frequent mention of the Mastersons in his diary and throws much light on the early careers of Bat, Jim and Ed.

Ed Masterson

Raymond reached Dodge City on November 16, and on Friday, November 22, joined the three Masterson boys in buffalo hunting on Kiowa creek which runs through portions of present Ford, Kiowa, Clark and Comanche counties. For the next six weeks the boys endured biting cold, loneliness and lice-eating Indians, but they were successful in killing and butchering as many as 20 buffalo a day. By January 1, 1873, they apparently had had enough and headed for Dodge, where they arrived on January 3. Bat may have returned earlier than the others, at least he is not mentioned in camp after December 20, 1872.

On January 6, 1873, Raymond, Ed and Jim, having sold their buffalo meat, started for Sedgwick county by wagon. The trip was uneventful except, perhaps, at Larned where Henry Raymond recorded that "a fair Senorita asked me to Invest A note with her. . . ."

To pass the time the boys shot at telegraph poles in a spirit of competition. At Great Bend, Ellinwood and Peace (now Sterling) they stopped to buy cookies, crackers, cheese, etc. Finally, on January 12, they arrived at the Masterson farm. There they stayed until February 18, 1873, when Henry and Ed, at least, returned to Dodge City.

The boys stayed at the ranch of Thomas C. Nixon but nearly every evening ventured into town to enjoy the music and company at a dance hall. On February 26 Ed got a job at the restaurant of James H. Kelley. Bat was apparently still in Dodge for he is mentioned several times in Raymond's diary.

In July and August the friends hunted buffalo together again but had returned to Dodge City by September 10, 1873. Two months later Henry Raymond hopped a freight out of Dodge and headed for Sedgwick county. The young buffalo hunter did not record whether any of the Masterson boys accompanied him but by the next spring Ed and possibly Jim were there to attend the wedding of Henry's brother, Theodore, to school teacher Ida Curtiss. The Wichita *Eagle*, April 30, 1874, reported the event:

M. T. Kopf writes us from Grant township an account of a happy matrimonial affair, in the following language: "On Tuesday, the 21st inst., we had the pleasure of witnessing the first marriage that was ever solemnized in this township, at the residence of E. B. Jurd, esq. The happy pair were Mr. Theodore D. Raymond and Miss Ida E. Curtiss, of Grant township, and the knot was tied by the Rev. Mr. Ashley, of Sedgwick, at 12 o'clock precisely. . . .

In the evening a cotillion in honor of the event was given at Mr. Lindsay Mitchell's where all 'tripped the light fantastic' in the 'merry mazes of the dance' until midnight's witching hour, when we all returned to our homes with light and happy hearts. Among others present at the wedding in the morning and the party in the evening were . . . the fair belle of Sunny Dale Miss Nellie Masterson and her charming sister Minnie . . . the genial Dr. Ed. Masterson; that old buffalo slayer, 'Cheyenne Jim,' [Masterson?]. . . . "

For the next three years no contemporary information relating to Ed Masterson has been located. His name reappears in the spring of 1877 when he was named a Dodge City police officer. His first arrest was accomplished on June 6, the day after he had been appointed.[1] His prisoner was Robert Gilmore, or Bobby Gill as frontier towns knew him, and the newspaper report of the events leading to the arrest is reprinted in the section on Bat Masterson.

WHY THE WEST WAS WILD

It is not certain whether Ed Masterson was originally appointed assistant marshal or merely policeman. On June 9, 1877, the Dodge City *Times* said: "Ed. Masterson has been appointed Assistant Marshal of this city. He is not very large, but there are not many men who would be anxious to tackle him a second time. He makes a good officer." Elsewhere in that same issue and again on June 16, the paper referred to him as policeman. On the latter date the *Times* said: "The new policemen, Ed Masterson and Joe Mason, are covering themselves with glory, and their prompt and efficient action cannot be too highly commended."

By July 3, at least, Ed Masterson had been named assistant marshal to serve under Marshal L. E. Deger and over Policeman Joe Mason. Deger, Masterson, and Mason each earned $75.00 a month.[2]

Ed Masterson was instrumental in easing the trouble between Marshal Deger and Mayor James H. Kelley when the two broke into open conflict on July 20. This story is reported in the section on Deger.

By this time followers of these sketches doubtless have become accustomed to the frequent eruptions of humorous journalese so characteristic of several of the cowtown editors. This account of a session of the Dodge City police court, as described by the *Times*, August 11, 1877, should measure up to the expectations of even the most sanguine:

THE JUDGE AND THE C---S.

"The Marshal will preserve strict order," said the Judge. "Any person caught throwing turnips, cigar stumps, beets, or old quids of tobacco at this Court, will be immediately arranged before this bar of Justice." Then Joe [Policeman J. W. Mason] looked savagely at the mob in attendance, hitched his ivory handle a little to the left and adjusted his moustache. "Trot out the wicked and unfortunate, and let the cotillion commence," said his Honor.

City vs. James Martin.—But just then a complaint not on file had to be attended to, and Reverent John Walsh, of Las Animas, took the Throne of Justice, while the Judge stepped over to Hoover's [George M. Hoover, purveyor of wines, liquors and cigars!]. "You are here for horse stealing," says Walsh. "I can clean out the d----d court," says Martin. Then the City Attorney [E. F. Colborn] was banged into a pigeon hole in the desk, the table upset, the windows kicked out and the railing broke down. When order was restored Joe's thumb was "some chawed," Assistant Marshal Masterson's

292

nose sliced a trifle, and the rantankerous originator of all this, James Martin, Esq., was bleeding from a half dozen cuts on the head, inflicted by Masterson's revolver. Then Walsh was deposed and Judge [D. M.] Frost took his seat, chewing burnt coffee, as his habit, for his complexion. The evidence was brief and pointed. "Again," said the Judge, as he rested his alabaster brow on his left paw, "do you appear within this sacred realm, of which I, and only I, am high muck-i-muck. You have disturbed the quiet of our lovely village. Why, instead of letting the demon of passion fever your brain into this fray, did you not shake hands and call it all a mistake. Then the lion and the lamb would have lain down together and white-robed peace would have fanned you with her silvery wings and elevated your thoughts to the good and pure by her smiles of approbation; but no, you went to chawing and clawing and pulling hair. It is $10.00 and costs, Mr. Martin."

"Make way for the witnesses," says Joe, as he winks at the two c---s that comes to the front, and plants one on each side of Mr. [W. N.] Morphy, who appears for defendant—"A thorn between two roses." It was the City vs. Monroe Henderson, all being "n----s" except the City Attorney and Mr. Morphy. The prosecuting witness, Miss Carrie, looked "the last rose of summer all faded and gone" to ----. Her best heart's blood (pumped from her nose) was freely bespattering the light folds which but feebly hid her palpitating bosom. Her starboard eye was closed, and a lump like a burnt bisquit ornamented her forehead. The evidence showed that the idol of her affections, a certain moke named Baris, had first busted her eye, loosened her ribs and kicked the stuffing generally out of Miss Carrie. That Carrie then got on the war path, procured a hollow ground razor, flung tin cans at defendant, and used such naughty, naughty language as made the Judge breathe a silent prayer, and caused Walsh to take the open air in horror. But the fact still remained that defendant had "pasted" her one on the nose. The City Attorney dwelt upon the heinousness of a strong giant man smiting a frail woman. Mr. Morphy, for defendant, told two or three good stories, bragged on the Court, winked at the witnesses and thought he had a good case, but the marble jaws of justice snapped with adamantine firmness, and it was $5.00 and costs. Appeal taken.

It was Carrie's turn next to taste the bitter draughts brewed in our Police Court. She plead "Guilty, your Honor, just to carrying that razor in my hand. 'Deed, 'deed, your Honor, I never had it under my clothes at all." Carrie received an eighteen dollar moral lecture and a fine of $5.00 and costs, and Court stood adjourned.

In all of the above excentricities, and during the exciting scenes that broke into the stillness of "that hour of nights black arch the key stane" at divers evenings of the week, the city was not wanting in an efficient peace officer, and as a coincidence worthy of mention, assistant marshal Edward Masterson seemed to be always on time to quell the disturbance, and to bear away to that home of the friendless (the dog house) the noisy disturbers of the peace. Mr. Masterson has made a remarkable record during the month as the docket of the Police Court will bear testimony.

The *Times* editor was still in a playful mood when, on August 18, 1877, he reported:

Mr. Evans, of Quindaro, Mr. Webster, of Wyandotte, Mr. Evarts, of Ann Arbor, and Messrs. [M. W.] Sutton, [D. M.] Frost and Ed. Masterson, of this city, held a moonlight picnic at Fort Dodge Thursday evening [August 16]. Their conveyance was a four horse ambulance, decked with bunting and drawn by four horses. They sang songs, acted charades, held moot court, the evening's exercises closing with prayer by the deacon and a song called "put me in my little bed," all the musicians joining in the chorus.

On September 3, 1877, Masterson, with Marshal Deger and a citizen named Anderson pursued and captured a horse thief. This *Times* article is included in the section on L. E. Deger.

About September 15, Ed Masterson was reported to have discouraged a couple of the boys from fisticuffs:

Stonewall Jackson and Kinch Riley disagreed this week as to the proper mode of dividing certain "winnins," amounting to the enormous sum of $2.00. After discussing the matter fully they concluded to resort to the dog method of deciding quarrels, and prepared to fight. But just as they were about to begin Ed. Masterson informed them that the most peaceable place to fight was down on the reservation, owing to the stringency of the city laws. The fightists went down to the reservation, followed by a large crowd, but when they got face to face on the battle field their courage weakened and neither would strike the first blow. Thus a good item was spoiled.[3]

Ed's younger brother, Bat, who had been under sheriff during the summer and who was now also on the city police force, helped the assistant marshal attempt to arrest A. C. Jackson, a fun-loving Texas cowboy, on September 25. The story of Jackson's escape is in the section on Bat Masterson.

Late in September Ed Masterson was involved in another unsuccessful pursuit. This time the lawman was after the culprits who had robbed the Union Pacific at Big Springs, Neb., on September 18, 1877. The article reporting the attempt was included in the section on C. E. Bassett.

On October 2, 1877, the police force was reduced so that only Marshal Deger and Assistant Marshal Ed Masterson remained.[4] On November 5 half of the police force was put out of commission when the assistant marshal was shot by Bob Shaw. This gun play was described in the Dodge City *Times* of November 10:

FRONTIER FUN.

Frank Shaw Tries to Remedy His Grievances with a Revolver, and Gets Left.

A Deputy Marshal's Pluck.

Last Monday afternoon one of those little episodes which serve to vary the monotony of frontier existence occurred at the Lone Star dance hall, during which four men came out some the worse for wear; but none, with one exception, being seriously hurt.

Bob Shaw, the man who started the amusement, accused Texas Dick, alias Moore, of having robbed him of forty dollars, and when the two met in the Lone Star the ball was opened.

Somebody, foreseeing possible trouble, and probable gore, started out in search of Assistant City Marshal Ed. Masterson, and finding him hurried the officer to the scene of the impending conflict.

When Masterson entered the door he descried Shaw by the bar with a huge pistol in his hand and a hogshead of blood in his eye, ready to relieve Texas Dick of his existence in this world and send him to those shades where troubles come not and six shooters are not known.

Not wishing to hurt Shaw, but anxious to quiet matters and quell the disturbance officer Masterson first ordered him to give up his gun. Shaw refused to deliver and told Masterson to keep away from him, and after saying this he again proceeded to try to kill Texas Dick. Officer Masterson then gently tapped the belligerent Shaw upon the back of the head with the butt of his shooting iron, merely to convince him of the vanities of this frail world and to teach him that all isn't lovely even when the goose does hang antitudilum. The aforesaid reminder upon the back of the head, however, failed to have the desired effect, and instead of dropping, as any man of fine sensibilities would have done, Shaw turned his battery upon the officer and let him have it in the right breast, the ball striking a rib and passing around came out under the right shoulder blade, paralyzing his right arm so that it was useless, so far as handling a pistol was concerned. Masterson fell, but grasping his pistol in his left hand he returned the fire giving it to Shaw in the left arm and the left leg, rendering him hors du combat.

During the melee Texas Dick was shot in the right groin, making a painful and dangerous, though not necessarily a fatal wound, while Frank Buskirk, who, impelled by a curiosity he could not control, was looking in at the door upon the matinee, received a reminiscence in the left arm, which had the effect of starting him out to hunt a surgeon. Nobody was killed, but for a time it looked as though the undertaker and the coroner would have something to do. The nerve and pluck displayed by officer Masterson reflects credit both upon himself and the city, which has reason to congratulate itself upon the fact that it has a guardian who shirks no responsibility and who hesitates not to place himself in danger when duty requires.

On another page the paper reported: "Assistant City Marshal Ed. Masterson, who was shot last Monday while attempting to make an arrest, has so far recovered as to be up and around. To-morrow evening he will start to Wichita to spend a week or two visiting his parents."

The shootout caused Bob Shaw to forsake the West for his native Georgia:

Mr. Bob Shaw, whom we noticed last week in connection with the shooting scrape, in which Officer Masterson was wounded, had so far recovered as to be able to start for his home in Georgia a few days ago. Shaw is not a desperado as would seem from this incident. Parties who have known him say he never was known to make a six-shooter play before this. Dr. Galland, under whose medical treatment he so rapidly recovered, has a high regard for him. Mr. Shaw's family are highly respectable people, and he has concluded to quit the far west and go back to live under the parental roof.[5]

Masterson made a rapid recovery from his wound and about November 19 returned to Dodge City. The *Times*, November 24, 1877, reported: "Assistant Marshal Masterson returned from Wichita the first of the week. He is recovering from the wound received in the recent shooting affray, and will soon be able to resume his duties as an officer." On page four the *Times* said: "Ed. Masterson's wife has returned, she came from Hays on a horse."

At the December 4, 1877, meeting of the city council of Dodge City Larry Deger was discharged as city marshal and Ed Masterson promoted to the position. The *Times*, December 8, reported the council's actions:

On motion of John Newton the office of City Marshal was declared vacant, the Mayor thereupon appointed Edward J. Masterson to the said Marshalship, which appointment the Council confirmed.

The petition of D. M. Frost, F. C. Zimmermann, S. Keller, P. G. Reynolds and others protesting against the removal of L. E. Deger was upon motion laid upon the table. . . .

The following bills were presented and allowed: Edward J. Masterson salery as asistant Marshal and medical treatment of wounds received in the arrest of Shaw, $93.00. . . .

Editorially the *Times* had this to say of the change:

City Marshal Edward Masterson receives the congratulations of his many friends without a show of exhultation. Notwithstanding the fact that considerable feeling was manifested against the removal of Mr. Deger, no one accuses Mr. Masterson of seeking the position. In fact he preferred to retain his old position as Assistant, which gave him the same salary and engendered less responsibilities. As an officer his reputation is made, and it is a good one. . . .

Charles E. Bassett, sheriff of Ford county, was named assistant to Masterson.[6]

The arrest of an army deserter netted the marshal spending money in January. The *Times*, January 19, 1878, reported: "Marshal Masterson, Monday last [January 14], arrested a deserter by the name of A. J. Brusten, who was delivered to the commanding officer at the Fort. Ed. will receive $30 for this neat work."

Horse thieves, deserters, and drunken cowboys were not the only trouble makers with whom the city marshal had to contend. The *Ford County Globe*, January 29, 1878, reported a less exciting type of delinquency:

Several of our over grown-babies emulated themselves, at the theatre last week, by throwing beans at some of the colored people present. If they have no respect for the colored population, they ought to have for themselves.

———

Marshal Masterson stopped some nonsense at the theater, Saturday night, by calling out the names of the participants, and telling them to stop. Correct Edward, repeat the dose.

In February "Marshal Masterson and Adam Jackson attended a court-martial at the Fort this week," and "Marshal Masterson took advantage of the pleasant weather and dried his lime kiln [city jail] blankets last Tuesday." [7]

As an opposition paper the recently established *Ford County Globe* felt constrained to criticize the police force:

THE FESTIVE REVOLVER.

Some of the "boys" in direct violation of City Ordinances, carry firearms on our streets, without being called to account for the same. They do it in such an open manner, that it don't seem possible that our City officers are ignorant of this fact.

There must be some reason for it. What is it? Is it because they belong to the "gang," or because they intend to harm none but anti-gang men? An honest man attending to his own business, doesn't require the constant companionship of a six-shooter, to make him feel easy and safe. We think there is something rotten with a man's conscience when he parades the streets with an exposed six-shooter, knowing that he is violating law with impunity, simply because he is a friend of the marshal or policeman. We understand that Mayor Kelley has instructed the police force to rigidly enforce the ordinance against the carrying of firearms, for which he deserves great credit.[8]

However, the *Globe* was capable of encouragement as well as criticism. On March 12, 1878, it said: "Some of our officers displayed great courage, and justice, in raising h-ll in the south side dance hall, last Sunday." But criticism still received more type space:

We have heard more complaint during the past few days about parties being "held up" and robbed, on our streets, than ever before. How long is this thing to continue? We have one more policeman on the force now than ever before at this season of the year. It therefore seems strange that midnight robberies should be more prevalent than ever before. There is something wrong somewhere, and the people are beginning to feel that there is no legal remedy. We would like to see the town smell worse of dead highway robbers than hell does of sinners.

If there is any place in this country that needs the attention of our officers of the law, its the robbers roost across the dead line.

Also on March 12 the *Globe* printed this story:

Thursday last [March 7], a poor bare-footed girl, came tramping into Dodge; with a year-old babe in her arms. Her garments were tattered and torn, her babe naked; and her story such as would ring tears from the heart of a stone, it ran thus: "I have since I was five years old, been living with my uncle Mr. Smith, who now resides on the Pawnee, about thirty-five miles north of Dodge. My uncle has since my earliest recollections ill treated and abused me, he has always kept me isolated from other society than that of himself and family. About nine months ago I gave birth to a child, my uncle was the father of the child; he having by coercion seduced me; on the day before my arrival in Dodge, my uncle was absent from home, I took my babe in my arms; and started for Dodge. I am afraid of my uncle, because he threatened to kill me if I ever ran away from him."

On Saturday morning, the uncle arrived in Dodge searching for the girl. He says that the girl's story from beginning to end is false, and stated that she stole from him when leaving his house, $180, which was done up in a newspaper, and placed under the floor for safe keeping.

The Police arrested Mr. Smith, on a charge of disturbing the peace, but on promise of his leaving the girl alone in her glory, and departing from Dodge at once, he was permitted to go.

The sympathy of our people are decidedly with the girl, who is a buxom young woman, aged seventeen. Strong talk was made on the streets against Smith, "tar and feathers," "black-snake whips" and "cold water baths," were among the remedies advocated for his application. He, however, made good his departure, and all is now quiet on the "Rackensack," so far as the Smith family is concerned.

On March 15, 1878, Ed Masterson teamed with Bassett and brother Bat, who by then was sheriff of Ford county, to capture two train robbers. The articles reporting this appear in the section on W. B. Masterson. Ed went along with the prisoners to Emporia, where they were taken for safety's sake. He returned on March 17. The Dodge City *Times*, March 23, 1878, reported: "City Marshal Masterson returned home last Sunday morning, after conducting the two train robbers to Emporia, where they were safely lodged in jail. At all the stations along the road crowds assembled to see the robbers."

Things began to get lively as spring came on. "Our police force were kept jumping till three o'clock yesterday morning, corraling disturbers of the peace. The result was a full calaboose of soldiers for Police court yesterday," said the *Globe*, March 26, 1878. The *Times*, March 30, reported: "A prize fight was indulged in by two pugilists in the outskirts of the city this week. Three rounds were fought when both pugilists weakened and fled at sight of the City Marshal. The one-armed slugger received a slight scratch under his left blinker. Victory, in dispute." And on April 6 the *Times* stated: "A tall man with a hooked nose was placed in the calaboose yesterday by Marshal Masterson. Having nothing else to do he amused himself cremating the blankets."

Masterson wanted to put Dodge's vagrants to work on the city streets. The Dodge City *Times*, March 30, 1878, reported his intentions:

UTILIZING TRAMPS.

City Marshal Masterson contemplates organizing a tramp brigade for the purpose of clearing the streets and alleys of the filth and rubbish that has been accumulating for a year or so. There are about thirty tramps now sojourning among us, all of whom have no visible means of support and are liable to arrest under the vagrant act.

On April 9, 1878, calamity struck the cowtown. Twenty-six-year-old Marshal Edward J. Masterson was killed in the performance of his duty. The *Ford County Globe* got out an extra the next day from which this account was published in the Topeka *Commonwealth*, April 12, 1878:

DEATH OF MARSHAL MASTERSON.

The Dodge City Globe extra, of the 10th, has the following about the death of Marshal Masterson.

At ten o'clock last night, City Marshal Edward Masterson, discovered that a cow boy who was working for Oburn of Kansas City, named Jack Wagner, was carrying a six-shooter contrary to the City Ordinance. Wagner was at the time under the influence of liquor, but quietly gave up the pistol. The Marshal gave it to some of Wagner's friends for safe keeping and stepped out into the street. No sooner had he done so than Wagner ran out after him pulling another pistol, which the Marshal had not observed. The Marshal saw him coming and turned upon Wagner and grabbed hold of him.

Wagner shot Marshal Masterson at once through the abdomen, being so close to him that the discharge set the Marshal's clothes on fire.

Marshal Masterson then shot Wagner.

About this time a man named Walker got mixed up in the fight. He, it appears, was boss herder for Oburn, and Wagner was working under him. He also got shot once through the left lung, and his right arm was twice broken.

Marshal Masterson walked across the street to [George M.] Hoover's saloon, where after telling that he was shot, he sank to the floor. He was immediately removed to his room, where in half an hour he expired.

Walker and Wagner were nearly all night insensible, and none thought that either of them could live through the night. However, morning has come and neither are dead; both are in a very precarious condition and their chances for recovery very small.

The city is in mourning; every door is draped with crape; business is entirely suspended till after the funeral of Marshal Masterson, which will take place at two o'clock p. m., and will be attended by everybody in the city.

Marshal Masterson will be buried in the Military Cemetery, at Fort Dodge.

The *Globe* elaborated in its somberly black-lined issue of April 16, 1878:

SAD NEWS.
MARSHAL MASTERSON HURRIED HENCE BY A MURDERER'S HAND.
A PUBLIC CALAMITY.

On the evening of the 9th inst., at 10 o'clock P. M., six pistol shots "rang out," on the night, on the south side of the R. R. track in Dodge City. Hurrying to the spot to ascertain the cause and result of the shooting, we found them to be as follows: A party of six "cow-boys" who had arrived in town in the evening, had been enjoying themselves with dancing and drinking, some of them evidently getting too much liquor for their own and the City's good. Marshal Masterson and Policeman [Nat] Haywood, being the custodians of the public peace of the City, were present, prepared to prevent any disturbance or trouble among the boys. One of the boys named Jack Wagner, becoming more intoxicated than the others, got to be very noisy. About this time the City Marshal observed that he was carrying a six-shooter, contrary to a City Ordinance, and proceeded to disarm him, which he accomplished without much trouble, and turned the pistol over to Wagner's Boss, A. M. Walker.

The dance went on and all appeared to be peace and harmony. The Marshal stepped out the front door to the side-walk where he again met Wagner, and saw that Wagner was again in possession of his pistol. He at once attempted to take it from him, a scuffle ensued, a general rush was made from inside the Hall to the sidewalk; Policeman Haywood stepped forward to assist the Marshal, but just as he did so, two other "cow men" drew their pistols upon him and held him in position. One of them snapped a pistol in his face, which fortunately missed fire.

About this time a pistol was discharged, and Marshal Masterson was shot through the abdomen.

Five shots followed in quick succession. A general rush was made from the scene, and all was over.

Wagner being shot ran into [A. J.] Peacock's saloon and fell upon the floor, where he remained until carried away by his friends. He was fatally shot through the abdomen. He died on the evening of the 10th, and was burried on the hill near town at 4 P. M., on the eleventh.

Walker, the Boss herder, ran through Peacock's Saloon, and fell some distance in the rear of the saloon, from whence he was carried by his friends to a room over Wright, Beverly & Co's store, where he now lies in a very precarious condition, shot once through the left lung and twice through the right arm.

Marshal Masterson walked across the street and entering [George M.] Hoover's saloon, in the agonies of death he said to George Hinkle, "George, I'm shot;" and sank on the floor. His clothes were still on fire from the discharge of the pistol, which had been placed against the right side of his abdomen and "turned loose." Making a hole large enough for the introduction of the whole pistol. The ball passed completely through him, leaving him no possible chance for life. He was carried to his brother's room, where in half an hour he died.

Everyone in the City knew Ed. Masterson and liked him. They liked him as a boy, they liked him as a man, and they liked him as an officer.

Promptly at 10 o'clock on the morning of the 10th every business house in the City closed its doors which remained so until 6 o'clock, P. M. Crape draped almost every door in the City. Never before was such honor shown in Dodge, either to the living or dead.

The Dodge City Fire Company, of which Edward J. Masterson was a much respected member, took charge of the remains, and refused to permit any of the friends or relations of deceased to sustain any of the funeral expenses. Every vehicle in the City was employed for the use of the funeral attendants. Funeral services were had at the Fireman's Parlor, where the ladies discoursed appropriate music, and the Rev. O. W. Wright delivered a sermon. The funeral procession started from town at 3 o'clock P. M. and was formed as follows: The City Council in a body; next, came the hearse containing deceased; next Sheriff [Bat] Masterson, the only living relative of the deceased who could be present at the funeral, because of the family residing in the Southern part of the State and not having time to get here to attend; next, came the Fire Company, sixty strong, uniformed and in mourning; next, came buggies and wagons containing ladies and gentlemen; then came many horsemen. The procession marched to the Military Cemetery, at Fort Dodge, where the last sad rites were performed to one of the best and most generous men that God ever fashioned. Rev. O. W. Wright performing the burial services.

Four "cow boys" were arrested as accessories to the murder of our Marshal, but all were after the fullest and most complete investigation discharged by Judge R. G. Cook, as it was established that they were to blame only for being in bad company.

Wagner when dying said that he shot Marshal Masterson, and there is now but little doubt in the minds of any but that it was he who killed our Marshal.

Our Fire Company met in their new parlor, on the evening of the 12th inst., for the purpose of paying their respects in an appropriate manner to the memory of their deceased brother. After due consideration, the following preamble and resolutions were unanimously adopted, and spread upon the Journal:

WHEREAS, One of the most beloved of our number, Brother Edward J. Masterson, has been called from us by the voice of Death. Sadly, and with hearts filled with deep sorrow do we mourn the loss of our brother. Now that he is no more we vividly call to mind his many noble and generous qualities. In the bosom of man the Creator never caused a more true and brotherly heart to beat; ever ready to perform a kind act, he bore malice toward none and held the firm friendship of all. We feel that his death is a calamity that can never be repaired. His place among us cannot be filled. Long will we cherish him in memory as one who was near and dear to us all. And be it

RESOLVED, That as a mark of our high esteem and universal respect for our deceased brother, our place of meeting and our fire implements be draped in mourning, and that we wear a badge of crape for thirty days from the date of his death. This we do in honor of the dead. Also

RESOLVED, That we extend our heart felt sympathy to the afflicted relatives of our deceased brother and instruct the Secretary of this Company to forward copies of the foregoing preamble and resolution to their address. And to furnish both City papers with a copy thereof for publication.

The Dodge City *Times,* April 13, 1878, also carried a story and an editorial about the murder on its front page:

THE PISTOL.
MURDER OF EDWARD J. MASTERSON CITY MARSHAL.
THE ASSAILANTS SHOT—ONE OF THEM DEAD.
DODGE CITY IN MOURNING.

On Tuesday evening, about 10 o'clock, Edward J. Masterson, Marshal of Dodge City, was murdered by Jack Wagner and Alf Walker, two cattle drivers from near Hays City. The two cow boys were under the influence of bad whisky and were carrying revolvers. Early in the evening Marshal Masterson disarmed Wagner; later Marshal Masterson and Deputy Marshal Nat Haywood tried the second time to disarm Wagner. While in the act Masterson was shot in the abdomen. Walker in the meantime snapped a pistol in the face of Officer Haywood. Masterson fired four shots, one of them striking Wagner in the bowels from the left side. Walker was struck three times, one shot in the lungs and his right arm horribly shattered with the other shots.

302

The shooting occurred on the south side of the Railroad track. Marshal Masterson cooly walked over to the business side of the street, a distance of about 200 yards, and upon reaching the sidewalk he fell exhausted. He was taken to his room where he died about 40 minutes afterwards.

Wagner and Walker were removed to Mr. Lane's room, where the former died at about 7 o'clock Wednesday evening. Walker is lying dangerously wounded, with no hopes of his recovery.

Some of the flying shots grazed the faces of one of our citizens and a cattle man. The shots were fired almost simultaneously, and the wonder is expressed that more death and destruction did not ensue, as a large crowd surrounded the scene of the shooting.

The officers were brave and cool though both were at a disadvantage, as neither desired to kill the whisky crazed assailants.

The death of Marshal Masterson caused great feeling in Dodge City. The business houses were draped in mourning, and business on Wednesday generally suspended.

Elsewhere we give the expression of sympathy and ceremonies following this terrible tragedy.

THE MURDER.

An Officer has been stricken down in the discharge of his duty. The deep feeling of gloom that pervades this community over this sad affair, leaves us opportunities for calm reflection and judgment. A life that periled itself, that others might enjoy safety from the assassin's bludgeon, while in the discharge of duty, has been slain in cold blood. The avenging hand though too struck back that the penalty might be swift and unerring.

The loss of Edward J. Masterson, the late murdered City Marshal, has cast a gloom through which is felt the realizing sense of buckling on the armor unto death. The general sympathy and respect for the deceased is deep and heartfelt. As an officer he was vigilant, courageous and conscientious of the important trust in his hands. As we knew him he was kind, civil and steadfast—combined with those qualities that make a brave man, the true friend and good citizen.

While we commend the good qualities that possessed our deceased friend, and deplore the tragic end that so summarily disposed him—and through our sorrows and reverence for the departed, let us go forth girdled with common fraternity for our bodily protection; armed with resoluteness and courage; and guided solely in the axiom: Self-preservation is the first law of human nature.

A frontier life stimulates all the qualities of manhood—the true, the good and the bad. The reckless denizen of the plains is at the mercy of an outraged people. As we see the draped doors, the solemn faces, and the cold, quiet air of remorse, we see depicted that steady determination to give no quarter to the ruthless invader of our lives, peace and prosperity. While we give utterance to our feelings in kindly sentiment, we shall find no mawkish sentimentality in guarding the future conduct of those whose utter disregard of their own lives jeopardize those whose lives are worth living for.

We can forget the animosities engendered through the ordinary courses of life, that we may doubly arm ourselves, by strengthening the picket lines, and filling to the maximum the ranks of the reserves.

There will be no slow work in protecting the lives of this people against cold-blooded assassination.

On an inside page of the same issue the *Times* ran Masterson's obituary:

EDWARD J. MASTERSON.

Died—In this city, on Tuesday, April 9th, in the 26th year of his age, Edward J. Masterson, City Marshal.

The subject of this sketch was born in Henryville, Canada East, on September 22d, 1852, and removed to Wichita, Kansas with his parents in 1869, where he continued to reside until attaining his majority when he left his home and became one of the first inhabitants of this city.

In May 1876 [June 5, 1877] he accepted the appointment of Assistant Marshal, and in the December following [December 4, 1877], having displayed marked adaptability for the position, he was promoted to the Marshalship, in the discharge of the duties of which he continued until his unfortunate death.

Possessed of a geniality of temperament, a kindness of heart and a richness of personal bravery, he had many warm friends and admirers.

As an officer he followed the dictation of duty, striving at all times for its honest and complete discharge and gaining for himself the dignity and respect that of necessity followed from his determined intrepidity.

He died in the service he performed so well, and has added one other to the list of those who, living, were so many representatives, each of his day and generation, but who dead, belong to all time, and whose voices ring down the ages in solemn protest against the reign of violence and blood.

The city council passed a resolution of respect and sympathy:

PROCEEDINGS OF THE COUNCIL.

Now on this 10th day of April, 1878, at the City of Dodge City comes D. D. Colley, C. M. Beeson, James Anderson, Walter Straeter and John Newton Councilmen thereof, and, whereas the Mayor of said city being absent, and there being no President of the Council; on motion of John Newton D. D. Colley was chosen acting President of the Council; and on motion of James Anderson D. D. Colley was elected President of the Council.

The following resolutions were presented by C. M. Beeson and unanimously adopted:

Whereas, Edward J. Masterson, Marshal of the City of Dodge City, was on the night of April 9th, 1878, killed in the lawful discharge of his duties, be it

Resolved by the Council of the City of Dodge City, that in his death the city has lost an officer who was not afraid to do his duty, and who never shrank from its faithful performance; a worthy servant and an upright citizen.

Ed Masterson

RESOLVED that we offer our heartfelt sympathy to his many friends both here and abroad; and that these resolutions be spread upon the journal of these proceedings; and that the Clerk be directed to forward a copy of the same when printed to his parents at Wichita.

D. D. COLLEY, Pres't. of the Council.
E. F. Colborn, City Clerk.[9]

The April 13, 1878, edition of the *Times* was filled with items of interest concerning the shooting:

Marshal Masterson lived about forty minutes after he was shot and died surrounded by many of his warmest friends. He remained conscious to the last and passed away apparently without pain or dread.

When prepared for burial his remains were visited by many of our most worthy ladies. His face was that of one who had been called away in the midst of his slumber.

The parents of Marshal Masterson reside near Wichita.

INCIDENTS OF THE SHOOTING.

After Wagner was shot he rushed into the saloon and fell to the floor in an almost senseless condition. Walker, upon receiving his wound, ran out back of the saloon and fell to the ground. The excitement was so great and the place where the shooting occurred (out on the sidewalk) being dark, no one hardly knew what was the matter until after the firing ceased. Marshal Masterson talked but very little after he was shot.

SUPPOSED ACCOMPLICES.

An hour after the shooting warrants were issued and Sheriff Masterson arrested the four associates who accompanied Walker and Wagner into the city. They were examined Wednesday and Thursday before Justice Cook, a large number of witnesses were sworn but no evidence was brought out of sufficient strength to convict them as accomplices in the killing of Marshal Masterson, and they were released. Their names were John Hungate, Thomas Highlander, Thomas Roads and John Reece. The examination was ably and thoroughly conducted by County Attorney Sutton, assisted by his partner Mr. Colborn. Messrs. [H. E.] Gryden, [D. M.] Frost and [W. N.] Morphy defended the prisoners. Although there was a crowd of people standing within a few feet of the shooting when it occurred, not one of them saw the affair from beginning to end.

JOHN WAGNER.

Mr. John Wagner, who received his death wound at the time Masterson was killed, died on Wednesday evening about sundown. He was 27 years old and about the average size, blue eyes and light complexion. Before he arrived in town he informed some of the men with him that he had been lost from his

305

mother for eight years. Some time ago he received a fall from his horse, which it is thought rendered him partially insane. He was buried Thursday evening on the hill west of the city.

ALFRED WALKER, who was shot at the time of the killing of Marshal Masterson, is still lying very low at Mr. Lane's rooms. There is a prospect of his recovery.

Bat Masterson and his friend, Attorney M. W. Sutton, spent several days with the Masterson family in Sedgwick county. The *Times,* April 20, 1878, said:

County Attorney Sutton and Sheriff Masterson arrived home from Wichita last Wednesday morning. The Sheriff spent several days with his parents and brothers and sisters, who received the news of the death of Edward—who was the eldest son, and greatly beloved—with great grief; they have the sympathy of this entire community.

The Dodge City *Times* kept the town informed of Walker's progress. On April 20, 1878, it reported: "Alfred Walker, who was wounded at the time of the shooting of Marshal Masterson, is still in a critical condition, but will probably recover if mortification can be prevented," and on June 1:

Alfred Walker, who has been confined to his bed ever since the unfortunate shooting scrape last April, was removed to Kansas City last Friday [May 24], where he is still under medical treatment. We learn that his father, who accompanied him, took suddenly ill this week and died at Fort Scott. He had left his son at Kansas City and started for his home in Texas when something like cramp seized him and the result was fatal. He was a highly respectable old gentleman and had many friends among those who knew him.

A year after Ed Masterson was killed Dodge City had obtained a respectable cemetery of its own and the body of the slain marshal was brought back "home." The *Times,* April 19, 1879, reported:

The body of Ed. Masterson, the city marshal, who was murdered in this city a year ago, was removed from the Fort Dodge Cemetery, Monday, and placed in Prairie Grove Cemetery. A monument will be erected over his grave. The disinterment was conducted by P. L. Beatty, the Dodge City Fire Department foreman.[10]

1. Dodge City *Times,* June 9, 1877.   2. *Ibid.,* July 7, August 11, September 8, October 6, November 10, December 8, 1877; January 5, February 9, March 9, April 6, May 11, 1878.   3. *Ibid.,* September 15, 1877.   4. *Ibid.,* October 6, 1877.   5. *Ibid.,* November 17, 1877.   6. *Ibid.,* December 15, 1877.   7. *Ibid.,* February 9, 23, 1878.   8. March 5, 1878.   9. Dodge City *Times,* April 13, 1878.   10. Prairie Grove cemetery later was converted into a residential section and the bodies were for the most part removed to Maple Grove cemetery. Local residents of Dodge City say that the body of Edward J. Masterson was not identified when the move was made, and further that Bat Masterson, then a New York newspaperman, had tried to locate Ed's grave so that a monument could be erected but it could not be found.

MASTERSON, JAMES P. (1855-1895)

James Masterson, third in age of the Masterson brothers, was also the third member of the family to serve on the Dodge City police force. Jim was not a newcomer to Dodge when he was appointed. He had been in the town off and on since the fall of 1872 (*see* the section on Ed Masterson). In February, 1878, he was in Dodge again, back from a long buffalo hunt. The Dodge City *Times*, February 23, 1878, mentioned his return: "Jim Masterson, brother of Bat and Ed, returned from a buffalo hunt this week. He had been absent nearly four months."

The younger Masterson was hired as a policeman in early June, 1878; his first salary payment indicating June 1 to be the exact date of his appointment.[1] The local newspapers, however, did not report his employment until June 11, when the *Ford County Globe* stated that "Policeman Trask has resigned and Jim Masterson has taken his place on the force." In any event, within two months of the death of Jim's brother Ed, city marshal of Dodge, another Masterson was wearing a badge.

The Dodge City police department in the summer of 1878 consisted of Marshal Charles E. Bassett, Assistant Marshal Wyatt Earp, Policeman John Brown, and Policeman Jim Masterson. The marshal's salary was $100 while all the others earned $75 a month.[2]

The first activity in which Jim Masterson is reported to have participated occurred in the early morning of July 26, 1878. There is an even chance that it was Jim Masterson and not Wyatt Earp who shot George Hoy that night. Both of the officers emptied their pistols at the fleeing cowboy making it impossible to state positively which fired the bullet that dropped the herder. The *Times* article reporting the scrape is reprinted in the section on Wyatt Earp. The *Globe*, July 30, 1878, said:

SHOOTING AFFRAY.

On Friday morning about three o'clock two Texas boys, having saddled their horses and started for camp, passed down Bridge street by the Comique Hall. As they arrived at the rear end they commenced shooting into the hall, firing about five or six shots, all of which passed across the stage or into the ceiling of the room. At the time the shooting commenced there were at least 150 people in the house all enjoying themselves immensely. Fortunately no one was, as usual, in the boxes of the Theater, everybody being down on the dancing floor, and owing to this fact no person inside the house was hurt, because the balls all passed too high to hit anyone on this floor. A general scamper was made by the crowd, some getting under the stage, others running out the front door, and behind the bar; in the language of the bard, "such a gittin up stairs never was seed."

Our police force was promptly on hand, and they, together with several citizens, turned their pistols loose in the direction of the flying horsemen, who by this time had nearly reached the bridge.

In the morning the fruit was gathered in and consisted of Geo. Hoyt [most newspaper articles reported his name as Hoy] with his arm broken in two places. He, it appears, was one of the horsemen who did the first shooting, and was wounded by one of the many bullets fired after him, while fleeing from the disturbed peace of the community which at that time was "up on its ear." He claims not to have done any shooting; be that as it may he was in bad company and has learned a lesson "he wont forget soon." We learn from Dr. T. L. McCarty, his physician, that amputation will not be necessary.

Hoy died from his wound on August 21, 1878.[3]

John Brown was relieved from the police force on August 6, 1878, leaving Bassett, Earp, and Masterson,[4] all of whom may have been involved in another episode reported on August 20 by the *Globe*:

Another shooting affair occurred on the "south side" Saturday night. It appears that one of the cow boys, becoming intoxicated and quarrelsome, undertook to take possession of the bar in the Comique. To this the bar keeper objected and a row ensued. Our policemen interfered and had some difficulty in handling their man. Several cattle men then engaged in the broil and in the excitement some of them were bruised on the head with six shooters. Several shots were accidentally fired which created general confusion among the crowd of persons present. We are glad to chronicle the fact that none were seriously hurt and nobody shot. We however cannot help but regret the too ready use of pistols in all rows of such character and would like to see a greater spirit of harmony exist between our officers and cattle men so that snarling cayotes and killers could make their own fights without interesting or draging good men into them.

Officer Jim Masterson, along with Assistant Marshal Earp, was on duty the night Dora Hand was shot. Though the two were soon at the scene the killer escaped. The story of Dora Hand's death is included in the section on Bat Masterson.

On December 3, 1878, the city council of Dodge City, probably because the end of the year's cattle season had arrived, reduced the expenses of the police force from $250 to $200 a month. The salaries of Earp and Jim Masterson were cut to $50 while Bassett's remained at $100.[5]

Jim Masterson was concurrently a deputy sheriff of Ford county, serving under his brother Sheriff Bat Masterson. A *Times* article,

Jim Masterson

January 11, 1879, which commended his efficiency in that position, is printed in the section on C. E. Bassett.

As a deputy sheriff Jim aided Bat in guarding seven Cheyenne prisoners whom the sheriff brought from Fort Leavenworth to stand trial for certain atrocities they were alleged to have committed in September, 1878, during the last Indian raid in Kansas. The complete story of the Cheyenne prisoners appears in the section on Bat Masterson.

During Jim Masterson's absence at Leavenworth J. J. Webb filled his position on the police force.[6]

On April 9, 1879, the city council, in anticipation of the coming cattle season, raised the salaries of the assistant marshal and the policeman, effective April 12, to $100 a month each. In addition an officer was allowed $2 for each arrest he made.[7]

Jim took a week's vacation in May. The *Times*, May 10, 1879, reported: "Officer James Masterson spent a week at his home, near Wichita."

Later in May Masterson and Earp faced down seven drovers in order to collect a bill for a colored man. The *Times* article covering this is included in the section on Wyatt Earp.

Another shooting scrape between cowboys and police rent the air on the night of June 9, 1879:

THE WORK OF THE PISTOL.

Last night the police undertook to disarm a squad of cow boys who had neglected to lay aside their six-shooters upon arriving in the city. The cow boys protested and war was declared. Several shots were fired, and one of the cow boys was wounded in the leg. The balance of the cow boys made their escape.[8]

Much of the wild life in Dodge had its locale in that portion of the city south of the Santa Fe tracks. The editor of the *Ford County Globe*, June 24, 1879, described a typical "good time" in that place:

A HIGH OLD LONESOME.

The boys and girls across the dead line had a high old time last Friday [June 20]. They sang and danced, and fought and bit, and cut and had a good time generally, making music for the entire settlement. Our reporter summed up five knock downs, three broken heads, two cuts and several incidental bruises. Unfortunately none of the injuries will prove fatal.

Apparently the police often considered such goings on routine and did not interfere.

Although a Las Vegas, N. M., correspondent of the *Globe*, October 28, 1879, reported that Jim Masterson was in that town on October 16 the salary record of the policeman did not indicate an absence from duty in Dodge City.[9]

Wyatt Earp left Dodge City early in September, 1879, and about the first of November Marshal Bassett also resigned. On November 4 Policeman Jim Masterson was promoted to the chief marshalship. Neil Brown was named assistant marshal and the two earned $100 a month each.[10]

Dodge City police activities did not make the newspapers during the winter of 1879-1880. On May 8, 1880, the Dodge City *Times* mentioned that both Masterson and Brown had been reappointed to their respective positions by the newly elected council at a meeting held on May 4. Their salaries remained at $100.

The tenth United States census was enumerated in Dodge as of June 22, 1880. Jim Masterson's name appeared on page 19 of the Dodge City section. He was listed as being 24 years old, employed as city marshal, and living with one Minnie Roberts, a 16-year-old concubine.

Things remained quiet in Dodge all during the cattle season of 1880. Not one incident involving the city marshal was reported by the papers for the remainder of the year. Apparently the town was so tranquil that the city fathers thought $100 a month was too much salary for services received so on October 5, 1880, a reduction was ordered. From November 1, 1880, Marshal Masterson and Assistant Marshal Neil Brown each received $50 a month salary.[11]

At last, on January 4, 1881, the quiet of Dodge was broken, not by drunken cowboys, hot headed gamblers or vociferous dance-hall girls but rather, because of a home triangle situation. The *Times*, January 8, 1881, reported:

A SHOOTING SCRAPE.

The still air of Tuesday evening, about 8 o'clock, was broken by the report of pistol shots; and it is well to add the affair created little or no excitement. J. Q. Stultz is a painter by trade, and eighteen months ago, with his wife, domiciled under the same roof with A. H. Snyder, a carpenter. There was a family rupture, Stultz leaving for Nebraska, and Mrs. Stultz for Illinois. They both returned to this county some weeks ago, Mrs. Stultz instituting suit for divorce. The wife came into town Tuesday, and her appearance brought both Snyder and Stultz to her stopping place. Words brought out pistols, both men firing, when the injured and enraged Stultz chased Snyder up the street east of

310

the signal office; and while the trembling form of Snyder lay prostrate on the ground the outraged and indignant Stultz fired several shots over the disturber of his family relations. No shot took effect but Snyder had a close call, the powder blackened his face. Both men were arrested.

As the causes which led to this trouble will probably be shown at the present term of the District Court we forbear making further comment.

The police and Mayor Kelley staged their own show on March 30, according to the *Globe* of April 5, 1881:

> The agent of the Adams Express Co., at this place, Mr. Ruby, was taken out to the railroad water tank last Wednesday, and drenched with water by Mayor [James H.] Kelley and his policemen, for writing an article to an Iowa newspaper reflecting discreditably upon said officials.

What had Mr. Ruby written to cause him to receive a full cascade from the railroad water tank, with the mayor probably pulling the rope? Here is Ruby's correspondence as it appeared in the Oskaloosa (Iowa) *Herald,* March 17, 1881:

KANSAS CORRESPONDENCE.

DODGE CITY, KANSAS, March 4, 1881

EDS. HERALD—Weather warm and pleasant, snow all gone, roads dusty and farmers getting ready for spring work. Ice moved out of river first of week.

The principal topic at present is discussing the temperance law lately passed by the Legislature. The opinion of most people here is that it will not affect the whiskey business here as public opinion is so strong against the law. During conversation between a lawyer and saloonkeeper yesterday the former said: "We want to keep quiet [and] not agitate the question just yet, but organize and then call mass meetings and show our business men and mechanics how the law is going to work against their interests. If they try to enforce the law, if I had a hundred dollars to spend, I can defeat it, as I have never yet seen a jury in this town that I could not carry with me for that amount." This lawyer [Harry Gryden] is present city solicitor. A responsible citizen says he has boasted that he has made over fifty dollars per week by not prosecuting the gamblers and cuthroats here. He was formerly a U. S. revenue officer in southern Indiana but immigrated to Kansas in a hurry, as climate there was unhealthy for him. The mayor is a flannel mouthed Irishman and keeps a saloon and gambling house which he attends to in person. The city marshal and assistant are gamblers and each keep a "woman"—as does the mayor also. The marshal and assistant for their services (as city officials) receive one hundred dollars per month, each. The sheriff [George T. Hinkle] owns a saloon and the deputy sheriff [Undersheriff Fred Singer?] is a bar tender in a saloon.

The mayor and a "bruiser" from Texas had a kind of prize fight the other night, in which the mayor got severely punished. The marshal

311

and friends stood by with drawn revolvers to see fair play. No arrests are made except for killing or attempt to kill unless strangers should come in whom they think has plenty of money. They will arrest him on slight pretext and bleed him. The ex-chairman of the Board of County Commissioners [A. J. Peacock?] runs a saloon and dance hall, where the unwary are enticed, made drunk and robbed. Six men were knocked down and robbed one night last week. There was a novel suit in justice's court last week—men pleaded guilty to charge of assault and battery, as was also proven by several witnesses. Squire got mad, fined lawyer for prosecution ten dollars for contempt, dismissed case stating there was no cause for action. Taxed the costs ($17.50) to prosecuting witness and in default of payment committed him to county jail. There seems to be no energy or pride among the citizens as regards improving the looks or comfort of their property and surroundings. They all seem to be reaching for the almighty dollar and a majority of them are not particular how they get it either. There are many good people here, but the bad ones are so numerous we almost lose sight of the good. If any of your readers anticipate immigrating to Kansas, advise them to shun Dodge City as they would the yellow fever, measles, smallpox and seven year itch combined, as I think they would all be preferable in a civilized country to residence in this town. My opinion of this place is pretty much the same as that of a certain Santa Fe conductor. A drunken Texas cowboy boarded his train east of here and when he called "tickets" Texas responded "hint got none." "Where are you going?" "Goin to ___hic___hell." "All right, give me fifty cents and get off at Dodge." However, I came here with the intention of staying a certain length of time which I intend to do if they don't raise my hair before I get ready to leave.

M. C. RUBY

Mayor Kelley and the entire city council (W. C. Shinn, W. H. Harris, C. S. Hungerford, Mike Sutton, and T. J. Draper) were defeated for re-election on April 4, 1881. The defeat cost Masterson and Brown their jobs for within two days the new administration declared their positions vacant and proceeded to appoint new police officers.[12]

A few days after he had been discharged from the police force Jim Masterson became involved in a slight shooting scrape with bartender Al Updegraff. Masterson, along with A. J. Peacock, owned the Lady Gay saloon where Updegraff plied his trade. Peacock had sided with Updegraff in a controversy concerning one of Jim's friends and ultimately Al and Jim took ineffective pot shots at each other.

Either Jim or a friend is said to have telegraphed Bat Masterson, who was then in the Southwest, to come to his brother's aid. The former sheriff of Ford county arrived in Dodge City a few minutes before noon, April 16, 1881, and immediately went gunning for Peacock and Updegraff. A lively Front street battle ensued in which Updegraff and several noted buildings were perforated. Bat was arrested and fined $8 for disturbing the peace. He was told, however, to leave the town and and return no more. The complete story appears in the section on Bat Masterson.

As a postscript to the affair the Dodge City *Times*, April 21, 1881, said: "Jim Masterson and Charley Ronan [who was also involved in the incident] have gone west to grow up with the country."

Jim Masterson returned to Dodge sometime later. In January, 1889, he was one of the Dodgeites involved in the Gray county seat war. This action is described in the section on William M. Tilghman.

Later that same year, 1889, Jim went to present-day Oklahoma and was one of the first settlers in Guthrie. He served as a deputy sheriff of Logan county, in which Guthrie is located, and in 1893 was appointed a deputy United States marshal by E. D. Nix. Jim was still a deputy marshal when he died on March 31, 1895. The Guthrie *Daily Oklahoma State Capital*, April 1, 1895, said:

JIM MASTERSON DEAD.
A Well Known Figure in the West Dies of Quick Consumption.

Jim Masterson, a first day settler of Guthrie and a well known figure about town, died last night about 11 o'clock. The cause of his death was quick consumption. He was conscious to the last. He was even out Saturday; but last night about 10 o'clock he called to have some of his friends come to see him, and died an hour later.

The deceased was at one time a well known figure in western Kansas. He was one of the marshals of Dodge City during its cowboy days and was reputed to be a brave man. He came to this city the first day and has been acting as deputy marshal since. He was considered here the bravest of all the marshals. Whenever a big raid was to be made on any stronghold of outlaws, like that at Ingalls,[13] he was always asked to be one of the party. When every man would flinch, he would still be found in the front rank. Every man has his virtues and his faults. Jim Masterson was a man who never went back on a friend, and never forgot an obligation. He never pretended to keep up the conventional social amenities; but yet there was a man whom money could absolutely never make break a trust, and who would have done a kind act to a man on the gallows after all the world had given him the cold shoulder, and where there was no chance of any personal reward. Many who walk the conventional paths of social life are not as honorable in their obligations to their fellow men as he was. He was so proud

313

that in his last moments he would not let his condition be known to his relatives. He is a brother of Bat Masterson, a man of national reputation as a backer of athletic sports, and quite rich, but he would not apply to him for aid.

The body will be shipped to relatives in Wichita in the morning for interment.

1. Dodge City *Times*, July 6, 1878. 2. *Ibid.*, July 6, August 10, September 7, October 5, December 7, 1878. 3. *Ibid.*, August 24, 1878; *Ford County Globe*, August 27, 1878. 4. Dodge City *Times*, August 10, 1878. 5. *Ibid.*, December 7, 1878; January 11, April 12, 1879; *Ford County Globe*, April 15, 1879. 6. *Ford County Globe*, February 17, 1879. 7. *Ibid.*, April 15; Dodge City *Times*, April 12, May 10, June 7, July 12, August 9, September 6, October 11, November 15, 1879. 8. *Ford County Globe*, June 10, 1879. 9. Dodge City *Times*, November 15, 1879. 10. *Ibid.*, November 15, 1879; January 17, February 14, March 6, April 10, May 8, July 10, August 7, September 11, October 9, 1880; *Ford County Globe*, November 18, 1879. 11. Dodge City *Times*, October 9, December 11, 1880; April 14, 1881. 12. *Ibid.*, April 7, 1881. 13. This battle at Ingalls, Okla., between United States peace officers and members of the Doolin gang, occurred September 1, 1893. For accounts of the fight eleven miles east of Stillwater, Okla., see Evett Dumas Nix, *Oklahombres, Particularly the Wilder Ones* (Eden Publishing House, St. Louis, 1929), pp. 103-116, and Glenn Shirley, *Six-gun and Silver Star* (University of New Mexico Press, Albuquerque, 1955), pp. 85-97.

MASTERSON, WILLIAM B. (1853-1921)

Bat Masterson was a resident of Dodge City in its earliest days. The story is told that he, along with brother Ed, subcontracted to build a portion of right of way for the Santa Fe in the late summer of 1872 between Fort Dodge and what was to become Dodge City. The story goes on to say that the contractor, a man named Ritter, failed to pay the brothers and Bat, when he finally located him, extracted their pay at point of gun.

The story may be based on fact, for on April 15, 1873, according to diarist Henry H. Raymond, an old friend of the Masterson family (*see* the section on Ed Masterson), "Bat took Ritter prisoner I [Raymond] went on train [and] got his valice. . . ."

Raymond had come to Kansas in November, 1872, and almost immediately joined Bat, Ed and Jim Masterson on a buffalo hunt. For the next 13 months he kept a day-by-day record of his activities and often he also recorded the activities of the Masterson boys. From the start Raymond indicates that William B. was referred to as "Bat," a fact of some interest since for years a few Western historians have believed that Bat earned his nickname by using a cane to subdue his opponents. They claim Bat used it only

314

after the winter of 1876 when he was wounded by Sgt. Melvin A. King in a Sweetwater, Tex., brawl that left him somewhat crippled.

Modern-day descendants of Henry Raymond say that the Raymond family thought Bat's middle name was Bartholomew which was shortened to Bart (a fact substantiated by the diary), and subsequently to Bat.

Raymond's brief diary records Bat in and out of Dodge City as late as October 24, 1873. The next time he can be located with certainty is on June 27, 1874, the day of the Battle of Adobe Walls in the Texas Panhandle. One of the most famous Indian fights in the West, it was described by a participant in a letter appearing in the Leavenworth *Times*, July 10, 1874:

FROM THE FRONTIER.

FIVE DAYS FIGHTING ON THE CANADIAN, AND TWENTY-FIVE RED SKINS KILLED.

HUNTERS CORRALLED—HERDERS DRIVEN IN—
STOCK RUN OFF—BRIDGES BURNED—MEN MURDERED.

THE LATEST AND MOST RELIABLE NEWS FROM THE SEAT OF THE INDIAN WAR.

Yesterday the mails from the South brought full and complete particulars from the scene of the Indian troubles. Not only have the infernal red skins been skirmishing along the Kansas border, but they have skipped out of the Territory on both sides, and on the Canadian, in the Texas Pan Handle, they have been giving the hunters a lively game. Over a hundred hunters and teamsters have been corralled there since the 27th of June, and have been fighting the red devils tooth and nail. The first of the week a courier reached Dodge City bearing dispatches from the imprisoned men, and also an account of the killed and wounded. The letter was addressed to Mr. A. C. Meyers, partner of one [of] the imprisoned men and reads as follows:

ADOBE WALLS, TEXAS, July 1, '74.

DEAR MYERS:—We have been attacked by Indians, and corralled since June 27th. The attack was made early in the morning, and the battle lasted about three hours. Ike Shadler and brother, Billy Tyler and Mr. Olds were killed. The latter shot himself accidentally.

The hunters are all sick of hunting, so they say, and are apt to leave without a moment's warning; but I am willing to stay if I can get enough men to guard the place. The bastions and corral were useless to us; we had to do our fighting from the store. About 25 or 30 Indians were killed—we found 11. I have put the place in a state of seige. If you can get an escort of 50 men, send [A. J.?] Anthony's or all the horse teams you can get. If things quiet down so that the boys will stay, I will send a dispatch. Indians in sight all the time. All the hunters are in except about 30, and we are expecting them to-night. The corral is full of horses; we have 38. We are well armed, and can stand off 500 Indians. There were 200 of them. We were completely taken by surprise. Our men behaved like heroes. If the Indians had come one hour later, we would all have been killed, as Dixon and Jim Hanrahan and their men would have been started on a hunt, leaving the place with only 17 men, and only half armed. I killed one Indian that I know of, and I don't know how many more, as I was shooting at them with my 40 at from forty to sixty yards, for twenty shots. I took one scalp. Fred Myers killed two Indians; they rode around us to the corral and got off their horses, and fought as brave as any men I ever saw. We had 150 Indians around our place at one time. Their intention was to take the place, and probably the hunters as they come in. All the men are of the opinion that the Indians are waiting for reinforcements, and then give us another rattle, but we are fixed for them.

FRED LEONARD. . . .

The little trading center was not wiped out, however. The Leavenworth *Daily Commercial,* July 26, 1874, reprinted the story of their homecoming from Dodge City's first newspaper:

THE INDIAN WAR.

NEWS FROM THE CANADIAN.

FROM THE DODGE CITY MESSENGER.

The Hon. James Hanrahan and party arrived in Dodge City on the 17th inst., direct from the Canadian. They bring with them some fine trophies of the fight they had with Mr. Lo, in the latter part of June. The trophies consist of head-and-tail gear of savage chiefs.

There are four war bonnets, with all of the gew-gaws attached—feathers, birds, and a number of scalps—together with the scalp of some poor woman hanging to one of the bonnets. Bows and arrows, and lances fixed up in gorgeous Indian style. The paraphernalia belonged to chiefs who led the savages at the attack on the hunters. The shields are made of the neck of buffalo hides, and which are capable of withstanding arrows or small shot, but could not prevent the hunters' bullets from dashing through in search of the Indian. The trophies are ugly looking, and it is no wonder that stock is easily stampeded at the sight of such horrid things.

The party in coming up kept off the main route so as to avoid meeting any number of Indians—and they succeeded in getting through without being molested.

The following are the names of the men that comprised the Hon. James Hanrahan's party, and who done some tall Indian fighting:

James Hanrahan,	Joshua Fredericks,
M. Welsh,	J. W. McKinley,
Wm. Dixon,	Joseph Craig,
Arth Abercrombie,	W. W. Murphy,
Frank Brown,	George Wilkes,
Wm. Ogge,	Chas. Wright,
Wm. Thornhill,	John McCabe,
O. Sheppard,	Phillip Cisk,

316

M. Coffee,	Sylvester Lilly,
Bat Masterson,	Tom. O. Keefe,
John Clark,	Chas. O'Brien,
Martin Gallaway,	Rankin Moore,
George Aiken,	Dave Campbell,
Sam Smith,	Clark Teneyke,
Joe Plummer,	Jim Saunders,
Jack Williams,	Wm. H. Johnston,
James Carlyle,	Hiram Watson.
Henry Wirtz,	

One of the earliest descriptive stories of the battle appeared in the Leavenworth *Times,* November 17, 1877, and was reprinted in the Dodge City *Times,* November 24:

THE ADOBE WALLS FIGHT.
ONE OF THE MOST MEMORABLE INDIAN BATTLES ON RECORD—TWENTY-NINE AGAINST FIVE HUNDRED—A BRAVE RESISTANCE.

The following description of the Adobe Walls fight is from the pencil of Mr. John Coulter, of the Leavenworth *Times,* who visited this city recently:

DODGE CITY, November 13.

EDITOR TIMES:—The details of that memorable and wonderful fight at Adobe Walls, in the Pan Handle of Texas on June 27th, 1874, between a party of twenty-nine white men and some five hundred Indians, has never yet found its way into print. It was a thrilling episode, more wonderful than any ever pictured in a dime novel, and has the advantage over the average Indian story of being true, as several of the leading men of Dodge City, who were present in the fight, and among them Sheriff elect of this county, Mr. W. B. Masterson can testify.

ADOBE WALLS

is situated in the Texas Pan Handle, in a little bottom just between the two forks of Adobe Creek which empties into the Canadian river, the Walls lying in the triangle described by the forks of the creek and the Canadian, and consisting of two stores, a blacksmith shop and a saloon, the town, if it could be so called, having been founded in the spring. The stores were those of Chas. Rath & Co., and Leonard and Myers; the blacksmith shop belonged to Tom Kief, and the saloon was kept by James Hanrahan. On the 5th of June Hanrahan's party left Dodge for Adobe Walls, and on the 7th, at Sharp's Creek, seventy-five miles below Dodge were

ATTACKED BY A BAND OF CHEYENNES

who run off all their stock. Just after this skirmish they were joined by a wagon train, which accompanied them to the Walls, arriving there but a short time before the fight took place. On the morning of the 27th, about 3 o'clock, the day of the battle, the party sleeping in the saloon building, consisting of James Hanrahan, William Dixon, formerly General Miles' chief of scouts, and now chief of scouts at Fort Elliott, Texas, W. B. Masterson, now Sheriff elect of Ford County, Kan., Michael Welsh, Oscar Shepherd, ——— Johnson, ——— McKinney, ——— Bermuda, ——— McCabe and William Ogg, were startled by the falling of a portion of the roof, which had given way. The men, awakened by the crash, jumped up apprehending that they had been

ATTACKED BY INDIANS,

but discovering the real state of the case proceeded to make the needed repairs. One of their number, Billy Ogg, went out to get the horses, which were picketed a short distance from the building, but discovering the Indians charging down from the hills he was forced to leave the stock and run for the house. The Indians, as nearly as could be estimated, were nearly five hundred in number, and comprised braves from the Kiowas, Comanches, Cheyennes, and Southern Apaches. The Indians, for weeks previous to the attack upon the Adobe Walls, had been

MURDERING EVERY WHITE MAN

they came across, and it was their intention to clean out the Walls as a part of the programme. The store of Leonard & Meyers had a stockade built around it, and the party holding it were Fred Leonard, now one of the prominent business men of Dodge City; Frank Smith, William Tyler, who was killed during the fight, Hiram Watson, Samuel Smith, Charles Armitage, an old man named Keeler, Henry Wert and Moccasin Jim. In Rath & Co's store were Jas. Langton, now in the Sutler's store at Fort Dodge, William Eba, George Olds, who accidently shot himself the day after the fight, Andy Johnson and Thomas Kief. The Indians charged down upon the little garrison in

A SOLID MASS,

every man having time to get under shelter with the exception of the two Schaddler brothers, who were sleeping by their wagons a short distance from the Walls. Both were killed and their bodies mutilated. The Schaddlers were just about to start with a load of hides for Dodge City, when they were killed. The red devils charged down right to the very doors and windows of the houses, and the gate of the stockade, but were met by such a galling fire that they were forced to retire. So close were they that as the brave defenders of the Walls shot out of the doors and windows they planted the muzzles of their guns in the very faces and breasts of the savages, who rained a perfect storm of bullets down upon the houses. For

TWO TERRIBLE HOURS

did the Indians, who displayed a bravery and recklessness never before surpassed and seldom before equalled, make successive charges upon the walls, each time being driven back by the grim and determined men behind, who fired with a rapidity and decision which laid many a brave upon the ground. But one man was killed in the stockade, Billy Tyler, who

318

was shot in the left side of the neck while in a sitting position, looking out of the stockade gate, the ball passing entirely through his body and coming out under the right arm. The Indian who gave Tyler his death wound was scarcely fifteen feet from him at the time. At the end of two hours the Indians, finding it a losing game, withdrew to the hills, keeping up a bombardment upon the stockade all the time. In the afternoon, and while the bullets were coming down upon them like hailstones, Masterson, Bermuda and Johnson came out of the stockade and found ten Indians and one negro who were lying out on the bottom. These were all who were known to have been killed, but subsequent Indian reports, made by savages who were driven into the agencies by General Miles in his campaign of the summer of 1874, showed that some

SEVENTY INDIANS WERE KILLED

or died of wounds. The weather at the time of the fight was intensely hot, and to be struck by a bullet was certain death, as the wound immediately began to mortify and death was a matter of but a few hours. The Comanches in the Adobe Walls fight were led by Big Bow, the Kiowas by Lone Wolf and the Cheyennes by Monimick, Red Moon and Gray Beard. Gray Beard was afterward captured and taken to Fort Leavenworth with other chiefs in 1875, and while, with others on their way to Florida attempted to escape and was

KILLED BY THE GUARD.

The Indians were shortly afterwards completely subdued by General Miles. The Miles expedition started from Fort Dodge on the 6th of August and on the 30th fought the reds on the Red river. Masterson, who participated in the Adobe Walls fight, went out with the expedition as a scout under Lieut. Baldwin, of the old 5th, and was with Baldwin at the time of the capture of the Germain children.

Thirty-nine years after the fight, Bat wrote to author Frederick S. Barde and explained what he knew about the Negro found lying dead on the battlefield. A copy of the letter is in the manuscript files of the Kansas State Historical Society:

Office of the
Advertising Manager
THE MORNING TELEGRAPH
Long Acre Square
New York

October 13, 1913.

FREDERICK S. BARDE, ESQ.,
Guthrie, Oklahoma
My dear Mr. Barde:—
I forgot to tell you in my Saturday letter about the negro bugler at the Adobe Walls. What probably gave rise to the belief that he was a

deserter from the Tenth Cavalry was the fact that he was familiar with many of the bugle calls and executed them in first class style.

We had in the building I was in two men who had served in the army and understood all the bugle calls. The first call the negro blew was a rally which our men understood instantly. The next was a charge and that also was understood and immediately the Indians came rushing over the hills in a fresh attack. Every bugle call he blew was understood by the ex-soldiers and were carried out to the letter by the Indians, showing that the negro had the Indians thoroughly drilled in this particular department of the army service.

The negro was killed late in the afternoon of the first day's fighting as he was running away from a wagon owned by the Schadler brothers, both of whom were killed in this same wagon. The negro had his bugle with him at the time he was shot by Harry Armitage. Also he was carrying a tin can filled with sugar and another filled with ground coffee under each arm. Armitage shot him through the back with a 50 calibre Sharp's rifle as he was making his escape. That ended the negro bugler.

Very truly yours,
(s) W B MASTERSON

The battle of Adobe Walls was part of a general Indian outbreak which resulted in the formation of an Indian territory expedition under the command of Col. [Bvt. Maj. Gen.] Nelson A. Miles. The expedition formed at Fort Dodge about the first of August, 1874, and there, on August 5, Bat signed on as civilian scout. Billy Dixon, who had also been at Adobe Walls, joined the scouts on August 1. Bat, Billy and most of the other scouts were paid at the rate of $75 per month with $50 bonuses for carrying dispatches through Indian-infested country. Bat, however, apparently did not earn one of these premiums.

The detachment of scouts, under the command of Lt. Frank D. Baldwin, was part of the force directed by Maj. [Bvt. Lt. Col.] Charles E. Compton which also included four companies of cavalry and one of infantry. On August 11 this group left Fort Dodge and headed south for the Texas Panhandle. Two days later the remainder of the expedition pulled out. In his report dated Fort Leavenworth, March 4, 1875, Colonel Miles detailed the actions of Baldwin's detachment until it rejoined the main force:

From the crossing of the Beaver, near Kiowa Creek, a scouting party of forty-nine (49) men, under command of Lieut. Baldwin, proceeded along the line of the Palo Duro to Adobe Walls, on the Canadian River, arriving there in time to repulse a second attack upon that place, made by a small band of Indians, who retreated southeast, burning the prairie grass behind them.

320

From Adobe Walls this force moved down the Canadian, surprised a small party of Indians near the mouth of Chicken Creek, killed one and wounded another, and rejoined the main command . . . twelve (12) miles west of the Antelope Hills, August 24th.

Lieutenant Baldwin left Adobe Walls at 8:50 a. m., August 20, 1874, and headed down the Canadian on its north bank. Twenty miles from the Walls he crossed to the south bank and shortly thereafter four of his scouts, who were acting as advance or point, had the skirmish with two Indians which was mentioned in Miles' report. That evening Baldwin wrote in his diary:

The Indian signs are fresh and a great many evidences are seen proving that they are in this vicinity in large numbers and we will probably see plenty of them before we rejoin the command. I sent McGent and Masterson to the main command with despatches to night. They left camp at 9 this evening and as I supposed the Head Quarters to be about 55 miles from here on Wolf Creek gave them until 12 o'clock mid-night to-morrow which I think is abundant time. . . .

For the next several weeks the scouts were continually being used to reconnoitre for Miles and to serve as flankers on columnar movements. Skirmishes were had with the Indians with some regularity and with varying intensity. On November 8, 1874, Baldwin, in command of Co. D, Fifth infantry; Co. D, Sixth cavalry and the scouts, attacked a large party with such success that the Indians abandoned most of their camp property and two small white captives, Julia and Adelaide German, who had been captured near the Smoky Hill on September 11, 1874.

Most of Bat's biographers have stated that he was present when the little girls were recovered, but this hardly seems likely since official records of the office of the quartermaster general indicate that he was discharged from his position as scout on October 12, 1874, four weeks before.[1]

In a letter dated December 18, 1874, Bat's old buffalo hunting friend, Henry H. Raymond, wrote: "I hear that Bat has got a job at camp supply [at the junction of Wolf and Beaver creeks in present Woodward county, Okla.], of counting mules, night and morning." By March 1, 1875, Bat had drifted back to Dodge City, where he was listed in the Kansas state census as a 24-year-old teamster who was born in Kansas but who had moved to this state from Illinois. Obviously the enumerator was in error. Bat was born on November 24, 1853, which would have made him 21 years old in March, 1875. Neither was Bat born in Kansas but probably in eastern Canada, though his death certificate lists his birthplace as the United States. The Masterson family did, however, move from Illinois to Kansas sometime around 1870.

Contemporary records fail to indicate Bat's whereabouts between March, 1875, and the spring of 1877. Within this time, however, Bat was supposed to have had his altercation with Sgt. Melvin A. King over the affections of one Molly Brennan. The story goes that the trooper one night surprised Bat and Molly in an after hours' meeting in a Sweetwater, Tex., saloon, and commenced shooting. Molly threw herself in front of Bat to protect him and received one of the shots. Though Bat was wounded, too, he was able to return the fire and kill the sergeant. For several months thereafter, the story goes on, Bat supported himself with a cane which also served as an auxiliary weapon and became the cause of the legendary Masterson nickname.

As with many "legends" this story is based on a little fact for on February 11, 1876, the Jacksboro (Tex.) *Frontier Echo* reported: "Telegraphic News: King, of H. Company, 4th Cavalry, and a woman, Molly Braman, killed at San Antonio by a citizen."

The muster roll of Co. H, Fourth cavalry, now on file in the National Archives, indicates that King died at a cantonment on Sweetwater creek, Tex., January 25, 1876, from the effects of a pistol wound received January 24. The wound was not received in the line of duty.

More than a year passes before a mention of Bat again appears in the newspapers. The Masterson about whom the Dodge City *Times*, April 28, 1877, was speaking in this article however, might have been Ed or Jim:

Dodge City is bracing herself up for the cattle trade. Places of refreshment are being gorgeously arrayed in new coats of paint and other ornaments to beguile the festive cow boy. Masterson & Springer's place can scarcely be recognized since the bar has been moved and operated upon by Mr. Weaver's brush. The graining is finely executed. Charley Lawson's orchestra are mounted on a platform enclosed by and tastefully ornamented with bunting.

On May 6, 1877, the *Times* reported that the city council had, on May 1, approved certain saloon licenses. Masterson's name appeared again:

Petitions properly signed and recommending the following parties as suitable persons to engage in the keeping of dram shops were presented and accepted:

322

Garis & Tilghman, McGinty & Deger, Dunham & Dawson, Beeson & Harris, Springer & Masterson, A. J. Peacock, Beatty & Kelley, G. M. Hoover, Rule & Smith, Cox & Boyd, Langton & Newton, H. J. Fringer, H. B. Bell, Colley & Manion, Chambers & Foster, Henry Sturm.

The first definite identification of Bat Masterson in available local newspapers concerned some trouble he had with the Dodge City police force. On June 6, 1877, he tried to prevent the arrest of Bobby Gill (Robert Gilmore), a persistent and ubiquitous cowtown character. The *Times,* June 9, described Bat's attempt:

THE GANG CORRALED.
THE OPENING OF THE CATTLE TRADE CELEBRATED IN THE DOG HOUSE.

Bobby Gill done it again. Last Wednesday was a lively day for Dodge. Two hundred cattle men in the city; the gang in good shape for business; merchants happy, and money flooding the city, is a condition of affairs that could not continue in Dodge very long without an eruption, and that is the way it was last Wednesday. Robert Gilmore was making a talk for himself in a rather emphatic manner, to which Marshal Deger took exceptions, and started for the dog house with him. Bobby walked very leisurely—so much so that Larry felt it necessary to administer a few paternal kicks in the rear. This act was soon interrupted by Bat Masterson, who wound his arm affectionately around the Marshal's neck and let the prisoner escape. Deger then grappled with Bat, at the same time calling upon the bystanders to take the offender's gun and assist in the arrest. Joe Mason appeared upon the scene at this critical moment and took the gun. But Masterson would not surrender yet, and came near getting hold of a pistol from among several which were strewed around over the sidewalk, but half a dozen Texas men came to the Marshal's aid and gave him a chance to draw his gun and beat Bat over the head until blood flew upon Joe Mason so that he kicked, and warded off the blows with his arm. Bat Masterson seemed possessed of extraordinary strength, and every inch of the way was closely contested, but the city dungeon was reached at last, and in he went. If he had got hold of his gun before going in there would have been a general killing. . . .

Ed. Masterson accomplished his first official act in the arrest of Bobby Gilmore the same afternoon.

Next day Judge [D. M.] Frost administered the penalty of the law by assessing twenty-five and costs to Bat . . . and five to Bobby.

The boys are all at liberty now.

James H. Kelley, then mayor of the town, returned some of Bat's money. The *Times,* July 7, 1877, said: "The Mayor, with the consent of the Council, remitted the fine of $10.00 assessed against the defendant in the case of city vs. W. B. Masterson."

During the summer of 1877 Bat served as under sheriff of Ford county, his superior being Charles E. Bassett, sheriff. On August 2 the county officers pursued one William Samples who had just killed Enos Mosley up on the Saw Log. The *Times*, August 4, 1877, reported their failure:

Sheriff Bassett, Under-sheriff Masterson, Al. Updegraff [with whom Bat was to have a near fatal altercation in just four years] and one of the herders started out soon after the news came to town, and spent two days scouring the country in search of Samples but failed to get trace of him.

Samples, however, was finished off next day by cowboy friends of Mosley.

There is little doubt that a degree of enmity existed between Bat and Larry Deger, especially since the affair in June when Deger had given Bat a pistol whipping. It seems probable, then, that this was the reason Bat used his authority as under sheriff to force Deger to resign as deputy sheriff, a job he held concurrently with the position of city marshal. The *Times*, August 4, 1877, simply stated: "Marshal Deger resigned his position of Deputy Sheriff this week, at the request of Under Sheriff Masterson."

In early August Bat visited John "Red" Clarke at his ranch on the Cimarron river.[2] In September he arrested a horse thief. The *Times*, September 8, 1877, stated: "Under Sheriff Masterson arrested a man this evening who had stole a horse near Granada last week and sold him to a man near Offerle. The prisoner 'put up' and was released."

Nine days later, September 17, Bat was instrumental in preventing bloodshed which might have resulted through mistaken identity. The protagonists, of all people, were a Dodge City policeman and the sheriff of Edwards county, neither of whom recognized the other. Let the Dodge City *Times*, September 22, 1877, tell the story:

SWINDLERS.
THEY COME FROM KINSLEY AND TRY TO SWINDLE THE GOOD PEOPLE OF DODGE.

Last Monday three men came up from near Kinsley with a wagon and team. They stopped at Rath & Co's. store and ordered a supply of provisions, saying they were going out hunting. Having no gun, they wanted to trade a gold watch and chain to Mr. Wright for a gun in his store. Mr. Wright, in the goodness of his nature, told them all right, he would take the watch just to accommodate them and help them get outfitted. They took the goods and gun and loaded them in the wagon, the whole purchase amounting to about $120. But instead of calling around at the office to settle and turn over the watch, they silently drove out of town taking a southerly direction. As soon as their absence was discovered at the store, and that they had really skipped out, one of the employees Mr. Strauss, was sent to overtake and remind them of the little bill they had left behind unpaid. He overtook them several miles south of here and asked them to come back or give him the amount due. They asked him if he was an officer, and he said he was not. They were not very obedient; did not like to come back and would not give up any money. After fooling for some time they said they would give him the watch, which they did, and he returned home.

Being positive that they did have money, and being convinced that they had not done exactly the square thing, Mr. Wright sent Under-Sheriff Masterson out to overhaul them again. Masterson overtook them, and in his amiable manner bulldozed them out of all the money they had, amounting to about $25. The watch and chain being worth about $75, the $25 in cash added left Rath & Co. out only $20, which they concluded to look out for when the hunters returned. They could have taken the gun, but this would have left the hunters without means of hunting, so they were allowed to keep it.

But the joke of this transaction—if joke it be—was the fact that on this same evening Sheriff McCanse, of Edwards county, arrived with two deputies, after this same party of hunters, charging them with having taken the watch and chain and the wagon in about the same manner as they took the goods from Rath & Co. As McCanse and his men came riding up the road on their way here, they passed the residence of Mr. J. E. Van Voorhis, who has been searching for some horse thieves of late. Mr. Van Voorhis saw the sheriff and his men riding rapidly, and it being about dark he immediately took them to be the thieves he was looking for, and hitching his horse to his buggy gave chase, following close at their heels until he reached this city, where he immediately informed our sheriff and police, and pointed out the supposed thieves, who were then putting up their horses at Anderson's livery stable. Under Sheriff Masterson and Policeman Mason immediately rushed over to the stable. Masterson met one of the men, took his pistol and made him a prisoner. Mason pointed two ivory-handled guns at another, and completely covered him. The last man they met was Sheriff McCanse. Mason seized his revolver, but McCanse did not like the idea of losing his gun, and held on to it. It was very opportune that Masterson came up just then and recognized McCanse, as our Joe might have had trouble in arresting him. But we firmly believe that if McCanse had not been identified, our Dodge City "braves" would have captured the Edwards county crowd without losing a man. It was all a mistake, and the principal part of the joke is on Mr. Van Voorhis.

That same evening McCanse and his men went on south after the hunters, whom they captured without any resistance a few days drive south of here, and took them back to Kinsley.

One of the hunters gave him name here as Samuel Miller, but other parties say his name is Gooddale. There were two others with him.

In spite of the not too amiable feelings between the under sheriff and City Marshal Deger the former was appointed a special policeman on the city force on September 17. The Dodge City police department then consisted of Marshal L. E. Deger, Assistant Marshal Edward J. Masterson, and Policemen Joseph W. Mason and William B. Masterson. The terminal date of Bat's employment as a city officer is not known, although on October 2, 1877, he was paid $25 for his services. At the rate of $2.50 per day, based on Mason's salary, this would mean that Bat served ten days or from September 17 to September 27.[3]

The only recorded action in which Bat participated as a city policeman was the attempted arrest of A. C. Jackson, a "gay and festive" cowboy. The Dodge City *Times*, September 29, 1877, reported the gunplay as follows:

RANDOM SHOTS.

Mr. A. C. Jackson is a gay and festive Texas boy, and like all true sons of the Lone Star State, he loves to fondle and practice with his revolver in the open air. It pleases his ear to hear the sound of this deadly weapon. Aside from the general pleasure derived from shooting, the Texas boy makes shooting inside the corporate limits of any town or city a specialty. He loves to see the inhabitants rushing wildly around to "see what all this shooting is about;" and it tickles his heart to the very core to see the City Marshal coming towards him at a distance, while he is safe and securely mounted on his pony and ready to skip out of town and away from the officer.

The programme of the Texas boy, then, is to come to town and bum around until he gets disgusted with himself, then to mount his pony and ride out through the main street, shooting his revolver at every jump. Not shooting to hurt any one, but shooting in the air, just to raise a little excitement and let people know he is in town.

In order to put a stop to this, the carrying of concealed weapons within the city limits has been prohibited, but this has only partially stopped the practice. Several times this summer the town has been thrown into excitement by the firing of revolvers in the middle of the streets, and the marshals have become very much aggravated over the matter, and determined to put a stop to it if possible.

Last Tuesday [September 25] the sound of the revolver was heard several times in quick succession. The police were on the alert in a moment, and everybody rushed toward where the sound came from. Men hatless and women with their back hair down hastened to see whether their absent friends were safe. But all this excitement was caused by Jackson indulging in his favorite amusement of shooting. However, he came out loser, and that is some consolation. He was riding down Front street, and about opposite Beatty & Kelley's he commenced to shoot. He had shot two or three times, when the police got their eyes on him. Bat Masterson ordered him to halt, but nary a halt would he. He says, "I am going to skip out for camp," and bang! bang! went his gun. Bat had a gun too, and he immediately brought it to bear on the festive cow-boy's horse. Instantly after Bat shot Ed. got in a shot. The horse seemed to scringe, but being spurred on dashed out of town and off toward camp. Two more shots were fired after him, but without effect. Bat then mounted a horse and gave chase, but when he was about to hail the shootist again, he found that his own revolver had not a load in its chambers. So what else could he do but return? Jackson's horse proved to be mortally wounded, but the noble animal carried its rider a mile or two from the city at a rapid gait, and then fell to the ground and rose no more. Jackson "hoofed it" the balance of the way to the camp. This will probably serve as a slight check to the practice of shooting "just for fun" inside the city limits.

On September 27, Bat, as under sheriff, accompanied Bassett and J. J. Webb in a futile search for Sam Bass and his Union Pacific train robbers. The Dodge City *Times* story of this chase was included in the section on Bassett.

With the approach of election time Bat became interested in the office of sheriff of Ford county. His friend and the current holder of the position, Charley Bassett, was prohibited by the state constitution from succeeding himself for a third term. His enemy (or at least not a friend), Larry Deger was also interested in the job. What better chance, then, not only to add to his already impressive laurels as a peace officer but also to humble his Dodge City foe by winning the race for sheriff?

So it was that in the Dodge City *Times*, October 13, 1877 (the same issue in which Deger announced himself as a candidate), Bat placed this announcement:

At the earnest request of many citizens of Ford county, I have consented to run for the office of Sheriff at the coming election in this county. While earnestly soliciting the suffrages of the people, I have no pledges to make, as pledges are usually considered before election to be mere clap-trap. I desire to say to the voting public that I am no politician, and shall make no combinations that would be likely to in anywise hamper me in the discharge of the duties of the office, and should I be elected will put forth my best efforts to so discharge the duties of the office that those voting for me shall have no occasion to regret having done so.

Respectfully,

W. B. MASTERSON.

The Shinn brothers, W. C. and Lloyd, who owned and edited the Dodge City *Times*, threw Bat a plug in that same issue, October 13, 1877:

Mr. W. B. Masterson is on the track for Sheriff, and so announces himself in this paper. "Bat" is well known as a young man of nerve and coolness in cases of danger. He has served on the police force of this city, and also as under-sheriff, and knows just how to gather in the sinners. He is qualified to fill the office, and if elected will never shrink from danger.

On October 27 the Lady Gay Saloon was the scene of a "Peoples' Mass Convention." The purpose was to nominate candidates for the coming election. Both Larry Deger and Bat were suggested for sheriff, but when the vote was taken, Masterson was the choice. This, however, did not discourage Deger and he ran anyway. When the ballots were counted after the polls closed on November 6, 1877, Bat had beaten his opponent by three votes.[4] (For more information on this election see the section on Lawrence E. Deger.)

D. M. Frost, a political opponent of Bat's, was at that time police judge of Dodge City. On December 4, 1877, Bat, R. M. Wright, P. L. Beatty, H. M. Beverley and others presented a petition to the city council asking that Frost's office be declared vacant since the judge no longer resided in the city and consequently was not eligible for the position. The Times, December 8, noted:

At the last meeting of the Council a petition was presented asking that the office of Police Judge be declared vacant, by reason of the fact that Judge Frost resided on his claim and not in the city, but the Judge informed the council that he had ceased to reside on his claim and was a resident of the city, whereupon the petition was laid upon the table.

It was at this same council meeting that Bat's brother, Ed, was appointed city marshal.

Though Bat did not assume the duties of his office officially until January 14, 1878, he did act as sheriff of Ford county in opening the January term of the district court on January 2.[5] After Masterson was sworn the Times January 19, 1878, reported:

NEW OFFICERS.

W. B. Masterson on the 14th assumed the duties of the office of Sheriff, to which he was elected last November, succeeding Chas. E. Bassett who has held the office for a period of four years, and who has made many friends. Mr. Masterson, on assuming the duties of his office appointed Chas. E. Bassett under-Sheriff, Simeon Woodruff, a respectable and trustworthy citizen and formerly of the East End, Deputy Sheriff, also our old friend Col. John W. Straughn for Jailor. These appointments will meet with the approbation of our people, and indicates that Bat intends to do his duty and that to with a view to the best interests of the county.

Within two weeks fate gave the young sheriff an opportunity to rise toward glory, and resourceful Bat Masterson was not found wanting. It all started at four o'clock, Sunday morning, January 27, 1878, at the Santa Fe railroad station in Kinsley, 37 miles up the line from Dodge. Five men, with faces blackened to avoid recognition, stepped out of the darkness and confronted young Andy Kinkade, the night operator, ordering him to throw up his hands. The story is told by the Kinsley *Valley Republican*:

At a few minutes before 4 o'clock this (Sunday) morning, five desperadoes having faces blackened entered the office of the R. R. depot at this place, saluting the night operator, Andrew Kinkade, who was at his post, with a "good morning," at the same instant "covering" him with revolvers, and demanding the money in the office. Mr. Kinkade with a remarkable presence of mind replied that there was no funds at his command, at the same time opening an empty money drawer. The leader of the gang ordered Mr. K. to "open that safe, d----d quick, too," at the same time shoving two cocked revolvers in his face. Mr. Kinkade informed the party that he did not have the key— Gardner had charge of it and they could go to him at the hotel—adding that the funds had gone east on the train a few hours before. Mr. Kinkade bravely stood at his post defending two thousand dollars in hard cash of the company's funds, which had he faltered would have been taken. The west bound Pueblo express was approaching, and something must be done. The five well armed highwaymen, confronted by a boy, were foiled. They threatened to blow his brains out if he did not open the safe. Kinkade had a small derringer in his hip pocket, and cocking it attempted to draw it, when one of the highwaymen, noticing his move said: "No, you don't—hand that over," and he laid it down on the counter. Kinkade knew the hotel men would be there to meet the train in a few moments, but when he was ordered outside and marched down the platform his only fear was that he could not inform the conductor of the danger. Shouting to Blanchard, of the Eureka [hotel], to "go back, these men are armed," one of them attempted to strike him. As the train drew up Mr. Kinkade escaped, crossing the track in front of the engine, followed by a shot. Running down the train he informed conductor Mallory of the danger. Blanchard was taken in charge, but made his escape and armed himself. A dozen shots were fired into the train, which the robbers stopped after it had pulled out 100 yards. Again the train started and was stopped two miles up the track, where it was detained 20 minutes and 20 shots exchanged. The town was aroused. In company with eight or ten others we boarded a hand car and started to the rescue. The train moved off before we reached it, and we saw the mounted robbers, six or eight in number, well mounted, approaching. They crossed the track toward the river, and three or four shots were fired at them. A large party well mounted started in pursuit at once. A telegram from Dodge City at 6 a. m. states that conductor Mallory, engineer Anderson and expressman Brown held the fort and lost nothing.[6]

Monday, January 28, the *Republican* issued a second extra in which this appeared:

REPUBLICAN OFFICE,)
Monday, 5 p. m., Jan. 28.)

Supt. Pettibone, who arrived this morning from the east, received a telegram from Dodge City stating that Lieut. Gardner with a detactment of U. S.

329

troops from the Fort, captured six of the train robbers on Mule creek yesterday, killing one. We present the report for what it is worth, and will add that we believe it to be sensational. It was ascertained yesterday that the robbers crossed the river 12 miles above Kinsley, and went south through the hills. C. L. Hubbs, ex sheriff McCanse, E. A. Noble and N. Billings have just returned from the pursuit. They crossed the river at daylight yesterday morning, after which they saw no trail, riding to the head of the Kiowa. The fog was so dense this morning they returned after riding 115 miles. Sheriff Fuller, Clute, Welles and "Calamity Bill" were in Dodge City at 3:30, consulting with Pettibone. A party of eight well mounted and armed left here at 4 o'clock this morning, determined to follow the trail. It has transpired that the robbers left the train near the depot, and conductor Mallory stopped two miles out to ascertain if the messenger was safe and examine the train. The firing was signals of rejoicing over the escape. The robbers had left their horses near the tank at midnight, intending to rob the 1:30 express east, when it stopped for water. It did not stop. Thus foiled they planned the robbery of the Company's safe at the depot, and as a forlorn hope attacked the express car of the train west. Then in the darkness they ran two miles to their horses, closely pursued by the hand car party, when they mounted and escaped. We received orders this morning from Supt. Morse to strike posters offering $100 reward each for the capture of the masked robbers "dead or alive."

LATER.—Sheriff Fuller just returned on a special train from Dodge. Lieut. Gardner with a detactment of U. S. troops in hot pursuit of robbers south of the river.[7]

The *Republican* issued a third extra on Tuesday, January 29:

At this writing the highwaymen have not been captured, neither do we harbor faith equal to a grain of mustard seed that they will be taken in. There was perhaps a blunder on the part of our officials and posse in not mounting in hot haste and pursuing the disappointed night riders immediately. Yet we cannot censure, for the surroundings offer a broad margin of justification. The attack was unexpected as an earthquake. The excitement ran high. It required time for men of nerve to realize the situation and act intelligently. Sheriff Fuller started in pursuit with a well armed party as early as possible. The blunder in not crossing the river was perhaps excusable, as no trail could then be traced. The failure of the sheriff of Ford County to co-operate with the Kinsley party was as it appears to us inexcusable, and the excuse assigned is "too thin." The attempt—feeble indeed—on the part of certain parties to implicate citizens of Edwards county in the diabolical plot is contemptable, and we hurl it back. The deliberate and well planned scheme of the foiled robbers signally failed, and our officials and citizens—including the brave boy who firmly stood at his post at the depot—did nobly. Without the hope of reward further than the performance of duty, a score of our best citizens have for three days and nights been in pursuit, exposed to the wintry storm. We congratulate the Santa Fe Company on the result of the raid, and that the masked marauders failed in their efforts is due in the main to the excellent discipline and moral courage of the employees and the fact that the company has wisely prepared for emergencies. If these frontier night marauders have any ambition to raise a stake in the future, they are advised to give the Santa Fe a wide berth if they don't want to get hurt.[8]

Referring to the *Republican's* censure of Sheriff Masterson the *Ford County Globe,* February 5, 1878, had this to say:

The Kinsley Republican extra of Jan. 29th, says that the failure of our Sheriff to co operate with the Kinsley posse, in hunting the train robbers, was inexcusable; and the excuse he assigned is a little "too thin." Now Mr. Republican, we don't know what you mean by his excuse, but have this to say: Our Sheriff is not in circumstances that will warrant him in incurring the expense necessary to hire horses, employ a posse of men, and pay their expenses, even to hunt train robbers whose crime was committed in a neighboring county; unless, those expenses are guaranteed by somebody. We are personly not on squeezing terms with our sheriff, but when as an officer he is unjustly assailed, we feel it our duty to defend him, as well as any other officer in our county. We know that he has the stuff in his make up to be a good officer, and when he does right we will be found telling him so with the same spirit of justice that will guide us to tell him he is wrong, when we consider him so. We think that our Sheriff's hunt for the train robbers has accomplished more than the hunt of all the other possees, even if his departure was not heralded with blasts of trumpets, news paper extras, &tc.

The *Globe's* last sentence referred to Bat's successful pursuit of two of the robbers. The Dodge City *Times,* February 2, 1878, first told of his achievement:

TWO KNIGHTS TAKEN IN.

AND FURNISHED QUARTERS IN FORD COUNTY JAIL.

THEY ARE CAPTURED BY STRATEGY, MY BOY.

SHERIFF W. B. MASTERSON AND HIS HEROIC POSSE BAG THE
GAME WITHOUT A SHOT.

PERILOUS ADVENTURE WITH GRATIFYING RESULTS.

THE DETAILS OF THE PURSUIT AND CAPTURE.

There was a slight ripple which disturbed the usual quiet of Dodge City yesterday evening about 6 o'clock, and increased in volume as the startling announcement spread over the city bearing the gratifying intelligence that W. B. Masterson, Sheriff of Ford county, and posse had returned from a four days hunt, bringing with them two of the gang that made the raid on the town of Kinsley and attempted the robbery of the railroad agent and the western bound express train. The programme for this successful capture was well laid, and what may have appeared as indifference and tardiness has since shown to be a matured and well devised effort to follow a successful capture. The prudence and strategy is highly commendable. The nerve skill and energy of Sheriff Masterson and gallant posse is recorded as a brilliant achievement and is receiving just tribute for so daring a venture accomplished so adroitly and maneuvered with the skill of a warrior.

Sheriff Masterson started on this trail Tuesday afternoon from Dodge City, and went as far as Crooked creek, 27 miles, the first day. The party was snowed in and had to lay over one day. Next day went 35 miles further to Lovell's cattle camp, on mouth of Crooked creek, 55 miles from Dodge City, arriving there at sundown, and remained there next day until afternoon. The storm was terrible about 5 p.m. when four men approached the camp, two of them being the subsequently arrested parties. When within a few hundred yards of the camp they discovered the Sheriff's buggy and horses, and asked the other two, who were cattle men, what strange outfit that was. One of the cattlemen recognized a horse from Anderson's stable, and told them so. They hesitated, the boss herder telling them to come on, which they finally did, when [John J.] Webb, one of the Sheriff's men, went out to meet them, and told them he was on his way to Geo. Anderson's. They came in with Webb, and were decoyed to a dug out where the Sheriff and his party were concealed. Bat stood up behind a post, and came out from his concealment and presenting his pistols told the two outlaws to throw up their hands, which they did, when Kinch Riley, one of the Sheriff's posse, searched them, and took away a Colt's 45, Smith & Wesson's improved. After Riley had taken a pistol from each and supposed that was all, Sheriff Bat Masterson saw that one of the men had another, and when he went to take it the prisoner tried to hold on to it. They also had guns, one a 40 Sharp's sporting rifle and the other a 45 calibre Government carbine.

The prisoners wanted to know what was the matter. The Sheriff replied that they were arrested on a charge of attempting to rob the train. They made no answer nor did they deny what was charged.

The arrested parties are two well known desperadoes, but quailed under the intrepid, cool and daring movements of Sheriff Bat Masterson. Ed. West, the older of the two, is about twenty-six years old, and is a notorious thieving character; Dave Ruddebaugh is about twenty-three years of age, and has lead a wild career in crime. They may have to answer to a catalogue of crimes. The prisoners are safely secured in the Ford county jail, but will be placed to the charge of the authorities of Edwards county.

The sheriff's party composed himself, J. J. Webb, Dave Morrow and Kinch Riley. They were under the direction of the Adams Express Company, by whom the pursuit was arranged, and the well devised and executed capture reflects credit, good judgment and bravery upon all who engaged in it.

There are four others who were engaged in the train robbery. Their capture is only a question of time.

Harry Lovell had three good horses stolen Wednesday night, and his cattle men were on the return of a search for them, accompanied by those two robbers whom they met on the way, when they were apprised by the Sheriff and his posse.

The prisoners will be conveyed to Kinsley tonight, and a preliminary trial had immediately.

332

Bat's "gallant" posse was composed of an interesting group. John Joshua Webb served as a Dodge City policeman, as a Ford county deputy sheriff, and as a leader in the struggle between the Santa Fe and the Denver & Rio Grande for control of the right of way through the Grand Canyon of the Arkansas. In 1880 he was made marshal of Las Vegas, N. M., and in that capacity shot and killed a man for which act he was arrested, tried, and sentenced to die. Peculiarly enough, one of the several attempts Webb made to escape was abetted by Dave Rudabaugh, the man he had helped Bat Masterson capture.

Dave Morrow, known as "Prairie Dog Dave," was an old timer in Dodge. He also served as a Dodge City policeman as well as a Dodge township constable. Prairie Dog Dave and Bat Masterson continued their Dodge City friendship for many years.

Kinch Riley had been a companion of Bat's in the Adobe Walls fight in June, 1874. The Dodge City *Times*, September 20, 1879, said of him: "He . . . had been wounded and bruised in a number of personal encounters. He has undergone many severe trials and exposures, and made many narrow escapes. . . . He was brave and kind. . . ."

The *Ford County Globe*, February 5, 1878, gave more particulars of the capture:

THE TRAIN ROBBERS!
FORD COUNTY TO THE FRONT AS IT SHOULD BE.
AND W. B. MASTERSON MAKES A GOOD BEGINNING.

The attempted train robbers spoken of in our last issue, caused a number of parties to start in pursuit. Sheriff Masterson of our county, with J. J. Webb, David Morrow and Riley having struck a "scent" ambushed themselves on last Thursday at Mr. Lovells cattle camp, some 65 miles south of Dodge City. After some hours waiting two horsemen cautiously approached from the north east. Their motions indicating their fear of coming up. Mr. Webb with concealed revolver went out to meet them, after some talk they came within shooting distance when Masterson springing out with leveled rifle sang out his well known "throw up your hands." West at once complied, but Reudebaugh reached for his revolver; the click of Webb's gun at close quarters changed his mind, however, and both surrendered and were disarmed. Each carried a rifle and two revolvers, all best quality. The party arrived in Dodge City about 6 o'clock P. M. Friday evening, having stopped all night during the storm in camp. Capt. J. M. Thatcher, the general agent of Adams Express Company, and who has been managing the pursuits, with his attorney, interviewed them the same night. The result we are not at liberty to divulge but it was conclusive to Messrs. Thatcher and Gryden. A special train at once went to Kinsley returning at 11 A. M. on Saturday with necessary documents and the prisoners were at 3 P. M. in charge of a large posse conveyed to Kinsley by special train. Kinsley was reached at 4:30 P. M., the town having turned out en masse to receive them. We have forgotten to mention that Wm. Tilghman was also arrested just before the train left. The three prisoners were brought into the spacious court room, which was densely filled with the curious. Reudebaugh and West being shackled together. Justice Willey presided. The prisoners having been promptly turned over to the court, Mr. Gryden opened by explaining his connection with the case, and asked that Reudebaugh be first put on trial. Reudebaugh (who is positively identified by Mr. Kingkade the operator, as the man who disarmed him and who conversed with him over five minutes,) was perfectly cool, and with the tact of an old hand waived a preliminary examination, and was held in $4,000 bail for his appearance at the June Term of Dist. Court. Reudebaugh is a good looking specimen of the border ruffian, and was cool and collected throughout the arguments of the attorneys on the question of amount of bail.

Edgar West was next brought in, he is tall, and low browed, with black mustache and hair and "looks the villain" he too waived an examination and was held in $4,000 bail.

Wm. Tilghman who is we believe, merely held on suspicion of being a "wire puller" for the party, declared himself ready for trial. The State not being ready his case was continued ten days, and his bail fixed at $4,000. The prisoners were all remanded to the jail of Ford County where they were safely lodged in charge of jailor Strong [Straughn] at 10:30 P. M.

Sunday afternoon Messrs. Gryden and Phillips, took a special for Kinsley and returned during the night with warrants for three more of the party, but whose names we are unable to obtain. There are no new developments up to the hour of going to press.[9]

On February 5, 1878, Sheriff Masterson arrested one James McDuff, accused of horse thievery. The *Times*, February 9, stated:

ARREST OF A HORSE THIEF.

The successful efforts of Sheriff W. B. Masterson, in his recent capture, has been followed by another arrest remarkable in skill and judgment. The unanimous accord of praise, in speaking of Sheriff Masterson, as being the right man in the right place, evinces also the hope that the career of crime will not stalk naked hereafter in this section of the Arkansas Valley. The feeling is indulged in a better security of life and property through the vigilance of our officers. The spell has been broken and the heretofore difficult task of apprehending outlaws regarded out of the question, since the band of outlaws has been shattered.

We mentioned a few days ago that Mr. Miles Mix had lost a span of horses. Obtaining clue, Sheriff Masterson boarded the train Tuesday morning for Las Animas, where he found one James McDuff, a notorious character, and promptly arrested him, having searched for his man under the bed in a dance house. To accomplish this purpose Sheriff Masterson took in tow another well known character, who, to avoid incarceration, disclosed the hiding place of McDuff.

334

The stolen horses were disposed of by McDuff for small sums of money. The recovery of only one of the horses seems probable, the other have been run off.

Sheriff Masterson and Mr. Mix returned Wednesday night with the prisoner, who has been furnished accommodations in the Hotel de Straughn.

This is but the prelude of the interesting drama on the boards, and the sequel will develop some startling characters in the clutches of the officers.[10]

The Kinsley *Valley Republican* thought McDuff was connected with the attempted train robbery. On February 9, 1878, it said:

The notorious MacDuff, known as "Duffy," was arrested by Sheriff Masterson's party in a cellar at West Las Animas Tuesday evening, and brought to Dodge yesterday. The network of evidence has been so ingeniously thrown around the entire gang that they can't escape. Important developments are pending which will be made public at the earliest moment consistent.

The Dodge City *Times*, February 9, 1878, reported:

BOUND OVER.

James McDuff, arrested on a charge of horse stealing, was bound over in the sum of $2,000, in default of which he was returned to jail. The prisoner is charged only with horse stealing, but an attempt was made to take him to Kinsley, and Sheriff Masterson, acting under advice of the County Attorney M W Sutton, refused to give up the prisoner. The "interview" was had as well in Ford county, inasmuch as the prisoner was arrested on a warrant issued in this county, and his detention here frustrates any cheap notoriety, as the law will take its course, thieves ferreted, and justice prevail.

Receiving a lead that more of the robbers were holed up on the Llano Estacado, Bat recruited another posse and rode south on February 10. The *Ford County Globe*, February 12, 1878, said:

Sheriff Masterson, Chas. E. Bassett, J. J. Webb, John Clark and H. Lovell, started Sunday morning, for the prairie in quest of more of the gang of train robbers. We don't know that our boys will be successful in capturing any more of the gang, but we do say that no better posse ever undertook such a duty. We know that every man in the party has the sand and nerve to go where any other man on earth dares to go. If the robbers are not captured it will not be for want of bravery, coolness or strategy, on the part of Sheriff Masterson or his posse. Wishing them success, we await further developments.

In reply to the *Ford County Globe's* February 5 defense of Bat's actions, the Kinsley *Republican* merely stated: "We give Sheriff Masterson of Ford due credit for his activity in pursuing and capturing the brigands. He did his duty finally and no more." The *Globe*, which reprinted the item February 12, 1878, merely appended a polite "thank you."

By February 9 the *Republican* appeared ready to bury the hatchet with the Dodge City newspapers. On February 16 it said:

THE ROBBERS' RAID.

Sheriff Masterson of Ford county started for the staked plains last Sunday with a well armed posse for the purpose of capturing the raiders yet at large, where it is reported they are fortified in a "dug out" determined to resist arrest. Masterson can and we believe he will bring them back dead or alive—it matters little which. Reudebaugh and West, two of the brigands, are now behind the bars of the Emporia dungeon, thanks to the efficiency of Ford county officials. Much light has been thrown on the diabolical scheme of the raiders which will yet be ventilated. Let every official or agent do his whole duty until the end is reached. The question is not whether the officials or attorneys of Edwards or Ford counties shall receive the major part of credit for their efforts, but rather shall any guilty man escape? We confess that we were disposed to think ten days ago that justice would be cheated but the raiders have been hunted to their dens, and if they are gathered in as we now have reasons for believing they will be, faithful officials will receive due credit no less than our brave citizens who generously went forth in pursuit, and we shall not stop to inquire what the means used to accomplish the end. It is enough for us to know that the guilty are to be brought to justice and the good name of our own county vindicated from aspersions from sources of questionable reliability. . . .

On February 15 G. H. Syburt came into Dodge with news of Masterson's progress. The *Times*, February 16, 1878, reported:

PURSUING THE ROBBERS.
SHERIFF MASTERSON HEARD FROM.
WITHIN TWO HOURS RIDE OF THE BRIGANDS.
A PROBABLE DEADLY ENCOUNTER.

G. H. Syburt came in yesterday evening from Lovell's camp, having left there two days ago. Sheriff Masterson and posse arrived there on the 12th. Three of the attempted train robbers, Mike Roarke, a fellow named Mack, and one name unknown, had left the vicinity of Lovell's camp only two hours before the arrival of the Sheriff. The Sheriff and party immediately followed [in] pursuit, trailing the robbers to Beaver creek, Sybert went with the Sheriff twelve miles out from Lovell's, where the Sheriff and party intended staying all night, when Syburt returned yesterday as we have stated.

The Sheriff and posse had kept in advance of their provision wagon, and so closely were they on the trail of the robbers that they were 30 hours without provisions.

Roarke said at the camp that he understood he was charged with the attempted train robbery, and that officers were in search of him, but he was ready for them at any time. Would meet them at any place. They might send the whole city of Dodge and he would fight them anywhere.

Beaver river is about 80 miles south of Dodge City in the stock range, in a strip between Kansas and Texas, the neck of the Indian Territory.

Sheriff Masterson and party, C. E. Bassett, J. J. Webb and Miles Mix, left here Sunday. They were well armed and equipped.

Roarke is a desperate character, and may give Sheriff Masterson a severe struggle. A capture without a bloody encounter, seems almost improbable.[11]

Bat Masterson

The sheriff and his posse returned home on February 22. Next day the Dodge City *Times* described their unsuccessful chase:

RETURN OF THE SHERIFF.
THE ROBBERS SCATTER AND HIDE IN THE BREAKS OF THE CANADIAN.

The party started from Dodge City on the 10th, consisting of Sheriff Masterson, C. E. Bassett, J. J. Webb and Red Clarke; went to Walker's Timber, on Crooked creek, the first day, then to Lovell's camp. On the way to Lovell's they met one of Lovell's men, who told them that Mike Roark and Dan Webster had been at the camp that morning, and had only left three or four hours before, for Shepherd's camp, fifteen miles further south. The posse at once started for Shepherd's camp, and when they arrived there found that Roark and Webster had left a few hours before for their own camp, on a tributary of the Beaver, about thirty-five miles further. The boys took a hasty dinner and hurried after the robbers, their trail being plainly visible. Night overtook the party on the Cimaron river, and it was impossible to see the trail, but they still traveled in the direction the robbers had taken until they reached a branch of Beaver creek, about midnight. Here they expected to find the robbers encamped and alighting from their horses they cautiously made their way down the stream to Beaver, about five or six miles further, but failed to discover any sign of the robbers.

Keeping on down the Beaver they soon struck the robber's trail again, and followed it in a southeasterly direction for about fifteen miles; here they found a deserted camp in a plumb thicket. From this camp the robbers had taken a wagon and more stock, making a much plainer trail. The trail seemed to indicate that two more men had joined the gang here. Following this trail they went through the head breaks of the Kiawa or Medicine Lodge creek, then west to Jones & Plummer's ranche on Wolf creek, where the robbers, feeling themselves too closely pursued, had left their wagon, harness and camp equipage and struck out on horseback. The robbers had left this camp about fifteen hours before our party arrived. They had gained one night's travel owing to the fact that the Sheriff and party could not follow their trail at night, while the robbers traveled both day and night. After leaving Jones and Plummer's ranche, the robbers were trailed some distance to where they entered the breaks of the Canadian river, in Texas, and here they seemed to have seperated as their trail was lost. The Sheriff and his men after a fruitless search had to give up their game. The place where the robbers have taken refuge is one of the wildest and most broken countries in the world, and affords a perfectly safe retreat for the robbers. They can here find hiding places where all the advantage is on their side in such a search. The Sheriff and his posse were absent thirteen days and did some hard riding, traveling between five and six hundred miles.[12]

As luck would have it Bat was soon able to capture two more of the robbers. The arrests were made right in Dodge City, March 15, the *Times* reported on March 16, 1878:

337

GATHERING THEM IN!!
Two More Train Robbers Captured!!
They Come Into Dodge City to Get "Information."
Sheriff Masterson, Under Sheriff Bassett
and Marshal Masterson Kindly Take Them In.
They Are Arrested After a Short Chase.

Tom Gott alias Dugan, and Green, two of the gang who attempted the robbery of the train at Kinsley some weeks ago, were arrested at about nine o'clock last night, on the bottom just on the outskirts southwest of Dodge City, by Sheriff Masterson, Under Sheriff Bassett and City Marshal Ed. Masterson.

At about nine o'clock, Officer Nat Haywood, returning from his rounds on the south side of the railroad track, reported to Sheriff Masterson that he had seen Tom Gott alias Dugan, at one of the dance houses, the officer not then knowing that Dugan was charged with the attempted railroad robbery. Sheriff Masterson immediately summoned Under Sheriff Bassett and Marshal Masterson, who were at his side, and the three officers started in quest of the two fugitives. Arriving at Anderson's stable the officers were informed that two men had just passed by on the south side of the stable and were making their way up the bottom. The officers proceeded in haste and were soon within sight of the robbers, who, observing they were being tracked, put out on a brisk run. The clear moonlight night afforded an easy chase, and the officers soon pounced upon their victims and which proved to be a desired catch. The robbers showed some resistance, but one of them found his revolver entangled in his clothing.

The prisoners were taken to the jail and locked up. Dugan stated that they had left three horses hitched to a tree about a mile west of the city. Subsequently the three officers above named made a scour of the country and found two horses and a mule, all saddled, and strapped to each was a carbine, and a Creedmore rifle.

There were evidently four in the party, the other two being the notorious characters Mike Roarke and one Lafeu. It is said that all four were in town during the evening, and they came to ascertain the condition of affairs, having so long been uninformed, and little fearing a capture they boldly ventured to a less frequented part of the city. But the officers of this city and county are vigilant and quick to do their duty. They know no fear and will beard the lion in his den.

The officers scoured the surrounding country for Mike Roarke and Lafeu, but these worthies with their well known sagacity eluded the pursuit, having made a dash in and out of the environs of Dodge City in their stealth, and stillness of the night.

Marshal Masterson took the two prisoners Gott and Green to Kinsley this afternoon, where they will have a preliminary examination. Gott or Dugan is about 22 years of age and Green is 25 years old. Last year they were engaged in driving on the plains, and are well known to the citizens of the city.

A party under charge of Sheriff W. B. Masterson, consisting of himself, Under Sheriff C. E. Bassett, J. J. Webb and Jas. Masterson, left this city to-day and will follow the supposed trail of Roarke and Lafeu. Their capture is highly probable. These two are the remaining ones of the gang of six who attempted the train robbery. In all events their capture is but a question of time.[13]

Unfortunately "the Sheriff's posse, that went out last Saturday, hunting for Mike Roarke, who was supposed to be in the neighborhood, returned without success." [14]

On March 23, 1878, the Dodge City *Times* described the trip to Kinsley and the disposition of the prisoners:

THE TRAIN ROBBERS.

BOUND OVER AND TAKEN TO EMPORIA FOR SAFE KEEPING.

Last Saturday afternoon a special car, with Superintendent W. H. Pettibone as conductor, and Frank B. Lowe as engineer, left the Dodge City depot for Kinsley carrying Greene and Gott, the two train robbers, and James Duffy, a prisoner bound over on the charge of horse stealing. The officers in charge of the prisoners were City Marshal Edward J. Masterson, Col. D. D. Colley and Ben Springer, special deputies. Accompanying the officers and prisoners were M. W. Sutton, County Attorney and attorney for the railroad company, Major Dick Evans, Ex-Mayor Hoover and Lloyd Shinn of the TIMES.

Duffy was taken along more on account of the opportunity the trip afforded for giving him a good airing than anything else, his confinement being very close and dark in the county jail.

As the people at Spearville had not yet learned of the capture of the robbers, and did not know what the special car contained, no demonstration was made. At Offerle the train was compelled to wait half an hour to allow the west bound freight to pass, during which time several parties visited the car and took a look at the prisoners—this being the first news they had received of the capture.

Arriving at Kinsley everything was quiet about the depot, the Agent having apprized no one of the expected arrival. But as the prisoners were being marched up to the Justice's office, handcuffed together, a crowd gathered round to "see what they could see." The Justice's office being very small but few spectators were allowed inside.

Justice Willy read the complaint to the prisoners and they both waived an examination and plead not guilty. We understand they agreed to do this before the hearing came on, so as not to make any trouble on the part of the prosecution.

County Attorney McArthur, and Sheriff Fuller of Edwards county were there promptly to attend to their duties, and both seem to be good, honest officers.

The two prisoners, Greene and Gott, are men of more than ordinary natural intelligence—especially Greene. It is said that he ranks next to Mike Roarke as a leader of the organized gang. He has an intellectual countenance, eyes rather sunken, protruding forehead and rather a stupid disposition. Gott is more boyish and talkative.

Not a particle of doubt exists as to their guilt, as Sheriff Masterson, from descriptions &c., has had them spotted ever since the robbery.

To prove the daring of their character we give the following:

Immediately after their examination they were placed in an upstairs room and a Deputy Sheriff left to guard them; Duffy was also in this room, but was not handcuffed as the other two were. One of the robbers seeing the Deputy Sheriff near the window, ordered Duffy to slip up and pitch him out, thus giving them a chance to escape. Duffy refused, whereupon the two men—who were handcuffed to-gether by one arm—approached the officer to perform the act themselves, but he was on the alert and foiled the attempt.

The Dodge City party remained in Kinsley only about an hour—just long enough to see what a busy, growing, beautiful town it is, and to greet a few old friends, such as Flick, Brewer Clute, Hubbs' Milner and others. We returned by moonlight all roosting on Frank B. Lowe's engine, and had a jolly ride.

Marshal Masterson and Sheriff Fuller took Green and Gott on down to the Emporia jail the same evening.

On March 28 "Sheriff Masterson of Ford county, was in the city [Kinsley] . . . consulting with Mr. Herrington, attorney of the alleged train robbers, in reference to disposition of property that he captured with them." [15]

The trial of the four accused prisoners was to be held in Kinsley on June 17, 1878. But first they had to be brought from Emporia where they had been taken for safety's sake. Bat left Dodge on June 14 to perform that deed. The *Times*, June 15, 1878, reported:

TRIAL OF THE TRAIN ROBBERS.

Sheriff W. B. Masterson left last night for Emporia. He will be followed by Jos. Mason, Al. Updegraff, Thomas Campbell and Frank Richards, who will act as guard in conveying the attempted train robbers from the Emporia jail to Kinsley. The District Court meets at Kinsley Monday. Dave Ruddebaugh, Ed. West, Tom Gott and J. D. Green, charged with the attempted train robbery at Kinsley, on the night of January 27th, 1878, will be tried at this term of the court in Kinsley. The prisoners have been confined in the Emporia jail since their preliminary examination.

Because of flooding in the Arkansas valley the trial was not commenced until June 19. The Kinsley *Graphic*, successor to the *Republican*, reported the proceedings on June 22, 1878:

Bat Masterson

EDWARDS CO. DISTRICT COURT.

"Graphic" Report of Proceedings of the June Term of Court—
Trial of the Railroad Robbers—
Confession of Dave Rudabaugh—
West, Green and Gott Plead Guilty and Sent Up Five Years—
A "Big Week" of Excitement in Kinsley.

By reason of the floods down the Valley Judge [S. R.] Peters did not arrive until late Tuesday evening. . . .

State of Kansas vs. David Rudabaugh et al. Issue robbery first degree. The following motions were made: By defendants for State to elect which of two counts they would go to trial on. Stood on first, Robbery of Kingkade of pistol. Motion by defendants to strike information from files on account of there having been no preliminary examination for offence charged in information. Overruled, Def'ts excepted. Defendants motion that information be stricken from files because it had not been sworn to. Overruled and exceptions noted.

Thomas Gott brought into Court. Affidavit for continuance filed on account of the absence of material witnesses. Affidavit adjudged sufficient and admitted as deposition. Separate trial demanded as to Thomas Gott, who was arraigned and plead not guilty. After some delay a jury was secured composed of the following citizens: J. E. Crane, A. L. Kendall, G. W. Wilson, J. F. White, W. L. Hunter, Walter Robley, J. T. Carter, S. S. Hart, J. D. Verney, Geo. N. Wear, S. T. Reed, N. L. Mills. The prosecution was ably conducted by County Attorney MacArthur, assisted by Capt. J. G. Waters, and M. W. Sutton of Ford county, and the defense well managed by B. F. Herrington of the Edwards county bar, and A. A. Hurd of Great Bend. The following witnesses were called to the stand and testified: Andrew Kingkade, David Rudabaugh, W. H. Pettibone, J. W. Mallory, James Duffy, Charles Palmer, J. M. Anderson, H. A. Brown, W. F. Blanchard, Thomas Palmer, John Slatterly and James Hammond. The story of the 'raid,' as related by the several witnesses was the same that we published through 'extras' at the time, but there was a sensation when Dave Rudabaugh's confession was given in testimony, and the confessed outlaw related the story of how the brigands deliberately planned their diabolical scheme on Wolf Creek, in the Pan Handle country, to come to Kinsley and rob the Santa Fe train. The preparations made to carry out their plans; the route they came; the places assigned each man by their leader Rourke; how they were foiled in their original plan of robbing the east bound train; their attack on the night operator and attempt to rob the express car, their escape, wanderings and final capture, as told, would make an interesting chapter of crime on the frontier.

The Plea of Guilty.

On the convening of Court yesterday morning, it was whispered that the prisoners West, Green and Gott had been advised to plead guilty. They were brought into Court, the charge read, and each of them responded "guilty." The Judge then interrogated each of them regarding their past lives, their families, etc., after which he addressed them directly for half an hour upon the lives

341

they had led, the laws they had violated, and the sentence it was his duty to pass upon them. The Judge stated that the most unpleasant duty he as an officer had to perform was that of passing sentence upon young men. The punishment though severe would cause other hearts to suffer. That mother whose love could not be fathomed, whicl. could not be expressed in words; those loving sisters and brothers—they would be disgraced. The disposition in our society to encourage crime among our young men who are thrown on their own resources here in the West, and from whom a kind word is withheld ofttimes, was severely condemned by the Judge. After speaking words of encouragement, importuning the prisoners to despair not but then to resolve to lead different lives and be men, each of them was sentenced to five years at hard labor in the State penitentiary at Leavenworth. At 1 p. m. Sheriff Fuller, assisted by A. Menny, W. Barkman and V. D. Billings, started for Leavenworth with the prisoners on a special train. Rudabaugh was taken as far as Newton, where he was released. Thus endeth the first chapter.

In the same issue of the *Graphic* some incidentals of the trial were given:

The handsome young Sheriff of Pawnee, Mr. Christy, and Sheriff Masterson of Ford, the brave and popular young official of the frontier, have been with us this week.

Kingkade's story of the 'raid' implicated Rudabaugh as the ringleader.

Rudabaugh testified that he was promised entire immunity from punishment if he would 'squeal,' therefore he squole.

Some one has said there is a kind of honor among thieves. Rudabaugh don't think so.

There was less difficulty in securing a jury in the robbery case than was anticipated.

Rudabaugh explained that he did not pursue Kingkade and 'the other man,' as they seemed to be needing no help to get out of the way.

While the three prisoners sentenced were doubtless the least guilty of the six engaged in the raid, yet their punishment was just.

In answer to the question of the Judge, 'Had you a pleasant home?' two answered 'yes,' one 'no,' two have mothers living, one a father who was present, and all had brothers and sisters.

Mike Rourke and two companions, one of whom was named Tilman (which might have been the cause for the arrest of Dodge City's William M. Tilghman) were discovered 11 miles south of Ellsworth in October, 1878. Rourke was promptly captured and placed in jail at Junction City but no record was found of his ultimate fate.[16]

Rudabaugh, who by turning state's evidence against his former comrades, secured his own release, turned up in Dodge City in March, 1879. The *Ford County Globe*, March 18, reported:

Dave Rudebaugh, who was arrested as one of the Kinsley train robbers, but turned state's evidence and was discharged, arrived in this city last week from Butler county, where he was a witness against Mike Roarke. Rudebaugh is looking for a job of work and intends to earn his living on the square.

In April, 1880, Rudabaugh attempted the rescue of J. J. Webb from a Las Vegas, N. M., jail and then turned to riding with William "Billy the Kid" Bonney. The year 1882 saw him ambushing Wyatt Earp in Arizona. By 1885 he was in Mexico, soon to die, beheaded, at Parral. For more information *see* the sections on J. J. Webb and Wyatt Earp.

If one may judge from notices in the newspapers, the Kinsley train robbery crowded nearly everything else out of Sheriff Masterson's schedule. However, the Dodge City *Times*, March 2, 1878, hinted that Bat and his friend, County Attorney Mike Sutton, would shortly make a number of other arrests:

LOOK OUT.

Recent developments indicate that Sheriff Masterson and County Attorney Sutton will soon fasten the clutches of the law upon a band of unsuspecting horse thieves. "Let no guilty man escape."

If the arrests were made they were not reported in either of the town's newspapers.

On March 16, 1878, the *Times* reported that "Sheriff Masterson returned last Sunday from a trip to Topeka and other points East." The Topeka *Commonwealth*, March 6, 1878, merely stated that "W. B. Masterson, sheriff of Ford county, and Harry E. Gryden, of Dodge City, are at the Tefft." The reason for the visit remains unknown.

The sheriff found a stolen horse on March 23. The *Times*, March 30, 1878, reported:

CAPTURE OF STOLEN HORSES.

Mr. H. Spangler, of Lake City, Comanche county, arrived in the city last Saturday in search of two horses that had been stolen from him last December. He described the stolen stock to Sheriff Masterson who immediately instituted search. On Monday he found one of the horses, a very valuable animal, at Mueller's cattle camp on Saw Log, it having been traded to Mr. Wolf. The horse was turned over to its owner. The Sheriff has trace of the other horse and will endeavor to recover it.

The Ford county board of commissioners awarded Bat $78.25 travel fees on April 8, 1878, possibly reimbursing him for expenses incurred in chasing the train robbers.[17]

Death threw a punch which left Bat Masterson reeling on the night of April 9 when his brother Ed, city marshal of Dodge, was shot by drunken cowboys. Bat responded promptly by arresting four supposed accomplices of the dead and wounded murderers. For the story of Ed Masterson *see* the section devoted to him.

Grief-stricken, the young sheriff, accompanied by his friend Mike Sutton, headed for Sedgwick county to visit the Masterson parents. Within five days he was back at his post in Dodge City,[18] and within hours of his arrival was on the prowl for some stolen horses. The Dodge City *Times*, April 20, 1878, reported:

MORE HORSE STEALING.
THE THIEF CAPTURED AND COMMITTED TO JAIL.

Last Wednesday [April 17] Mr. M. A. Couch and three other gentlemen arrived in this city from Walnut creek, forty miles north of here, in search of four horses that had been stolen from them on the day previous. They immediately applied to the County Attorney for information and assistance, stating that they had tracked the horses to this city. Sheriff Masterson was sent for, and in company with Couch and party instituted search for the stock, which, luckily, they succeeded in recovering. Two of the horses were found in the river bottom southwest of the city and the other two were found in Mr. Bell's livery stable, where they had been placed the night before. The owners of the horses were very much pleased upon recovering their stock, and proposed starting immediately for home without making any search for the thief; but the Sheriff with an eye to giving his thiefship punishment for his wrongs, made search and discovered men whom he supposed to be guilty. Swearing out a complaint himself he arrested Henry Martin and William Tilghman. Henry Martin was brought before Justice Cook on Wednesday and examined. There being strong evidence against him he was bound over in the sum of $2,000, in default of which he was sent to jail. Mr. Tilghman's examination took place Thursday before Justice Cook. It was generally supposed he would be bound over also, but he was released by the court. He was defended by Mr. Gryden, assisted by Mr. Frost. Both prisoners were ably prosecuted by County Attorney Sutton, and we are glad to observe the interest manifested by both the County Attorney and Sheriff in bringing horse thieves to justice.[19]

Thursday, May 16, was a busy day for Bat. First he and John Straughn prevented a proposed jail break by discovering and confiscating the tools of escape. The *Times*, May 18, 1878, recorded:

NIPPED IN THE BUD.

Sheriff Masterson and Jailor Straughn have been unearthing some implements of jail delivery. Thursday a brace, a rod of iron and some small wedges were found in one of the cells of the jail supposed to have been passed in the night previous. There is a poor chance to make a break under the present official management. The officers have argus eyes.

Thursday night Bat captured a horse thief. The same issue of the *Times* (May 18, 1878) reported:

HORSE THIEF CAUGHT.

Sheriff Bat Masterson Thursday night arrested one Geo. Foster, charged with stealing a horse belonging to J. W. Duncan, living on Smoky river, at Hays crossing, on the 29th of April. The horse was not recovered. The prisoner has been placed in charge of a couple of officers and taken to Ellis county for examination. Horse thieves find hospitable reception at the hands of Sheriff Masterson. He is an excellent "catch" and is earning a State reputation.

Law enforcement did not occupy all of Sheriff Masterson's time. For instance he was active in the Dodge City Fire Company and at one time served as a member of that organization's finance committee with Chalk Beeson and Deputy U. S. Marshal H. T. McCarty. Bat's under sheriff, Charles E. Bassett, was first assistant marshal of the volunteer fire fighting unit.[20] Other and more frivilous social activities attracted the young sheriff also. On June 8, 1878, the Dodge City *Times* recorded that Bat and a local belle had attended a grand ball at Spearville with several other well known Dodge Citians:

THE SUMMIT HOUSE OPENING.

Our Spearville neighbors gave a grand entertainment last night, it being the occasion of the formal "warming" of the magnificent hotel at that place, the Summit House, J. McCollister, proprietor. There was gayety and beauty there, the staid bachelor and the festive young man, the buxom lassie, the comely maid and the village belles. A sumptuous board was spread to which the guests responded with alacrity and avidity—especially those from Dodge City. Major McCollister demonstrated his ability to keep hotel.

The merry dance was kept up until a late hour. Music was furnished by Beeson's Orchestra, and was pronounced excellent by the Spearvillians. The tollowing Dodge City people were present and tipped their light and heavy pedestals:

Mayor [James H.] Kelley and lady; Mr. and Mrs. M. Collar; Mr. and Mrs. [Chalkly E.] Beeson; Mr. and Mrs. [S. E.?] Isaacson; Mr. and Mrs. J. Collar; Sheriff Masterson and lady; D. M. Frost and Miss Lutie Chambliss; Mr. and Mrs. C. S. Hungerford; John B. Means and lady. Our home folks arrived this morning much elated from the night's revelry.

But where news of Bat's activities was concerned business predominated. On June 15, 1878, the *Times* reported that he had captured two more suspected horse thieves:

Two suspicious characters named Andy Payne and E. W. Qilleur [*sic*], charged with stealing stock from the estate of Sanders & Couch in the Pan Handle, were arrested this week by Sheriff Masterson. They will have their preliminary trial next week. Col. Straughn entertains them.

Being an "opposition" paper, the *Ford County Globe* often censured Bat and County Attorney Sutton for alleged misuse of their positions. Such an opportunity knocked with the arrest of Quillin [?] and Payne [?]:

W. E. Quillin and Henry Pagne who have been held here since the 12th inst., by the arbitrary exercise of power by our county officers, were turned loose yesterday because there never existed any cause for holding them. They were compelled to pay $18 livery bill on their stock before they got it from the custody of the Sheriff who had taken possession of the same at the time they were arrested. We are surprised that the boys were not retained in custody till they paid their board during the time of their incarceration.21

To its credit, the *Globe* also noticed the good work. In the same issue, June 25, 1878, it reported:

Messrs Sutton and Masterson compelled two of the show case institutions to disgorge some of their ill gotten gains last week, and recovered the same to the parties who had been robbed. We cannot understand how any of our county farmers can be so green as to come to Dodge and go up against those cut throat games, yet they do it nearly every day.

The Dodge City *Times*, being pro-Sutton and Masterson, was outspoken in its praise of the two county officers: "We quite agree with the generally expressed opinion that 'Judge Sutton and Bat Masterson are the right men in the right place.'" "County Attorney Sutton and Sheriff Masterson are using all fair and honorable means as officers to bring criminals to justice. All law abiding people commend them for the honest discharge of their duties." 22

In July Bat used a slick ruse to capture another wanted man. The *Times*, July 27, 1878, reported:

Sheriff Masterson captured a fugitive from justice from Ft. Lyon this week after the most approved style. He received a telegram from the authorities asking him to look out for a man named Davis on the eastward bound train. Masterson went down to the train, and among the crowd of passengers singled out a suspicious looking man, and approaching him said: "Hello, Davis; how do you do?" The stranger was completely off his guard, and answered to the name at once, thinking he had met an old friend. The Sheriff immediately gave him lodging in jail until he could be sent back to Lyon, where he had been sentenced to the penitentiary for three years.

The furnace-like weather of southwest Kansas began to have a telling effect on Bat as the summer dragged on. Finally he decided to visit the spa at Hot Springs for relief. The *Times,* August 3, 1878, told of his going:

Sheriff Masterson, who has not had good health during the late hot weather, having at times been confined to his bed with attacks of something like vertigo, started last Thursday morning [August 1] for a visit to Hot Springs, Arkansas, where he will remain three or four weeks. We hope he will have a pleasant time and return restored to perfect health.

Bat was back on the job by August 12. The *Times,* August 17, 1878, told of his capturing a horse thief that day. For a reprint of the item and of another Masterson commendation *see* the section on William Duffey.

During the whole of its career as a cowtown, Dodge was bothered with confidence men whose numbers must have been legion. The year 1878 was no exception and as fast as one group was run out of town another was there to take its place. Toward the end of summer Sheriff Masterson arrested two such operators on complaint of a man named E. Markel. As luck would have it, a deputy allowed the two to escape, which prompted this long statement in the Dodge City *Times,* September 14, 1878:

THE CONFIDENCE OPERATORS.
Shoving the Queer—
Arrest of Two "Land Agents"—
The Subsequent Flight.

For sometime past Dodge City has been cursed with a class of confidence operators, who have plied all the arts of deceit in gulling the unsophisticated and unwary. A batch of these bold operators fled the town during the summer, but their places were occupied by another class who resorted to other means to fleece the unsuspecting stranger. The class who have lately been carrying on their nefarious schemes in Dodge suddenly came to grief Tuesday night.

Their manner had been to represent themselves as land agents. To pursue this purpose they were present upon the arrival of all railroad trains. By graceful and winning ways and tolerably fair representations they gained the confidence of the credulous stranger. Once in their toils the poor deluded victim was at their mercy. The straw that broke the camel's back was laid Tuesday evening [September 10]. The confidence men succeeded in roping in one E. Markel, an illiterate gentleman from some backwoods, and inducing him to exchange greenbacks for what purported to be $20 gold pieces. Upon discovering the cheat, Markel caused the arrest of one Harry Bell, the leader of the gang, and a bold and successful guy that sailed under the sobriquet of "Kid."

347

The warrant was placed in the hands of Sheriff Masterson, who arrested the men and placed them under charge of Deputy [William] Duffy. Duffy had been on service the night previous, and feeling the need of rest turned the prisoners over to an incompetent guard. The guard was not vigilant, and while indulging in nature's sweet restorer, the prisoners saw the opportunity to escape justice, and boldly "lit out," taking the 5 o'clock morning train for the west.

The citizens of Dodge City naturally felt indignant Wednesday morning when they learned that the birds had flown, and were free to express feelings of censure against the Sheriff for a direlection of duty, in either not placing the prisoners in jail or else putting them under a proper and sufficient guard until a preliminary trial should be had. Bell made the most solemn protestations against the charge of guilt, and assured the Sheriff that he would make no attempt at escape if not placed in jail.

The pieces purporting to be gold were made of some base metal, plated, and did not resemble gold or the device of gold coin. A person with ordinary intelligence would not have been gulled with such a trick. It matters not, the pieces were represented to be gold, and a charge of obtaining money under false pretenses could have been sustained.

The people of Dodge City have borne with these outrages long enough. There has been an under current of sentiment working and the climax had been reached when no mild measures would have been used to rid the community of this intolerable nuisance. By these operations it had become known abroad that "land agents" and "business men" of Dodge City were robbing the innocent straggler in the modern Nineveh. It was in this manner, by falsely representing themselves as "land agents" and "business men" that these robbers succeeded in gaining the confidence of their victims. Various swindling operations have occurred lately, but the parties victimized rarely "squealed," and hence the operators have gone on unmolested.

We haven't much sympathy for the man who permits himself to be duped by a stranger; but we presume it is a misfortune not to know all the wiles and tricks in human ingenuity. Again, the unsophisticated and probably better knowing ones, tempt the hidden hand to feather their own nests.

But these swindling operations were bringing the town into greater discredit, and forebearance was ceasing to be a virtue. It is therefore necessary for the honor, credit and character of Dodge City that a solemn protest be entered against such practices. We hasten the conclusion by stating that circumstances have probably done the best thing to further the riddance of these men, and cannot regret the course of the bold confidence operator in his flight west—if he will only stay away, and we believe he will. It would be "warm" to return.

The *Ford County Globe*, September 17, 1878, used the escape as an opportunity to chastise not only the sheriff and his men but also the Dodge City *Times*:

CAPTURE AND ESCAPE.

On Tuesday evening last [September 10], two of those notorious and well known confidence men, Bill Bell and "The handsome Kid," who have been for

Bat Masterson

the past few months working the unsophisticated land seekers who visited Dodge, were captured upon the complaint of E. Markel (a respectable and honest man who had come here for the purpose of securing a home), charging them with passing off upon him something purporting to be a $20 gold piece, which in reality was a gilded "spiel marke." The evidence was so conclusive, and witnesses so numerous to the transaction, that Bell and "The Kid" were "booked" for the Penitentiary if they stood trial. They tried to compromise, but without avail; then they tried to talk Judge Cook into a small bail bond, but the Judge, seeing his duty in the premises, said, "$2,000 each with the best of security." A commitment was made out and placed in the hands of the Sheriff, who, instead of listening to the commands of the commitment, or the mandates of the law, "to put his prisoners in jail," placed them in care of his Deputy, Duffey, who permitted them to walk the streets in his charge. Next morning the prisoners were gone! without any explanation except that they had escaped from "Red," who had been employed to guard them. Who is "Red?" Does anybody know him? The only information that we can get concerning him is that he is one of the "confidence gang." If this is true he was evidently the right kind of a man to guard his pals—from justice. We have now told the facts as they are understood, by us, we do not wish or desire to censure anybody unjustly, our aim in the premises is to lay bare the facts as they exist, knowing well that our readers are competent to form their own opinions, arrive at their own conclusions and censure those who deserve it. The GLOBE has and will always be found, commending an officer when he does his duty, but it will not praise an officer for not doing his duty, it is not that kind of an institution. Dodge City is already cursed with an institution of that character, which, in its existence of two and a half years, has never dared to question the correctness of the doings of any officer in Ford county, and God knows it has had many an opportunity to do so. We know it is the duty of any journal, that expects the people's patronage, to labor for the best interests of the community wherein it exists, by exulting over the good deeds of its officers and condeming their official faults, and we believe that a journal that will not do so, is tainted with a hankering after the "flesh pots" of office, or is controlled and managed by cowardice.

A meeting of the citizens was held in the school house, on Thursday evening, for the purpose of discussing the confidence question, at which there was not a very general attendance of citizens, but confidence men and their sympathizers were on hand in full force. Messrs [F. C.] Zimmerman and Collar being called upon, said, that the officers had not and were not doing their duty in relation to the confidence men. W. N. Morphy [editor of the Ford County Globe] said that the officers could stop the nuisance if they desired to do so. Messrs. [Edward F.] Colborn (City Attorney), Bobby Gill [Robert Gilmore] and E. O. Parish defended the officers by saying that they were the best officers whom God in His wisdom had ever created, (for which, oh, Lord, make us truly thankful). The meeting very nearly broke up in a row but didn't, and finally a peaceable adjournment was had. The citizens of the town at present feel that legally they are helpless, because they cannot have the law enforced; they also feel that they ought to take the law in their own hands and drive confidence

349

men from the town. What will be done we cannot tell but we hope that the question will soon solve itself. The officers claim that they have always lacked the support of the citizens. We cannot understand how they can expect the support of the citizens unless they show themselves more worthy of it than they have heretofore done. What Ford county needs is a complete change in judicial officers and the ballot box is the place to get it. Remember this, voters of Ford county, and vote against any and every man who has not done his duty in driving out the confidence curse from our midst.

Perhaps to escape from it all temporarily, Bat took in the fair at Kansas City. With him were A. B. Webster, W. H. Harris, A. J. Anthony, Robert M. Wright, and Charles E. Bassett. They were gone during the week ending September 24, 1878.[28]

In its 14 years as a rough frontier town Dodge never had a better year in the accepted TV Western tradition than it did in 1878. First there was the success of Sheriff Bat Masterson and his posse in capturing two of the Kinsley train robbers. Then two others were arrested right in town. The shooting and death of City Marshal Edward J. Masterson quickly followed in April. Deputy United States Marshal H. T. McCarty was shot and killed in the Long Branch saloon in July and Cowboy George Hoy died at the hands of Policemen Wyatt Earp and Jim Masterson a few days later. In September the flight of Dull Knife and his small band of Cheyennes across western Kansas toward their former home in the north threw Dodge City into a panic. It was all there—plenty of cowboys, Indians, train robbers, killers, sheriffs, and marshals. The climax, or perhaps the anticlimax, of it all came early in the morning of October 4, 1878. On that day Actress Fannie Keenan, or Dora Hand as she was sometimes called, was mistakenly shot and killed by an unknown person.

Fannie's Dodge City story begins with this item from the *Ford County Globe*, July 30, 1878:

COMIQUE.

This favorite place of resort is at present giving to its patrons the best show or entertainment ever given in Dodge. They have Billy and Nola Forrest, Dick Brown and Fannie Garretson, May Gaylor, Belle Lamont, Fannie Keenan, Jennie Morton, and that unequalled and splendidly matched team [Eddie] Foye and [Jimmie] Thompson. All the members of this troupe are up in their parts and considerable above the average in ability. . . .

Two weeks later Fannie was at Ham Bell's. The Dodge City

Times, August 10, 1878, reported: "Hattie Smith and Fannie Keenan take a benefit at Ham Bell's Varieties next Wednesday night [August 14]. They are general favorites and will be sure to draw a crowded house."

Miss Keenan apparently did not rejoin the troupe at the Comique as her name did not appear in the almost weekly notices given the theater by the *Globe.* If she remained at Bell's that fact is not indicated by the papers. After the August mention in the *Times,* Miss Keenan's name did not reappear in the local papers until October 5, 1878, when the *Times* reported her death:

ANOTHER VICTIM.

THE PISTOL DOES ITS WORK.

THE KILLING OF DORA HAND,

ALIAS FANNIE KEENAN.

At about half past four o'clock this (Friday) morning [October 4], two pistol shots were fired into the building occupied by Dora Hand, alias Fannie Keenan. The person who did the firing stood on horseback at the front door of the little frame [house] south of the railroad track. The house has two rooms, the back room being occupied by Fannie Keenan. A plastered partition wall divides the two rooms. The first shot went through the front door and struck the facing of the partition. The remarkable penetration of a pistol ball was in the second shot. It passed through the door, several thicknesses of bed clothing on the bed in the front room occupied by a female lodger; through the plastered partition wall, and the bed clothing on the second bed, and striking Fannie Keenen on the right side under the arm, killing her instantly. The pistol was of 44 calibre, nearly a half inch ball.

The deceased came to Dodge City this summer and was engaged as vocalist in the Varieties and Comique shows. She was a prepossessing woman and her artful winning ways brought many admirers within her smiles and blandishments. If we mistake not, Dora Hand has an eventful history. She had applied for a divorce from Theodore Hand. After a varied life the unexpected death messenger cuts her down in the full bloom of gayety and womanhood. She was the innocent victim.

The pistol shot was intended for the male occupant of the bed in the front room, but who has been absent for several days. The bed however was occupied by the female lodger at the time of the shooting, and narrowly escaped the ball that went through the bed covering. The cause for the shooting is supposed to be for an old grudge. The officers are in pursuit of the supposed murderer, to whom circumstances point very directly.

Three days later, October 8, 1878, the *Ford County Globe* printed its version of Fannie's death:

MIDNIGHT ASSASSIN.

DORA HAND, ALIAS FANNIE KEENAN,
FOULLY MURDERED WHILE IN BED AND FAST ASLEEP.

JAMES KENNEDY, THE SUPPOSED MURDERER, ARRESTED AFTER RECEIVING A DANGEROUS WOUND AT THE HANDS OF THE OFFICERS.

On Friday morning, about 4 o'clock, two shots were fired in a small frame building, situated south of the railroad track and back of the Western House, occupied by Miss Fannie Garretson and Miss Fannie Keenan. The building was divided into two rooms by a plastered partition, Miss Keenan occupying the back room. The first shot, after passing through the front door, struck the floor, passed through the carpet and facing of the partition and lodged in the next room. The second shot also passed through the door, but apparently more elevated, striking the first bed, passing over Miss Garretson, who occupied the bed, through two quilts, through the plastered partition, and after passing through the bed clothing of the second bed, struck Fannie Keenan in the right side, under the arm, killing her instantly.

The party who committed this cowardly act must have been on horseback and close to the door when the two shots were fired. From what we can learn the shots were intended for another party who has been absent for a week and who formerly occupied the first room. Thus the assassin misses his intended victim and kills another while fast asleep who never spoke a word after she was shot.

James Kennedy, who it is supposed did the shooting made good his escape, and the following morning the officers went in pursuit of him, returning Saturday night with their prisoner, whom they met and on refusal to surrender shot him through the shoulder and with another shot killing the horse he was riding, thus capturing him. What evidence the authorities have that Kennedy is the man who did the shooting we are unable to learn. Below we give the verdict of the coroner's inquest:

STATE OF KANSAS, FORD COUNTY, ss.

An inquisition holden at Dodge City, in said county, on the 4th day of October, A. D. 1878, before me, a justice of the peace for Dodge township, said county (acting as coroner) on the body of Fannie Keenan, there lying dead, by the jurors, whose names are hereunto subscribed. The said jurors, upon their oath, do say: That Fannie Keenan came to her death by a gunshot wound, and that in their opinion the said gunshot wound was produced by a bullet discharged from a gun in the hands of one James Kennedy.

In testimony whereof, the said jurors have hereunto set their hands the day and year aforesaid.

P. L. BEATTY, Foreman.
JOHN B. MEANS,
J. H. CORNELL,
W. STRAETER,
THOS. McINTIRE,
JOHN LOUGHEED.

ATTEST: R. G. Cook, justice of the peace, acting coroner, for Dodge township, said county.

352

L. C. HARTMAN, special policeman, whose exchange of shots with Luke Short marked the opening of the 1883 Dodge City "war." (A Beeson restricted photo.)

LUKE SHORT, part owner of the Long Branch saloon, imported gun-fighter pals to reinforce his Dodge City position. (A Beeson restricted photo.)

A. B. WEBSTER, an early resident of Hays and former mayor of Dodge City, was a leading spirit in the anti-Short faction. (A Beeson restricted photo.)

THOMAS MOONLIGHT, Kansas adjutant general, represented Governor Glick at Dodge City during Short's trouble with local authorities.

TOP ROW   Will Harris - Luke Short - W. B. Masterson - Wᵐ Tilghman
                                        Bat
                                        Sheriff   *City Marshall*

LOWER ROW   Chas. Bassett - Wyatt Earp - Frank McLain - Neal Brown
                  Sheriff   *City Marshall*   *Asst. City Marshall*

THE DODGE CITY PEACE COMMISSION

Opposed by the governor, and the touted superior fire power of ousted Luke Short's recruited army of assorted gunslingers, Dodge City administration forces knuckled under, and Short was allowed to return. Before disbanding, several of the victors posed for a picture (June, 1883) which long has been labeled "The Dodge City Peace Commission."

The most widely used print (*opposite page, top*) is that showing only seven members, though the photograph is obviously, and crudely, retouched.

Another version (*left*) contains the correct number but William M. Tilghman, who had little part in the trouble, has been substituted for W. F. Petillon.

The third and correct version (*above*, and see p. 562) shows Petillon at the right. The men have been identified as (back row, *from left*): W. H. Harris, Luke Short, W. B. Masterson, W. F. Petillon; (front row, *from left*): C. E. Bassett, Wyatt Earp, M. F. McLain (or McLane), Neil Brown.

NICHOLAS KLAINE, editor of the Dodge City *Times,* was antagonistic to Luke Short.

D. M. FROST, editor of the *Ford County Globe,* was friendly to Short.

MICHAEL W. SUTTON, local Santa Fe attorney, turned prohibitionist and finally outsmarted his old friend Bat Masterson, a wet, in the liquor war of 1886.

HARRY GRYDEN, a Dodge City lawyer, was made major of militia and ordered to keep the peace "at all hazards." (A Beeson restricted photo.)

VOX POPULI.

DODGE CITY, KANSAS, NOVEMBER 1, 1884.

SALUTATORY.

: The Vox Populi makes its bow to the voters of Ford county this morning, and in launching its little craft feels the grave responsibility it has undertaken. It has carefully weighed the many vicisitudes that it will encounter while gliding over the murky and turbulent waters of the great "Arkansas." Its object is, however, to permit no obstacle to impede its onward course. Its columns will be made to sparkle with native wit and ability. Its political sentiments will be Republican of the Conklin stripe. Canting hypocracy will not be one of the features of the Vox Populi. It has unfurled its banner to the gentle Kansas zephyr, with the avowed-intention .. exposing political and moral characters of many of the candidates seeking the suffrage of our voters at the coming election. Its political warfare upon those whom it opposes will be bold and untrammeled. It asks no favors and will give no quarters. Its columns will be chaste and readable. No man, woman nor child need have any hesitancy about reading the Vox Populi.

EDITOR.

THE prospects for a large immigration to Ford county this fall and winter is very flattering, and it behooves us as citizens to take every measure and pains to please and benefit the settlers. Let us try to help them; try to make their new homes pleasant for them, not rob them or take advantage of their ignorance of our ways of dealing. As citizens then let us go work for the best interests of our country, county and town.

LET Burns go back to Naperville, and tell the people there, who were generous enough to purchase him a pauper ticket to Dodge City that the people here don't want him.

UNION CHURCH SHOW COMBINATION.

Grand aggregation of living and fossil relics.

We have concluded to exhibit to the present age a rare collection of old fossils and living wonders,

At Dodge City, Nov. 4th, 1884.

To no previous age has ever been exhibited the first of our rare curiosities known as Klaineus Homo, a species of former man now extinct, but the only fossil remains of which we have secured at a great cost (of about $1700 in cash and $400 in accounts). It was first discovered buried in mud in one of the valleys of the State of Missouri. When the natives beheld it such terror was spread among them, that it was swiftly transferred to the borders of civilization in Kansas. Geologists in examining the signs of the regions where it was found have concluded that it was a voracious species, addicted to killing each other as one Tom Little was killed some years ago.

Our next rare gem is a peculiar kind of winged thing, allied in habits to the tame Magpie and Crow, but in appearance like unto a bird the ancients worshipped, called the Swan. Said bird has been known to take valuable papers from one Ferrier in Spearville, and appropriate them to a fraudulent use.

We next exhibit a marvelous amphibious creature known as Sutton-a-cuss Gymnatus or the electrical. To whatever object it comes in contact, it transmits a shock such that the victim seldom recovers (in his purse). It is also allied to the chamelion, changing its color to correspond to the object it approaches. It has been known to be

on one day red like wine and on the next allied to water. It will pay you to see it.

We have next on the list a species of Badger, prowling by night and having a fang of chemical properties, by the use of which the hardest iron is softened and it has even been known to open a safe in a mill by that means.

Now we bring before you the greatest of living wonders, a cross between the Chimpanza and Baboon--nature recoils at such an object. Naturalists claim it to be the greatest of existing curiosities. It has been exhibited to the bald heads of Europe with immense success. He was captured in the wilds of Illinois in a bear trap which accounts for its lameness—for many years being the terror of women and children in the above state; at last he made a swift exodus to this community. He is now partly civilized and always does the bidding of his master who are now on exhibition, his specialty is to limp at will, and when it limps it indicates that he wants something.

VOTE for B. F. Milton for county attorney, who is a gentleman and possessed of a character that is above reproach.

Ford county does not want the scum and filth of other communities for county attorney, such is Burns the Republican candidate.

Had it not been for the good women of Dodge City, the father of the Republican candidate for Probate Judge would actually have died from starvation.

E. D. Swan would be a nice man to have charge of the poor widows and orphans of Ford county, after turning his aged and decrepit father out upon the streets to die of starvation.

Whether armed with gun or pen, Bat Masterson was a formidable adversary. On November 1, 1884, he issued at Dodge City a political newspaper, *The Vox Populi*, which conveyed the suggestion that all his opposition were trash, and worse. After his full slate of local candidates was elected, Bat promptly wrote

(Continued on p. 358)

ᴄᴏₜₑ ᵍᵒ𝐱 ᵖᵒᵖᵘₗᵢ.

Published by the

VOX POPULI PUBLISHING CO.

W. B. MASTERSON, - EDITOR

SUBSCRIPTION, - $10.00 PER ANNUM

DODGE CITY, KANSAS, NOV. 1ST, 1884

Vote for J. W. Rush for State Senator.

THREE HUNDRED majority is what Milton and Crumbaugh will have over their filthy opponents in Dodge precinct on November 4th.

CRUMBAUGH is a gentleman and deserves the support of every decent man in Ford county, which is more than can be said of his opponent.

THE "gang element," as the old Missouri vulture calls them will show the hermaphodites that the Times is supporting what influence they have on election day.

WHAT an exalted opinion Gen. Caldwell and Mr. Lathey must have formed of the Republicans of Ford county, judging from the committees that received them; Zimmermann and Galland.

The Burns and Swan managers have advised them to keep away from portions of the county where they are not known, as this circumstance would certainly blight what little hopes they have of winning.

HORACE GREELY once said that "politics makes strange bed-fellows." The old sage comes very near hitting the nail on the head, judging from where we saw Col. Prouty and Perry Wilden last night. Gentlemen we advise you to disenfect yourselves this morning.

LET the voters of Ford county see that E. D. Swan is not elected probate judge by the same means that he secured an appointment for justice of the peace at Spearville some years ago, by misrepresentation and the names signed to a petition he county commissioners 'ing them to his petition to or.

county see that the name of J. W. Rush appears on his ticket. Remember that the state central committee have indorsed him.

The Times says Burns has the "requisite qualifications and experience for county attorney." Heavens! how we must have been mistaken, we thought he only possessed the requisite qualifications and experience of a tramp.

THE SPEAKING.

THE speech General Caldwell delivered in this city on last Thursday night was a master piece of oratory. His clear and concise manner of speaking showed him master of the different issues under discussion. His scathing arraignment of the Democratic party made many Democrats who were present squirm and twist in their seats. The magnificent showing that he made for the Republican party since their ascendency to power, had a telling effect on many who were inclined to be lukewarm, and no doubt many who were indifferent as to the result of the pending contest, will walk straight up to the polls on next Tuesday morning and cast their vote for Blaine and Logan. The speaker dwelt at some length on the beneficent effects of protection to our homes, industries and particularly to American labor. He showed that the country had gained in wealth from fourteen billion of dollars in 1860 to nearly fifty billion of dollars in 1884, or nearly four times as much in the twenty four years of Republican administration under a protective tariff as what it was during seventy years of free trade policy under Democratic rule. He also showed by official figures direct from the United States treasury that the loss of money on every thousand dollars received by the Government, exceeded five dollars under Democratic rule, while it did not exceed thirty-eight cents under Republican administration and asked with such a record for the party was the cry raised by the Democratic papers throughout the land, to turn the rascals out, a just one. General Caldwell is one

City, in fact we know of no better one in Kansas.

THE editors and managers of the VOX POPULI have been, are now, and always will be opposed to anything that the editors, or managers of the Dodge City Times advocate. They intend to wage a persistent and relentless warfare upon any and all things emanating from this source. Their opposition to this scapegoat faction is just and right; no decent newspaper or set of men with the least claim to respectability could do otherwise. The editor of the Times is, and always has been a scurrilous and unscrupulous vagabond; his treacherous and fiendish acts drove him from Missouri; the same purile mendacity that characterized him in Missouri, and stamp ed him as a villian of the deepes dye, has manifested itself in Kansas The goddess Nemesis, who so effectually squelched him in Missouri will crush him here. His days are short The time has about arrived when he will fold his government blanke and seek the shelter and assistance of a friend, as he did when he lef Missouri for Dodge City. His on that the gang must go' will soon r coil upon his own vile and putric carcass with such force that he wil be left the shattered and pestilen remnant of an obliterated faction "The gang," as this vile wretch see fit to call the element that oppose him in Dodge, will sweep him an his little coterie of venomous reptile that answer to his beck and call, an grin and acquiesce in all he says an writes into the eternal depths of pe dition. The slurs and vile utter ances of the Times which has be hurled and heaped with such unstir ed persistency upon those who wou not permit this refugee Missouri to black their boots, have only a ded staunch and unswerving me bers to their ranks. He begins realize his position; he feels the co of an inexorable enemy tight around him, and makes one despe ate dash to avoid what must be evitable sooner or later.

VOTE the ticket at the head of columns straight, and get good to fill the various offices.

(Continued from p. 357)

the paper's obituary: "The Vox Populi is no more. . . . [It] said nothing that it is sorry for, and with this declaration it says good day."

Only one issue of *Vox Populi* was published and only one copy is known to have survived. The paper is owned by Mrs. Merritt L. Beeson, who courteously permitted the reproduction of its four pages here, while reserving all reprinting rights elsewhere.

Swan, Burns, Klaine and Sutton combination will be left out in the cold on election day.

Aug Crumbaugh is the man you want to cast your vote for for Probate Judge. He is worthy of your suffrage.

VOTE for Milton and Crumbeaugh and force the crawling reptiles who are their opponents, to crawl in their holes.

THE rule or ruin principles of the Times won't work; people are being educated above individual interests in public affairs.

NOTWITHSTANDING the strenous effort being made by the safe blowers John Groendyke will get there by his usual majority.

IT is with the utmost disgust that we see the reptiled editor of the Times try to lead the Republican party to ruin and defeat.

IT makes the editor of the Times shake in his boots to mention the North Wing of the Normal school located at Warrensburg, Mo., to him.

DODGE CITY and Ford county has long borne an unenviable reputation, and its inhabitants should see that insult is not added to injury by voting for such trash as Burns and Swan.

Will the voters of Ford county support a man for Probate Judge who could wantonly permit his poor old father to suffer for the necessaries of life? Such a man is E. D. Swan.

WE think it would be better policy for Bro. Klaine to make good his little shortage with the city treasurer, than trying to place himself at the head of the Republican party of Ford county.

THE voters of Ford county ought to come up to Dodge City and ascertain how Burns and Swan stands in this community. We venture to say that they will return home and cast their ballot against those two worthies.

the dark days of war, let us do so D. M. Rose, the candidate for clerk of the district court on the republican ticket, is to-day a victim of disease contracted while in the army. He is the soldier's candidate and will receive their united support. Let every citizen be he veteran or not march in solid front to the polls and cast a ballot for Mr. Rose. His qualifications for the office are beyond question. He is a genial gentleman, modest and retiring in disposition, and only through earnest solicitations of his friends would he allow his name to come before the convention for nomination. Now that he is a candidate, let us give him a rousing majority on Tuesday next.—Larned Chronoscope.

THE manly and honorable course of D. M. Frost agaist whom the executive committee decided in the senatorial contest, is most commendable. Prior to submitting the case for arbitration he made appointments for meetings in different portions of the district. On Friday the day after the decision was rendered Mr. Rush received a telegram from Mr. Frost asking that he meet him at Ness City on Saturday evening. He proposed to keep his appointments, but instead of a Frost they would have a Rush meeting. This same spirit seems to prevail all over the district; the most ardent supporters of Mr. Frost are now working for Mr. Rush with a good will. The chances for a division in the republican ranks are thus done away. It is a happy termination of the vexed question.—Larned Chronoscope.

OLD Nick Klaine has repeatedly been branded as a thief, liar and murderer, yet he never whimpers, or attempts to deny any of the accusations. We expect that proof of his being a rapist, barn burner and a poisoner of his neighbors horses could be obtained without much effort.

There will be a little pile of rubbish on Nov. 5th. A board nailed on a stick set up there will read—sacred to the memory of Nasty B. Klaine, buried by the side of his twin babes. "Bobby and Ezra."

How poor was little Bobby Burns,
That people paid his way?
About as poor as he is vile,
That's what the people say.

How came that he got the votes,
That elected him one day?
He limps and squints, and has sore eyes,
Upon election day.

Vox Popvli is in for a free bridge.

Vote for Jack Jernigan and kill off a Klaine henchman by so doing.

Give Boss Petillon the grand bounce, and vote for L. E. McGarry for clerk of the district court.

A good honest government is all we ask, and must have honest men in office. Our ticket, we believe, fills the bill.

The Vox Popvli is for keeping the county lines just as they now stand, and thus save an extra expense to the tax payers.

If old Nick Klaine would pay as much attention to the speedy distribution of the mail as he does to the reading of postal cards that comes through the postoffice, there would not be so much kicking.

We want every settler on the south side to look to their interests on election day, and vote for such officers that will keep the county intact just as it now exists, and vote for men that will give them free passes over the Dodge City bridge. Remember that the Burns, Swan, Klaine and Sutton combination are against these two great interests to the tax payers.

In the event that Shoup being elected to legislature next Tuesday, a vacancy will occur in our board of county commissioners, as Mr. Shoup the present incumbent from the 3rd commissioners district will undoubtedly resign. It is to be hoped that the people of the 3rd commissioner district will be careful whom they recommend for appointment to fill the vacancy, as the two remaining commissioners in conjunction with the county clerk will make this important appointment, they should see that no man gets the appointment that will be dictated to and controlled by Zimmermann who has done about as he pleases with the present board of county commissioners. They should recommend a man who has some judgment and will power of his own, and not a pliant tool who will be bulldozed and handled by Zimmermann, who is no more fit to be chairman of the board of county commissioners than a jackass. His Election was a disgrace and a stain upon the people of Ford county. It requires a man of some intelligence to manage the affairs of our growing and prosperous county, and not a man who will be actuated by selfish and mercenary motives, such as has characterized Zimmermann's official conduct, since his installment as chairman of the county board.

The people of Ford county do not want any more such appointments as that made by Zimmermann when he intrusted the building of the new court house wing to the squirrel headed Elliott. Nor do they want any more thousand dollar appropriations for the repairing of the bridge across the Arkansas river at Cimarron, which was a direct stealing of the peoples money. The law required the board of County Commissioners, in this instance, to advertise this work, and secure bids for the performance of the same; and that the one making the lowest bid should be entitled to the contract. Yet Mr. Zimmermann disregarded the law and awarded the contract to his pet suckling, Mr. Elliott. We advise the people to look into this matter and see that no more mistakes are made in this direction.

A candidate is certainly out of luck that has old Nick Klaine supporting him. One puff from the columns of his foul sheet would defeat the best man in Ford county for any office that he would be an aspirant for.

Down with machine politicians and their nominees.

Turn in and elect our ticket by a rousing majority.

Bat Masterson

Fannie Garrettson, Miss Keenan's housemate the night of her
death, also had performed in St. Louis. Knowing their Missouri
friends would want to hear the details, Miss Garrettson almost
immediately wrote J. E. Esher, their former employer. Her letter,
and some explanatory material, were published in the St. Louis
Daily Journal, October 11, 1878:

FANNIE KEENAN.
HOW A VARIETY SINGER MET HER DEATH IN KANSAS.
DELIBERATE CRIME BY A COLD-BLOODED ASSASSIN.
AN INTERESTING LETTER GIVING THE DETAILS OF THE TRAGEDY.

On Saturday morning last the telegraph brought the news of the accidental
killing at Dodge City, Kan., of Fannie Keenan, a variety actress, well known
in this city. For the past two years she had been employed at Esher's
varieties, on Fifth street, at various times, and her last engagement in St.
Louis was at the Tivoli varieties. About two weeks ago she left for Dodge
City for the purpose of making arrangements for her approaching marriage.
She was formerly married to a musician named Theodore Hand, but obtained a divorce from him in Indiana. Hand arrived in St. Louis on Tuesday
morning, and for the first time heard of the death of his former wife. Fannie
Keenan was thirty-four years of age at the time of her death, and was well-
known to the variety profession throughout the country. She had appeared
in every variety theater in the south, and came to this city two years ago
from Memphis. She was universally popular among her associates, and,
as one of her acquaintances remarked, "had not an enemy in the world."
When she arrived in Dodge City she went to live with Fannie Garrettson, also
a variety performer, who recently appeared in Esher's varieties, and met her
death as stated in the following article taken from the Dodge City *Times*
[the article printed on p. 351 of this section, from the *Times* of October 5,
1878, was here reprinted by the *Journal*]:

The following letter was received on Tuesday by J. E. Esher, from Fannie
Garrettson, who is referred to in the above report as the "female lodger:"

DODGE CITY, KAS., October 5, 1878.

MESSRS. ESHERS:

DEAR FRIENDS:—No doubt ere this you have heard of the very sad and
fatal end [of Fannie Keenan, one of the most] fiendish assassinations on record.
Although the bullet was not intended for poor Fannie, yet she was the innocent
victim, and so it is invariably. Any one gets it but the one for whom it is
intended, and particularly in this wretched city. This is now the third or fourth
instance and still nothing is done. But the man who perpetrated this deed will
never exist for a judge or a jury, as the officers have sworn never to take him
alive. They were offered a big reward to get him but they declined to
accept it, for they were only too well pleased to get the order to start after
him. He is either a half breed or half Mexican; but let him be what he may
I know him to be a fiend in human form or some one else who will go at such

an hour, and attempt to take the life [of] any individual, and knowing at the same time there were other occupants in the same house and occupying the same bed. It shows what a fiend he must be and that he regarded no one's life. The party he was after is the mayor of Dodge City [James H. Kelley] I have written to you about. My room was the front one and Fannie occupied the one back of me. Both our beds stood in the same positions, mine being a higher bedstead than hers. There were four shots fired, two in the air and two penetrating through the door leading into my room. One was fired very low, hitting the floor and cutting two places in the carpet. It then glanced up striking the inside side piece of the bedstead, the one I occupied. It penetrated through these and through the plastering and lath and part of the bullet was found on the floor. They said it was a forty-five caliber. The one that did the horrible work was fired directly lining for my bed and had the one whom they were after been there, the probability is there would have been three or four assassinated. Certain there would have been two, probably Fannie and myself. But I was alone. The mayor has been very sick for two or three weeks, and last Monday he was obliged to go to the hospital to the post [Fort Dodge] where he could be under the best of treatment.

There is no very good doctor in town, and consequently people who have any means go to the post, as the doctor there [W. S. Tremain] is considered the best. But these parties who were in search of the mayor were not aware of that, as they had been away from town, and only came in that evening. Of course he did not dare to make any inquiries, as they all knew he held a grudge towards the mayor. But you can rest assured his aim was a good one. The death-dealing messenger penetrated through the bed clothes that covered me, and so close to me that it went through the spread, then the heavy comforter that covered me, and the sheet that was next to me, cutting a hole through all, and again passing through the clothes the same way only nearer to the wall, and then penetrating through the wall and passed between Fannie's fifth and sixth ribs. I suppose tearing her heart into atoms.

Poor Fannie, she never realized what was the matter with her. She never spoke but died unconscious. She was so when she was struck and so she died. She closed her eyes as though she was going to sleep. The only indication of any pain were the moving of the head once or twice on the pillow, a few gasps and her sufferings were over in this world. Peace to her soul. I think she died happy, as her look was such; but what a horrible death! To go to one's bed well and hearty and not dream of anything and be cut down in such a manner, without a chance to breathe a word. She was killed between the hours of 4 and 5 and was buried yesterday between the same hours, everything being done that could be, and every respect and honor shown her to the last, the leading gentlemen of the city officiating at her funeral and following to her lonely grave.

They have gone in search of the fellows who committed the deed and yesterday evening were within five or six miles of them, but I am afraid the trouble has not ended, as some twenty of the Texas men went out after the officers and there were only six of them. This man has been allowed more privileges than the rest of them because he has plenty of money, and now he has repaid their liberality. Well, I want to leave here now, while my life is safe; I think I have had enough of Dodge City.

With kindest wishes and rembrance to all, I will close, hoping you will write on receipt.

Very respectfully,

FANNIE GARRETTSON.

The posse that captured Jim Kennedy consisted of some of the West's most famous lawmen. The Dodge City *Times*, October 12, 1878, told of the chase in detail:

THE CAPTURE OF JIM KENNEDY.

THE SUPPOSED ASSASSIN OF DORA HAND alias FANNIE KEENAN.

THE PRISONER WOUNDED IN THE LEFT SHOULDER.

In last week's TIMES we detailed the circumstances of the killing of Dora Hand alias Fannie Keenan, at about half past four o'clock Friday morning. There were few persons up at this unseasonable hour, though all night walkers and loungers are not uncommon in this city, and the somber hours of that morning found one James Kennedy and another person gyrating in the dim shadows of the flickering light of the solitary opened saloon. Four pistol shots awakened the echoes in that dull misty morning, and aroused the police force and others. Pistol shots are of common occurrence, but this firing betokened something fatal. Assistant Marshal [Wyatt] Earp and Officer Jim Masterson were soon at their wits' end, but promptly surmised the upshot of the shooting. Shortly after the firing Kennedy and his companion were seen in the opened saloon. The arrival of the officers and the movements of the two morning loungers threw suspicions in their direction. Kennedy mounted his horse [and] was soon galloping down the road in the direction of the Fort.

It was believed the other person knew something of the firing though he had no connection with it. He was arrested and placed in jail; in the meantime expressing his belief to the officers that Kennedy did the shooting. There were some other reasons why the officers believed that Kennedy did the shooting, and accordingly a plan for his capture was commenced, though the officers did not start in pursuit until 2 o'clock in the afternoon. The party consisted of Sheriff Masterson, Marshal Basssett, Assistant [Marshal] Wyatt Earp, Deputy [Sheriff] Duffy and Wm. Tilghman, as intrepid a posse as ever pulled a trigger. They started down the river road, halting at a ranch below the Fort, thence going south, traveling 75 miles that day. A heavy storm Friday night delayed the pursued and pursuers; but Saturday afternoon found the officers at a ranch near Meade City, 35 miles south west of Dodge City, one hour in advance of Kennedy who said he was delayed by the storm in his proposed hasty exit to his cattle ranch at Tuscosa, Texas. The officers were lying in wait at Meade City, their horses unsaddled and grazing on the plain, the party avoiding the appearance of a Sheriff's posse in full feather, believing that they were in advance of the object of their search, but prepared to catch any stray straggler that exhibited signs of distress.

Their patient waiting was rewarded about 4 o'clock Saturday afternoon [October 5], when a solitary horseman appeared on the distant plain approaching the camp. The officers had apprised certain parties to give no heed of their presence, and from them it was afterwards learned that Kennedy had made diligent inquiries concerning the whereabouts of supposed horsemen. To these inquiries Kennedy received negative replies. The cautious manner in which he approached the camp led the officers to believe that he snuffed the danger from every movement forward. He halted when within a few hundred yards of the camp, apparently dreading to proceed further. Seeing that he would approach no nearer, the officers thrice commanded Kennedy to throw up his hands. He raised his arm as though to strike his horse with a quirt he held in his hand, when several shots were fired by the officers, one shot striking Kennedy in the left shoulder, making a dangerous wound; three shots struck the horse killing him instantly. Kennedy was armed with a carbine, two revolvers and a knife. He was brought in Sunday and placed in jail, where he is receiving medical treatment, though he lies in a low and critical condition.

A preliminary examination will be had as soon as the prisoner is able to appear in court.

Kennedy's examination was held about two weeks later. The *Globe*, October 29, 1878, reported the results:

FREE AS AIR.

Kennedy, the man who was arrested for the murder of Fannie Keenan, was examined last week before Judge [R. G.] Cook, and acquitted. His trial took place in the sheriff's office, which was too small to admit spectators. We do not know what the evidence was, or upon what grounds he was acquitted. But he is free to go on his way rejoicing whenever he gets ready.

On December 9 Jim Kennedy's father arrived in Dodge to take his boy back home. The *Globe*, December 10, 1878, said:

Yesterday morning's train brought to our city Capt. M. Kennedy, of Corpus Christi, Texas, father of J. W. Kennedy, who received a severe wound at the hands of our officers some time ago, and has since that time been confined to his room at the Dodge House. Mr. Kennedy came here with a view of taking his son back home with him should he be able to endure such a long journey.

Before he was able to return to Texas Kennedy had to undergo a serious operation which the *Globe* described on December 17, 1878:

SURGICAL OPERATION.

On yesterday quite a difficult as well as a dangerous surgical operation was performed on J. W. Kennedy, who had been shot through the shoulder some two months ago, which necessitated the taking out of a piece of bone some four or five inches in length before the wound could be successfully healed. Mr. Kennedy was taken to Fort Dodge about a week ago, at which place he would have better attention. Dr. B. E. Fryer of Fort Leavenworth was brought here to assist in this operation, and on last Saturday he, assisted by Drs. Tremaine and T. L. McCarty, took from the left shoulder of Mr. Kennedy several shattered bones, one being nearly five inches in length. The doctors experienced considerable difficulty in stopping the blood but finally succeeded. Though considerably exhausted from the slight loss of blood as well as from the shock experienced, Mr. Kennedy showed remarkable fortitude and nerve and said afterward that he would not die from the effects of the operation. Just how the case will result is hard to conjecture, but life is hanging on a very slender cord. But as he is receiving the best of medical attention we predict for him a speedy recovery.[24]

Jim Kennedy undoubtedly lived, for in November, 1880, it was rumored that he had shot and killed Wyatt Earp on Sand creek, in Colorado. The *Times'* notice of this rumor was reprinted in the section on Earp.

While Kennedy was still in jail the Dodge City *Times,* October 12, 1878, listed the prisoners which the sheriff was then holding as evidence that he and Mike Sutton were more than doing their duty:

STRAUGHN'S BOARDERS.

Sheriff Masterson, Deputy Sheriff Duffy and County Attorney Sutton, and the officers "everybody" "damns" are assisting Jailor Straughn in keeping a boarding house. There are six prisoners boarding at public expense. They are charged, as follows:

Thos. O'Hara, charged with murder in the first degree; the killing of H. T. McCarty.

H. Gould, alias Skunk Curley, assault with intent to kill; on Cogan, of Great Bend.

Dan Woodward, the same charge, made on Frank Trask.

James Skelly, robbery.

James Kennedy, murder in the first degree; killing of Fannie Keenan.

Arthur Baldwin, in default of a fine.

On October 15, 1878, the *Ford County Globe* mentioned that "Sheriff W. B. Masterson has taken up quarters in the front room of the GLOBE building" on the corner of Bridge avenue and Chestnut street.

Bat was interested in Republican politics and on several occasions attended local conventions as a delegate. On November 5, 1878, the *Globe,* a political opponent of Bat's, noticed that he and several other Dodgeites had been campaigning in eastern Ford county:

Messrs. Wright Sutton, Masterson, Duffey, Mueller, Straeter and a half dozen others, returned Sunday morning from an electioneering tour through the east end of the county. We presume they told the dear people exactly how to vote.

A state, county, and township election was held on November 5, 1878, at which a sheriff was not to be elected since that officer was chosen in odd numbered years. The "gang" to which Bat belonged walked off with most of the local offices. The *Globe*, November 12, 1878, summarized:

CAPTURED.

On Tuesday a "gang" took possession of the good ship "Ford" at a well-known landing on the Arkansas river, with the intention of going upon a piratical voyage of two years. The victory of the pirates was an easy one. Some of the owners had been chloriformed, some were bought, some were scared; the true men were overpowered. Amid "lashins" of free whisky the following officers were unanimously elected:

Pirate Captain—Mike Sutton [re-elected county attorney].

Sutler and paymaster—Bob Wright [elected state representative].

Chaplain—"Old Nick" Klaine [elected probate judge].

The crew was then sworn in as follows: John O'Haran, James Scully, Kinch Riley, James Dalton, under the charge of Boatswain Bat Masterson.

The ceremonies were celebrated by a grand Cyprian ball. After which Chaplain "Old Nick" Klaine [editor of the Dodge City *Times*] closed the exercises by giving out the following from the "Gospels Hymns,":

"Free from the law, O happy condition."

Bat arrested another horse thief on November 22 at Pierceville, a small town in present Finney county near the Gray county line. The *Times*, November 30, 1878, reported the capture:

HORSE THIEF CAUGHT.

Sheriff Masterson, on Friday last, at Pierceville, 40 miles west, arrested one W. H. Brown, having in his possession a horse stolen from John N. Stevenson, six miles north of Speareville, on the 19th. The prisoner had a preliminary examination Saturday and was bound over in jail. There are seven prisoners in jail charged with various offenses. This looks like business on the part of the officers.

Bat's career as a peace officer soon suffered a setback when four county prisoners escaped from jail on December 6. The *Ford County Globe*, December 10, 1878, told of the flight:

JAIL DELIVERY.

FOUR PRISONERS ESCAPE FROM CUSTODY—
ONE OF THE PRISONERS CAPTURED "ON THE FLY."

For the first time in over a year we are called upon to chronicle the escape of prisoners from our county jail. The particulars of the manner in which the escape was effected are as follows: At the last meeting of the Board of

366

County Commissioners the jailor was authorized to alter the door of the jail, by cutting one of the bars and making a small hole that food and water could be handed in to the prisoners, without making it necessary to unlock and open the jail. This the jailor undertook to do last Friday.

The work of sawing the iron bar was commenced, and one of the prisoners, on the inside, was allowed to assist, which is a very common thing when work is to be done about the jail. After the sawing had been partially completed, the jailor found something lacking in the completion of the work which necessitated his visiting the blacksmith shop. He took the saw away from the prisoners, and examined the bar that had been partially sawed, striking it with his hammer to see that it was not too weak to be safe. It seemed to be only sawed about a third off, and confident that all was secure, the jailor went to the blacksmith shop, where he was detained some time. This gave the cunning prisoners the opportunity they desired, for instead of sawing the bar as the jailor supposed, and as it appeared from the outside, they had, whenever opportunity offered, drawn the saw across the inside of the bar, cutting it more than half into from the inside.

As soon as the jailor had gone one of the prisoners procured a heavy piece of board, which he had managed to get hold of, and using this as a lever, succeeded in breaking the bar where it had been sawed. This done, it was only the work of a moment to bend the bar and break it at the other end. Thus a means was afforded of escape, and four of the prisoners silently and cautiously availed themselves of the opportunity. Their names were H. Gould, awaiting trial for murder, and W. H. Brown, Frank Jennings and James Bailey, charged with horse-stealing. They immediately "struck out for tall timber," each taking the course that suited him best. The alarm was, however, given in a short time, strange to say, by one of the prisoners in jail, who with his companion, John O'Haran, made no attempt to escape, both being lame, and not very good roadsters.

On hearing the disastrous news the sheriff and his deputy immediately mounted horses and scoured the country around town in search of the fugitives. Their prompt search proved partially fruitful in the capture of Gould, about a mile from town, hid in a buffalo wallow on the prairie. Had it not been for the approach of darkness, the escape being in the afternoon, the officers would probably have secured all the prisoners. They, however, continued their search through the night and the next day, but the prisoners having taken to the prairies and hills, no trace could be found. The search is still in progress and we hope for success.

The officers feel the misfortune keenly. The sheriff, whose conduct in the capture and detention of horse-thieves, has been so frequently complimented of late, was greatly exercised over the news of the escape and made every effort to regain the prisoners. The feelings of the jailor can be better imagined than described, as this is the first misfortune he has had since he has held the office. He blames himself for not having used more care or left some one to guard the door during his absence. While every citizen deplores this occurrence, no suspicion of complicity rests upon the officers.

The jailor, Col. Straughn, who was immediately in charge of the prisoners at the time of the escape is a man of undoubted honesty and fidelity to his office, and although this outbreak might have been avoided by greater care, yet a thousand other men in a like position would probably have thought and acted just as he did. It will be a warning for the future.

LATER.—Another of the prisoners, Frank Jennings, was captured this morning at Kinsley, and sheriff Masterson has gone down to secure the baffled fugitive.

The Dodge City *Times*, December 14, 1878, gave the credit for recapture of Gould to Bat's brother Jim:

A JAIL DELIVERY.

Notwithstanding the caution used in guarding the jail, through a careless and unguarded moment last Friday afternoon, four prisoners made their escape, one of them, Skunk Curley, being captured that evening by Officer James Masterson.

Jailor Straughn had sawed one of the iron bars of the jail door, intending to arrange an aperture through which to hand the prisoners their food. While absent "down town" for a bolt to complete his job, the prisoners slipped the sawed bar and made their escape, though there were several parties in the jail building. The remaining prisoners gave the alarm which was not heeded in time. As soon as Sheriff Masterson was informed of the jail delivery he and a large party started in pursuit and search, which was keep [*sic*] up that night and until Sunday; but without success, excepting the early capture we have above stated.

The three prisoners evidently concealed themselves in some of the breaks nearby, for that night two men attempted to raid the corral of Nichols & Culbertson. A mare belonging to C. S. Hungerford was stolen from Wolf's camp several miles north of the city. The mare was probably stolen by W. H. Brown, one of the escaped prisoners, as a person answering his description was seen in that vicinity early in the evening.

The names of the escaped prisoners are: W. H. Brown who was charged with stealing Mr. Stevenson's horse near Speareville; Frank Jennings and James A. Bailey were charged with stealing horses from Hardesty and Smith, and were arrested by Geo. Pease at Fort Elliott.

Two more of the escapees were captured by the sheriff of Edwards county. On December 11 Bat journeyed to Kinsley and brought them back to Dodge. The *Times*, December 14, 1878, said:

CAPTURED.

Frank Jennings and James A. Bailey, two of the prisoners who escaped from the jail on Friday last, were captured at Kinsley by Officer Cronk, and brought to this city Wednesday by Sheriff Masterson, and placed in the Ford county jail.

W. H. Brown is the only fugitive.

Our officers felt considerably hurt over the jail escapade. We believe no one censures them; and we trust that double caution will be used on the part of the jailor.[25]

Wednesday night, the same day he brought Jennings and Bailey back to Dodge, Bat embarked on another man hunt. This time, accompanied by a few soldiers from Fort Dodge, he was after brigands who had stolen eight mules from a government supply train. The *Times*, December 14, 1878, reported:

GOVERNMENT TRAIN RAIDED.

A Government train of two wagons and eight mules was "raided" Tuesday night at their camp on Bluff creek, 37 miles south, and eight mules stolen. The train was en route to Camp Supply, and was in charge of soldiers. Sheriff Masterson and Lt. Guard, of Fort Dodge, with a couple of men, left Wednesday night in search of the stolen property and the capture of the thieves.

Horse thieving is a little too bold and frequent to be longer endured without more stringent measures than a short term in the penitentiary. Some of these bold operators will some fine evening be taken in the most approved and summary style.

"Some of these bold operators" did not include the men Bat and the lieutenant were chasing, for the next week the *Times*, December 21, 1878, told of their unsuccessful pursuit:

Sheriff Masterson and posse returned this week from a fruitless search after the thieves who raided the government train. The snow storm caught them the next day after they were out.

Lieutenant Guard, with whose detachment Bat traveled in search of the thieves, made this detailed report upon his return to Fort Dodge:

FORT DODGE KANSAS.
Dec 24" 1878

To THE
POST ADJUTANT: SIR:

In compliance with Special Orders No 156 dated Fort Dodge, Ks. Dec 11" 1878, I in charge of a detachment of one Non Com Officer and six privates, Co. "G," 19" Inf and one private Co. "F," 19" Inf, mounted and with three pack mules, left this post at sunset on the 11" instant in pursuit of horse thieves. We proceeded up the Arkansas river to a point about twelve miles from this post, then crossed the river and travelled in a southerly direction to near the head of Mulberry Creek, where a dry camp was made at 2 oclock A. M. on the 12" instant, distance travelled 25 miles. At day break on the 12" inst. we marched to Gantz Ranch on Crooked Creek, a distance of fifteen miles from the Camp, a halt was made for the purpose of cooking breakfast, after breakfast every thing was prepared for a start, when a severe wind and snow storm prevented our leaving, as there was no timber or shelter on the course I wished to take, within thirty miles, of the place where we then were. I thought it unsafe to start until the storm had ceased.

The storm continued all the remainder of the 12" inst and until 11 P. M. on the 13" inst. On the morning of the 14" inst we started for Lovells Cattle camp on Crooked creek a distance of thirty miles from Gantz, in a southeasterly direction. We found the country covered with snowdrifts which made it almost impossible to search ravines on the way. Camped at Lovells that night. The next day the 15" marched to a point on Beaver Creek, I. T. about forty five miles west of Camp Supply.

Ravines, on Crooked Creek, Cimmaron River, and Beaver Creek were searched as well as the snow drifts would permit. Distance traveled on the 15" thirty miles, direction West of South.

On account of rations and forage giving out, I was compelled to go into Camp Supply. We arrived at that Post on the night of the 16" inst. having travelled forty five miles.

The horses being tired and stiff with cold and the long march, a rest of two days became necessary. Left Camp Supply for Fort Dodge on the 19" inst. Marched to Cimmaron River, distance travelled thirty seven miles. On the 20" inst marched to Bluff Creek, distance twenty eight miles. On the 21" inst arrived at Fort Dodge Distance travelled twenty two miles.

The weather was intensely cold throughout the march.
Distance travelled two hundred and thirty two miles.

> Very respectfully
> Your obedient servant
> A. McC. GUARD
> 2" Lieut 19" Inf.[26]

The Dodge City *Times*, December 21, 1878, reported that Bat had appointed another deputy sheriff:

DEPUTIES APPOINTED.

County Attorney Sutton has appointed L. W. B. Johnson Deputy County Attorney. Sheriff Masterson has appointed A. S. Tracy Deputy Sheriff of Ford County. The new appointees are residents of Foote township, Foote county [now Gray county], attached to Ford county for municipal and judicial purposes. These gentlemen are well qualified to fill the responsible positions.

Bat attended a gay social event on Christmas day. The *Ford County Globe*, January 1, 1879, described the festivities:

THE BAL MASQUE.

The first masquerade ball of this season was given on Christmas night by the Dodge City Social Club. The grotesque masquers assembled at the Dodge House, where the ball was given, and participated in the amusements laid out for them, unknown to each other, until 12 o'clock, when the order was given to "show up" which occasioned a considerable amusement, as many had so completely disguised themselves that even their most intimate friends failed to recognize them. This was one of the most real enjoyable dances given for a long time, and was attended by a very harmonious class of our society. Messrs. Webster, Marshall, Connor and Willett were the committee on management and the music was under the superintendence of Mr. Geo. Hinkle. Messrs.

Bat Masterson

Cox & Boyd, the proprietors of the Dodge House, made themselves particularly agreeable and their guests correspondingly comfortable. Champagne and wine flowed freely, but not to excess, and a merrier Christmas night was never enjoyed in Dodge. As near as our reporter could distinguish the following is a list of those who were present and participated: . . . W. B. Masterson and Miss Brown. . . .

As far as Sheriff Masterson was concerned the year 1879 started off auspiciously. On New Year's day he journeyed to Trinidad, Colo., after one of the West's most wanted men, Dutch Henry.

This man was then considered to be one of the most successful horse thieves, escape artists, and all round outlaws in the West. His fame approached that of Jesse James and the Younger brothers back East. Naturally the capture of such a character would be quite a feather in any lawman's hat.

Officers of Trinidad arrested Henry on Bat's telegraphic request. When it was found that no money was offered the Trinidad police were reluctant to turn the prisoner over to Bat. The Dodge City *Times,* January 4, 1879, said:

DUTCH HENRY.

Sheriff Masterson learning that Dutch Henry was under arrest at Trinidad, proceeded to that place Wednesday. He telegraphed County Attorney Sutton as follows: "Sheriff wont deliver up Dutch Henry unless I pay him $500. He says he can get that fer him in Nevada." So Mr. Dutch Henry is high priced and the silver State can take him.

Three days later, January 7, the *Ford County Globe* announced that Bat had brought Henry to Dodge:

CAUGHT AT LAST.

THE RENOWNED DUTCH HENRY, THE OUTLAW CHIEF, HAS FALLEN.

Hearing that this great king of outlaws was in the hands of the Las Animas county officers, at Trinidad, Sheriff Masterson went up last Wednesday to see what he could see, and, if possible, secure the prisoner and bring him to Ford county to answer for the many "irregularities" in his conduct toward the owners of horseflesh in this vicinity. The following is from the Trinidad Enterprise, which explains what action was taken there:

"Dutch Henry," the man who seems to be wanted in different states and territories for a variety of crimes, such as horse-stealing, mail robbery, and even murder, and of whose arrest here we gave an account in yesterday's Enterprise, was brought before Judge Walker to-day, upon complaint of Sheriff Wootton, that he is a fugitive from justice in Ford county, Kansas, charged and indicted for grand larceny. The sheriff of Ford county, Mr. W. B. Masterson of Dodge City, was present as a witness. Mr. Caldwell Yeaman appeared for the prosecution, and Mr. Salisbury for the defense. We learn that in the

371

course of the proceedings there was some sparring between one of the attorneys and the visiting sheriff from Dodge, in which the legal gentlemen became considerable excited by unwarrantable mention of "unmentionable" matters by the witness. Now it is generally the witness who gets badgered and excited, and it may be well enough for gentlemen of the legal persuasion to happen upon a witness who can give them an opportunity to know how it is themselves. The result of the examination was that "deutcher Heinrich" was bound over to appear at the March term of the district court, and it was ordered that in default of bail he shall be confined in the Bent county jail. A motion was made by the prisoner's counsel that the case be referred to Judge Henry in chambers at Pueblo, and Justice Walker took the matter under advisement. "Dutch Henry" is rather a genteel looking man for a horse-thief, road-agent and murderer. He has black hair and eyes, black moustache, long face and Roman nose. His eyes are bright and penetrating, and indicate quick intelligence. He is dressed in a good suit of black, white shirt and other corresponding clothing.

Sheriff Masterson arrived with Dutch Henry in charge last Monday morning and how he obtained possession of him we will relate below. Masterson received news that Dutch Henry was at Trinidad in company with Charley Morrow, Mysterious Dave [Mather?] and others, and had been there several weeks. Masterson telegraphed the officers to arrest Henry, which they did, and after doing so telegraphed to various parties to find out what reward was offered; but they were disappointed in finding any reward whatever. Then they agreed to release Henry if he would pay expenses of arrest, etc., which Henry agreed to do, and would have done [so] had not some stock men prevailed upon the officers to hold the prisoner until news could be received from Ford county. As soon as Masterson arrived Henry was tried on the charge of being a fugitive from justice, and bound over in the sum of $500 bail, in default of which he was ordered committed to the jail in West Las Animas. Masterson desired to bring the prisoner to Dodge, but having no requisition from the Governor of Kansas, was in a bad fix, and when the subject of bringing him here was first spoken of Henry made a talk for himself, in which he took recourse to threats of exposure, etc. This made Masterson all the more determined to bring him and he finally succeeded in making an arrangement by which he was given possession of the prisoner, and he is now safely ensconced in our jail. When the officers went to arrest the notorious Henry he was in a saloon watching a pool game, and was evidently off his guard, making no resistance whatever. He is now suffering from sickness, and has very little to say to any one. His trial will take place as soon as the witnesses for the state can be subpoenaed.

DUTCH HENRY.

A GLOBE representative visited Dutch Henry in the county jail this morning. Henry was lying on a mattress, and on inquiry as to his health said he was feeling better than on the previous day, but was still far from well. He talked very composedly and when his probable trial was referred to did not seem uneasy in the least. Said he thought the officers arrested him more to make capital for election purposes than anything else. (This may be a little policy talk, but we give it as part of his conversation.) He says he had been at Trinidad several weeks and was well acquainted with everybody there, including the sheriff and officers, and never had any suspicions of any intent to arrest him, and never carried arms; was not armed when the officers arrested him. Says he was thinking of going into business at Las Vegas, New Mexico. He spent last summer catching wild horses, and last fall killed and dried a load of buffalo meat which he sold in New Mexico. He says his character as a horse-thief is greatly over-estimated, and it has become the custom of all the thieves in the country to saddle their crimes upon him. Says he never stole a white man's horse in his life. Says there are many old settlers here who have known him heretofore and who he thinks will not believe all the stories told about him. For these parties he seems to have a warm regard and says he has saved Dodge from ashes several times, when some of his associates wanted to burn the town to get revenge for treatment from some of the citizens. Of his early history Henry has but little to say, as he does not wish his friends in his eastern home to identify him. During a recent visit home, where he remained several months, he frequently received papers from the west, containing accounts of horse-stealing, etc., which was all charged to Dutch Henry, while in reality he was a thousand miles away. He says he could make some revelations but does not wish to, and will not if he is treated fairly.

The appearance of Dutch Henry is that of an educated German-American, and his language is very slightly broken. His career opened in the west in 1867, when he joined the Custar expedition, since which time he has been a roving plainsman. He says no one in the west knows what his real name is. His examination, on the charge of stealing Emmerson's mules, about a year ago, takes place as soon as the witnesses arrive. Parties who claim to know say that Henry's real name is Henry Borne.

The Dodge City *Times*, January 11, 1879, reported:

DUTCH HENRY.

The ubiquitous individual who wrestles with horse flesh, under the well-known sobriquet of "Dutch Henry," is again in the toils. He was brought to this city and placed in jail by Sheriff W. B. Masterson, Sunday night last [January 5]. Dutch Henry was arrested in Trinidad, Colorado, and the subjoined account is taken from the Trinidad Enterprise. Sheriff Masterson deserves a great deal of credit for the venture, and it is only one of the many successful official moves he has made since holding the important office of sheriff.

Dutch Henry has become famous in the western States and Territories, and has made many bold and successful escapes from justice. He has broken jail and escaped from officers no less than three times within a year; but he has found himself within the iron grasp of a vigilant and brave officer, and will no doubt receive a sentence for one of his many crimes.

How Bat got possession of the prisoner without the payment of a reward and without a gubernatorial requisition, will probably be explained in one of the pages of a yellow-backed story book, which will detail the mysteries and crimes of the early settlement of this border. We are not curious to know just now. History will give us all the enlightenment we care to know. That is one of the things we hand down to posterity. But here is the interesting account from the Enterprise. It seems Bat was a match for that squalid lawyer. . . .

From this point the *Times* reprinted the same *Enterprise* article that the *Globe* used on January 7.

Two short items from the Trinidad *News* were copied in the *Globe* on January 14, 1879:

Considerable merriment was created in Justice Walker's court on Saturday, during the hearing of Dutch Henry's case, by Sheriff Masterson of Dodge City, Kansas, insinuating that the attorney for the defense, Mr. Salisbury, had left Kansas under a cloud. The answer made by the sheriff was under oath, and may have caused some to believe that there was truth in it. But we happened to overhear Mr. Masterson say to a party of friends that night that there was not a word of truth in it; that he was driven into a corner by Salisbury, and had to say something to let himself out. We make this statement not because we have any reason to think that any person would seriously believe that there was anything in it, but because it is due to Mr. Salisbury that any false impression should be removed.

Dutch Henry has left Colorado and returned to Kansas. He agreed to waive his rights and to save the trouble and delay of having a requisition made upon the governor by the governor of Kansas. Accordingly he went east with Sheriff Masterson on Sunday morning. Of course he was not ironed, and was really not a prisoner. If he should undertake to violate his promise and to walk off while still in Colorado a serious complication might arise. He would have a strict legal right to do so, but it is hardly probable that Sheriff Masterson would consent to follow a policy of masterly inactivity in such an emergency. It is more probable that he would himself become a violator of the law, and would make Henry his prisoner whether he "could" or not.

On January 11, 1879, the *Times* said that "they tried to habeas corpus Dutch Henry before Judge Peters, but it didn't take," and "the preliminary trial of Dutch Henry will be had before Justice Cook this Saturday." The *Globe,* January 14, 1879, reported Henry's examination:

A large crowd assembled at the Court House yesterday to hear the preliminary examination of Dutch Henry, who was arrested on a charge of grand larceny about a year and a half ago, but who at that time made his escape through the key-hole of the jail door. He was again arrested and brought here from Trinidad, Col., by Sheriff Masterson. He waived a preliminary examination and the court bound him over for his appearance at the next term of the district court in the sum of $600, in default of which he was committed [to] jail.[27]

Henry was tried at the adjourned term of the Ford county district court. The *Times*, January 25, 1879, recorded:

Dutch Henry's trial occupied two days of the time of the court, and Thursday night the jury brought in a verdict of not guilty. The prisoner was charged with horse stealing. Insufficient evidence and barred by statute of limitations, though the latter point was negatively decided by a jury, probably led to the prisoner's acquittal. Colborn and [Thomas S.] Jones conducted the prosecution and [H. E.] Gryden and Hurd for the defense.

So Henry was released. He eventually traveled to Wichita where he was arrested by Deputy United States Marshal C. B. Jones and delivered to the sheriff of Shawnee county to answer another charge of jail breaking.[28] Thus continued the career of Dutch Henry *ad infinitum.*

Back in Dodge City—the January, 1879, term of the Ford county district court was convened by Sheriff Masterson on January 7. The *Times*, January 11, 1879, reported the early days of the session:

DISTRICT COURT.

The January term of the Ford County District Court, S. J. Peters, Judge, presiding, convened Tuesday afternoon. The following officers were promptly at their posts:

County Attorney—M. W. Sutton.

Sheriff—W. B. Masterson.

Clerk—H. P. Myton.

Tuesday afternoon the time was occupied in the usual preliminaries required for the working order of the court.

Wednesday morning, the case of James Skelly, charged with stealing a horse and gun, was taken up. The prisoner was found guilty of the charge.

Wednesday afternoon, the trial of Dan. Woodard, charged with assault with intent to kill, took place. The prisoner was defended by H. E. Gryden. The prosecution was conducted by County Attorney Sutton, who made a vigorous and able argument against the "pistol practice" in Dodge City. The jury was out but a short time and brought in a verdict of guilty. The defense moved for a new trial.

Frank Jennings, charged with horse stealing, was found guilty.

James A. Bailey plead guilty to the same charge.

H. Gould, alias Skunk Curley, plead guilty to the charge of assault with intent to kill.

In the case of Thomas O'Haran, charged with the murder of H. T. McCarty, a motion for a change of venue was filed [*see* the section on McCarty].

The trial of M. A. Sebastian was being had Friday, but up to the time of going to press no verdict had been reached. Sebastian and Bill Brown are charged with stealing twenty-seven sacks of corn. The trial of Brown will follow that of Sebastian.

The next cases on the docket are those of G. U. Holcomb and G. A. Watkins, charged with stealing cattle.

The trial of Dutch Henry will close the criminal docket. This may not be had until the adjourned term of the court [*see* p. 375].

The sentences of the several convicted prisoners will be passed before the adjournment of court.

The following attorneys were in attendance: E. F. Colborn, Thomas S. Jones, H. E. Gryden, Nelson Adams, Geo. A. Kellogg, D. M. Frost, Judge [J. C.] Strang, Judge W. R. Brown.

There was a large attendance during the entire session of court. Many of the spectators were interested parties, as jurors, witnesses, &c.

The large criminal calendar suggests the "probability" of an "endeavor" on the part of the officers to do their duty. To an unprejudiced person, somebody has been making things lively. Sheriff Bat Masterson, Under Sheriff Bassett, and Deputies Duffy and [James] Masterson, have evidently earned the high praise accorded to them for their vigilance and prompt action in the arrest of offenders of the law.

The energy of the indomitable and untiring worker, County Attorney Sutton, is manifested in the successful prosecution of these cases. Mike certainly "got to the joint" in his accustomed and able manner, and is deserving of the many good words spoken in his behalf for his efficient services in the cause of justice.

The court adjourns this Saturday evening, until week after next, when the remainder of the criminal cases will be tried and the civil docket disposed of.

On Saturday, just before the court was adjourned, Judge Peters passed sentence upon the six who had been convicted. The *Ford County Globe,* January 14, 1879, reported:

THE WAY OF THE TRANSGRESSOR.

To all who witnessed the scene in the court room last Saturday evening, the proof was positive that "the way of the transgressor is hard." The room was crowded with curious spectators, who had heard that the convicts were to be sentenced that evening, and as sentences in this community have been almost as rare as angels' visits in the past—few and far between—it was natural for the people to assemble as they would to witness a contest in the arena. The Judge was seated at his desk, his grave and solemn countenance told that his thoughts were stern and decisive. Groups of attorneys conversed in low whispers within the railing, all of whom, save one—the prosecutor—had failed to get the ear of the jury, and their spent eloquence was as pearls cast before swine—trampled and trod upon. In a row in front of the Judge sat the six sinners for whom they had labored; all were convicted, and from their features every ray of hope had fled. The whispering was hushed in the room as Judge Peters finished writing, laid aside his pen and reflecting for a moment, said, "James A. Bailey, you may stand up." The first of the six slowly rose to his feet. He was a man of fine appearance, and to questions propounded by the Judge, answered that he was born and raised in New York; was 42 years of age; had received an education, and before coming west was employed as traveling salesman for his brother. When asked if he had any reason to offer why sentence should not be pronounced, he said he had none, as he had plead guilty; but in view of the fact that he was already advanced in years, he hoped the Judge would not sentence him to a long term, as he would be unable to survive it. He asked that the fact of his being under the influence of liquor be considered in mitigation of his crime.

He had stolen a horse.

Frank Jennings was next called up. He was from Pennsylvania; was 26 years old; had been in Kansas five months; has a mother living; by profession a house carpenter. Was under the influence of liquor. Begged the Court to treat him with leniency. His offense was horse stealing.

James Skelley, convicted of stealing a gun. Was 27 years old; been in the west two years; from Illinois; parents both living; by trade a glass blower; uneducated. Was under the influence of liquor; hoped the Court would be lenient.

H. Gould, assault and battery with intent to commit murder. Mr. Gould wore a smiling countenance, and did not seem to fully comprehend his situation. Was a native of Kansas; by occupation a herder of cattle; age, 24 years. Was influenced by liquor. In view of his tender years he asked the court to be merciful.

Mr. Sebastian, charged with stealing 26 sacks of corn, was the only one of the six who claimed to be innocent, 31 years of age.

Mr. John Brown, charged with the same offense as Sebastian, said he supposed, from the evidence he was guilty. Was 36 years of age and by trade a butcher. Was intoxicated at the time of the theft.

After the prisoners had all been thus questioned, Messrs. Gryden, Jones and Kellogg, in behalf of their respective convicted clients, argued to the Judge, and directed his attention to the "brightest spots" in the lives and acts of the criminals, and asked that mercy be shown them. The Judge then passed the following sentences, the date of imprisonment to commence Jan. 7th, 1879; Bailey, two years and six months; Jennings, two years and six months; Skelley, two years and three months; H. Gould, two years and three months; Sebastian, eighteen months; Brown, two years and three months.

The remarks of Judge Peters on this occasion were very appropriate, and the advice he gave should be followed by all who heard it and witnessed this sad scene. It was long after lamplight when court adjourned, and the crowd dispersed, free to go where they pleased, while the doomed six filed out under heavy guard to seek what comfort they might within the narrow bounds of their lonely prison cells.[29]

"Sheriff Masterson, City Marshall Bassett, [County] Commissioner [A. J.] Peacock, and District Clerk [H. P.] Myton started to the Leavenworth penitentiary last Saturday evening [January 11] with the six prisoners," said the *Globe,* January 14, 1879.

About the time he delivered the six prisoners to Leavenworth, Bat revoked the appointment of his deputy sheriff in Spearville township. A local correspondent of the *Times* reported, January 18, 1879:

The action of Sheriff Masterson in revoking the appointment of Murray Wear as Deputy, is approved by all citizens in this township, and all are satisfied that he could make no better selection than to choose the portly L. M. Depuy as the successor of Wear.[30]

In the same issue, January 18, 1879, the *Times* recorded the fact that "Sheriff W. B. Masterson has been appointed Deputy U. S. Marshal."[31]

After the adjourned session of the January, 1879, term of the Ford county district court, Bat had more prisoners to take to the state penitentiary. The Leavenworth *Times*, January 28, 1879, said of the sheriff:

FORD COUNTY'S CONTRIBUTION

SHERIFF MASTERSON AND UNDER-SHERIFF BASSETT BRING UP ANOTHER INSTALLMENT OF DODGEITES TO THE STATE PENITENTIARY.

Sheriff W. B. Masterson and Under Sheriff Bassett, of Ford County, arrived on Sunday [January 26] from Dodge City with another installment of prisoners for the State Penitentiary, turning their charges safely over to the authorities of the prison. During Sheriff Masterson's term of office he has contributed liberally to the State's boarding house and has kept things as straight as a string in his county. He is one of the most noted men of the southwest, as cool, brave and daring as any one who ever drew a pistol. He was with Gen. Miles' expedition in 1874, and was present at the time of the capture of the Germain children. He was also one of the twenty-six who defended the Adobe Walls in 1874, against some eight hundred Indians, and although he has been in many a tight place he has always managed to save his scalp. Under-sheriff Bassett is also well-known, and has a good record. They left for Kansas City Sunday afternoon.

The *Times'* brief mention of the 1874 battle at Adobe Walls provides another example of the speed with which fact is often turned into something unrecognizable. An on-the-scene report four days after the battle began said that 200 Indians were at the place and over 100 buffalo hunters and teamsters outfought the 150 warriors who were pressing them (*see* pp. 315, 316). Three years later when some of the defenders were interviewed (pp. 317-319), their number was reduced to 29, while attacking Indians were increased to 500. In another 14 months, as reported above, the ratio became

378

26 defenders vs. 800 Indians. Now, books and articles often set the number of attacking Indians at 1,000 or more! Thus exaggeration runs away with a story, leaving a reasonable facsimile of truth by the wayside.

"M. W. Sutton, W. B. Masterson, C. E. Bassett, tarried in Topeka, after safely lodging the prisoners in the Leavenworth prison. They are Senator lobbying," said the Dodge City *Times*, February 1, 1879.

From Topeka Bat visited his home near Wichita, returning to Dodge February 10, 1879.[32] On his way to Leavenworth Bat had stopped at Kinsley and placed this notice in the *Edwards County Leader*, February 6, 1879:

NOTICE OF APPLICATION FOR PARDON.

Notice is hereby given that on the 14th day of February, A. D. 1879, application will be made to his excellency John P. St. John, Governor of the State of Kansas, at the executive office in the capitol building in the city of Topeka, in the state of Kansas, to pardon and set at liberty one Thomas Gott, who was convicted of an attempt to rob the Atchison, Topeka & Santa Fe Railroad Company, at the June term of the district court held within and for Edwards county, Kansas, in the month of June, A. D. 1878.

Dated at Kinsley, Kansas, this 28th day of January, A. D. 1879.

W. B. MASTERSON,
Sheriff Ford County, Kansas.

Although the petition asking for Gott's pardon has not been located, letters written by Governor St. John indicate that the petition was received, that the pardon was considered but that it was turned down. In a letter to Sheriff Masterson dated June 25, 1879, the governor gave Bat this rather confusing explanation: "I have examined into the application of Gotts for pardon but cannot find it consistent now with my duty to turn him loose at present. The fact is the population in the penitentiary is increasing so fast that I am compelled to go very slow about issuing pardons."[33]

In February, 1879, there began in Kansas a phenomenon somewhat akin to the war crimes trials of the post World War II era. In September, 1878, the last Indian raid was made through Kansas by a group of Cheyenne expatriates who were attempting to return from their reservation in the Indian territory to their former home in Dakota territory. Led by Dull Knife and Little Wolf, the Cheyennes threw the western portion of Kansas into a frenzy of excitement by their depredations, which included at least 40 Kansas deaths. The small band eventually was captured north of Kansas and the last Indian raid in the state was over. Western Kansas pioneers, fearful of further attacks, proposed stringent measures to forestall them. One solution was to punish, as criminals, the braves who were known to have participated in the raid.

Accordingly, on November 11, 1878, Gov. George T. Anthony had written the Secretary of War:

> On mature reflection, and with thoughtful reference to the demands of law and justice, as well as the ends of public safety, I feel it an imperative duty to call upon you for a surrender to the proper officers of the civil courts of the State of Kansas, for trial and punishment under its laws, the principal chiefs, "Dull Knife," "Old Crow," "Hog," "Little Wolf," and others, whose identity can be established as participants in the crimes of murder and woman ravishing.
>
> I believe there is a precedent for this demand, in the surrender to the civil courts of Texas of "Satana" and one other chief in the year 1872. But if there is no precedent public necessity and simple justice would, I believe, be ample justification for this demand.[34]

On December 31, 1878, Maj. Gen. John Pope, commander of the Department of the Missouri, wrote this answer to Anthony's plea:

> I have the honor to inform you that I have received orders from the War Department to turn over to the civil authorities of Kansas, such of the Cheyenne prisoners en route to this place [Fort Leavenworth] as can be identified as the criminals who committed murders or other crimes during the raid of the Indians through Kansas in September last. As it is desirable not to keep these Indians here longer than necessary, I have to request that such persons as may be needed for the identification of the criminals be sent to meet the Indians on their arrival here. . . .[35]

County Attorney M. W. Sutton, on January 15, 1879, had sent the governor, now John P. St. John, a letter enclosing warrants for the arrest of Dull Knife and other Cheyenne Indians and requesting a requisition on the governor of Nebraska for their deliverance. St. John answered that the Indians were in the custody of United States military authorities and were soon to be in Leavenworth for identification. Possibly because of this early request on the part of Ford county, the trial of the Indians was to be held in Dodge City. At any rate, on February 6, 1879, the governor sent this telegram to Sutton:

> All that is left of Cheyenne raiders will be at Leavenworth soon—What can be done from your section of the state to aid in Identifying them—Answer by mail.[36]

380

Mike's answer was handed to the governor by Bat Masterson:

COUNTY ATTORNEY'S OFFICE
DODGE CITY KANSAS, FEB 11TH 1879

To HIS EXCELLENCY
JOHN P. ST. JOHN.
GOVERNOR OF KANSAS.
DEAR SIR.
This will introduce to you the bearer W. B. Masterson Sheriff of Ford County, who has the witnesses with him to identify the Cheyenne Indian prisoners.

He comes to you for instructions, as to the manner of proceeding in this matter of identification, a subject which is new to me, and that I do not thoroughly understand, and hence am unable to advise upon.

I would suggest, if not improper, that the Adjutant Genl accompany him to Ft. Leavenworth, and assist him in the matter.

Respectfully yours—
M. W. SUTTON
County Attorney.[37]

Bat must have visited the governor on February 12 for on that date St. John telegraphed for passes which would provide Masterson and his four witnesses transportation from Topeka to Leavenworth.

The Dodge City *Times,* February 15, 1879, published a resume of what had thus far been accomplished and identified Bat's four companions:

IDENTIFYING THE CHEYENNES.

The remnant of the Cheyenne band arrived this week at Fort Leavenworth, from Fort Robinson, Neb. This remnant comprises that portion of the Cheyennes that escaped the slaughter at Camp Robinson, a few weeks ago. There are seven bucks in the band, together with fourteen squaws and papooses. These Indians are the remaining ones of the band that made an incursion through Kansas last September. Their operations of murder and depredations are familiar to our readers.

It will be remembered that a few weeks ago County Attorney Sutton filed complaint against Dull Knife and his band for the murder of five persons, who were killed during the raid. The complaints were filed with the Governor, who is aiding County Attorney Sutton in bringing the murderers to justice. The prisoners are in the hands of the military authorities. With a view of transferring the prisoners to the civil authorities, an identification of the murdering savages has been required. For this purpose, Sheriff W. B. Masterson left Tuesday night for Fort Leavenworth. He was accompanied by Deputy Sheriff C. E. Bassett, James Masterson, Capt. A. J. French and Kokomo Sullivan, who, it is believed, can identify the prisoners. These gentlemen are all old timers on the plains, and are familiar with Indians and Indian ways. Kokomo Sullivan (the first name is a sobriquet,) was a long time engaged as a scout. Capt. French experienced an episode with the Indians last September, as they passed Meade City. The Indians did not harm the inhabitants of the village, but killed Washington O'Connor as they were retiring from the settlement. The Captain concluded he had marvelously escaped murder, as Dull Knife and his band were on their murdering and depredating tour. Jim. Masterson has had experience with Indians. Bassett's long experience on the plains and knowledge of Indians, will be of service in the identification. Sheriff Masterson has had many engagements with Indians, and will be able to discriminate with good judgement. The party stopped over at Topeka, Wednesday [February 12], for instructions from the Governor, and the next day proceeded to Fort Leavenworth. They will probably return by the time this matter appears in print before our readers. If the Sheriff succeeds in making a proper identification of the Indian prisoners, they will be turned over to his charge and brought to Ford county for trial, which prosecution will be conducted by County Attorney Sutton.

The prisoners were heavily ironed and are now at Fort Leavenworth. The trial of these savages will add no little to the zest of an exciting life on this frontier, and will generally excite comment and interest.

At Fort Leavenworth identification was made and a transfer from military to civil control accomplished. The Leavenworth *Times,* February 16, 1879, reported:

DUSKY DEMONS.

THE CHEYENNE ROBBERS AND MURDERERS FALL AT LAST
INTO THE HANDS OF THE CIVIL AUTHORITIES.

THAT THEY WILL NEVER AGAIN RAVISH WOMEN
AND KILL CHILDREN IS A CERTAINTY.

THEY WERE TAKEN AWAY YESTERDAY TO BE LODGED
IN THE FORD COUNTY JAIL FOR TRIAL.

Yesterday morning there gathered a throng of people about the Union Depot whose faces were a study; they had heard much of the atrocities committed by the renegade Cheyennes in Meade, Ford and other counties, and many of them being old frontiersmen said little. Their eyes betokened curiosity to see the devils who had desolated so many homes, and the firm set of lips of the "old timers," when their names were mentioned, indicated anything but a friendly feeling.

THE PRISONERS.

At ten o'clock, Lieut. Pardee, of the Twenty-third Infantry, in command of a strong guard of soldiers, arrived at the depot with the prisoners, seven in number, the guard and the prisoners being in government wagons, drawn by four mules each. The command was halted at the corner of Cherokee and Front streets, and the soldiers ordered to get out of the wagons and keep

CLOSE TO THE PRISONERS

while they were being transferred. The crowd of interested spectators meanwhile became so dense that it was necessary for the soldiers to use some force to keep the more eager men back. Lieut. Pardee, after examining a warrant presented by Adjutant General [P. S.] Noble, of Kansas, the following Indians were delivered from the military to civil jurisdiction:

Wild Hog, Old Crow, Big Head, Left Hand, Blacksmith, Porcupine and Nosey-Walker, making seven in all who had been identified except Old Crow, as participators in the crimes of murder, rape and robbery charged in the warrant. General Noble then transferred the prisoners to Sheriff W. B. Masterson, of Ford county, who took them in charge, and conducted them to one of the passenger rooms in the Union depot, all being in irons, except Old Crow. The latter is said by the army officers to have been a valuable, faithful and trustworthy scout of the Government, and one who bears a good reputation, and that belonging to the Crow Indians could have had no hand in the depredations of the Cheyennes.

WILD HOG,

who is reputed to have been the worst of the band, in getting out of the wagon was forced to use a long piece of board for support, being yet weak from a recent attempt to commit suicide by stabbing himself with a pair of shears. The others all alighted nimbly as could be possible shackled as they were.

IN THE DEPOT.

After they had been elbowed through the crowd into the passenger room, they were all seated in a row and it required all the patience that Sheriff Masterson's posse possessed to keep the crowd at a comfortable distance without force. Sheriff Lowe who was present knew some of the captives having at one time furnished them with beef, and in consequence had some conversation with them as did a TIMES representative. Mr. Lowe bought them some clay pipes, which after being filled were smoked by the prisoners with evident enjoyment.

One of the party, after passing the pipe to another, endeavored to say that he was no Cheyenne; that he was the baby of Three Bears, a noted Sioux. Old Crow, who is really an intelligent looking old fellow, had little to say, although he seemed to understand all that was going on about him. Wild Hog took a piece of silver, cut to represent the sun and attached to a chain from his neck, and handed it to Mr. Lowe, who read the words "Wild Hog," that were engraved on one side. He pretended to know no English, but Mr. A. J. French, who was one of the sheriff's posse, says he can speak the language very well.

The remainder of the prisoners seemed much broken down and sat with their heads resting in their hands, to all appearances unmindful of the excited audience about them. They were put on the train at 10:40 and under the care of Sheriff Masterson, his two brothers,[38] Mr. A. J. French and Mr. Bassett, City Marshal of Dodge City, left for Topeka, from which place they will be conveyed to Dodge City, for trial, which will not take place until some time next June.

Traveling by way of Lawrence, Bat reached Topeka the first day and remained in that place overnight. The Topeka *Commonwealth*, February 16, 1879, described the journey that far:

DULL KNIFE'S BAND.

The Indians who have lately been turned over to the county authorities of Ford County for trial were brought from Leavenworth yesterday, and placed in the Shawnee County jail over night. They are in charge of Sheriff W. B. Masterson, of Ford County, who is assisted by City Marshal Bassett, of Dodge City. The Indians are seven in number—all that remains of Dull Knife's band of ninety-one. The rest were killed at the time these were captured. Their names are Wild Hog, Old Crow, Big Head, Left Hand, Black Smith, Porcupine, and Nose Walker.

Big Head had one hand shot away and carries his arm in a sling. Left Hand and another were wounded in the legs, and limp painfully. All are heavily ironed, either hands or feet or both. They are strong, hard-looking men, with repulsive features, suggestive of their being murderers, as charged. The prosecution will probably be made for complicity in the outrages. Mr. Masterson and Mr. Bassett say positively that these are a part of Dull Knife's band. They were encamped at Dodge about a year, and they had frequent opportunities for becoming acquainted with them.

They are in a very desperate condition of mind, and would, it is thought, commit suicide if they had a chance. They will therefore not be allowed to use a knife and fork, but will convey the fare of the Hotel de Disbrow to their mouths with their dirty fingers.

The arrival of the Kansas Pacific train from the east was eagerly waited for by a crowd of probably one thousand people, who had come to see the "real live wild Indians." The prisoners were put into one of Terry's busses and conveyed to the jail.

Sheriff Masterson says that at Lawrence he had much trouble, and was obliged finally to fight his way. The first man he struck happened to be the City Marshal, who retaliated by taking Batt in charge. Explanations followed, and matters rightened. The prisoners will be taken to Dodge to-day via the Santa Fe.

The *Ford County Globe*, February 17, 1879, reported the band's arrival in Dodge City:

THE CHEYENNE PRISONERS.
PITTIFUL REMNANTS OF A ONCE POWERFUL BAND.
THEY ARE BROUGHT TO DODGE CITY FOR TRIAL.

The seven Cheyenne Indian prisoners arrived from Fort Leavenworth last Monday morning, in custody of W. B. Masterson, Sheriff of Ford county, assisted by City Marshal Chas. E. Bassett and Deputy Sheriff James Masterson. The train arrived about 5 o'clock and there being no carriage in waiting to receive our distinguished visitors, the motley band was compelled to walk up to the jail, a distance of several hundred yards. This was the longest walk they

384

had taken since leaving Leavenworth and it proved too laborious for the delicate health of one of the wounded chieves, who, after limping and struggling along for some distance, sank helplessly to the ground, where he remained until a wheelbarrow was procured, upon which he was placed, and carted to his destination.

The Indians were placed in the jail, where they still remain, their hands and feet closely shackled. They sit in a row upon the damp floor of the dim dungeon with sorrow and despair deeply engraven upon their manly countenances. All hope of future happiness in this wicked world has forsaken their breasts. Death in any form would be welcomed by them as a healing balm to their bleeding hearts. In this desperate state of mind they would commit suicide if the least opportunity presented itself. But not the least murmur or sign of complaint escapes them. Believing, sincerely, that the bloody deed with which their hands are stained, was committed in the sight of their Great Spirit, and sanctioned by that Deity, they will never repent. As they have no interpreter, they do not attempt to converse or make known their desires, save that they are anxious to have their wives and children near them. As is truly characteristic of the noble race, they wish it to be said of them, after their death, as uttered by the immortal Logan, "there runs not a drop of my blood in the veins of any living creature." Their preliminary examination will take place in a week or ten days. Wild Hog is the principle chief. He accepts the situation with the dignity of a conquered General and receives the fruits of disaster with a countenance stern and unyielding.

Below we publish extracts from Leavenworth and Topeka papers [printed above] indicating great excitement manifested by the semi-civilized natives of those towns. At every station a mob of hoodlums assembled and made such demonstrations in their eagerness to see the Indians that Sheriff Masterson was compelled to use physical means in preventing his pets from being trampled upon. At Lawrence the mob was almost overpowering, and our officers were involved in a fight which resulted in victory for Dodge City, as usual. The Mayor, City Marshal and a large portion of the able bodied braves of Lawrence undertook to capture Masterson and his outfit, but were repulsed in a very neat and workmanlike manner. The Indians think a great deal of the Sheriff and heartily welcome him when he visits their prison. In this most trying hour of the noble Indian's life it is a remarkable fact that his appetite remains intact, and he feasts heartily three times a day. Sheriff Masterson and Marshal Bassett have a very high opinion of both Governor St. John and Gen. Pope, from whom they received very gentlemanly treatment.

There is less curiosity to see the captured Cheyennes among the citizens of Dodge than any town in the State. The sentiment here is that curiosity would be better exercised in getting close enough to see the Indian when he is on the war path—close enough to get a sight on him with a rifle or six-shooter. Our people are not the kind to turn out en masse to gaze at sick and wounded prisoners, and the arrival of seven thieving Mokes would have excited just about the same interest.

As our readers are familiar, the charge against these Indians is that of murder, committed during their raid through Kansas last fall.

The Dodge City *Times*, February 22, 1879, pursued the same line as did the *Globe* in praising the officers and people of Dodge and condemning those of Leavenworth, Lawrence, and Topeka:

THE CHEYENNES.

THEIR SAFE ARRIVAL IN DODGE CITY AND CUSTODY WITHIN JAIL WALLS.

Sheriff W. B. Masterson and party, consisting of the City Marshal, Charles E. Bassett, officer James Masterson, Capt. A. J. French and Kokomo Sullivan, arrived in Dodge City Monday morning, having in charge the seven Cheyenne prisoners who were lately brought to Leavenworth from Fort Robinson. There was no demonstration in Dodge City whatever that awaited these prisoners, though their arrival was duly heralded. A solitary policeman, outside the usual depot attendants and passengers, was the only person who welcomed the gentle savage with a bloody stick to a safe lodgment in the Ford county jail. The prisoners were taken from the cars quietly and noiselessly, and thence to quarters in the jail, where they now remain.

The names of these red gentlemen, who some months ago paid the environs of Dodge City a visit, and who threw the city and country into such a tremor of excitement, are given in pure English as follows: Crow, Wild Hog, Tall Man, Old Man, Run Fast, Young Man and Frizzle Head. They are fine specimens of the genus Indian—stalwart braves—apparently comfortable under their distressing circumstances.

Some of these prisoners are suffering from wounds received during the slaughter at Camp Robinson. The wounds are not dangerous, however, and under proper treatment, which they are receiving, they will shortly recover. Wild Hog has an ugly wound in the left breast, caused by his own hand, while attempting to take his own life.

The prisoners are under the immediate charge of the humane jailor, Col. John W. Straughn, who will liberally provide for them in the comforts of prison fare, and such accommodations as are usually given prisoners. We visited the jail on Monday, in the capacity of a reporter, but we made no inquiries, and will give only such facts as we have learned through other sources. We know our anxious readers will look for elaborate details, but they must be content to feast upon a few bare facts. We have saved the labor of interviewing Mr. Lo, because we believe his broken English would afford little knowledge of his depressing condition. We know the prisoners will be kindly treated and amply provided for. An Indian is contented with a full stomach and plenty of tobacco. These luxuries will not be denied them. They will go far to render their condition comfortable, and thus allay any apprehension regarding an escape.

Sheriff Masterson and party speak in the highest terms of Governor St. John and Adjutant General Noble, for their kind treatment and assistance rendered them in executing the identification of the Cheyenne braves. Gen. Pope also treated the officers and identifiers with courtesy, and they are profuse in words of praise. But a couple of incidents occurred which marred the otherwise harmonious trip. The Sheriff of Leavenworth county and the Marshal and Mayor of Lawrence were more eager to pay homage to the stinking savage than render assistance to the officers. The ill-treatment and discourtesy by these officers is roundly condemned by Sheriff Masterson and party. Were they engaged in a similar service in Dodge City, no pains would be spared to make their work agreeable. But the infuriated mob, so anxious to feast upon a red savage, may in a measure be overlooked. It is not often such a curiosity is gratified, and while Sheriff Masterson and his menagerie of wild Indians were passing through the country, it is not to be wondered that somebody "beat" his way to the show. And it happened to be the officers we mentioned.

The officers' account of the trip from Leavenworth to this city exhibits the morbid curiosity which seizes the noble denizen further down the plain. At every station, and far into the night, great crowds congregated at the depots, all eager to get a glimpse of the gentle savage. This was extremely embarrasing and annoying, and gave the party much trouble. The Indian took it, no doubt, as a great ovation intended for him. It is a proof of what penchant the American has for strange things, even if such things be no more than Indian savages and murderers. But it only excites the dread of these beings and renders fear more susceptible. How different with the people who have more knowledge of savage crimes and butchery. Not a ripple of excitement was observed as the Indian prisoners entered the village.

Mr. Lo, however, is not caring for all this. His inquiries are for Mrs. Squaw and Master Papoose. When the Indian dies he wants his family about him. He may little know the course he is to pursue; he awaits, nevertheless, with intense solicitude, having no knowledge, probably, what it all means. He is aware that he is disgraced by being in captivity. Could he wipe out that disgrace he would rapidly hie himself to the happy hunting grounds. The utmost precaution will be used, and to avoid suicide, the now tranquil savage will be carefully watched and no implement more dangerous than an iron spoon placed within his reach.

The preliminary trial of these prisoners will take place as soon as witnesses reach here. The examination will be conducted by County Attorney M. W. Sutton, whose recent successful prosecutions have been the admiration of a law-abiding people and a terror to evil-doers.

The chains which bound the Cheyenne prisoners belonged to the state of Kansas and not until he was reminded by Adjutant General Noble did Bat remember to return them to Topeka. He sent this letter of apology:

DODGE CITY KANSAS FEB. 20" 1879

P. S. NOBLE ESQ
Topeka, Kansas
FRIEND NOBLE

I am In receipt of your letter this morning and I am Sorry I was So dilatory in Sending back the hand cuffs and leg Irons however I have Expressed them to your address [to]day and hope you will receive them all right. the Indians are all well and in good spirits but want their Squaws and papooses, which I am in hopes they may get

I am very respectfully
W. B. Masterson,
Sheriff Ford County [39]

The Cheyennes were given their preliminary examination in Dodge City but were granted a change of venue to Lawrence. On June 26, 1879, Governor St. John sent Bat passes on the railroad to transport the braves and five guards to their new place of trial. Bat and Charley Bassett returned to Dodge on June 29. The case against the Indians was dismissed for lack of evidence in October, 1879, but their Ford county incarceration had a telling influence on the November election for sheriff.[40]

While Sheriff Bat Masterson was in eastern Kansas securing the Cheyenne prisoners two of his jail prisoners escaped in Dodge City. The *Globe*, February 17, 1879, said:

JAIL DELIVERY.

Last Saturday [February 15] evening about 8 o'clock two prisoners escaped from the Ford county jail and, like the Arab, folded their tents and silently stole away. Their names are G. U. Holcomb and Geo. Watkins. They were both under arrest for stealing about 75 head of cattle from Dunham & Ward, south of Cimarron station. The means by which they escaped was a follows: They were not considered desperate men and were accordingly allowed to remain in the outer prison during the day time. The iron cells or cages into which they were placed at night are about seven feet high and reach to within one foot of the ceiling of the jail. The ceiling is ordinary pine ceiling. On the day in question one of the prisoners secured some kind of a knife and climbing on top of the cell cut a hole through the thin ceiling and also through the floor above. Through this hole the two men crept and found themselves in the County Treasurer's office, which was unoccupied. They then gently opened the window on the east side of the room which opens out on an old shed on the east side of the Courthouse. Climbing out on the roof and from thence to the earth, they found themselves free men, with darkness to assist them in their escape.

It is a great wonder that prisoners have not taken advantage of this mode of escape from the jail before this, as the work of cutting a hole through two thicknesses of pine boards could be accomplished in one hour's time. By all means the county jail should be lined overhead with iron or something that would be proof against an ordinary pocket knife. Holcomb is a lawyer who practiced some time in Cimarron. Watkins was also a resident of Cimarron where his family now reside. Watkins was foolish for escaping, as he would not have been sentenced for more than a year, and then could have returned to his family. Now he is a fugitive and if he attempts to go to his family or have them come to him he will almost certainly be recaptured. His wife spent

388

several weeks here and worked hard to secure leniency for her husband. She went to the cattle men from whom he had stolen the cattle and plead with them until she aroused their sympathy and made them promise to deal gently with her erring husband.

We cannot see any occasion to censure the officers. The commissioners should either make the jail more secure or employ a guard to watch the prisoners.[41]

Bat recaptured Holcomb on February 21. The *Ford County Globe,* February 25, 1879, reported:

A JAIL BIRD CAPTURED.

G. U. Holcumb, who escaped from the Ford county jail about ten days ago, was captured in Pueblo, Col., by Sheriff Masterson. The sheriff received news that Holcumb was traveling west by freight and took the first train in pursuit. When he arrived at Sherlock, fifteen miles this side of Lakin, he learned that Holcumb had boarded the freight a few hours ahead. Masterson went on to Pueblo, where he arrived about the same time Holcumb did, and after a short search found him in South Pueblo. He immediately took the young truant under his wing and placed him in the Pueblo jail until the next train went east, when he escorted him to Dodge. The Pueblo officers were very obliging and offered all the assistance they could. Holcumb said he was expecting some money by mail to Pueblo and as soon as it arrived he intended to light out for the mines and mountains of Leadville. Alas, how his fond hopes were shattered.[42]

A week later, on February 26, Bat took Holcomb to Topeka to appear before the supreme court. The Topeka *Commonwealth,* February 28, 1879, told why:

Geo. Holcom, who was brought here by Sheriff Masterson, of Dodge City, on Wednesday, was taken before the Supreme Court yesterday on a writ of *habeas corpus.* The charge against him is stealing eighty head of cattle, in one of the Counties attached to Ford County for judicial purposes. The stock was driven into Ottawa County, and Holcom arrested. The legal point to be decided was the legality of the act attaching the County referred to, to Ford County, and so, the right of Ford County officials to detain him.

The *Commonwealth* mentioned the case again on March 1, 1879:

AN IMPORTANT CASE.

The *habeas corpus* case before the Supreme Court, which we mentioned yesterday morning, is likely to be a most important one, affecting persons who have heretofore been arrested for misdemeanors in the counties attached to Ford County for judicial purposes, and in case Holcom is released, the decision will cause the release of the remaining members of Dull Knife's band of Cheyennes, now in jail at Dodge City, awaiting trial. It is evident that if Ford County has no jurisdiction over the counties attached for that purpose to it, there is no county in the State which has. Nelson Adams, of Larned, is the attorney for Holcom. The State asked and obtained two days' time in which to file briefs. The opinion will be delivered today perhaps, and perhaps not until Monday. Hon. J. G. Mohler, of Salina, has been retained to defend the Indians.

Bat brought his prisoner back to Dodge City on March 5. The Dodge City *Times,* March 8, 1879, said:

THE HABEAS CORPUS CASE.

Sheriff Masterson returned from Topeka Wednesday morning, with the prisoner, G. U. Holcomb, who had been taken before the Supreme Court under a writ of habeas corpus. The point the prisoner's attorneys wished to determine was the constitutionality of the act attaching unorganized counties to Ford county for judicial purposes. This matter involves the legality of the conviction of prisoners who were tried at the last term of the District Court, and the arrest of those now awaiting trial. The matter for the State was presented to the court by M. W. Sutton, County Attorney, and Gen. H. B. Johnson, of Topeka. The court will render a decision on the 31st of March.

The opinion of the court, delivered by Associate Justice David J. Brewer on April 25, 1879, was that "the petitioner [Holcomb] is not entitled to his discharge, and must be remanded to the custody of the sheriff of Ford county; and it is so ordered." [43]

Holcomb was not tried at the June term of the Ford county district court. His ultimate fate remains unknown.

The March, 1879, resignation of County Commissioner George Cox revealed the less than cordial relations which existed between the commissioners and Sheriff Masterson, a situation which had not before been mentioned in the papers. The *Globe,* March 18, 1879, reported:

RESIGNATION OF GEO. B. COX.

By reference to the official proceedings of the Board of County Commissioners, it will be seen that Geo. B. Cox, chairman of the Board, has resigned and that his resignation has been accepted. The cause of his resignation, as he states in his letter, is a lack of harmony between other county officers and the Board which, he says, would deter him from discharging his official duties. For a long time the relations of the Sheriff and the Board have not been amicable, and frequently high words have been spoken. Mr. Cox being naturally of a very retiring disposition and not, like most men in office, always ready to maintain his opinions and enforce his ideas at all hazards, just quietly resigns and will have nothing more to do in an official capacity. Many will regret very much to hear of his resignation, as he is a leading business man, a large property holder and a man in whom the people have confidence. His place on the Board will be supplied by J. B. Means, the County Clerk, until the Board see fit to appoint some one to fill the vacancy, or an election is held.

Bat Masterson

When the Santa Fe railroad contested right of way through the Grand Canyon of the Arkansas—the Royal Gorge—with the Denver and Rio Grande Western, Bat Masterson was asked for help. The *Ford County Globe*, March 25, 1879, failed to mention how the sheriff of a Kansas county could legally aid a private corporation in another state:

TROUBLE AHEAD.

Last Thursday evening [March 20] Sheriff Masterson received a telegram from officers of the Atchison, Topeka and Santa Fe road at Canon City, asking if he could bring a posse of men to assist in defending the workmen on that road from the attacks of the Denver and Rio Grande men, who were again endeavoring to capture the long contested pass through the canon. Masterson and Deputy Duffey immediately opened a recruiting office, and before the train arrived Friday morning had enrolled a company of thirty-three men. They all boarded the morning train, armed to the teeth, Sheriff Masterson in command, and started for the scene of hostilities.

The Denver News of Wednesday published an item to the effect that trouble is again brewing between the Atchison, Topeka and Santa Fe folks and the D. & R. G. road with regard to the right of way through the Grand Canon of the Arkansas. Litigation has been pending several months, and the News declares that the Rio Grande people want to break the recently entered into lease, and if the decision of the U. S. court is in their favor they will hold the canon. The Santa Fe folks are arming their men with weapons and making every arrangement to repel with force any attempt of the Rio Grande people to take possession of the canon upon order of the court. On Saturday last a train left the end of the Santa Fe's track for Grand Canon loaded with provisions, tents and a force of men, ostensibly laborers. Since that time until yesterday a number of cases of ammunition were sent after the men, and the intent of this action is clearly plain. The whole proceeding has been conducted with great secrecy, and to keep the knowledge of it from the Rio Grande men a new force of employees was put in charge of the trains.

If the decision of the Supreme Court is in favor of the Rio Grande, the managers of the road are going to take possession of the canon. They had a little experience in hold-out against an armed Santa Fe force some time ago, and stood the siege pretty well. Gen. Palmer is at Colorado Springs, aware of every move taken by the Santa Fe people, though they are carrying them on so secretly.

"Sheriff W. B. Masterson and thirty men left Dodge Saturday last [March 22], for Canon City, where they were called in anticipation of railroad troubles, but we do not hear of any," said the Dodge City *Times*, March 29, 1879.

On April 5 Bat and his boys came back to Dodge for a weekend. The *Globe*, April 8, 1879, reported:

Sheriff Masterson and several of the boys returned from Canon City last Saturday evening, where they had been guarding the canon through which the A., T. & S. F. road is building its branch from Canon City to Leadville. The boys report having had an easy time, nothing to do, plenty of chuck and $3 a day from the railroad company. They spent Sunday in the city and went back on Monday to resume their duties. So far there has been no trouble, and about five miles of the road is completed. About 100 men are employed just to see that no attempts are made by the Rio Grande men to drive the A., T. & S. F. workmen from the disputed canon.

The local papers did not state whether Bat went back to Colorado with the men. Possibly he did, for his name does not appear in the Dodge City press until May 10, 1879, when the *Times* told how he saved Wyatt Earp from possible extinction and escaped assassination himself a short time later:

UNRULY MISSOURIANS.

There was a little brush Monday evening [May 5], which, however, terminated with only a few bruised heads. Three movers, on their way to Leadville from Clay county, Mo., under the influence of bad whiskey, undertook to "take the town." While Assistant Marshal Earp was attempting to disarm [them] and [was] leading an unruly cuss off by the ear, another one of the party told his chum to "throw lead," and endeavored to resist the officer. Sheriff Bat Masterson soon happened on the scene and belabored the irate Missourian, using the broad side of his revolver over his head. The party was disarmed and placed in the cooler. Tuesday night an attempt was made to assassinate Sheriff Masterson. The three men who caused the difficulty the night before, assembled in the rear of a store building, Tuesday night, and sent word by a colored boy that a man wished to see him. The negro "smelt a mouse," and put the Sheriff on his guard. Officer Duffy shortly afterwards arrested one of the) men. These fellows remarked that they "had run things in Missouri," and believed they could "take" Dodge City, but admitted that they were no match for Dodge City officers. Dodge City is hard "to take." the pistol brigands find in it a "warm berth."

On June 10, 1879, the *Ford County Globe* stated that Bat had again gone to Canon City:

BOUND FOR THE CANON.

In response to a telegram from headquarters of the A. T. & S. F. railroad, Sheriff Masterson opened a volunteer recruiting office in this city, and half an hour from the receipt of said telegram he was whirling westward with an engine and one coach containing sixty men, at the rate of forty miles an hour.[44]

Having left on June 9, Bat and his posse returned on June 12. The Dodge City *Times*, June 14, 1879, reported:

Sheriff Masterson and party of fifty men returned from Pueblo on Thursday morning. He had been placed in charge of the railroad property there, but surrendered his authority upon writs being served by U. S. officers. The Denver & Rio Grand has possession. And "our boys" didn't smell any powder. Their voice is for peace.

More routine sheriff's duties now occupied Bat's time. On July 1 he delivered another prisoner to the state penitentiary. The *Globe*, July 8, 1879, said: "The only prisoner sentenced this term was Vanderhoff, for stealing $25 of Mrs. D. B. Lewis. He went 'up' for one year. The Sheriff took him 'down' last Tuesday." [45]

The Leavenworth *Times*, July 6, 1879, apparently was a little confused by all the Mastersons when it reported:

James Masterson, the sheriff of Ford county, who knoweth not the name of fear, brought E. Vanderhoff to the penitentiary as his Fourth of July party, and turned him over. He has one year for grand larceny.

On July 22, 1879, the *Ford County Globe* reported that "W. B. Masterson, last week, purchased a house and lot of G. M. Hoover on 2nd avenue," and on August 2 the *Times* said that "Sheriff Masterson has taken a few days' visit to Wichita." [46]

Bat was soon back in Dodge and once again on the trail of horse thieves. The Dodge City *Times*, August 30, 1879, reported in its Spearville column:

A valuable team of horses was stolen on Sunday [August 24] from James Vandermark, six miles south of town. The owner and a neighbor, J. B. Gray, traced the thief across the river and then hurried to Dodge City, soliciting the aid of Sheriff Masterson, who at once recognized the rascal by the description given him, and is confident of his capture. On his advice the Board of County Commissioners offered a reward of $50 for the apprehension and conviction of the horse thief.

County Attorney Sutton, Sheriff Masterson and Register Muller were down the road Wednesday [August 27] to make arrangements for the capture of horse thieves.

Another of Bat's prisoners had made a successful break for freedom on August 25 but this time not for long. The *Times*, August 30, 1879, put the blame on the board of county commissioners:

A prisoner broke from the Ford county jail on Monday last, but was promptly captured. We are not surprised at this, for the walls of the jail are barely security against the escape of prisoners. With a board flooring above for a roof, and a dirt floor underneath, unless there is a constant and vigilant watch, the prisoners are liable to escape with little effort on their part. The prisoner on Monday escaped by digging a hole under the door. Some time ago two prisoners escaped by cutting a hole through the board floor above. The wretched and insecure condition of the jail is a matter that demands the serious attention of the Board of County Commissioners. Upon them alone rests the responsibility of the security of the prisoners; for the insecure jail is no fault of the sheriff's officers, who are liable for the safe custody of the prisoners. The people naturally look to the sheriff and deputies for a proper discharge of their duties; but under the present management of affairs the officers are almost rendered powerless. The entire community is at the peril of horse thieves and robbers. To the community the sheriff's officers are the protectors of the lives and property. These officers should have such means at their command to carry out the responsible duties of their trusts. The proper thing just now for the Board of Commissioners to perform, is to repair the jail quarters and render them fit for the confinement of prisoners.

Horse thieves again were on the young sheriff's agenda late in August. The *Times*, September 6, 1879, reported the capture of four:

CAPTURE OF HORSE THIEVES.

Sheriff Masterson and officers captured in the city, Friday last [August 29], two horse thieves, who had stolen stock nine miles north of Great Bend. The prisoners had a preliminary examination before Justice Cook, and were held over in the sum of $800 each, but were subsequently taken to Great Bend, where they will no doubt be held for trial. A third person engaged in stealing with these two, managed to elude the vigilance of the officers and escaped. The prisoners gave fictitious names before their trial, thus attempting to avoid identification.

On Sunday two more persons were arrested, charged with horse stealing, and having in their possession fourteen head of horses, supposed to be stolen, which they had secreted on the range south. The prisoners were taken before Justice Cook, on Monday, but the trial was postponed for ten days.

On Wednesday Sheriff Masterson received a dispatch from J. B. Matthews, at Fort Griffin, Texas, telling him to hold the two men arrested by him on Sunday. The prisoners' names are Charley and Jack Lyon, and they had eight horses stolen from Matthews. These horses are in possession of the Sheriff.

Horse stealing has taken a fresh start in the country, and since the wholesale conviction of thieves last winter that crime had not been on the rampage until within the past few months. The officers of Ford county are on the alert and watch with a vigilant eye every suspicious character lurking in our midst.

"County Attorney Sutton and Sheriff Masterson went to Great Bend, Wednesday last [September 10], to be present at the trial of the horse thieves," said the Dodge City *Times*, September 13, 1879.

Bat visited Topeka on September 15, this time bringing with him an unfortunate person sentenced to the state hospital. The Dodge City *Times*, September 20, 1879, stated:

Louis Snizek, the person adjudged to be insane, was taken by Sheriff Mas-

Bat Masterson

terson to the Insane Asylum, at Topeka, on Monday morning last. Snizek's
case is a hopeful one, and he may soon be entirely cured of lunacy.[47]

"Messrs. [C. M.] Beeson, Masterson and [G. M.] Hoover have
gone to Kansas City to attend the fair," recorded the *Globe,* September 23, 1879.

In early October Bat was on the trail of some reward money
which he apparently never obtained:

Dodge City   Kan
Oct 2nd   1879

Gov. JOHN P ST JOHN
Topeka   Kansas
Dr. Sir,
Will you be so kind as to inform me in regard to the reward offered for one
Dan Henson—alias Cherokee Dan. . The reward was offered by Ex. . Gov. .
Geo. T Anthony. . Amount $500.00 five Hundred Dollars. . I think I
can arrest him with some little Expence and if the reward is Still Standing
I will make an Effort. . it was for the murder of one F. U Wyman in
Commanche Co. Kan
You will oblige me by an immediate answer

Very respectfully
W. B. MASTERSON
Sheriff
Ford Co   Kan [48]

On October 7, 1879, Bat wrote another letter to the governor this
time asking for information concerning the reward offered for John
"Scotty" Scott who murdered William Taylor on June 3, 1873. W.
H. Ward, the governor's secretary told Bat the $500 reward was
still in effect.[49] There is no record of Bat's capturing Scott, one of
Dodge's earliest murderers.

As November approached, the newspapers of Dodge City featured
more and more election news. On September 16, 1879, the *Globe*
contained this letter from a subscriber:

CANDIDATES FOR SHERIFF.

Speareville, Kan, Sept   14.
EDITOR GLOBE:—Will you be kind enough to let the farmers of the east end
of Ford county know through the columns of your paper who the candidates
are that are seeking the office of Sheriff this fall, besides Masterson? We
have enough of the Masterson rule.

SUBSCRIBER.

For the information of our subscriber we will say that as yet we have heard
the name of but one man mentioned, aside from the present sheriff, and that
is George T. Hinkel, of this city, who would make an excellent officer. He is
not seeking the office, but would certainly make a strong candidate.

The *Times*, long a pro-Masterson organ, immediately came out with this rebuttal:

SPEAREVILLE, KAS., Sept. 17th.
To THE EDITOR OF THE TIMES.

In reply to a communication published in the last issue of the Ford County Globe, in reference to candidates for the office of Sheriff, we beg to state that the most diligent inquiries among farmers and settlers in this neighborhood have thoroughly convinced us that W. B. Masterson is beyond doubt their choice for the office. Judging from the fact, that no one acquainted with the excellent success with which he has so far discharged the duties of his office, could be induced to cast his vote for another candidate; and the high esteem and respect with which Masterson is regarded by all authorities, not only in this, but in other counties of this State as well, is sufficient guarantee of his superior qualifications for the office. Outside of a few soreheads, only the friends of evil-doers desire the election of a man who will as Sheriff be less dangerous to them and their associations.

W. H. LYBRAND.[50]

Bat was nominated on an Independent ticket to run for re-election. The *Times*, October 25, 1879, said of the candidate for sheriff:

THE INDEPENDENT NOMINEES.

The Independent Convention, held at Dodge City, on Saturday last [October 18], was composed of the representative men of Ford county. Each precinct was fully and fairly represented by first-class and honorable men. The harmony of the proceedings and the unanimity by which the nominees were accepted, is a guarantee that there will be a triumphant success at the polls.

W. B. MASTERSON, the nominee for the office of Sheriff, is the efficient incumbent of that office. Bat is acknowledged to be the best Sheriff in Kansas. He is the most successful officer in the State. He is immensely popular and generally well liked. Horse thieves have a terror for the name of Masterson. He was the unanimous choice of the convention, and will be elected by a heavy majority. Every hater of horse thieves will rejoice over Bat's triumphant election; and the friends of good order and peace will contribute to his success.

The election was hotly contested. Bat's opponents used the expensive Cheyenne Indian trial as a major issue against his re-election. The *Ford County Globe*, a determinedly anti-Masterson paper, opened the ball with this preparatory statement of October 21, 1879:

AT LIBERTY.

As will be noticed by an article from the Lawrence Tribune on the fourth page of this paper, the Cheyenne Indians have been released from custody and are now at liberty. A large number of witnesses were present and the defendants were ready for trial. The prosecution was almost entirely abandoned, only a faint effort for a continuance being made. There is a suit now pending against Ford County for a large bill of costs in this case, and as will be seen by the proceedings of the Board, J. G. Waters, of Topeka, has volunteered his services to defend the county against paying these costs, amounting to several thousand dollars. The suits against the county are brought by W. B. Masterson, Sheriff.

Next week, the *Globe* began to take pot shots at Masterson and his Independent cocandidates:

Just think of Ford county having to pay $4000 for the simple arrest of seven lousy Cheyenne Indians and that without even an effort to convict them. Hoover is against all such frauds. Don't his vote show it on Sheriff's bills?

Masterson and Sutton made it hot for the Nations Wards whom they so cunningly conspired against, and brought to Ford county for the people to look at. They now desire to make it hot for the poor tax payers of the county, by getting them to pay the bills incurred in their innocent amusement. The Governor has gone back on them. He hasn't any funds on hand to give them so they have to fall back on the dear people of Ford county. Let them appeal to the Secretary of the Interior, Carl Schurz.[51]

Other expenses must have played a part in the campaign for on October 25, 1879, the *Times* said: "Bat Masterson is Sheriff of thirteen unorganized counties. Of course it costs something to run so much territory."

In northeast Ford county the Speareville *News,* October 25, 1879, also used the Cheyennes as ammunition against the Independent ticket:

Mr. Masterson has already received about three hundred dollars on the Cheyenne Indian account, and he and some others have instituted suit against Ford county for twenty-one hundred dollars more. Joe Waters, attorney for the Santa Fe, has volunteered to defend the county. Where is Mr. Sutton?

R. B. Fry, new editor of the *News,* pulled no punches in his campaign against Bat. On November 1, 1879, he published several items designed to injure the sheriff's chances at the polls:

DODGE-OZED.

The little Bull dozed on us the other night, because we saw proper to use our influence against him in the coming election, by using such weapons as he has deliberately placed in our hands. And we here emphatically reiterate that we never have, to our knowledge, nor never will support a man for an official position the second time, that during that time, has been a law breaker himself. And now voters' for the "Doze" "I am going to make this a personal matter and follow you up and if I hear you saying any thing more about me I will shoot you through the g-t-s, and when I come, you be prepared". Personally we have nothing against Mr. Masterson, officially we have; and whenever Mr. Masterson or any other man places themselves before the public, they become public property, and we shall handle them as such, in accordance with their deserts.

N. B.—For the want of space, and the respect we entertain for our patrons, we omit the obscene portion of the "doze."

We understand that "Bat Masterson" is going to shoot his way into the office of sheriff. This manner of conducting a canvass may do in Mississippi, but not in Ford county; many that had intended to support "Bat" will not do it now.   H.

We understand that Mr. Masterson has introduced the Yazoo plan in Ford county.   D.

There is a report being circulated that J. M. Stevenson had to pay Mr. Masterson for hunting and catching his horse, and thief. We are informed by Mr. Stevenson that such is not the case, it is also substantiated by Mr. Myton, who was present at the time Mr. S. offered to pay him. We make this voluntary correction, through justice to Mr. Stevenson, and Mr. Masterson as well, notwithstanding we are opposing Mr. M's reelection, we propose to be fair in the matter, and use such weapons, only, as he has forged himself.

Mr. Stevenson himself came to Bat's aid through the Dodge City *Times*, November 1, 1879:

I desire to inform the people of Ford county that all parties circulating the report that Bat Masterson charged me $25 or any other amount, for the finding and return of my stolen pony last fall, is telling an unmittigated falsehood as was ever uttered by any evil-minded persons. My transactions with Mr. Masterson have always been perfectly satisfactory. I expect to vote for him and work for his election.

JOHN M. STEVENSON.

SPEAREVILLE, Oct. 29, 1879.

The combination was too great, however, and the Independent ticket went down to defeat on November 4, 1879. Bat was beaten in all six of Ford county's voting areas. His final tally was 268 votes to George T. Hinkle's 404. Whether Bat was beaten as an individual or because he was one of the "gang," as represented by the Independent ticket, is a matter of open speculation. At any rate the entire party fell, soundly defeated by the "Peoples'" ticket.

The *Times*, November 8, 1879, mused over the blow:

There is a good deal of speculation as to the causes of the late defeat in Ford county, of the Independent ticket. The reasons given would fill a large volume; but we conjecture the most powerful influence was in the beer keg; and of course people fighting for honesty and reform wouldn't use money.

398

Bat Masterson

According to the *Times*, November 15, the Peoples' party was not the only group glad to see the defeat of Sheriff Masterson:

Since the success of the Peoples' ticket horse thieves have become emboldened. A fine span of mules was stolen from J. H. Werner in the Windthorst settlement, a few nights ago. The thief had previously held a parley with the owner of the mules, and the thief expressed satisfaction over the defeat of Sheriff Masterson. That night the mules were stolen.

Bob Fry of the Speareville *News* continued to publish articles detrimental to the character of Bat Masterson even after the election was over. Two of them appeared in the November 8, 1879, issue of the *News*:

We hear that Bat. Masterson said he was going to whip every s-- of a b---- that worked and voted against him in the county.

The above was given us on the best authority and taking into consideration the source of our information and the fact that two or three citizens already have been fearfully beaten, by himself and friends, would give the above statement a credence, that but few would attempt to deny. We publish in this issue, a statement of Chas. Roden, one of the men that he should have assaulted, of the manner in which he was attacked, also after he had went out on the street, he was searched for pistols and his discovery afterwards, that his pocketbook was missing, carries with it a degree of conviction that the above threat was made and deliberately being carried out. We have talked with several of Mr. M['s]. supportors and everyone without an exception, condemn such a course on his part. The question remains, if the above reports are true, how long will the citizens of Ford County permit this to go on.

(CORRESPONDENCE)

SPEAREVILLE, Nov. 6, 1879.

EDITOR NEWS: Being in Dodge City on a visit in company with some ladies, and while walking down Main street and in front of Col. Jones office. Mr. Jones called me in to have a little talk. When all at once Sheriff Masterson came in, stepping in front of me and said: "You have been doing good work down in the East end," and before I had time to reply, he struck me several times; after I had got out on the street, some official, I believe it was the sheriffs brother, searched my pockets, he said to see if I had any pistol, but did not find any. When I got ready to go home I felt in my pocket for my pocket-book to pay my bills and found it gone. I would advise every person from the East-end, that voted the Peoples' ticket to be on their guard.

CHAS. RODEN.

It seemed that Mr. Roden was telling something less than the truth for on November 15, 1879, the *News* published a letter from Col. T. S. Jones, a prominent Dodge City attorney and owner of

399

the office in which the altercation took place, which placed a different light on the matter:

EDITOR SPEAREVILLE NEWS: In justice to myself, as well as to Mr. Masterson I wish to correct some erroneous impressions as to the difficulty which took place between Mr. Chas. Roden and Sheriff Masterson in my office a few days since, an incorrect report of which was given in the last Speareville NEWS signed by Roden containing statements untrue and unjust.

Mr. Roden and myself were engaged in a friendly conversation when Mr. Masterson entered my office, in response to an invitation extended him during the early part of the afternoon, as I wished to see him in reference to a matter of business. Roden was standing up and in the act of leaving, when Masterson came in, they met face to face and to all appearances the greeting between them was mutually friendly, soon after which a conversation commenced between them, in which Masterson accused Roden of using language against him before the election, which was untrue and which he had no right to do. Roden replying, that was alright.

They then assumed the attitude of beligerents, Roden putting his right hand in his rear pocket, evidently for the purpose of intimidating Masterson and making him believe he intended something more serious. Masterson immediately seizing him by the hand dealt him several severe blows, saying at the same time "pull it, if you can." Roden finally made an unceremonious exit from the scene of strife into the street and from thence into Mr. Mueller's shoe shop. Masterson was unarmed. While fighting is to be deprecated, frankeness impels me to the belief, that in this instance, there was a merited rebuke visited upon the person of the wrong-doer. Your

T. S. JONES.

The above communication from Col. Thomas S. Jones of Dodge City puts a different feature on the case. The columns of the NEWS are always open for controversy in a courtous manner.

A footnote to the character of Bat's accuser, Charles Roden, was printed in the Speareville *News* just two weeks later, November 29, 1879. Roden, it seems, had been engaged in thievery at Spearville, storing the loot in his house. When arrested he gave bond to appear the next day but skipped town singing, according to Editor Fry, "Oh! for a lodge in some vast wilderness."

Of course, Bat was not one to take the accusations of Bob Fry charitably. He sent this rebuttal through the editor of the Dodge City *Times*, November 15, 1879:

TO THE EDITOR OF THE TIMES.

In answer to the publication made by Bob Fry of the Speareville News, asserting that I made threats that I would lick any s-- of a b---- that voted or worked against me at the last election, I will say it is as false and as flagrant a lie as was ever uttered; but I did say this: that I would lick him the s-- of a

400

Bat Masterson

b---- if he made any more dirty talk about me; and the words s-- of a b---- I strictly confined to the Speareville editor, for I don't know of any other in Ford county.

W. B. MASTERSON.

Bat's retort had its effect. The *Times*, November 22, 1879, reported that "Bob Fry, of the Speareville *News*, exhibited to the Hon. Nelson Adams, while on the train going west the other evening, a self-cocking pistol, that he was carrying for Sheriff Masterson. Better hitch yourself to a cannon, Bob."

Next, Bat was caught up in the tangle of jurisprudence. The *Ford County Globe*, November 18, 1879, reprinted an article from the Buckner (later Jetmore) *Independent* and added some comment of its own:

THE HORSE THIEVES RELEASED.

It seems that there were some thirty horses stolen from Milton Harrison, of the Pan Handle, who with a few companions followed and found the horses in the vicinity of Hays City, in the possession of W. B. Rogers and four other men, who were and are supposed to be the thieves who stole the horses from the Pan Handle. He took his horses and the thieves and arrived at Hays City on election day; lodged the prisoners in jail and had them detained a couple of days.

For some reason unknown to us and to the sorrow of every law-loving citizen, Mr. Harrison and party pursued their journey without obtaining the proper papers to take the prisoners to Texas, and arrived at Dodge City on the evening of the 13th inst. They turned the prisoners over to W. B. Masterson, sheriff of Ford county, who, Mr. Harrison says, promised to return them to him. But the prisoners succeeded in getting the ear of M. W. Sutton, the County Attorney of Ford county, who filed a petition before the Hon. Probate Judge of said county, asking for a writ of habeas corpus. The said sheriff made the following answer.

STATE OF KANSAS, Co. of Ford.

To the Probate Court: I hereby state that I hold the within named parties without any authority whatever; that I have had no commitment of them.

W. B. MASTERSON,
Sheriff.

We are informed that the sheriff did not notify Mr. Harrison that the writ was served on him until some time after the prisoners had been released.

This release may be justifiable under the law, for the reason that Mr. Harrison ought to have obtained, to say the least, a warrant, if not a requisition at Hays, to give him the authority to remove the prisoners. But notwithstanding Mr. Harrison did not fulfill the requirements of the law, his intentions were undoubtedly to do so, and we look upon it as Mr. Masterson's express and official duty to have notified Mr. Harrison of the writ, and we can not understand why he did not so do.—Buckner Independent.

The above detailed statement as given in the "Independent" is substantially correct as far as the theft is conserned, and the arrest of the guilty parties and lodging them in our jail for safe keeping as well as the release that followed. We think that there are other officers that are equally as liable for this wholesale jail delivery as Mr. Masterson, our Sheriff. We find that the county-attorney Mike Sutton lent a willing hand to assist these thieves out of their trouble—instead of informing Mr. Harrison that he was doing an illegal act and instructing him how to proceed, so that he might bring to justice the parties who had robbed him out of all he possessed; instead of counseling the thieves,—we say it would look much better if Sutton had been on the other side of the question, but he was not, as the facts in the case will show.

He filed with the Probate Court, N. B. Klaine, publisher of the Times, (a man that talks about "rings, fraud," etc.) an affidavit setting forth the illegal restraint and incarceration of these thieves, and prays that a writ of habeas corpus issue from said court so that these parties may have a hearing and show cause why they should not be released. The court promptly issued said writ and a hearing was had, and, of course, the parties were released, as they say, "on the ground that they were illegally held and that no one appeared against them." That, also, may be true. Not a single attorney in the city knew anything about this case outside of Sutton. The probate court didn't even continue the case sufficiently long to get word to the party that brought them here so that he might give an explanation of his acts, and we doubt very much whether Mr. Klaine cared to do so.

The whole transaction was done after night or so early in the morning that none but the trio know what was being done in this honorable (?) court. At all events it was done before the time had arrived for Mr. Harrison to go to the Sheriff and reclaim the parties he had turned over to him for safe keeping and when he did go, imagine his surprise, when he is informed by the Sheriff that they had been legally released. Klaine may possibly be enabled to explain to the people in his next issue that this was a square deal, right and just and all that sort of thing; but we venture the assertion that this is a far greater ring than he would have the people believe was inaugurated at the late election.

Bat answered the charges in the Dodge City *Times*, November 22, 1879:

A CARD.

"We are informed that the Sheriff did not notify Mr. Harrison that the writ was served on him until some time after the prisoners had been released."

The above quoted words are from the Buckner Independent and commented on by the Ford County Globe. In response thereto, I will say that I had a writ of habeas corpus served on me in the evening about 5 o'clock, and issued by the Probate Judge of Ford county, commanding me to have the defendants B. W. Rogers et al, before the Probate Court at ten o'clock the following day, and to show by what authority I held the above named defendants; and I will state here my reasons for not informing the parties plaintiff in the above cause: that when the hour of ten o'clock came the following day, that none of the parties plaintiff could be found, with the exception of one, and he was in such a beastly state of intoxication that he could not be aroused; and I am positive that if I had been able to have got him on his feet he would not have known the difference between a writ of habeas corpus and a Texas steer. When he turned the prisoners over to me he conducted himself in a turbulent and quarrelsome manner.

The defendants told me while in my charge that they were willing to be turned over to some legal and responsible officer, and be taken back to Texas for trial; that they had not stolen the horses, and were prepared to prove it; but they did object to being turned over to a drunken mob, and be taken out and hung without jury or trial, as the party in charge had threatened to do so as soon as they were far enough away from Dodge to be safe.

W. B. MASTERSON.

Retaliation of a sort occurred on November 30 when Bat swore out a warrant for the arrest of the *Globe* editor, D. M. Frost. The *Globe,* on December 2, 1879, was the first to report the arrest:

ARRESTED.

Again the GLOBE has a choice morsel of news for its readers. The election excitement had about subsided, the Times had exhausted its stock of weeping and wailing, and a quiet spell seemed inevitable, when, on Sunday evening last, W. B. Masterson, Sheriff of Ford county and Deputy United States Marshal, relieved the monotony by arresting D. M. Frost, one of the editors of this paper, on a United States warrant, issued by United States Commissioner R. G. Cook. The complaint, or information upon which the warrant was issued was signed and sworn to by W. B. Masterson, and charges Mr. Frost with having violated that portion of the United States Statutes which prohibits the buying or selling of stolen government property. The date of the transaction is something over a year ago, at which time it is alleged that Mr. Frost received some government stores from Sargeant Evarts, an employee of the Quartermaster's department at Fort Elliott, Texas.

Mr. Frost was taken before his Honor, United States Commissioner R. G. Cook, who set December 18th as the time for holding the preliminary examination, and required the defendant to give a bond for his appearance on that day in the gentle sum of five thousand dollars. The value of the goods alleged to have been purchased was about one hundred and forty dollars. The bond was given with neatness and dispatch, and it would have been just as promptly forthcoming had it been fifty thousand instead of five.

We do not know whether it is the intention of the prosecuting parties to hang the defendant on a sour apple tree, burn him at the stake, or imprison him for life in the bastile on a bread and water diet, but it is evident that they would "smile all over their faces and half way down their backs" to see him in either of the above predicaments, as their love and affection for him is not of that tender and sympathetic nature which is said to have existed in the breast of the Saviour when he sacrificed his life to save a lost and ruined community.

403

The affair is liable to cause Mr. Frost considerable trouble and expense, but his vast fortune will be poured out like water from the clouds to secure his vindication. But if, on the other hand, it shall be proved that he has been systematically plundering the government of the United States and wearing government socks purchased from one of the brave defenders of his country, then we shall be tempted to place our right hand upon our left brest and swear a mighty oath that the human race has lost its virtue, the devil is a saint and "things are not what they seem."

The GLOBE will endeavor to keep its numerous intelligent readers posted on the progress of the case and large posters will be struck announcing the locality and hour for the hanging to take place.

And now in conclusion we will suggest that if the great and good Nancy Balderstone of the Times wishes to offer an exhortation on the subject of honesty, morality and the degeneration of our race, the present is a fit moment for him to "shoot his little wad."

The Dodge City *Times*, December 6, 1879, went to great pains to report the arrest as if the principal were not the editor of a rival newspaper but merely another unfortunate:

ARREST OF D. M. FROST.

D. M. Frost, editor of the Ford County Globe, was arrested on Sunday last by W. B. Masterson, Deputy U. S. Marshal, and taken before R. G. Cook, U. S. Commissioner, to answer to the complaint sworn to by W. B. Masterson, which alleges that on the 1st day of May, 1878, D. M. Frost did obtain 300 pounds of white lead, two gallons of varnish, three kegs nails, a lot of stationery, to the value of $127 54, the property of the United States; and that he did unlawfully, wilfully, feloniously, knowingly steal, take this property contrary to the statutes, peace and dignity of the United States, obtaining said property of Jos. Evarts, a soldier of the 19th Infantry, employed and entrusted with the care of said property belonging to the United States; said Frost knowing that said Evarts was a soldier and employed by the Government, that said Jos. Evarts had no right to sell the property of the United States; and that Frost did conceal and aid to conceal, with intent to convert to his own use, the articles mentioned; that said property had been embezzled and purloined by Jos. Evarts, said Frost knowing said property had been embezzled, purloined and stolen; said Frost knowing it to be the property of the United States.

Frost gave bail in the sum of $5,000, for his appearance before Commissioner Cook, on the 18th of December, to answer to the charges set forth in the complaint, when a preliminary examination will be had. Jos. Evarts, the soldier mentioned, is now serving a sentence of three years imprisonment in the military prison at Fort Leavenworth. His trial took place at Fort Elliott only a few months ago.

Frost was indicted by a grand jury at Topeka on April 14, 1880. On August 18, 1880, a petition signed by prominent Dodge City residents was presented to Charles Devens, attorney general of the

Bat Masterson

United States, asking for a dismissal of the charges. The ultimate fate of the case is not known, but to all appearances it did not injure the career of D. M. Frost.

In December, 1879, Bat learned that the county clerk, John B. Means, had forged county scrip in the sheriff's name. The *Times,* December 27, recounted the story:

FORGED COUNTY SCRIP.

John B. Means has resigned the office of County Clerk. The reason for Mr. Means' sudden termination of the office so close to the end of his term, was from the fact that he had forged two pieces of county scrip; one for the sum of $256 60, in favor of W. B. Masterson, Sheriff, "for services in conveying prisoners to the penitentiary." Another piece of county scrip, for the sum of $278 25, in favor of Hamilton & Co., stationers. How the discovery of the forgery transpired may be briefly stated as follows: On Monday night [December 22] Means was pretty well "boozed," as the saying is, and was bantered to make a bet on a game of billiards; and not having the "needful" he drew forth the first mentioned piece of scrip and called the game. This was a grand mistake—undoubtedly the wrong piece of scrip was put up as a wager. Some cunning eye noticed the large amount for which the scrip was drawn, and the name of W. B. Masterson being thereon, suggested the fact that "Gid" was dealing in "crooked" county indebtedness.

Sheriff Masterson was immediately apprised of the circumstance; and confronting Means inquired if any of his bills had been allowed for which he had not yet received the county warrant. Means replied no. Masterson then demanded the piece of scrip bearing his name, saying it was a forgery. Upon further investigation it was found that Means had the second piece of scrip above described, which also proved to be a forgery.

The two county commissioners residing here were immediately notified, and they peremptorily demanded Mr. Means' resignation. An examination of the scrip book did not disclose the forgeries, because the forged pieces were issued on numbers properly drawn. Means states that these two pieces are the only ones "out" that have a crooked imprint. The name of "A. J. Peacock, Chairman," was signed by him, which he states was done at a time when several parties were waiting to have scrip filled out, and he signed several blank pieces in order to facilitate business. The name of "C. H. Lane, Treasurer," in the registry of the scrip is a skillful forgery.

The scrip purports to have been issued on the 6th of July and registered on the 11th of that month. Mr. Means fully exonerates Mr. Peacock of any knowledge in the matter, and says that gentleman signed blank scrip at his request, as he desired to fill out scrip for jury fees. No one had complicity in this fraudulent scheme.

His intention was to dispose of these forged pieces of scrip after his term of office expired; but being well up in his "cups" he inadvertently unearthed his own rascally action. Gid is not a shrewd forger. The State and not the county

WHY THE WEST WAS WILD

pays the Sheriff for conveying prisoners to the penitentiary. He should have carefully concealed the forged pieces. "They will not do to bet on."

Means makes an humble confession of his guilt. He is really to be pitied; and we exceedingly regret that we are compelled to make these statements of his conduct. But poverty stared him in the face. He is broken down physically; is subject to epilepsy and boozeism. The man's deplorable physical condition excites sympathy, and for this reason no prosecution will probably be made; notwithstanding the offence is a grave one, and one deserving punishment.

We presume the Board of County Commissioners will present a complaint to the District Court which will be in session week after next.

Means was not jailed for his misdeed but was permitted to leave the city. By late January, 1880, he was as far west as Santa Fe, N. M.[52]

Apparently the effort of Joseph G. Waters to defend the county against payment of Sheriff Masterson's Indian bills failed, for on January 5, 1880, the board of county commissioners allowed Bat over $1,000 expenses in the case.[53]

On January 6, 1880, Bat opened the January term of the Ford county district court [54] and then on January 10 departed on his last official duty as sheriff of the county. The *Times,* January 17, 1880, said:

Sheriff Masterson went to Leavenworth Saturday night last, having in charge George Parker and Fred L. Baldwin, charged with horse stealing, and convicted at the last term of the Ford county District Court. They were sentenced to twelve and sixteen months imprisonment respectively.

Ex-Sheriff W. B. Masterson and Ex-Deputy Chas. E. Bassett, returned from the Leavenworth prison, having safely lodged the two prisoners, Baldwin and Parker. This is Bat's last official act as sheriff.

Early Dodge Citians were famed for the jokes they pulled on one another and on strangers who seemed to ask for the full treatment. A "practical joke" on a so-called "doctor of medicine," was recorded in the *Ford County Globe,* February 17, 1880:

IN AND OUT OF DODGE.

EXPERIENCE OF A SCIENTIFIC M. D. ON THE LECTURE PLATFORM.

PISTOLS, POWDER AND PRIVATE DISEASES.

Dodge City has been shaken from center to circumference during the past week by the advent of a gentleman of distinction who bore the unassuming name and title of Meredith, M. D. He was what the boys would call a "daisy." The general outlines of his outward appearance did not indicate that

406

he had ever finished his education with foreign travel, or that he had at any time during his earthly career peregrinated with a circus—therefore he was not thoroughly posted on the modes and costumes that prevail in chaste and civilized cities with advanced ideas, such as Dodge possesses, and to all appearances is wonderfully proud.

The Doctor had written to some of our citizens wishing to know whether Dodge would be a good field for his line of science, which he designated as Phrenology and the treatment of certain diseases which it is not here necessary to mention in detail. He was encouraged to come, and recommended to Major James Dalton and Mr. Luke McGlue as prominent citizens who would be likely to take a deep interest in his cause. Immediately after his arrival he determined to deliver a lecture defining his particular sphere that the public might understand his great mission and come unto him to be cured and to have their organs examined.

The old Lady Gay dance hall was engaged for the occasion and thither at early candle-lighting a large concourse assembled. Mr. W. B. Masterson, Esq. was chosen to act as chairman and introduced the speaker in a few neat and well chosen remarks.

Dr. Meridith opened his address by saying that he had not intended to deliver a lecture, but "at the urgent solicitation of numerous prominent"—

"You lie!" shouted some one in the audience.

Chairman Masterson rebuked the insult, and when order was restored the doctor began again. Proceeding further in a like manner, he was again interrupted by an insulting remark from one of the audience, and it was only by stern commands and threats of annihilation that the chairman brought the house to order.

Again the Doctor proceeded and was just wading deep into a scientific problem when a loud, profane and fiendish yell from Luke McGlue turned the house into an uproar of excitement, and all efforts to restore order were in vain.

Just at this critical moment a southside exhorter with one eye in a sling made an effort to drag the orator from the stand, whereupon Chairman Masterson drew from beneath his coat-tails a Colt's improved, nickel plated, size 44 shooting instrument and formed himself in a hollow square in front of the horrified Doctor, determined to defend or die! A crash was heard—the lamps went out instantaneously, windows were smashed, missiles flew through the darkness, the air was filled with demoniac yells and shooting commenced in rapid succession. In the language of the poet we may well exclaim

"What a row was that, my countrymen!"

It was only after all the ammunition in the house was expended that the murderous carnival ceased and a lamp was lighted by which to remove the dead and wounded. But the dead and wounded had ere this time escaped and even the Doctor was nowhere to be found. Search was made, and at last he was discovered coiled up under the speaker's stand with his hands over his marble features and a ghastly bullet hole through the crown of his hat.

The meeting adjourned sine die.

The gold fields in Colorado attracted Bat following the completion of his term as sheriff. On February 28, 1880, the *Times* reported: "W. B. Masterson, formerly sheriff of Ford county, left for Leadville Wednesday morning [February 25], where he will remain a short time. Bat has many friends who wish him a successful career, and trust he may shortly return." [55]

The young ex-sheriff returned to Dodge on March 6 or 7, depending on whether one consults the *Times* or *Globe*. "W. B. Masterson returned from Leadville last Sunday and gave a glowing account of the immense business of that mushroom city and the richness of its mineral surroundings," said the *Globe*, March 9, 1880. "W. B. Masterson returned from Leadville on Saturday last. Bat says there is going to be some big openings in the Gunnison country. Things are getting to a solid basis in Leadville. It takes money to make money," reported the *Times*, March 13, 1880.

On March 10, 1880, Bat donated $20.00 to the defense of his friend J. J. Webb who was accused of murder in Las Vegas, N. M. Of 42 donors, Bat was one of four who gave such a large sum. [56]

Bat continued his interest in politics. He attended the county Republican convention on March 20 and the state convention at Topeka on March 31. He was firmly for Grant, the *Globe* indicated. [57]

"W. B. Masterson has gone to take a look on the Gunnison country. We hope he will 'strike it big,' " said the *Times*, April 17, 1880. [58]

On May 4, 1880, the *Globe* repeated a rumor involving Bat: "A report reached the city yesterday from Colorado that Ex-Sheriff W. B. Masterson had made a big commotion up about Buna Vista by a dexterous use of his revolver. As the report has not been confirmed we can give no particulars."

The gold bubble soon burst for Bat. On May 29, 1880, the Dodge City *Times* mentioned a letter he had written concerning the value of the Gunnison country:

W. B. Masterson writes to M. W. Sutton that he is in Denver and will probably return to Dodge City this week. He says "the Gunnison is the worst fraud he ever saw. There are no mines anywhere near Pitkin or Gunnison City, the closest being Ruby City, and there is three feet of snow in the streets, and it will be impossible to do anything there before the middle of July." Bat advises his friends to keep away from the Gunnison country, if they have any show of making a living, where they are living.

"W. B. Masterson returned from Colorado Tuesday morning [June 1]. Bat. does not give a glowing acount of the Silver State," said the *Times,* June 5, 1880.[59]

Bat arrived in Dodge just in time to be enumerated in the tenth United States census. His occupation was listed as laborer, his age as 25 years. The census taker also stated that he was living with one Annie Ladue, a 19-year-old concubine. The date of the enumeration was June 22, 1880; the enumerator—it should be pointed out—was W. C. Shinn, brother of one of the *Globe's* coeditors, Lloyd Shinn.

On July 6, 1880, the *Globe* reported that "W. B. Masterson has gone to Ogalala, Nebraska." According to Robert M. Wright, an old time Dodge resident—the Wright of Wright, Beverley & Co.— Bat made the trip at the instance of his friend Ben Thompson to rescue Ben's brother Billy who had been wounded in a gun fight in that Nebraska cowtown. This was substantiated several years later by Thomas Masterson, Jr., Bat's brother.[60]

It was recorded in the local press, Dodge City *Times,* June 26, 1880, that Bill Thompson was wounded in an Ogallala gun battle:

Wm. Thompson had a difficulty with a Texas man in Ogallala, a few days ago. A number of shots were fired. Billy received five shots. He was not dangerously hurt.

It was also recorded that when Bat came back to Dodge City he shared his wagon with Bill Thompson. The *Times,* July 17, 1880, reported his return:

W. B. Masterson arrived from a visit to Ogallala, this week. He says Nebraska is dry and many people are leaving the State. He came by wagon, and was accompanied by Texas Billy Thompson. The latter has recovered from his wounds.

Beyond that the Dodge City newspapers had nothing to say about Bat's "rescue mission" to Ogallala. Latter-day writers, however, have contended it was a daring whisking away of a man from under the law's snout.

Bat's name did not again appear in the papers of Dodge City until December 7, 1880, when the *Globe* said that "Ex-Sheriff W. B. Masterson arrived in the city a few days ago." The *Times,* December 11, stated that "he lives in Kansas City. Bat was welcomed by a host of friends."

Apparently Bat remained in Dodge for about two months and

then on February 8, 1881, left for Tombstone, Ariz., "where he expects to remain next summer." [61]

The Dodge City *Times*, February 24, 1881, reported that "C. M. Beeson received a letter from W. H. Harris, who states that W. B. Masterson arrived at Tombstone, Arizona. The old Dodge boys are seeking fortunes in the gold fields of Arizona."

In April, 1881, Bat was suddenly called home to Dodge to aid his brother Jim, now ex-marshal, in a difficulty with Al Updegraff and A. J. Peacock. The *Ford County Globe*, April 19, 1881, printed the first of many articles on the affair:

THE FESTIVE REVOLVER.
AGAIN ITS MUSICAL VOICE IS HEARD IN THE LAND.
SHOOTING ALL ALONG THE LINE AND ONLY ONE MAN HURT.

Last Saturday [April 16] about noon one of the most daring and dangerous shooting scrapes took place that Dodge City has ever experienced.

The facts as near as we can gather them are about as follows:

A. J. Peacock and James Masterson have been partners in the dance hall and saloon business in Dodge City, and for some time past their business relations have not been as smooth as polished glass.

A few weeks ago Mr. Al Updegraff was employed as bar tender in the dance hall, and it seemed he was a strong friend of Peacock's.

Something occurred last week which caused an open quarrel between Masterson on the one side and Updegraff and Peacock on the other. Pistols were drawn and several shots fired, but no one was hurt.

It appears that immediately after this quarrel Masterson telegraphed to his brother, Bat Masterson, in New Mexico, asking him to come to Dodge and help him out of his difficulties. In response to the invitation Bat came on the first train, arriving here last Friday morning about 11:50. About the first objects that met his eyes were Peacock and Updegraff walking across the street. He followed them up, hailed them, and immediately the shooting commenced. Masterson fortified himself behind an embankment near the railroad track, while Peacock and Updegraff took shelter behind the corners of the calaboose building. Both sides continued to shoot for about three or four minutes, during which time the excitement along the street was rather lively, as the shots from the calaboose party were in direct range with the stores and business houses. One bullet passed through the front of Dr. McCarty's drug store, one through the Long Branch, and one through the front of G. M. Hoover's wholesale liquor store. Some unknown party was at one time seen to fire two or three shots from a point to the right of Masterson's position, at the Peacock party, and then disappeared to be seen no more. It is asserted, and is probably true, that several shots were fired by other parties along the street at Peacock and Updegraff. When the shooting, which lasted but a few minutes, had ceased, it was found that the pistols of Masterson and Peacock were empty, while Updegraff had one shot left. Updegraff was

410

the only man hurt. He was shot through the lungs, the ball passing entirely through his body. The wound was at first thought to be fatal, but there is now fair prospect of his recovery.

Masterson was arrested by the city officers and fined in the police court for disturbing the peace. A State warrant was issued later in the evening for several parties connected with the affair, but they were allowed to leave town, with the understanding that they were not to return.

Great indignation was manifested and is still felt by the citizens against the Masterson party, as the shooting was caused by a private quarrel, and the parties who were anxious to fight should have had at least a thought for the danger they were causing disinterested parties on the street and in business houses.

Such was the nature of the affair that the officers thought best not to undertake the process of criminal prosecution, although many advised it. At any rate the citizens are thoroughly aroused and will not stand any more foolishness. They will not wait for the law to take its course if such an outrage should again occur.

A correspondent's article appeared in several Kansas newspapers. The following copy was printed in the Caldwell *Commercial,* April 21, 1881:

THAT LITTLE AFFAIR AT DODGE CITY.

Dodge City, Kas., April 17.—The new administration, with A. B. Webster at its head, has taken charge, and law and order is the watchword. This, however, was sadly violated yesterday, when a remarkable fight and killing occurred. It seems that for some time trouble has been brewing between A. J. Peacock, Al. Updegraff and James Masterson, proprietor of the Lady Gay dance hall. This culminated several days ago in Masterson being shot at a number of times and slightly wounded. The Mastersons have a fighting reputation, the eldest, Edward, having been killed while Marshal, and all having been shot and wounded at divers times. W. B. Masterson, who is the "boss," and has been Sheriff of this county and Marshal of this city, was telegraphed for at Tombstone, N. M., to come and settle the trouble. He came at noon yesterday, and while taking a drink with some friends seen Updegraff and Peacock crossing the railroad. He immediately followed them, and, coming within twenty feet, said: "I have come over a thousand miles to settle this. I know you are healed; now fight."

All three immediately commenced firing, Masterson having the advantage of a slight embankment at the railroad track, while Peacock and Updegraff retreated to the corners of the city jail and fired from there. Two other parties opened fire from the saloon on the north side, while Masterson, thinking he was fired on from behind, laid down to reload, when he again commenced firing. Updegraff, who was shot through the right lung, retreated, and Mayor Webster, with Sheriff [Fred] Singer, coming up with shotguns, compelled Masterson to give up his pistols. This happening in the heart of the city, with over a hundred people in sight, it is remarkable that only one was killed and two wounded. While lying down to reload, a bullet threw the dirt into Mas-

411

terson's mouth, and rebounding struck James Anderson in the back. Several bullets entered the saloons and business houses, and there were many narrow escapes. The Mastersons were arrested, pleaded guilty, fined $10 and costs, paid their fines and left on last night's train for the West. Fifteen extra police were on duty last night, but now all is quiet. It was the most determined fight made since the days of "Wild Bill" (Jim Hicok) and his celebrated fight at Springfield.

Even Bat's long time supporter, the Dodge City *Times*, could find little excuse for his actions this time. On April 21, 1881, the *Times* said:

Al. Updegraff, who was shot in the street recontre Saturday last, is recovering slowly, and will soon be well. The shot entered the lower part of the right lung, and shattered the ribs. The cause of the shooting arose from trouble between the proprietors of the Lady Gay dance hall. Al. is barkeeper of the house. He was shot by Bat. Masterson, who came up from New Mexico to take his brother's part. The firing on the street by Bat. Masterson, and jeopardizing the lives of citizens, is severely condemned by our people, and the good opinion many citizens had of Bat. has been changed to one of contempt. The parties engaged in this reckless affray were permitted to leave town, though warrants were sworn out for their arrest. Bat. Masterson, James Masterson, Chas. Ronan and Tom O'Brien were the accused, and there is good reason to believe they will never darken Dodge City any more. We believe the authorities did perfectly right in permitting these men to go. If they will remain away there will be no more trouble in Dodge City. Should they return they will be prosecuted.

By April 21 Updegraff was well enough to write a letter explaining his version of the affair to the *Ford County Globe*. It was published on May 10, 1881:

THE TRUE STATEMENT OF THE SHOOTING AT DODGE CITY.
MEDICINE LODGE INDEX.

DODGE CITY, KAN., APRIL 21, 1881.

EDITOR GLOBE: There having been several statements published relative to the shooting that occurred here, in which I was wounded, and as my relatives and friends live in your city, I desire to make a brief statement of the affair for the purpose of correcting the erroneous statement heretofore published, that all concerned may know that I am not entirely to blame for it all. When I arrived here from Medicine Lodge I went into the employ of Peacock & Masterson, as bar-keeper. During the time I was so employed a friend of Masterson's robbed a woman of $80 by entering her room while she was absent. I advised her to have the party arrested, which she did, through the proper officers. Masterson thereupon came to me and insisted that I should make the woman withdraw the complaint, which I refused positively to do. He, Masterson, thereupon informed me that my services as bar-keeper was no longer needed, and I must quit. Mr. Peacock, the other member of the

412

firm, thereupon insisted that I should stay, as I was right. Masterson having claimed to be a killer, then undertook the job of killing me, and attempted it on the following evening by coming into the saloon and cocking his revolver in my face. I got the best of him by a large majority, and notwithstanding his reputation as a killer, he hid out and was next morning arrested upon my complaint.

He or his friends then telegraphed an inflamatory dispatch to his brother, Bat Masterson, who arrived in due time, and met Mr. Peacock and myself midway between the two front streets and without any warning to us, commenced shooting at us. We of course returned the fire and soon drove Bat Masterson behind the railroad embankment where he lay down out of range of our fire. We were then fired at by parties from the saloon doors on the north Front street, from one of which I was shot through the right lung, now six days ago. I feel that I will soon be around again, and will not die as the party wished me to. The parties who participated in the affair against me were by the citizens bounced out of town, and I invite anyone who doubts this statement, to correspond with any respectable man in this place, who, I am satisfied will corroborate this statement.   Respectfully yours,

AL. UPDEGRAFF.

In view of Bat's writing ability it is unfortunate that he did not offer for publication an explanation of his side of the shootout.

Bat again received notice in the May 24, 1881, issue of the *Globe* after his picture had appeared in the *Illustrated Police News:*

It must be very consoling to W. B. Masterson's friends to see his photograph by the side of a darky who is to be hung for murder, both of which figure very prominently in the late issue of the Illustrated Police News.

Bat was in Pueblo, Colo., when he received this letter which the *Times* reprinted June 9, 1881:

REACHING TO THE BOTTOM.

The following letter, which was addressed to W. B. Masterson, S. Pueblo, has been handed us for publication. The contents will be well understood by the citizens of Dodge City:

DODGE CITY, Kas., June 4, 1881.

DEAR BAT: I am sitting in Kelley's; we have just took a drink, and Jim says to drop you a word—the damn town has been torn up over the telegram of your coming. Webster telegraphed to Sargent and the shot gun brigade was up all night. They consisted of Webster, Singer, Bill Miller, Deger, Tom Bugg, Boyd, Emerson, Bud Driskill, Hi Collar, Peacock, Updegraff and others. Nate Hudson refused to support them. Kelley and myself will be up one of these days to see you. I have an annual and have written for a pass for Kelley. Dont give away what I tell you Bat; it is damn hard for me now to stay here, because I have pronounced myself in your favor; so has Kelley and Phillips, Mose Barber, Dave Morrow and several others. You ought to hear Old Dave ROAR. Charley Powell is here, the same good fellow as of old. Kelley is look-

413

ing over my shoulder and says "tell him Sutton is at the bottom of it all, damn him."

Yours as ever,
H. E. GRYDEN.

The letter created so much interest in Dodge City that the *Times* printed it again on June 16, 1881, along with a version in rhyme:

REACHING TO THE BOTTOM.

Last week the following appeared in the TIMES. As there was considerable demand for the paper and we were unable to supply the call for extra papers, we reproduce the letter with a paraphrase in rhyme, written by a well known bard who was present last week. The "take off" is in the writer's most happy vein, but he does not claim literary distinction on account of this local sensation.

[The letter above appeared here.]

The following lines in rhymes were written for the TIMES, and they will make you laugh until you feel sore, when you hear the roar:

"Better Walk 100 Miles to See a Man than Write a Letter."—VAN BUREN.

Dear Bat: I am sitting in Kelley's
And we are filling our bellies
With something to drink;
That is fair, we think.

Jim says to send you word,
For we have just now heard
That the damned town is humming
With the news of your coming;
They say that "the shot gun brigade"—
(Kelley bring me a lemonade,)
Was up all the night;
It was a hell of a sight
To see Webster, Singer and Bugg
Each biting off the very same plug,
And Deger, Boyd and Miller,
Fill up their glasses and swill'er
Down, while Driskill, Peacock and Collar
Were enough to make you holler.

Nat Hudson I know does not belong,
You hear me sound my gong.
I'll try my best and be up some day,
And from the looks of things I'll come to stay;
I'll get a pass for Kelley to ride on,
As sure as my name is Harry Gryden.

It's damned hard for me to stay here,
At night, by day in constant fear—
Have to stand them off for beer,
And the shot guns are always near.

414

And you may bet your belly
That I and Kelley,
And I state it flat,
Are for you, Bat;
And so is Morrow,
To his own sorrow;
And there is Barber,
They will not harbor,
Because he is sound and true
For truth, freedom and you.

It would make you sore,
To hear old Dave roar.
Let's have some beer;
'Charley Powell is here,
He is not wise as he becomes older:
Kelley looks over my shoulder,
And says to send you a kiss,
And tell you, at the bottom of this,
Is that sinner and glutton,
Whom you know as Mike Sutton.

So be kind to yourself and clever,
And I am, Gryden, as ever.

Bat was becoming a legend in his own time. His skill with a six shooter was known throughout the West and, as with all legends, his prowess seemed to increase each time his story was told. One absurd yarn was printed in the New York *Sun* and reprinted in the *Ford County Globe*, November 22, 1881:

A MILD-EYED MAN,
WHO HAS KILLED TWENTY-SIX PERSONS.
LETTER TO NEW YORK SUN.

At Gunnison, Col., last August, while waiting for the small hours of the morning to come around, we were entertained with narratives illustrating the customs of the country, given by Dr. W. S. Cockrell, Lieutenants Febriger, Wagner and Wetherill, gentlemen connected with the United States army, and others familiar with life and death in the western wilds.

Dr. Cockrell, on being asked whether the reports of killing affrays were not greatly exaggerated, replied that some of them were, while in other cases the truth had never been told.

"There is a man," remarked the doctor, indicating a medium sized, mild-eyed person, who stood in the doorway looking into the billiard room of the Tabor House, "who has killed twenty-six men, and he is only twenty-seven years of age. He is W. B. Masterson, of Dodge City, Kan. He killed his men in the interest of law and order. Once he shot seven men dead within a few minutes."

"How?"

415

"While in a frontier town news was brought to him that his brother had been killed by a squad of ruffians just across the street. Taking a revolver in each hand, for he shoots readily with both, in this manner (the doctor here crossed his right wrist over his left in the form of an X), he ran over to avenge his brother. The murderers became terror-stricken when they saw him coming, and hastily locked the door. Masterson jumped square against the door with both feet, bursting it open at the first attempt. Then he sprang inside, firing immediately right and left. Four dropped dead in a shorter time than it requires to tell it. The remaining three ran for their horses in a vain attempt to escape from the town. He followed them up so closely that before they reached the outskirts all three had bitten the dust."

"At another time," continued the doctor, "two Mexican half-breeds, a father and son, became very troublesome in the mining camps. They were the sharpest shots in the country, working together with a precision that made them invincible. As soon as one had emptied the chambers of his revolvers, he would reload under cover of the other. Many a miner had they murdered and relieved of his outfit and treasure. A standing reward of $500 was offered for their bodies or their heads. Finally, Masterson resolved to kill the half-breeds. They occupied a cabin in a little clearing in an almost inaccessible place in the mountains. One morning, hours before daybreak, Masterson crept to the verge of the clearing with a repeating rifle in his hands. Hidden by a friendly bush, he reclined on a sack that he had brought from his horse, which he had fastened in a glen a mile away.

"Shortly after sunrise the door of the cabin opened wide enough to permit the shaggy head of the old man to protrude. After sweeping the boundaries of the clearing with searching eyes, the head was slowly withdrawn. In a few minutes the head reappeared, followed by a body with a belt of pistols strapped around its waist and a rifle slung over its shoulder. The old man carried a water pail, and at his side walked the son fully armed. Masterson covered the old man with his rifle over a path to and from a spring at a hundred yards or so from the cabin at right angles. The father and son were conversing earnestly, seemingly unwilling to re-enter the cabin, before the door of which they stood for some time. Thirty minutes passed, which seemed hours to Masterson, before he could obtain what he considered a favorable shot. Finally, the old man made a move which uncovered his son. Masterson took advantage of this opportunity, and the young man fell to rise no more. Before the smoke revealed from whence the shot had come the old man was a corpse alongside of his boy. Cutting off their heads, Masterson placed them in his sack, and started to exhibit his trophies in order to obtain the promised reward. A two-days' ride under a hot sun swelled and disfigured the heads so that they were unrecognizable, taking advantage of which the authorities refused to pay the reward."

After the story had appeared in the *Sun*, the Kansas City (Mo.) *Journal* interviewed Bat who was then a visitor in the city. The interview was published in the issue of November 15, 1881:

Bat Masterson

BAT'S BULLETS.

A Talk With the Frontiersman Who is "On His Third Dozen," Or At Least Is Said to Be.

BAT. MASTERSON IS REFERRED TO—SOME OF HIS MORE TRAGICAL EXPLOITS. The gentleman who has "killed his man" is by no means a *rara avis* in Kansas City. He is met daily on Main street, and is the busiest of the busy throng. He may be seen on 'change, and in the congregations of the most aristocratic churches. He resides on "Quality hill," or perhaps on the East Side, or again in the five story buildings which bear in letters of living light at the doorway: "Furnished rooms for rent, 15¢, 25¢, 50¢, and $1.00 per night—reductions to regular lodgers." This ubiquitous individual may be seen almost anywhere. He may be found behind the bar in a Main street saloon; he may be seen by an admiring audience doing the pedestal clog at a variety theater; his special forte may be driving a cab, or he may be behind the rosewood counters of a bank.

If he has been here any great number of years, his "man" was

PROBABLY A PIONEER,

and died in the interest of "law and order"—at least so the legend runs. And no one dares dispute the verity of the legend, for behold the man who executed a violator of the law without waiting for the silly formalities of a judge and jury, mayhap now sits in a cushioned pew at an aristocratic church, and prays with a regularity, grace and precision only equaled by his unerring arm with a revolver, the great Western civilizer.

The gentleman who has killed his man is therefore a ubiquitous individual in this city, and may be met at every corner. He is usually quiet in demeanor, sober and thoughtful in aspect, somber in dress, and the last man on earth one would suspect of having notches on the butt end of his pistol. He may take a drink occasionally, but seldom gets drunk. He plays a game of pool at times, but never quarrels over the game. He perhaps goes down to West Kansas and tackles the tiger, but when there are loud words over the cloth of green he is not the man who utters them. He is quiet—fatally quiet. Your gentleman who has dropped his man is a blue eyed or gray eyed man in nine cases out of ten, and his hair and beard are brown, unless grizzled or whitened with the frosts of the many winters which have come and gone since the glories of the old Santa Fe trail began to wane.

Your gentleman who has dropped his man is, therefore, no uncommon individual, but when you see a man who has entered upon

HIS THIRD DOZEN,

it is about time to be civil, for he may begin to fear that material is about to run out, and may have an uncontrollable desire to hurry up and finish that third dozen. Such a gentleman was introduced yesterday evening to the iron-clad reporter of the JOURNAL, and the person referred to is none other than the famous H. [*sic*] B. Masterson, of Dodge City—known, by those whom he has not shot, as "Bat" Masterson. Mr. Masterson (it is well to be respectful) was met at the door of a Main street restaurant about 8 o'clock last evening. He was in company with Mr. H. E. Gryden, prosecuting attorney of Dodge City.

417

An introduction all round followed, and the reportorial magnet was applied to Mr. Masterson to draw out whatever reminiscences he was willing to relate of his crusade in the interests of law and order. It may be well first to describe

MR. MASTERSON'S APPEARANCE.

He is a medium sized man, weighing perhaps 150 pounds, and reaching five feet nine inches in hight. His hair is brown, his rather small mustache of the same tint, and his smooth shaven cheeks plump and rosy. His eyes are blue, and gentle in expression, his attire modest but neat, and withal he is about as far removed in appearance from the Bowery frontiersman as one could well imagine. Strange as it may seem, he is grave and quiet in demeanor, and polite to a fault. This latter characteristic was evidenced not only in his demeanor to the news man, but to an impertinent admirer (!) who wished him to go down the street and confine his attentions to him.

In answer to a very leading question, Masterson said he had not killed as many men as was popularly supposed, though he had "had

A GREAT MANY DIFFICULTIES"

and had in fact been tried four times for murder in the first degree and acquitted each time.

"How about shooting some Mexicans, cutting off their heads, and carrying the gory trophies back in a sack?"

"Oh, that story is straight, except that I did not cut off their heads," replied Bob [sic]. He then related the account of the "affair," which is in substance as follows:

A Mexican half breed and his son became very troublesome in the camp where Bat was then sojourning. They were good shots, and always worked together. They had murdered many a miner, and relieved him of his outfit and dust. A reward of $500 was offered for their heads, and Masterson, both for the sake of the money and for the purpose of ridding the camp of their dreadful presence, concluded to annihilate them. [The remainder of the story was similar to that published in the Sun except that the sack upon which Bat rested while waiting for day light was changed to a blanket and that Bat was not mentioned as having cut off the heads of the two desperadoes. The Journal article then continued:]

On May 14, 1878, his brother Ed. was

MURDERED IN DODGE CITY.

Ed. had tried to arrest a man named Walker for some offense, and had grappled with him, seizing him by both shoulders. Walker was known to be a dangerous man, and meanwhile a desperado named Wagner had come to the rescue, "Bat" heard of the trouble, and rushed to his brother's relief. Meanwhile an army of roughs had gathered to the rescue of Ed.'s prisoner, and affairs looked dark. Just then Bat arrived, and taking in the situation, he shouted, "Ed., shove him away from you." At that moment Walker drew a pistol and shot Ed through the body, inflicting a wound from which he died in about fifteen minutes. Bat immediately began firing. His first bullet laid Walker low, his second struck Wagner in the breast and glanced around, inflicting a dangerous but not fatal wound. His third and fourth shots laid

418

low two more of the mob, and three more were forever forbidden to come to Dodge City by Masterson. They walked out of town and never returned.

IN APRIL, 1881,

Bat's second brother was killed in Dodge City by two men named Updegraff and Peacock. These men remarked after the killing: "The Mastersons were born to run." Bat was then in Tombstone, Ari., and was telegraphed of his brother's murder. Though eleven hundred miles away from the scene of the tragedy, he packed his grip that day and started for Dodge City. On his arrival he learned that one of the men had said "the Mastersons were born to run," and this infuriated him more even than the death of his brother. The story is related in a very few words. Bat Masterson shot Peacock and Updegraff dead, disproving, at least, the assumption that "the Mastersons were born to run."

Regarding his exploit in Texas with the soldiers, Mr. Masterson was quite reticent. In answer to a direct question he said, "I had a little difficulty with some soldiers down there, but never mind, I dislike to talk about it." It is popularly supposed that he

ANNIHILATED A WHOLE REGIMENT

and this belief is strengthened by the fact that there was an urgent call for recruits about that time. Only West Point graduates escaped, and being officers they sought places of safety early in the engagement.

Alluding to the killing of Ed. Masterson, Mr. Gryden said: "The man walked some distance before he fell. I saw him coming, and in the darkness of the evening he seemed to be carrying a lighted cigar in his hand. I remarked to a friend that the cigar burned in a remarkably lively manner, but as the man drew near we saw that the fire was not at the end of a cigar but in the wadding of his coat. He fell dead at our feet.

THREE YEARS AGO

a gang of men attempted to rob a Santa Fe train near Dodge City. Bat, who was sheriff of that time, pursued them, and single handed and alone brought in three of the robbers at the muzzle of his revolver."

H. [*sic*] B. Masterson, the subject of the above sketch, came to Kansas in 1869. He is now but twenty-seven years of age, so that he was a mere boy of fifteen when he reached the state. For a time he shot buffalo for the government. In 1876 he was elected deputy marshal of Dodge City, and in 1878 sheriff of that county. He is a wonderful shot, and possesses the rare ability to shoot with equal precision with either hand. When he has a large audience to entertain he crosses his wrists like a letter X, and enters the action firing with two revolvers at once.

Masterson leaves the city to-day, but will return in a few days and make a brief sojourn here. Whether he has killed twenty-six men as is popularly asserted, cannot be positively ascertained without careful and extensive research, for he is himself quite reticent on the subject. But that many men have fallen by his deadly revolver and rifle is an established fact, and he furnishes a rare illustration of the fact that the thrilling stories of life on the frontier are not always overdrawn.

It is interesting to note that of the stories which could be checked, only the death of Ed Masterson falls anywhere near the truth—at least he did die. If Bat really told the other stories he obviously enlivened them in true Western story-telling style, perhaps in the same spirit as in later New York days when he would occasionally purchase a second hand revolver, notch the butt and give it away as his authentic "peacemaker."

The Atchison *Champion*, November 17, 1881, brought the whole thing back into focus with this amusing editorial:

TOO MUCH BLOOD.

THE CHAMPION is the last paper to discourage any citizen in a worthy pursuit, or to deprive any Kansan of the fruits of his honest toil, or of honors earned; but really the newspaper correspondents east and west credit some of our people with more bloodshed than rightfully or reasonably belongs to them. We do not stickle about a few tubs full of gore, more or less, nor have we any disposition to haggle about a corpse or two, but when it comes to a miscount or overlap of a dozen, no conscientious journalist, who values truth as well as the honor of our State, should keep silent. To credit unjustly a man with having killed thirty or forty people when his accomplished book-keeper, with the undertaker to check off, can only find two dozen has a tendency to bring Kansas statistics into disrepute, and also to discourage some humble beginner in the field of slaughter who has as yet sent only four or five to act as foundations for the daisies.

Somebody out at Pueblo, in a letter to the New York *Sun*, started the story that ex-Sheriff "Bat" Masterson, of Dodge City, had killed twenty-six men, and was as yet only twenty-seven years of age, with a long life of usefulness before him. Two of the men were Mexicans, whom Mr. Masterson bagged at one hunt, and whose heads, we are informed, he cut off and carried to Dodge City to sell for whatever the market price was at that time. Mr. Masterson being in Kansas City since, in company with the celebrated romancist, Mr. Harry Gryden, a Kansas City paper comes out with the *Sun's* story greatly renovated, repaired and generally beautified. Mr. Masterson is represented as modestly disclaiming the statement that he decapitated the two Mexicans. The reporter had got ahead or, rather, two heads of him there, but, while he wished no public reception, brass band, or anything of that sort, he *was* the bright and morning star that had shone on twenty-six graves, besides a fight with a fragment of the United States army, which had led to Gen. Sherman's earnest request for more men.

Now this may all be so, but we "allow" that twenty six men is a good many. They would make a string about one hundred and fifty feet long, or well on to half a cord. Incorporated, they would make a city of the third class in Kansas, and the crowd largely outnumbers the Democratic vote in some counties, though not much "deader" than that party in some localities. Twenty-six, two dozen with two "brought forward!" It may be all right, but it seems too much for a small man only twenty-seven years of age, and we call for a re-count.

From Kansas City, Bat was next heard of in Denver. The Leavenworth *Times*, May 21, 1882, stated that "Bat. Masterson has been regaling Denver newspaper reporters with the stories of old times in Dodge City, when Bat. was city marshal, and had a private graveyard staked off especially for unruly cowboys."

In August Bat was in Trinidad. The Dodge City *Times*, August 3, 1882, mentioned that Bat had sent a letter of introduction to Luke Short:

Two Chinamen are added to the population of Dodge City. They are directly from Trinidad, and brought with them letters of introduction from Bat Masterson to Luke Short. They engage in the washee business. There are four gentlemen of the Celestial Kingdom now residents of Dodge. All are pursuing the wash business. Mr. Fred Wenie provided the new arrivals with quarters. Fred is chief mogul among the Chinese. He speaks their language fluently. But he can't go their diet of rats, mice and rice.

By 1883 the Dodge City *Times*, which had once been such a staunch supporter of Bat's, and the *Ford County Globe*, his one time political enemy, had reversed their positions. This switch became apparent with the *Times* of February 8, 1883:

Bat Masterson rescued a prisoner who was in the hands of an Iowa officer, at Trinidad, some days ago. Bat tried the means of false papers, but failing in that, he took the prisoner by force. There are some people in this city who would like Bat to return. We think Trinidad is more congenial to him.

The *Times* item naturally stirred up the Irish in Bat Masterson who immediately wrote a blistering reply which was published in the *Globe*, February 20, 1883:

EDITOR GLOBE:—Sir: Having noticed a short squib in the last issue of the Dodge City Times in refference to myself and as it was evidently written with a view of doing me a malicious and willful injury, I deem it as a duty devolving on me to refute the malicious statement contained in that short paragraph. I am actuated in writing this explanation of the rescue referred to by the editorial nonentity of the Times in order to give what friends I have left in Ford county who read the Times an opportunity to judge for themselves whether my statement or that of the Times is correct.

I am accused by old Nick of the Times of having rescued a prisoner from the custody of an Iowa sheriff by force and that I first tried to get possession of the prisoner by means of false papers and finding this could not be done, I resorted to force, which is as infamously false as it is ridiculous. I will dispose of the whole statement by saying that I had no false papers of any kind, and that I did not demand the prisoner from the Iowa sheriff or attempt to take him by force, and furthermore had nothing whatever to do with the prisoner, but simply went to the train in company with Miles Mix a deputy sheriff of Chaffee county, Colorado, who had a copias warrant for the arrest of the prisoner on a charge of murder committed in Chaffee county two years ago. I was solicited by Mix to accompany him to the train which I did as a matter of friendly courtesy and nothing more.

Mr. Klaine can ascertain the truth of this statement by referring to any official in this place, or to sheriff Landes of Iowa, if he feels so disposed, but I am satisfied he has no desire to do so, as he has never been accused of either telling or writing the truth by anyone who knows anything of his Missouri or Kansas reputation. He concludes his scurrilous article by saying that some residents of Dodge City are anxious that I should return but adds that Trinidad is a more congenial place for me. To this I will say that I have no desire to return to the delectable burg, as I have long since bequeathed my interest in Dodge City and Ford county to the few vampires and murdering band of stranglers who have controled its political and moral machinery in the last few years. In conclusion I will say that Dodge City is the only place I know of where officials have taken people by brute force and without the sanction of law, and that on all such occasions the officials who committed the unlawful act never failed to receive a laudatory puff from the long haired Missourian who edits the Times.

Respectfully,

TRINIDAD, COL., Feb. 12th, 1883 W. B. MASTERSON

In May, 1883, the Dodge City "war" broke out between Luke Short and the authorities of Dodge. Before it was settled Luke had enlisted the aid of such personages as Wyatt Earp and Bat Masterson. The difficulty was involved and the settlement long in coming, but by June 10, 1883, Bat and Wyatt were on the Santa Fe headed west after completing their mission. For the complete story of the war, including the part played by Bat, *see* the section on Luke Short.

Toward the end of summer Bat returned to Dodge in a more peaceable frame of mind. The *Ford County Globe,* September 4, 1883, noticed his coming: "Ex-sheriff Bat Masterson arrived in Dodge City a few days since. We understand he will engage in the mercantile business at this place."

It is doubtful that the mercantile business interested Bat as much as the approaching election. On October 16 sheriff candidate Pat Sughrue made a statement in the *Globe* that, contrary to rumor, if he were elected Bat Masterson would not be appointed under sheriff, "not that Mr. Masterson wouldn't be fully competent and acceptable. . . ." Bat, it seems, was considered a resident of Colorado by Sughrue and not available for the position.

Apparently Bat took an active part in the election through

422

the pages of the *Globe*. At least the *Times*, November 1, 1883, thought so:

BAT MASTERSON

Col. Bat Masterson, a well known character in the west, has discarded his former illegitimate business and has adopted newspaper writing as a profession. While Col. Masterson's literary effusions do not have moral or religious tendencies, they are chaste productions in a literary way. The fine artistic style in which Col. Bat wields the pen is adding fame to his already illustrious name. Col. Masterson is now associate editor of the Ford County Globe, and the last number of that paper bears ample evidence of this statement. The Globe has long needed a brainy editor, and the substitution of brains for adipose tissue is certainly commendable, and must be highly appreciated by the readers of that journal. As a newspaper writer Bat is gaining distinction.

The *Globe*, November 6, 1883, answered:

We are charged with having an associate editor, to-wit: Mr. Masterson, and from the showing the Time's man gives the distinguished gentleman, we feel somewhat flattered. But as Mr. Masterson has left the city, the GLOBE will be rather a tame paper this week. Yet we have managed to put together a few sentences that may not set well on the opposition.

Though Bat had left Dodge he returned for election day with another ex-police officer. The *Globe*, November 13, 1883, reported:

W. B. Masterson, formerly sheriff and ex-city marshal, and Wyat Earp, ex-city marshal of this city quietly and unostentatiously dropped in onto our inhabitants early last Tuesday morning [November 6], and their presence about the polls on that day had a moral effect on our would-be moral element, that was truly surprising. It is needless to say every thing passed off quietly at the city precinct on election day.

A few days later Bat headed for Texas. The *Times*, November 22, 1883, suggested he was going as another "peace commission" to aid the gambling element:

Gen. Bat Masterson, and Col. Luke Short, (the latter returned here for one day,) left on Friday morning [November 16] for Ft. Worth, Texas. The authorities in Dallas and Ft. Worth are stirring up the gambling fraternity, and probably the celebrated "peace makers" have gone there to "harmonize" and adjust affairs. The gambling business is getting considerable "shaking up" all over the country. The "business of gambling" is "shaking" in Dodge. It is nearly "shook out" entirely.[62]

From Texas Bat went to Trinidad, Colo., where he was engaged in a controversy which was only partially explained by the Dodge City *Democrat*, January 12, 1884:

The always interesting, newsy and saucy Trinidad News, contains some letters signed W. B. M. and a reply from City Marshal Kreeger concerning the arrest of the alleged murderer, Hibbard. We are informed by under sheriff Fred Singer, that the statement of facts made by W. B. M. are verbatim et literatum, true. Yes, says Fred, and more too. But we enter our protest, and hope the News will chastise "Bat" for his deplorable carelessness in spitting out the truth about the "great and good." It was his great fault, here, and made him enemies, but the predominating streak in Bat's corporosity is that like Jim Bloodsoe, "he wouldn't lie and he couldn't flunk, I reckon he didn't know how."

In a controversy through the Trinidad *Press*, "W. B. M." shows himself almost as adept with the pen as he undoubtedly is with the six-shooter—a dual accomplishment much appreciated on the frontier. Won't "Freddie" take a hand in the writing as well as the chase?

Early in February Bat returned to Dodge. The *Democrat*, February 9, 1884, noticed his coming:

Col. Bat. Masterson, no doubt scenting a democratic victory in the breeze, dropped down from Trinidad on election day [township elections held February 5]. Bat looks as smooth, pretty and guileless as of old, and was heartily welcomed by his innumerable friends.

A few weeks later he again visited the Kansas cowtown. Said the *Democrat*, February 23, 1884:

The genial ex-sheriff, Bat. Masterson, is down amongst us. He was, we understand, drawn as a member of the Grand jury, soon to convene at Trinidad. Bat., who is constitutionally opposed to secret inquisition and condemnation courts, avoided serving as a juror by a visit to old Dodge. Better come to stay, Bat. What a genial City Attorney or rare old Police Judge you would make, eh?

By the time this notice appeared in the *Democrat*, May 3, 1884, Bat seems to have returned to Dodge City to stay:

Bat Masterson has the reputation of being able to face a six-shooter without flinching, but when a football pasted him a gentle reminder under the left ear last Tuesday evening, he gracefully retired.

The same issue of the *Democrat* reported that Bat was one of the founders of a Dodge City base ball club and was serving as its vice-president. Other interested parties included Sheriff Pat Sughrue, Robert M. Wright, A. B. Webster, and W. H. Harris. On May 17, 1884, the *Democrat* said that the driving park association, which was planning a gala Fourth of July celebration including a genuine bull fight, had named Bat to its committee on foot racing. Bat gained a little experience in the racing game by judging a contest on June 21. The *Globe*, June 24, 1884, reported the result:

A three hundred yard foot race for a purse of $1,000, between a white man named Sawyer and a colored man named Hogan, of this city, took place last Saturday afternoon [June 21], on the railroad track below the depot. Hogan won the race by about three feet, and deceived a great many who had their money up on the white man. Over three hundred people turned out to witness the race, among whom were quite a sprinkling of the fair Demi-monde. "Bat" and "Til" [William M. Tilghman?] were the judges, therefore everything was on the square, and no grumbling was heard by the losers.

Though Bat was officially interested only in the foot racing aspect of the celebration he personally was so dissatisfied with the results of, or perhaps more correctly the judging of, the horse race that he wrote a fiery letter to the Topeka *Commonwealth* which was published July 6, 1884. The letter is particularly interesting in that it represents the earliest known attempt on the part of W. B. Masterson to write a descriptive sports article:

DOINGS AT DODGE.

A LIVELY HORSE RACE, IN WHICH DISSATISFACTION
EXISTS OVER THE DECISION OF TWO JUDGES.

DODGE CITY, July 4, 1884.

TO THE EDITOR OF THE COMMONWEALTH.

The Dodge City Driving Park and Fair Association was opened on the 2d, the first thing on the programme being a three hundred yard horse race for purses amounting in the aggregate to $150, divided into two purses, first money $100, and second $50. This race turned out to be the most interesting event of the day, as there were three entries in the race, and the horses were probably the fastest for that distance of any three in the country. The little sorrel horse, Billy Burt, and the bay mare, Lulu Mc, entered by Joe Blackburn, of Gainsville, Tex., are two of the fastest quarter horses in this or any other country. Arthur Gilson's big sorrel, Lazy Bill, was the other entry.

The horses were brought up to the score and "tapped" off, Blackburn's little sorrel, Billy Burt, getting about thirty feet the worst of the send off, but notwithstanding this, and also the fact that Gilson's horse fouled him by running him into the fence, he ran a dead heat and passed under the wire with his nose along side the Gilson horse, Lulu Mc leading them about one length and a half, taking first money, but instead of the race being declared a dead heat between the two horses, and as the Hon. R. M. Wright, who was one of the judges, said it certainly was the other two judges gave the second money to the Gilson horse, thereby committing one of the most flagrant injustices ever perpetrated on a race track.

It is needless to say that the two judges who rendered this decision were prejudiced and favorable to the Gilson horse. Those who are charitably inclined attribute this action to ignorance of the rules in horse racing, while a great many are loud in their denunciation of the two men whom they claim were so biased that they were willing to stultify their honor and manhood in order to gratify their preferences. The latter is undoubtedly the case, as they both had money bet on the horse. If the directors of the association are not more careful in selecting judges, they will give this organization a bad reputation abroad. Drs. Cockey and Chouteau may be very efficient in rendering relief to any one afflicted, but their heads are too small for judges on a race track. The association had better dispense with the services of those two foptailed nonentities.

B. W. MASTERSON.

Bat made the social columns too. The *Democrat,* July 5, 1884, included a short item: "Olney Newell, of the Trinidad *News,* and his two children, were guests of Mr. and Mrs. Bat Masterson." This constitutes the first mention of a Mrs. Bat Masterson. Perhaps it was only a playful notice since other mentions—or mentions of other Mesdames Masterson—appear later.

Bat, apparently, came to know racing, for on July 19, 1884, the *Democrat* reported that "Bat Masterson and Walter Hart won $2,500 at the Newton races."

Also on July 19, the Dodge City *Kansas Cowboy,* carried this advertisement:

LOST.

Knights of Pythias watch charm. $5.00 will be paid for it if returned to
BAT MASTERSON,
Lone Star Saloon.

Along with an active interest in sports, gambling, and social fraternities Bat still had a yen for politics. The Dodge City *Times,* July 24, 1884, mentioned that Bat, heretofore a stalwart Republican, had switched to Democrat George W. Glick in the upcoming gubernatorial race:

Such men as Sheriff Sughrue, Judge R. G. Cook, Bat Masterson, and a dozen others, the backbone of the Republican party in this county, say they will support Glick for governor.—Dodge City Democrat.

We regret that the "backbone" has become weakened by this bolt. If the party can worry through the summer with a weak backbone probably a November breeze will stiffen the demented anatomical member.

When T. C. Nixon was killed by Mysterious Dave Mather on July 21, 1884, Bat was one of the first to arrive on the scene. For the testimony Bat gave at the preliminary examination *see* the section on Mather.

Habeas corpus hearings were held in the Mather case on August

16 at Larned. While there Bat came under the observations of the editor of the Larned *Weekly Optic* who wrote on August 22, 1884:

Mr. W. B. Masterson—better known as "Bat"—was in this city last Saturday in the capacity of a witness in the Mathers-Nixon murder case. He is a very quiet, unassuming little gentleman, with large, mild blue eyes, a frank and open countenance that at once inspires respect and confidence, and a most genial disposition. Add to this the ease and dignity of an educated and polished gentleman, and you have a pen picture of the most famous "killer" in the west. He was the center of all eyes while here, and many expressed surprise at his mild appearance—no doubt expecting to see a man in every respect just the very opposite.

And midst all Bat retained his reputation as one who was ready to defend himself with anything handy. The Dodge City *Cowboy*, September 27, 1884, reported a refurbishing of this reputation:

A LITTLE MELEE.

Quite a little "unpleasantness" occurred in a saloon in this city. We could not learn the cause of it, nor that there was any cause. There was a trial, however, and that developed the fact that one Mr. A. J. Howard, who is a cook in a restaurant, determined to make mince meat of Mr. Bat. Masterson, and consequently he selected as a very appropriate instrument for that purpose a carving knife from a foot to eighteen inches long. As he commenced the assault some person hallowed to Bat. that he had a gun. Then the stalward form of Masterson rose in its majesty. Fortunately perhaps, Bat. was unarmed. He seized "the first opportunity" and a chair, and went for his assailant, knocking him down. It was well for the safety of the chair and Mr. Howard's head that some person intervened. The affair drew quite a crowd, and for a moment, considerable excitement. The finale was that Mr. Howard was arrested, and brought before Esq. Cook, who gave him a good moral lesson and a fine of $25, and costs. Mr. Howard evinced considerably intelligence and claimed to be a lawyer as well as a cook. But for the want of the requisite funds, Esq. Cook "cooked the goose" of the cook by sending him to the lockup to work out the fine.

Back in the world of politics, the Ford county Republican convention held in Dodge City on October 8, 1884, next attracted Bat's attention. At this meeting he, along with W. H. Harris, ranching partner of Chalk Beeson, was named to the committee on permanent organization.[63]

In the October 21, 1884, issue of the *Globe*, now the *Globe Live Stock Journal*, an article signed by one "Coal House" cast political aspersions on R. E. Burns, Republican candidate for county attorney, E. D. Swan, candidate for probate judge, N. B. Klaine, editor of the Dodge City *Times*, and several others. The *Times* of October

23, 1884, accused Bat Masterson of writing the article. True to form, Bat was not long in answering the charge through the pages of what the *Times* called the "Gambler's *Gazette*":

DODGE CITY, KAN., Oct. 25, 1884.

ED. GLOBE LIVE STOCK JOURNAL:

I see by the last issue of the Dodge City Times, that I am accused of being the author of the article signed Coal House, which appeared in your last issue, and also that I am honored with the title of being the "boss gambler of the west."

As to the article I have this much to say, that any time the good (?) deacon of the Times or any of his scurvy outfit feel desirous of refuting any of the statements contained in Coal House's article I will consider it as an imperative duty, to sustain every allegation contained therein by the affidavit of every responsible man in Dodge City, and if I fail to do this, I will write an apology to every individual named in said article, and cause the same to be published in all the papers published in this city. There was not anything said in the article referred to that cannot be proven, and if Deacon Klaine, Burns, Schmoker, Swan, or the pestiferous cur who adorns (?) the editorial tripod of the Clipper, don't think I can furnish the necessary amount of documentary evidence to sustain my position in the matter, let them turn their monkey loose, and see whether or not I will be forthcoming.

As to being the "boss gambler of the west," I will say, that I have no desire to usurp a title that the sapient scribe at the Times office bestowed upon one of our worthy citizens, a long time before he became a defaulter in Dodge City.

W. B. MASTERSON.[64]

On November 1, 1884, Bat issued a small newspaper called the *Vox Populi* which was devoted to the political issues of the approaching election. Only one edition was published and this was probably printed on the press of the *Globe Live Stock Journal* which gave editor Masterson a flattering review November 4, 1884:

We are in receipt of the first number of the Vox Populi, W. B. Masterson, editor, which in appearance is very neat and tidy. The news and statements it contains seem to be somewhat of a personal nature. The editor is very promising; if he survives the first week of his literary venture there is no telling what he may accomplish in the journalistic field.

Only one copy of Bat's paper is known to have survived and this is held by the Beeson Museum, Dodge City. A reproduction of the entire issue appears on pp. 357-360.

November 4, 1884, saw the election of those candidates favored by the *Vox Populi*. There was no more need for it so Bat wrote its obituary which was published in the *Globe Live Stock Journal*, November 11:

Bat Masterson

DODGE CITY, KAN., Nov. 8, 1884.

ED. GLOBE LIVE STOCK JOURNAL:

The Editor of the Vox Populi through the medium of the GLOBE LIVE STOCK JOURNAL wishes to return thanks to the people of Dodge City and Ford county for the many favors received, and the courtesies extended to the Vox Populi and its editor, during the latter's brief sojourn in the journalistic field.

The Vox Populi is no more. Its mission in this world of progress and usefulness is performed. While its existence was comparatively of short duration, the wonders it performed was simply miraculous. The blows it dealt to the venomous vipers whom it opposed had a telling effect as the returns from the different voting precincts has indicated, not one of this puerile outfit have been elected. Not one of the candidates that the Vox Populi supported was defeated. The cry of the Times, that the "gang must go," recoils on its idiotic editor with the force of a cyclone. No one but an idiot would have uttered such nonsense in the first place. It must be apparent to "Old Nick" by this time that the gang is quite numerous; it also must be obvious to him that they are not inclined to "trot in his class of political nags." The Vox Populi said nothing that it is sorry for, and with this declaration it says good day.

EDITOR.

In postscript the *Globe Live Stock Journal,* November 18, 1884, commented on the opinion of the Trinidad *News*:

Bat Masterson is the editor and proprietor of a daily paper at Dodge City called the Vox Populi. Bat is an easy and graceful writer and possesses real journalistic ability. The News will be glad to hear of his making a howling success—Trinidad News. Yes, the Vox Populi was a howling success, that is, if we know anything about that kind of success, for the howling over the only issue of that paper still goes on. Bat with his paper was on the winning side in the election.

After the election Bat took a trip to St. Louis, Mo.,[65] but returned to Dodge City on November 29 just in time to be the reported victim of a different type of confidence game. The Dodge City *Times,* December 11, 1884, warily—but with obvious delight—told of Bat's being taken:

ANOTHER VICTIM.

TO THE EDITOR OF THE TIMES.

It had been hoped that the day of confidence swindlers had come to an end, but it seems that in this as in many other long wished for reforms, we are disappointed, and the confidence fiend still plies his nefarious trade in our midst gulling the innocent and cheating the verdant out of their honest (?) earnings.

Only last week there appeared upon our streets a young man, apparently about twenty-five years of age, accompanied by a boy who perhaps had seen seventeen summers—honest farmer looking sorts of fellows who might have been taken for a couple of Hoosier tenderfeet who had located claims somewhere in this Great American Desert, and had come into town to obtain a sup-

429

ply of beans and bacon. They had a common farm wagon, drawn by a pair of mules, such as is often seen here, and in addition a third mule hitched behind the wagon. Wandering apparently aimlessly about the town with mouths open and a smile that was childlike and bland, they came in contact with our enterprising fellow citizen, Bat Masterson, and in an easy green off hand sort of a way made some inquiries in regard to banking and finance, and from that the conversation drifted to agricultural and stock topics, and finally to the pulling qualities of mules in general, and this party's mule in particular, until our e. f. c. was induced to make a bet as to the pulling powers of the greenie's mule. The preliminaries were arranged, the mule was hitched to the load and walked away with it as easy as its green (?) owner did with our enterprising fellow citizen's money.

Such things ought not to be. If green horns are allowed to come in here, and swindle our unsophistacated people out of their money what are we coming to? What do we keep policemen for? If it is not to protect our citizens from being fleeced by the superior abilities of the country green horns. This fellow knew that Mr. Masterson's business had been of a financial nature nearly all his life, and that he knew no more about the pulling powers of a mule than the mule did of the ten commandments. The city has been disgraced, the character of one of our business men smirched and the perpetrator of the vile deed is still at liberty—Let him be hunted down, and let his fate be a warning to every granger that Dodge City will protect its citizens from the avaricious greed of the settlers, even if the Glick Guards have to be called out.　　　　　　　　　　　　　　　　　　　　　　　　　SCRIBE.

The Nixon-Mather murder case, mentioned before, was granted a change of venue to Edwards county and the trial held at Kinsley. Bat was one of the witnesses. The actions of the assistant prosecuting attorney riled Bat and he was not long in giving vent to his disgust. In a characteristic letter to the Kinsley *Graphic*, January 9, 1885, Bat settled the attorney's hash:

BAT SPEAKS OUT.

DODGE CITY KANSAS January 2.

ED. KINSLEY GRAPHIC:—Being one of the members of the Dodge City delegation that recently paid their respects to your little burg, as witnesses in the Mather case, I deem it but justice to your citizens to express our sincere thanks for the many courtesies extended to us while enjoying the hospitality of your city. This I do in behalf of the entire delegation who were witnesses for the defense. It is true there were some of the boys who felt a little mift at the remarks made to the jury about them by the learned gentleman who conducted the prosecution, but after considering the matter carefully from an impartial and I might add charitable standpoint, his pungent reflections upon their character and veracity are pardonable and consequently are forgiven. The fact that he is but recently from Missouri, and the further fact that gentlemanly deportment and a strict adherance to professional etiquette are not generally practiced in the lower courts of that sweet and verdant land that gave birth to the Fords

430

and Liddells, this conduct is not to be wondered at. His stigmatizing all of the witnesses for the defense, as being pimps and prostitutes can only be considered in one light, (to-wit) the utterances of a coarse, vulgar, and untutored mind.

Mr. Vandivert in all probability was considered a good lawyer in Missouri. It doesn't require much material to gain such a distinction there, but to a casual observer in Kansas, he certainly lacks many of the elements that constitute a gentleman. This frequent allusion to pimps and prostitutes, would lead the ordinary person to believe that he posessed a greater knowledge of this class, than he did of law, for he scarcely ever referred to the latter. The ordure with which he besmeared the jury was fully appreciated judging from the verdict [not guilty]. This utter failure to induce the jury to stay out more than thirty minutes should be taken by this incipient deciple of Blackstone as a lesson to guide him in the future, and should cause him to pay more attention to law, and less to blackguardism.

Wishing you all a happy New year, I am respectfully yours,

W. B. MASTERSON.

Bat, said the *Globe Live Stock Journal,* January 13, 1885, "gives his opinion right out in meetin'."

With W. H. Harris, Bat went to Topeka around the middle of January, 1885, probably to witness the inauguration of John A. Martin as governor and the start of the new state legislature.[66]

From Topeka Bat may have gone on to Kansas City but he was back in Dodge by February 12 when he answered a letter from an Iowa lady regarding the now famous town. The woman had been advised to write to "Reverend Masterson" for information. In replying Bat couldn't help unloading on a doubtlessly surprised Iowan his opinion of the arch enemy who referred to him as "Reverend." Bat's letter was published in the *Globe Live Stock Journal,* February 17, 1885:

The following letter is one in answer to a letter to W. B. Masterson, from a lady in Iowa, who says she was recommended to him as a minister, by the Post Master of this, Dodge City. She is desirous of coming here to live, and was making inquiry about the town and county:

DODGE CITY, KAN., Feb. 12th 1885.

MRS. C. LeBEAU, Harlem, Iowa.

MY DEAR MADAM: On my return from Kansas City last night where I had been for ten days, I found your letter awaiting me. I was somewhat astonished to find that you had addressed me Rev.; unfortunately, perhaps for me, I have not the honer of being a member of the clergy, and there is probably no man in this part of Kansas farther from it. I am a gambler by profession, and our esteemed (?) Post Master knew this to be so when he referred you to me. Our P. M. in doing what he thought a very smart trick, only demonstrated what has long been accepted as a fact in this community, relative to himself; (to-wit), that he lacks many of those elements that constitute a gentleman; he should at least, in my judgement, have considered you a lady and treated your letter of inquiry with the consideration that a lady is entitled to from a gentleman.

The name of our Post Master is N. B. Klaine, he is also editor of a nasty sheet published here, under the caption of Dodge City Times. He is a blatant prohibitionist, and a deacon in the Baptist church. A strictly moral man and a gentleman, as his letter refering you to me would indicate. There are several first class physicians here, all of whom are gentlemen, and any of whom he could have referred you to with a greater degree of propriety than myself. I herewith send the names of our most prominent physicians: T. L. McCarty, C. A. Milton and T. J. Wright. By addressing either of the above named gentlemen you can undoubtedly obtain the desired information.

I am respectfully,
W. B. MASTERSON.

As the Globe said on another page, "Bat Masterson has his failings like other white folks, but he is a gentleman and does not sail under false colors."

On March 1, 1885, the Kansas state census was enumerated in Dodge City. Bat was listed as being 30 years old with farming as his occupation. Bat's younger brother Tom, 26 years old, was also in Dodge, according to the census, and practicing as an attorney. Jim apparently had not yet returned to his former home.

Bat continued to hound his foe, Nicholas B. Klaine, nipping his heels whenever he had the chance. The Kinsley *Mercury*, June 6, 1885, condensed another skirmish:

The Topeka *Commonwealth* of June 3rd, contains a letter written by some person in Dodge City and signed Tanous, in which the details of a postoffice robery in that moral city are given and among other things that the article contains is a very strong reflection against Klaine, the postmaster and editor of the *Times*, intimating that he was a party to the robery. The reader is warned by the newspaper publisher that he is not bound to believe the statements contained in the letter. The handiwork of the Rev. Bat Masterson is apparent in the letter. Klaine has our profound sympathy. He is surrounded by a terrible hard gang and while he holds his own with them pretty well, they are always after him.

Later in the month an incident occurred which resulted in publicity reminiscent of that given the famous "war" of May, 1883 (this is discussed in the section on Luke Short). Little was said in the Dodge papers but much was printed outside. Since Bat played a minor role in the affair it will be mentioned only briefly.

The trouble began with the arrival of one Albert Griffin, a Kansas pioneer, editor of the Manhattan *Nationalist,* prohibitionist and officer in the State Temperance Union. Griffin had visited Dodge to lecture on the evils of whisky but once in town he attempted to obtain an injunction against the open saloons. Failing in that he began a campaign of public denouncement censuring County Attorney Mike Sutton, District Judge J. C. Strang, the Dodge City and Ford county police officers, and even Gov. John A. Martin for their lassitude in enforcing the prohibition amendment. Prohibitionist papers in Topeka helped spread Griffin's charges with vitriolic condemnations of the "sporting fraternity" of Dodge City. Of course, Bat Masterson was among those mentioned.

On July 2, 1885, in a foreword to Griffin's story of the Dodge City trouble, the Topeka *Capital* said that Bat was at the head of 300 ruffians who were bent on driving Griffin from town or, if they failed in that, killing him. The former Ford county sheriff was described as being "one of the most disreputable characters in the west." According to Griffin's own statement, however, Bat was the one who protected him from the mob which was actually led by a saloonkeeper named Sheridan.

In a prepared statement published in both the *Capital* and *Commonwealth* on July 2 Griffin stated:

Bat Masterson, the reputed leader of the lawless elements of Dodge City, had voluntarily called on us and stated that neither Colonel [A. B.] Jetmore [who was in Dodge as a representative of the attorney general to investigate the saloon business] nor myself should be molested, and when the assault was made on Dr. [S.] Galland [owner of the Great Western hotel at which Griffin was staying and an ardent local prohibitionist, according to Griffin], he went out and ordered the mob to go across the street. . . . Bat Masterson stayed in front of our room for half an hour or more, and sent the men back as they attempted to come and they finally retreated across the railroad. So far as I know, Mr. Masterson steadily did all he could to prevent any attack being made upon us, but said to me that he would not be responsible for what would happen to the citizens of the place who had taken a prominent part in the movement for the closing of the dram shops, against whom he also evidently entertains the bitterest of feelings.

Safely home, Griffin wrote in his own Manhattan *Nationalist,* July 10, 1885:

Bat Masterson is a professional gambler who has killed two or three men and shot several others. He is smart and has many elements of a leader, but is unquestionably a vicious man. He did not want Assistant Attorney Jetmore or myself killed, and the reason he is said to have given his associates was that "they could not afford to bring down upon themselves the vengeance of the

State government and the State Temperance Union." We had never had any personal intercourse, and, as he supposed we were simply operating as a matter of business . . . he probably felt no enmity toward us individualy, and as he had already "made a long record" he had nothing to gain and everything to lose by permitting an attack on us.

Nevertheless, we would, in all probability, have been killed but for the accidental fact that he happened to be in our room when the mob made its rush for our quarters. While he was with them the rioters obeyed him implicitly, but when out of his presence they were ready to follow any ruffian who proposed to *do* something. I do not suppose Masterson is one of those human tigers whose chief delight is shedding blood, but no one who knows his history and studies his face would feel safe to have in his power a friend against whom he holds a grudge. The very fact that he has the qualities of "good fellowship," "occasional generosity," "steadfastness to friends," "fluency of speech" and "cool courage," make him all the more dangerous a man in such a community.

T. J. Tate, under sheriff of Ford county, stated in an interview with a reporter of the Topeka *Commonwealth* that on the evening in question he "met Bat Masterson, who had been sworn in as deputy sheriff, and told him to see that the boys did not create any trouble. He [Bat] then went over to Griffin's room. . . ."

Later in the evening Tate saw a crowd in front of the Great Western hotel and upon inquiry was told that Dr. Galland had struck Sheridan, apparently without provocation, and Sheridan had subsequently knocked the physician down. "Bat Masterson," said Tate, "was over there and the trouble there was over very quickly." [67]

Griffin's desire for publicity was the cause of the trouble, according to District Judge J. C. Strang of Larned. In a letter to Gov. John A. Martin, July 5, 1885, he wrote:

Griffin wants to close them [the saloons] with a proclamation, or with a great hurrah—with the State Temperance Union on the ground, & the Atty-Genl. and Judge of the district Court present, to do the bidding of the representative of the said Union, so he can send out an Associated Press dispatch to the world saying Albert Griffin organizer for the State Temperance Union has closed the Saloons in Dodge.

Judge Strang felt that the end of the cattle trade would soon enforce prohibition better than could the courts, the governor and the state militia combined. He continued:

Dodge City is in a transition state and will come all right soon of itself. The quarantine law [prohibiting the entrance, between March and December, of Texas cattle "capable of communicating . . . what is known as Texas, splenic or Spanish fever" into Kansas] passed last winter is quietly

434

working out the salvation of Dodge City. The festive cowboy is already becoming conspicuous by his absence in Dodge, and ere long he will be seen & heard there, in his glory, no more forever. The cowboy gone the gamblers and prostitutes will find their occupations gone, and, from necessity, must follow. The bulk of the saloons will then die out because there will be no sufficient support left, and the temperance people can close the rest as easily as they could in any other city in Kansas.[68]

Judge Strang was right. The *Capital,* August 6, 1885, confirmed his opinion:

There are silent but irresistible forces at work to regenerate Dodge City. The passage of the Texas cattle bill, the defeat of the trail bill [providing for a national cattle trail just west of Kansas] and the rapid settlement of the country south and southwest of Dodge, have destroyed that place as a cattle town. The cowboy must go, and with him will go the gamblers, the courtesans, the desperadoes and the saloons.

The most eloquent obituary for cowtown Dodge City, however, might have been this reminiscent item in the *Globe Live Stock Journal,* January 13, 1885:

A fashion item says that leather belts are in favor. They were in favor here at one time. Perhaps there was a difference in them, ours were stuck full of cartridges, and were very popular.

In spite of Albert Griffin's denunciation of Bat, the deputy sheriff remained popular at home. At a Fourth of July celebration "a gold chain was voted to the most popular man, amid much good natured rivalry, and was voted to W. B. Masterson. The prize was to have been a gold headed cane, which we understand is yet to be given to Mr. Masterson as soon as it gets here from the east where it was ordered." [69]

On July 24 Bat ordered a fancy pistol from the Colt company. The letter he wrote is preserved in the Connecticut State Library:

OPERA HOUSE SALOON.

CARY & WRIGHT, PROPRIETORS.

Dealers in Imported Wines, Liquors and Cigars.

DODGE CITY, KAN., July 24th 1885
COLTS F. A. MG CO

HARTFORD CONN
Gents
please send me one of your Nickle plated Short 45. Calibre revolvers. it is for my own use and for that reason I would like to have a little Extra paines taken with it. I am willing to pay Extra for Extra work. Make it very Easy on trigger and have the front Sight a little higher and

thicker than the ordinary pistol of this Kind. put on a gutta percha handle and send it as soon as possible. have the barrel about the same length that the Ejacting rod is.

28-B Express-COD

Will forward Thursday July 30/85

      P. S. duplicate the above order by sending [words torn from sheet].

Truly yours

W. B. MASTERSON.

M.

"W. B. Masterson went up to Pueblo Saturday [July 25], expecting to return to-day," reported the *Globe,* July 28, 1885.

Instead of returning Bat moved on to Rawlins, Wyo., where on August 1 he refereed a prize fight. The *Globe,* August 11, 1885, said:

W. B. Masterson returned last Thursday [August 6] from a trip to Denver and Rawlins, Wyoming. At the latter place, the first inst., he acted as an umpire for [John P.] Clow, in the Clow and Hynds prize fight. He says there were special trains run from various parts of the country, and a good many parties present from long distances. There was no less than twenty thousand dollars bet on the fight, which was won by Clow, the sixth round. The Denver News publishes a full account of the fight, and says Masterson makes a ready umpire.

Though he had again journeyed to Denver in October, according to the Dodge City *Democrat,* October 17, 1885, Bat was back home in time to aid this unfortunate ex-soldier mentioned by the *Democrat,* October 24, 1885:

Probably the most pitable sight that has been seen on our streets was a young man lately discharged from the U. S. army, who is in the last stages of consumption and only kept alive by stimulents furnished by the saloon men of our city. He was trying to get home but had no money. This was told to W. B. Masterson last Tuesday evening, and he in company with two others proceeded to canvass what is called the "rough element" of the town, for funds to send the man to his home in Flint, Michigan. Mr. Masterson raised in less than half an hour $22,00 [*sic*], which was turned over to the man, who could not find words to express his gratitude. It was a touching sight, one that will not soon be forgotten. It is a well known fact, that whenever there is a contribution to be raised this element is the first to go down in their pockets and the most liberal givers. "Surely charity covers a multitude of sins."

The relationship of Bat and Clow continued through the fall. On October 23, 1885, they attended the races at Kinsley with Bill Tilghman, Charley Heinz, Ben Daniels, and Neil Brown. [70] A few days later Bat was found helping a fellow Dodge Citian escape a Kinsley process server. The *Globe*, November 3, 1885, reported:

While at Kinsley last week, we heard that a prisoner had been taken away from an Edwards county officer at Dodge City, by a mob, in which was two officers. We were greatly surprised at the statement, and on returning made enquiry, and W. B. Masterson made the following statement to us of the whole affair. A Dodge City man, by the name of Phelps, obtained a license to run a game of chance at the Edwards county fair; the last day he heard that he was going to be arrested, so left town, and sent back word he would pay the association for his license. Terry, a deputy sheriff from Kinsley, came up here and arrested Phelps, who offered to pay the officer thirty eight dollars, being the amount due the association and the officers cost; Terry would not take the money. Masterson telegraphed A. D. Cronk that he would pay that amount of money to settle, and Cronk answered all right that is satisfactory, but the prisoner will have to come down and settle with the county attorney. The boys say that means the heaviest fine the law would allow, so they wanted in some way to settle without Phelps going down there.

Just before train time Terry and his prisoner were at the depot, and Masterson went over there alone, and spoke to the officer, saying he would like to speak to him a minute; Terry walked around the telegraph office leaving his prisoner alone, and when he came back his prisoner was gone. Terry then came over on Front street and laughing, said, "boys you played it pretty fine, but I don't care, only I would like to get Cronk's money." He gave deputy sheriff Singer his warrant for Phelps, and in the afternoon went out to the fair grounds to see the glove contest; on returning to town he went up to Phelp's room over Cary's and spent over an hour talking to Phelps; what they said, nobody knows, but Terry came down stairs, hunted deputy Singer up, and took the warrant for Phelps, without making a explanation. Deputy Singer would have arrested Phelps on sight. Terry was with Phelps an hour or two after he had made his escape, why didn't he take him to Kinsley, nobody interfered in any way. There was no mob, one man, and only one, went to Terry to effect a settlement, and he walked off and left his prisoner.

We do not claim that Dodge City is the most moral place on earth, but we claim, know and can prove, that no officer ever came to Dodge City with proper authority after a man, but what our officers, if they knew of it, or were called upon, did not lend the visiting officer every assistance. If Terry had, on his arrival here, made known to one of our officers, his business, as he ought to have done, Phelps would have gone to Kinsley on the first train, even if it had been necessary to make a cordoroy road of dead men to walk on from Front street to the depot.

In early December Bat and Clow journeyed to Barber county where the fighter was scheduled for an exhibition bout with another pugilist named Ed Smith. Bat left a pleasant impression with both of the Medicine Lodge papers; the *Cresset*, December 3, 1885, said of him:

Bat Masterson, who has become famous as the leading killer of the west, is here this week making arrangements for a sparring exhibition between an Englishman by the name of Smith; and the champion pugilist of Colorado. . . . Speaking of the manager, Bat Masterson, considering his reputation, his general appearance is somewhat surprising. He certainly hasn't the appearance of a man who is said to have sent enough men up the golden stair to start a fair sized cemetery. He is a man of about the medium height, rather strongly built, with a fair complexion and a mild blue eye, this in a general way describes Bat Masterson, who is famous all over the west for his skill with a revolver, and, who is said to have put the light out of more than a score of men. It is said to his credit that he has never been known to take a cowardly advantage of an opponent, and, that the most of, if not all, of the men he has killed were more of an ornament to a graveyard than to society.

The *Barber County Index,* December 4, 1885, thought that Bat was a "plain, unassuming young man, with lots of horse sense and a very pleasant conversationalist." Could be Bat's statement that "Medicine Lodge is the best town he has ever struck in Kansas," didn't hurt his Barber county popularity.

On March 10, 1886, Bat made an astonishing switch from his previous pro-saloon feelings to inaugurate a determined crusade against the venders of alcoholic beverages. The Dodge City *Democrat,* March 13, was perplexed at Bat's actions:

Deputy Sheriff Bat Masterson has filed complaints with the county attorney against all of the saloon men and druggists in the city with the exception of Sturtevant, Garland and McCarty. Warrants have been issued and the parties have been arrested. The saloons are all closed now and the prohibitory law apparently enforced. How long this state of affairs will continue to exist is hard to tell and the object of the move will probably develope in the near future.

The Dodge City *Times,* March 11, 1886, said the action had roots in the coming city election:

CLOSED.

The saloons in Dodge were closed yesterday morning, complaints against the saloon-keepers having been made by W. B. Masterson. This step was produced by the candidacy of A. B. Webster for Mayor. Several saloon men signed the petition calling upon A. B. Webster to become a candidate for Mayor, and in consequence of this some feeling has been engendered. If Mr. Masterson will carry out his prohibition movement successfully he will have the gratitude of a generous public.

The *Globe Live Stock Journal,* March 16, 1886, agreed with the *Times* and offered a more detailed explanation:

Bat Masterson

A CHANGE OF BASE.

A petition published in the GLOBE of last week, so numerously signed by our citizens, asking ex-Mayor Webster to become their candidate for mayor at the forthcoming election, caused quite a flurry in our city as soon as it made its appearance in print, and aroused to action certain individuals who, heretofore were counted on in supporting him rather than to place themselves in direct opposition to his candidacy. While the present opponents were aware of the fact that he would be largely endorsed by the business men of the city, they did not count that one-half of the saloon druggists would also endorse him, which they did, thus leaving the other half to fight their own people and business, with great odds against them; made up of the neutral element, with a united temperance faction at their back.

This brought about a revolt within their own ranks, and ex-Sheriff W. B. Masterson and present deputy sheriff of Ford county, entered complaint against every saloon-drug store in the city, and going even further than this, including two legally licensed druggists who, he claimed were violaters of the prohibition law under which the complaint was made. Of course, arrests soon followed and all have given bonds for their appearance at our present term of district court, which convenes this day. This closed the saloons, and what the end will be, we, of course, at this time, cannot say any further than this. The ball has been started by one they counted as their friend, and even should he be inclined to hedge, the cases will not be dropped, as we are assured by the county attorney, but will be vigorously prosecuted to the end.

Ex-sheriff Masterson did not stop in his raid on saloon men, but has filed a complaint against a number of gamblers as well. He says he is going to make a general clean up in Dodge.

Prohibitionist Mike Sutton, Bat's old-time friend but long since his antagonist, sized up the situation and quickly wrote the following confidential letter (now in the archives of the Kansas State Historical Society) to the attorney general:

LAW OFFICE OF M. W. SUTTON.　　　DODGE CITY, KANSAS, 3-10" 1886

    S. B. BRADFORD
       Atty Gen. Topeka Kan.
        DEAR SIR.
           A very remarkable state of affairs exists in this city now, and as I promised to keep you posted I shall endeavor to make matters plain. There has been a faction in control of the affairs of this City composed of the very worst element that ever infested a place, and there are two other factions in this city,—one the Prohibition Party, in favor of the enforcement of all laws alike. There is another Element or party that is in favor of all laws excepting the gambling laws and laws against prohibition. The worst element or party is controled by Masterson and Bob. Wright and is under their control. Outrages have been so frequent that the saloon element is in rebellion against the "Gang" or the sure thing confidence games & holding up crowd, i. e. have taken strong ground against Wright-Masterson and their mob of confidence

men and thugs. The Prohibition crowd to which I belong has encouraged the anti-thug element and they have nominated Webster, a druggist for mayor. this has been done upon a platform which is that Wright and his gang must go. Masterson has declared that if his crowd is not to be permitted to violate the laws and rob people the saloon men shall not be permitted to carry on their nefarious schemes in selling whiskey and has made complaint against whiskey men right and left and now no whiskey can be obtained here. The Co. Atty who would not prosecute when you urged him to—who would not do his duty when the Governor desired it—who would not entertain the complaints has upon the complaint of Masterson against the saloons decided to entertain it. The saloons are closed and prohibition reigns supreme. Now this break of Masterson is to force the saloon men to accept his man for mayor and drive Webster off the track. So soon as he accomplishes this feat he will withdraw the complaints. The Co. Atty. will consent and the affair will be ended. The game can only be defeated by your appearing on the field and informing the Co. Atty. that the cases must stand. The complaints must be pushed. (You) get to be an atty. of record, and let the courts know that the cases must not be dismissed. General, now is the opportunity. We pray you come next train.

M. W. SUTTON.

Private and confidential.

Thus Bat seems to have outsmarted himself. However, the Spearville *Blade* of March 19, 1886, still reflected the prevailing opinion that " 'Bat' Masterson seems to be a bigger man just now than Attorney General Bradford, as he has succeeded in closing the Dodge City saloons, which was more than Bradford could do —or did do."

On April 1, 1886, the Dodge City *Times* reported that "Bat Masterson and his gang went west on the afternoon train of Sunday [March 28]. Where the next base of operations will be made we are not informed."

Denver was the destination and from there Bat returned to visit Dodge in September and October of that year.[71] Perhaps his September visit was in the company of Nellie McMahon with whom he had allegedly eloped a few days before. The Denver *Rocky Mountain Daily News*, September 22, 1886, reported the love affair:

NELLIE McMAHON, WIFE OF LOU SPENCER,
THE COMEDIAN, ELOPES WITH W. B. MASTERSON.

In the Superior court yesterday Mrs. Lou Spencer filed a suit for divorce from her husband, Louis Spencer. In her complaint she alleges as a cause failure to support, brutality and habitual drunkenness.

440

The case was made very sensational last evening by the discovery that Mrs. Spencer, better known as Nellie McMahon, had eloped with W. B. Masterson. The couple left the city in the afternoon, and are now supposed o be located in Dodge City, Kan.

A reporter put about last night for the full details of the sensation. Lou Spencer, the negro [black face] comedian, who has been convulsing the audiences at California hall for a week past, was sought out and pumped for the particulars of this recent domestic trouble. He talked with ease on the subject and told all the particulars.

"The trouble commenced Saturday night [September 18?]," he began. "I saw my wife sitting on Bat Masterson's knee in a box during the performance. I went to the door and called her out, and asked her what she was doing. Masterson spoke up and said that if I had anything to say to the lady I might tell it to him. I reminded him that the lady was my wife, when he struck at me with his pistol, and I struck back with my fist. Then we were arrested and taken down to the station, where we were both released and I went back to work. A dozen times my wife called me to her and asked me to forgive her, after the affair, and I told her there was nothing to forgive. Nellie kept on at her work Sunday and Monday nights and I knew nothing being up until to-night when I heard she had gone off with Masterson. We lived together happily for three years. Her charges in her complaint for divorce are all false, for she has been out of employment for five months and I have supported her. Masterson and others have been talking around my wife ever since we commenced here and with this result."

Spencer does not seem much put out because his wife has run away "with a handsomer man." He is a good negro comedian, who has held good positions in Haverly's and other large minstrel companies.

His wife, Nellie McMahon, is a beautiful woman, with a fine wardrobe and a sweet voice. Her singing has made her famous to some extent. She once sang in this city with the Kate Castleton Opera company, and was as much distinguished by her capabilities as any other member of the company.

W. B. Masterson is well known in this city. He is a handsome man, and one who pleases the ladies.

The affair has been sufficient a sensation to create a great stir about California hall.

It is questionable whether Bat married Mrs. Spencer, for a few years later, November 21, 1891, he married Emma Walters with whom he spent the remainder of his life.

Early in 1887 it was rumored that Bat Masterson had been hired to represent the city of Coronado during the county seat contest in Wichita county. The fears of the opposing town, Leoti, were presented in a letter to Gov. John A. Martin and in a dispatch to the New York *Sun*, a copy of which was reprinted in the *Wichita County Herald*, Coronado, February 24. 1887. The latter is still another example of how Bat's reputation was enhanced by inaccurate story telling:

BAT MASTERSON.—
A Leotian's Idea of Him.
[Leoti Dispatch to New York Sun.]

On Thursday the electors of this (Wichita) county will decide at the polls whether the county seat will remain here or be removed to Coronado. The fight is one of the bitterest that was ever waged in the West. It began long ago, and was decided temporarily in favor of Leoti, but since then the people of Coronado have rallied and, with the assistance of certain outsiders, they threaten to carry the day. Wichita County is some distance from Dodge City, but it is to that town that the Coronadoers look for the power which will enable them to overcome the natives. Since he retired from the desperado line, Bat Masterson has become something of a figure in frontier politics. It is only a little while ago that he was mixed up in a case of intimidation and fraud in his own county, and was summoned before the Supreme Court as a witness. Bat espoused the cause of the People's ticket in Dodge City, and by remaining at the polls all day terrified many men so that they refused to vote at all or voted as he wished. The result was the success of his party. The defeated candidates carried the matter to the Supreme Court and declared that Bat Masterson had killed a man on every birthday since he was a lad. Bat was sent for, and as he reached Topeka he was ushered into the presence of the Court. He needed an introduction, because of all the men in the room he was perhaps the most docile in appearance. Rather under the average height, he was sinewy and bronzed, but in dress and demeanor he was the peer of any one then before the Court. When asked by the Court if he had killed thirty-eight men, he said he had not, unless Indians were counted. He had killed a good many Indians. He had never killed a man except in self-defense. "I don't let any body shoot at me," he said. "If folks let me alone I never hurt them."

Bat's Dodge City killings have all had some connections with his brothers. Once when Bat was in Dodge City out of a job his brother Ed was Marshal. Hearing that ten or fifteen cow-boys were down at the Lady Grace saloon Ed went there for the purpose of enforcing an ordinance prohibiting the carrying of concealed weapons. Going into the place he commanded all there present to move up to the bar and deposit their guns with the barkeeper. All did as requested, and as Ed turned to leave he was riddled by five or six bullets from the second round of pistols which the cow-boys still retained. It so happened that Bat was passing and hearing the firing he entered the saloon, saw his brother's body on the floor, and proceeded immediately to settle the account. The result of his sudden appearance was the death of two cow-boys and the wounding of several others, all of them who were able starting for the Territory on a jump. At another time, when Jim Masterson was Marshal of Dodge City, Bat received word from his old friend, Wyatt Earp, who was then Marshal at Tombstone, that he had his hands full out there and would like a little help. Bat accordingly left Dodge City and for some months he was busy clearing out the rustlers of the Southwest.

He had hardly finished his work in this quarter when his brother Jim telegraphed him that two men named Updegraff and Peacock were in Dodge City running the town and threatening to clean out all the Mastersons that ever lived. At this Bat started for home, and, though warned by telegraph that Updegraff and Peacock would be at the depot on his arrival, he came right on to Dodge City and got off in broad day light, without a companion. About forty of the friends of Updegraff and Peacock were at the depot but Bat ignored them, and started for the town on foot. He had gone only a little ways when he saw Updegraff and Peacock coming toward him on the tracks. Bat drew his two revolvers and stood still watching them. Their friends all armed, gathered in a crowd at the depot awaiting the outcome. Presently Updegraff and Peacock ran behind a freight car and opened fire on Bat. The latter was entirely exposed, but he was the coolest man in town. His two assailants fired very frequently, but Masterson reserved his lead, and shot only as one of the others exposed himself. Updegraff and Peacock both fired from the same corner, and as they showed their heads Bat would shoot. His aim was deadly, but though he splintered the edge of the car every time, he did not hit either of his enemies.

At last Updegraff endeavored by a quick move to get a good shot at Bat, exposing himself as he did so, and quicker than a flash both of Bat's revolvers spoke. Updegraff dropped dead in his tracks with two bullets in his heart and Peacock started to run. Bat might easily have killed him, but refrained from doing so on the ground that he and Peacock used to be good friends and he could not understand what had set him against him now. The feeling of the crowd toward Bat changed at once in view of the result of the battle, and he was escorted up town, where he had a royal reception.

Since this fight Bat has had no serious encounters. He has become something of a sportsman and a good deal of a politician. At the last election in Dodge City Bat was out on a campaign tour and got a little under the influence of liquor. Approaching a saloon which was filled with people of both sexes, Bat stopped at the door, and, with a revolver in each hand, shot holes in half a dozen bottles on the bar. Then, striding in, he looked around and said: "Seeing there is nobody to drink with me, I'll take something by myself."

Pouring out a big drink he swallowed it and went away. Every man and woman in the place had stampeded as soon as he appeared.

The fact that he and his crowd are to be imported by the people of Coronado has caused intense excitement here, and every body is preparing for the worst. No man now goes out without his guns, and even the farmers go around with rifles and revolvers strapped to them. The election will be a bloody one if Bat takes part in it in the style which has made him celebrated at Dodge City.

To his majesty the Devil as a boon companion we recommend the author of the above dime novel chapter.

In the first place, Ed Masterson was not shot in a bar-room, but on the streets and afterwards entered a saloon to expire in a few moments. Secondly, Updegraff was not killed, but severely wounded. He died with smallpox one year afterwards.

The author of the above would attempt to lead the people to believe Masterson to be a drunken desperado, while it is a note-worthy fact that he was always on the law and order side, and his victims thugs, toughs and gamblers. He is inclined to be temperate, instead of intemperate.

We have not heard of Masterson or any one else coming to this county to take a hand in the election before reading the above—and would have opposed such proceedings had we known it—but after last Thursday's proceedings [in which toughs broke up voter registrations] we believe all good citizens in the county would welcome him and his friends with outstretched arms, for they would then feel safe in going to the polls, knowing that every legal voter could exercise his right of elective franchise without being covered with guns. Less than twenty men are the cause of all the trouble in this county.

If a fair election is held we are willing to abide the results, but if bull-dozing and Southern tactics are resorted to we will fight it to the end in the courts. If Bat Masterson is in this county on the day of election we can assure our readers he will not be here at the request of the citizens of this city.

Judging from available contemporary records it would appear that the *Herald* was correct—Bat had no part in the Wichita county seat war. He was in and out of Dodge several times that year, though. One visit was mentioned in the *Globe Live Stock Journal,* June 14, 1887:

W. B. Masterson, ex-sheriff of Ford County, came up from his home at Wichita last week to pay his Dodge friends a visit. Bat, as he is familiarly called, has been quite sick of late from the effects of which he has not yet fully recovered.

On October 23, 1887, he was staying at the Delmonico Hotel, registering Lamar, Colo., as his home town.[72] He was in Dodge on November 9 when in a letter to the Kansas City *Times* he denied taking part in still another county seat war. The Garfield *Call,* an active participant in the fight reprinted the letter on November 18, 1887, and added a postscript:

MASTERSON HAD NO HAND IN IT.

To THE KANSAS CITY TIMES.

DODGE CITY, KAN., Nov. 9.—In reply to a special telegram sent to the *Times* from Cimarron, Kan., on November 7, and appearing in the *Times* on No-

444

vember 8, wherein it is made to appear that I was taking an aggressive part in the Garfield county seat fight, I wish to say that I was not in Garfield county, and have taken no part, directly or indirectly, in the county seat election in said county.

W. B. MASTERSON.

This is one more of the Cimarron and Ravanna lies that they were using for electioneering purposes exposed, and it will only take time for many more of them to come to light.

In 1892 Bat was at the Colorado mining town of Creede. The Leoti (Kan.) *Standard*, March 3, 1892, reported that "Bat Masterson, well known in western Kansas, is the city marshal [at Creede]."

Lute Johnson, a correspondent for the Denver *Republican*, described Bat's activities in Creede and added an erroneous version of the Dodge City "war." The article has been preserved by the State Historical Society of Colorado in the "Lute Johnson Scrapbook," v. 1, pp. 24, 25; the exact date is unknown:

But Masterson is generally recognized in the camp as the nerviest man of all the fighters here [among whom was Bob Ford, slayer of Jesse James]. He has a record for cool bravery unsurpassed by any man in the West. He is managing the saloon and gambling house of Watrous, Banninger & Co., a rich Denver firm who have opened a branch here. Their bar receipts average $650 a day. There is no telling how much they rake off the gaming table every twenty-four hours. Every gambling device known to the West is carried on in their house, and every table is literally full night and day. Masterson walks around the house about sixteen hours out of the twenty-four, and knows everything that is going on. He is a short, thick man of 38. He wears a corduroy suit of lavender color, and a plain black tie, without jewelry of any kind. He is an Illinoisan by birth, but has been in the toughest sections of the West for twenty years. There is no blow or swagger about him. He is of unusually pleasant address, and his language is that of a man of uncommon education. His deportment and bearing are such that, despite the fact you know his record, you could never summon hardihood enough to ask him about some of his escapades. But all the toughs and thugs fear him as they do no other dozen men in camp. Let an incipient riot start and all that is necessary to quell it is the whisper, "There comes Masterson."

Masterson has been living a quiet and uneventful life at Denver for the past ten years, serving most of the time as a deputy sheriff of Arapahoe County. He has never been a desperado in the sense of other men with whom his name has been connected. He doesn't stand accused of train robbery and such like deeds of lawlessness. But many is the man who did commit these deeds that he has met and vanquished. He has been in nearly every rough town of the West since 1872 as a gambler "on the inside," as the sports term it, and he has come through many a shower of bullets unscathed, but his pistol has caused innumerable of the "opposition" to bite the dust. Perhaps the most doggedly dangerous man he ever encountered was A. D. Webster, of Dodge City, Kan. Webster in the palmy days was running a saloon and gambling house in Dodge. So was Masterson, and out of this business rivalry sprang an animosity between the two men. In a town election Webster defeated Masterson for Marshal. Not content with his political victory, Webster declared boldly that he and Masterson could no longer live in the same town. The day after the election the defeated candidate went to visit Luke Short another nervy man, in Texas. While away he heard of the threats Webster had made, and the railroads couldn't bring him back to Kansas fast enough. Some of the Marshal's friends saw Masterson on the train going out of Kansas City west, and wired him this brief, but ominous message:

"Masterson on the train bound for Dodge."

That was enough for Webster. He knew that it meant the fight of his life. He rallied the boldest of his friends around him, armed them to the teeth, and awaited the train's arrival. The Marshal's posse were in Webster's saloon close to the depot. To get to his own place Masterson was compelled to walk right by the saloon that was for the nonce a veritable arsenal. He knew the men were in there. The doors and windows were thrown wide open, and he saw the devilish gleam of their shotguns and pistols. But it didn't phase him. He stalked boldly up to the saloon with a six-shooter in each hand, looked into the door, and walked leisurely on to his own place of business, a half block away. His audacious nerve saved him. If he had faltered in his walk he would have been riddled with slugs and buckshot. The next day the friends of Webster and Masterson got them together, and unarmed they rode to a secluded spot on the outskirts of Dodge, patched up their differences, and lived together in the same town until Webster died of pneumonia.

After Dodge City, Denver became Bat's main center of interest in the West. It was from there that he wrote to his old friend of buffalo hunting days, Henry H. Raymond:

W. B. MASTERSON, President	JOHN W. CONDON, Vice-president	GUS TUTHILL, Treasurer	NELSE INNES, Secretary

OFFICE OF
OLYMPIC ATHLETIC CLUB
1320 Sixteenth Street.
All communications should be addressed to
W. B. MASTERSON, President.

DENVER, COLO., July 23— 1899

MR. H. H. RAYMOND
Vally Center   Kansas
MY DEAR FRIEND
Your letter relative to the Jester affair was received by me some days ago.

Since you spoke about the case I recall the killing of a man near big

446

hollow who had attempted to kill some one for his team. I can not now recall the names of any one connected with the tragedy excepting Mike O'Brien who I believe killed the man in the vicinity of big hollow. I remember the killing more from the fact that the Coyotes had dug up the body which remained exposed for some days and was finally reburied by some bufalo hunters. I read some thing recently in the papers regarding the Jesters but as I had entirely forgotten the case you referred to I paid no attention to the matter.

I am glad you wrote me and I assure you that I will always find time to write to old friends when ever they write to me.

I have been intending to run down home for a brief visit for some time but some how or an other conditions would arise that have prevented me from doing so.

The letter head will indicate my business at present it is easy and lucrative and I find that I can stand a whole lot of that just now. I am 45 years old and in the best of health but fleshy. I weigh 200 pounds and I find that a moderate amount of exercise will not reduce the adipose tissues as it used to do.

I hope you and your family are well and that you are as prosperous as it is possible for a person to be in Kansas.

Should you write again give me Theodores address.

> I am yours
> W. B. MASTERSON
> 1825 Curtis st.[73]

In later years, Bat forsook the West and moved to New York, where he became a sports writer and a secretary with the New York *Morning Telegraph*. On October 25, 1921, he died, quietly, at his desk.

The Kansas City (Mo.) *Daily Drovers Telegram*, November 4, 1921, paid him this last tribute:

> BAT MASTERSON. . . .
>
> A plainsman bold has just passed out,
> A man of the Last Great West;
> Fighter and hunter and great old scout,
> They have laid him away to rest.
> There's a sigh in the heart of the
>   Last Great West,
> A sigh for the days that have gone,
> For these are the men whom the West
>   loved best,
> They are quietly passing on.
> Cowboy and rider and Indian scout,
> Men of the gun and the spur,
> The Last Great West is calling out
> "Come where the breezes stir,

447

Come and sleep on my grass-grown
West,
Come and sleep in the Last Great
West."

DODGE CITY, KAS.
                                                        —E. M. BOON.

Bat Masterson, Indian fighter, death defier and once ruler of Dodge City, Kas., died in New York last week. "Bat" is said to have had the reputation of having killed 27 men with his trusty Colt in the days when the gun was mightier than the pen. His career as sheriff at Dodge City was filled with thrills and the progress of civilization caused him to seek adventure in the East as a sporting writer, where he died.

1. A copy of Colonel Miles' report and portions of the diary of Lt. Frank D. Baldwin are included in "Papers of Maj. George W. Baird, 1871-1891" (microfilm), manuscript division, Kansas State Historical Society. Masterson's employment record may be found in "Records of the War Department, Office of the Quartermaster General, Reports of Persons and Articles Hired, Indian Territory Expedition, 1874-1875," National Archives. 2. Dodge City *Times*, August 11, 1877. 3. *Ibid.*, September 22, October 6, 1877. 4. *Ibid.*, November 3, 10, 1877. 5. *Ibid.*, January 5, 1878. 6. Reprinted by the Kinsley *Valley Republican*, February 2, 1878, from its extra of January 27, 1878. 7. Kinsley *Valley Republican*, February 2, 1878. 8. *Ibid.* 9. *See, also*, Dodge City *Times*, February 9, 1878, and Kinsley *Valley Republican*, February 9, 1878. 10. *See, also, Ford County Globe*, Dodge City, February 12, 1878. 11. *See, also, ibid.*, February 19, 1878, and Kinsley *Valley Republican*, February 16, 1878. 12. *See, also, Ford County Globe*, February 26, 1878. 13. *See, also, ibid.*, March 19, 1878, and Kinsley *Valley Republican*, March 23, 1878. 14. *Ford County Globe*, March 19, 1878. 15. Kinsley *Valley Republican*, March 30, 1878; *see, also*, Dodge City *Times*, March 30, 1878. 16. *Ford County Globe*, October 29, 1878. 17. Dodge City *Times*, April 13, 1878. 18. *Ibid.*, April 13, 20, 1878; *Ford County Globe*, April 16, 23, 1878. The Mastersons had two farms in Sedgwick county. One consisted of 160 acres in Garden Plain township; it was the N. E. ¼ of Sec. 15, T. 27 S., R. 3 W. Bat's father, Thomas Masterson, paid $500 for the place in May, 1875. The other farm was in Grant township, the E. ½ of the S. W. ¼ of Sec. 24, T. 25 S., R. 1 E. 19. *See, also, Ford County Globe*, April 23, 1878. 20. Dodge City *Times*, January 12, 1878. 21. *Ford County Globe*, June 25, 1878. 22. Dodge City *Times*, June 29, 1878. 23. *Ford County Globe*, September 24, 1878. 24. *See, also*, Dodge City *Times*, December 21, 1878. 25. *See, also, Ford County Globe*, December 17, 1878. 26. "Records of the War Department, United States Army Commands, Fort Dodge, Kansas, Reports and Journals of Scouts and Marches, 1873-1879," National Archives. Microfilm copy in manuscript division, Kansas State Historical Society. 27. *See, also*, Dodge City *Times*, January 18, 1879. 28. Topeka *Commonwealth*, March 4, 1879. 29. *See, also*, Dodge City *Times*, January 18, 1879. 30. *See, also, ibid.*, January 11, 1879; *Ford County Globe*, January 14, 1879. 31. *See, also, Ford County Globe*, January 21, 1879. 32. *Ibid.*, February 11, 1879; Dodge City *Times*, February 15, 1879. 33. "Governors' Correspondence," archives division, Kansas State Historical Society. 34. *Ibid.* 35. "Marking an Epoch—the Last Indian Raid and Massacre," *Eighteenth Biennial Report of the Board of Directors of the Kansas State Historical Society*, p. 30. 36. "Governors' Correspondence," archives division, Kansas State Historical Society. 37. *Ibid.* 38. Possibly the *Times* was mistaken in saying Bat's two brothers accompanied him. James Masterson was along but there is no record of Tom being with them. The fourth member of the party, as identified by the Dodge City *Times*, February 15 and 22, 1879, was Kokomo Sullivan. 39. "Correspondence of the Adjutants General," archives division, Kansas State Historical Society. 40. "Marking an Epoch—the Last Indian Raid and Massacre," *loc. cit.*, pp. 21-31; "Governors' Correspondence," archives division, Kansas State Historical Society; *Ford County Globe*, July 1, October 21, 1879. 41. *See, also*, Dodge City *Times*, February 22, 1879. 42. *See, also, ibid.*, March 1, 1879. 43. "In

the Matter of the Petition of George H. Holcomb, for a Writ of Habeas Corpus," *Kansas Reports*, v. 21, pp. 628-637. 44. *See, also,* Dodge City *Times*, June 14, 1879. 45. *See, also, ibid.,* July 5, 1879. 46. *See, also,* Ford *County Globe*, August 5, 1879. 47. *See, also, ibid.,* September 16, 1879; Topeka *Commonwealth*, September 16, 1879. 48. "Governors' Correspondence," archives division, Kansas State Historical Society. 49. *Ibid.* 50. Dodge City *Times*, September 20, 1879. 51. *Ford County Globe*, October 28, 1879. 52. Dodge City *Times*, January 10, 31, 1880. 53. *Ford County Globe*, January 13, 1880. 54. Dodge City *Times*, January 10, 1880. 55. *See, also, Ford County Globe*, March 2, 1880. 56. Dodge City *Times*, March 13, 1880. 57. *Ibid.*, March 20, 1880; *Ford County Globe*, March 30, 1880. 58. *See, also, Ford County Globe*, April 20, 1880. 59. *See, also, ibid.,* June 1, 1880. 60. George C. Thompson, *Bat Masterson; the Dodge City Years* (Fort Hays Kansas State College Studies, Language and Literature Series No. 1, 1943), p. 36. Thompson held an interview with Thomas Masterson, Jr., on November 4, 1937. 61. *Ford County Globe*, February 15, 1881. 62. *See, also, ibid.*, November 20, 1883. 63. *Globe Live Stock Journal*, October 14, 1884. 64. *Ibid.*, October 28, 1884. 65. *Ibid.*, November 18, 1884. 66. *Ibid.*, January 13, 1885. 67. Topeka *Commonwealth,* July 4, 1885. 68. "Governors' Correspondence," archives division, Kansas State Historical Society. 69. *Globe Live Stock Journal*, July 7, 1885. 70. *Ibid.*, October 27, 1885. 71. *Ibid.*, September 28, November 16, 1886. 72. Hotel register in possession of Mrs. Merritt L. Beeson, Dodge City. 73. Copy in manuscript division, Kansas State Historical Society.

MATHER, DAVE (1845?-_____)

Dave "Mysterious Dave" Mather was one of those colorful frontier characters who was equally comfortable on either side of the line dividing lawlessness from order. The first time his name appeared in the newspapers of Dodge City, for example, he was consorting with the West's most intrepid horse thief, Dutch Henry Born. The *Ford County Globe,* January 7, 1879, reported that "Dutch Henry was at Trinidad in company with Charley Morrow, Mysterious Dave and others, and had been there several weeks. . . ." (This article was reprinted in the section on W. B. Masterson.)

Mather was in Las Vegas, N. M., later in the year and was suspected of having attempted to rob a train on August 14. The Las Vegas *Gazette*, November 4, 1879, reported the outcome of his trial and that of another famous ex-Dodgeite:

Several cases involving the question of complicity in and accessory to the various stage and train robberies were disposed of in Justice Morrison's court yesterday morning. David Radabaugh [Rudabaugh] and Joseph Martin were accused of stage robbing some weeks [ago and] were brought in and arraigned. Plead not guilty and in the absence of any prosecution were discharged. This case seems to be involved in mystery. The prosecution failed to appear, and the evidence was of such doubtful

449

character that it was uncertain as to whether a case could have been made against them or not.

Dave Mathers, accused of being accessory to the train robbery of August 14th, was arraigned. Plead not guilty. The prosecution having failed to appear, the prisoner was released and his bonds canceled. This seems to have been a case of malice as the prosecutor had no evidence whatever to sustain his charge. These two case were being held under warrants sworn out by one Texas Frank and Frank P. Whitfield. The case of Thomas Geary and Patrick H. Fleming, accused of complicity in the train robbery of October 14th, was continued until today at ten o'clock by request of the prosecution, they wishing to look into the matter a little farther before the case was brought to trial.

Apparently Dave was some sort of police officer in the area. This article from the *Gazette,* November 22, 1879, would indicate such:

Night before last, while the soldiers were stationed in the town, several of the boys went over to the new town and imbibed a little too much benzine and consequently became noisy and boistrous. They were arrested by the officers of the new town, loaded into one of Hutchinson and Company's hacks and started for the jail. One of them, however, broke away and started to run. Mr. Mathews [Mather?] ordered him to halt, but he refused to obey, whereupon he was pursued and fired at some five or six times, one of the shots taking effect in the thumb. He was then taken and lodged in the jail.

The duty of an officer is a delicate one and should be criticized as little as possible. Yet the offense committed by the soldiers seems to be rather too small a one to justify such promiscuous shooting. Not only was the life of the offender in danger, but also the lives of those on the streets, and even in the houses in the immediate vicinity. Officers as well as others should be careful about the use of firearms.

Mather was a constable, at least, and on one occasion had to kill to preserve order in his bailiwick. The Las Vegas *Daily Optic,* January 26, 1880, said:

A WRONG PLAY.
JOE CASTELLO PULLS HIS PISTOL ON DAVE MATHER AND IS KILLED.
AN UNFORTUNATE AFFAIR.

Last night, between the hours of ten and eleven o'clock, the sharp report of a pistol rang out on the night air in front of McKay's restaurant. The city being full of wild rumours about the return of the cowboys, and as it was known that three mysterious individuals rode into town after dark and asked permission to

450

Mysterious Dave Mather

SECRETE THEIR HORSES

in a blacksmith shop, not wishing to take them to a stable and have them unsaddled, everybody was sure that the bloody work of Thursday night, a night never to be forgotten in Las Vegas, was to be repeated. The streets were soon alive with

PANIC-STRICKEN HUMANITY,

who stood in groups fearful to approach the scene of the shooting lest their own lives might be sacrificed. However, as but one shot was fired, followed by the

DYING GROANS OF A MAN,

the crowds took courage and approached the prostrate form of Joseph Castello, a telegraph operator, who, about a year ago, was employed as clerk by Mr. Neely, a contractor in the Raton Pass.

PARTICULARS

Castello arrived in Las Vegas yesterday morning, having in charge a squad of men, who came from Kansas to work on the railroad extension. Some of his men indulged in frequent potations during the day and grew quarrelsome. This was particularly true of two men who had been separated by the deceased in the afternoon and he was endeavoring to prevent trouble between these two men when he met his death. As the crowds began to gather around the angry men, Castello drew his revolver as if to keep anyone off him and soon another pistol

GLISTENED IN THE MOONLIGHT

in the hands of one of his own men. At this juncture, Dave Mather appeared upon the scene and commanded the parties to put up their weapons as we had had trouble enough of late. Instead of complying with this request, Castello suddenly pointed

HIS MURDEROUS WEAPON

at Dave Mather, and with a cocked pistol in his hand, threatened to shoot the officer if he advanced another step. Dave knew his duty and knew the consequences that would result from a delay of action, so he advanced, and in the twinkling of an eye, almost before the breathless bystanders had time to see a movement on his part, he drew his trusty revolver from its place and

FIRED ONE SHOT

at the determined man, the ball taking effect in Castello's left side below the ribs, penetrating the lung, and ranging downward, passing through the stomach and liver. Of course the man could not live. He was carried to H[yman]. G. Neill's [also known as Hoodoo Brown] office where Dr. Russell Bayly was summoned and remained until six o'clock this morning when Castello breathed his last. It was impossible to save his life, but every human effort was put forth to make his dying moments as easy as possible.

THE DECEASED

Joseph Castello was aged about 22 years and was formerly employed in the construction of the St. Louis and San Francisco road. While not a slave

451

to drink, yet he was not averse to going out with the boys. Had he been duly sober on the night of his death, the sad event, which may send a mother with gray hairs to her grave, might not have occurred. His mother resides at No. 2, 128 Biddle Street, St. Louis.

THE CORONER'S INQUEST

We, the jury, sworn to inquire into the facts concerning the death of Joe Castello, now lying dead before us, find that deceased came to his death by a pistol shot fired from a pistol in the hands of D. H. Mather, constable, in the discharge of his duty as an officer; and that said shooting was justifiable and in self protection.

E. G. ARMENT
W. H. BENNETT
WM. L. GOODLETT

E. W. ZEBBEN
WM. N. MORAN
M. S. BRADLEY
H. G. NEILL, Acting Coroner

Jan 26, 1880

On March 9, 1880, the Dodge City *Ford County Globe,* quoting the Las Vegas *Optic,* said that James Allen, who had shot and killed one James Morehead in Las Vegas, "was arrested by Officer Dave Mather, the writer accompanying him into the dining room, where Allen was found quietly preparing the tables for dinner."

Mather must have quit his peace officer job in Las Vegas to go gold hunting in the Gunnison country. The *Ford County Globe,* April 27, 1880, mentioned that he, along with Charley Bassett and two other prospectors, had left Dodge City "in search of 'greener fields and pastures new.' " The Dodge City *Times,* May 1, 1880, was more explicit: "Chas. E. Bassett, 'Mysterious Dave' Mather and two others left Saturday [April 24], in a wagon well equipped, for the Gunnison country."

Perhaps New Mexico beckoned Dave back. On November 16, 1880, the *Globe* again copied an article from the Las Vegas *Optic,* this time about an escape from the city jail. The *Optic,* November 10, had ended its article with this statement: "The friends who assisted in the escape are the dreaded gang of 'killers' who infested Las Vegas last winter and made times lively for newspaper reporters. Dave Rudabaugh, 'Mysterious Dave,' 'Little Allen,' Bennett and others . . . are known to be the most desperate men on the plains."

The next year Dave was in Texas, located first at San Antonio and then at Dallas and Fort Worth. The *Optic,* April 6, 1881, said of him:

Mysterious Dave Mather

We have been shown a letter from "Mysterious Dave" Mathers, who is now in San Antonio, Texas. In it he sends regards to all of his friends except George Burton [the operator of a restaurant], who probably regretted his departure from Las Vegas (in dollars and cents) more than anybody.

In Fort Worth Dave was arrrested for theft. The Fort Worth *Democrat-Advance*, January 27, 1882, stated the case:

MYSTERIOUS DAVE.

Dave Mathews, alias "Mysterious Dave," was arrested here night before last, charged with stealing a gold chain and ring belonging to Georgia Morgan, a copper-colored coon who is proprietress of the famous "Long Branch" house of Dallas.

It seems, from Georgia's statement, that she and Mysterious Dave had been on very intimate terms, and that David had taken advantage of her confidence and stolen from her a gold ring and chain, and that he had then left the wicked city of Dallas and taken up his abode with the good people of Fort Worth.

Georgia came up here with anger in her face and a big butcher knife and a huge pistol in her hip pocket, with a desire to interview her Davy.

Not being used to seeing a female armory walking on the streets, Georgia was captured and placed in the calaboose, to be kept as a curiosity. Yesterday morning she appeased the injured dignity of this city by the contribution of $8.25 of her hard earned cash, and was allowed to go her way. But not so with Dave. As stated before, he was arrested by Officers Neely and Sands, who took him off the departing train while it was running. He was released by the city authorities yesterday morning but taken in charge and lodged in jail by the sheriff who will take him to Dallas this morning. We would not venture an opinion as to Dave's guilt or innocence, as it would be a rather precarious investment to bet on Georgia's word. The prisoner is from New Mexico and is known to some of the officers here. Indeed some of them say that he has been in the employment of Marshal Farmer during his stay here.

Mather was still in Texas in March, 1883, when this letter was written to Kansas Gov. G. W. Glick concerning him:

MANCHACO TEXAS   March 29 83

HIS EXCELLENCY GOVERNOR OF KANSAS

is there any reward offered by your State for a man is a desperado and gambler goes under the name of Mysterious Dave I have been told he is wanted in Kansas for Murder I do not know his real name but I can get him at any time   please answer if he is wanted   address

J C MARTIN
Manchaco
Travis co
Texas

453

The letter and Governor Glick's answer are both on file in the archives of the Kansas State Historical Society:

April 2-nd, 1883.
J. C. MARTIN, Esq.,
Manchaco, Texas.
Dear Sir:
Your letter of March 25-th [sic], inquiring whether the Governor of the state of Kansas offered any reward for a murderer whom you call "Mysterious Dave," is at hand. I have no information upon that subject. If I could learn the name of the individual, something might be learned in relation to the matter.
I am sir,

Your obedient servant,
G. W. GLICK

According to the *Ford County Globe*, June 5, 1883, Mather was appointed assistant marshal of Dodge City about June 1, 1883. His salary was $75 per month but on July 6, 1883, the city council raised his pay to $125. The marshal, Jack Bridges, received $150 under the new pay scale. At the end of the cattle season both salaries were dropped to $100.[1]

The appointment of Mather to the police force did not meet with universal approval. One disturbed Dodgeite wrote this letter to Governor Glick:

June 30th 1883
To
GOVERNOR GLICK
From J. De Grass of Dodge City Kansas
Dr Sir I write to you for protection which is due every Citizen of the U. S. I applied to the Justice here for a warrant to arrest a man and also called on an Officer for Assistance and he Cooly told me he would put me in the Lock up if I spoke of the Affair again. I was assaulted and abused on the Public Streets because I was not a Blackleg and gambler by the Officer and one of his Subordinate's They are running this town and a Decent Family Cannot be Tolerated by them or their Minions the aforesaid officer was taken from a Cold Deck Table and made Assistant Marshal inside of a few hours and no question's asked. I am a Stranger here only been here 6 week's but came to Settle and try to gain an Honest living for my Wife and Children I have been threatened and my Liberty has been Intimidated by a man who should give us their assistance and the other man has been held up to the public as a hero because he has the reputation of being a bad man and he has done his Man as they term it here the Town is being run by such a Class and the State of Kansas or anyone does not say Boo. I sincerely trust that you will give me your assistance or at least take some Steps to allow me to protect myself if

only my Life as he has already Killed one Man in Cold Blood and got out of it and I am in danger of my Life here hoping to hear from you I Remain Your

Obedient Sevt.
JAMES DE GRASS
Dodge City
Kans.

P. S. the man that Struck me had a gun in his pocket at the time and I was not armed as I never carry Arms. he is around the Town now and I am sick in Bed with the Doctor's attending me.[2]

Assistant Marshal Mather's first Kansas newspaper appearance by office and name—though misspelled—added no luster to his career. The role he played was of a minor nature. The *Ford County Globe*, September 25, 1883, reported:

THE CITY vs. JOHN SHERIDAN.

About a week ago our city attorney filed a complaint against John Sheridan, charging him with vagrancy, which came before Police Judge Bobby Burns. The case was called and considerable evidence was offered to show that John Sheridan had visible means of support, and that he had employment at the very time he was charged with vagrancy. It was also in evidence that Sheridan had been a gambler and had paid his monthly tax for that privilege; that on or before the first day of September he notified the city marshal that after the first of said month he would no longer follow the profession of gambling and hence could not be called on to pay a tax to the city, as he had found other employment. He was legitimately employed by Spencer & Drew to take charge of a certain shipment of cattle from here to Kansas City; he made one trip and returned to Dodge and arranged for another trip.

While he was waiting for the time to roll around for this second shipment of stock, he was arrested and brought before the city extortion mill and fined ten dollars and costs, amounting to $25.60. He refused to pay the fine and costs and was jailed,—placed in the county jail and locked up in a cell with a darkey; finding that the only relief he could get would be to pay the fine and costs, he did so and was released. In connection with the above facts we desire to say that the only evidence against this man was assistant marshal Dave Mathews, who testified that he was "loitering about saloons and had no employment or means of support so far as he knew," or against positive evidence, not only of ready means at his command for his support, but that he was actually employed in a legitimate avocation of life, and in no sense a vagrant, as charged. But the court held that he was a vagrant and that he must shell out or go to jail. This is reform with a vengeance. If a gambler gives notice that his game is closed, and that his employment is to be changed, and it is actually done, what right has a court to declare a fellow mortal a vagrant, a tramp, or anything else they failed to prove him to be. What can be the motive of these exalted dispensers of justice?

In addition to being on the city police force, Mysterious Dave also served as a deputy under Sheriff Patrick F. Sughrue. It was in this capacity that Dave took a small posse to Coolidge on September 29 in search of train robbers. The Dodge City *Times*, October 4, 1883, reported the incident:

TRAIN ROBBERS
ATTEMPT TO ROB THE CANNON BALL AT COOLIDGE.
ENGINEER JOHN HILTON KILLED—FIREMAN GEORGE FADEL BADLY WOUNDED.

Saturday morning Dodge was thrown into a high pitch of excitement by a report that a gang of roughs had attempted to rob the westward bound cannon ball at Coolidge that morning, and that engineer Hilton and fireman Fadel were killed.

It was soon learned that John Hilton was dead and his body at the Fireman's Hall, and George Fadel was at Coolidge badly wounded, and dying. A short time after he was reported dead, but we are glad to say that he is still alive and will undoubtedly recover.

The cannon ball in charge of conductor Greeley and engineer Hilton pulled into Coolidge shortly before one o'clock. After standing some ten minutes three masked men, heavily armed, appeared upon the platform, and while two of them attacked the express car one of them mounted the engine. One of them ordered Hilton to "pull out," and at the same instant sent a ball through his heart. The next instant he placed his pistol almost against George Fadel's face and fired, the ball going in the cheek and coming out of the neck. The express messenger, Peterson, promptly returned the fire into his car and repulsed the robber; several shots were then fired at the conductor, when the villains withdrew.

Dave Mather, of this city, was speedily notified to gather a posse and start in pursuit, which he did, leaving here about 4 o'clock a. m. on a special train. Another special from the west brought Sheriff Parsons and deputies from Bent county, Colo., into Coolidge about the same time. Acting in concert with Sheriff Parsons, Mather arrested two men during the day, Luny and Chambers, and the next morning Dean and Harry Donnelly were arrested at Garden City and brought down on the cannon ball, and lodged in jail.

Engineer Hilton's body reached the city on the train he ran from La Junta to Coolidge, and Fadel was taken to the hotel in Coolidge, where he remained until Tuesday, when he was brought to his brother's residence in this city. Upon his arrival here a TIMES representative obtained from him the following account of the shooting:

The train arrived at Coolidge on time and laid there some six or eight minutes, the time being occupied by Hilton and himself in oiling the engine, Hilton on the right and he on the left. This brought him next to the platform, and when nearly done his attention was drawn to a man standing on the platform by the side of the tender. This man had his hat pulled well down over his face, and as Fadel got on the cab he followed, Hilton being already up.

At this instant Hilton had his hand on the lever about to start, in response to the signal already given by Conductor Greeley. The stranger had a pistol

456

now in each hand, and pointing one at Hilton ordered him to "pull out," at the same moment firing, and Hilton fell, realing backwards and falling in the gangway. Almost simultaneously he fired from the other revolver at Fadel, who fell by the side of Hilton. He lay for a few moments insensible, and then regaining consciousness attempted to revive poor Hilton, who was dead, having been shot through the heart, the ball going in the shoulder and coming out the side. Fadel was shot in the cheek, the ball passing by the base of the ear and out the back of the head.

Of the four prisoners now in jail it is thought that at least two were implicated in the shooting, and the others were present to aid. But of course no investigation can be had until Fadel has recovered sufficiently to take the stand, as he thinks he can positively identify the man who did the shooting.[3]

The four suspected train robbers were tried and freed in short order. Notice of their trial and dismissal appeared in the *Ford County Globe,* October 9, 1883:

THE COOLIDGE TRAIN ROBBERS.

Judge Cook's court was in session each day since last Monday, before whom were arraigned four parties brought here charged with complicity in the attempted train robbery at Coolidge a week ago Friday night. The names of the individuals are Mack Dean, Harry Doneley, Lon Chambers and Jim Looney. County Attorney J. T. Whitelaw prosecuting, and H. E. Gryden defending three of the prisoners, and E. D. Swan the other. The case has been continued from day to day and but little evidence has been developed up to Saturday as to who the real parties were in this drama. The cases were again called yesterday and dismissed for want of evidence.

About the middle of November, 1883, Mather journeyed to Texas after William Byrd, an accused cattle thief out on bond who had failed to appear when summoned before court. Byrd's Dodge City bondsmen sent Mysterious Dave after him, but, if the *Ford County Globe,* November 20, 1883, were correct, Dave was not too anxious to capture his man:

WILL THE "BYRD" RETURN?

Just now a great effort is being put forth by the bondsmen of Wm. M. Byrd, charged with cattle stealing, to have him returned and again incarcerated in our jail in order that he may be here when the next term of court convenes, in February next, as it is feared he may again fail to put in an appearance when his case is called for trial the second time. If this question is to be left with Byrd himself, we do not hesitate in saying as we did before, "he will not be here." But as an officer has been dispatched for him, armed with a requisition from the Governor of this State to the Governor of Texas, it is generally supposed that he will be brought back,—that is he might have been had the officer that was sent for him kept himself and business out of print. But as soon as he arrived at Kansas City an associated press dispatch is made up for the

Kansas City Times,—it being the only paper that published it—purporting to have been sent from Austin, Texas, and to the effect that Dave Mathews, of Dodge City, had arrived in that city with a requisition on the Governor of that state for the arrest of Wm. M. Byrd, a notorious cattle thief, and that he had his man, etc. The peculiarity of this special to the Times is that Mathews was in Kansas City on the very day when the supposed special came from Austin.

Why this was done is not known to us. It certainly would not have been done by an ordinarily cautious and prudent officer before he had his man secure, as it might give him the very information he would not care to have him receive, to-wit: That an officer was after him, and thus give him another chance for his freedom. On the other hand if the officer wanted to impart such information, this was an excellent method to resort to. The question is daily asked us "will Mathews get his man?" Not under such broad-gauged tracks that he is making in his questionable efforts in endeavoring to secure him. We haven't the slightest hesitancy in saying that we don't believe that Wm. M. Byrd will ever come back, and more particularly with Dave Mathews; so Byrd's bondsmen must content themselves with Mathews' return.

On November 27, 1883, The *Globe* was able to confirm its own prediction: "Dave Mathews returned home yesterday from his trip to Texas, but minus the 'Byrd,' who is still in the bush. We said HE WOULD return without him, and so he did." [4]

Byrd did not escape completely, however, for in June, 1884, Sheriff Pat Sughrue "found his man" at Fort Worth and returned him to Dodge for trial.[5]

A more favorable report of Mysterious Dave's activities appeared in the Dodge City *Times*, December 27, 1883:

Patsey Barrett, the boy enticed from his home in Topeka, by Crider, alias Hull, was returned to his brother, who furnished transportation for the boy. Assistant Marshal Dave Mather is entitled to a good deal of credit for the feeling and interest shown in this case, and his exhibition of humanity will certainly weigh considerably in his favor.

On January 5, 1884, the Dodge City *Democrat* reported that Mysterious Dave had thwarted a break from the county jail:

Chas. Ellsworth, the accomplished young horsethief and jail breaker, was on Thursday morning discovered by deputy sheriff Mathers in possession of a vial of aqua fortis and a small saw. Dave, prying his detective nose further into the matter, discovered that the vial of strong-water was purchased by a female resident of the court house from Gallagher's drug store. Dave will probably reconstruct matters about the bastile?

In February Dave ran for constable of Dodge township. The election was held on February 5 and he was defeated by Nelson Cary and O. D. Wilson, thus placing third in the field of five.[6]

458

Mysterious Dave Mather

Dodge City's annual municipal election was held April 7, 1884, and George M. Hoover was elected mayor over George S. Emerson by a large majority. The new city council met in special session on April 10 and approved Mayor Hoover's appointments to the police force. William M. Tilghman replaced Jack Bridges as city marshal and Thomas C. Nixon assumed Mysterious Dave's post as assistant. No policemen were appointed.[7]

Dave still held his deputy sheriff's appointment, however, for on June 4 "A man named Frank Denson stole a mule from S. O. Aubery, in this city on Wednesday, and took it to Lakin and sold it. Deputies Mike Sughrue and Dave Mather captured the thief at Cimarron. Judge Cook held him in $1,000 for trial, and he is now in jail." On June 28, 1884, the Dodge City Democrat stated further that Dave, as deputy sheriff, had accompanied three other officers who were taking prisoners to the state penitentiary.[8]

On the night of July 18, 1884, the new assistant marshal took a pot shot at the old assistant marshal. The Democrat reported the incident on July 19:

ANOTHER SHOOTING.

About 9 o'clock last night the city was thrown into considerable excitement by the report that Deputy Marshal Thos. Nixon had shot ex-Marshal Dave Mather. Investigation showed that Nixon had fired one shot from his six-shooter at Mather from the foot of the Opera House stairs, Mather at the time standing at the head of the stairs. The bullet went wild, and struck in the woodwork of the porch. Mather's face was considerably powder burned, and the little finger of his left hand was injured by a splinter. The shooting was the result of an old feud, and as both men tell different stories about the shooting, and there were no witnesses, it is impossible to state who provoked the quarrel. Sheriff Sughrue promptly disarmed Nixon and he was taken to jail. Mather claims to have been unarmed, while Nixon claims Dave reached for his gun before he attempted to draw his own. Mather says he will make no complaint, but from all appearances the end is not yet.

Nixon gave bonds before Judge Cook in the sum of $800 for his appearance at the next term of court. The charge is assault with intent to kill.

Three days later Nixon was dead, shot by Mysterious Dave. The Globe Live Stock Journal, July 22, 1884, reported the homicide:

THE MURDER.

Ass't. Marshal Thomas Nixon Killed by Dave Mathers.

At about 10 o'clock last evening, while assistant Marshal Thos. Nixon was on duty at the corner of Front street and First Avenue, Mysterious Dave, (Dave Mathers), who keeps a saloon in the Opera House, came down stairs and deliberately shot him through.

459

The facts as near as we could learn are as follows: Mathers came down the stairs from his saloon and on his arrival at the foot he called to Nixon who was standing at the corner, and as Nixon turned around Mather commenced shooting at him, firing four shots, two of them striking him in the right side, one in the left side and one passed through the left nipple, killing him instantly.

Mather was immediately disarmed and lodged in jail. A cow boy, whose name we could not learn, was hit in the leg and severely wounded by a ball that had passed through Nixon's body.

Thomas Nixon was one of the oldest citizens of our city, coming here years ago to hunt the buffalo. He was made assistant marshal at the election last spring and has been an officer in our city off and on for several years, being once city marshal. He was well liked by all who knew him and a vast number of friends will miss Tom from his accustomed beat on front street. He leaves a wife and two children to mourn the loss of a loving husband and kind father.

Of Dave Mather we have but little to say. He is known at Las Vegas and wherever he has been as a dangerous man to have a quarrel with. He was once assistant marshal in this city, up to last spring when Tom Nixon took his place. While constable at Las Vegas, he killed several men, and killed his man while in a quarrel at Mobeetie, some time ago. After he had killed Nixon he said "I ought to have killed him six months ago," and as they had not been on good terms for a long time it is supposed that it was the result of an old feud.[9]

The preliminary examination of Mather was held July 31, the *Globe Live Stock Journal,* August 5, 1884, reported:

THE MATHER MURDER CASE.

The case of the State of Kansas vs. Dave Mather, who shot and killed Assistant Marshal Tom Nixon in this city on the night of July 21st, on preliminary examination was called up before Justice [W. H.] LyBrand. County [city] attorney H. E. Gryden prosecuted and Messrs. [T. S.] Haun, [E. D.] Swan and [M. W.] Sutton appeared for the defense. Considerable sparring and cross-firing was indulged in by the attorneys present on sundry motions, such as the separation of witnesses on the part of the state, which of course was all proper enough, but when it came to a similar treatment of witnesses for the defense the attorneys for the prosecution were astonished to find that there were no witnesses docketed for the defense and it was further claimed that possibly they would have none, yet desired to reserve the right to call a dozen or more should they need them. The court decided the question by ordering the witnesses for the state to be called and sworn, after which they were to be separated; the defense was not compelled to present their witnesses at this stage of the proceeding.

Just before the evidence on the part of the state was introduced county attorney [J. T.] Whitelaw was upon his feet and appealed to the court that all newspaper reporters be excluded from the room. He was afraid to have the testimony go abroad for the flimsey pretext that the reading of the same would so bias and prejudice the minds of the people of the county against the defendant, Mather, that it would be impossible to get an impartial jury in the county on the final trial of the case; that unless they would promise not to report the evidence he would move their expulsion from the court room. This was certainly an unwarranted as well as unheard of procedure on the part of the high functionary who claims to be the prosecuting attorney.

But he was met by the only representative of the press present, and by one that had seen this gag rule enforced by border ruffians during the early period of Kansas history, when Missourians made our laws as well as our law officers, the same being the Hon. John Speer, who at present is managing the Cow-boy, and to whom we are indebted for the full and complete testimony. He informed the court that it was a simple duty he owed to his employer, Col. [S. S.] Prouty and the readers of the Cow-boy that caused him to be there, and no selfish desire of his own. He knew not what other representatives of the press might be there and within the hearing of his voice, who perhaps desired the same facts that he himself was seeking. The GLOBE, he said, had made a promise that it would have a full and complete report of the proceedings, and as present manager of the Cow-boy, he did not propose to be outwitted in this matter. The court promptly sat down on Mr. County Attorney by allowing the reporters to retain their seats. (Applause in the gallery.)

The following witnesses were sworn: Dr. [C. A.] Milton, Fred Boyd, Bud Gohins, H. V. Cook, Andrew Faulkner, and Archie Franklin.

Dr. Milton was the first witness called. He stated, in reply to interrogatories, that he practiced about two and a half years in Ford County, and was a graduate of Rush Medical College, Chicago. He had examined the body of Mr. Nixon. He found seven wounds and one ball under the skin, which showed four shots in the body. The examination was not thorough enough to make a definite statement. Some things he could state positively and others only to the best of his knowledge.

I found a ball lodged in the skin of the body under upper portion of right arm. Probably all fatal—three certainly; the one which came out near the nipple must have passed through the heart and been instantly fatal. He did not anticipate answering minutely as a witness or he should have made a post mortem. Made examination about ten o'clock of next day after he was shot, July 22d.

Mr. Boyd sworn:

On the night of the 22d he was in the opera house. I was there at the time of the shooting of Thomas Nixon. I did not see the deceased when he was shot. I saw his back. I was about 8 rods and 10 feet distant. When I first noticed him he was standing talking, and I heard his name called—Tom. I looked around. He was standing leaning against the east door looking in to the right—against the north door. He had his left hand on his hip—the right hand against the door. Here he described his position as looking into the door at the game. Immediately the report of a revolver followed. Nixon exclaimed "Oh! I am shot" or "Oh! I am killed." I think he said I am killed. He turned before the revolver was fired. There was nothing in either of his hands as I could see. Nixon fell immediately on the first fire, and there were three shots in quick succession. He fell to the ground before the last three shots were fired. Tom Nixon neither drew nor attempted to draw any weapons. When he fell he was out of my sight I did not see the party who fired at the time; but I did some time before.

Cross examined:

I was standing south of center of the gambling table towards the door at the time of the shooting. I had stood there five or ten minutes—perhaps not over five. Al Rudy was standing with me. We had just met as I heard the name "Tom" called. I came from the oil-house, there. I did not discover Nixon till his name was called. I can't say how long he stood there. I don't know where or from what direction he came there. The first call "Tom," Nixon did nothing—he was called twice—at the second call he turned around. Here he described his left hand behind his back—right hand elevated and elbow crooked. He turned to the right. On first shot he turned around outside of the door from where he was standing. It wasn't over a breath from when he turned around till I heard the second shot. I did not see his back then. As he turned around I just got a glimpse of his back, and then he was out of sight. Yes, I said the other three shots immediately followed the first. I did not see Nixon when he fell. He fell immediately after the first shot. I heard him fall. It was after first shot he said "I'm killed;" when I heard that I moved ten or fifteen feet north toward the restaurant door, and remained 10 or 15 minutes. I swear positively I saw Tom at the door before any shot was fired.—I am positive I cannot be mistaken—I swear positively.

Andrew Faulkner sworn:

I was in Dodge City on the night of the 22d July. I was at the opera house, sitting outside of the saloon. I was at the head of the stairs of the opera house the time Tom Nixon was killed. I did not see him until after the first shot was fired. I saw him a second or two afterwards—did not know who it was—but found afterwards it was Tom Nixon. He was lying down when I saw him at the east door of the house. I could not see the whole body. I only saw one man around him that I know—took him to be Dave Mather. He was four or five feet from Nixon—this defendant here was the man I took him to be. When I first saw him he was standing with a revolver in his hand pointed downward, and afterwards I herd three reports of a revolver. Mather after the shooting, walked to the foot of the stairs and came up the steps. I recognized him, and it was Dave Mather. He had a revolver in his right hand as he was going up the stairs. There were four shots fired. I walked right down afterwards and looked at the dead man, he was Tom Nixon.

Cross examined:

Yes, I saw his body lying on the side walk. That was after the first shot. The man's head lay upon the door step, his feet out to the sidewalk. I saw his body at first from his feet to here (the witness putting his hand on his waist) I was standing at the head of the stairs against the banister looking into the window. When I first looked at the body it had not been moved. He was lying on his right side, and back, his feet due east or a little north of east.

(At this point the court adjourned to the residence of Mr. Cook, who was sick.)

[H. V. Cook] Sworn: I was at the opera house the night Tom Nixon was killed. Tom Nixon was close to the east door walking up to it. I saw Dave Mather. I saw Tom Nixon when the defendant shot him. Defendant said "Oh, Tom" immediately preceding the shooting Nixon was then walking toward the door of the saloon—the east door. He turned to the right when Mather spoke to him. As he wheeled Mather shot. When Mather shot him I did not see anything unusual in Nixons hands and he had nothing in his hands after he fell. He made no demonstration I could see. He fired four shots at Nixon. When he fired the three last shots Nixon was lying on the floor. He fell immediately on his firing the first shot. He advanced as he fired the three last shots till he came within four feet of Nixon. Mather then left. I think he went up stairs—at least I saw a person go up I took to be him. Tom Nixon came from the north to the door.

Cross examined:

The exact locality where I stood was on the east edge of the sidewalk. I did not stand there; I moved this way (north) probably got ahead 12 feet when the last shot was fired. Nixon was not leaning up against the door, he was walking and turned. Nixon was struggling a little when he got the last three shots. He fell on his left side and back. His feet were north east, on left side, struggling. Nixon was 18 inches or two feet from the door when he received the first shot. The last three shots after he was down. He did not step up and lean against the door before he was shot. Mather was 10 or 12 feet north from the place where he first shot.

Re-examined by State.

He fell on his left side and back, I am not positive—it might have been the reverse. It is possible he might have leaned against the door, but he must have done it quick, if so, and when I was not noticing him. I did not hear Nixon speak at all after he was shot.

Re-crossed-examined:

It was a very short time he leaned against the door if at all. He might have been. I saw one shot fired, and passed on, but stopped when I heard the other. I did see him lean against the door when the first shot was fired. He was now about 12 feet distant.

Adjourned to restaurant, to take the testimony of Archie Franklin, the cowboy who was shot accidentally by one of the balls, and was unable to appear in court. This witness was found in bed and is still suffering pretty severely.

Archie Franklin sworn:

The night Tom Nixon was shot I was standing leaning up against one of those upright pieces that hold the portico at the opera house. I had been there about 10 minutes. A young fellow of the name of Bud Gohins was standing with Tom Nixon was a little north of me—he was walking along. I couldn't say he was facing north or facing the man that fired at him. He was making no demonstrations of any kind towards defendant when first shot was fired. Both spoke but I did not understand either one. Mather fired four shots. Nixon did not fall after the first shot. He fell between the second and third shots. The second shot hit me. Mather advanced after the first shot was fired. I could not say he shot him after the first shot. Mather told him before he shot that he was going to kill him. That was before the first shot was fired, and he immediately commenced to fire. Nixon had no weapon of any kind at that time. He made no effort to get his gun that I saw.

Cross examined:

I first saw Mr. Nixon that night at the dance hall, over here. The next time I saw him was right down at the corner where the shooting was done. I went with him from the dance hall to Wright & Beverlys. Then I sat down. He sat down. We sat together 15 or 10 minutes. Potter came along the man I was working for, and we got some money from him, and walked down the street together. I next saw Nixon at the corner where the shooting was. We came from the west, and when he was shot he was coming from the west. When he was on the corner Mr. Nixon came down to that corner. As I got a little east past the door, he, Mather, came walking around the corner before I heard them exchange any words. Mather was then at the foot of the stairs. Tom advanced about two steps toward Mather, and Mather towards him, and then he commenced shooting. He told him just before he shot, that he was going to kill him. I cannot tell exactly what, but he didn't say he would "go him one," I will swear to that. I wouldn't swear to the part I did not understand. I don't swear he did not say he would go him one, in that part I did not understand. The exact words were, he would kill him. I kind of think he said "you have lived long enough," but I do not know it well enough to swear to it. Mather spoke first. I can't tell how many were there. I was leaning against a sidewalk post, about the center of the walk going north and south. Bud Gohens stood right beside me. There was no man on the east of the side walk near me. There might have been after the shooting commenced, I should judge Nixon was about five feet from the door.

Re-direct:

It is not probable Nixon could have leaned up against the door without me seeing him, he fell right by the door, could not say which side.

Bat Masterson sworn:

I was among the first to get to the body of Nixon after he was killed. I think I was the first to take hold of him. He was lying on his right side and back, and had his feet to the northeast, his head southwest, his left hand down by his left leg, his right hand up. That was just a minute after the last shot was fired. He had his revolver on him. He was lying on it. It was partially drawn out. He had no other weapons that I saw.

Cross-examination.

He had a leather scabbard made for a short Colt's revolver, heavy leather. The revolver was put in with the handle reversed. His legs from the knee down were slightly drawn up. His head lay on the door sill:

P. F. Sughrue sworn:

I was the officer that arrested the defendant. It was a Colt's 42 that he shot Nixon with.

Cross-examination.

I did not see the pistol at the time it was being shot. I did not see the shooting.

The defense offered no testimony.

464

After a long discussion on the question of admitting the prisoner to bail, the court over-ruled the motion and remanded the prisoner to jail for trial in the district court.[10]

The Topeka *Commonwealth*, August 3, 1884, included some observations on the defendant in its description of the examination:

The prisoner was brought in by Sheriff Sughrue, and as he was seated by the side of THE COMMONWEALTH reporter, we had a good opportunity of observing his demeanor. He was calm and collected, and being unrestrained, the best observer of human nature could not have selected him as the man whose life was in jeopardy. He is known to the plains men as "Mysterious Dave," was born in Connecticut, and claims to be a lineal descendant of Cotton Mather. He has been a resident of Dodge City, off and on, for several years, and has served both as Marshal and Assistant Marshal of the city. He has acted in similar capacities at other pioneer cities and mining camps, and is reported to have killed several men, but I could not hear that the charge was made that he had ever before killed a man except in the discharge of his duties. It is said that at Las Vegas he came near hanging by a mob and was saved greatly through the instrumentality of a present citizen of Dodge City. . . . The firm of Mather & Black formerly ran a dance hall in the opera house, which was suppressed, and he laid its suppression to Nixon. Nixon was an old citizen of Dodge, a buffalo hunter before the city had "a local habitation or a name," and had quite a number of men in his employ. Though rough, he is generally spoken of as a warm-hearted man and had many friends here.

During the trial, Mather sat quietly and apparently little concerned, whittling the edge of his chair, but to a close observer evidently taking every word. Observing a reporter of THE COMMONWEALTH present, he turned and advised us to give him a fair show when the other side of the story came to be told. This remark was made in an as nonchalant a manner as if we had been reporting the [recent] bull fight. . . .

The Dodge City *Kansas Cowboy*, August 16, 1884, made some comparisons between the Mathers, Dodge City Dave, and his noted kin, Cotton:

THE MATHER FAMILY.

"Since Dave got the drop on his man," his great-great-great-several-times-great-grandfather, old Cotton Mather, has become a person of historical interest. As soon as he told us who he was, we knew his family. Old Cotton is dead, or ought to be by this time. He was an eminent divine of New England, and was very active in putting down witchcraft at Salem in 1692, and wrote a book on witchcraft, in which he proved conclusively there were numerous and divers witches around Salem who were doing more deviltry than his descendant, Dave, ever did in Dodge City, or in the "great boundless west." He was, however, a man of great influence, piety, and usefulness, and with remarkable industry, wrote 382 works. His *Essay to do Good* was among his best, and was highly commended by Benjamin Franklin. In his witchcraft works, he claimed that persons possessed as well as devils, were familiar with foreign and dead languages without classical education. Spiritualists claim the same in regard to mediums to-day, but David and his contemporaries show no disposition to hang them; but when a man got "possessed" in Dodge Dave pulled his little gun, and put an end to him.

We do not know whether old Cotton was so much to blame for hanging the witches as most people imagine at this day. It was a strange infatuation. But it must be remembered that Sir Mathew Hale, one of the greatest jurists and purest of men, tried witches and even Blackstone said that to deny their existence was to deny revelation. For ought we know there may be witches in Dodge, for one of old Cotton's arguments in favor of witchcraft we see all around us, that people act queerly and seem to be possessed of spirits, and speak if not in dead in devilish languages. We have seen the witches of night around us with more devils in them than Mary Magdalena, and some of them look as pretty as the original Mary, when she donned her new hat and red stockings. In the afternoon and evenings they seem more "possessed" with spirits than any other period, unless it be near the midnight hour. The moon seems to affect them, and they sing "meet me by moonlight alone," but they are not so very particular about being alone either. The favorite hymn of the Dodge witches is

Blessed is the man who hath a little jug,
And in it some good rum,
Who passeth it about,
And gives his neighbor some.

Toward the end of August Dave was freed on bail. The *Cowboy*, August 23, 1884, reported his release:

DAVID MATHER RELEASED.

Judge [J. C.] Strang granted a writ of *habeas corpus* in the case of David Mather charged with the murder of Nixon, and after a hearing of testimony decided that it was a bailable case, and fixed his bond at $6,000. The bond was promptly given, Messrs. Digger, Drake, Emerson, Crane, Crawford, Bullard, Haun and Sutton filling the bond. They are of the best, most solid and substantial men of Ford county, representing a capital of more than $100,000. David is therefore again at large among the people. He seems to have had no difficulty in getting a bond.[11]

At the October, 1884, term of the Ford county district court Dave Mather's case was granted a change of venue to Edwards county. He was to be tried at the December term of that court, in Kinsley.[12]

Meantime it was reported that Mysterious Dave had been killed in Washington territory. The Dodge City *Times*, November 20, 1884, quoted and commented on the rumor as printed in the Larned *Optic*:

The Las Vegas Optic says a brother of Dan Mather, who is employed at a brickyard in that city, is in receipt of a letter from Washington Territory, announcing that "Mysterious Dave" was recently shot and killed by a party who quietly followed him all the way from Dodge City. It will be remembered that Dave was released from jail at the latter place on $10,000 bail.—Larned Optic.

Dave was in the city Saturday and was looking hale and hearty. He is engaged in some business at Coolidge in the west line of the State. He has not been out of the State of Kansas for some months.

Commenting on the same rumor the Dodge City *Democrat*, November 15, 1884, said: "We heard from Dave yesterday, he is 'just as well and hearty as ever he was in his life,' and is stopping at Coolidge, Kansas."

The jury in the case of State of Kansas vs. Mather rendered its verdict on December 30, 1884, after deliberating only half an hour. The Dodge City *Times*, January 8, 1885, reported the trial:

THE MATHER TRIAL.

Dave Mather, who was charged with killing City Marshal Nixon, in this city, in July last, was acquitted before a jury in the District Court at Kinsley last week. The trial occupied the time from Monday morning until Wednesday night, at 10 o'clock, at which time the jury returned a verdict of acquittal, after being out 27 minutes. The jury was composed of the very best men of Edwards county. The case was ably prosecuted by the State, being represented by Robert McCanse, county attorney, assisted by Samuel Vandivert, Esq. The defense was represented by M. W. Sutton, of Dodge City, and T. S. Haun, of Jetmore. Messrs. Sutton and Haun devoted considerable time in the preparation of the defense, and have won fame by their indefatigable and successful efforts. The reading of the verdict by the court was interrupted by demonstrations of approval by the audience. Of the trial the Kinsley Mercury says:

The trial of the case of the state against Mather was commenced on Monday and after a trial of two days and a half the jury returned a verdict of not guilty. The verdict was undoubtedly a proper one as the weight of the testimony showed that Nixon was the aggressor in the affray and that Mather was justified in shooting.

The Kinsley Graphic says:

The jury in the case Dave Mather found the defendant "not guilty" after a very few minutes deliberation. The State was represented by County Attorney McCanse and his partner, Mr. Vandivert. The defendant appeared by M. W. Sutton and T. B. Haun. The jury was a good one, and the verdict is generally regarded as the right thing under the evidence.[13]

The 1885 Kansas state census, enumerated as of March 1, listed Dave Mather a farmer, 40 years old, and a resident of Dodge City.

On May 10, 1885, Mysterious Dave was involved in another shooting, this one resulting in the death of an Ashland resident named Dave Barnes. The *Globe Live Stock Journal*, May 12, 1885, was the first to report the incident:

467

A DESPERATE FIGHT.—
ONE MAN KILLED AND THREE WOUNDED.

Sunday evening, at half past eight, the quiet of the city was broken by the sharp quick reports of fire-arms in the saloon known as Junction's, and to those in the immediate vicinity it was evident that a desperate battle was going on within. It was some time after the firing ceased before any one ventured in, when it was found that David Barnes was shot dead, James Wall, who had nothing to do with the trouble, wounded in the calf of his right leg, C. P. Camp, who was in the door, shot through both legs, and Dave Mathers cut across the forehead, the ball passing out through his hat.

The origin of the trouble as near as we can learn from the many reports, which cannot be given as facts until an investigation is made by the courts, are, that Dave Mathers and Dave Barnes were playing cards for money. Mathers won the first game and Barnes the second, when Mathers got up from the table and took the money. Barnes claimed the money was his, and said he was not treated fair. One word brought on another until Mathers made for Barnes when Sheriff Sughrue, who was present stopped him; a moment afterwards Mathers struck Barnes, and almost instantly a dozen shots were fired with the result above stated, but by whom at this time cannot be said. When the firing commenced Sheriff Sughrue caught John Barnes, a brother of the man that was killed, just as he was drawing his revolver, and held him until the firing ceased, when he arrested Cyrus Mathers, a brother of Dave, and locked him up in the county jail, and in a few minutes after arrested Dave Mathers and locked him up with his brother.

Owing to the fact that our district court convenes the ninth of next month the jury already being drawn, and the many conflicting reports, we refrain from expressing an opinion as to who is guilty of the murder, or in fault in the first place. From the statements made by parties present the firing was so rapid and the excitement so great it could not be told who all were engaged in the shooting.

The Coroner's court investigating the trouble has adjourned until Thursday.

The Dodge City *Democrat's* story of the shooting, May 16, 1885, included statements of the murdered man's brother and Sheriff Sughrue:

SUNDAY'S SHOOTING.

On last Sunday evening about 9 o'clock, a dispute arose in the Junction saloon between Dave Mather and David Barnes, over a game of cards. They were playing "seven up" at fifty cents a game, and after three games had been played, Mather got up and putting the money that was on the table in his pocket, walked over to the bar. Barnes followed him and claimed the money. Mather then struck him. Immediately the shooting commenced which resulted in the killing of Barnes, and the wounding of Mather in the head, John Wall in the leg, and C. C. Camp shot through both legs. Sheriff Sughrue happened to be there at the time, and no doubt saved two [or] three more from

468

getting killed, as every body who had a pistol was firing. After the shooting was over the sheriff arrested Dave and Josiah Mather and lodged them in jail.

As yet nothing has been produced to show who killed Barnes, or who commenced the shooting. It is claimed, however, that after Mather struck Barnes, he (Barnes) drew his pistol and fired, striking Mather in the forehead, and that a dozen shots were fired within the next ten seconds. Below we give what the brother of the deceased has to say, also Sheriff Pat Sughrue.

STATEMENT OF JOHN BARNES.

My brother told me Saturday evening that he would have to come in to prove up on some land. I came in with him on Sunday. We got here about 3 o'clock. We stopped on the other side of the bridge. We came over to the city to get our mail. My brother said: "We will go down street and see if I can find Doc Neil," who was a friend of my brother. A little boy was with us, by the name of Frank Eastman. We went into a saloon opposite the railroad track, the second door from the corner. My brother went back to look at a game of keno and afterwards came back to the counter. He was talking to two men. I do not know what they said, but heard my brother say: "I will play one or two games for pastime." One of the strangers went behind the bar and got some cards and checks. My brother and the stranger sat down to the table and commenced playing "seven up." They were playing for a dollar a game. The name of the man was Mather or Matthews, I do not know which. My brother won the first game, the other man the second and my brother the third. After my brother went out on the game the man picked up the money with his right hand and shoved the cards over to my brother with the left, then got up and walked around the table and back of my brother. My brother got up and backed away, and said: "I want my money." The man then jumped toward my brother and tried to get his hand inside of his coat. My brother pulled his coat together with both hands, the man then struck him. My brother fell back considerably and his hat fell off; he may have caught himself on his right hand. My brother had his money purse in the inside pocket of his vest or coat, I do not know which. He had exposed his money when he started to play cards.

When my brother was struck I stepped up and said to this man: "That man has some friends here and he can't be robbed in such a manner." He shoved me back and said: "What have you got to do with this?" I then attempted to pull my revolver which I carried in my hip pocket, when a man caught my hand just as [I] got hold of it, and told me to hold up. Some one caught hold of my other hand and the man had hold of my revolver with both hands. I did not know that he was the sheriff, and thought that if I gave up the revolver he would kill me. He told me he was the sheriff. I heard a ball go by my head, and turned to see where my brother was. I saw him standing at the door with his side toward me acting like he was trying to get out, and then he fell down, easy like. I think that about five shots were fired, and that three revolvers fired at once. The man that was playing with my brother stood about eight feet from me and about fifteen feet from my brother. When I turned to look this man was facing my brother and had his arm out, pointing toward him. I do not know whether he had a gun or not. The man behind the bar was duing something with his arms, and either had one or both of them stretched out. My brother was twenty-four years old this coming birthday. He sold groceries at his residence and had followed that business for six years.

STATEMENT OF SHERIFF SUGHRUE.

Last Sunday evening as I [was] passing the Junction saloon I saw quite a crowd inside, and I went in. A large number were playing keno, and Dave Mather and a stranger were playing "seven up" at a table by themselves. They seemed to be laughing and talking to each other, and I stood behind the stranger and watched the game for a while. They were playing for fifty cents a game, and I believe had played three games, at the end of which Dave Mather got up from the table and picking up the money with one hand threw the cards over toward the stranger with the other. Mather walked around the table and the stranger got up and backed off a little. The stranger then told Dave that he wanted his money, as he had won it fairly. Mather then struck the stranger, and at the same time seemed to be trying to get his hand in the inside of the strangers coat. I said to Mather: "Here, that won't do!" Just then some one in the back part of the room cried out, "Look out, he is pulling a gun!"

I turned around and saw a man trying to get his gun out. I rushed at him and grabbed his hand and revolver at the same time. The shooting then commenced. The man that I was holding did not know me. I could not see who [was] doing the shooting while wrestling with the man. I told him I was the sheriff, and he finally let go of the gun. I then turned around and saw the stranger who was playing with Mather, standing at the door, and in a few seconds he fell to the floor. Josiah Mather was behind the bar, and had a gun in his hand. While I was looking he fired three times in the direction of the stranger at the door. I immediately arrested Josiah Mather. Dave Mather had a gun on when I arrested him but it was loaded and no empty shells were in it. I then learned that the name of the deceased was David Barnes, and the man I took the gun from was John Barnes.

The preliminary will take place next Monday afternoon, and it is hoped that more light may be thrown on the case.

Deceased and John Barnes lived in Clark county, about eight miles from Fowler City, and deceased sold groceries at his residence. He leaves a wife and two children.[14]

An inquest was held on May 11 and 14 and reported in the *Globe Live Stock Journal,* May 19, 1885:

STATE OF KANSAS, }
County of Ford, } ss

An inquisition holden at Dodge City, in Ford county, on the 11th and 14th days of May, 1885, before me, R. G. Cook, J. P., Dodge township, Ford county, and acting coroner of said county, on the body of D. Barnes, there lying dead, by the jurors whose names are hereto subscribed.

The said jurors on their oaths do say that the deceased, D. Barnes, came to his death on the 10th day of May, 1885, from a gun shot wound received at the hands of David Mathers and Josiah Mathers, by means of revolvers by them fired, and that the said shooting was feloniously done.

In witness whereof the said jurors have hereto set their hands this 14th day of May, 1885.

Foreman, H. C. BAKER,
A. C. LANGLEY,
A. McCLEOD,
ANDY FALKNER,
G. T. LOGAN,
B. J. JACKSON.

Attest: R. G. COOK, Justice of the Peace, acting as Coroner.

The Mathers' preliminary examination was held on May 22. The Dodge City *Democrat* reported the hearing next day:

THE SHOOTING.

The preliminary trial of David and Josiah Mather took place yesterday, but nothing, to the testimony given at the coroner's inquest, which appeared in our last issue, was shown. Several witnesses were examined, and their testimony was all about the same. The case shows that D. Barnes was killed at the Junction saloon, and that himself and brother had gone there armed. That D. Barnes had shot at Dave Mather, (the ball going through his hat), with the intention to kill. That John Barnes attempted to pull a revolver but was hindered by the sheriff. That Josiah Mather was seen shooting over the bar. That Dave Mather was not seen to fire a shot.

That is all that has been produced so far, and the case will be very difficult to unravel. There is liable to be more light thrown on it, however, at the trial which takes place at the next term of court in June. . . .[15]

On June 11, 1885, the Dodge City *Times* said:

David and Josiah Mather, charged with murdering D. Barnes at Dodge City two or three weeks ago, after being committed to jail without bond were brought before Judge Strang at chambers in Kinsley, Tuesday upon habeas corpus. After hearing the testimony presented in support of the petition for the writ, the court permitted each of said defendants to be discharged on bond in the sum of three thousand dollars. The defendants are held for bail which they will probably be able to give.—Kinsley Mercury.

Mather apparently was able to raise the required bond for on August 4, 1885, the *Globe Live Stock Journal* reported that he was in Topeka:

Fred Singer and Dave Mathers, alias 'Mysterious Dave,' were registered at the Windsor Hotel on the 31st ult, while Mike Sutton was booked at the Copeland. We failed to see any notice of either having been interviewed by Topeka newspaper reporters.

In the same issue the *Globe* carried this item from the Kinsley *Mercury*:

471

The murderer, Dave Mathers, left Dodge City last Wednesday night as Jeff Davis left the Southern Confederacy—in boots petticoats and hoopskirts. It had come time to kill Dave, and not desiring to be present on that occasion he disguised himself as Jeff Davis and took his hoops in hand and walked. His whereabouts will probably be known when it comes time for his next killing.—Kinsley Mercury.

Dave did leave the city, but not in petticoats, the reports of his going, like others from this city, become wonderfully magnified as they travel from home.

Next, Mather, perhaps not so surprisingly, became a lawman again. The Dodge City *Times*, August 20, 1885, recorded his appointment in a Barber county town:

Dave Mather, on Friday last was appointed City Marshal of New Kiowa, and at once entered upon the duties of the office. Dave was marshal at Dodge City, and also assistant marshal for a long time. Dave makes a good officer.[16]

The Mather brothers apparently never stood trial for the murder of Barnes, escaping that ordeal by jumping their $3,000 bonds. The *Globe Live Stock Journal*, December 8, 1885, reported the act: "In the Mathers case they failed to appear, and their bonds were forfeited."

1. *Ford County Globe*, July 17, 24, August 14, September 11, 1883; Dodge City *Times*, November 15, 1883. 2. "Governors' Correspondence," archives division, Kansas State Historical Society. 3. *See, also, Ford County Globe*, October 2, 1883. 4. *See, also*, Dodge City *Times*, November 29, 1883. 5. *Ford County Globe*, June 10, 1884; Dodge City *Times*, June 12, 1884. 6. "Ford County Commissioners' Journals," v. A, p. 444; Dodge City *Democrat*, February 2, 9, 1884. 7. Dodge City *Times*, April 10, 1884; *Ford County Globe*, April 15, 1884. 8. Dodge City *Democrat*, June 7, 1884; *see, also*, Dodge City *Kansas Cowboy*, June 28, 1884. 9. *See, also*, Dodge City *Times*, July 24, 1884; Dodge City *Democrat*, July 26, 1884; Dodge City *Kansas Cowboy*, July 26, 1884. 10. *See, also*, Dodge City *Democrat*, August 2, 1884; Dodge City *Kansas Cowboy*, August 2, 1884; Dodge City *Times*, August 7, 1884. 11. *See, also*, Dodge City *Kansas Cowboy*, August 9, 1884; Dodge City *Democrat*, August 16, 1884; Larned *Weekly Optic*, August 22, 1884. 12. *Globe Live Stock Journal*, October 28, 1884; Dodge City *Democrat*, December 20, 1884. 13. *See, also*, Dodge City *Democrat*, January 3, 1885. 14. *See, also*, Dodge City *Times*, May 14, 1885. 15. *See, also, ibid.*, May 28, 1885; Dodge City *Democrat*, May 30, 1885. 16. *See, also*, Dodge City *Democrat*, August 22, 1885.

MEAGHER, MICHAEL (1844?-1881)

In the spring of 1871 Wichita was a rapidly growing trading center, officially less than one year old. Though the Chisholm trail ended at Wichita, the cattle trade had bypassed the town and continued on north via Joseph G. McCoy's trail extension to Abilene.

Declaring he would have shot even "if it had been Jesus Christ," Billy Thompson gunned down Ellsworth Sheriff C. B. Whitney, August 15, 1873.

FRED SINGER, twice marshal of Dodge City, was also a deputy U. S. marshal and under sheriff of Ford county. (A Beeson restricted photo.)

SADIE RATZELL was the indirect cause of Joseph McDonald's death at the hands of Marshal Singer in July, 1881. (A Beeson restricted photo.)

TOM SMITH was Abilene's first chief of police. His career ended in 1870 when he was nearly decapitated by a crazed, ax-wielding settler.

J. H. "DOG" KELLEY and C. S. HUNGERFORD. Kelley was a Dodge City mayor and lover of fine hunting dogs, hence his nickname.

Views of Ashland in 1886 (*above*), and in 1887.

BILL SMITH, candidate for Wichita city
marshal, slugged it out with Wyatt Earp in
a pre-election brawl in 1876.

DAVE ST. CLAIR, gambler, killed cowboy
Bing Choate in Dodge City, July 6, 1884.
(A Beeson restricted photo.)

PAT and MIKE SUGHRUE, twin brothers, led twin careers as sheriffs of
adjoining Ford and Clark counties during the 1880's.

BILL TILGHMAN, Dodge City saloon owner, police officer, rancher, and gun-slinging warrior in county-seat fights, left Kansas in 1889 to resume his police career in Oklahoma.

Kansas artist Henry Worrall's drawing of Texas Longhorns being loaded on cars of the Kansas Pacific at Abilene, 1871.

CHAUNCEY B. WHITNEY was one of the courageous band of scouts who withstood repeated Indian attacks at Beecher Island in 1868. He survived, only to be gunned down in Ellsworth five years later.

BILLY THOMPSON, who shot Sheriff C. B. Whitney, August 15, 1873, while in a drunken rage.

BEN THOMPSON, a brother, brazenly took over Ellsworth's Main street while Billy made his escape.

GOVERNOR'S PROCLAMATION.

WHEREAS, C. B. Whitney, Sheriff of Ellsworth County, Kansas, was murdered in the said county of Ellsworth, on the 15th day of August, 1873, by one William Thompson, said Thompson being described as about six feet in height, 26 years of age, dark complexion, brown hair, gray eyes and erect form; and Whereas, the said William Thompson is now at large and a fugitive from justice;

NOW THEREFORE, know ye, that I, Thomas A. Osborn, Governor of the State of Kansas, in pursuance of law, do hereby offer a reward of FIVE HUNDRED DOLLARS for the arrest and conviction of the said William Thompson, for the crime above named.

IN TESTIMONY WHEREOF, I have hereunto subscribed my name, and caused to be affixed the Great Seal of the State. Done at Topeka, this 22d day of August, 1873.

(L. S.)

THOMAS A. OSBORN.

By the Governor:
W. H. SMALLWOOD, Secretary of State.

Reward poster for the capture of William "Billy" Thompson.

The quartet which gunned its way into the Medicine Valley Bank at Medicine Lodge on April 30, 1884. *Left to right* in the center: John Wesley, cowboy; Henry N. Brown, marshal of Caldwell; Billy Smith, cowboy; Ben Wheeler, assistant marshal of Caldwell. Shortly after this picture was taken, Brown was shot and the others were hanged by "persons unknown!"

Not until May, 1872, when the Wichita and Southwestern provided rail connections to the Santa Fe main line at Newton, did Wichita achieve status as a major cowtown and cattle shipping center. Those first years were not ones of tranquility and even tenored growth, however. From the time the town was incorporated, July, 1870, until its elevation to a city of the third class, April, 1871, at least three marshals were appointed only to resign or leave for unexplained reasons. Nor was death on the city streets unknown, as the shooting of J. E. Ledford (which was detailed in the section on Jack Bridges), February 26, 1871, testifies.

Becoming a city of the third class meant that an election had to be held to replace the board of trustees with a mayor and city council. Shortly after the election, the new mayor, E. B. Allen, and the council appointed William Smith marshal of the town. Three days later, on April 13, Smith resigned; the council then appointed Mike Meagher. The assistant marshal was Meagher's brother, John. In addition two policemen were appointed, Bradford Dean and Adam Roberts.[1] Each of the officers was formally notified of his selection and was required to complete an oath of office. That of Marshal Meagher was typical:

WICHITA KANSAS
April 13th 1871

MR MICHAEL MEAGHER
SIR
You have this day been duly appointed *City Marshal* in and for the city of Wichita by the City Council of said City. You will proceed at once to be duly qualified.

E B ALLEN
Mayor of the City of Wichita

Attest
O. W. BROMWELL
Clerk

THE STATE OF KANSAS)
County of Sedgwick)
City of Wichita)
I Michael Meagher do solemnly swear that I will support the constitution of the United States, the constitution of the State of Kansas, and faithfully discharge the duties of the office of City Marshal in and for the City of Wichita, so help me God.   MICHAEL MEAGHER
Subscribed and sworn to before me this 13th day of April A. D. 1871.
W. B. HUTCHINSON, Deputy Clerk [2]

The first city council of Wichita lost little time in making preparations for the suppression of lawlessness and disorder. On April

481

15 motions were carried which instructed the city attorney, D. C. Hackett, "to draft an Ordinance prohibiting the carrying of deadly weapons concealed or otherwise," and by which "the City Marshal and two members of the Council (to be selected by the Mayor) [would] be appointed as a committee to ascertain the probable cost of building a suitable City Jail or Calaboose. . . ." On April 29 the council authorized the marshal to "procure six suitable badges to be worn by himself, Asst. Marshal & Policemen." [3]

The fifth and sixth badges were put to use on May 7, 1871, with the appointment of Policemen William E. Reid and Charles W. Allen. On May 25 another man was added when Daniel Parks was named second assistant marshal. The same day, however, the resignations of Bradford Dean and Adam Roberts were accepted.[4]

The contract for building the city jail was let on June 1, 1871, early construction to be paid for by poll and dog taxes.[5] So quickly was the work accomplished that by June 22, 1871, the Wichita *Tribune* was able to say: "Our saloon keepers sell the drinks, and next week Marshal Meaher will be ready to cell the drinker's.— In the new calaboose."

At a meeting held June 28 the council authorized acceptance of the new jail provided the "committee on calaboose" judged it satisfactory after a careful inspection.

With a new jail open for business and five men on the police force the city council apparently felt ready to enforce its ordinances. At the June 28 meeting Mike Meagher was instructed

to procure at the expense of the City two pine boards 3 X 4 feet and have the following inscribed thereon.

NOTICE.

All persons are hereby forbidden the carrying of firearms or other dangerous weapons within the city limits of Wichita under penalty of fine and imprisonment.

By Order of the Mayor

M MEAGHER

City Marshal

The Marshal is furthermore instructed to have one of the boards erected at the River ford at the foot of Douglas Avenue and the other near the Harris House or some prominent place near the Emporia Road.[6]

The summer of 1871 was apparently peaceful enough. One of the main police duties was the rounding up of stray hogs. As the sum-

Mike Meagher

mer progressed the force experienced a heavy turnover in personnel, including all positions except that of marshal. On August 16 Assistant Marshal John Meagher resigned and upon the recommendation of the marshal Policeman Simon K. Ohmert was promoted. Others who served on the force included George D'Amour and Charles Bratton.[7]

On November 15, 1871, Emil Werner, a local saloon keeper, filed a letter with the city council protesting the treatment he had received at the hands of the Wichita police force:

To His Honor the Mayor & Councilmen of the City of Wichita

I Emil Werner your petitioner would respectfully beg leave to represent to your Honorable body that on the 25th day of October A. D. 1871, Michael Meagher, City Marshal, S. K. Ohmert, Deputy Marshal & Charles Bratten, policemen, Entered my saloon situated on Main Street, No. 17, Wichita, Kansas, and arrested and took from thence a Soldier who was sleeping at one of my tables. In a short time they returned and Charles Bratten entered the saloon the other two, viz: Meagher & Ohmert remaining at the door. Bratton spoke to me, telling me, that I would get myself into trouble, selling liquor to men and getting them drunk. I replied that I paid license for selling liquor, and that what I paid to the city, helped to pay his Salary. He (Bratton) without any further provocation, struck me with a revolver and knocked me down and before I could get up the others (Meagher & Ohmert) rushed in, and all three of them struck me with revolvers and sling shots and took me off to the Calaboose, without Coat or hat, tearing my shirt off of my back, locking my door and taking possession of my keys.

I was finally released upon the payment of the sum of $5.00 into the City Treasury, together with the costs of Suit. Amounting in all to Eight Dollars. Now therefore I would respectfully request your Honorable Body to examine into these Statements that I have here made, and if you find them correct & true, to remit & repay the fine & costs imposed upon me, Otherwise to act as in your judgment you deem best

And this your Petitioner humbly prays

Emil Werner.

Wichita Nov. 15th 1871.

Apparently little came of Emil Werner's protest. At the council meeting of December 6, 1871, it was decided that "action on the petition of Emil Werner complaining of certain acts of the City Police be indefinitely postponed."[8]

In spite of the fact that it was not stimulated by the Texas cattle trade, Wichita was a fast-growing city. Before the next annual election it was elevated to city of the second class, and by law the city marshal was elected by the people, not appointed by the council. The Wichita City *Eagle*, April 12, 1872, reported:

THE CITY ELECTION

The City election in Wichita, under the special act making it a City of the second class, on the 2nd passed off pleasantly and with no particular excitement, and no trouble of whatever character. The men chosen to fill both the offices of the city and school board are among our most substantial and leading men, in which we congratulate our citizens. The following are the names of those chosen for the various positions and are taken from our contemporary the *Vidette.*

Dr E. B. Allen was elected Mayor, J. M. Atwood, Police Judge, . . . M. Meagher, Marshal, . . . S. K. Ohmert and George D'Amour, Constables.[9]

On April 12, 1872, only a month before the Wichita and Southwestern guaranteed the town temporary supremacy in the Texas cattle trade, the Wichita *Eagle* described the place as a model of propriety:

The Sabbath day is as strictly observed—Sunday as quiet, upon the streets of Wichita, as in any town of the west. It is remarked by strangers, who, almost unanimously, wonder and congratulate. No drunkenness or street brawling can be seen or heard at any time, notwithstanding the place is a frontier town not three years old, containing all the elements, excepting those of drunkeness and rowdyism, to be found usually in frontier towns. For this moral state of affairs much is due the city government and the wholesome manner in which its ordinances are administered, as also, to the intelligent and moral element that predominates in the society of the place. None others than members of the police force are permitted to carry arms. Upon each avenue leading into the city is a large sign prohibiting the carrying of deadly weapons under penalty of both fine and imprisonment. We can assure all who contemplate making this live city their home, immunity from all danger, and from even disagreeable disturbances.

Six weeks later the railroad had arrived and things were immediately different. Foreseeing a riotous summer's cattle season, the *Eagle,* May 24, 1872, suggested:

It must be evident to every one that the police force of this city should be uniformed, that is, the members should be compelled to wear such a suit as would be recognizable upon the instant. Another thing, each man's beat should be prescribed and in that quarter he should stay except when called upon for assistance by the chief or some other member. We have seen men whooping full of whisky and no police in sight. It is also evident that ways and means must be devised for doubling up the force for at least two or three months during the summer. Should our authorities fail in holding their present power woe will be the sure result.

The newspaper's advice was heeded to an extent. On June 7, 1872, the *Eagle* reported that more men had been hired for the force:

Mike Meagher

The city council at their meeting on Wednesday night appointed two additional men on the police force of the city, viz: Geo. D'Amour and D. F. Parks. Two secret police were also appointed for a certain duty. The council also incorporated a certain piece of ground near the bridge and extended police authority over it.

A few days later the city council commissioned even more policemen. The minutes of the city council record the appointments:

On motion of Mr Schattner the following resolution was adopted

Resolved that the Mayor be empowered to appoint as special police men the men acting as toll keepers on the bridge whose duty it shall be to take possession of and safely keep all fire arms carried by parties crossing the bridge into the City of Wichita said policemen to receive such salary as may be paid them by the bridge company. . . .

Resolved that the Mayor be empowered to purchase fifty brass copper or tin checks to be supplied to said toll keepers and it shall be the duty of the said toll keepers upon receiving any fire arms from any person crossing the bridge into the City of Wichita to give one of the checks for the same and upon the presentation of which when leaving the City the party owning the fire arm shall be entitled to receive the same.[10]

Much of the time of the police force continued to be taken up with the collection of fines, shooting stray dogs, and other routine duties. Occasionally things would get lively but usually were stopped before they could get well developed. The Wichita *Eagle*, June 14, 1872, reported such an incident:

The efficiency of our police was exemplified on Wednesday night [June 12]. Mike Meagher, city marshal, went into a saloon and took a knife from a fellow's girdle that looked like a butcher's cleaver elongated. There were two together, and they had concluded to stand him off, but finally were persuaded not to do so.

A week later the *Eagle* reported a similar happening:

A fellow that said he would get away with a policeman before night, kept his word. We saw them going toward the calaboose early in the evening. Several of them have got away with the police the same way this week.

The only incident of continued interest that summer of 1872, was the arrest, escape and re-arrest of a man named Sam Teets whom Mike Meagher had captured for the authorities of a Pennsylvania town. The crime charged, seduction, was of minor importance in light of the strange transactions carried on through legal channels. The Wichita *Eagle*, July 26, 1872, reported the first arrest:

One Samuel Teats was arrested here on Saturday [July 20], by Marshal Mike Meagher, upon a telegram from the sheriff of Alleghany, Penn. Teats is charged with seduction, under a promise of marriage, which is a crime under the laws of Pennsylvania punishable by imprisonment in the penitentiary. We understand that Meagher had previously received a descriptive letter from the authorities in Alleghany, which enclosed a photograph, so there remains little room for mistake. The reward offered for his arrest was $1,000. Teats was taken before 'Squire Van Trees and in default of proper bail was committed to prison until such time as the Pennsylvania authorities can be heard from.

Further developments were reported in the *Eagle*, August 2, 1872:

Last week we noticed that one Samuel Teats had been arrested by Mike Meagher, upon a telegram from Alleghany City, Penn. Within a day or two after the arrest, a man representing himself as B. F. Clark, chief of police of the above city, made his appearance, provided with a requisition from the governor of Pennsylvania. The night of Clark's arrival Teats, with other prisoners, was furnished tools, and, but for timely discovery, would have made his escape in a few minutes. The next night Clark hand-cuffed Teats and put him aboard the north-bound train. While he was procuring his tickets his prisoner walked out of the car and out into the dark and liberty. The pretended chief made no attempt to recapture his bird, but took the train and left. There is a strong suspicion that all is not as it should be. A thousand dollars had been offered for the arrest of Teats, a per cent. of which Clark forked over to Mr. Meagher. We believe the latter officer has addressed the city authorities of Alleghany upon the subject.

A week later, August 9, 1872, the Teets affair was again on the *Eagle's* pages:

The B. F. Clark great detective embroilment caused some little talk and feeling among our citizens and officers. The associate dispatches, as also Clark's affidavit, both of which set forth that our officers connived at Teets' escape, are a complete tissue of lies, colored only by circumstantial truths. Unfortunately for the great shyster detective, some half dozen of our best citizens were perfectly cognizant of all that occurred at the depot. John Meagher, the sheriff [elected November 14, 1871], Mike Meagher, city marshal, J. C. Morehouse, deputy sheriff, and Jim Antrim, policeman, are too well known, and have had their courage and honor too often tested, for the affidavit of a cowardly sneak to affect them in Wichita. Clark was either bribed by Teets or scared out of his wits, and from the fact that Teets offered $500 for his release, and the other fact that Clark had a long private conversation with his prisoner, our people entertain but little doubt that Clark was bought. The Pittsburgh *Dispatch* divines the whole matter in the following brief paragraph, which, although misapprehending the facts as far as our officers are concerned, lays Mr. Clark, the pusillanimous coward, wide open:

"While we do not doubt that the town officials of Wichita, Kansas, when Chief Clark went to receive the prisoner Teets, acted very strangely and did all they could do to prevent his being brought away, we cannot help feeling surprised that an experienced detective like Mr. Clark should have left his

prisoner in charge of any one for a moment, especially on so trivial an excuse
as that of purchasing a ticket. He surely ought to have known that none of
the other officers had any authority to hold Teets, after he had been delivered
to him and receipted for."

On August 16, 1872, the *Eagle* reported the end of the Samuel
Teets case:

The Teets affair has had at last a practical solution, and a solution that
proves our boys not only honest, but entirely too sharp for the boobies who
undertook to slander them. After all the blowing that was done, the boys
quietly made up their minds that Mr. Teets should be put into the hands of
the governor of Kansas. To this end they went quietly to work. Nobody
suspicioned anything, or knew that the boys were up to anything until Mike
Meagher and George D'Amour came marching into town the other night with
the escaped bird. He had been caught at a camp on the high prairies, fifty
miles northwest of Wichita, near Hutchinson. The old calaboose was not to be
trusted, and Mr. Teets now lies in the Topeka jail awaiting orders from the
governor of Pennsylvania. The boys have been at great pains and expense in
maintaining their honor against the foul slander of Clark, and we congratulate
them upon the happy turn of affairs.

It is possible that Mike Meagher held a commission as either a
township or county officer in addition to his office of city marshal
for on August 9, 1872, the Wichita *Eagle* reported that he had
made an arrest far from the boundaries of the town: "Mike Meagher
rode sixty miles day before yesterday and arrested two persons
who had stolen a team of horses from a Missourian."

In October Mike again stopped a disturbance before it had a
chance to make much headway. The *Eagle*, October 10, 1872,
said: "Our efficient city marshal, with his usual promptness and
unflinching bravery, on last Tuesday [October 8] quelled a disturbance which was fast assuming dangerous proportions by
promptly arresting and lodging the leaders in the calaboose."

Two weeks later Mike prevented a fight between two Wichita
lawyers from taking disastrous proportions. The *Eagle*, October
24, 1872, stated:

A slight difference of opinion arose between two law partners of our city,
on Tuesday afternoon [October 22], which they concluded to decide with
their muscle. After taking several rounds on the sidewalk in front of their
office, and failing to come to any definite decision, they were invited by the
city marshal to postpone further trial until the opening of the police judge's
court next morning.

As the *Eagle* said in the same issue: "As far as we know, we believe the boys who look after the good order of the city are seldom complained of."

Within two months, however, a local gambler found something to complain about. It was explained in his petition to the Wichita city council:

To THE HONERABLE MEMBERS OF THE COUNCIL OF THE CITY OF WICHITA.

Your petitioner I Thayer states that in the year 1872 he was running a room for gambling purposes & paying for the privilege therefore into the City Treasury of Wichita City the Sum of fifty dollars per month. Your petitioner further states that having paid said sum of money to said city he was allowed to run his the said Gambling room that during this time the Marshal of said city demanded the further sum of twenty five dollars which sum was paid the said marshal. Your petitioner states that it was stipulated & agreed upon that it was to cost your petitioner no more than fifty dollars for running said gambling rooms. that the said city of Wichita was not Entitled to the further sum of twenty five dollars which your petitioner paid to said city of Wichita, wherefore your petitioner prays that said twenty five dollars be remitted to him, or be applied on his saloon license for the month of February 1873.

I THAYER [11]

Except for the disappearance of Assistant Marshal George D'Amour (which was covered in the section on D'Amour) police business in Wichita was slow indeed until well into the spring of 1873. True, the annual city election in April enlivened the scene somewhat but the new mayor, James G. Hope, and the city council, in retaining Meagher in the marshal's office (his post was once again appointive), removed the trauma of change from the police department. Except for William Dibbs, who was named policeman, all were veterans in the business. Dan Parks, the new assistant marshal and W. E. Harwig, policeman, had both served on the Wichita force before. Meagher, of course, was beginning his third term.

In May, Mike nabbed two robbers from eastern Kansas. The *Eagle*, May 15, 1873, reported:

Two criminals, Clark Whisner and Tom Preston, who robbed a store at Twin Springs, Linn county, last week, were arrested by Marshal Meagher, ironed and in the calaboose within an hour after their arrival in town. The only means he had for identifying the thieves was a letter which he had received from the authorities of Linn, which speaks well for his efficiency and discretion as an officer. Wichita is a poor rendezvous for rogues.

A few days later Meagher prevented possible bloodshed. The *Eagle*, June 5, 1873, stated:

A drunken man assaulted Mr. Fox, the omnibus agent, last Thursday night [May 29], with a pistol. The owner of the pistol would have figured in the hearse at a funeral next day, but for the opportune appearance of the city marshal.

Apparently Mike Meagher sought to resign from the police force but his resignation was laid over at the July 9, 1873, meeting of the city council. At the meeting of July 16 a motion was made to increase the marshal's salary but this too was postponed. Judging from later salary payments neither the resignation nor the increase was approved.[12]

On July 24, 1873, the police force came in for some criticism from the Wichita *Eagle*:

Two horse races occurred last Saturday [July 19], upon one of which $800 was staked. Of course the decision was unsatisfactory, and much loud talk during the evening was indulged in upon the street, especially at the postoffice crossing on Douglas avenue, where three or four fellows on horses blocked up the walk and cursed and swore, and used vile epithets at a fearful rate, regardless of passing ladies. We noticed two policemen in the crowd who never raised a hand to clear the walk, to stop the oaths or to make an arrest. At last John M. Steele [Mike Meagher's brother-in-law] stepped forward and told the horsemen to clear the track.

On Christmas day, 1873, Wichita was thrown into a frenzy of excitement by what appeared to be an accidental fire and death. Subsequent investigation indicated, however, that neither the fire nor the death was accidental. For weeks the case of the "Christmas Cremation" was the big news in Wichita and little else in the way of police activity was reported upon. Though Mike Meagher was city marshal at the time of the fire the role he played in the drama was small and his name appeared in the cast only infrequently. Finally the climax was reached and two young men, Arthur Winner and Joseph W. McNutt were convicted of the murder of one W. W. Sevier and sentenced to be hanged. The most active police role was taken by an ex-policeman, William Smith, and further details of the crime appear in the section devoted to him.

Possibly because of the excellent job of detection done by Smith in the Christmas cremation case he was appointed Wichita city marshal by the mayor and city council who were elected in April, 1874. Thus on April 15, 1874, Mike Meagher, after serving three years, was no longer on the city police force.[13]

For a while Mike stayed in Wichita, then went into the Indian territory. He was in Wichita when the *Eagle,* May 7, 1874, reported:

Ex-Marshal Mike Meagher, with a long whip in hand, and astride of a vicious kicking mustang, to which was attached a shaky buggy containing two men, presented such an unusual scene as to frighten a pair of long eared mules, attached to a lumber wagon, into a stampede, for which the colored driver was arrested and fined $3.00 and costs for reckless driving; all of which had the effect to heighten the usual stir on Douglas avenue of our lively city, on Tuesday afternoon [May 5].

Mike then went south but was back in Wichita early in June. The *Eagle,* June 11, 1874, noted his visit:

Our ex-marshal, Mike Meagher, put in an appearance in Wichita last week. He has been milling around through the Indian Territory and the western part of the state. Mike made a good officer, and has hosts of friends in the city where he stood so long as its chief sentinel.

Meagher served as a deputy United States marshal that summer but no record has been found of the terminal dates of his appointment. As a deputy marshal he was mentioned only twice by the Wichita newspapers. The *Eagle,* June 18, 1874, said:

Deputy U. S. Marshal Mike Meagher arrested Frenchy last Sabbath evening in this city, and started for Fort Sill, Indian Territory, with his prisoner last Monday morning.

The second article appeared the following week and once more dealt with "Frenchy":

Mike Meagher, U. S. deputy marshal, returned from Ft. Sill last Monday [June 22], having safely delivered French into the hands of the U. S. officers. This French acknowledged that he had himself been, and had put the Indians up to much of the devilment of the last year. He is a desperate character, and it is supposed he had a hand in the murdering of that young doctor at the fort last spring. Sheriff [P. H.] Massey showed us a letter yesterday which made inquiries about French. It was from the great spiritualist E. V. Wilson, and announced that French's father's vessel had arrived in New York 9th inst., it appearing that his father was a sea-captain sailing out of the port of New York. The time French was in Wichita he had two stolen horses and it is supposed that he was on his way east. These facts we gain from Meagher and Massey.[14]

While Mike was acting as a deputy U. S. marshal, the Topeka *Commonwealth,* June 14, 1874, reported that he was first lieutenant in a newly formed militia company then engaged in scouting possible Indian difficulties along the southern Kansas border.

With the return of spring and the city elections approaching

490

Mike Meagher

once again Mike began to eye the office of Wichita city marshal.
In 1875, as in 1872, the marshal was to be elected by the people.
Both Mike Meagher and incumbent Smith made a bid for the
office in the *Eagle* of April 1, 1875. Mike announced:

EDITOR EAGLE:
At the earnest solicitation of business men, and the urgency of many Texas
men, by letter, I take this opportunity of announcing myself as a candidate
for the office of city marshal, at the ensuing spring election.

Respectfully,
MIKE MEAGHER

A third candidate for the office was Dan Parks who had served
as assistant marshal since 1873. When the election was over,
April 5, 1875, Mike had won easily, garnering 340 votes to Parks'
311 and Smith's 65.[15]

The newly elected mayor, George E. Harris, and city council
met on April 21, 1875, naming John Behrens assistant marshal and
Wyatt Earp and James Cairns policemen.[16]

Mike had hardly begun his fourth term as marshal when he captured two horse thieves. The Wichita *Beacon*, May 5, 1875, reported the arrest:

Last week city marshal Meagher received a postal card from Kalida, Woodson county, giving the description of a mare and three horses that had been
stolen from Mr. Stewart, a farmer living four miles this side of Kalida. Taking
a turn about town, the marshal struck the trail of two men whose actions excited his suspicions, and tracing them up he found that they had a couple of
horses at a livery stable, on Douglas avenue. The horses corresponding to the
description given on the postal card, Mike took possession of them, and afterwards arrested the two men, who gave their names as Thos. Cook and Charley
Glosfelter. The fact of their arrest was telegraphed to the Sheriff of Woodson
county, who arrived here on Thursday night, accompanied by Mr. Stewart.
The men and stock were identified, taken possession of, and on Saturday morning departed for Woodson county, where they will probably receive a full
reward for their love of horse flesh and their fondness for traveling at the
expense of others.

The cowboys who frequented Wichita's entertainment areas were
no respecters of the Sabbath. The Wichita *Eagle*, May 27, 1875,
told of one such herder who successfully eluded the city's police:

The three shots that were fired on Main street between the Occidental and
Empire last Sunday night [May 23], were showered into the innocent air by
a hilarious party of the name of Higinbotham, who was a horse back, and
heavily armed for the sport. The police chased him to the corporate limits,
but could go no further.[17]

491

On August 11, 1875, the *Beacon* reported that

Mike Meagher received a telegram from the sheriff of Douglas county, Tuesday of last week, requesting the arrest of a colored man, named Jesse Harrington, for stealing a horse near Lawrence. The arrest was made but no response to the information sent the sheriff having been received up to Saturday night, Mike released his prisoner Sunday morning [August 8].

Also in August the city council relieved James Cairns from the force. The *Eagle* reported the action on August 12: "The city authorities have reduced the police force. This was wise. They might have done the same thing months ago, which would have been wiser." Remaining on the staff were Meagher, Behrens and Earp.

Toward the end of August, 1875, 32-year-old Mike married a 24-year-old Ohio girl named Jenny. The city little suspected Mike of romantic intentions as the *Beacon*, September 1, 1875, indicated in this article:

The marriage of Mike Meagher was quite a surprise, but an agreeable one, to his many friends here. That our popular city marshal should go off and "do so," without consulting some of the old "roadsters," was unexpected by them, to say the least. We wish him, for ourselves, a long, brilliant and happy wedded career with a life lived long enough to get up a full force of his own.[18]

Several disturbances of minor importance kept the police force busy in September. A lady of questionable virtue enlivened Main street on September 10, the *Beacon* reporting on September 15, 1875:

A soiled dove got her guzzle full of whisky last Friday and with a fast team drove single handed up and down Main Street, swearing and howling like a wolf. She was finally gathered by a "nabbing guy," following third on the boose register, under charge of loose and "laskivious" conduct.

The next night, Saturday, again saw Main as a place of lively spirits. The *Beacon* reported in the same issue (September 15):

A Main street dive furnished a sufficient amount of generic force to create a first class sceance last Saturday night, which was afterwards transferred to the cooler. The register showed enough names for a full game of eucher. Several of this party were married and reported themselves as lost on a hunt, but didn't tell what kind of a hunt.

In reporting similar disturbances the next week, the *Beacon* September 22, 1875, felt the police were not fully performing their duty:

Several night brawls of a disgraceful character, have occurred lately, between the hours of 12 and 2 o'clock. The scene dragged in front of the Occidental Hotel last Saturday morning [September 18] was of this kind.

Mike Meagher

Aside from thefts and even burglaries, such might not be worth mentioning, if they did not raise a question as to the whereabouts of our night police. Several citizens have complained of this already, and have intimated in a disreputable way as to the whereabouts of the police at these hours. When our officers do their duty no one is so quick to give them the meed of praise as the BEACON, and it is our equal duty to condemn them for any dereliction.

In November Mike Meagher arrested Bill Potts with the assistance of Wyatt Earp (*see* the section on Earp) and Ed Hays with the assistance of John Behrens (*see* the section on Behrens). The *Beacon* said of the latter capture:

> One Ed. Hays came riding down from Little Rattlesnake, Tuesday, "smoothing his horse's chestnut mane," and all unaware that Mike Meagher knew of his coming, had his description, and true to his nature would, and did have him safely lodged in jail before night, charged with passing counterfeit money at Big Bend.[19]

After Potts was tried, and released, Meagher served another warrant on him. The *Beacon* reported the second arrest on November 17, 1875:

> Bill Potts and the two colored men, an account of whose arrest was given in last week's issue, were brought before Justice Misner on Wednesday last [November 10], on a writ of *habeas corpus* and released. Marshal Meagher immediately served a state warrant on them, and they are now under charge of the sheriff. The stolen cattle belonged to a Mr. Saunders, of Fort Sill, for whom these men were working. Mr. Saunders arrived here on Friday night last.

Meagher was re-elected to the office of city marshal on April 4, 1876, in spite of the difficulty his policeman, Wyatt Earp, had caused shortly before the election by striking the rival candidate, William Smith. (*See* the section on Earp.) Mike won a handsome majority over Smith, the votes totalling 477 to 249.[20]

This year, Mike's last on the Wichita police force, was a quiet one except for the disorder that ended with Mike's first killing. It happened on New Year's day, 1877, and was reported by the *Eagle,* January 4:

ANOTHER FATAL OCCURRENCE.

> Our city was on New Years night, the scene of one of those sudden, distressing and fatal occurrences, the first recital of which sends the blood back upon the heart and pales the cheek of the stoutest listener, and wherein a life at full tide was short cut off and the spirit of its possessor sent unheralded back to its author. Sylvester Powell, for some time past in the employ of the Southwestern Stage Company as the driver

of the city 'busses, in company with Albert Singleton, was making a day of it on New Years. In a spirit of recklessness and venture, the two took possession of E. R. Dennison's pony which was standing in front of Mayor [James G.] Hope's, sometime in the afternoon. He spoke to them in a jocular way when Powell picked up a neck yoke and struck Dennison a wicked and severe blow upon his arm, disabling it. Following this, Singleton menacingly told Dennison that it wouldn't be healthy for him to make any complaint of the outrage, whereupon Dennison had Powell arrested and conveyed by the City Marshal, Michael Meagher, to the city calaboose.

Later in the evening, W. A. Brown, the passenger agent of the Stage Company, paid his fine and procured his release. No sooner was he free than Powell made dire threats against the life of Meagher, swearing that he would put daylight through him on sight. Meeting Policeman McIvor about 9 o'clock in front of Hope's, Powell inquired for Meagher, accompanying the inquiry with the assertion that Mike had spent his last day on earth, or words to that effect. But a few moments afterward he discovered the Marshal at the water-closet in the rear of Hope's saloon when, without a word, he pulled a revolver and in the uncertain light of the moon, commenced shooting; one shot taking effect in Meagher's leg below the knee, and another passing through the breast of his coat. The few feet that separated them was closed in a moment, and while Meagher was attempting to wrench the weapon from the maddened man's grasp, it was discharged again, the ball grazing Meagher's hand, thence through a window and into the casing of an inside door to the sample room. Powell broke away and ran around into the alley between the New York and Centennial Blocks. Meagher ran around the front way encountering Powell in front of Chas. Hill's drug store when, without waiting for any more attempts upon his life, he raised his pistol and shot once. The ball took effect in Powell's heart and he fell and died without a struggle, a victim of his own murderous rashness. Coroner Munger being notified soon after, a jury consisting of E. J. Jenkins, M. R. Moser, Mr. Dabertz, Harry Vantrees, Will Crawford, and Squire Fitzgerald, was empaneled who found the cause of death as above stated.

Powell has a mother, brother and sister and other relatives living in Lawrence in this State, also a brother living in St. Louis, who were telegraphed to at once, and some of whom will doubtless reach here today, Wednesday [January 3]. Powell's confederate, Singleton, was missing soon after the fray. Powell was a young man of ordinarily quiet habits, but it is said a perfect demon when excited by drink, as the police of the city, as well as the inmates of certain houses, can testify. He remarked an hour or so before the fatal meeting, to one of the police force, that should any of their number meet him that night at a given house or in any way interfere with him, that such an one would never see the light of another day. The assertion has been made twice in our hearing that the deceased had killed two men, one with a pair of brass knuckles.

494

In all the trying and exceedingly dangerous positions into which Mr. Meagher has been thrown as an officer in times past, he never before resorted to arms to protect his own life. During the earlier days of our town, when it was infested with bands of known desperadoes and murderers, and upon occasions when deadly weapons were cocked and leveled within a foot of his face, he always succeeded by his imperturbable coolness to not only come off without a scratch, but to hold and confine his assailants without resort to deadly means, and although we have neither seen or talked to him since the fatally sad encounter of Monday night, from our knowledge of the man's character we know he regrets as much as anyone, the sad issue.

An examination was set to be heard before Squire [D. A.] Mitchell on Tuesday evening and again on yesterday morning, but as no one appeared against the Marshal we suppose that ends it.

We should have said that as Powell broke loose from Meagher he shot at him the fourth time, which shot was returned by Meagher as he ran.[21]

Wichita's cattle business had begun to fall off sharply after the season of 1874. In both 1875 and 1876 shipments declined approximately one-half each year. By 1877 only 4,102 head were shipped out. With increased settlement around the older established routes the cattle trails were shifting westward to avoid the barbed wire of the nesters. Dodge City was fast becoming the most popular shipping center and in the years that Wichita's trade fell off, Dodge's increased by even greater percentages. For a while it seemed that the northern end of the Chisholm trail was doomed to a certain death but in the spring of 1880 it was given a transfusion by the completion of the Cowley, Sumner & Fort Smith railroad to Caldwell. From that time until the end of Kansas' trail-driving days Caldwell was booming, boisterous and bloody, aptly named by her residents, "the Border Queen."

Sometime before the completion of the railroad Mike Meagher had moved the scene of his own operations to Caldwell. He had served out his term as Wichita city marshal but between April, 1877, and April, 1880, transferred his loyalties to the Border Queen. On April 5, 1880, ten weeks before the first steam engine puffed into town, Mike was elected mayor.[22] He was Caldwell's third chief executive.

One of Mike's first official acts was to appoint a police force. The mayor nominated William Horseman, marshal; Dan Jones, assistant marshal, and James Johnson, policeman. All of the appointments were confirmed by the council.[23] (*See* the sections devoted to each of these persons.)

495

On June 5, 1880, the United States census taker enumerated the city of Caldwell, listing Mike Meagher on page 18. Mike then was 37 years old; his brother John, 35, was also listed as being in the town. Both were born in Ireland.

When George Flatt was killed on the night of June 19, 1880, Mayor Mike Meagher, the city marshal, and several others were soon on the scene. Little could be done, however, for Flatt died instantly and the assassin was unknown. (*See* the section on Flatt.) A few days later Mike and his police force were arrested by county authorities, charged with complicity in the Flatt killing. The Caldwell *Commercial*, July 1, 1880, reported:

THE CITY GOVERNMENT ARRESTED.

Last Friday [June 25] Sheriff [Joseph] Thralls came down with three or four deputies and warrants for the arrest of Mike Meagher, Mayor of the city, Wm. Horseman, City Marshal; Frank Hunt, James Johnson, Policemen; Dan Jones, Constable; and Geo. W. McFarland and R. H. Collins, charged with complicity in the killing of Geo. Flatt. The Sheriff also summoned Hugh A. Ross, Dr. [D.] MacMillan, Dan Rogers, Charles Spear and William Thompson, as witnesses on the part of the prosecution. No information could be obtained as to whether these arrests were made on a verdict rendered by the Coroner's jury or at the instigation of outside parties.

Hasty preparations were made by prisoners and witnesses, and at 2:20 the party boarded the passenger train and went to Wellington. Arriving there they found that County Attorney Wilsie was sick and that no examination could be had before Tuesday. Steps were at once taken to sue out a writ of habeas corpus, which was done on Saturday and trial under the writ set for Monday before Judge Evans.

On Wednesday evening the trial closed, resulting in the discharge of all the parties except Horseman and Hunt. Warrants were immediately issued and the entire party re-arrested, but on second thought the Justice of the Peace issuing the warrants discharged Mr. Collins.

At noon to-day Meagher, Johnson, Jones and Collins came down, Collins to stay, but the others to return by the afternoon train. What the result of all this will be it is impossible to say, but, if we are correctly informed, the whole thing has the appearance of a put up job. So far no evidence has been offered —except that given by Thompson, a boy employed in the Varieties, who swore that he had been offered money to testify as he did; and the testimony of a man named Sexton, living at Missouri Flatts, who acknowledged that he had offered Thompson $50 to testify against the parties—against any of the parties charged.

We are told that the Justice of the Peace—whose name we have forgotten— was indignant because the case was taken out of his hands and brought before the Probate Judge, and for that reason he issued the second batch of warrants. Be that as it may, all accounts agree that he showed an unusual personal interest in having any or all of the parties held for the killing of Flatt, regardless of evidence or any thing else.[24]

Meagher's second examination was held July 3 before Justice of the Peace I. N. King at Wellington. Though Meagher was discharged, Horseman, Hunt, Jones, and Johnson were bound over for the next term of the district court. The Caldwell *Commercial,* July 8, 1880, indicated there never were any valid grounds for the arrests, that the whole thing was a money making scheme on the part of Wellington officials:

We have endeavored to obtain the evidence given in the trial before the Probate Judge and also before the Justice of the Peace, but have been unable to do so. Statements of its purport have been given by several who were present at both examinations, and from these statements we believe the desire on the part of the officials at Wellington was to bring business to their town and make money out of it rather than to discover who killed Flatt. It looks not only like a money making scheme, but also a scheme to cast odium upon the city of Caldwell, and to injure it in so far as could be done by conveying the impression that our people were a set of thugs and assassins. . . .

Like other well known frontier characters, Mike was only human, and even the exalted office of mayor did not restrain him from engaging in a business common to his kind. On August 2, 1880, for instance, Mike was arrested for running a keno game. He was fined $5 and costs by Police Judge James D. Kelly.[25]

Meagher did not run for re-election in 1881 but on July 18 he was nominated for city marshal. The nomination was rejected by the city council.[26] There were those in the city who still wanted Mike to be marshal, however, and on July 21, 1881, the *Commercial* said:

Mike Meagher has taken to the saw and plane. Several of our citizens who know his qualifications for the position, have been anxious to have him appointed City Marshal, but Mike says he has had enough of that kind of business and believes he will stick to his present job.

But next week, on July 28, the *Commercial* announced Mike's appointment: "At the request of Mayor [W. N.] Hubbell, M. Meagher consented yesterday to act as City Marshal for the present."

Mike served as marshal of Caldwell for only five days. At a council meeting held August 1, 1881, the mayor placed both Mike's name and that of James Roberts in nomination for the position. Roberts received three council votes to Mike's one.[27] Thus was settled, temporarily, a police problem which had been before the mayor and city council for weeks. The *Commercial,* however, did not think highly of the decision, saying on August 4 that "we presume [the council] feel as proud as peacocks over the wisdom and able statesmanship they have exhibited in settling the vexed question for the time being at least."

The problem reappeared in October and Mike was again offered the marshal's position. He declined, however, as did George Brown and Dan Jones. The man finally selected was John Wilson.[28]

A few weeks later Mike Meagher was cut down by an assassin's bullet. It happened on December 17, 1881, and was reported by the Caldwell *Post,* December 22:

WAR ON THE BORDER.

Two Men Killed and One Wounded.

A Desperate Fight With Outlaws.

To begin at the beginning of this affair, one would have to get into the secrets of men's hearts; so we will only begin at the apparent beginning. One Jim Talbot who has been around the city about a month, gambling, drinking, bullying, and attempting to bulldoze every one, was the leader of the party. He has a wife and little boy and girl living on Chisholm street, in this city, and came up the trail with Millett's herd this fall. On Friday night at the play he became very much incensed at the writer hereof, and swore he would kill him before he left the city. He repeated the threat on Saturday morning on the streets; but one editor was too sharp for him, and was out of his way. The aforesaid editor was not aware that the threat had been made until after the shooting on the street had occurred.

With Talbot on the drinking spree during the night were Jim Martin, Bob Bigtree, Tom Love, Bob Munsen, Dick Eddleman and George Speers. Speers did none of the shooting, but was in the act of saddling one of Talbot's horses when he was shot. Talbot, Martin, Bigtree, Munson and Doug Hill were standing holding their horses near Speers, waiting for him to saddle up.

After the fighting in the city, and Mike Meagher and George Speers were killed, the five outlaws—Jim Talbot, Bob Bigtree, Bob Munson, Jim Martin, and Doug Hill—rode off to the east of town, across the railroad track. Some one of the citizens fired at and killed a horse from under one of them. He got up behind one of the other men. A party of citizens organized, mounted horses and started in pursuit.

The outlaws met a man bringing hay to town, with a lead horse in the rear of the wagon. They cut the horse loose and rode it off. At W. E. Campbell's they got two more horses, those they were riding having been wounded. The party of citizens got sight of them just before they crossed Bluff creek into the I. T. There were five of the outlaws then, but after they appeared on the prairie beyond, there were only four. They followed at a break-neck pace, both parties keeping up a constant fire for about twelve miles.

Mike Meagher

The outlaws headed for Deutcher Bros.'s horse ranch on Deer creek, intending to get fresh horses there, but were so closely pressed by the pursuing party that they could not make the change and get away. When they reached the ranch the citizens were only a few hundred feet away. The outlaws passed on to the bluff and creek about six hundred feet south of the ranch, dismounted and took to the brush and rocks, firing all the time at the citizens. The citizens finally drove them over the bluff and into a canyon, where there had been a stone dugout. Into this three of the outlaws went, threw up breast-works of stone, got behind them and would bang away at any one who showed an inch of his person to their view.

The citizens surrounded the gulch and kept up a constant firing at the fort, but without effect. One of the outlaws took refuge up in a small gulch leading to the west, and was not seen until he fired at W. E. Campbell, who was sliding down the hill on his face to get a commanding point above the fort. The outlaw's ball took effect in Campbell's wrist, passing between the two bones. Another ball passed through his clothes six or seven times, and made a small flesh wound on the thigh. This disconcerted the citizens to a certain extent, and, it being dark, they could do but little good in fighting. Being above the outlaws, they were splendid marks for their fire, while the outlaws were in the shadows, so that their position could not be distinguished. Had the fourth man been anywhere else in the gulch the citizens could have taken them in; but his position covered every point that the others were exposed from; in fact, he held the key to the situation. Thirty minutes more daylight would have told the tale for the outlaws; or had Campbell escaped the fire of the villain that shot him, he could have killed the other three in as many minutes, as his position commanded the fort in every corner. The two parties were not over seventy-five feet apart at any time during the battle, while Campbell's man was not over twenty-five feet from him when he shot. Johnny Hall got a bullet through the top of his hat, missing his head about an inch.

Reinforcements arrived at the ranch from town about ten o'clock. Pickets were formed around the gulch, but the outlaws had flown before that time. There were only about fifteen men at the place during the evening fight, and most of them returned to town as soon as Campbell was shot, leaving only six men to guard the gulch and over thirty head of horses. The horses required the attention of at least four men, for they were what the outlaws needed.

The morning round-up revealed the fact that the outlaws had escaped. The entire party, except Sheriff Thralls, Frank Evans, Bob Harrington, Jim Dobson, Sam Swayer, Mr. Freeman, A. Rhodes, another man and the writer hereof, came to town. About thirty-five came in, leaving the small party to look up the outlaws, inform the camps below to look out for stolen stock, etc. Our party visited two or three camps on Deer creek and started home. We met several parties coming out from town, most of them for fun, others for business. They all returned before night.

A party of fifteen was organized by the Mayor and started out Sunday evening to guard certain cow camps to see that no horses were stolen from them. The outlaws traveled six or seven miles, or possibly ten, Saturday night. Two freighters were camped on Bullwhacker creek about eighteen miles

499

south of this city Sunday night, when Talbot's party, five in number this time, rounded them up and took five horses from them. Two of the party were bare-headed, and one had a slight wound in his foot. The outlaws started south.

The freighters came in Monday about two o'clock, when Sheriff Thralls, with a posse, started in pursuit. Another party of freighters passed the outlaws near Pond creek during the night. The outlaws were going south.

A party was organized Tuesday evening and started to Cantonment to intercept them there. Mr. George Brown was in charge of the party.

SYNOPSIS OF EVIDENCE

before Coroner's jury concerning the death of Mike Meagher:

Dr. Noble's evidence was to the effect that Meagher died from the effects of a gunshot wound through the lungs, the ball passing through the fleshy part of the right arm, thence through the body, producing death in about twenty-five or thirty minutes from the time of the infliction of the wound. Dr. West assisted in the *post mortem* examination, and verifies Dr. Noble's evidence. John Wilson, City Marshal, says, in his evidence, that early in the morning (Saturday) Mike Meagher came to his residence and asked him to come down town and stop a riot; that Jim Talbot and party were wanting to kill him. He came down town with Meagher, went to Moores Bros.' saloon, arrested Tom Love for firing a revolver in the building. Bill Mankin, Bob Munson, Dick Eddleman and Jim Talbot were with him, armed with revolvers, needle guns and Winchesters. "I started to take Tom Love to the calaboose, when he resisted. I called Mike Meagher to assist me, when the party made a rush for us and made an attack upon Meagher. Meagher went up the Opera House stair way, and I stood at the bottom. Jim Talbot and Tom Love were loudest in their threats against his life. I stopped at entrance of stairs, and told them I would shoot the first making the attempt. Had been compelled to release Love in the meantime. The party then dispersed.

"About one o'clock I arrested Jim Martin, who was still armed; took him before Judge Kelly, who fined him. Started him to York & Co.'s with Assistant Fosset to get money. He passed down on street, where Love, Talbot, Munson and Eddleman took the prisoner away from Fossett. Talbot started to run south, turned around and fired two shots at me. I followed down sidewalk on east side, passed through alley way south of Pulaski's store, Mike Meagher with me. Stopped in alley back of store. Jim Talbot commenced firing at us from north of Opera House on sidewalk with Winchester rifle. No one was with him. Saw Talbot take aim in the direction we were in. I took hold of Meagher and warned him to look out. I heard the report of the gun, and Meagher said, 'I am hit, and hit hard.' Took hold of him and helped him to a box. Then left him and went with Hubbell to laundry back of Hubbell's, and began firing at Talbot, Bob Bigtree and three others who were on horses returning fire as citizens. Talbot took a six-shooter from Meagher in the morning in Meagher's saloon."

Ed. F. Rathbun said: "I was with Meagher and Wilson at the rear of Pulaski's store. We were firing at Bob Bigtree near the Chinese laundry, they returning our fire. I looked north toward the M. & D. Bank building. Saw

500

Mike Meagher

Talbot standing with a Winchester rifle aimed at Meagher or myself. Saw the smoke issue from the gun, heard the report and saw Meagher begin to sink down. Said, 'Good God, Mike, are you hit?' He said, 'Yes; tell my wife I have got it at last.' Mike was standing with his six-shooter in his right hand and rifle under left arm, aiming at Talbot. I assisted him to the south side of Pulaski's store, from where he was removed into the barber shop."

W. D Fossett: "I was crossing Main St. with Jim Martin in my custody, when Talbot and gang came up to us. Talbot said that Martin need not pay his fine if he did not want to. Wilson saw that two of the party were armed, and ordered them to give up their arms. They refused and scattered. Talbot ran down the street, turned and fired two shots at Wilson, ran between the building east, yelling to the boys to get their Winchesters. He ran to his residence, got his gun, came up 5th street to the rear of Opera House, and began firing at me. I was then at rear of Hockaday's store. Meagher and Rathbun were near me. Doug Hill and Bigtree were firing at me from the east, and Talbot from the north. After the heavy firing ceased up town, I saw Munsen and Bigtree come from Talbot's house, armed with Winchesters."

George S. Brown says: "I was standing on the street about eight o'clock in the morning. Saw Wilson arrest Tom Love. Mike Meagher came to his assistance. Talbot's gang and Comanche Bill rushed in and began to threaten Meagher. They went up street and a short distance. Meagher stepped up the Opera House stairs. Was in the rear of my shop when the fight was going on in the afternoon. Saw Talbot shoot at me from rear of Opera House. Ball struck barrel near me. I returned into my shop."

W. H. Reily says: "I was in the street. Saw Wilson arrest a man for shooting off his revolver. Meagher came to Wilson's assistance. Before they got away with prisoner an armed party of men came down street and took prisoner from officers. Talbot remarked, 'Meagher is the man we want, and Meagher is the man we will have.' This happened about 8 o'clock in the morning."

Richard Wilson says: "About 2 o'clock p. m. I was at George Kalbflesch's stable. During a lull in the fighting Doug Hill, Bob Bigtree, Bob Munson, Jim Martin, Dick Addleman, Jim Talbot, and two others came to the barn, presented rifles and ordered us to saddle horses. They chose four horses and made us saddle them. They took an extra saddle with them. After they left Dick Addleman presented a revolver and ordered us to saddle a horse for him. We refused. He put up his revolver, asked us to not give him away, and left."

Andy Caylor's evidence verifies that of Richard Wilson's with reference to taking horses.

Nellie Whitson says: "I saw Jim Martin run to Talbot's house. Doug Hill and Bob Munson came soon after. The door seemed to be locked. Talbot told the boys to break the door in. They did so. Immediately they came out armed with guns. In the morning a lot of men, Jim in the number, came to our house. Jackson and Comanche Bill were with them, and were trying to get them to lay down their arms and be still. They all did so except Jim Talbot, who for a time refused and swore he would kill Mike Meagher before he left town, if it cost him his life. The guns were taken to Talbot's house.

They then left, except Tom Love and Comanche Bill, who went to sleep. About 1 p. m. Talbot, Hill and Munson came back, woke Love and Bill up. Took Love up town with them. Bill would not go with them. When Doug Hill quit firing at Bill Fossett, he directed his fire at two men in the rear of Pulaski's store. After his last shot I saw this man stagger and fall. I saw Rathbun pick him up."

Edward Heiflinger said that he saw Comanche Bill take a pistol away from Love, who was trying to shoot Meagher in his saloon early in the morning.

William Mankin (Comanche Bill) says: "On Saturday morning, about sunrise, I, with Challes, Dave and George Speers, Jim Talbot and five others, were in Robison's saloon, talking and drinking, when John Wilson came in and asked the boys to keep quiet. He asked me to keep them quiet. I wanted them to go with me to breakfast at the Clifton House. Munson objected. Finally got them to go. Got the guns away from the boys, except Jim Talbot. I also got two revolvers from the party. The party were seated at the table. Jim Talbot would not come in. Jim said: 'Boys, they have arrested one of the boys; let's take him away from them.' They started out of the hotel with their guns. I went with them up the street to the Opera House stairs, where two of the boys had their guns down on Meagher. I took them away from them or got them away. I got them to give up their guns. Talbot insisted on having the guns taken to his house, which was done. Tom Love laid down on my bed after the others left. I went to sleep, and woke up when I heard the firing. Before I went to sleep, I went up town to see Wilson, he asking me to do so. Went to Meagher's saloon, where I was sworn in as special police. Did not fire a shot all day, as I had no arms of any kind."

The Coroner's jury returned a verdict to the effect that Mike Meagher came to his death from the effect of a gun shot wound from a gun in the hands of Jim Talbot, and that Bob Bigtree, Jim Martin, Tom Love, Dick Eddleman, Bob Munson and Doug Hill were accessories.

Warrants were issued for the arrest of the above named men. Tom Love and Dick Eddleman were arrested Tuesday and sent up to Wellington. The others escaped into the I. T.

Up to a late hour last night no news had been received from the outlaws below, nor from the Sheriff Thralls party. The party that started out Tuesday evening returned Wednesday morning, six men being too small a party to try a racket with the five outlaws.

Mayor Burrus offers a reward of $500, Sheriff Thralls $200, W. E. Campbell $200 and J. M. Steele, of Wichita, $200 for the outlaws, dead or alive.[29]

Mike's body was taken to Wichita for burial. Two days later, December 22, 1881, the Wichita *Eagle* printed a glowing tribute to the former marshal:

A BRAVE MAN GONE.

When the history of the daring spirits of the Kansas border are written up, there will be found few brighter than he whose mortal remains were consigned to the grave in this city yesterday. With nothing of the dare-devil or reckless

502

Mike Meagher

bravado in his composition, nevertheless Mike Meagher did not know the meaning of personal fear. As marshal of this city in the day when one-half of our residents were of the worst desperadoes between the Missouri and the Rio Grande, large numbers of whom boasted the blood of fellow beings, reckless, red-handed manslayers, whose only notion of heroism was embodied in the expression that "he had killed his man," Mike Meagher, by his consummate coolness and wonderful bravery, preserved the lives and property of our people. Many a time and oft has he faced death upon these streets with a bravery, fortitude and composure beyond the power of words to describe. He has fallen at last, fallen only at the hands of an assassin—at the hands of one who has threatened his life for years, but who would never have accomplished his awful work in an open field and equal chances. The brave spirit before whom murderers have quailed and mobs slunk away, was freed only by deadly stealth. Kind of heart, gentle as a child, generous and open in all things, always helpful and never overbearing, his life was a heroic ideal. His remains were brought to this city by Captain J. M. Steele, his brother-in-law, attended by his sorrowing wife and relations, and were buried on Tuesday, being followed to the grave by a very large concourse of people, most of whom were his fast friends in life, and who regret and mourn his untimely taking off. "After life's fitful fever he sleeps well."

Not often does one hear both sides of such rows as that which resulted in the death of Mike Meagher, especially when the "other side" has made a successful escape. The Caldwell fracas was an exception, however, for on January 12, 1882, the killers wrote an indignant letter to the Kansas City (Mo.) *Times* explaining things as they saw it. The letter was copied in the Caldwell *Commercial*, January 26, 1882:

THE CALDWELL COW BOYS

PUT IN A DEFENCE FOR THEIR RECENT FIGHT DOWN THERE.

TO THE KANSAS CITY SUNDAY TIMES.

IN CAMP, January 12.—We have noticed through the columns of your paper the account of the so called cut-throats. You are aware of the fact that every story has two sides, so we wish to inform the readers of the *Times* that we have been very basely misrepresented. In the first place we were not drunk at the time of the fight. In the next place we never rode into the city of Caldwell. We had been in town about one month and had always abided by its laws, and as far as helping ourselves to anything it is false. We never molested any thing that was not our own. As for Meagher when he was killed we were not mounted. He had two six shooters in his hands at the time he was shot; and more he went to Hubbell's store and borrowed the pistols. It seems to be the general opinion that Meagher was a leading man in Caldwell. Do you know his business? He was nothing more than a saloon keeper and ran a keno table. Just a few days before the row he was arrested and had to give bond for selling whisky in Caldwell. It has been published that the row

503

grew out of the killing of George Flat, this is also false. It never entered our minds.

The very reason the row came up was that the honorable Marshal of Caldwell, John Wilson, was on a protracted drunk and stationed a posse of men in the Exchange saloon and told them to shoot every man that moved—that is, cowboys—then arming himself with two pistols, and then throwing them down on every one of the cow boys, telling them to throw up our hands, which we refused to do. He then withdrew his weapons and proceeded to organize a mob to take or kill us. We went and got our guns and marched to the front and engaged in a fight, which lasted about an hour. We then went and got our horses and started to leave town and then we were fired on from every and all concealed place imaginable. The second skirmish lasted about thirty minutes and then we were forced to ride. We were pursued by about 100 armed men. They at length got us rounded up in a washout and there we stayed until night; then we got together and left. After the mob had dispersed Wilson turned to shoot one of the boys in the back, and this is why the row came up. George Spears was shot by the town mob. He had no hand in the fight whatever. He was a friend to the cow boys and that was the cause of his death. He was just as honorable a citizen as Caldwell had. The Assistant Marshal acknowledged that Wilson was drunk, and that if he (Wilson) had let things alone every thing would have been all right and there would have been no row.

We did take the freighters' horses and told them that we would return their horses in six or eight days, and on the seventh day we took them back. They told us that if they were situated in the same position that they would do the same thing and did not blame us. Caldwell citizens seem to think that Talbot was one of Billy the Kid's gang. This is a bare falsehood, he has never seen the Kid and has never had any acquaintance with him whatever. We notice that it was stated we had a fight at a ranch on Wagon creek; this is a mistake; we never was at Wagon creek and took saddles and horses. We never took any horses but the freighters. We are willing to go and stand our trial if we thought we could get justice, but this we know we cannot get. This is the true facts of the row.

[Signed]   JIM TALBOT,
DUG HILL,
BOB MUNSON,
JIM MARTIN,
BOB BIGTREE.

On January 24, 1882, Tom Love, one of the two who were captured shortly after the Meagher murder, was acquitted at his preliminary examination in Wellington.[30] Dick Eddleman, the other prisoner, escaped from the Sumner county jail four days later. The Caldwell *Post*, February 2, 1882, reported his flight and recapture:

Mike Meagher

JAIL DELIVERY.

Dick Eddleman, who has been confined in the county jail in Wellington for some time for participation in the Talbot riot, succeeded in walking out Saturday evening while the guards were feeding the prisoners. The cage door was open and Eddleman climbed upon the cell and was locked out when the cage was shut. Deputy Sheriff Thralls missed his man at bed time, and, supposing he had skipped for Caldwell, procured a team and drove to this city and notified his brother, Sheriff Thralls. They together drove north on the road towards Wellington. When out about three miles they met Eddleman on horseback, and commanded him to halt; he heeded not the command, but skipped out at a lively pace.

The Sheriff's party fired upon the escaped prisoner, and suppose they wounded the horse, as, after he had gone a short distance the horse was unable to go faster than a walk. The prisoner wandered around the north part of town for a short time, then went around to the north-east part of town where he unsaddled his horse and turned him loose, then struck off in a northwesterly direction. The Sheriff's party soon rounded him up over by the Avery place, brought him into the city and sent him up to Wellington in charge of Deputy Sheriff Thralls. Eddleman will probably get about seven years for breaking jail and stealing a horse. This will be rather rough on the boy if he could have escaped the charge of participating in the Talbot riot. It was rather convenient this time for Sheriff Thralls that he was at his branch office in this city.

Doug Hill was arrested in 1887 and placed on trial for murder. He pleaded guilty to manslaughter in the fourth degree, was convicted, and given six months in the county jail. Jim Talbot, the supposed leader of the bunch, did not stand trial for the crime until 1895. His first trial ended in a deadlocked jury and in the second he was acquitted. He returned to his home in Ukiah, Calif., where in the late summer of 1896 he was killed by an unknown assassin. It was rumored that Talbot, whose real name was James D. Sherman, was killed by his wife's lover.[31]

The fate of the remainder of the gang remains unknown.

1. "Miscellaneous Papers," Records of the City of Wichita. 2. Ibid. 3. "Proceedings of the Governing Body," Records of the City of Wichita, Journal A, pp. 44, 46, 55. 4. Ibid., pp. 75, 76; "Miscellaneous Papers," Records of the City of Wichita. 5. "Proceedings of the Governing Body," Records of the City of Wichita, Journal A, pp. 78, 81. 6. Ibid., pp. 89, 90. 7. "Miscellaneous Papers," Records of the City of Wichita. 8. "Proceedings of the Governing Body," Records of the City of Wichita, Journal A, p. 128. 9. See, also, ibid., p. 159. 10. Ibid., pp. 186, 187. 11. "Miscellaneous Papers," Records of the City of Wichita. 12. "Proceedings of the Governing Body," Records of the City of Wichita, Journal A, pp. 316, 320; many routine official records bearing the name of Mike Meagher have not been included in this sketch since their presence would contribute little in proportion to the space they would require. 13. "Proceedings of the Governing Body," Records of the City of Wichita, Journal A, p. 371; Wichita Eagle, April 23, 1874. 14. Ibid., June 25, 1874. 15. "Proceedings of the Governing Body," Journal B, p. 42. 16. Ibid., p. 44; Wichita Weekly Beacon, April 28, 1875. 17. See, also, ibid., May 26, 1875. 18. See, also, "United States Census," 1880, Caldwell, Sumner county, Kansas, p.

18.   19. November 10, 1875.   20. "Proceedings of the Governing Body," Records of the City of Wichita, Journal B, p. 103.   21. See, also, Wichita Weekly Beacon, January 3, 1877. 22. Caldwell Post, April 8, 1880.   23. Ibid., April 15, 1880.   24. See, also, ibid., July 1, 1880.   25. "Police Court Docket," Records of the City of Caldwell.   26. Caldwell Commercial, July 21, 1881.   27. Ibid., August 4, 1881; Caldwell Post, August 4, 1881. 28. Caldwell Commercial, November 3, 1881.   29. See, also, Caldwell Commercial, December 22, 1881.   30. Caldwell Post, January 26, 1882.   31. Caldwell News, April 18, 25, September 19, 1895, September 3, 1896; Caldwell Messenger, April 30, 1956.

MORCO, JOHN (_____-1873)

In the summer of 1873 there were five "Jacks" manning the Ellsworth police force, a situation that was not to endure for long. John W. "Brocky Jack" Norton, one of Wild Bill Hickok's policemen at Abilene in November, 1871, was city marshal. John "Happy Jack" Morco, John S. "High Low Jack" Branham, John "Long Jack" De-Long and Short Jack were policemen. Possibly Ed Hogue was called Short Jack in keeping with the other nicknames for when these policemen had been appointed on June 11, 1873, Hogue was among the number.[1] There were no other policemen on the force besides these four and Norton.

As had some of the other frontier peace officers, whose careers have been mentioned in these sketches, Happy Jack started out on the wrong side of the law. He had been arrested in Ellsworth for vagrancy on June 5, 1873, but Police Judge V. B. Osborne found him not guilty.[2] Less than a week later, June 11, he was made a policeman.

Judging from the Ellsworth police court docket Happy Jack was one of the most active officers in the city. Few of the arrests were of any consequence, though one is of interest in light of developments later that summer. On July 1, 1873, Morco arrested Billy Thompson who, on June 30, "did then and there unlawfully and feloniously carry on his person a deadly weapon commonly called a revolver, and was unlawfully in a state of intoxication and was unlawfully disturbing the peace and did unlawfully assault one John Marcho."

Thompson pleaded guilty to being drunk and to carrying a pistol; he was fined ten dollars and costs of $15.[3]

On July 15, Happy Jack and the marshal rode over to Fort Harker, four miles east, and arrested a thief. The Ellsworth *Reporter,* July 17, 1873, stated:

POLICE ITEMS.—John Smith and another man whose name we did not get, were arrested about sunrise Tuesday morning, for breaking into Davis' store. Smith had a preliminary trial yesterday, and will have some more today. It is reported that he has been engaged in extensive steals in the Territories. Smith was captured by "Brocky Jack" and "Happy Jack," at Fort Harker, after a careful, determined chase and search on horseback. It is supposed that Smith's companion escaped, and that the second man arrested will be discharged.

On July 19, 1873, Happy Jack was requested to resign as was his fellow officer High Low Jack Branham. Ten days later, however, a petition signed by 77 persons was presented to the city council asking that Morco be reinstated. Happy Jack resumed his place on the police force that same day, July 29, 1873.[4]

Ellsworth county Sheriff Chauncey B. Whitney was murdered by Billy Thompson on the streets of Ellsworth on August 15, 1873. Billy's brother, Ben, would not surrender his weapons until Happy Jack had been disarmed since the Thompson brothers seemed to have a bitter grudge against Morco. The full story of the killing appears in the section on Whitney.

Because of their apparent inefficiency during the Whitney-Thompson episode, the entire police force of Ellsworth was discharged by the mayor. Later that same day the city council met in special session to pass on the mayor's actions. On first motion the mayor's course was not approved but on a reconsideration he was sustained. The mayor and council then appointed a new police force. Mayor Miller offered John DeLong's name for marshal but the council turned him down. Miller's second choice was Ed Hogue and this time the appointment was approved. For policemen the mayor and council named Ed Crawford, DeLong and Happy Jack Morco.[5]

Twelve days later, August 27, 1873, the entire police force was again relieved. This time Morco was not reappointed.[6] Happy Jack journeyed to Salina where he was arrested on an order from Ellsworth. The *Saline County Journal,* September 4, 1873, reported the situation as follows:

"Happy Jack," ex-policeman of Ellsworth, whom the wayward Texans especially dread, was arrested upon a dispatch from Ellsworth, last Thursday evening [August 28], on the eastern bound train, after it had stopped at our depot. We are informed that there is a division of feeling among the Ellsworth people as to how their present troubles with lawless Texans should be managed—one party advocating enforcement of the laws on every occasion, the other clamoring for great leniency towards Texas law-breakers, whose trade they desire to retain. The latter party has lately obtained the ascendancy and through their influence Jack was removed from office, as the Texans had threatened to withdraw their herds from Ellsworth provided it was not done. Upon his discharge Jack was asked to give up his arms—to comply with a city ordinance which would not permit him to carry weapons. This he refused to do, as desperadoes were awaiting the first favorable opportunity to take his life, and he was only safe when armed. To avoid what he considered was personal danger he jumped on to the train and came to Salina, when he was arrested as above stated. He was confined in jail for a day or so and then was released. Several parties from Ellsworth came by carriage and demanded that he should be turned over to them unarmed, which our officers refused to do, suspecting some intended foul play. Since Jack has been domesticated in Salina he has been the center of attraction.

Happy Jack returned to Ellsworth on September 3 and next evening was killed by Policeman Charles Brown. His death was recorded in the Ellsworth *Reporter*, September 11, 1873:

"HAPPY JACK" KILLED.

Last Thursday evening during the time between early twilight and dark, we heard the report of a revolver, and a second report the next instant told us that it might "mean something."—These shots were for "Happy Jack," and before the sound of them had died way upon the evening air, "Happy Jack" was not of this world. He was shot through the heart and he died without a struggle, a word or an audible groan. The circumstances causing his death are somewhat difficult to get at, but as nearly as we can ascertain, are as follows:

It will be remembered that Happy Jack was discharged with the balance of the police force about three weeks ago. Jack remained here for several days thereafter and then went to Salina. On arriving there he was arrested on an order from the authorities here, for carrying off a pair of pistols. He was kept in prison a day, and no one appearing against him, was released.—These pistols that he was accused of taking, belonged to John Good, and are said to have cost $100. At the request of Mayor Miller, policeman Brown went to Salina to give in his testimony, as he had some knowledge of the matter.—Brown wanted a warrant, but was told that none was needed. Accordingly he went to Salina. But no trial was had; Good, for some reason, hurried back to Ellsworth.

At Salina, Brown advised Jack not to come to Ellsworth, telling him that he would send him anything he wanted, and he did express his things to Salina after reaching home.—But Happy Jack was determined to come, against

508

Happy Jack Morco

the advise of his friends at Salina, and the entire population seemed to be his friends; at Brookville where he stopped and purchased ammunition he was also told to keep away, but he said "he was good for all his enemies up there." He arrived here during the night on the freight train. During the following day, Thursday, he was on the street armed with his revolvers, but making no trouble. —He refused to give up his arms, however, with an oath, and threatened to "make way" with some one before morning. Repeatedly he was urged to obey the ordinance but he was obstinate and determined to die rather than surrender his revolver. As night was coming on the police for the last time approached him and told him he must give up his revolvers. Still persisting he was shot, the first ball passing thro' his heart; as he was falling a second shot went through his head. He fell to the ground in front of the sidewalk and died without a struggle.

Thus ended a career that is sure to come to all who live such lives as he claims to have led. Happy Jack came here last spring from California. He claimed to have fought the Modocs, to have killed twelve men in Portland, Oregon, in self defence. His wife, who came here with a theatrical troupe from Wichita recently, says that it was four men he killed—that he used to get drunk and abuse her—that one time she called for help while they were living in Portland and that Jack shot four good citizens who came to her relief. He was put in jail but managed to escape. It was at this time that he had his arm broken. Jack and his wife had not met for several years, and she was three days in town before he recognized her.

We write the above with the desire to do full justice to all. It is possible that fuller particulars may be gained in time. Policeman Brown has always had our respect, and he denies most emphatically that he was "hired or asked to kill Happy Jack," claims that he was obliged to do it; that to have arrested him would have cost his own life. We are sorry for the unfortunate event. Jack was a man, and not without good qualities. But he invited his fate; it came quickly and he is at rest.

Jack's friends back in Salina thought he had been purposely murdered. The *Saline County Journal*, September 11, 1873, said:

"Happy Jack" has met the fate of many like him—"died with his boots on." We gave an account of his arrest and release at this place, last week. Last Thursday he returned to Ellsworth. While there, he is reported to have acted properly and shown no disposition to disobey the laws. But he would not give up his arms, though the city ordinance was strict in that respect. He considered that his life hung by a brittle cord when deprived of his weapons, (as the Texans were undoubtedly ready to take advantage of his being unarmed) and he acted as nine out of ten would have done under like circumstances. The demand by policeman Brown to give them up was not acceeded to, and Jack was brutally murdered, as we think, by this cowardly officer. One bullet went through his brain and another through his heart. Justice would demand that Brown should be tried for murder. In the unsettled state in which Ellsworth is now in, it is not probable that the murderer will be brought to trial.

Jack may have been too reckless in re-visiting Ellsworth, but under no circumstances can a murder of this kind be justified.

A coroner's jury acquitted Policeman Brown. (*See* the section on J. Charles Brown.)

1. "Minutes of the City Council," Records of the City of Ellsworth, p. 87; Ellsworth *Reporter*, July 3, 1873. 2. "Police Court Docket," Records of the City of Ellsworth, June 5, 1873. 3. *Ibid.*, July 1, 1873. 4. "Minutes of the City Council," Records of the City of Ellsworth, pp. 94, 96, 97. 5. *Ibid.*, pp. 98, 99. 6. *Ibid.*, p. 102.

PHILLIPS, JOHN W.

On April 4, 1881, Caldwell elected a new mayor and city council. As was usually the case with a change of administration the old police were relieved and a new force appointed. The man chosen to fill former City Marshal James Johnson's spot was John W. Phillips. The appointment and confirmation by the council were made April 11, 1881.[1] A few days later "Newt Miller . . . [was] appointed deputy City Marshal under Mr. John Phillips. Mr. Miller is an old hand at the business and makes a good officer," according to the Caldwell *Commercial*, April 21, 1881.

Not long after the new administration was under way an economy drive threatened to force the marshal from his office. The *Commercial*, June 23, 1881, included editorial remarks on the situation in its regular city council column:

CITY COUNCIL.

Council met on Monday night [June 20], Mayor [W. N.] Hubbell in the chair. . . .

The salary of the City Marshal was reduced from $60 to $50 per month, to take effect on the 1st of July.

The present Marshall, John Phillips has stated that he would resign if the Council reduced his salary; and we don't blame him. If he attends to his duties in the manner a marshal should, he is worth to the city every cent of $60 per month. If he does not he would be a dear man at any price. A man who would take the position of marshal of a town like Caldwell for $50 per month is not worth his salt any place, a fact the present so-called economical Council will ascertain before their term of office expires. While extravagance should not characterize the financial policy of a city like Caldwell, all attempts to run it upon the principal governing a peanut stand will only result in failure and a greater cost than if a fair, liberal course had been pursued. The true policy in regard to employing public servants should be the payment of a respectable salary in the first place and then a rigid exaction of prompt and faith-

510

John Phillips

ful services. Any other policy is putting a premium upon lawlessness and rowdyism.

The salary reduction stood in spite of the *Commercial's* remarks and on June 29 the council accepted Phillips' resignation. The *Commercial,* July 7, 1881, said:

Caldwell is without a City Marshal, John Phillips having resigned and turned over his badge of office. The facts connected with this state of affairs are about as follows: At the organization of the present city government, Mr. Phillips agreed to accept the Marshalship at $60 per month and no less. On that basis he was appointed by the Mayor and council. Now the council comes in and says the salary paid is too high and reduces it to $50 per month, payable in city scrip. To this Mr. Phillips objects and hence his resignation. Of course the City Council can do as they please about such matters, but we ask the members of that body, if as individuals they had made a bargain, would they feel like going back upon it whenever the fancy suited them? and if they did how long do they suppose their credit as individuals would last? Not a boot black in town would trust them for a shine, and they couldn't buy a pint of peanuts without first depositing the colateral.

Of course, if they were dissatisfied with Phillips as a city marshal, they had a perfect right to discharge him. But they had no right to do it by a reduction of salary after making a contract for a specified amount per month.

It may be the council can find a man who will take the position at the reduced salary, but we venture the prediction that the person accepting it under existing circumstances will turn out to be a costly piece of municipal furniture. It is possible he may be an ornament to society and an evidence of good taste on the part of the council, but he will neither be very useful nor reflect credit upon their judgment of men.

The *Commercial's* prediction was correct—the city had quite a time finding someone suitable to work for the salary. After much delay the mayor nominated John Brown for marshal at a meeting held on July 18. The appointment was rejected by the council. The mayor then named Mike Meagher but again the council refused confirmation. The meeting adjourned with Caldwell still lacking a marshal. On July 27, 1881, the mayor appointed Meagher marshal until a permanent appointment could be made. At last, on August 1 the city administrators settled on James Roberts (*see* the section on Meagher).

Four days before the settlement the *Commercial,* July 28, 1881, had said:

The City Council did not make a regularly written contract with John Phillips when he accepted the position of City Marshal. They did make an implied contract, however, by confirming his appointment by the Mayor after he (Phillips) had stated that he would not accept the place unless the council

511

would allow him $60 per month in cash, or what was equivalent to cash. When Phillips was appointed there was nothing said about $50 for the marshalship and $10 for doing street commissioner work; at least the records of the City Council don't show it. Phillips was appointed and confirmed City Marshal without reference to performing the duties of street commissioner. Afterwards he agreed to fill that place, with the understanding that the members of the council would do the work among themselves. When Messrs [L. G.] Bailey, [L.] Thrailkill and [H. C.] Challis, as a majority of the council, reduced the marshal's salary they did it, not for the purpose of saving money on the street commissioner business, but in order that they might make a vacancy for some particular pet, well knowing that Phillips would not serve for $50 in city scrip. The street commissioner excuse was only an after thought, suggested by the statement published in the COMMERCIAL two weeks ago.

The councilmen above mentioned have sought in every way to hamper the Mayor in his management of the police force, and in that course they seem to have been impelled more by a desire to gratify their personal feelings than to subserve the interests of the city. But we have written sufficient on the subject at this time, and we close by recommending said councilmen to be honest in their contracts, as councilmen, and to avoid, if possible, seeking to excuse themselves for doing something which needed no excuse, if their own consciences told them they were right.

It was as a private citizen that John Phillips performed the odious task of exhuming the body of brothel-keeper George Woods in May, 1882. Woods had been killed on August 18, 1881, in the manner described in this article from the Caldwell Commercial, August 25, 1881:

THE KILLING OF GEO. WOODS.

About 8 o'clock on Thursday night of last week the sharp report of a revolver startled the general quiet of the city, and shortly after the news circulated that George Woods, the proprietor of the Red Light dance house had been shot and killed.

The account of the occurrence as given by the inmates of the house was about as follows: It appears that a young fellow named Charlie Davis, who came to Caldwell from Texas some time last fall, had been keeping a girl, an inmate of the house [which also served as a brothel], who goes by the name of Lizzie Roberts. Davis had endeavored to induce the girl to leave the house and live with him. On Thursday night he went down there to get her to leave, and told her she must go with him. She refused, and Woods said she should not go unless she wanted to. Davis asked Woods what he had to do with it, at the same time calling him an opprobious name. Woods replied, saying that he had a great deal to do with it, and ordered Davis to leave the house. Davis immediately pulled out his revolver and fired at Woods, the ball striking the latter between the breast bones and a few inches above the naval, going clear through his body and lodged in a partition a few feet behind where Woods was standing. Woods immediately grappled with Davis,

512

seized the revolver and attempted to get it away from the latter. In the struggle the two got out of the front door and a few feet from the house, when Davis succeeded in getting away and ran up town, where he gave himself up to a policeman. Woods walked into the house and toward the back door, near which he laid or fell down, saying that he was killed. He was placed upon a cot in the room and Dr. [W. A.] Noble sent for, but the bullet had done its work and he only lived a short time after.

On Friday morning Judge Kelly summoned G. G. Godfrey, I. B. Gilmore, L. Thrailkill, S. H. Horner, H. C. Unsell and Wm. Morris as a coroner's jury and held an inquest upon the body. The testimony of the witnesses examined was taken down at length, but we were requested not to publish it. The jury rendered a verdict that George Woods came to his death from a pistol shot fired by the hands of Charlie Davis.

Davis, after giving himself up, finding that Woods was dead or about to die, concluded not to remain, and before provisions could be made for his safe keeping gave his custodians the slip and got away. As there seems to be a sudden and great desire for the enforcement of all penal laws upon our statute books, we presume vigorous efforts will be made for his recapture and punishment.

Of the two men, Woods and Davis, little need be said at this time.

Woods was well known in Wichita, Caldwell and Hunnewell. He had for several years kept a brothel in the first named place, removing to Caldwell last year, where he opened up the Red Light, and this spring set up another house in Hunnewell. Outside of his business he was generally well liked by those who knew him, and was said to be honorable and upright in all his business transactions. The occupation he followed was not such as to make him a very useful or ornamental member of society and his violent death is only regarded as a natural result.

Of Charlie Davis we know but little. We have seen him about town for nearly a year, and always as a quiet man. It is said by those who know him that he was not quarrelsome, seldom got under the influence of liquor, and never made a practice of carrying weapons. It is claimed by some that he was intoxicated on Thursday night, and by others that he was duly sober. Be that as it may, he has perpetrated a crime which will practically make him a wanderer upon the face of the earth, and perhaps bring him to a violent death.

Grave robbing was the charge which caused John Phillips and others to open the coffin of George Woods. The *Commercial,* May 18, 1882, carried the story:

ROBBING THE DEAD.
ARREST OF DAVID SHARP.
CHARGED WITH OPENING GEORGE WOOD'S GRAVE
AND TAKING A DIAMOND PIN FROM THE BODY.

On complaint entered by Margaret Wood [George Woods' widow], Dave Sharp was arrested on Tuesday morning [May 16], charged with opening the grave in which George Wood's body was buried and taking from the corpse a diamond pin. An examination of the accused was had before J. D. Kelly, Esq., and the accused held to bail in the sum of $1,000 for his appearance at the next term of the District Court. He gave bail, Henry LeBreton becoming his bondsman.

The circumstances which led to the arrest of Sharp we understand to be about as follows: Last winter, shortly after the shooting matinee in which Mike Meagher was killed, a girl who goes by the name of Minnie, and who lived at the Red Light at the time of the shooting, informed Mag. Woods that Blanche, another of the demi-monde, who was living with George Spear at the time the latter was killed [at the same time Meagher was shot], had told her, while they were in Kansas City that George Spear and Dave Sharp had opened George Wood's grave and taken the diamond pin from the body. The statement of the girl Minnie was given little attention until a few days ago, when Mag became impressed with the idea that the girl's story must be true, and on Monday night she had an interview with Blanche in which the latter gave all the details connected with the affair.

Blanche's story was to the effect that one night shortly after Wood was buried George Spear and Dave Sharp started out with a spade and some tools; she inquired as to where they were going when Spear answered that they were going sky-larking. Not satisfied with the reply she followed the men, who took a direct course for the cemetery; arriving there, and finding the grave, they built a small fire by the side of it and began to dig away the earth. When they were fairly at work, Blanche went up to them and from that time was a close spectator of all that transpired. When the earth had been removed to the box which contained the casket, they broke the top off with a hatchet, then broke the lid and glass of the case, removed the diamond pin from the shirt front on the body, and then filled in the earth, never taking any trouble to fix the casket so that the dirt would not fall in upon the body.—They also threw in the pieces of burning wood and coals of the fire they had kindled and all returned to town.

After the arrest of Sharp, and at the request of Mag Woods, John Phillips, Mr. Robinson, Jack Fossett and some others went to the cemetery to take up the body and examine it. Drs. Noble and [W. B.] Brengle also accompanied the party. The surface of the grave showed indications of having been disturbed, and as the removal of the earth proceeded, they found a piece of the lid of the coffin, then the coals and burnt wood of the fire, and finally the broken box and the broken coffin. The coffin was taken out of the grave, the body removed from it and a strict examination made. There on the shirt front were the markes of the pin, so that Blanche's story had been confirmed so far.

Sharp denies having anything to do with robbing the dead and claims that Blanche's story is a lie. However, time will tell, but the present appearance of things looks rather billious for David.

David Sharp was acquitted of the crime on June 10, 1882.[2]

John Phillips was appointed marshal of Caldwell a second time on

John Phillips

May 5, 1884, replacing Henry Brown who, with his assistant marshal, Ben Wheeler, had been killed for attempting to rob a bank in Medicine Lodge on April 30, 1884. Marshal Phillips chose Bedford B. Wood to be his assistant. The Caldwell *Journal*, May 8, 1884, concluded its report by saying "both are good men and will make splendid officers. Here's our ☞, boys; shake."

The two were apparently efficient officers. During the cattle season of 1884 they made over 150 arrests most of which involved boisterous drunks, prostitutes, gamblers, and other routine or minor criminal elements.[3] The Caldwell paper had little in the way of excitement to report in the city police field but on October 16, 1884, the *Journal* relieved the monotony with this article:

DRUMMERS TAKEN IN.

A pair of very "fly" Chicago drummers came down last week bent on doing the "boys" up and painting the town red. Their first break was to "drop their wad" on the wrong horses, and leave themselves without the money to liquidate.

The boys caught on to their style and proceeded to give them one of the old fashioned Caldwell deals.

Denhollem's [J. C. Denhollem, dealer in coal] safe was broken open during the night while these "fly ones" were peacefully reposing in their beds, but the boys saw a chance for some fun and improved it. Phil. Bond was into the game and with John Phillips after him rushed to the victim's room, calling upon them to get up and give themselves up, or the door would be broken open and they probably be hanged for safe blowing. Phillips emphasized the order by tremendous kicks upon the door. The door flew open and the "fly" ones were disclosed [in] their night robes, pale as ghosts, trembling like leaves. Joe Harris exclaimed, "My Got, boys I didn't do this! Before Got, I'm innocent, don't hang me! Vere is Ed. Hewins [vice-president of Caldwell's Stock Exchange Bank], he goes on mine pond! Don't let them gentlemen in here to kill me," etc. The other one, Eli Kohn, was putting in about as good time as Harris, imploring for mercy and protesting his innocence. Phillips told them Hewins was not in town, and if he was he would not stand in with thieves and burglars; that they must go to jail at once. The breakfast hour at the jail was over and they could have nothing to eat until supper, as they did not feed burglars but once a day in this town. By this time they had crawled into their clothes and were being marched down stairs, where they were met by an angry looking mob, who insisted upon their being hanged at once to save trouble and expenses. This was too much for them and their pleadings for mercy and protestations of innocence were simply too much for the crowd to longer stand and a roar of laughter, such as only can go up from a Caldwell gang, went echoing off in many directions, but the main body of it landed in a neighboring saloon, followed by the victims and the crowd. About $25 paid

515

the bill at the bar, and the Lone Star clothing house put up money for the boys to get home on.

Joe Harris said, while the boys were drinking, "Dot vellow offer there," pointing to Kohn, "was the vorst scart veller I effer saw. I was not scart at all," and all the while he was about the color of a last year's slicker and shaking so his glass almost fell from his fingers. Those Chicago drummers will not return here soon to illuminate the town with a carmine hue to any alarming extent. It was pretty rough on them, but then they deserved it.

The most exciting incident in the police career of John Phillips was the shooting of Oscar Thomas on November 15. The Caldwell *Journal,* November 20, 1884, reported the roles played by the marshal and his assistant:

CALDWELL AGAIN TO THE FRONT.
OSCAR THOMAS MEETS HIS DEATH BY
REFUSING ARREST.

The quietness of this city was disturbed about 6 o'clock last Saturday evening by a couple of reports from a gun and upon looking to see from whence the noise came we saw a crowd of men rushing to the store of Witzleben & Key, on the corner of Main and Sixth streets, and thither we went with the eager crowd, bent on learning the cause of all the disturbance, and upon reaching the center of attraction, we saw, with horror, a man wallowing in his own blood, in the rear end of the store. At first none seemed to know very much of the man, or the circumstances that surrounded the case, but those who did were unwilling to say very much, and various and wild were the rumors concerning the cause. About the only thing that could be learned at that time was, that the unfortunate fellow was Oscar Thomas, and was shot by our City Marshal and deputy in refusing to be arrested.

From the evidence given at the inquest and what we could learn concerning him, it appears that Thomas had been at work for the Washita Cattle Company, and came into town a week or so ago. Like many of that wild class of cowboys when they are in town, think they must carry their arms the same as in the Territory, so, accordingly, he went armed with a dirk knife and six-shooter, and sometimes two. When noticed by his friends in that condition, they remonstrated with him and tried to get him to lay them off, or he would get into trouble. His only answer seemed to be that he would carry them if he wanted to, and that no man or officer could take them from him, and that he was tired of this way of life and would as soon pass in his checks now as to live. When under the influence of liquor he became very abusive and his own companions had no control over him. At last, becoming so bad, the officers were notified of the case and were put on their guard; also that he would be a very bad man to handle. The officers, through his friends, tried to get him to leave town, but to no avail.

Thomas' whole spite seemed to be on Witzleben & Key [A. Witzleben and B. W. Key, general outfitters, successors to York, Parker and Draper Mercantile

John Phillips

Co.], because they refused to sell him goods on credit, and at different times he was in the store only to create a fuss with them or their clerk. And at the time of being shot was in an abusive altercation with Mack Killibraw, the clerk, who, not wanting to bear any more of the abuse, caught up an axe and would have axed him to retract, but it was taken from him by Mr. Witzleben, whereupon he, Thomas, attempted to draw his arms, and Mack grabbed hold of his hand to keep him from doing so, at the same time asking him not to draw his gun on him. At this instant City Marshal, John Phillips, came to the scene of action by a call, and, walking up to Thomas with drawn revolver saying, "Throw up your hands," whereupon he turned around facing Phillips, but did not comply with the order. Again he was ordered to "throw up," but instead of doing so he made a pass for his arms, whereupon Marshal Phillips fired, and Thomas partially dropped down behind the counter. In the meantime Assistant Marshal, Bedford Wood, came in at the side door and taking in the situation, came to the rescue, Thomas not complying to another request to "throw up his hands," was ordered by Marshal Phillips to fire, which Wood did, the ball piercing his, Thomas' head. Thomas falling to the floor was then disarmed of a 45-calibre six-shooter and a four-inch dirk knife.

Drs. Noble and Goddard made an examination of the wounds, reported them fatal and that life would soon be extinct. The first ball entering the left breast opposite the lower end of the sternum, passing directly through and coming out on the right of the spinal column, the second ball a little to the left of the median line of the union of the two parietal bones with the occipital, coming out at the middle part of the forehead, lacerating the brain in its course.

In a short time Thomas was removed to the city jail building, where he remained until life became extinct at 9 o'clock Sunday morning.

After the inquest was held over the body Monday by T. H. B. Ross, Justice of the Peace, it was buried in the cemetery at this place. And Tuesday afternoon the jury brought in the following verdict:

STATE OF KANSAS, }
Sumner County. } ss.

An inquisition holden at Caldwell, in Sumner county, on the 17th and 18th days of November, A. D. 1884, before me, T. H. B. Ross, a Justice of the Peace of Caldwell township, in said county, acting coroner of said county on the body of Oscar Thomas, then lying dead, by the jurors whose names are hereunto subscribed. The said jurors, upon their oaths, do say that said Oscar Thomas came to his death about nine o'clock A. M., on Sunday morning, on the 16th day of November, A. D. 1884, from two gunshot wounds, and that the weapons which produced his death were six-shooters, 45-calibre, loaded with leaden bullets and gun powder, and were held in the hands of John Phillips, marshal, and Bedford Wood, assistant marshal, of Caldwell, where said wounds were produced. And that said killing was not felonious, but justifiable and commendable and that said officers were acting in the line of their duty as officers of the city of Caldwell and in a careful and prudent manner. In testimony whereof the said jurors have hereunto set their hands this 18th day of November and the year aforesaid.

I. N. COOPER,
W. MOORES,
T. L. CRIST,
M. M. BARNARD,
JAS. M. KERR,
S. H. HORNER.

ATTEST: T. H. B. Ross, Justice of the Peace, Caldwell township, Sumner county, Kansas, acting coroner of Sumner county, Kansas.

T. H. B. ROSS,
Justice of the Peace.

Some citizens of Caldwell thought that Phillips and Wood had killed Thomas unnecessarily. The Caldwell *Journal,* November 27, 1884, defended their action:

There are some in the city who do not think that the verdict of the jury in the Oscar Thomas case as reported last week was entirely justifiable, but we are prepared to state that the number can be counted on the fingers of one hand. The citizens of Caldwell deprecate the killing of any one, but when it becomes a necessity for some one to be killed, or else we lose a good officer, they one and all say, save the officers and let the other fellow take care of himself, obey the laws or take the consequences. The evidence in the case shows that Thomas had his hand on his six-shooter when commanded by the officers to throw up his hands, and was attempting to draw it when first fired upon, after being commanded to surrender. That he did not surrender when called upon after the first shot was fired and that the officers had every reason to believe that their lives were in jeopardy, when they fired the second shot. No officer is called upon to take extreme chances on losing his life when in the discharge of his duty. He is not then acting for himself but for the country at large. If he takes desperate chances and is killed he does not sustain the only loss that is had, but the community who placed him there is a loser by reason of its servant being removed and the laws broken. Our officers did their duty and our citizens upheld them in this case, as they will in all others when they do their duty and use reasonable precautions in making arrests of dangerous men to prevent bloodshed. The jury's verdict is the verdict of the people in this case.

After the shooting of Thomas the police life of John Phillips returned to its former routine ways. On December 2, 1884, he arrested William Williams and George Schnover for being drunk. The *Journal,* December 4, 1884, said:

A couple of "plain drunks" were brought in town from the outskirts Tuesday by the City Marshal in an express wagon. Caldwell officers are kind to the weary and way fallen sinners and hauls them in a wagon when they get too tired to walk.

518

The two were fined $3 and costs each the next day in police court.[4]

So routine had police business become that Caldwell papers ceased to mention the marshal's name in the next few months though he continued on the force until the middle of the summer when he was replaced by his assistant Bedford Wood.[5] The season of 1885 was the last that Texas trail herds entered Kansas, and Caldwell, like Dodge City, no longer needed the type of policemen she once had.

1. Caldwell *Commercial,* April 7, 14, 1881. 2. *Ibid.,* June 15, 1882. 3. "Police Court Docket," Records of the City of Caldwell, May-October, 1884. 4. *Ibid.,* December 3, 1884. 5. *Ibid.,* summer, 1885.

SHORT, LUKE L. (1854-1893)

The story of Luke Short in Kansas is also the story of the Dodge City "war." Though by his own statement Luke had been in

Luke Short

Dodge City some two years before the difficulties began, his name appeared in the city papers only intermittently, the earliest known mention being nine months before the trouble broke out. That first news item appeared in the Dodge City *Times,* August 3, 1882, and is reprinted in the section on Bat Masterson.

Luke next made the newspapers when he purchased Chalkley Beeson's interest in the Long Branch saloon. The *Ford County Globe,* February 6, 1883, carried the first of a series of notifications:

DISSOLUTION NOTICE.

This is to certify that C. M. Beeson, and W. H. Harris doing a saloon business in Dodge City, Kansas, under the firm name of Beeson & Harris, has this day been dissolved by mutual consent. Mr. Beeson selling his interest in the business

519

to Luke Short who will continue the business with Mr. Harris and who assume all the liabilities of the late firm and collect all outstanding accounts due the same.

C. M. BEESON
February 6th 1883.
W. H. HARRIS.[1]

Shortly after the transfer, Luke's new associate was nominated to run for mayor of Dodge City. At a voters' mass meeting in the court house on March 17, Harris was suggested for mayor and Pat Sughrue, T. J. Tate, Nelson Cary, Henry Koch, and Charles Dickerson for councilmen. Among Harris' supporters were former mayor James H. Kelley, Clerk of the District Court W. F. Petillon, and the *Ford County Globe.*[2]

A few days later, on March 19, a similar meeting named an opposition ticket backed by Nicholas B. Klaine's Dodge City *Times,* Mike Sutton, Former Rep. R. M. Wright, and Mayor A. B. Webster. This ticket included L. E. Deger for mayor and H. B. Bell, H. T. Drake, H. M. Beverley, George S. Emerson, and Henry Sturm for councilmen.[3]

The election was accompanied by much vilification, especially on the part of the *Times* which assured Dodgeites that should Harris be elected the town would become a snug harbor for all the robbers, drunks, con men, and general ne'er-do-wells in the area. The *Globe,* in contrast, seemed content to let the election take whatever course it chose and used most of its political space condemning Editor Klaine for his vitriolic attacks. Perhaps Klaine's tactics paid off. When the votes were counted on April 3 Larry Deger had defeated Harris 214 to 143.[4]

Three weeks later the new city administration passed two ordinances which were to have a profound effect on both Luke Short and Dodge City. The first dealt with prostitution:

(Published April 26, 1883.)
ORDINANCE NO. 70.
AN ORDINANCE FOR THE SUPPRESSION OF VICE AND IMMORALITY WITHIN THE CITY OF DODGE CITY.
Be it ordained by the Mayor and Council of the City of Dodge City:
Section 1. Any person or persons who shall keep or maintain in this city a brothel, bawdy house, house of ill fame, or of assignation, shall upon conviction thereof be fined in a sum not less than Ten nor more than One Hundred Dollars.
Sec. 2. Any person whether male or female, being an inmate or resident of any brothel, bawdy house, or house of ill-fame in this city, shall upon conviction thereof be fined in a sum not less than Five nor more than Fifty Dollars.

Sec. 3. Any person or persons as defined in sections one and two of this ordinance found upon the streets or in any public place within the corporate limits of the city of Dodge City, for the purpose of plying or advertising her or their calling or business as defined in section one and two of this ordinance, shall upon conviction thereof be fined in a sum not less than Five nor more than Fifty Dollars.

Sec. 4. The general reputation of any such houses mentioned in the foregoing sections, or of its inmates and residents, shall be prima facie evidence of the character of such houses or persons.

Sec. 5. All ordinances or parts of ordinances inconsistent herewith are hereby repealed.

Section 6. This ordinance shall take effect [and] be in force from and after its publication in the Dodge City Times.

Passed by the council April 23d, 1883,

Attest, L. C. HARTMAN, City Clerk.

Approved April 23d, 1883. L. E. DEGER, Mayor.

The other ordinance dealt with vagrancy:

(Published April 26, 1883.)

ORDINANCE NO. 71.

AN ORDINANCE TO DEFINE AND PUNISH VAGRANCY.

Be it ordained by the Mayor and Councilmen of the City of Dodge City.

Section 1. Any person who may be found loitering, loafing or wandering within the corporate limits of the city of Dodge City without any lawful vocation or visible means of support, shall be deemed guilty of vagrancy under this ordinance, and may be fined in any sum not less than Ten nor more than One Hundred Dollars.

Sec. 2. Any person who may be found loitering around houses of ill-fame, gambling houses or places where liquors are sold or drank, without any visible means of support or lawful vocation, or shall be the keeper or inmate of any house of ill-fame or gambling house, or engaged in any unlawful calling whatever, shall be deemed guilty of vagrancy under this ordinance, and may be fined in any sum not less than Ten nor more than One Hundred Dollars.

Sec. 3. All ordinances or parts of ordinances inconsistent herewith are hereby repealed.

Section 4. This ordinance shall be in force and effect on and after its publication once in the Dodge City Times.

Passed the council April 23d, 1883.

Attest: L. C. HARTMAN, City Clerk.

Approved April 23d, 1883. L. E. DEGER, Mayor.[5]

On Saturday night, April 28, two days after the ordinances became effective, arrests were made under their provisions. These arrests were of women ostensibly employed as singers in the Long Branch. No one seemed to question that their real occupation was prostitution; what caused the subsequent trouble was the apparent partiality with which the laws were enforced. The *Ford County Globe,* May 1, 1883, reported:

The annual revolutionary spirit was again exhibited on our streets yesterday. Wars and rumors of war, was the out-cry all along the line. The smouldering volcano broke forth on this day and wiped out the wicked and the ungodly, they having to flee from the wrath that was to come. It was a hot day for the vagrant, the gambler and the inmate of the house of ill fame, but they must yield to the majesty of the law or take the consequences. All day, armed groupes of officials, both city and county, might have been seen by the least inquisitive, and the very determined look of their countenances indicated to the most confiding that they meant business, and business it was. In order to show why this determined stand was being made by the authorities, we must go back to the passage of sundry ordinances by the new city council, to which some exception was taken by those whom it seemed to press down upon most heavily the same being "an Ordinance for the Suppression of vice and Immorality within the city of Dodge" and another "to Define and Punish Vagrancy" passed April 23d 1883. It was not the ordinance itself that was objectionable to those it was calculated to reach but the partial manner of its enforcement as they think, which caused the trouble.

Saturday night the first arrest was made under the new ordinances, the same being that of three women in the long branch saloon. This was peaceably accomplished and without any resistance so far as we are enabled to learn. Yet, later in the night, Luke Short and L. C. Hartman met upon the street and paid their respective compliments to each other by exchanging shots, fortunately no one was hurt. Hartman, it seems, was a special who helped to make the arrests. Short was one of the partners of the saloon from which these women were taken. It was claimed by the proprietors that partiality was shown in arresting women in their house when two were allowed to remain in A. B. Webster's saloon, one at Heinz & Kramer's, two at Nelson Cary's, and a whole herd of them at Bond & Nixon's dance hall, and if this is true, it would be most natural for them to think so and give expression to their feelings. No doubt they spoke unpleasant words toward our city government, that may have caused them to rise in their majesty and cause the arrest on yesterday of Luke Short, Thomas Lane, saloon keepers, and half dozen others known by the professional name of gamblers. All were hustled into the city bastile without any resistance on their part, and were allowed to languish there until the arrival of their choice of trains, both east and west come along, when they were invited to take passage without any further ceremony or explanation. The women who had been jugged Saturday, were all brought up before his honor Bobby Burns and he imposed a heavy fine on each one of them for their disregard of the law.

Thus the smouldering volcano has burst forth in all its fury, and has stricken terror to the hearts of the inhabitants that so closely surround it and causes one to reflect as to whether or not it will be followed up by a St. John cyclone and sweep away in its train the dispenser of ardent spirits, and thus give us another evidence of the moral and temperance element of our citizens and show that the righteous must and shall prevail in the city of Dodge.

522

Luke Short

On May 3, 1883, the *Times* told its version of the difficulty:

ENFORCING THE LAW.

The city has been under an intense commotion for several days, growing out of the ordinance in relation to the "Suppression of gambling and prostitution." On Saturday night an additional police force was put on, and the work of enforcement was commenced. Three prostitutes pretendedly employed in Harris & Short's saloon, as "singers," but employed evidently to evade the ordinance in relation to prostitution, were arrested and put in the lock-up. This action engendered bitter feeling, and City Clerk Hartman who was on the police force, was afterward met by Luke Short, and his assassination attempted. Short fired two shots at Hartman, the latter replying with one shot, none of the shots taking effect. Short was arrested and placed under $2,000 bonds. Mayor Deger, learning that a conspiracy had been formed, which had for its object the armed resistance to the enforcement of the law and consequent murder of some of our best citizens, organized a police force on Sunday, and on Monday the plan was carried out. Luke Short was the first one arrested and placed in the calaboose. Subsequently, five others were arrested, as follows: W. H. Bennett, a former New Mexico desperado, Dr. Niel, a Mobeetie gambler, Johnson Gallagher, a gambler, and L. A. Hyatt, a gambler. These men, Hyatt, being retained a couple of days, were given the "choice of trains," and on Tuesday, under orders of Mayor Deger, were sent out of town. Short, Lane and Gallagher went east, Bennett went west, and Niel went south.

As a precaution, about one hundred and fifty citizens were on watch Monday night, and a large police force is still held on duty night and day. Mayor Deger, the police force and the citizens of Dodge City are determined that the lawless element shall not thrive in this city. No half-way measures will be used in the suppression of either lawlessness or riot. Mayor Deger is a resolute, fearless and obstinate officer. All good and law abiding citizens are standing by him in this trying emergency.

It must be understood that no foolishness will be allowed in the conduct of city affairs. Let the people employ their pursuits peacefully. And evildoers must stand the consequences of their lawless conduct.[6]

Of the three gamblers who boarded east bound trains, Tom Lane, at least, stopped in Topeka and sought legal counsel. The Topeka *Daily Commonwealth,* May 4, 1883, reported his failure:

WILL SUE DODGE CITY.

Mr. Lane, One of the Men Run Out of Town, On the War Path Against the City.

Mr. Lane, one of the men who were ordered out of Dodge City recently, was in town yesterday and applied to one of the prominent attorneys of the city to commence an action for damages against Dodge City. He claims that he has lived in Dodge since 1876, never had a law suit or any trouble except once when he paid a fine for fighting, and that there is no reason why he should not be allowed to remain there and conduct his business, saloon

WHY THE WEST WAS WILD

keeping, as before. He admits that two of the men were bad characters, and says that the others were forced to leave on account of the unfriendly feeling of the mayor toward them, resulting from the recent election. The attorney did not take the case, and Mr. Lane took the train for Dodge City in the afternoon. He says that he intends to stay there, if he can; that he will not fight a mob, but that if he has to go, he will sue the city.

On May 3, 1883, the *Commonwealth* had said:

A gentleman who knows the crowd that was driven out of Dodge City, as announced in our special dispatches yesterday, says that some of the men are now in this city. The number includes all classes of roughs, and it is possible that some of them were implicated in the burglaries here. It is also a fact that there are several Kansas City thieves in town.

Luke had established himself in Kansas City and was kept informed of the local situation by letters from friends in Dodge. Otto Mueller, a saloon owner, wrote on letterhead stationery bearing the name of W. H. Harris' Bank of Dodge City:

DODGE CITY, KAN., May 5th 1883

FRIEND LUKE:

I intended to write you before this, but did not know your address until informed by Myton this morning that a letter directed in care of "Marble Hall" [522 Main street, Kansas City, Mo.] would reach you.

The situation here in town is unchanged except so far as relates to public opinion, which is gradually but steadily changing in your favor. All your friends are at work with a determination which is bound to win in the end. Of course every movement must be made with the greatest care and caution, and as many are too timid to express themselves, it will naturally require time, before the organization that style themselves "the Vigilanters" will be convinced that they must give way to public opinion. And a beautiful lot of reformers they are, these vigilanters, under the leadership of their captain, Tom Nixon of Dance Hall fame. But no matter how slow, you may rest assured that this time will surely come. As the heat of passion subsides and men begin to look over the past more calmly, they can not help to see that a great wrong has been committed and many are frank enough to admit that fact. Men of good standing in this community, against whom nothing can be said, but who take little interest in the management of public affairs, feel that they are not safe in the enjoyment of their life and property in a place where such outrages may be committed without the interference of the authorities, and feel more alarmed when they begin to realize the fact that the outrages here committed not only without interference, but under the guidance of the municipal government, whose duty it should be to protect even those charged with the commission of a crime against violence.

Harris feels very downhearted, but is untiringly at work to set matters right. You can form no idea how your enemies watch him at every step and move. No train passes this station without being searched and watched by the Vigilanters for Contraband. Harris and his friends feel confidant that Bob

524

Wright on his return to town will take the lead against the suppression of further outrages, and I think also that he is the best man for it. Our best men in town will back him, and I think that before long the *"Reformers"* will be compelled to surrender and lay down their arms. Do not feel discouraged, but feel confident that Harris will spare no effort to have everything fixed right and that your friends will assist him all they can. I will write again and keep you advised as times goes on.

Yours very sincerely

OTTO MÜLLER.[7]

Luke wrote to Dodge City the same day. George Hoover, a wholesale liquor dealer and representative in the Kansas legislature, answered:

Dodge City, Kansas, May 7th 1883

MR. LUKE SHORT, Kans. City.

FRIEND LUKE.

In reply to your letter of 5th inst. I am sorry to say that the excitement is more intense now than ever and growing more so every day as the powers that be now in Dodge, are determined that what they have already done and what they propose to do, should any one else displease them shall stick. The Governor and all his power to the contrary notwithstanding and it would not be safe for Harris to appear in your petition in any shape for he was very nearly one of the selected ones. Nor for any of your friends to do so, for it would not only compel Harris to leave but also any who would appear in the matter should a petition *be signed* by the *few* who would have courage enough so to do, it would avail nothing for it would be immediately followed by one to the contrary—signed by numerous people which would make the one in your favor appear as nothing—for though *you have* many friends here and deserve them yet they would fear to sign a petition in your favor knowing that it would jeopardize themselves.

You know how a Governor acts. With the church element, the Railroad officials and part of the so called immoral element against you he would not interfere in the rulings of a city or mob ruling. My advice to you would be to either sell your interest in Dodge or else employ some one to look after your interests here and make up your mind to abandon Dodge at least during the present administration. Much as I would like to see you at your own place I think this the only safe plan for both yourself and friends.

Very truly Yours

G. M. HOOVER.[8]

Short apparently sought legal assistance from Larned attorney Net Adams who wrote:

LARNED, KAS. May 8 1883

DEAR LUKE

Yours Just received on my return from Stafford. Pete Harding was here yesterday he says the Shot Gun brigade are still boarding the trains. They wont let any body stop Lon Hyat stoped here two days & went back but he could not get off Lane is at Cimeron & Corn H[ole]. Johnny [Johnson Gallagher] is also out they are still running things with a high hand. I shall go up there in few days Pete Harding says public opinion is growing against them fast there. I don't know exactly what I will do yet with them. Think strong of suing the whole out fit to gether with the W. U. Telegraph Co. & sue here, but dont know yet. I will be ready at any time to go and do anything I can for you. But if I were you I believe I would wait for a week or 10 days yet & let matters die down a little. They swear vengence against you as I understand it, and are watching everything to work Harris so I am informed. Let me hear from you again soon & will write more.

Respct

NELSON ADAMS

Hyat made a rucket over Harris when he was fined, but I think he is making terms. Dont Let the Devils Know that I furnish information

NET [9]

The Dodge City *Times*, May 10, 1883, expanded on the attempted return of Hyatt:

Two of the men who were ordered out of town last week returned here on Thursday night. Hyatt stepped off the train on the south side of the track, but was confronted with about a dozen pistols presented to him. He gladly returned to the car and too gladly pursued his journey west. Lane did not get off the train here but at Cimarron, twenty miles west, where he continues to hold forth. Lane would like to make terms and return to Dodge and behave like a good citizen, but we believe there is no disposition to accept his profered repentance and promises.

By this time things had progressed sufficiently for newspapers over the state and in the East to print summaries of the events. Depending on the source of information, the papers were either pro Deger or pro Short. As an example, it is not difficult to determine the side on which the Kansas City (Mo.) *Evening Star*, May 9, 1883, had cast itself:

RUFFIANS REGIME.

A STARTLING STATE OF THINGS AT DODGE CITY.

The fact, that for the past ten days a very remarkable and startling state of affairs has existed at as well known a point as Dodge City, Kas., and that all mention of them has been kept out of the press, the matter, in short, entirely suppressed from the outside world, is an excellent illustration of what western lawlessness can do and the state of society in some of the border towns. That trouble of a serious nature has existed there can be surmised from the fact that prominent Kansas City attorneys left to-day for Topeka to petition Gov. Glick in the interest of Dodge City property owners that the town be placed under martial law.

The difficulty, which began only a little over a week ago, is but the culmination of a long standing feud between two elements of the place. Dodge City has long enjoyed the reputation of being a hard place. It was one of the few points in Kansas where saloons run openly and gambling is legitimized. The headquarters of the cowboys and cattle men of that vicinity, the majority of the institutions are designed for their especial selectation.

Just before the last city election the mayor was a man named Webster, the proprietor of a dive, half saloon and the other half gambling house and variety hall. He was a representative of the tougher element of the sporting fraternity. The head of the other faction was W. H. Harris, of Harris & Short, proprietors of the Long Branch saloon. Harris represented the quieter and more reputable element and there was bitter feeling between the two.

At the last election Harris was beaten in the race for mayor by one Deger, Webster's candidate, and since then it has been conceeded that it was only a matter of time when all of Harris's sympathizers would be driven out of the town. Thus Dodge has been hovering on the brink of trouble for a long time. About ten days ago it came. Mr. Short, who is Harris's partner, and a police officer, had a shooting affray. Neither were hurt, and the evidence showed that Short was fired on first. He was nevertheless placed under bonds, and next day thrown into jail. The marshal of Dodge, who made the arrest, is Jack Bridges, a well known character, who formerly lived here and traveled principally upon having "killed his man."

A short time later five gamblers were arrested, and also jailed. That night a vigilance committee was formed with Tom Nixon, the proprietor of one of the hardest dance halls that ever existed in the west, at the head. This crowd repaired to the jail and notified the prisoners that they must leave town next morning and that they would be given their choice of trains going east or west. Meantime the vigilantes took possession of the town.

The correspondent of the Chicago *Times* [Dodge City Attorney Harry E. Gryden] and other leading papers were notified that they must not be permitted to send any telegrams in reference to the situation and a body of armed men watched the arrival of each train to see that there was no interference. A lawyer from Larned, sent for by one of the prisoners was met by a vigilante who leveled a shot-gun at his head and told him not to stop. He passed on. Next morning the five gamblers were put on a westward bound train and Short left for Kansas City where he is at present.

The trouble has by no means yet abated. The place is practically in the hands of the "vigilantes" and the situation is more serious from the fact that the mayor is acting with them and it was he who notified the prisoners that they must go. The trains are still watched and armed men guard the town, while a list of others who will be ordered out has been prepared. Every source of reliable information indicates that Dodge is now in the hands of desperadoes, and that incident to the ejection of Short and the others, the lives and property of citizens are by no means safe. For this reason martial law is being asked. That there will be trouble of a very serious character there, is anticipated.

From Kansas City Luke went to Topeka to see the governor. The Topeka *Daily Capital,* May 11, 1883, reported:

A MAN FROM DODGE.

KANSAS CITY, May 10.—Luke Short, the most prominent of the six men who were expelled from Dodge, came to this city and left to-night for Topeka, where he intends to lay his case before Gov. Glick. He claims that the authorities had no right to expel him from town, but if he has violated any laws he should be permitted to remain there and answer the charges.

A PROMINENT CATTLE MAN ALSO.

A prominent cattle dealer who resides in Dodge City, said in an interview here to-night that he believed the whole trouble was simply a war upon the gamblers; that the citizens had determined to have a more orderly state of society, and had, therefore, compelled certain parties to leave. He said that they had a similar experience about three years ago, and that there is nothing especially remarkable in the present movement. The law cannot reach these cases, and consequently the people are obliged to take the law to a certain extent in their own hands.

As Luke visited Topeka, another Dodgeite was summoned there by Gov. George W. Glick. This man was W. F. Petillon, a prominent Democrat and clerk of the district court. The Dodge City *Times*, May 10, 1883, said:

W. F. Petillon has gone to Topeka in response to a telegram from the Governor. Some affairs of state need the diplomacy of statesmen. We suppose the Governor's intercession is desired on behalf of affairs in Dodge. The Governor will not interfere with our local laws and the manner of disposing of them. He might execute the State laws which would then render local laws of no use and no consequence.

In the capital city Luke presented Governor Glick with a petition which he had drawn up in Missouri. It was corroborated by Petillon:

To HIS EXCELLENCY. HON. GEO. W. GLICK, GOVERNOR OF KANSAS:

The Petition of Luke L. Short, respectfully represents to your Excellency that he has resided at Dodge City Kansas for nearly two years; that he is a member of the firm of Harris and Short of said city, that his said partner is vice President of the Bank of Dodge City and has large business interests at said place.

Your Petitioner further states that during his said residence in Dodge City he has ever been in the peace of the state, and have not been charged with any crime until the 30th day of April 1883 when he was arrested charged with an assault upon one L. C. Hartman of said city; that he was entirely innocent of said charge, and gave bond in the sum of $2000 to answer the same on Wednesday the [second] day of May, 1883. That he caused the said Hartman to be arrested on a charge of assaulting your petitioner and the trial of said Hartman on said charge was set for hearing for Wednesday the 3rd day of May 1883.[10]

Luke Short

On Monday [11] the 2nd day of May 1883 your petitioner was again arrested but on what charge your petitioner was at the time and is now ignorant. That no warrant was read or shown to him on the occasion of this arrest, and your petitioner was denied bail. Doctor S. Galland of said city offering to Execute a bond for any amount for your petitioner's release, but said offer was refused; that about five oclock of the evening of said 2nd day of May and while your Petitioner was in custody in the calaboose a band of armed men led by Larry Deger, Mayor of said city came to said Calaboose and ordered your Petitioner to leave said city and never to return, and then and there threatened your petitioner with great personal danger, upon a refusal so to do, and also informed him that if he returned he would do so at his peril.

Your Petitioner then & there remonstrated with the said Deger and his followers, and averred that he was guilty of no crime against the law; that he was ready & willing to meet any and all charges in the courts, where he would satisfy all of his innocence, that he was under bond to appear to answer the charge, in this petition before mentioned, that he had a prosperous business in said city and that no reason existed for any such extraordinary proceeding, but the said Deger and followers would not listen to your petitioners remonstrances, and repeated their demands, that he must leave.

Your petitioner avers that by reason of the aforesaid threats, he was put in fear of his life, and he verily believes that had he remained in said city, he would have been murdered; that upon advice of friends he left said city the next morning; that while your petitioner was confined in the calaboose he was not allowed to see counsel, and when his regular counsel, Mr. Dryden attempted to see him, he was refused admittance, and his life was threatened if he further attempted to see your petitioner that after said Dryden was refused admittance to your Petitioner, Mr. Harris your Petitioners partner telegraphed to Nelson Adams Esq of Larned Kansas to come to said city to act as your Petitioners counsel. that when said Adams arrived at 11 o clock of day, he was met, as your Petitioner is informed and believes by said Deger and his band of armed men and ordered not to stop, on pain of his life and said Adams returned to his home.

Your Petitioner further states that the leading parties of the band that came to said Calaboose and intimidated your petitioner were Larry Deger, Fred Singer, Thomas Nixon, A. B. Webster, Brick Bond, Bob Vanderburg, Jack Bridges, Clark Chipman, L. C. Hartman and these were followed by about twenty five others all being heavily armed.

that said Deger is Mayor. Fred Singer, under sheriff, Thomas Nixon, a proprietor of a Dance Hall in said city. A. B. Webster, proprietor of a saloon & gambling house, Brick Bond, a proprietor of a dance hall. Bob Vanderburg a special policeman. Jack Bridges, a Marshal. Clark Chipman, Assistant Marshal. L. C. Hartman special policeman.

Your petitioner further avers that the cause of said act of violence was not anything that your petitioner had done against the law, but arose from political differences and Business rivalry; that many of the best and most prominent business men of said city stand ready & willing to become personally responsible to the state for your petitioners good behavior, that he has no desire to return

529

to Said city for the purpose of violating the law, but simply for the purpose of protecting his business interests. But that the parties above mentioned threaten your petitioners life if he returns and still maintain the same attitude of defiance to the law, and unless your Excellency as conservator of the Public peace acts in the premise your Petitioner is wholly without remedy. Wherefore your petitioner humbly prays your Excellency to take such action as to your Excellency may seem appropriate, to protect your petitioner from the unlawful violence of the above mentioned parties—to the end that he may return and remain in safety—and prosecute his business holding himself amenable to all lawful action of the authorities—

STATE OF MISSOURI)
COUNTY OF JACKSON)   LUKE L. SHORT

Subscribed & sworn to before me, the undersigned Notary Public this 10th day of May 1883. My commission expires June 30th 1884—

CHRISTOPHER HOPE
Notary Public

W. F. PETILLON—Clerk of the District Court of Ford County Kansas, says that he has read the foregoing petition of Luke L. Short; that he is personally cognisant of the facts stated therein and that they are true, according to his best Knowledge information and belief.

W. F. PETILLON

STATE OF MISSOURI)
COUNTY OF JACKSON)

Subscribed and sworn to before me the undersigned Notary Public within and for said County and state this 10th day of May 1883. My Commission expires June 30th 1884.

CHRISTOPHER HOPE
Notary Public.[12]

Luke's visit with Governor Glick apparently had some results. Though no copy has been found, Glick must have telegraphed the sheriff of Ford county asking the situation in Dodge. Sheriff Hinkle's telegraphic answer was:

Received at Topeka, Kan. 6:30 pm.   May 11, 1883.
DATED DODGE CITY, Ks.
To HON. G. W. GLICK:

Mr. L. E. Deger our mayor has compelled several persons to leave the city for refusing to comply with the ordinances. No mob exists nor is there any reason to fear any violence as I am amply able to preserve the peace. I showed your message to Mr. Deger who requests me to say that the act of compelling the parties to leave the city was simply to avoid difficulty and disorders. Everything is as quiet here as in the capital of the state and should I find myself unable to preserve the present quiet will unhesitatingly ask your assistance.

Resp'y
GEO. T. HINKEL,
Sheriff [13]

A few minutes later Glick received a similar telegram from Robert M. Wright and Richard J. Hardesty:

Received at Topeka, Kan. 6:35 pm   May 11, 1883.
DATED DODGE CITY, KS.
To Gov. G. W. GLICK:
    Our town and county never was more peaceable and quiet than it is at present notwithstanding all reports to the contrary.

R. M. WRIGHT
R. J. HARDESTY [14]

Before the three Dodgeites had been heard from Governor Glick had alerted two companies of the Kansas National Guard, company H at Sterling and company K at Newton. The commanders of each company wired back that they were ready for immediate service.[15]

The receipt of Sheriff Hinkle's telegram, instead of placating Governor Glick, obviously incensed him. He replied:

GEO. T. HINKLE,   May 12th, 1883.
    Sheriff Ford County,
        Dodge City, Kansas.
MY DEAR SIR:
    Your telegram to me of the 11th is at hand. I am glad to be assured by you that you are able to preserve the peace of Dodge City, and of your county. The accounts of the way things have been going on there are simply monstrous, and it requires that the disgrace that is being brought upon Dodge City, and the State of Kansas, by the conduct that is represented to have occurred there, should be wiped out. Your dispatch to me presents an extraordinary state of affairs, one that is outrageous upon its face. You tell me that the mayor has compelled several parties to leave the town for refusing to comply with the ordinances. Such a statement as that if true, simply shows that the mayor is unfit for his place, that he does not do his duty, and instead of occupying the position of peace maker, the man whose duty it is to see that the ordinances are enforced by legal process in the courts, starts out to head a mob to drive people away from their homes and their business.
    It was the mayor's duty, if he did anything, to have appointed and sworn in special policemen to protect citizens, and if he could not do it, to have called upon you, or have called upon me, for assistance to aid him in executing his duties as mayor, and in preserving the peace of his town. It is represented to me by affidavits, and by statements, that the best men in Dodge City have been threatened with assassination, and with being driven away from their homes, if they raised their voices against the conduct of this mob. Now if this is true, it is your duty to call to your assistance a respectable number of people, sufficient to enforce the law, and protect every man in Dodge City, without any reference to who he is, or what his business is, and if he is charged with crime, or the violation of law, to see that he has a fair trial before a proper tribunal, and that the sentence of the law is executed by you or by the authorities, according to the command of the court.

It is also represented to me that this mob is in the habit of going to the trains armed, searching for people that may be coming to their homes, and for the alleged purpose of driving any persons away, or threatening their lives, who may seek to return to their homes, and to their business. The further statement is also made to me that instead of its being disreputable characters that were driven away for the purpose of peace, it is simply a difficulty between saloon men and dance houses, and that the mayor of the town with his marshal has taken sides with one party against the other, to drive them out of business, and instead of the mayor enforcing the ordinances against lewd women visiting saloons, it is reported to me that he has called to his assistance those who were running dance houses with women in them, and entered saloons to drive out men who were keeping other saloons, and that he has set himself up as the judge as to who may violate the ordinances and who shall not, and that he proposes to permit certain parties to violate the ordinances of the city, while others are driven from their homes for violating ordinances, and not prosecuting others according to law for the violation of the ordinances.

I hope this is all untrue, and that the mayor has not been guilty of any such offenses. I cannot believe these statements of the mayor of Dodge City, as I believe him to be a clear-headed, honorable gentleman, and would not become a party to such transactions, or permit any such things to be done. I hope to learn from you that he has been wrongfully represented to me. His own good name, and the good name of the state, that is placed in his hands for protection, certainly would be sufficient inducement to him to see that such charges could not be truthfully made.

It is represented to me also that at this very time, and ever since this pretence of the mayor that he was trying to enforce two ordinances against women visiting saloons, that he has prohibited it only as to one saloon, made arrests in one case, and permitted that ordinance to be violated every day and every night, to his own personal knowledge, and that of the marshal and police officers of the city, by other men who were running saloons where women are permitted to visit, and sing and dance.

Now Mr. Sheriff, I desire to remind you that your duty as a public conservator of the peace, and also having authority over and above the mayor of Dodge City, if he fails to discharge his duties, that it is your duty to see that these things are not permitted and are not tolerated, and that no citizens shall be interfered with, that no citizen shall be driven away from his home, that the mayor of Dodge City shall not pick out men and say that the ordinances shall be enforced against them, and shall not be enforced against others.

It is also represented to me that citizens who have been driven away from home attempted to return to their homes, and were again driven off. Now if this state of affairs is to continue, you can see what disgrace it will bring upon your city, upon your county, and upon the state of Kansas. The demand is made upon me, and is coming to me from all parts of the state, that it is a disgrace that must be wiped out. It is also demanded and charged by parties who are now demanding the enforcement of the liquor law, that every saloon and dance house in Dodge City must be suppressed, and there is coming up almost a universal demand over the state, that it shall be done, if I have to

Luke Short

station a company of troops in the city of Dodge, and close up every saloon, and every drinking place, and every dance house in that city.

I am also informed that one of your deputies was aiding in this mob. If this is so, Mr. Sheriff, your duty to yourself, your duty to the public, and your duty under the law, and even decency requires, that you shall dismiss that man at once. If these things cannot be suppressed now, it is your duty also to notify the judge of your district of the state of affairs, that he may come there and invoke the judicial power of the state for the protection of those people.

I desire also to inform you that I expect you to see now that the peace of Dodge City is preserved, that the life and property of every individual there is fully protected, and that any person who desires to return to his home and to his business, must be protected by you, and must not be permitted to be molested while he is in the lawful discharge of his business, and conducting himself in a peaceable quiet manner. If anybody attempts to interfere, if they refuse to prefer legal charges in a proper court, and permit them to be tried in a proper manner, it is your duty to at once notify me, and I will see that those parties are taken charge of in a manner that will satisfy them that they must preserve the peace of the state, and behave themselves as good citizens.

I ask you in addition to this, that you call together the good citizens of Dodge City, lay this matter before them, ask them to come to your assistance, to aid you in preserving peace, and preserving order and the quietude of the town, and the consequent preservation of the good name and reputation of the state. This outrage has been heralded all over the United States, not only to the disgrace of your town, but to the whole state of Kansas. If they offer to furnish you assistance, and will respond to your call I will order a sufficient amount of arms and ammunition into your custody, so that you can have any assistance that you require.

If this is not sufficient, a company of troops will be at once ordered to Dodge City, and placed under your command and control, so that you shall have full authority and full power to preserve the peace and protect every individual that may be in the city. If this is not sufficient, proceedings will be commenced, for the purpose of at once installing officers in power who will discharge their duties honestly and faithfully to the public. Please give me a full careful and correct statement of the condition of affairs now, and say to me whether people who have been driven away will be permitted to return to their homes. Use the telegraph freely at my expense, as I have a train ready, and a company of troops ready to go to your city on a moment's notice.

I desire you also to read this letter to the mayor of Dodge City, and say to him that I invoke his assistance to aid you in preserving the peace of the town, and that I hope that the representations that have been made to me about his conduct are untrue. I should regret to hear or to know that the mayor of a city of the state of Kansas should so far forget the duties of the high office that he fills as to permit himself to become a party to a mob, and head anybody, or any crowd of individuals, in trampling upon the rights and privileges of other citizens. The good name of the city demands that it shall not be true, and the reputation of the state requires that no man occupying that position should

533

be guilty of such conduct, or should permit such things to be tolerated in his city. Say to him in addition to this, if he cannot preserve the peace with the police force that he has, it is his duty to discharge every one of them, and appoint a new set of men who will act in preserving the peace, and if he cannot do this, to notify me, and I will furnish him with men who will act. I hope that all the difficulty has blown over, that there will be no more excitement or trouble over this matter.

I have assured parties who have written to me, and who have appealed to me for protection and aid, that they might be permitted to return to their homes, that the sheriff of the county would see that they were protected. You have a right to call out all the men that you want to aid you in this, and in doing it, you will be simply doing your duty to the state, and maintaining the good name and reputation of your city, your county and the state of Kansas. The peace of the city is with you, Mr. Sheriff, and I expect it to be safe in your hands.

I am, my dear sir,

Your obedient servant,

G. W. GLICK
Governor of Kansas

GEO. T. HINKLE,
Sheriff Ford County,
Dodge City, Kansas.[16]

Even after this letter Sheriff Hinkle seemed not to understand that driving persons out of town rather than trying them for their crimes, whether real or imaginary, in the courts, was an unlawful act. His next telegram to Governor Glick still upheld the actions of the mayor:

Received at Topeka, Kan. 11:15 am   5/12 1883
DATED DODGE CITY, KS.
To HON. G. W. GLICK:

Your message recd this am. I will continue to do all in my power to preserve order in the community yet I cannot become responsible for the actions of any individual. Mr. Short's expulsion from the city is the direct result of his own action and the feeling of the people generally is very strong against him. The city is as quiet now as it has ever been but I fear that if Mr. Short returns trouble will ensue. It is evident that but one side of the matter that caused these men to leave [the] city has been presented to you and would respy suggest that you ask a statement of facts from prominent men of our city among whom I will name Hons. R. M. Wright; G. M. Hoover; J. T. Whitlaw, County Atty.; R. J. Hardesty; Geo. B. Cox; F. C. Zimmerman; N. B. Klaine and numerous others.

Respectfully

GEO. T. HINKLE
Sheriff [17]

534

The Topeka *Commonwealth*, May 12, 1883, carried its regular daily resume of the troubles but also included an interview with an unnamed "gentleman from Dodge City":

"What about these women?" asked the reporter.

"They are a necessary evil. The cattle men who come to the town expect to meet them. They are not the wives of gamblers, as has been stated. They have never insulted a lady yet and only show themselves at night."

"D. M. Frost, who publishes a paper there [the *Ford County Globe*], was denouncing the mob, when he was threatened with death if he didn't keep still.

"Dr. Chateau [A. S. Chouteau], who is a friend of Short, went with him to the calaboose when he was arrested and while returning, was denouncing Short's arrest without a complaint. Mayor Deager said afterwards that the bullet which was aimed at him was only stopped because he (Deager) put his thumb under the hammer of the pistol and prevented its discharge. When asked why he didn't arrest the man who was going to shoot, he replied: 'He was one of our party.'"

Luke and W. F. Petillon were interviewed in the Topeka *Daily Capital*, May 12, 1883:

THE MEN FROM DODGE.

THEIR MISSION TO TOPEKA, AND THEIR STORY OF THE TROUBLE—IT PUTS A VERY DIFFERENT FACE ON THE MATTER.

The editorial rooms of the CAPITAL were visited last evening by Mr. Luke Short, of Dodge City, and Mr. Petillon, district court clerk of Ford county, whose residence is the same. Mr. Short's name has appeared in the dispatches several times lately, as that of one of the persons expelled from Dodge City, in the interests of morality and good order. Learning that he was in Topeka yesterday, a reporter called at the Copeland, but finding him absent, left his card. In response he called during the evening, with Mr. Petillon, and jointly they gave a full statement of the controversy from their point of view, bringing forward a number of facts which have not been presented heretofore.

The narrative below is given substantially as drawn from these gentlemen in conversation, and solely on their authority, subject to all allowances which may be necessary, because of Mr. Short's personal interest in the matter.

THE SHORT AND PETILLON OF IT.

Mr. Short is a Texan, who came to Dodge some two years ago, and having been interested in the cattle business himself—as, indeed, he is still—he had an extensive acquaintance with other cattlemen and their employees. At Dodge he engaged in the saloon business with a man named Harris, and his friendly relations with the numerous Texans coming to Dodge has made Harris & Short's saloon the most popular and profitable one in the city. Mr. Webster, late mayor of Dodge City, is also a saloon keeper, and during his term of office removed from a more remote location to one next door to Harris & Short's "Long Branch," on Front street.

535

While Short's popularity has increased, that gentleman modestly stated, Webster's has declined, and finding it impracticable to secure his re-election to the mayoralty, Webster some weeks before election brought out Mr. Deger as a candidate, against whom Harris, Short's partner, was nominated. Deger had been a foreman for Lee & Reynolds, who are engaged in freighting, and had their place of business outside the city limits. About March 1st, however, it is said, Deger began boarding at the hotel in town, in order to gain a legal residence.

The night before election the construction trains of the Santa Fe railroad, manned by men residing at different places scattered along the line, were run into Dodge, and the next morning the men were all on hand, obtained control of the election board by filling vacancies under the forms of law, and voted. Thus Deger was elected by a majority of seventy-one in a poll of between 300 and 400 votes. Deger, Messrs. Short and Petillon declare, is a mere creature of Webster.

The saloons of Dodge City, these gentlemen say, are all of similar character including bars for drinking, gambling tables, and games of various kinds, arrangements for variety performances, or at least singing, and all employ women who are admittedly of loose character, and are provided with facilities for plying their business. In addition to the saloons there is a dance house, carried on by a man named Nixon, who was formerly an adherent of Harris, but shortly before election transferred his allegiance to the Deger-Webster party. His place is said to be of the lowest and vilest character.

Gambling is recognized and licensed by ordinances of the city, a "fine" of $5 a month being collected on account of each table, and the same amount being levied on every dealer of any game. An attempt was made in the common council to raise the tax to $12.50 a month, but it was not carried. An ordinance was passed, however, shortly after the accession of the new administration, prohibiting loose women from pursuing their solicitations in any public place.

As a collateral incident it is asserted the Webster-Deger party promised Nixon, in consideration of his support in the election, not only that he should be unmolested in his dance house business, but that he should have no competitor in the city.

The remainder of the article was merely a rehash of Luke's petition before Governor Glick, except that in the article Short claimed that "the sheriff of Ford county has taken no part in the matter. Mr. Short says that officer sent word to him that he (the sheriff) was a sufferer from heart disease and dared do nothing for fear excitement might prove fatal." [18]

On the afternoon of May 12 Luke had returned to Kansas City and Petillon was bound for Dodge bearing the governor's message to Sheriff Hinkle. The next day, Sunday, the governor received this telegram:

Luke Short

5/13   1883

Received at Topeka, Kan.
DATED DODGE CITY, Ks.
To HON. G. W. GLICK:
Your letter to Sheriff has been laid before committee of citizens. We judge you have been badly misinformed. Send adjutant genl. or some proper person to investigate before you act. Answer.

GEO. T. HINKLE, Sheriff; G. M. HOOVER; R. M. WRIGHT; R. W. EVANS; M. R. DRAPER; J. COLLAR; HENRY STURM; GEO. B. COX; J. T. WHITELAW, Co. Atty.; P. G. REYNOLDS; FRED T. M. WENIE, City Atty.; M. S. CULVER, Chairman Dem. C. Com.[19]

Also on Sunday, May 13, 1883, a well-known ex-Kansan arrived in Kansas City to aid Luke Short. His name was Bat Masterson. The Kansas City (Mo.) *Journal,* May 15, 1883, reported:

The troubles at Dodge City are assuming serious proportions, and the governor must interfere very soon or a terrible tragedy will undoubtedly result. The men driven out may be men who are classed with the sporting fraternity, but as far as known they are no worse than the men who have been chiefly instrumental in driving them out. But setting all question of comparative respectability aside, the whole affair resolves itself into a matter of victory for superior force, and not law. Luke Short, the chief of the band of men lately exiled, has his interests in the town, and claims he has been wronged. The vigilantes who drove him and his friends away assert that they are evil characters. Law has been set aside and force is the sole resort. Governor Glick has been attempting to preserve the peace, but so far has made no great progress. The sheriff acknowledges that he cannot protect the exiled men should they return, and so the matter stands at present.

Yesterday a new man arrived on the scene who is destined to play a part in a great tragedy. This man is Bat Masterson, ex-sheriff of Ford county, and one of the most dangerous men the West has ever produced. A few years ago he incurred the enmity of the same men who drove Short away, and he was exiled upon pain of death if he returned. His presence in Kansas City means just one thing, and that is he is going to visit Dodge City. Masterson precedes by twenty-four hours a few other pleasant gentlemen who are on their way to the tea party at Dodge. One of them is Wyatt Earp, the famous marshal of Dodge, another is Joe Lowe, otherwise known as "Rowdy Joe;" and still another is "Shotgun" Collins; but worse than all is another ex-citizen and officer of Dodge, the famous Doc Halliday.

A brief history of the careers of these gentlemen who will meet here tomorrow will explain the gravity of the situation. At the head is Bat Masterson. He is a young man who is credited with having killed one man for every year of his life. This may be exaggerated, but he is certainly entitled to a record of a dozen or more. He is a cool, brave man, pleasant in his manners, but terrible

537

in a fight, and particularly dangerous to the ruling clique, which he hates bitterly. Doc. Halliday is another famous "killer." Among the desperate men of the West, he is looked upon with the respect born of awe, for he has killed in single combat no less than eight desperadoes. He was the chief character in the Earp war at Tombstone, where the celebrated brothers, aided by Halliday, broke up the terrible rustlers.

Wyatt Earp is equally famous in the cheerful business of depopulating the country. He has killed within our personal knowledge six men, and he is popularly accredited with relegating to the dust no less than ten of his fellow men. "Shot-Gun" Collins was a Wells, Fargo & Co. messenger, and obtained his name from the peculiar weapon he used, a sawed off shot gun. He has killed two men in Montana and two in Arizona, but beyond this his exploits are not known. Luke Short, the man for whom these men have rallied, is a noted man himself. He has killed several men and is utterly devoid of fear. There are others who will make up the party, but as yet they have not yet arrived.

This gathering means something, and it means exactly that these men are going to Dodge City. They have all good reason to go back. Masterson says he wants to see his old friends. Short wants to look after his business. Earp and Holliday, who are old deputy sheriffs of Dodge, also intend visiting friends, so they say, and Collins is going along to keep the others company. "Rowdy Joe," who has killed about ten men, and is the terror of Colorado, goes about for pleasure. Altogether, it is a very pleasant party. Their entrance into Dodge will mean that a desperate fight will take place. Governor Glick has, up to the present time, failed to preserve order, and unless he takes some determined action within the next twenty-four hours, the men swear they will go to Dodge and protect themselves. For the good of the state of Kansas, it is hoped the governor will prevent violence.[20]

When news of Bat's arrival at Kansas City, and the rumor of the proposed visit from these celebrated "dead-eye" gunslingers reached the ears of Sheriff Hinkle he frantically wired Governor Glick:

8 pm   May 15, 1883

To HON. G. W. GLICK, Emp[oria]:

Are parties coming with Short for the purpose of making trouble? Answer quick.

GEO. T. HINKLE.[21]

Whatever the governor's reply Hinkle must have misinterpreted it for he assumed he was directed to enlist a large posse with which to greet Short on his arrival. Glick, however, denied that this was his intention. The Topeka Daily Capital, May 16, 1883, did little to clear matters up:

Luke Short

DODGE CITY AGAIN.
A RUMOR OF INTERVENTION WHICH GOV. GLICK DENIES.
THE EVICTED IN CONSULTATION—THOUGHT THEY
PROPOSE TO RETURN—DISPOSITION OF THE
PEOPLE OF DODGE—TROUBLE AHEAD.
UNDER WHAT LAW?

DODGE CITY, May 15.—Much excitement exists here to-night. The sheriff has been ordered by Gov. Glick to arm forty men and have them at the train, to see that order is preserved on the arrival of Luke Short, who is supposed to be on his way here. Short is a prominent whisky and sporting man, and was, by the authorities, forced to leave the city. He comes, it is said, on the Governor's permission, and things this evening look threatening.

(Governor Glick returned from Emporia at 2 o'clock this morning. He says he sent no such orders as stated above, but positively declined to say what directions he had given asserting it was a private matter between himself and the sheriff.)

CONFERENCE IN KANSAS CITY.

KANSAS CITY, May 15.—An informal committee of three citizens of Dodge City arrived this evening to confer with Luke Short, who is here with Bat Masterson, one of his friends. The members are G. M. Hoover, banker and Representative in the Legislature; R. M. Wright, merchant; C. M. Beeson, a prominent cattle man. They were in consultation with Short and Masterson all the evening. Being interviewed afterward they were very reticent, saying they would remain over to-morrow and would then reach some conclusion. Their mission is to effect a settlement of the present difficulty if possible and they brought letters to Short from Sheriff Hinkle who it is understood, says if Short returns to Dodge he (the sheriff) and the mayor will endeavor to afford protection, but that the feeling is very strong and he would advise Short not to come. One of the committeemen said that if Short were to go back he would probably be allowed to remain unmolested long enough to settle his business affairs, but if he should insist upon staying there there would most likely be trouble, and his life would be in danger. It is not known to-night whether Short intends to start to-morrow as intended, with his friends, who were to meet him at Topeka. The committeemen here are apparently urging him to give up the idea, or at least to wait a day or two in hopes of a peaceful settlement of the difficulties.

AN INTERVIEW WITH HIS EXCELLENCY.

EMPORIA, Ks., May 15.—A reporter of the Emporia daily *Republican* interviewed Gov. Glick, who was in this city this evening, in relation to the condition of affairs at Dodge City. The Governor said that the trouble there has grown out of a misapprehension in the management of local affairs, and the feeling between the parties has become so intensified that many of the citizens expect, not without cause, that serious trouble may follow. Governor Glick says the sheriff of that county, with whom he is in constant communication by telegraph, has ample means at his command with the aid of good citizens

539

to preserve the peace. The Governor expressed the hope that he would not be called upon to interfere in the settlement of their local difficulties and thinks that by a judicious course on the part of the local authorities peace will be maintained.

Meanwhile Sheriff Hinkle organized a posse and met the train which he thought carried Luke Short and Bat Masterson. The Dodge City *Times,* May 17, 1883, said:

THE SHERIFF'S POSSE.

Under orders from Gov. Glick, Sheriff Hinkel organized a posse of 45 men Tuesday evening, and upon the arrival of the "Cannon Ball" train proceeded to the depot, under the assumption that Short and Masterson were on the train destined for Dodge City. Yesterday the Governor telegraphed the sheriff to keep his men in readiness, in case of necessity. We trust the Governor's nerves have become quieted by this time and that he is tired of the Dodge City business. The Governor will be a very sick man before many days.

On the day that Luke and Bat were expected to arrive in Dodge a group of citizens of that place prepared a statement which they sent to the Topeka *Daily Capital.* The statement exhibited the sentiments of the pro-Deger group and was published in the *Capital,* May 18, 1883:

A PLAIN STATEMENT
OF THE RECENT TROUBLES AT DODGE CITY, KS.,
AS MADE BY THE OFFICIALS OF THAT CITY—SIMPLY
A DESIRE TO RID THEIR COMMUNITY OF
BLACKLEGS AND GAMBLERS.

DODGE CITY, Ks., May 15, 1883—There has been quite a commotion among the papers of Kansas City and Topeka, and while they would have the readers of their respective papers believe that Dodge is in the hands of a mob, and that the persons and property of peaceable citizens are in constant jeopardy from destruction, the city itself and its inhabitants have been pursuing the even tenor of their way, the city assuming an aspect peaceable—if anything, more so than it has for years. The doings of violence to person and property by the mob in Dodge City is all being done in Kansas City and Topeka through the press, while in fact Dodge City itself, the scene of all the lawlessness as stated, is quiet, orderly and peaceable.

The occasion for what the press have called trouble is only a repetition of what is found to be necessary about every two years in Dodge City; that is, a clearing out of an element composed of bold, daring men of illegal profession who, from toleration by the respectable portion of the community, are allowed to gain a prestige found difficult to unseat. This element has to be banished, or else the respectable people have to be bulldozed and browbeat by a class of men without any vested interest or visible means of support, who should

540

Luke Short

be allowed to remain in a decent community only by toleration, but who, instead, after gaining prestige, they undertake to dictate the government of the better class. This is the element which Dodge City has recently ordered out of town, an act which is done in every town of good government. The facts have been misunderstood, both to and by the press, and to the Governor. The true state of facts is about as follows:

At the last April election Deger and Harris ran for Mayor of the city. Harris is a gambler by profession and living in open adultery with a public prostitute, and the interest which he has in the town is merely of a local character. He could close up and settle his affairs in one day. The only real estate that he owns, and on which he pays taxes, is a small house in which he lives, and he would not own that only it is cheaper than for him to rent. It is worth about $400. He is a man whose character no respectable man in the community in which he lives would vouch for. He is a man that is recognized by the decent people as a sympathizer, friend and shielder of the gambler, thug, confidence man and murderer, who may be arrested by the authorities for offenses against the law. He is always to be found on their bond for recognizance, no matter how glaring the deed or heinous the offense for which they stand charged.

This man was the candidate for mayor representing the gambling element. Deger, who is a man of irreproachable character and honesty, is an old resident of the town and represented the better class of people and as a matter of course, as was conceded, he was elected by a large majority, but it was very apparent that Harris felt very sore over his defeat. It was also very apparent that he and some of his followers who were mostly composed of gamblers were going to buck against everything the new administration done.

At the first meeting of the new administration it was found necessary to pass and revise certain ordinances and among them was one to prohibit women of lewd character from loitering around saloons and upon the streets. This ordinance was passed upon the application of a majority of the business men including the saloon men, of the town. They also passed another ordinance in regard to gamblers, which they considered stringent, and loudly denounced it, and upon the application of a committee representing the gamblers, the councilmen made concessions, and in fact, made all the concessions asked, in order to preserve peace and harmony. The ordinance in regard to women, went into effect two days before the concession was made by the councilmen.

The first day and night the women obeyed the ordinance without a single exception, but the second night, which was the night of the concession made by the mayor and councilmen, Short, Harris, and another gambler, who were loud in their abuse of the ordinance, there being no women down town, went to a house of ill fame, and, according to their spoken words, forced two of the inmates down to their saloon to violate the ordinance, saying that they would pay the fines and costs assessed against the women. The women, after being tried and fined for the offense, had to pay their own fines and costs themselves, and when ordered to leave town, and after Short and Harris refused to pay their fines, as above stated, they made a statement, as above set forth, before the police judge, and since.

541

The officers, as was their duty, arrested the women and locked them up in the calaboose, for a violation of the city ordinance. After this arrest, Short, the partner of Harris, who is a gambler and an acknowledged hard character, attempted to assassinate L. C. Hartman, a special policeman who assisted in the arrest, by shooting at him from an obscure spot after night, which happened about as follows.

After making the arrest, Hartman walked down the principal street, and, when in front of a general store, which was closed, the front being dark, Hartman met Short and another gambler coming up the street. While passing by, Short and his companion, Short turned and drew a pistol and said, "There is one of the son's of -------; lets throw it into him," immediately firing two shots at Hartman from his six-shooter. Hartman, in his endeavor to turn upon Short, in some way fell to the ground. Short, supposing he had killed him, started to the saloon of one Tom Land, near by, but Hartman, immediately recovering himself, fired one shot at Short. Strange to say, neither of the shots fired took effect.

Short gave bonds in the sum of $2,000 and afterwards filed a complaint against Hartman, stating that Hartman had fired the first shot, half a dozen of Short's confederates being ready to testify that he (Hartman) had done so, although there are several reliable business men who witnessed the affair, who will testify that Short fired the two first shots as above stated.

The women were locked up. Short and Harris were bound they should not remain locked up all night, as is customary with prisoners when locked up by city authorities. By intimidating some of the city officers by threats, etc., they affected their purpose. In all these proceedings, Short was the leader and spokesman. He is the man who but a few weeks ago pulled out his pistol and beat one of our most respectful citizens over the head until he was carried home on a stretcher, and his life was despaired of for several days. He is a man who, on several occasions, has picked up chairs and broke them over the heads of men who, as it happened, had done something in his place of business that displeased him. He is a man that killed his man, an old gray headed man 57 years old, in Tombstone, Arizona, and has been run out of that and other places by the respectable people. He is a man who was an intimate friend of such men as Jack McCarty, the notorious and well known three card monte and confidence man, known all through the west as being a hard character, and who recently died near this place after being convicted of highway robbery and about to receive his sentence of ten years.

Harris and Short keep a saloon that is a refuge and resort for all confidence men, thieves and gamblers that visit the town, and the statements that have been made in regard to the place kept by Webster are false. He is regarded as a man of personal honor and integrity, and as mayor of the city, an office he held for two terms, he so conducted the affairs of the city, and made such vigorous war on bunko steerers, thugs and confidence men as to gain the gratitude and respect of every law abiding citizen of the place.

It was very apparent to the mayor and councilmen of the city that this element, with Harris and Short at their head, were going to violate, encourage, shield and protect all violators of the laws of the city, and that the probability was that there would be trouble in the city during the whole of their administration if they and their followers remained. Short had attempted to assassinate an officer in the discharge of his duty, had bulldozed the city officers, had violated, aided and abetted in the violation of the laws, and at a meeting of the mayor and a large number of citizens, including the council, it was, after due deliberation and consideration, determined to arrest Luke Short and his followers and let them leave town, and accordingly, he, with six other associates, were arrested on complaint and warrant and locked in the calaboose and precautions taken that they did not escape, and were allowed to leave town the next day. There was no mob violence used whatever. None but regular officers of the city made the arrest, but in case they were resisted there was sufficient force composed of armed citizens held in reserve to aid in the arrest.

It was afterwards ascertained by one of the parties arrested, who peached on the balance, that it was known by Short and party they were to be arrested, and as soon as the officers came to arrest them it was understood they were organized and that Short was to start the shooting and the balance of the party were to follow it up, but as stated by him "somebody weakened." The citizens understood the characters of the men they were dealing with and were prepared for them, and this was the occasion for the circulation that it was a mob. It was *bona fide* citizens armed to aid the officers if necessary in the enforcement of the laws.

Much of the confusion and misunderstanding regarding the situation in our city is due to the misrepresentations made to the Governor by one W. F. Petillon. Petillon is clerk of the district court and lives about six miles north of Dodge City on a claim of 160 acres. He had been recognized and identified as a Harris man some time before the election, which came about as follows: Jack McCarty had been arrested at this point for highway robbery, and had given bond for $2,000. Harris, as one of the bondsmen, and Short, having no property against which execution could issue, got a citizen worth some real estate to sign the bond and he (Short) deposited the amount to secure the party so signing. The bond was given for McCarty's appearance to be tried. McCarty appeared and in the course of the trial it was evident that from the evidence McCarty would be convicted. After conviction and before sentence, McCarty escaped.

When his escape became known, the clerk, Petillon, was applied to for the bond, he being the proper custodian of the papers in the case. Upon application, he could not give it, as he did not know where it was. He had it at the last day of court and was the one seen to have it last. The bond was never found, although he acknowledged it was properly filed, and it is impossible to obliterate from the minds of a great many respectable people here that Petillon knew why and where that bond disappeared. It has been a noticeable feature that since that time Petillon has been a firm believer and supporter of the Harris and Short combination. This is the kind of a man Governor Glick sends for, instead of sending for a proper representative as any reasonable, intelligent, discreet man should to investigate.

The condition of Dodge City at present is orderly and law-abiding, and the prospects are it will so continue if these men remain away. If they are allowed to remain it will be against the will and without the consent of a majority of the law-abiding citizens of this community, and if the Governor, through his interference and encouragement, forces these men back on us he does so at his peril, and if there is bloodshed as a result the responsibility will not rest entirely with the Governor, who, had he not given the matter encouragement, it would have passed unnoticed, as an occurrence frequent in all cities desirous of being law-abiding, and of good government.

Dated at Dodge City, Kansas, this 15th day of May, 1883.

L. E. Deger, Mayor,	R. E. Burns, Police Judge,
H. B. Bell,	N. B. Klaine, City Treasurer.
H. T. Drake,	L. C. Hartman, City Clerk.
Henry Sturm,	C. E. Chipman, Assistant Marshal.
George S. Emerson,	Fred T. M. Wenie, City Attorney.
H. M. Beverley,	J. L. Bridges, City Marshal.
Councilmen of Dodge City.	T. L. McCarty, City Physician.

On May 16, 1883, Luke and Bat returned to Topeka for another visit with the governor. The Topeka *Daily Capital*, May 17, reported their coming:

THE MEN FROM DODGE.

Luke Short, Bat Masterson and Mr. Petillon, of Dodge City, returned from their conference with friends at Kansas City yesterday, and are at the Copeland. Mr. Short is fully aware that his return to Dodge will be strongly objected to and that forcible means will be used to prevent his remaining any time. It is understood, however, that he intends soon to make an attempt.

That day, too, Sheriff Hinkle had learned that Short and Masterson would not make the attempt to re-enter Dodge via the Cannon Ball. At 1:20 A. M., May 16, 1883, this message arrived in Topeka:

To Hon. Geo. W. Glick:

Agreeable to your message I was at train with fifty armed men. No one came. Shall I hold these men in readiness for use?

Geo. T. Hinkle.[22]

Governor Glick's reply has not been preserved, but in answer to his own question Hinkle telegraphed this message to Topeka at 2:02 P. M. that same day:

To Hon. G. W. Glick:

Will have men ready to act if occasion demands. If Short returns peaceably and alone I can protect him and will continue to do all in my power to preserve order in the community.

Geo. T. Hinkle
Sheriff.[23]

By this time, after having heard from numerous parties on both sides, Governor Glick must have desired some first hand information

544

from an objective reporter. Possibly that was the reason Kansas
Adj. Gen. Thomas Moonlight turned up in Dodge City on May 16.[24]
Whatever his motives, Glick did not escape further visits from "committees" from southwest Kansas. One such group, composed of 12
Dodgeites, boarded the eastbound Santa Fe on May 16 with the intention of setting the chief executive straight in the matter of the
Dodge City troubles. The Dodge City *Times*, May 17, 1883, reported:

GONE TO SEE GLICK.

Twelve citizens left on the cannon ball train this morning for Topeka, where
they will appear before His Excellency George Washington Glick, Governor
of Kansas, and present him with the facts on the situation in Dodge City. The
Governor's counsel has been such men as Petillon and Galland, and he has
been wofully misinformed. His proffered protection to murderers has aroused
indignation. The following are the names of the citizens who left for Topeka:
R. J. Hardesty, G. S. Emerson, Elder Collins, R. E. Rice, S. A. Bullard, P. G.
Reynolds, S. Mullendore, T. L. McCarty, Henry Sturm, A. Dienst, F. J. Durand,
L. W. Jones. They will return tomorrow afternoon.[25]

On May 18, 1883, the Topeka *Daily Capital* made an attempt to
draw reason from confusion but only added to the complexity by
including an interview with Luke:

MOONBEAMS ON DODGE.
THE ADJUTANT-GENERAL ON THE GROUND—
A COMMITTEE IN TOPEKA—
EXPRESSIONS FROM ALL SIDES.

It was learned yesterday that Governor Glick had commissioned Col. Tom
Moonlight Minister Plenipotentiary to Ford county, to negotiate a treaty by
which peace might be restored to that distracted community, and that Col.
Moonlight was on the ground.

THE SHERIFF'S INSTRUCTIONS.

A reporter of the CAPITAL yesterday called Gov. Glick's attention to the
statement in the dispatches of yesterday morning, that:

"The sheriff, Geo. T. Hinkle, by order of the Governor, met the 11 o'clock
train with fifty armed men to protect Luke Short and his companion, who was
understood to be the famous Bat Masterson, formerly sheriff of this county,
but now outlawed by the city officials."

The Governor again said he had given the sheriff no such orders. He had
simply reminded that officer that it was his (the sheriff's) duty to preserve
the peace of the community; had advised the sheriff to call to his aid a sufficient number of good citizens and had assured the sheriff that he would be
supported by the authority of the State if necessary.

In response to explicit inquiries Governor Glick said he had directed the
sheriff in no respect whatever as to the details of his action or the means to

be taken to preserve the peace—had not advised him to organize and arm a posse of any specific number of men, and had only suggested particular watchfulness about the railroad station on the arrival of trains.

The Governor added a statement that as a result of his counsel, Mr. Short, and his immediate friends, had relinquished the idea of returning to Dodge City at present, and had pledged himself to use his influence to preserve peace and good order in that place.

MR. SHORT ADMITS IT.

At a later hour in the day Mr. Short was found at the Copeland, and on inquiry he admitted that he had given the pledge referred to by the Governor and would make no effort to return to Dodge City, at least at present.

The sheriff, Mr. Short said, had given assurance that ample protection would be afforded him in doing so. But Mr. Short continued, "If the sheriff is sincere in saying so, why has he not put some of my friends on his posse? Instead of doing that he has called to his assistance men known to be my bitterest enemies. I would as soon trust myself in the hands of the mob as to the protection of the sheriff's posse." Mr. Short said he was convinced that the plot for his assassination was perfected, and that his life would be the forfeit if he revisited Dodge City.

He said he expected to remain in Topeka some days yet, but was not questioned and made no statement in relation to his intentions for the future.

Mr. Short, who has been observed by many on the streets of Topeka during the last week, would hardly meet, in his personal appearance, the expectations of many who have heard and seen him described as a "red-handed desperado." He is a man rather under medium hight, but well built and firmly knit, with nothing in his features or complexion to indicate irregular or dissipated habits. He is cleanly-shaved, excepting only a natty little moustasche, and is dressed with great care and in good style. He sports a magnificent diamond pin, and yesterday twirled between his fingers an elegant black walking stick with a gold head. The CAPITAL knows little of his past history, and can say nothing as to his claim to the reputation which has been given him, but there is no doubt he is able to take care of himself in almost any kind of a crowd.

A COMMITTEE FROM DODGE.

Mr. S. A. Bullard, J. F. Durand, R. E. Rice and other gentlemen, making a committee of twelve representative citizens of Dodge and Ford county, arrived in Topeka yesterday afternoon and called upon Gov. Glick. They had an extended conversation with him, as a result of which they became satisfied that peace would be maintained, and the interests of all good citizens protected. Mr. Short will be assured that he will be permitted to return to Dodge and remain there ten days for the purpose of closing his business. During that time he will be perfectly safe against molestation of any kind.

The gentlemen of the committee called at the CAPITAL office for the purpose of extending their thanks for the course it had taken in this matter, expressing their gratification at the fairness with which it had been discussed, and at the assistance it had given in reaching a satisfactory solution of the difficulty.

The Atchison *Globe* says: "F. C. Zimmerman, of Dodge City, one of the largest general merchants in the State, in a private letter to Howell, Jewett &

546

Co., says; 'I suppose you have heard of the Dodge City trouble. The facts are that we are having no trouble at all, except that the decent people are driving out the bunko men, and disreputable citizens generally. These men complained to Gov. Glick, who now wants to send them back under the protection of the militia. Every decent citizen of Dodge City is indignant at the Governor's action, who did not consult the respectable people about the matter, receiving his information entirely from the other side. Everything is peaceable and orderly here, and you may say as much to the newspapers.' "

The Topeka *Daily Kansas State Journal*, May 18, 1883, introduced a new angle when it reported that the Dodge City ladies might petition the governor for Luke's return:

A NICE YOUNG MAN.

Luke Short over whom all this Dodge City excitement and sensation has been created, don't look like a man that would be dangerous to let live in any community. In fact he is a regular dandy, quite handsome, and Dr. Galland says, a perfect ladies man. He dresses fashionably, is particular as to his appearance, and always takes pains to look as neat as possible. At Dodge City he associates with the very best element, and leads in almost every social event that is gotten up. Dr. Galland thinks the ladies will yet be heard from in Mr. Shorts behalf. They have been very anxious to get up a petition among themselves to send the governor and it will probably come yet.

On the same day the Topeka *Daily Commonwealth* published a short interview with several of the 12 apostles out of Dodge City:

Col. Hardesty said that Dodge City was no more excited than Topeka; that the trouble exists chiefly in the newspapers outside. That he had friends on both sides; was an outsider so far as the row is concerned and didn't know much about it.

Meeting another member of the committee, a reporter said he had been informed that Sheriff Hinkle was disposed to preserve the peace and asked whether he would protect Short.

"No," said the committeeman, "Short has been ordered out of town by the citizens and will not be permitted to return."

"What are the charges against him?" asked the reporter.

"Disobeying the ordinances."

"Why don't you try him in the courts there and punish him?"

"Well, he is a bad man generally. He was ordered out of town a year ago, and allowed to return on promise of good behavior. But he is a bad man to have around, and we don't want him there, and won't have him. Our proceedings may not be just exactly according to law, but it's a custom, and he can't return."

"What will be done if he attempts to return?"

"He will be ordered to go on. If he does all will be well. If he resists the order and tries to come back there may be trouble. But I guess all will be peaceably settled."

Short said last night that he should go back; just when he don't know, nor how. If he don't have an escort he will have to go under cover, and can't tell how long it will take him to get there. If he persists in this intention, and carries it out there may be trouble yet, but Gov. Glick says he thinks all will be settled in a few days.

After hearing the committee of 12 from Dodge City, Governor Glick sent this letter to Sheriff George Hinkle:

May 17th 1883

GEO. T. HINKLE
   Sheriff of Ford Co
      Dr Sir
         I understand from the Com-tee of gentlemen, who called on me today that you seem to have understood me as requiring you to protect Luke Short. My advice and directions to you should be understood as requiring you to keep the peace between all parties. I have not regarded Short in this trouble at all, but only the peace and quiet of Dodge City and I have wanted to aid you and support you in doing your duty as the chief peace officer in the county, and in the discharge of that duty I offered you assistance to be under your control and under your orders alone till you advised me that you could not preserve the peace and in that case I would give you more assistance. I am well pleased with your course and the vigilance as to which you have acted & I can assure you shall have my support in the good work that the Gentlemen say you have done and the faithful manner in which you have acted in the discharge of your duty.

Your obt svt
G. W. GLICK
Governor [26]

At this point the Santa Fe railroad, perhaps at the governor's suggestion, instructed its Dodge City representative that he owed it to his company to assume a position of strict neutrality:

ATCHISON, TOPEKA, & SANTA FE RAILROAD CO.
LAW DEPARTMENT.

GEORGE R. PECK,
   General Solicitor

TOPEKA, KANSAS, May 17, 1883

HON GEO. W. GLICK
   Governor
DEAR SIR—
        I have sent telegram—copy enclosed—to Mr. Sutton at Dodge City. Shall be glad to do anything in my power to aid in restoring quiet.

Yours
G R PECK

Luke Short

The telegram Peck had sent to Mike Sutton read:

ATCHISON, TOPEKA, & SANTA FE RAILROAD CO.
LAW DEPARTMENT.

Telegram via R. R. Line

GEO. R. PECK,
General Solicitor.
TOPEKA, KANS., May 17, 1883

M. W. SUTTON
Dodge City,
Parties will not return to Dodge. Considering your relation to the Company and our large interests at Dodge City I think you should hold yourself aloof from both parties to the existing troubles. Do everything you can to allay the excitement, and to prevent any hostility to the company.

GEO. R. PECK.[27]

In the afternoon of May 17 Governor Glick began to receive telegraphic reports from Adjutant General Moonlight. Unfortunately the governor's answers have not been preserved. Moonlight's first wire arrived in Topeka at 2:25 P. M.:

To Gov. G. W. GLICK:
Luke Short to return alone to settle up private business within ten days or until official release of his bond for McCarty and his own bond in city case. All parties agree hereto.

THOMAS MOONLIGHT, Adjt. Genl.
L. E. DEGER, Mayor
GEO. T. HINKLE, Sheriff

Five minutes later a second wire arrived:

To Gov. GLICK:
Short can be protected from public attack but not from private assault. The agreement gives safety. Is best for all concerned and only safe course.

THOS. H. MOONLIGHT.

The adjutant general sent his final wire which arrived in Topeka at 9:06 P. M., May 17:

To Gov. GEO. W. GLICK:
Short has a right to come to his home. There will be no open riot or assault. The sheriff will do his duty but cannot protect against private attack. This is Short's danger. The agreement secures Short publicly and privately. It will be the beginning for reconcilliation & harmony will follow. I implore you to accept this beginning and time will do the rest. The Sheriff is earnest but should excitement continue he cannot secure men to do his bidding. I again implore you to advise Short to return on the agreement. All his friends say so and they ought to know. I leave for home in the morning unless you order otherwise. Let me know.

THOS. MOONLIGHT.[28]

The *Ford County Globe*, May 22, 1883, had this to say about Moonlight's visit:

COL. THOMAS MOONLIGHT, the Adjutant General of the state, was in the city all day Thursday, to ferret out, if possible, the late trouble in our midst, and we believe on his return, will show to the governor that the people of our fair hamlet are not half so bad as they were represented to be through the press of the east. In fact, he made diligent search and inquiry, irrespective of persons, cliques and combinations, and impartially listened to all who had anything to relate concerning the trouble that is supposed to exist. We know not what his report may be, but we feel confident that he will do justice to our people and that he will in a great measure refute many of the very exagerated reports that have been spread broadcast over the land, concerning the insurrection of our inhabitants. Justice is all we want and all our people can reasonably ask for.

On May 20, 1883, the Topeka *Commonwealth* published a letter from an anonymous Dodgeite refuting the statement published in the *Capital* on May 18 and signed by Mayor Deger and officials of Dodge City. Though much of the letter was merely a rehash of the pro-Short position, some new material was introduced:

THE FACTS IN THE DODGE CITY MATTER.
REPLY TO CAPITAL ARTICLE OF MAY 18th.
DODGE CITY, KAN., May 18, 1883.

TO THE EDITOR OF THE COMMONWEALTH:

It is an old saying and a true one that "Might makes right," and judging by the affairs in Dodge City we almost believe the "old saw." The article in the Topeka Daily Capital of Friday, May 18th, signed by the mayor and city officers, but publicly fathered by A. B. Webster, misrepresents entirely the affairs in our city. All who live in Dodge City and know the ins and outs of its business know that this feud originated in the jealousy of Webster against the Long Branch saloon, kept by Harris & Short. Webster, as mayor, having shown himself tyrannical and overbearing, found it was impossible for himself to be re-elected. He therefore imported a man who lived outside of the city, an old friend of his from Hays City, named L. E. Deager. Deager is an old "compadre" of Webster's, and well understood for years to have been his tool. The election resulted in favor of Deager, owing to the importation of illegal railroad votes by M. W. Sutton, the railroad attorney, who is a nephew of Webster, assisted by Drake, a self-constituted guardian of railroad voters. . . . [The paper here repeated the alleged agreement between Deger and Bond & Nixon concerning the operation of dance halls and the difficulty between Short and Hartman.]

A delegation picked and chosen by the Webster faction, headed by Captain Deinse, their chosen judge at the late city election, and composed of twelve men are now visiting Governor Glick on free passes furnished by the A. T. & S. F. railroad, through M. W. Sutton, local attorney of said railroad company. Some

550

Luke Short

of this committee don't live in or own a cents worth of property in the city. The cowardly attack on Mr. Harris in the said article has caused much comment. His large interests here in cattle and other business, his living here for seven years, his never having been charged with violating the law, make prominent citizens feel and say that the Capital article is venomous, scurrilous and unfair. It is stated in the Capital article that all his interests in Dodge City is a $400 house. It is well known and of record in the state that he is vice-president of Dodge City Bank and owns one-fourth interest in the same. He is also the owner of one-half of the well-known C. O. D. brand of cattle [Chalkley Beeson owning the other portion] and holds a large stock of bonded whisky in Kentucky, and could not wind up his affairs in six months without sacrificing thousands of dollars. He represents more wealth than all the signers of the Capital article combined.

Mr. W. F. Petillon, who is stigmatized and abused as a shyster from Chicago, is a man who came here with his family on account of their health and this climate. He has been here about six years, and has spent more money here than he has made. He is an active, energetic and aggressive politician and believes what he believes very strong. A democrat-dyed in the wool and always takes a strong stand for his friends. This, of course, makes him enemies, and bitter ones, and the cowardly charge of his malfeasance in office of destroying certain bonds in the McCarty case. The facts in the bond business are as follows: McCarty was found guilty by the jury on Friday evening, and on the same day a motion for a new trial was made by one of his attorneys, and a bond was also given by McCarty and approved by the judge, J. C. Strang, and the bond was kept by the judge and not filed with the clerk. On Monday the motion for a new trial was argued and overruled at 5:30 p. m. The court then adjourned until 7:30 p. m., at which time on the call of the case Mr. Gryden one of McCarty's attorneys, announced that he was unable to find McCarty. The court immediately took a recess, and deputy sheriffs were started to hunt McCarty.

Mr. Petillion during the recess of the court and while the hunt for McCarty was going on, happened in the office of M. W. Sutton, where he met Judge Strang and M. W. Sutton. Judge Strang asked him for the McCarty bond. Petillion told him he did not have the bond, and never had seen it. Then Judge Strang said, "I handed the bond to Sutton to-day, and he (Sutton) said, 'I threw it on your table while you were making out jurors' certificates and it fell at your elbow.'" Petillion then told them it was a careless trick, as he had not seen it. Judge Strang, Sutton and Petillion then went to the court house and searched for the bond and failed to find it. This is the statement of Petillion, which will be sworn to if necessary. . . .

A Lover of Justice and Law.

In the *Daily Kansas State Journal,* Topeka, May 23, 1883, Luke himself replied to the same Topeka *Capital* article of May 18, and applied the tar brush with vigor:

SHOTS FROM SHORT.

Topeka, Kan., May 21, 1883.

Editor State Journal:

I hope you will be obliging enough to give me sufficient space in your valuable paper to refute the malicious statement contained in the Topeka *Capital* of the 18th inst., under the caption of "Plain Statement" coming from Dodge City. It must be apparent to all those who have any direct knowledge of the circumstances that brought about the recent state of affairs at Dodge, that the article referred to was written for the purpose of justifying the parties who participated in running me away from the town; as not one word of truth appeared in the statement, which was unquestionably written by an adviser and principal director of the mob, and who is too cowardly to openly identify himself with them.

I simply refer to Mike Sutton, he who has been playing the part of "Judas" in this matter all through. He endeavors in his carefully prepared statement, which he had signed by all the city officials, to show that it was a fight between the city authorities on one side and the gamblers thugs, thieves and prostitutes on the other, which I denounce as a base, malicious falsehood, at least so far as my side of the question is concerned. Myself and Harris have never championed the cause of thieves, thugs and prostitutes since we had a business in Dodge City, which is more than can be said of those who have opposed us. They have published the lying article for the purpose of blackening the reputation of Mr. Harris and myself, in order to vindicate their own cowardly and dastardly acts. They speak of Harris not having any interest in the city, and that he only owns one little house, worth $400. To this I will say that he bought this insignificant little house and paid for it and did not obtain it as the writer of the "Plain Statement" obtained his, by jobbing and swearing a poor unfortunate creature into the penitentiary, as he did, in order to get possession of his little homestead.

They speak of Mr. Harris being a man without character and that he is living in an open state of adultery with a prostitute, which is an infamous lie, and I will venture to say that there is not a man in Kansas who knows Mr. Harris but will say that he is an honest and an honorable man, and a good citizen, and can buy and sell every man whose name appears on that official list. As to his living with a prostitute, I consider that a rather broad assertion to make and consider such things his own private affairs and no body's business. I can say however that if the accusation is true it is nothing more than what Sutton, Webster, Diger, Chipman, Hartman, and others of that outfit have done in the past, and are doing at present. Webster abandoned his family for a prostitute, Nixon did the same, and there are only those who cannot get a prostitute to live with, who have not got them, and it is a conceded fact by all who have any knowledge of Dodge, that all the thieves, thugs and prostitutes who have been in the town in the past two years have been directly and indirectly connected with the city government. These assertions I am prepared to prove in any court of justice in the world.

They go further on and state that I am a desperate character, and that not long since I murdered an old grey haired man in Arizona and that I have been run out of nearly every country I have lived in. Which is as infamous as it is false, as there is not a civilized country under the face of the sun that I can not go to with perfect safety, excepting Dodge City, and there is no law to prevent me from living there, nothing but a band of cut throats and midnight assassins, who have banded together for the purpose of keeping all those out of the place who are liable to oppose them at the polls, or offer them opposition in their business.

As to my murdering an old grey haired man in Arizona I was tried in a court of justice for any offence I committed there, and the records will show that it was a fair and impartial trial, and that I was honorably acquitted. The delegation who came here to see the governor, and who claim to represent the moral element of the town, was principally composed of tramps, who do not own a single foot of ground in the country, and never have, and I want to specially refer to the two leading spirits and spokesmen of said delegation, the Rev. Mr. Collins, and Capt. Dinst,—one an itinerant preacher, who by his peregrinations, through charitably disposed committees manages to eke out a miserable existence, and who, on the eve of the last municipal election at Dodge, sold the influence of his congregation and his own, for fifteen dollars; the other, Cap. Dinst, it is positively asserted by the most reputable citizens of Dodge City, was engaged in robbing a safe at the flouring mills owned and operated by one H. F. May. He is a man wholly without character, and cannot get employment of any description with any responsible parties.

They further maliciously and unjustly assail Mr. Pettilon because he had the temerity to visit the governor in my behalf, and in behalf of justice. They accuse him of stealing a bond, which he did not do, and which he is prepared to prove he did not do, as he never had the bond in his possession. It is a fine accusation for such a man as Mike Sutton to make against such a man as Pettilon.

There is not a responsible man in Ford county that believes Pettilon stole the bond, but there is not an honest man in the county but believes Sutton would steal a bond or anything else that he could get his hands on, and they base their opinions on his past record as an official of the county. Every inhabitant of the county knows that not over eight months ago he resigned his position as county attorney in order to accept a two thousand dollar fee to defend one of the most cold blooded murderers that ever appeared in any court of justice. He knew that by resigning he could defeat the ends of justice, as the man whom he had appointed in his stead was wholly incompetent to conduct a successful prosecution and the result was an acquittal and a red-handed murderer turned loose upon the world to repeat his crime. This man was not run out of town or molested by the city officials, who are so loud in their vaunted pretentions of justice.

They state in their article that I attempted to assassinate one of their police-men, and that I fired at him from a place of concealment, which shows it to be a lie on its face, for had I done as they say I did, it would be an easy matter for them to convict me, and they would only be too glad to do so had they the evidence to warrant a conviction, but on the contrary they knew their policeman attempted to assassinate me and I had him arrested for it and had plenty of evidence to have convicted him, but before it came to trial they had organized a vigilance committee and made me leave, so that I could not appear against him. And this is what they call justice and the law abiding element clearing out the lawless characters. If it be true, it is a sad commentary on Kansas justice and those who are supposed to execute the law.

I am invited to return on a pledge given me that I can remain for a period of ten days, and that during that time I will not be in imminent danger of being murdered, but that should I persist in remaining after the allotted time, they then would not be responsible for any personal safety. A very liberal concession on their part I must admit, but I will say for their benefit that I have no desire to accept their terms. I would be afraid of meeting with the fate General Canby met with when he accepted the invitation extended to him by the Modocs. I would sooner trust myself in the hands of a band of wild Apache Indians than trust to the protection of such men as Webster, Nixon and Diger, with Mike Sutton, in the background to perfect the plans of my assassination. When I return, it will be when they least expect me, and it will not be in answer to any invitation which they may extend to me.

In conclusion I will say that they may be able to keep me out of Dodge City by brute force without the sanction of law, but there are many towns in America that I will keep them out of, or make them show a valid cause for remaining.

Respectfully,
Luke Short.

After both sides had relieved themselves verbally, the maneuvering began. On May 21 Bat headed west but went beyond Dodge. Luke traveled to Caldwell. The Dodge City *Times*, May 24, 1883, told of Bat's passing:

Bat Masterson went west Monday night, passing this city on the cannon ball train. Some of the citizens of this place went on the train but they could not gain access to the sleeping car which contained the redoubtable Bat. No one in Dodge wants to offer Bat any harm so long as Bat offers no harm himself. The country has been anticipating some fearful things judging from the promulgation of the proposed movement of a notorious gang. But the denoument is just as the people of Dodge City anticipated. We suppose however, few people believed the statements in the Kansas City papers about the proposed action of the gang. And the chief shall flee unto the mountains of Colorado, where the lion roareth and the whangdoodle mourneth for its first born.

Of Luke the Caldwell *Journal*, May 24, 1883, said:

Luke Short, about whom the fuss at Dodge City was kicked up, arrived here on Monday. Mr. Short is a quiet, unassuming man, with nothing about him to lead one to believe him the desperado the Dodge mob picture him to be. He says the whole trouble arose from business jealousy on the part of Webster, Nixon and others. As to his plans he has nothing to say, but he is determined to take all legal measures possible to secure his rights.

554

For the next few days, until May 31, 1883, the Dodge City troubles simmered down. Then, at 3:00 P. M., this telegram heralded the re-eruption:

To GEO. W. GLICK, Govr.
Can you send Col. Moonlight here tomorrow with power to organize company of militia? I have ample reasons for asking this which I will give to Col. Moonlight so that he can communicate them to you.

GEO. T. HINKLE,
Sheriff.[29]

The "ample reasons" were probably embodied in the person of the celebrated individual mentioned in this *Ford County Globe* item of June 5, 1883:

Wyatt Earp, a former city marshal of Dodge City arrived in the city from the west, last Thursday. Wyatt is looking well and glad to get back to his old haunts, where he is well and favorably known.

The Topeka *Daily Commonwealth* of June 5, 1883, reported the impending battle:

MORE TROUBLE AT DODGE CITY.

SHORT AND HIS FRIENDS ORGANIZING FOR A
RAID ON THE TOWN—THE LIVELY TIMES
COMING IF THE PLANS ARE SUCCESSFUL.

It appears that there is to be more trouble at Dodge City and less talk than has been indulged in, if the news from there and the indications mean anything. The military organization under the name of the Glick Guards, which was effected a few days ago, is largely composed of men who are friends of Luke Short or enemies of the city administration of Dodge, and so great has been the objection since it was organized that Adjutant General Moonlight has issued an order suspending the organization for the present.

From a gentleman who came in from the west yesterday, we learn that an arrangement has been made for Short's return to Dodge, but that he cannot return peaceably, no matter how willing some of his old enemies may be. He does not trust them himself and will not come back without his friends, and so surely as the two forces meet there will be blood shed. Such is the opinion of men in Dodge and out of that town who should know whereof they speak. All the parties are tired of the life they are forced to lead on account of this trouble and want to end it. When they leave their places of business it is with six-shooters strapped upon them and eyes on the lookout for a hidden enemy. One man prominent in the late trouble said, "I can stand it no longer. It worries the life out of me, and I'm going to sell out and leave."

The rumor that Short intends to return with friends is confirmed by the following, which comes direct to THE COMMONWEALTH, and is reliable.

SHORT'S SCHEME.

—June 2

To THE EDITOR OF THE COMMONWEALTH:

Masterson, Wyatt Earp, and all the sports in the country, held a meeting at Silverton and decided to take Dodge City by storm. Short is at Caldwell but will meet the party at Cimarron, 18 miles west of Dodge, perhaps Sunday night or soon after. Horses will be taken at Cimarron and the whole party will rendezvous at Mr. Oliver's, two miles west of Dodge. Doc Holliday and Wyatt Earp are now secretly in Dodge City, watching matters. When the time for action comes a telegram will reach them worded as follows: "Your tools will be there at _____," giving the time agreed upon. The plan is to drive all of Short's enemies out of Dodge at the mouth of the revolvers.

This information is correct. I have it from undoubted authority, and h--l will be to pay at Dodge City soon. I think Gov. Glick has an intimation of it, but am not certain. . . . I write this so you will know all about it when the time comes, and can write intelligently."

As if to still further confirm the report, we learn that Earp and other friends of Short were registered at Kinsley on Sunday at the eating house. They probably left Dodge for further consultation with friends and are preparing to carry out the plan outlined above.

LATER.

About 9 o'clock last night it was rumored on the street that a fight had already begun at Dodge City and that Gov. Glick had information of it. A reporter called upon the Governor at once and found him in bed, unable to see visitors. Adjutant-General Moonlight was in the adjoining room and said no information had been received. He stated that the city and county authorities were amply able to take care of themselves and had not asked for assistance. The state could not interfere until they made application for help or said they were unable to preserve the peace. The sheriff has the custody of the arms belonging to the state and under ordinary circumstances ought to be able to take care of the city.

General Moonlight said he had no doubt there would be a fight between the factions, but that he had no information concerning any at that time.

The difficulty in obtaining news from Dodge is well known to our readers, but we hope to keep them posted and shall endeavor to do so.

The adjutant general, too, by this time was becoming a bit disgusted. In a letter to the sheriff he said:

June 4th, 1883.

MR. GEO. T. HINKLE,
   Sheriff Dodge City,
      Kans,

MY DEAR SIR;

Upon a petition (which was embraced in Special Orders No. 7) signed by 42 of your citizens, and a dispatch from yourself of May 31st, a company of militia was ordered organized, and a copy of the order furnished you. The Governor believed that it was your desire, and the desire of the good people of Dodge City, to possess themselves of a military organization for frontier protection, and as the arms and accoutrements were in Dodge City, the company was ordered mustered into service by Major [Harry E.] Gryden. Today a dispatch was received from Mayor Diger, Geo. M. Hoover, R. M. Wright and Fred Singer acting Sheriff, to stop organization of company on account of excitement.

The Governor desires the peace and quiet of Dodge City and the protection of all her citizens, and cannot understand the various changes of opinion and action among the citizens, as some who signed the petition sign the dispatch. However believing that it might be better to defer the organization for the present, the Governor so telegraphed you, as also Major Gryden, and Mayor Diger and others who signed the dispatch. I have always believed that you could convince the citizens of your county that they were injuring themselves by the bickerings and dissensions that have lately taken place, and have also believed that you could keep and maintain the peace; and the Governor desires me to convey to you this faith and trust in you, and that the arms and accoutrements of the State will be safe in your hands—

The cattle men will soon begin to throng your streets, and all your citizens are interested in the coming— It is your harvest of business and affects every citizen, and I fear unless the spirit of fair play prevails it will work to your business injury. Every man has his friends be he great or small, and I cannot but believe that there will be trouble unless the spirit of prosscription ceases to prevail in the council of the city government— I write to you frankly knowing your people and knowing the elements engaged on both sides and being particularly desirous for the wellfare and success of Mayor Diger, knowing his people as I have for a long time, I ask you to convey my feelings to Mayor Diger in this respect and wish upon you all a conciliatory policy for a house divided cannot well stand.

I am with much respect
THOMAS MOONLIGHT
Adjutant General.[30]

The *Commonwealth* was correct in stating that Earp and Luke Short had met in Kinsley on Sunday, June 3. The Kinsley *Graphic,* June 7, 1883, reported they had been in town:

Luke Short, Earp and Petillon were in Kinsley last Sunday and took the afternoon train for Dodge City, where they expect to be joined by Shotgun Collins and Bat Masterson. Unless the authorities of Dodge back down we may expect some lively news from that city this week.

The big news broke and the *Ford County Globe,* June 5, 1883, prophetically sized it up with this simple statement: "Luke Short returned to the city Sunday afternoon, and we believe he has come to stay."

By the evening of the day following Luke's return, Sheriff Hinkle despaired of peace settling over the town. In a telegram to Governor Glick he said:

I think it impossible to prevent a fight but we will try to arrest and lock up every one engaged in it. We stopped all gambling today. An agreement was made allowing Luke Short to return to Dodge City on condition he would send his fighters out of town which he has failed to do. I think a fight imminent.[31]

A special dispatch to the Leavenworth *Times*, June 5, 1883, explained Hinkle's reference to the prohibition on gambling:

GOING FOR GAMBLERS.

A POSITIVE PROCLAMATION.

THE DODGE CITY GAMBLING HOUSES CLOSED BY ORDER OF MAYOR DEGER— THE ALLEGED CAUSE OF THE ISSUANCE OF THE ORDER.

DODGE CITY, Kan., June 4. [Special]—Mayor Deger to-day issued a proclamation in which he ordered the closing of all the gambling places. This action on the part of the mayor was brought about by the failure of Short's friends in fulfilling the compromise agreed upon, which was to the effect that Short should return peaceably and that several hard characters here, in his interest, should leave town. Their failure to leave to-day caused the issuance of the proclamation. As soon as the proclamation was issued every gambling place in the city was promptly closed, and have remained closed until this hour. Whether the trouble will end here, it is hard to determine.

On the night of June 5, 1883, Maj. Harry Gryden wired the adjutant general: "Everything here settled. Parties have shook hands across the bloody chasm. A number of men with a record are here but all is lovely."

Gryden's telegram was received in Topeka at 8:23 A. M., June 6, 1883, just two minutes before this telegram of an entirely different nature, addressed to Governor Glick:

Our city is overrun with desperate characters from Colorado, New Mexico, Arizona and California. We cannot preserve the peace or enforce the laws. Will you send in two companies of militia at once to assist us in preserving the peace between all parties and enforcing the laws.

GEO. T. HINKLE, Sheriff   L. E. DEGER, Mayor
N. B. KLAINE, Post Master   GEO. S. EMERSON, Councilman
F. C. ZIMMERMAN   Hon. R. M. WRIGHT, Co. Commissioner.

The governor wired back: "Moonlight will go there on first train. Keep me fully advised of the situation." Moonlight wired militia major Harry Gryden: "Keep peace at all hazards—will be at Dodge tonight—meet me."

Twenty minutes after the adjutant general boarded the noon train for Dodge City this telegram was received by Governor Glick:

The difficulty is all settled. Shorts fighters have left town. I am satisfied we will not have any more trouble.

GEO. T. HINKLE,
Sheriff.[32]

Luke Short

Events were happening so quickly that the *Daily Kansas State Journal*, June 7, 1883, had difficulty keeping up with them in a single article:

A HOWL FOR HELP.

THE CITY OF DODGE SURGING TO THE FRONT AGAIN WITH ITS SENSATION.

Trouble at Dodge City is not over with yet. A call came to Governor Glick this morning, for assistance. It was signed by the sheriff, Mayor [omission] Bob Wright and others. They fear an outbreak from Luke Short and want militia to protect them. Adjutant General Moonlight went down on the noon train and will arrive there at 12 o'clock to-night. No action is to be taken by the governor, until he is heard from, further than that Sheriff Hinkle has been ordered to keep the peace. He has fifty Winfield rifles in his possession and one thousand rounds of ammunition. The general took a supply of ammunition with him, and if it becomes absolutely necessary, troops will be ordered at once to Dodge City. When Moonlight gets there and learns the true situation he will probably make the fur fly, one way or the other. Yesterday evening, an agreement was made between both factions at Dodge, that they would drop their differences and declare peace.

Short and his friends are there, and were parties to the compact. Short went back home Monday evening, by invitation of the citizens on condition that he give $1,000 bonds to keep the peace, which was done, and a man who is in this city now, that has stood steadily by him through the whole difficulty went his security. In an interview with him, the JOURNAL reporter learns that Short has proposed to act white this time, but the other side broke its pledges and is to blame—in fact has been from the start. A few hot headed officials, backed by half the gambling and sporting fraternity undertook to run the other half out, and the break is now having its reaction. They have found the game one that two can play at. The renewed hostilities this morning seem to be of a more serious nature than at any previous time, and the antagonizing element is sufficiently alarmed to want the aid of military interference and protection. There seems to be a general opinion, now very frequently expressed here, that a few of the ring leaders ought to be allowed to fight and kill each other off if they want to.

THE VERY LATEST.

Governor Glick received the following dispatch this afternoon: [the Hinkle wire announcing the settling of difficulties was reprinted here].

Those who have watched the row all along, are inclined to believe that this is no indication as yet that trouble is over. Another call for the "milish" is expected by tomorrow morning.

Bat Masterson told of his triumphant entry into the town now bursting with brotherly love in a letter which was reprinted in part in the *Daily Kansas State Journal*, June 9, 1883:

MASTERSON'S MUSINGS.

AMONG OTHER THINGS FROM DODGE "BAT" MASTERSON TELLS THE SITUATION.

All information from Adjutant-General Moonlight indicate that the war at Dodge City is actually over and peace has been declared sure enough. Luke Short, however, comes out on top as usual, and is again sporting in the playful sunlight beneath his own vine and fig tree.

Of the situation, as it is now, Hon. W. B. Masterson, ex-sheriff of Ford county, writes in a letter to his friends here as follows, under date of June 6th:

"I arrived here yesterday and was met at the train by a delegation of friends who escorted me without molestation to the business house of Harris & Short. I think the inflammatory reports published about Dodge City and its inhabitants have been greatly exaggerated and if at any time they did 'don the war paint,' it was completely washed off before I reached here. I never met a more gracious lot of people in my life. They all seemed favorably disposed, and hailed the return of Short and his friends with exultant joy. I have been unable as yet to find a single individual who participated with the crowd that forced him to leave here at first. I have conversed with a great many and they are unanimous in their expression of love for Short, both as a man and a good citizen. They say that he is gentlemanly, courteous and unostentatious—'in fact a perfect ladies' man.' Wyatt Earp, Charley Bassett, McClain and others too numerous to mention are among the late arrivals, and are making the 'Long Branch' saloon their headquarters. All the gambling is closed in obedience to a proclamation issued by the mayor, but how long it will remain so I am unable to say at present. Not long I hope. The closing of this 'legitimate' calling has caused a general depression in business of every description, and I am under the impression that the more liberal and thinking class will prevail upon the mayor to rescind the proclamation in a day or two."

Although the dove of peace had settled on Dodge City—gently, as is wont with doves—the news, nevertheless, took several days to reach all portions of the state. The Kansas City (Mo.) *Evening Star* did not have it on June 7:

KILLERS AT DODGE.

THE FAMOUS BAND ARRIVE THERE AT LAST.

The much talked of band of noted killers who were to congregate here and accompany Luke Short, the exile, back to Dodge City, Kas., are in part at least, at that place now. Advices from there state that Luke Short, Bat Masterson, Charley Bassett and Doc Holliday at present hold the fort and that trouble is liable to ensue at any moment. Mr. Bassett was here for quite a time and with Col. Ricketts at the Marble Hall. He is a man of undoubted nerve and has been tried and not found wanting when it comes to a personal encounter. But Masterson and Doc. Holliday are too well known to need comment or biography. A notice has been posted up at Dodge ordering them out and, as they are fully armed and determined to stay, there may be hot work there to-night.

Luke Short

By June 8 the Topeka *Daily Commonwealth* was reporting everything serene, in Dodge:

ALL QUIET AT DODGE.

DODGE CITY, June 7.—Adjutant General Thos. Moonlight has been here for the past twenty-four hours and has succeeded in effecting an amicable settlement between the warring factions. He will leave for Topeka to-night. The Short faction are in the ascendancy, so to speak, but are peaceably disposed. There is no danger of trouble. The organization of the militia company, which some days ago was stopped by the governor, will be perfected and the commissions of the various officers will soon arrive; so says Col. Moonlight.

On June 10 Bat and Wyatt Earp left Dodge headed west. Upon their going Mike Sutton probably felt he could now return to his place of business after being away for his health, kidded the Larned *Optic*, and quoted in the *Ford County Globe* of June 12, 1883:

MIKE SUTTON, my lord is an exoduster from Dodge. On the return of Luke Short and his friends, it didn't take Mike long to arrive at the conclusion that Kinsley was a much healthier locality, and that town is now his abiding place. Net [Nelson Adams] sends greetings to Mike, and a notification that Larned is quarantined against him. When Dodge becomes too hot for Mike Sutton h--l itself would be considered a cool place—a desirable summer resort.

In another column the *Globe* couldn't resist applying its own needle:

As soon as Bat Masterson alighted from the train on his late arrival into this city Mike Sutton started for his cyclone building on Gospel Ridge, where he remained until a truce was made.

In the same issue, June 12, 1883, the *Globe* thus summarized this so-called Dodge City "war," an event that was apparently destined to go down in history as a war to preserve the rights of "singing ladies," *i. e.*, until the above related facts could be assembled:

Our city trouble is about over and things in general will be conducted as of old. All parties that were run out have returned and no further effort will be made to drive them away. Gambling houses, we understand, are again to be opened, but with screen doors [probably ornate oriental type door shields designed to obscure the view from one room to another rather than fly screens] in front of their place of business. A new dance house was opened Saturday night where all the warriors met and settled their past differences and everything was made lovely and serene. All opposing factions, both saloon men and gamblers met and agreed to stand by each other for the good of their trade. Not an unlooked for result.

The mayor stood firm on his gambling proclamation, but as his most ardent supporters have gone over to his enemies, it will stand without that moral support he had calculated upon to help him in enforcing it. We have all along held that our mayor was over advised in the action he has taken and had he followed his own better judgment, and not the advice of schemers and tricksters who had selfish interests at stake, and not the best interests of this community, he would have fared much better. No one knows this now any better than himself. He has freed himself from that cropped-winged moral element and stands on the side of the business interests of Dodge. . . .

The *Globe*, June 12, 1883, also said, with what seems a bit of pardonable pride:

Within the past week the city had more distinguished visitors and more ex-city and county officers in it than we ever saw together at any one time. It was a regular reunion of old-timers. They all appeared to have some say about our late trouble and felt a deep interest in the future prosperity of our city.

The Dodge City *Times* struck a discordant note by listing the visitors as Shot Gun Collins, Black Jack Bill, Cold Chuck Johnny, Dynamite Sam, Dark Alley Jim, Dirty Sock Jack, Six-toed Pete, and Three Fingered Dave.[33]

Before Bat and Wyatt left town the group gathered for a now historic photograph (*see* pp. 354, 355). The *Times*, June 14, 1883, recorded the event:

The photographs of the eight visiting "statesmen" were taken in a group by Mr. Conkling, photographer. The distinguished bond extractor and champion pie eater, W. F. Petillon, appears in the group.

Just as Adjutant General Moonlight had promised, the local militia unit was commissioned and given the name "Glick Guards." Within its ranks were both former pro-Short and pro-Deger men. Truly, the Dodge City war was over. The captain of the unit was Pat Sughrue and the second lieutenant was James H. Kelley, both Short adherents. The surgeon, Dr. S. Galland was a former Deger man. In the ranks could be found Neil Brown, C. E. Chipman, W. H. Harris, W. F. Petillon, Luke Short, I. P. Olive, and William M. Tilghman.[34]

In August Luke had the police judge of Dodge City arrested. Possibly some remaining hard feelings of the troubles of May and June were the reason. The *Times*, August 23, 1883, reported:

ARRESTED.

Police Judge Burns was arrested and brought yesterday, before Justice Cook, on complaint sworn out by Luke Short, in which he is charged with misconduct in office and the collection of illegal fees. Judge Burns has incurred the enmity of those who unfortunately come under his official jurisdiction. He has spared no one, having inflicted heavy fines upon every one brought before him for violation of law.

There is a certain clique in this city that feel the legal halter drawing tighter and tighter, with an ultimate tightening of grasp never to be loosened. The law is coming down upon indecent conduct and illegitimate traffic, and the handwriting is so plain that some means must be used to thwart the swift and impending justice. The arrest of Judge Burns will not accomplish the purpose desired. On the contrary, law-breakers will feel the full power of justice. Threats of assassination will not deter the administration of the law.

Luke and his friend Bat Masterson journeyed to Fort Worth, Tex., in November, 1883. The Dodge City *Times* article reporting this is reprinted in the section on Bat. Luke had sold his interest in the Long Branch as had his partner, Harris. The *Ford County Globe*, November 20, 1883, carried their notice of dissolution:

A CARD.—We take this opportunity in informing our numerous patrons and friends that we have this day sold out our interest in the Long Branch saloon and billiard hall to Mr. [Roy] Drake and [Frank] Warren, who will continue the business and are authorized to collect and receipt for all accounts due us. Any accounts against the late firm will be settled by us. Thanking past patrons for their many favors shown us, and trust the new firm may receive a like generous treatment at their hands.

W. H. HARRIS.
LUKE SHORT.

November 19, 1883.

Perhaps Luke had seen opportunities in Texas and decided to transfer his operations to that locale. In another column the *Globe* had said:

Luke Short came up from Texas during the past week, spending several days here, during which time he sold his interest in the Long Branch and returns to Fort Worth, Texas, accompanied by W. B. Masterson.

On December 28, 1883, Luke returned to Dodge for a visit. The *Globe*, January 1, 1884, reported:

Luke Short and Chas. E. Bassett returned to the city last Friday looking well, and show that they have been kindly treated by their friends in the east. They will remain here until after the holidays.

Luke's friend, W. F. Petillon, now editor of the Dodge City *Democrat*, merely said in his issue of December 29, 1883: "Ex-Sheriff Bassett and Luke Short are in town, both looking as if the Missouri Sunday law agreed with their corporosities." The *Democrat*, May 10, 1884, again mentioned that Luke was in town: "Luke Short is here from Fort Worth. He will remain until after the

563

arrival of St. John and Campbell [ex-Governor John P. St. John and A. B. Campbell, ardent prohibitionists], as he is anxious to meet these learned gentlemen." Perhaps the last was written with tongue in cheek!

In the summer of 1884 Luke decided to sue the city of Dodge for throwing him out in 1883. Petillon announced the action in the *Democrat* of August 9, 1884: "Luke Short has now sued this city for $15,000 damages for the trouble he was put to sometime ago. Summons was served on our Mayor [no longer Larry Deger but now George M. Hoover], while at Larned last Monday." The city employed the county attorney to represent it in the case:

The city council have employed county attorney Whitelaw to appear for them, in the case of Luke Short against Dodge City, pending in the Pawnee county district court, and have agreed to pay him $250 retainer, and $740 additional if he wins the case, or reduces the judgment asked for to $500. Mr. Whitelaw agrees to furnish any counsel he may need to assist him in the defense.[35]

The case was eventually settled out of court.

The next time Kansas newspapers carried the name of Luke Short they were announcing his final days on earth. Luke, with his wife and his brother, Young Short from Kiowa, Barber county, checked in at the Gilbert hotel in Geuda Springs, Sumner county, about August 25, 1893. Geuda Springs was at that time a health resort, its springs reportedly containing health-restoring minerals. Luke was suffering from dropsy.

The springs did not help Luke, however, and in less than a month he was dead. The Geuda Springs *Herald*, September 8, 1893, recorded his passing:

Luke Short died at the Gilbert this morning of dropsy. The remains were embalmed by W. A. Repp today and will be shipped this evening to Ft. Worth, Tex. The remains will be accompanied by the wife and two brothers of the deceased.

The Dodge City *Democrat*, in its parting salute, September 16, 1893, went overboard when it said: "Thus ends the life of one of the most noted and daring men in the west." [36]

1. In 1877 the Long Branch saloon, on Front street, was owned by D. D. Colley and J. M. Manion. Chalkley Beeson and W. H. Harris owned the Saratoga five or six doors east of the Long Branch. About March 1, 1878, Chalk Beeson purchased from Robert M. Wright the building in which the Long Branch was located, possession to be "in a few weeks." Colley and Manion moved one door west into the Alamo saloon which had been operated by George M. Hoover, and H. V. Cook.

Fred Singer

The Alamo was actually a sample room and billiard hall run in conjunction with Wright, Beverley & Co.'s mercantile store next door west. The Alamo should not be confused with George M. Hoover's wholesale liquor house at No. 39 Front street, just east of the Long Branch.

Strangely, as these changes were made the saloon names stayed with the building, instead of following the prior owners.—*See* Dodge City *Times,* December 22, 1877; March 2, 1878.

2. *Ford County Globe,* Dodge City, March 20, 1883. 3. *Ibid.* 4. Dodge City *Times,* April 5, 1883. 5. Both ordinances were published in the official city paper, the Dodge City *Times.* 6. See, also, the Topeka *Daily Commonwealth,* May 2, 1883. 7. "Governors' Correspondence," archives division, Kansas State Historical Society. 8. *Ibid.* 9. *Ibid.* 10. *See, also,* Kansas City (Mo.) *Evening Star,* May, 1883; Kansas City *Journal,* May, 1883; Topeka *Daily Capital,* May, 1883; Topeka *Daily Kansas State Journal,* May, 1883. 11. Luke was confused; May, 1883, began on Tuesday. 12. "Governors' Correspondence," *loc. cit.* 13. *Ibid.* 14. *Ibid.* 15. *Ibid.* 16. *Ibid.* 17. *Ibid.* 18. *See, also,* Topeka *Daily Kansas State Journal,* May 12, 13, 1883. 19. "Governors' Correspondence," *loc. cit.* 20. *See, also,* Kansas City (Mo.) *Evening Star,* May 15, 1883. 21. "Governors' Correspondence," *loc. cit.* 22. *Ibid.* 23. *Ibid.* 24. Dodge City *Times,* May 17, 1883. 25. *See, also,* letter of Felix P. Swembergh to Gov. G. W. Glick, May 17, 1883, in "Governors' Correspondence," *loc. cit.* 26. "Governors' Correspondence," *loc. cit.* 27. *Ibid.* 28. *Ibid.* 29. *Ibid.* 30. "Correspondence of the Adjutants General," archives division, Kansas State Historical Society. 31. "Governors' Correspondence," *loc. cit.* 32. *Ibid.* 33. Dodge City *Times,* June 7, 1883. 34. *Ibid.,* August 30, 1883. 35. *Globe Live Stock Journal,* Dodge City, November 25, 1884. 36. For a fuller report on the life of Luke Short, *see* William R. Cox's *Luke Short and His Era* (Doubleday, Garden City, N. Y., 1961).

SINGER, FREDERICK (1852?-1890)

Fred Singer was another Dodgeite who held positions at nearly every level of governmental police responsibility. He had been a township constable before he was appointed under sheriff of Ford county by newly elected Sheriff George T. Hinkle on January 12, 1880. Singer was apparently well thought of in Dodge, for the *Ford County Globe,* January 20, 1880, called him "a straightforward, honest man" and added "we trust he may never give anyone cause to speak otherwise of him." [1]

Hardly had Singer entered upon the duties of his new office, however, when he came down with a severe case of diphtheria and was temporarily replaced by Ed Cooley. By February 10 the under sheriff was again on his feet and tending his duties. [2]

Fred Singer was probably 27 years old when he was sworn as under sheriff. The 1880 United States census, enumerated in Dodge township on June 6, listed him as being 28 years old, his wife Lula was 18. He was born in Wales, she in Missouri.

The first year of the Hinkle-Singer reign was a quiet one, most of their duties consisting of delivering prisoners to the state penitentiary at Leavenworth. The newspaper notices telling of these trips have been reprinted in the section on Hinkle.

On April 6, 1881, Fred Singer was appointed city marshal of Dodge. He and his assistant, Tom Nixon, were to replace Marshal Jim Masterson and Assistant Neil Brown whom the new city council did not see fit to retain.[3] One of the marshal's first performances reported in the local papers appeared in the *Ford County Globe*, May 3, 1881, and was somewhat less than the glamorous image in the minds of most latter day Western fans: "Marshal Singer was seen headed for the City Pound on the 1st inst., having a hog by the ear and a dog by the extreme appendage."

The new marshal also held a position on the county police force, and about the first of May traveled to Pueblo, Colo., to receive a prisoner, a railroad man, with the legendary name of John Henry. The Dodge City *Times*, May 5, 1881, reported:

John Henry, a railroad employee, was arrested last summer on a charge of grand larceny, but was discharged on a want of insufficient testimony. He was lately rearrested in Wyoming territory, by Deputy U. S. Marshal C. B. Jones, and the prisoner was brought to this city last week from Pueblo by Deputy Sheriff Fred Singer. John Henry made his escape from the train while in the temporary charge of a guard, but was soon recaptured. A preliminary examination was had and the prisoner was bound over. It is said sufficient evidence has been collected to warrant conviction.[4]

Another railroad man was arrested by Singer on May 16. The *Globe*, May 17, 1881, told of it:

Marshall Singer, on last night took in Charley McCollum, fireman on the switch engine of this city for relieving a brother railroad man of seventy-five dollars in cash and a gold watch and chain, which robbing occurred some time during the night. The watch and chain as well as a portion of the money was in possession of aforesaid individual, who is now awaiting his preliminary in the county jail.

Dodge City, now almost nine years old, was emerging from its days as a frontier village into the status of a full fledged city. At least it had reached the place where it was thought that the police should wear conforming uniforms. The *Ford County Globe*, May 31, 1881, said: "City Marshal Singer and Assistant Nixon came out in the standard uniform of navy blue last week, and their appearance is like that of metropolitan officers." And the *Times*, May 5, 1881, remarked: "Who says Dodge City isn't 'tony?'"

566

Still another railroader was the accidental victim of the marshal's marksmanship on July 22, 1881. The Dodge City *Times,* July 28, recounted the story:

Joseph McDonald was shot by Marshal Singer Friday night last and died three hours afterward. The circumstances which led to the shooting are as follows: The woman to whom Nate Hudson willed $3,000 sent word to the marshal that three men were prowling around her house, and from their suspicious actions she believed they were trying to rob her. Marshal Singer obeyed the woman's request, and when near the premises, in a thick growth of sunflowers, was commanded to halt by McDonald, the latter raising his arm horizontally, as though in the act of firing. The marshal apprehended some danger from this movement, and not knowing whether the man had a pistol or not, raised his weapon and fired, the shot striking McDonald in the hand and passing into his right side, causing death in three hours. The wounded man remarked that his brother shot him. He gave no account of his wandering in the vicinity of the woman's premises.

McDonald was in the employ of the railroad company, and in company with another man came down from Syracuse on Thursday, the day previous to the shooting. He was in questionable company on that day, though this circumstance had no bearing on the shooting, but there is an impression that robbery was the design. Marshal Singer's quick forethought and knowledge of frontier pistol practice, prompted him to make defense when halted in the darkness and almost hid from view of the person who commanded him to halt. The ball entering the hand and striking the right side at a direct angle would indicate that McDonald held his hand in the position ascribed by the marshal.

A coroner's jury was summoned and an inquest held over the body. The verdict was justifiable homicide.

The deceased was 23 years of age. The body was sent to Topeka, where the parents of the unfortunate young man live.

At the inquest held over McDonald's body, Marshal Singer had testified:

I am city marshal of Dodge City; was sitting in front of Peacock's in a chair between 11 and 12 o'clock. A little Mexican came and asked me to take a walk. I said certainly I will go. Started with him and got about half way over to Johnson's blacksmith shop; while we were walking together he said that May Ingram had been looking for Tom Bugg [a deputy sheriff] but did not think she had found him; that some parties had been prowling around Sarah Ratzell's house, and that she thought they were going to rob her. The Mexican said I had better go and get a gun. I told him no, that it was not necessary. We then went over to Mrs. Woodard's house, near Johnson's shop, where Sadie Ratzell was; Sadie and Tom Bugg were sitting on the porch when the Mexican and myself got there. I said to Sadie to come into the room that I wished to speak with her. Asked her if she had any money there; said no, that she had deposited it in town. Mrs. Peacock had before told me that the said Sadie had $875 in her trunk, and she was mighty foolish for keeping it there. I said to Sadie as she had a good deal of money and intended leaving very soon that she had better take only enough to defray expenses and take a check for balance, and then draw the same through some bank wherever she might be. Afterwards we walked out on the porch; I sat down on the porch; I believe she sat in a chair; I sat there about five minutes; I saw a man walking back of Johnson's shop, going northeast; I walked out to see who it was; I got within about thirty feet of him; he started out in the weeds and turned and threw his hand out, just as if he was going to shoot, and said, "Stand!" He said it very emphatically. When he threw up his hand and commenced to say the word I drew out my gun, and fired. I know Geo. Early [McDonald's companion] as one of the two fellows that I ordered out of town. The other fellow wore eye-glasses, and was fined in the Police Court.

Tom Bugg testified:

I am deputy sheriff; I was notified by Dutch Jake [a female of the sporting class] that May Ingram was looking for me. Jake said that May Ingram wanted me to go to the house where Sadie Ratzell was stopping; that two or three men had been around there since early after dark. Went up to the brick store with Brick Bond, thence to the dance hall, and from there to Johnson's house, on the corner; left Brick Bond at the last named place, when I went to the house and dwelling of Mrs. Woodard. We staid there about twenty minutes, when Bond left. I remained sometime afterwards. Mr. Singer and the little Mexican came after Mr. Bond had left. After Mr. Singer came I went with Mrs. Woodard over to Andy Johnson's house, while Mr. Singer remained at the house of Mrs. Woodard. I was gone with her four or five minutes before I returned to the place where I had left Singer. On my return I thought I heard some one going between Johnson's blacksmith shop. I popped between the two buildings, thence to Mrs. Woodard's porch. When I stepped on the porch referred to I heard some one say, "Halt!" or, "Stop!" A shot was fired immediately thereafter; the flash made everything dark. I then went in the direction of the firing; met Fred Singer, and asked him if some one had shot him, answered no; "I think I have shot some body." Asked him who, said he did not know. I then went to Mrs. Woodard's and got a match, returned to the man that was shot, lit some matches, turned him over and asked him his name and where he was shot, and he said through the breast and that his name was McDonald. Myself and others took him to the restaurant and from there to the southeast room of Hudson's dance hall. The man upon whom this inquisition is being held I identify as the man that was shot; saw one man moving near Mrs. Woodard's house in a suspicious manner about three-quarters of an hour before the shooting took place.[5]

After the shooting of McDonald, Marshal Singer apparently created no news, for the town's newspapers gave him little notice until his announced resignation was published in the November 1, 1881, issue of the *Ford County Globe*. The Dodge City *Times*, November 3, 1881, said:

Fred Singer

Fred Singer has resigned the office of City Marshal, and Mayor [A. B.] Webster has appointed B. C. Vandenberg to the position. Mr. Singer made an energetic and attentive officer. He was always on duty, and faithfully discharged his trust. Fred gave up the office in order to engage in more profitable business.

The work Singer chose was saloonkeeping. The *Times,* November 3, 1881, ran this ad:

OLD HOUSE—Fred Singer has taken charge of the "Old House," lately occupied by Mr. Webster. Fred is an excellent caterer to the taste of thirsty people. His place will be a popular resort in Dodge City. The Brower Bros. have opened a restaurant in the "Old House" and a "square meal" on the European plan may be had by the hungry and fastidious visitors.

Singer still held his county commission and a few months later he was called upon to arrest a soldier at Fort Dodge. The man was not to be found, according to the Dodge City *Times,* June 1, 1882:

A soldier broke open the city prison and liberated a fellow soldier confined there. A warrant was issued for the arrest of the soldier, and under-sheriff Singer and Marshal Vandenberg went down to the Fort to arrest the man, but he was either concealed or had flown. It was said he had deserted.

After a group of festive Kearny county cowboys had gaily shot up the Santa Fe's eastbound No. 6, at Lakin on October 18, 1882, Undersheriff Fred Singer rounded them up with the aid of a Ford county posse. Kearny county came under the undersheriff's authority since, being unorganized, it was attached to Ford for judicial purposes. The *Ford County Globe,* October 24, 1882, described the crime and the capture:

DESPERATE DOINGS
OF A PARTY OF COW-BOYS AT LAKIN.
THEIR CAPTURE BY A DODGE CITY POSSE.

When train No. 6, due in Dodge City at 12:45 p. m. pulled up to the depot last Wednesday, the coaches presented the appearance of having undergone a heavy seige, the north windows of the entire train being completely demolished, while the side of the cars underneath was perforated with numerous bullet holes, the result of an attack on the train by a party of cow-boys at Lakin, the particulars of which are as follows:

Frank Meade, who had been in the employ of the railroad company for some time past as night operator at Lakin, was discharged on Monday of last week, for drunkenness and general cussedness, and in company with a trio of friendly cow boys proceeded to drown his troubles in an overdose of conversational fluid. On the same day the party attended the funeral of a deceased cow-boy at Deerfield and while there attempted to board the engine of a freight train, culminating in a fight with engineer Norton, in which the cowboys and operator were badly worsted. The following morning the four returned to Lakin, vowing to shoot Norton on his next trip west, and for that purpose, armed with Winchesters and six-shooters kept a close surveillance over all trains arriving from the east, but failed to discover their man, as he had been notified of their intentions, and in consequence changed off at Garden City and returned to Dodge.

Wednesday morning, train No. 6 due at Lakin about 10 o'clock, was detained some twenty minutes in consequence of a broken draw-head. While the train men were repairing the damage, the friends of Meade mounted their horses and charged up and down the depot platform in veritable cow-boy style, whooping and yelling in demoniac glee, discharging their arms at the coaches, all of which were well filled with passengers, and clubbing in the windows with their revolvers. Four bullets entered the coaches, while dozens were imbedded in the wood work underneath the windows. A lady whose name we failed to learn was severely cut about the face by the smashing of a window at which she was sitting. The citizens of Lakin were completely terrorized and powerless against them, as they were known to be heavily armed and desperate men.

The facts of the attack were at once forwarded to Superintendent Nickerson who telegraphed Sheriff Hinkle to have a posse in readiness to proceed to Lakin by a special train immediately after the arrival of No. 6 at Dodge City. Upon receipt of the telegram, with the promptness characteristic of Ford county officials, Under Sheriff Fred. Singer and posse, consisting of Brick Bond, Al. Updegraff, Tom Bugg, R. G. Cook, Joe Morgan, Jack Marshall, Henry Smith, Ed. Bower, Charles Dowd and O. D. Wilson, all heavily armed; M. W. Sutton, representing the railroad company; Station Agent Graves, and Frank Wandress, representing the GLOBE, boarded the special, and immediately after the arrival of No. 6, took their departure for Lakin. The train was in charge of Conductor G. W. Stover; engine 25, Harry Forges at the lever. The run from Dodge City to Lakin, seventy-two miles was made in one hour and fifty five minutes, including a stop at Pierceville for water.

Upon arriving at Lakin, several horses were discovered tied in front of a store immediately in the rear of the depot, and as the posse left the car and made a run for the horses, two cow-boys made their exit from the building and with drawn revolvers attempted to mount the animals. But they were too late, for a dozen Winchesters in the hands of men who never failed in bringing a desperado to terms, were frowning upon them from every side, and considering discretion the better part of valor, they gracefully acquiesced to the command of "hands up" and were taken in charge of by the officers. Their names are John Rivers and Peter Corder, their occupation herders, and this, we are told, is the first affair of the kind in which they have been interested. When captured each had in his possession a six-shooter. They were taken into the waiting room of the depot, shackled together and guarded by a detachment of the posse.

At this juncture Tom Bugg, who had been in search of Meade, the operator and supposed instigator of the difficulty, emerged from the pump house with his trophy by the ear. Meade had been in a state of semi-oblivion throughout

570

the day by quaffing too freely of what the law forbids, and gave himself up without any resistance.

Upon inquiry, it was ascertained that the ringleader of the party, John Cass by name, was quartered in a house of ill-fame about a mile west of the depot, and Messrs. Singer, Bond, Updegraff and Morgan mounted the only available horses in the place and started in quest of their man, who they had been informed would not be likely to surrender without a fight, as he is considered the most reckless man and best shot in that section. They were discovered by the desperado when about a hundred yards from the house, and he at once mounted his horse and galloped toward the north, giving them a parting shot or two as he scampered over the prairie. The quartette of officers gave hot pursuit and returned the fire of the fugitive with a will. The chase was kept up for a mile or more with a rapid exchange of shots, when a well-directed shot from one of the officers crippled the horse of Cass in such a manner as to make him worthless for a long chase. Cass thereupon abandoned his horse and sought shelter in a dug-out about a mile north of the depot, and as he had shown himself as a man of superior fighting calibre, and was well armed, a consultation was held to consider the best means of dislodging him without endangering the lives of any of the officers. The dug-out was then surrounded and a brisk fire opened upon it, during which the horse of Cass, which was grazing in front of the dug-out door, was shot by the officers and rolled over dead.

As "a man from Texas" is no man without his horse, Cass gave up all hopes of escape at the death of the animal, and displayed a flag of truce through the door of the dug-out, following it himself a moment later. With hands up and under cover of the rifles, he advanced toward the officers, was safely corraled and searched. Besides the regulation Winchester and six-shooter taken from his person, there was fished from the depths of his saddle-bags a quart of Lakin fire-water, which in itself is quite a formidable arsenal, as we can vouch for its accuracy at forty yards or even less. During the running fight, Mr. Singer twice cut the fringe from Cass' buckskin leggins, while he in return came within an inch of taking off one of Mr. Singer's ears, and with another shot attempted to decrease the proportions of Al. Updegraff's nasal appendage, which he missed by only a hair's breadth. Cass is the "bad man" of the party, and it is rumored, with a strong ground of probability, that he is one of the parties implicated in the murder of Marshal Meagher at Caldwell early last spring.

The prisoners were given a preliminary examination before Justice Dillon, who bound them over in $1,500 each to the February term of the district court to answer to the charge of assault with intent to kill. Immediately after the hearing the prisoners were taken to the train, brought to Dodge City, and quartered in the county jail where ample time will be afforded them of dwelling on the vicissitudes of western life, and repenting the act which will in all probability place them for several years to come where the dogs won't bite or the pesky fleas annoy them.

Notwithstanding tne fact that the merchants of our city keep constantly on hand a well assorted stock of arms, ammunition and ready made coffins, Dodge has proved to be, under the present municipal administration, not only

571

a law-abiding but a law preserving community. Her officers are ever ready to protect the lives and property of citizens or corporations, which fact is fully appreciated by the railroad officials in their selection at all times and under all circumstances of Dodge City men for work requiring the administration of law and the capture of fugitives from justice.[6]

On February 17, 1883, Singer and Deputy Sheriff H. P. (or Charles) Myton delivered eight prisoners to the penitentiary.[7] A couple of weeks later they journeyed south to capture one Jack McCarty who was soon to die from smallpox. The Dodge City *Times*, March 1, 1883, stated:

Under Sheriff Singer, Deputy Sheriff Myton and Jos. Morgan were the parties who went after McCarty, but they abandoned him, and the remains were taken charge of by Tom McIntire, who brought the body to 5-mile Hollow, south of Dodge, where he buried the remains. The city authorities forbade the bringing of the body through the city. A simple board indicates the burial spot.

As a police officer Singer had a part in the famous Dodge City "war" of 1883. The small role he played is covered in the section on Luke Short.

Fred Singer was being mentioned as a candidate for sheriff as early as August, 1883. At that date, long before any nominating conventions had assembled, it was generally known that Singer and Patrick F. Sughrue would battle for the important office.[8] As election time neared the fight became heated, possibly because of the troubles of the preceding spring, for Singer was of the Deger faction and Sughrue was of the Short crowd.

On November 6, 1883, the day of the election, the regular edition of the *Ford County Globe* came out with two stories designed to injure Singer at the polls. The first had to do with his attempt to arrest Jack McCarty last winter:

ANOTHER CHAPTER IN THE HISTORY
OF THE OPPOSITION'S CANDIDATE FOR SHERIFF.

When McCarty was lying sick at a ranch south of Dodge City, Sheriff Singer, Mr. Chas. Myton and Jas Morgan were sent out to capture McCarty, under a promise of a three hundred dollar reward, made by the Kaiser of the Board of County Commissioners. A promise they had no more right to make them than the writer of this article, but the reward was paid and Ford county tax payers will have to pay their part of it. It may be a matter of news to some of our tax payers to know that the said Board of County Commissioners are personally liable for the said reward.

To return to our story, when Mr. Singer and his two assistants arrived at the ranch, thinking that discretion would be the better part of valor, halted, and the lady living at the ranch was hailed, and asked whether the said McCarty was there, she answered yes; they then asked her whether there were any guns in the house; she answered, plenty of them. They also asked her whether she thought that McCarty would make a fight, she said he would to a certainty. They, the posse, then told the lady of the house that if she would go in the house and would succeed in getting all the guns outside of the house, so that they could capture McCarty without taking any chances at all, they then would give her one hundred and fifty dollars, which would be half of the whole reward which they were to receive. She agreed to the said proposition and went to the house and put all the guns on the outside of the house, and the posse then had an easy capture, as McCarty was then lying on his death bed.

After they received the reward they must have forgotten their promise to the lady in question, as they still owe her the half of the said reward. If any one doubts the truth of the above, the lady is in town and will gladly make an affidavit to the above statements. A man or a party of men who would break their word to a woman under such circumstances will deserve defeat as an aspirant for any office.

The other was of a similar nature:

ONE OF FRED SINGERS OFFICIAL ACTS
AS A DEPUTY, UNDER SHERIFF HINKEL.

About three years ago, Singer and an assistant went down to Mrs. Brown's ranch, on Bear creek, (the place generally known as the soldier's grave,) for the purpose of arresting the notorious thief and bandit of the plains, named Jim O'Neill, (they succeeded in making the arrest,) but through the influence of Mrs. Brown, his mother, and the magical influence of about one hundred dollars, paid to Singer and his assistant, the redoubtable Jimmy was allowed to pack his grip and depart in peace. This is another bit of evidence as to how the sheriff and his deputies in the past few years have done their duty.

Apparently the items had the desired effect for Sughrue defeated Singer 488 to 343.[9]

Though he had been defeated at the ballot box Singer was continued as under sheriff while Hinkle remained in office. On December 19, 1883, he, with John Meagher (Mike Meagher's brother) and the marshal of Trinidad, Colo., captured a suspected murderer. The Caldwell *Journal*, December 27, 1883, reported the story:

ED. HIBBARD CAPTURED.

John Meagher, sheriff Singer, of Dodge, and City Marshal Kreager, of Trinidad, returned from Chautauqua county last Saturday with Ed. Hibbard, alias Ed. Lee, charged with the murder of a man near Trinidad, as stated last week.

The officers left this city Wednesday, went to Grenola, where they procured a team and started for the home of Hibbard's parents, near Wauneta, a small town about eight miles from Cedarvale. Arriving at Wauneta about 3 p. m., they went into the village store, which they found full of people, and Ed. standing by the counter, behind the stove, surrounded by a throng, to whom he was relating his western adventures. The officers knew him at a glance, and sheriff Singer at once stepped up to Ed. and taking him by the hand, said: "How do you do, Ed? I want you." Ed. reached for his revolver with his left hand, but by this time Meagher had him covered with a six-shooter, and he quietly submitted to being hand-cuffed, led out, and put into the wagon. In less than three minutes from the time the officers entered the store, they had their man and were on their return trip. Ed. claimed he did not know what he was arrested for, but at the same time requested the officers not to tell the people anything about it.

Shortly after passing Cedarvale, the party were overtaken by Hibbard's mother, who wanted to know by what right they were taking her son off in that manner. Ed. told her it was all right, the strangers were his friends, and that he would be back in a couple of weeks. This was satisfactory to his poor mother, and the party proceeded on their way, arriving here at the time above stated.

While at Cedarvale, on their return, a constable of that place stepped up to Meagher and told him that Hibbard was a hard case, that he, the constable, had carried a warrant against him for four years on the charge of horse stealing. It seems that about four years ago Hibbard left suddenly and went to Texas, where, it is stated, he killed a man. Thence he drifted to Colorado, where he ran across his uncle, stopping at his uncle's ranch until he killed the old man.

On being searched after his arrest, $105 in money was found upon his person, all that was left of the $1,100 taken off his victim, an old account book, with several leaves torn out, and the name "Reynolds" written on the inside of the cover. The writing was so worn that the initials could not be made out, but the name is supposed to be the name of the man killed.

Saturday afternoon Messrs. Singer and Kreager started for Trinidad with their prisoner, and he is ere this safely locked up in the jail at that place. There can be no doubt as to his guilt, and according to the laws of Colorado, he will suffer the penalty of his crime.

The Dodge City *Times*, December 27, 1883, reported that Singer had taken the prisoner on west:

Under Sheriff Singer left Monday [December 24] for Colorado with the prisoner Hibbard, who was arrested in the southeastern part of the state. Fred is an excellent officer, and does his duty faithfully.

With the end of the Hinkle sheriffship Fred Singer returned to private life, judging from the 1885 Kansas state census which listed him, March 1, as a 32-year-old merchant.

On July 31 he and Mysterious Dave Mather were in Topeka, staying at the Windsor hotel.[10] By September 1 he was again mentioned as a deputy sheriff. The Dodge City *Democrat,* September 5, 1885, told how he prevented a kidnapping:

A HALF-BLOWN ABDUCTION.

A bold attempt to abduct a child was made last Tuesday morning. The particulars, as we learned them, are as follows:

About three weeks ago Harry Logue, a well known gambler and general "rustler" of this place, parted from his wife. They had one child and he wanted it, and had threatened to kill her if she did not give it up. Last Tuesday morning he procured a rig and drove to the house where his wife was living. He went in and snatched the child from its mother's arms while she was in bed and ran out to the buggy, jumped in and started off south at a pace that astonished the natives. Mrs. Logue followed, screaming at every breath, calling on the people to get her baby. Deputy sheriff Fred Singer happened to be passing on a horse and immediately gave chase. He overhauled the gentleman just as he was driving on the bridge, and made him turn around and wend his way back amid the jeers of the populace.

It was an affecting sight when the babe was given into its mother's arms. She was wild with joy and hugged and kissed the innocent cause of all this excitement to her heart's content.

Half the population was out to see the chase, and all expressed their sympathy for the unfortunate mother, and all were glad when she got her child.

A month later Fred Singer was appointed deputy U. S. marshal for the district. "This was quite a compliment," said the *Globe Live Stock Journal,* October 6, 1885, "and the result of one of the finest endorsements ever sent out of this county. Everybody who is acquainted with Mr. Singer knows he will make a good officer." Singer's appointment was effective October 1.[11]

In another month, however, Singer was apparently replaced by H. B. Bell who was appointed about November 5, 1885.[12] No reason has been found for Singer's short term of office.

Singer was once again named marshal of Dodge City on September 23, 1886, by A. B. Webster. The *Globe Live Stock Journal,* September 28, 1886, noted the change in officers: "Mayor Webster on last Thursday morning made a change in the police force, removing Marshal [T. J.] Tate and Policeman [J. A.] Marshall, and appointing Fred Singer marshal and Nelson Cary assistant." Singer served until shortly after Mayor Webster's death, resigning May 10, 1887.[13]

Singer was one of several former Dodge City police officers involved in the county seat fight in Gray county, in January, 1889. The complete story of the street battle in which they were engaged is told in the section on William M. Tilghman.

1. *See, also*, Dodge City *Times*, January 17, 1880. 2. *Ford County Globe*, February 10, 1880. 3. Dodge City *Times*, April 7, 1881. 4. *See, also, Ford County Globe*, May 3, 1881. 5. *Ibid.*, July 26, 1881. 6. *See, also*, Dodge City *Times*, October 19, 1882. 7. *Ford County Globe*, February 20, 1883. 8. Dodge City *Times*, August 16, 1883. 9. *Ford County Globe*, November 20, 1883. 10. *Globe Live Stock Journal*, August 4, 1885. 11. *See, also*, Dodge City *Democrat*, October 3, 1885; Dodge City *Times*, October 8, 1885. 12. *See* the section on H. B. Bell. 13. *Globe Live Stock Journal*, May 17, 1887.

SMITH, THOMAS JAMES (1830?-1870)

"Bear River" Tom Smith was hired as Abilene's chief of police on June 4, 1870, his salary to be $150 per month plus $2 for each conviction of persons he arrested. Smith was originally employed for one month only but he stayed on the force until his death that fall. One policeman assistant was authorized, but the name of the person initially filling the position is unknown.[1]

The 1870 United States census for Grant township, Dickinson county, in which Abilene is located, listed Smith as 40 years old at the time of the enumeration, July 30, 1870. He was born in New York.

On August 9, 1870, the city council increased Smith's salary to $225 a month retroactive to July 4.[2]

Few items describing Smith's activities as chief of police or under sheriff have been preserved. One of these rarities appeared in the *Republican Valley Empire*, Clyde, August 2, 1870:

Under sheriff Smith, of Dickinson county, called on us on Monday [August 1?]. He had just returned from Brownsville, Nebraska, whither he had been in pursuit of Buckskin Bill, who stole horses at Abilene not long ago, an account of which we published. Bill had sold some of the stock at Pawnee City, and they attempted to prevent the sheriff from getting the property by telling him he had better get out, or he soon would have nothing to go out on. He does not speak in very favorable terms of Pawnee City—thinks that a man who has anything loose about him had better give the town a wide berth. The sheriff captured nearly all the stock. Foster, Bill's accomplice, was in jail at Nebraska City, having shot a colored man in a fracas. The sheriff says that he was aided by the officers and people of St. Joe, Atchison and Marysville. Bill was safely lodged in jail at Brownsville. He has a father there who is a prominent citizen and a worthy man, and who feels keenly the bad conduct of his son.

Smith may have been the officer who, a month later, arrested a Dickinson county murderer. The arrest was reported in the Abilene *Chronicle*, September 8, 1870:

576

MURDER.—On last Sunday [September 4] a terrible tragedy occurred at one of the dens of infamy, just suppressed north-west of town. It seems that a young man named Charles Fay, was visiting the house, when an altercation took place between himself and a man named Thomas Calloway. Another man named Warren Howell joined in the fracas and fired several shots at Fay. Fay was finally shot through the head, it is said by Calloway, and killed. C. C. Kuney, Esq. [police magistrate], caused an inquest to be held on the dead body, and the jury found that Fay came to his death by a pistol shot from the hand of Thomas Calloway, and also that Warren Howell aided and assisted in the murder. Howell was promptly arrested and lies in jail awaiting trial at the next term of the District Court. Calloway has thus far eluded arrest. The authorities would do well to offer a reward of $500 or more for his body. It is time that thieves and murderers be cleaned out of this part of the State. The people of Abilene, with scarcely an exception, unite in saying that the murder on last Sunday was a most cowardly, cold-blooded act. The murdered man did not offer to defend himself. It is said that he did not believe, until too late, that a murderous assault would be made upon him. The three men were from Texas. Heretofore the Texans have not been interfered with much, by the officers of the law in this locality, when they killed each other. But the time has come when violators of the peace must be punished, no matter where they may hail from. We know that every respectable Texan condemns lawlessness and violence, and is in favor of order and good morals—as are all intelligent, respectable men, whether from Texas or elsewhere. We believe that no citizen of Dickinson county has ever committed the crime of murder, and we hope that we shall never again be under the necessity of chronicling a murder perpetrated within the limits of the county.

A day or two after the killing Smith ordered the red light district to shut down. The same issue of the *Chronicle,* September 8, said:

CLEANED OUT.—For some time past a set of prostitutes have occupied several shanties, about a mile north-west of town. On last Monday or Tuesday Deputy Sheriff Smith served a notice on the vile characters, ordering them to close their dens—or suffer the consequences. They were convinced beyond all question that an outraged community would no longer tolerate their vile business, and on yesterday, Wednesday, morning the crew took the cars for Baxter Springs and Wichita. We are told that there is not a house of ill fame in Abilene or vicinity—a fact, we are informed, which can hardly be said in favor of any other town on the Kansas Pacific Railway. The respectable citizens of Abilene may well feel proud of the order and quietness now prevailing in the town. Let the dens of infamy be kept out, the laws enforced and violators punished, and no good citizen will ask more. Chief of Police, T. J. Smith and his assistants, and C. C. Kuney, Esq., deserve the thanks of the people for the faithful and prompt manner in which they have discharged their official duties. A grateful community will not forget the services of such efficient officers.

On October 23 an event occurred which eventually led to the death of the chief of police. The *Chronicle,* October 27, 1870, recorded:

FATAL AFFRAY.—We regret to learn that a fatal affray took place on last Sunday afternoon, near Chapman Creek, between two neighbors named John Shea and Andrew McConnell. The facts as related to us are substantially as follows:—It seems that McConnell had been out with his gun hunting deer, on his return he found Shea driving a lot of cattle across his (McConnell's) land. Some words passed between them, when Shea drew a revolver and snapped it twice at McConnell who stood leaning on his gun, and being on his own land. As Shea was cocking his pistol for the third time, McConnell drew up his gun and shot Shea through the heart, killing him instantly. McConnell went for a Doctor, and afterwards gave himself up, and had an examination before Esquire Davidson on last Tuesday, when a neighbor of both men, Mr. Miles, testified substantially to the above facts, and McConnell was discharged —the act having been done in self-defence. Shea leaves a widow and three children.

Later it developed that Miles and McConnell had taken liberties with the truth and a warrant was issued once more for McConnell. The Abilene *Chronicle,* November 3, 1870, continued the story:

HORRIBLE AFFRAY.—Last week we chronicled a terrible affair, which occurred on Chapman Creek, resulting in the death of John Shea at the hands of Andrew McConnell. McConnell gave himself up, and upon the testimony of a man named Miles was released, Miles swearing that the act was done in self-defence. But it afterward appeared to some of the neighbors, from unmistakable circumstances, that Shea was not the aggressor, and a warrant was issued for the re-arrest of McConnell. On Wednesday [November 2] of this week officers T. J. Smith, and [J. H.] McDonald, went out to McConnell's dugout to arrest him. Upon reaching the dugout they found McConnell and Miles. Officer Smith informed McConnell of his official character and that he had a warrant for his arrest, whereupon McConnell shot Smith through the right lung; Smith also fired, wounding McConnell; the two being close together grappled; Smith, although mortally wounded, was getting the better of McConnell, when Miles struck him on the head with a gun, felling him senseless to the ground, and seizing an ax chopped Smith's head nearly from his body. At this stage of the tragedy officer McDonald returned to this place for assistance. A posse was raised, and repaired to the scene of the murder, but McConnell and Miles had fled, and up to this morning had not been arrested. They were both wounded, and it is reported were in Junction City last evening. It is hoped that they will be speedily arrested. We give the above named particulars as we gather them from reports current in town.

The body of Mr. Smith was brought to this place last evening, and will be buried at 10 o'clock to-morrow. The sad event has cast a gloom over our town. Our citizens had learned to respect Mr. Smith as an officer who never shrank from the performance of his duty. He was a stranger to fear, and yet in the private walks of life a most diffident man. He came to this place last spring, when lawlessness was controlling the town. He was at once employed as chief of police, and soon order and quiet took the place of the wild shouts and pistol shots of ruffians who for two years had kept orderly citizens in dread

578

for their lives. Abilene owes a debt of gratitude to the memory of Thomas James Smith, which can never be paid. Although our people will never again permit the lawlessness which existed prior to his coming to the town, yet it will be a long time before his equal will be found in all the essentials required to make a model police officer.

Sacred be the memory of our departed friend and green be the turf that grows upon his grave. In years to come there will be those who will look back to the days when it required brave hearts and strong hands to put down barbarism in this new country and among the names of the bravest and the truest none will be more gratefully remembered than that of THOMAS JAMES SMITH, the faithful officer and true friend of Abilene.

Three days after their crime, Miles and McConnell were captured. The *Chronicle* article, November 10, 1870, reporting their unsuccessful flight is reprinted in the section on James Gainsford.

Knowing the local people could not render an objective verdict, after three special lists of prospective jurors had been exhausted, the court granted a change of venue to Riley county. The *Chronicle*, November 17, 1870, reported:

State of Kansas vs. Andrew McConnell and Moses Miles, charged with murder in first degree. One day and a half was consumed in trying to impannel a jury. Three special venues were exhausted without securing the requisite number of jurors. A change of venue to Riley county was finally granted by the court, and the prisoners conveyed to the Manhattan jail to await trial at the March term of District court for that county.

Tom Smith was buried in a two-dollar grave, gunsmith Patrick Hand was appointed his successor,[3] and the incident faded from the news until March, 1871, when Miles and McConnell were brought up for trial. The *Chronicle*, March 23, 1871, reported the result:

CONVICTED.—We learn the following particulars, relating to the trial at Manhattan of Miles and McConnell, for the murder of Marshal T. J. Smith. We are told by one of the attorneys that the evidence went to show that the officers in attempting to arrest the accused produced no warrant or authority; that the prisoners were in dread of a mob; that after they had Smith in their power—the officer whom he went to assist having fled—they brutally chopped him up with an axe. This fact alone caused the conviction of the prisoners. McConnell was sentenced to twelve and Miles to sixteen years confinement in the penitentiary. Thus ends one of the most horrible tragedies that has ever occurred in the State. When first arrested the prisoners were willing to plead guilty of murder in the second degree, which would have sent them to the penitentiary for life—but the prosecuting attorney would not permit such a plea, because public sentiment, at the time demanded the hanging of the prisoners. Twelve and sixteen years in the penitentiary seem long periods, but the condemned ought to be thankful that they get off with even such sentences. Never during their natural lives can they atone for their great crime.

Thirty-four years after Smith died, Abilene paid belated tribute to its former chief of police. His body was disinterred from its obscure grave in the Abilene cemetery and reburied near one of the main avenues of the grounds. On Memorial day, May 30, 1904, a huge natural boulder marking the new site was dedicated. Abilene's first mayor, T. C. Henry, returned from his Denver residence and delivered a stirring speech on Smith's Abilene tenure. But perhaps the finest—and certainly the most enduring—tribute was the sentiment expressed on the bronze plaque fastened to the boulder. It read:

THOMAS J. SMITH,
Marshal of Abilene, 1870.
Died, a Martyr to Duty, Nov. 2, 1870.
A Fearless Hero of Frontier Days Who
in Cowboy Chaos
Established the Supremacy of Law.[4]

1. "City Council Minute Book," Records of the City of Abilene, p. 29. 2. Ibid., p. 37. 3. Ibid., p. 43. 4. Abilene Daily Chronicle, May 31, 1904; Topeka Daily Capital, May 31, 1904.

SMITH, WILLIAM (1844-1908)

William Smith was born in Leicestershire, England, on April 22, 1844. When he was nine years old his family migrated to America and upon the opening of Kansas territory in 1854 moved to newly established Lawrence.[1] Sometime before the Civil War they moved to Wabaunsee, a Free-state town in present Wabaunsee county, 13 miles east of Manhattan. Here they took up farming.

On March 31, 1864, young Bill enlisted in Co. L, Eleventh regiment Kansas Volunteer cavalry as a private. He served until mustered out September 26, 1865, but saw no action against the Confederates since his company participated in Indian campaigns in western Kansas and western Dakota territory (now Wyoming).[2]

About September, 1869, Bill Smith and his half brother, Harry, moved to Wichita, taking a sawmill which they had been operating in Wabaunsee county during the previous year. The mill was set up in Wichita's present Riverside Park.

Smith took an early interest in law enforcement though he was defeated for sheriff in Sedgwick county's first election, November, 1870. Before the end of the year he was appointed a deputy United States marshal.[3]

On February 19, 1871, the new deputy marshal extended the strong arm of the law around the slender waist of Miss Mary Peck, marrying her in the Wichita Presbyterian church that Sunday. "The ceremony was witnessed by nearly every woman in Wichita," said the *Vidette*, February 25, 1871.

Smith, whose main occupation by this time was operating the Star Livery Stable, was possibly the fourth city marshal of Wichita. Like his predecessors he did not retain the position long; in fact Smith resigned only three days after he had been appointed. He was selected on April 10, 1871, by the governing body of Wichita;[4] his oath of office was dated April 11 and his letter of resignation was prepared on April 13. It read:

> WICHITA KANSAS
> April 13th 1871
>
> To His Honor
>   E. B. ALLEN
>   MAYOR OF THE CITY OF WICHITA
>   SIR.
>   In view of existing emergencies, having necessarily to leave the City for the space of at least fifteen days and having no competent person with whom I could entrust with the duties of City Marshal I hereby tender my resignation as Marshal of the City of Wichita and trust that yourself together with the City Council will accept the same.
>   I am Sir
>   Very respectfully
>   Your obdt servt.
>   WILLIAM SMITH
>   Marshal[5]

The next spring Smith again ran for public office and was elected a councilman for the fourth ward. The election had been held April 2, 1872.[6]

Some time later Smith obtained a commission as a Sedgwick county deputy sheriff under John Meagher, brother of City Marshal Mike Meagher. About June 6, 1873, the sheriff, Smith and Constable J. W. McCartney nabbed two mule thieves. The Wichita *Eagle*, June 12, 1873, reported:

Sheriff Meagher, Smith and McCarty, who went after the thieves who stole Mr. Wilkin's mules, returned on last Friday. They overtook the property and the "larkies" at Eureka, Greenwood county. The names of these patrons of mule flesh are Francis M. Carson and John Jefferson. They were found asleep in a barn, and the mules were staked out in the public square. They were terribly afraid of being brought back to Wichita, asserting that they preferred to die right there. At a preliminary examination Carson plead guilty and they were bound over for an appearance at the district court of the above mentioned county. As Judge Campbell's court sits there next week, these wayward boys will be pounding stone inside the penitentiary walls within two weeks. . . .

A week later McCartney and Smith again teamed up to arrest two suspected murderers. The *Eagle*, June 26, 1873, said:

Mr. King and his son, from Texas, who were arrested here last week by Constable McCartney and Deputy Sheriff Smith for the killing of a man in Clay county, Texas, were discharged by 'Squire D. A. Mitchell upon the ground of self-defense.

When John Meagher resigned as sheriff Gov. Thomas A. Osborn appointed Billy Smith to fill the vacancy September 15, 1873.[7] The *Eagle*, September 18, 1873, announced the change:

Following the resignation of Sheriff John Meagher, Deputy Sheriff William Smith was commissioned by the governor to fill the unexpired term. Wm. Smith has made an efficient and prompt officer, and we have no doubt but that he will prove faithful in his higher trust.

However, when Smith ran for the following full term in November he was defeated by Pleasant H. Massey 665 to 599.[8]

When district court opened on December 8, 1873, Sheriff-elect Massey attempted to assume the mantle of his office. Smith refused to yield, contending that his appointive term was still in effect and that Massey would not become sheriff until January, the regular time for swearing in county officers. The Wichita *Eagle* item covering this controversy is reprinted in the section on Massey.

Sheriff Smith was also active that December, attempting to locate Rowdy Joe Lowe who had skipped town slightly ahead of a warrant requiring his arrest. This episode has been reprinted in the section on Lowe.

Between four and five o'clock on Christmas morning, 1873, hungry flames began licking at the Main street millinery shop of Misses Annie Fardy and Kitty Hanley. The Wichita fire company and many private citizens battled desperately to keep the fire from spreading to other buildings and possibly consuming the entire frontier town.

Billy Smith

During the flurry of activity surrounding 73 Main street that morning Arthur Winner was discovered lying bloody and dazed, in his nightshirt, at the foot of the stairs leading to his quarters over the millinery shop. "In a few moments more the falling of the upper floor revealed amid the curling flames the white and ghastly face and the head of a corpse which soon fell with a dead thud to the joists below," the *Eagle*, January 1, 1874, reported. The body was thought to be that of Winner's partner, Joseph W. McNutt, with whom he had been sharing a bed shortly before.

As the winter progressed the fire was forgotten but the body was not. Subsequent developments indicated that McNutt had not died, and that the corpse was one W. W. Sevier, who had been killed in an attempt to defraud an insurance company which held a policy on the life of McNutt. Consequently a grand search was instituted for the person of Joseph W. McNutt. The man who found him, and returned him to Sedgwick county custody, was William Smith. A township constable, he had pursued McNutt on his own initiative. The Wichita *Eagle*, February 19, 1874, described Smith's success:

THE CHRISTMAS TRAGEDY.

On Tuesday, the 10th inst., intelligence was received at this place that McNutt was in Missouri, or, at least, it was supposed that it might be him. There was not much credit given to the statement, but Will. Smith, ex-sheriff of this county, had been "working up" the case for some time, and he concluded, from what he had gleaned, that he might possibly be there. Consequently he started in pursuit, leaving on the train that night, stopping off at Topeka to get a requisition from the governor of this state, proceeded to Leavenworth city, took the Chicago and Rock Island road to Plattsburgh, Mo., arriving at that place Thursday night. He immediately procured a horse and guide, riding all that night in the supposed direction of the criminal, visiting a number of small country postoffices, inquiring at each office whether a party by the name of Leahead procured mail there or not (for this was the name McNutt was going by). He finally came to the New Garden postoffice, in Ray county, and was told that a party by that name was getting mail at that office, and that he was working on a farm about one mile from there. Smith left his horse, borrowed a shot-gun of his informant for the purpose of killing chickens, he said, and proceeded to the farm.

On arriving at or near the farm house, which stood in a clearing, he espied McNutt in the back yard chopping wood. He passed around the farm to the east side, where stood a large barn. He went to the barn, keeping it between himself and his game; farther on, towards the house, about a hundred yards, and within twenty feet of where McNutt was chopping, stood a corn crib. He worked his way cautiously up to the corner of the crib, stepped out and leveled his gun on the chap, and told him to throw down his ax and hold up his hands, for he was his prisoner, which order he promptly obeyed, remarking while being handcuffed, "Well, you have got me at last." Smith said yes, he had been hunting him for some time. He was placed upon a horse and brought to Plattsburgh, arriving there on Sunday, and at this place Monday night. He denies the statements made by Winner in the main. Tuesday morning he was taken before Justice [E. B.] Jewett. His examination was put off until yesterday. We shall endeavor to lay before our readers in our next issue the evidence elicited at the examination.

Much praise is due to Will. Smith for the untiring energy and great sagacity displayed in capturing this man. What he did was in a quiet and unobtrusive manner. But very few in the town knew that he was trying to find McNutt, and it was a matter of great surprise to our citizens when it was announced Tuesday morning that Smith had got back with McNutt. But few men would have succeeded in ferreting out the whereabouts of this man, having no more to work upon than the mere name Leahead.

LATER.—He was again brought before Justice Jewett last evening. His attorneys, [W. E.] Stanley [later governor of Kansas, 1899-1903] and [J. M.] Balderston, appeared, asked that the case be postponed until next Thursday, which was granted.

The editor of the *Eagle*, March 5, 1874, was intrigued by the romantic aspect of the crime and capture:

No better evidence of the spirit of the people is necessary than to point to the manner in which the McNutt affair was unraveled and brought to the light of the world. There was almost nothing to work on at first, but as days rolled on, thread upon thread was woven into the net that was to entrap the guilty parties. We do not remember of reading of a more cool and deliberate murder than the one planned by McNutt and Winner. It reads like some romance we have read of the bandits of Bomerwald. Ned Buntline could weave from it a romance that would read as wonderful as any he ever spun. But the perpetrators of it are safe in the hands of the law, and if full justice is vouchsafed to them they will stretch hemp before long.

Winner is safe in the Cottonwood Falls jail, and McNutt is at present guarded by his captor, Mr. William Smith, and he could easier escape from a dungeon's wall than from such a man. McNutt is at "No. 11," Empire House. Mrs. McNutt is also guarded in the same Hotel. She seems to be fearfully agitated since the arrest of her husband and has attempted to kill herself by using poison, but was detected and frustrated. This we learn from a pretty reliable source, presume it is true.

In subsequent days both Winner and McNutt were convicted of their crime and sentenced to be hanged. These sentences were later commuted. William Smith, probably because of his excellent work in tracing McNutt, was re-elected constable on April 7 and appointed city marshal on April 15, 1874. Smith's city force included

Daniel Parks, assistant marshal; William Dibbs and James Cairns, policemen.⁹

A few days after his appointment Marshal Smith apprehended an escaped convict. The *Eagle*, April 30, 1874, said:

> City Marshal, Billy Smith, apprehended and arrested a convict one Thomas Hind on a telegram from Salina last week and confined him in jail. Hind was convicted for manslaughter in the third degree, at the above place, and sentenced by Judge Prescott to two years in the State Penitentiary. He was put into the custody of Sheriff Ramsey, of Saline county. While Ramsey was manacling two other prisoners Hind jumped through the door, shut in the hasp of the staple, and escaped, leaving the sheriff and his deputies prisoners. The night was very dark, and before the sheriff could make the situation known, his bird had flown and all efforts to capture him failed until he was picked up here by our boys. Wichita is a poor place for outlaws to flee to. Nearly every rough upon the border is known to our police force. Hind was taken away Tuesday morning.

On May 27, 1874, Marshal Smith was compelled to stand help-lessly by while the murderer of a Negro hod carrier made his escape. The Wichita *Eagle*, May 28, described the circumstances:

> ### A FATAL AND DISGRACEFUL AFFAIR.
> #### AN ATTEMPT TO MURDER A COLORED MAN.
>
> Yesterday afternoon, about twenty minutes to 2 o'clock, just before we commenced to make up our forms, a Texas man by the name of Ramsey stepped up to a colored man by the name of Charley Sanders, who was tending the masons at work upon Miller's building on Main street, and shot him twice, the first shot taking effect in the ear and the next about three inches below the nipple of the left breast. Simultaneously with the shooting a dozen revolvers were pulled by bystanding Texans, and Ramsey mounted his horse and fled down Main street, out Douglas avenue and across the bridge, followed by two or three hundred men, many of whom had revolvers in hand, but whether for the protection of the fleeing fugitive or his capture seemed doubtful to us until we were told it was for the protection of the shooting party.
>
> The city marshal was standing close by, but seeing it was a preconcerted job evidently, and being threatened with drawn weapons, he could do nothing.
>
> It appears that the Texas and the colored man had had a quarrel two or three night previous, for which both were arrested. The colored man is well known in the city, has a family, and is sober and a hard working man. Everything looks as though it was a regular preconcerted murder. He is still alive at this writing (an hour after the event), but bleeding badly inside, and he cannot possibly survive.
>
> It was only this morning that we warned our authorities in a three line item that the ordinance against carrying arms must be enforced, or we would have trouble in Wichita.
>
> Sheriff [P. H.] Massey with a posse started a few minutes ago after the man

who did the shooting. We believe the marshal and a posse are also going. He should be caught and tried, no matter what the expense, and every man who in any way aided or abetted the cowardly attack should be dealt with according to law. If the law and its officers are powerless, the sooner we know it the better. But they are not. A thousand men can be raised in Wichita and in this county, in three hours' notice, who will stand by their vindication.

In the mean time, in the name of the people and law abiding citizens, we call upon our mayor for a reorganization of his police force and a strict enforcement of the laws of the city, else our streets will flow in blood before the ides of November.

P. S.—An examination of the wounds reveals the fact that the ball that entered the breast went around on the outside of the ribs. The ball was extracted by the doctors, and there is a chance for the man's life.

P. S. No. 2—We were misinformed. The party was not followed by either the sheriff or marshal.

Two days after he was shot Charley Sanders died. Apparently his murderer was never caught.

Smith, it seems, did not rely entirely on his regular police to enforce the law, but reinforced them with a large reserve. The *Eagle*, July 16, 1874, praised him for its effectiveness:

In speaking of the special police force of this city last week and its organization [*see* the section on Sam Botts], we failed to give the proper credit, which failure was due to our ignorance. Our city marshal, Wm. Smith, organized the force, and it is of lawful effect. There is but little show or blow about our Billy, and he fails often in getting credit where it is really his due. He made an excellent and popular sheriff, and as city marshal we have no doubt of his success.

"A couple of soldiers came down from Dodge last Monday [August 3], after a deserter and horse thief named Percy whom our city marshal, Billy Smith had under arrest," reported the *Eagle*, August 6, 1874.

Because of a change in legal status Wichita could not appoint a city marshal in 1875 but instead had to elect one at the annual spring election of city officials. William Smith was one of the candidates. His opponents were Mike Meagher, another ex-city marshal (*see* the section on Meagher), and Dan Parks, his own assistant. When the election was over, April 6, 1875, Smith learned that he had run a poor third with Meagher garnering 340 votes, Parks 311, and himself 65.[10]

As a privately hired agent or perhaps as a deputy United States marshal, Smith pursued and captured a horse thief named Lee. The Wichita *Weekly Beacon*, September 29, 1875, told of the chase:

Billy Smith

The horse thief who was glimpsed by a party of freighters coming up from Arkansas City last week, of which mention was made in our last issue, was caught by his pursuers on the state line, twelve miles below Arkansas City, on the following Tuesday. The name of the thief is William Lee, he had been at work for H. C. Ramlow, in Park township up to Saturday. The horse he stole belonged to a colored man, a neighbor of Ramlow, by the name of Saunders. The horse had undoubtedly been spotted as he was a fine animal, a large iron grey, worth at least $125, a good traveler, sound in wind and limb. The colored man secured the services of ex-City Marshal Wm. Smith who started at 3 o'clock Monday morning in a light buggy accompanied by Mr. Ferguson, the partner of Pittenger in the livery business. The two struck the trail below El Paso, three relays of horses headed off their man in the timber near the Indian territory, night coming on, they called on farmers in the neighborhood, who turned out en mass, with shot guns and surrounded the victim, while Smith rode below that night yet, to the Kaw Agency and got out a squad of Kaw Indians to watch below. So he came to have Lee surrounded against morning. About day light Lee came out and went to a house for breakfast when he was arrested and brought in here Wednesday night and lodged in jail. He will slide by easy stages into the penitentiary.

Smith's service as a deputy U. S. marshal was mentioned at least once in the Wichita papers. The *Eagle*, October 28, 1875, recounted this humorous adventure:

Deputy United States Marshal, Wm. Smith, in pursuance of instructions from headquarters proceeded to Kingman county last week to execute some papers upon the Commissioners of that county looking to the payment of certain interest money due on bonds issued by that county, and now held by certain inflated eastern capitalists. For two mortal days Bill wandered over the dreary and uninhabited wastes of the once populous and flourishing municipality of Kingman, in the vain endeavor to find an inhabitant upon which to serve his process. Late one evening he struck the primitive domicile of an adventurous rooster who said he had been in the county long enough to vote, but as yet had found none of his neighbors. He was just the man, and the meat that our United States Marshal was in pursuit of and he forthwith pulled his papers and proceeded to read. One can better imagine than describe the feelings of that poor, lone settler, out there upon the confines of that eternal solitude when informed that he was held for the entire indebtedness of the said Kingman county, which amounted to about $60,000 in bonds besides interest. The affrighted prospector acknowledged that he had a good claim and some $300 in team and property and that he would gladly give up half of that for twenty-four hours' time in which to flee the impending doom. Bill says the next time [United States Marshal William S.] Tough wants any papers served in Kingman county he must send some fellow out a day ahead.

Next year Smith once again ran for the office of city marshal. While the campaign was in progress he and Policeman Wyatt Earp had a difficulty which resulted in a fight and Earp's leaving the service. (*See* the section on Wyatt Earp.) Whether or not the affair had any effect on the race for the marshalship is difficult to say; in any case, Mike Meagher once again defeated Smith, this time 477 to 249.[11]

In 1877 Bill Smith moved to Galena, Cherokee county, where he became one of its first mayors and, after 1898, postmaster. He died April 25, 1908, from Bright's disease.[12]

1. Galena *Evening Times,* April 27, 1908. 2. *Report of the Adjutant General of the State of Kansas, 1861-'65* (Topeka, 1896), p. 416; *Official Military History of Kansas Regiments During the War for the Suppression of the Great Rebellion* (bound with the Adjutant General's Report), pp. 198-220; George S. Burt, "The Wabaunsee Militia Company," *Kansas Historical Collections,* v. 11, pp. 604-607. 3. Wichita *Vidette,* November 24, December 29, 1870. 4. "Proceedings of the Governing Body," Records of the City of Wichita, Journal A, p. 35. 5. "Miscellaneous Records," Records of the City of Wichita, 1871. 6. "Proceedings of the Governing Body," Records of the City of Wichita, Journal A, p. 159. 7. Records of the Secretary of State, "Commissions, April 5-November 11, 1873," archives division, Kansas State Historical Society. 8. Wichita City *Eagle,* November 6, 1873. 9. "Proceedings of the Governing Body," Records of the City of Wichita, Journal A, pp. 369, 371; Wichita City *Eagle,* April 23, 1874. 10. *Ibid.,* April 1, 8, 1875; "Proceedings of the Governing Body," Records of the City of Wichita, Journal B, p. 42. 11. *Ibid.,* p. 103. 12. Galena *Evening Times,* April 27, 1908.

SUGHRUE, MICHAEL (1844-____)

Pat and Mike Sughrue were twins who for many years led strikingly similar lives as southwestern Kansas peace officers. For a while they served as sheriffs of neighboring counties. Pat was sheriff of Ford and Mike of Clark. Mike's career had begun in Dodge but a chain of circumstances led him to Ashland where he served first as city marshal and later sheriff.

Available records first show Mike Sughrue in August, 1861, when, already a veteran, he enlisted in Co. E, Seventh Kansas Volunteer cavalry. He gave his home town as Quincy, Ill. Re-enlisting in January, 1864, he was discharged June 28, 1865. Coincidently, William F. "Buffalo Bill" Cody was also a member of this regiment in its last year but served in Co. H.[1]

In the fall of 1881, Mike, who had been listed in the 1880 census as a teamster, ran for sheriff of Ford county. Nominated on the Independent ticket, Mike had four opponents: George T. Hinkle, Peoples' ticket; Samuel Gallagher, Female Suffrage ticket; E. P. Ott,

East End ticket; and D. M. Frost, Greenback. At the election November 8, 1881, Hinkle won by 35 votes over his nearest competitor.[2]

At the next county election Mike's brother Pat was elected sheriff and Mike was then appointed deputy and jailer.[3] He arrested a mule thief on June 5 according to the *Ford County Globe,* June 10, 1884:

> Last Thursday evening, Deputy Sheriff Sughrue arrested Frank, Tom and John Denson, on complaint of O. S. Aubery. A few days ago Mr. Aubery lost one of his mules and on Wednesday found the same with Mr. Mulligan, one of our citizens, who stated that he had purchased the mule from Frank Denson, giving a horse, silver watch, and revolver for the same. When arrested the Densons had six horses in all, among which was the horse that Mr. Mulligan had traded with them. As nothing could be found against Tom and John Denson they were released, and Frank Denson was held over for trial.[4]

Mike had some uneasy moments as jailor. The *Globe,* June 24, 1884, described a rather trying incident:

> On last Saturday evening [June 21] Deputies Sheriff Sughrue and E. G. Barlow, went to lock the prisoners up in separate cells which is the usual custom at night, Barlow going inside and Sughrue locking the door after him. After Barlow had got inside, one of the prisoners named Chambers, warned him that the others had put up a job to escape from jail, and to look out, and when Barlow had locked one of them up, the rest, eight in all, started for him, Denson, the horse thief throwing a blanket over his head. After searching his pockets for a revolver which they expected to find, they let him go, claiming it was a joke, and others thought so but it was not. Mr. Barlow, however, states that he had received several threats from the prisoners, and no doubt that if he had carried his revolver in with him that he would have been killed. Denson, the horse thief said that he would kill some one before he went to the penitentiary and was the leader in this break for liberty. Our deputies must be careful.

"Deputy Sheriff Sughrue arrested a man Tuesday morning [July 15] who had been firing his pistol in the court house building. The fellow was placed in jail. Such offenses ought to be punished severely. This man fired off several shots in the street near the court house," said the Dodge City *Times,* July 17, 1884.

The Dodge City *Democrat,* October 11, 1884, reported that "Deputy Sheriff M. Sughrue took a trip to Crooked Creek on last Thursday [October 9]. He traveled 60 miles, got his man, and done it all in ten hours."

On November 21 a series of events began to occur which eventually led to Mike's removal to present Clark county. The Dodge

City *Times,* December 4, 1884, copied from the *Clark County Clipper,* November 27:

TWO MEN AND A GIRL SHOT IN COLD BLOOD.

ONE OF THE MURDERERS HUNG.

Ashland has, since Friday last [November 21], been the scene of much excitement, which culminated Wednesday evening in the murder of Commodore Boggs and Daniel Adams, and the wounding of Miss Fannie Hankins. The circumstances connected with the affair, as nearly as can be ascertained at this time, are as follows:

The men who did the shooting were Joe Mitchell and Nels Mathews. Joe Mitchell came to this country about two weeks ago, it being reported that he had gotten into difficulty near Hazelton and was compelled to leave there. Nels Mathews had been about here for some three or four months and had no occupation during that time. They, together with two or three others, rode into town Friday afternoon and shot a fine grey hound, belonging to Ad Powers, they also shot out several window lights and broke the door of Roby & Lyon's Grocery.

The weather was quite severe Saturday and Sunday and they did not put in an appearance. Monday afternoon they came down from the saloon at Clark and commenced shooting at dogs. They then rode into many of the business houses with drawn revolvers. Did considerable shooting. Some shots were fired at our citizens. They roped and threw a pony several times and also roped a man from his mule he was riding. They constantly became more bold in their depredations. The next object of their cruelty was a man and a boy who were riding out of town in a wagon. They roped them several times but were unable to drag them from their wagon. Some words passed between them and Mathews beat both man and boy with his six shooter. Shortly after this they attempted to take a shot-gun from a young man named Frank Gage who objected, jumped back and drew down on Mathews, who then run into Roby's store, loaded his six shooter and followed Gage, but did not get an opportunity to shoot him. That evening they confined themselves to tearing down out houses.

Tuesday only three men were in the gang, there having been five the night before. Mathews, followed by Mitchell rode into Lee's restaurant and then shot through the door and front of the building while several persons were at dinner. Fortunately no one was injured. By this time the citizens had made up their minds to take the matter into their own hands, there being no officer nearer than Dodge City. Many shot guns and arms were in readiness that evening but the desperadoes had been warned and did not come into town, but rode over east and contented themselves with firing a few shots. Watch was kept in town until a late hour. One man who, it is said had been trying to keep Mathews and Mitchell from continuing their spree, left them in the afternoon.

Nothing occurred in town Wednesday to arouse suspicion until about half past five o'clock p. m., when a certain individual rode into town from the north and back again so quickly as to arouse the distrust of the poor fellows

590

who, so shortly after, met their untimely end. These very boys gave the alarm and in a few minutes their suspicion was verified.

Mathews and Mitchell rode up to the post office and Mathews mailed a letter. They then rode through town and over the bluff where the trail comes in from the East. They tied their horses in the clump of trees between Mr. Lowery's and Bear creek and went upon the hill between the dug-out and town. When Adams and Boggs passed and went down into Lowery's dug-out, where they were boarding, Mitchell and Mathews followed them. The dug-out had only two rooms; a main room and an ante room. Supper was spread and the table full of boarders. The victims were standing in the ante room together with Mr. Woods, Fannie Hankins and a little girl. Mitchell and Mathews stepped to the entrance and Mitchell, addressing Boggs, said: "here pard, we want to speak to you." He answered that he would not step out with them. Mitchell then grabbed him by the coat collar with one hand and raising his six shooter with the other, shot him in the stomach. At the same time Mathews shot Adams in the breast. Both boys probably made efforts to draw their revolvers, as one was found drawn and cocked, and the other partially drawn. Three or four shots were fired, one of which struck Fannie Hankins in the arm, inflicting only a flesh wound. It is thought that the shot was intended for her.

Immediately after the shooting the murderers took to their horses and rode rapidly toward Clark. Deputy Sughrue, who had been informed of the trouble, left Dodge at 11 a. m., and as good fortune would have it rode into Clark shortly after the shooting was done, and made for the saloon, thinking there was where he would find the men he was after. No one was there however, but as he passed out Mitchell rode up and Mr. Sughrue arrested him on suspicion. This was hardly done when Mathews rode up, having left a poor horse of his own and taken one belonging to Mr. Griffin. Mathews called to Mitchell to come on and Mitchell answered: "I can't, I'm arrested." Mr. Sughrue then commanded Mathews to halt, but he fired at him in reply upon which they exchanged three shots, and Mathews galloped away in the night. The deputies, Sughrue and [William] Thompson, then brought their prisoner to Ashland, where they were met by an excited throng. The extraordinary bravery and determination of the deputies is all that prevented Mitchell being taken from them and dealt with summarily. After the prisoner was secured, deputy Sughrue with a large force started in search of Mathews.

Everything had quieted down by midnight and the streets were deserted. A strong force guarded the prisoner and it was little thought that the people would take justice into their own hands. About three o'clock however, the room quickly filled with men and before there was any chance to resist, deputy Thompson and his assistants were overpowered. The prisoner was snatched out during the disturbance and daylight Thursday morning disclosed his lifeless body suspended from a beam of Bullen & Averill's lumber shed. He was cut down at 10:25 o'clock a. m. and an inquest held as follows:

An inquisition holden at Ashland, in Ford county,[5] State of Kansas, on the 27th day of November, A. D. 1884, before me, Geo. A. Exline, a Notary Public in and for said county, (such inquisition being held by me at the request of

William Thompson, Deputy Sheriff of said county, on account of the great distance to the Coroner, or a Justice of the Peace) acting as Coroner on the body of Joe Mitchell there lying dead, by the jurors whose names are hereunto subscribed.

The said jurors upon their oaths do say: That the person now here lying dead, was known by the name of Joe Mitchell; that he came to his death on the night of November 26th, A. D. 1884, at Ashland, Ford county, State of Kansas, by being hanged by the neck, by persons unknown to the jury.

H. B. WAKEFIELD,

J. R. GLEN,

C. E. RHODES,

C. M. BRUSH,

F. D. WEBSTER,

J. L. BLACKFORD.

ATTEST: Geo. A. Exline, Notary Public and acting Coroner, of Ford county, Kansas.

The victims of this cold blooded murder were both men of families and were here to make homes for themselves. They were very quiet, peaceable and law abiding citizens. Daniel Adams was twenty-three years old, he leaves a wife and one child. C. P. Boggs was twenty-four years old and also leaves a wife and one child.

B. W. Burchett, accompanied the remains to Mt. Savage, Center county, Ky., where their families are, for interment.

For want of space the finding of the Coroner's inquest is omitted. The verdict, however, was that they came to their death by pistols in the hands of Joe Mitchell and Nels Mathews.

Other facts connected with this foul tragedy may be expected next week.

Deputy Sheriff Michael Sughrue will remain with us. With him here we will have no further occasion for coroner's inquests.

Sheriff Pat Sughrue, whose brother has rendered us such efficient service, arrived Thursday night.

Mathews is still at large.[6]

The ultimate fate of Nels Mathews has not been learned.

Mike Sughrue had so impressed the people of Ashland with his efficiency that he was hired as the town's city marshal. The Dodge City *Democrat*, December 13, 1884, mentioned his large salary: "Deputy Sheriff M. Sughrue, has been engaged by the Ashland town company, at a salary of $175 per month, to keep order in that town."

Except for a visit now and then to his former home in Dodge, Mike Sughrue transferred his loyalties permanently to Ashland.[7] On March 2, 1885, he was injured while pursuing a murderer. The *Globe Live Stock Journal*, March 10, 1885, reported the unsuccessful chase:

A week ago last night, at a ranch [the 76 ranch near Bluff creek] ten miles from Ashland, this county, Fred Spencer shot and killed George Warwick. They had had a few words but no further trouble was expected, when, without

Pat Sughrue

a word of warning, Spencer shot Warwick twice, took what money his victim had and left. Both are young men, Spencer not being over nineteen years old. Deputy Sheriff Mike Sughrue was notified that night, and was soon in pursuit of the murderer, in company with Dr. Parks in a buggy; on the road to the scene of the tragedy, they were thrown out of the buggy and Mr. Sughrue had his shoulder put out of place, and one of his arms so badly bruised that he was unable to proceed farther. Sheriff Pat Sughrue was notified and went down to Ashland Wednesday returning Thursday, after putting two deputies on Spencer's trail, and seeing that his brother was getting along as well as could be expected after his injuries.[8]

On May 30, 1885, the Dodge City *Democrat* paid Mike a nice tribute:

M. Sughrue, the Marshal of Ashland, was in the city on last Thursday. He came after a man who had went wrong, and he took him back yesterday. When you want to catch a sharp send Mike after him, is all we have got to say.

When Clark county was organized in May, 1885, Mike Sughrue was elected its first sheriff. A few months later, in November, 1885, he was re-elected to a full term.[9] From here on he will be abandoned as his subsequent career is not in the scope of this cowtown series.

1. *Report of the Adjutant General of the State of Kansas, 1861-'65* (Topeka, 1896), pp. 233, 234, 247.   2. Dodge City *Times,* September 8, 15, November 10, 1881.   3. *Ford County Globe,* Dodge City, February 12, 1884.   4. *See, also,* Dodge City *Democrat,* June 7, 1884; Dodge City *Times,* June 12, 1884.   5. In 1883 and 1884 present Clark county was part of Ford, the county was re-established and organized in 1885.   6. *See, also,* Dodge City *Democrat,* November 29, 1884; *Globe Live Stock Journal,* Dodge City, December 2, 1884.   7. Dodge City *Democrat,* January 10, February 21, March 21, April 25, 1885.   8. *See, also, ibid.,* March 7, 1885.   9. *Ibid.,* June 20, November 14, 1885.

SUGHRUE, PATRICK F. (1844-1906)

Pat Sughrue, a blacksmith by trade, was serving as a lesser police officer in Dodge City as early as March, 1877. The Dodge City *Times,* March 24, 1877, gave him incidental notice in this article concerning an episode in the love life of that notorious cowtown character Robert Gilmore:

POLICE COURT.

The case of Dodge City vs. James Manion, carrying deadly weapons, in the city limits, was the great attraction last Monday afternoon [March 19]. The high position Mr. Manion occupies in social and business circles of this community undoubtedly went far towards exciting unusual interest in the case, and when court opened there was not room enough inside for half of the would-be spectators.

After close investigation, both at the trial and on the outside, we ascertained the following facts, which gave rise to the case:

Miss Susy Haden, a beautiful Creole maiden of this city, has for some time past been casting fond and loving glances upon our modest but susceptable young friend, Bobby Gill. The rich, creamy complection, dreamy black eyes and glossy, raven ringlets of the fair enchantress were too much for Bobby, and last Sunday night he cast his fortune and affections at her feet. A little after midnight the report was circulated among the boys that Robert was basking in the enervating luxury of Susy's presence, and a party of convivial spirits, including the defendant, repaired to Susie's home, with mischievous design to ruthlessly drag the gentle Bobby from the genial glow of the balmy smiles of his lady love—just for fun! It was cruel sport to thus tear apart two loving hearts which were no doubt entwined at that time in a loving embrace, but when Dodge City boys start in for fun and mischief, they don't stop to think about the sentimental features of the case.

The rumor proved true, and when the boys entered the Castle de Coon, Bobby was there in person "with both hands," and himself and Susy were occupying positions relative to each other of such a delicate nature as to entirely prohibit us from describing in these chaste and virtuous columns.

Suffice it to say that Mr. Gilmore was dragged from the downy couch, and when he made a hostile protest the defendant in the above entitled case had a very formidable gun four inches long, which he "banged and bluffed around" in a manner which Bobby despised.

Mr. P. Sughrue, the night watchman, happened around about this stage of the game and took charge of the gun, when the party broke up and each retired to his virtuous couch.

The Court said he thought fifteen dollars and costs would be about right.

A couple of months later Pat's humanity was not repaid in kind when a tramp whom he had befriended not only attempted to steal from him but also tried to kill D. D. Colley. The Dodge City *Times*, May 12, 1877, carried the story on its front page:

MURDEROUS ASSAULT.

A DESPERATE TRAMP ATTEMPTS TO KILL COL. D. D. COLLEY.

Dodge City is just now especially favored by the tramp fraternity. It seems to be the jumping off place for the Westward bound tramp (they invariably travel toward the setting sun). Some weeks ago one walked into town rejoicing in the name of John W. Charlton. He was six feet high in his soleless boots, and robust, muscular and healthy, as the professional tramp always is. He soon discovered that there was another "Jack Charlton" in the city, and rushed into the TIMES office with the request that if the other Jack Charlton ever had to be mentioned we should leave out the name for fear it might be mistaken for himself by his friends. After taking this precautionary measure to preserve his fair name from polluting stains, he began to cultivate the acquaintance of Mr. P. Shugrue, who was moved with compassion by his destitute condition, and furnished him bed and board until such time as he

Pat Sughrue

could obtain employment. Pat also gave him a new pair of shoes and supplied him with a shot gun that he might amuse himself killing ducks until he found work.

Week after week passed by and still Mr. Shugrue's guest reveled in idleness. Finally Mr. Shugrue took the matter in hand himself, and soon secured a good situation for his protege under Mr. Frolic. An expression of melancholy sadness came over Mr. Charlton's face when he learned of the toil in store for him; but Mr. Shugrue persuaded him to try it, and for one day he submitted to being reduced to the position of a servile hireling. His proud spirit, however, rebelled against an occupation so inferior to his exalted ideas, and in the evening he demanded his time and abandoned the job. The receipts of the day enabled him to drown his sorrows in the flowing bowl. Visions of duck shooting with Shugrue's gun flitted through his mind, and again he felt that happy days were yet in store for him; that life was not all a dreary desert. Vain anticipation; delusive expectation! For no sooner had Mr. Shugrue learned that our tramp had boldly shaken from him the shackles of toil than he cruelly drove him from the genial fireside and smoking viands which were so necessary to his comfort.

Such insolence could not fail to provoke Mr. Charlton's indignation; his chivalrous nature cried out for vengeance, and the next morning during Mr. Shugrue's temporary absence from the blacksmith shop he sneaked in and took what tools he could secrete in his pockets, under his coat and in his bosom. As he was leaving the shop Mr. Shugrue met him and noticed the end of a long file sticking from one pocket, the handle of a hammer protruding from another, while a pair of tongs and a few bars of pig iron were partly exposed below his coat tails. His late benefactor at once commenced applying a cowhide boot to our hero's person, and every kick made an implement drop. Supposing all the plunder had been disgorged Mr. Shugrue gathered up the tools and started for the shop. Charlton then drew a heavy sodering iron from his pocket and, sneaking up behind Shugrue, aimed a murderous blow at his head. The action was observed by a bystander, and Mr. S. was warned just in time to escape. C. then publicly registered a vow to burn the city to ashe, but Marshal Deger escorted him to the dog house, where he remained until evening, when he was released on condition that he would leave town. Between 9 and 10 o'clock the same night Harry Boyer saw him skulking and hiding between Webster's store and Beatty & Kelley's restaurant.

About half-past 11 the same night Col. Colley passed through the alley where our bloodthirsty tramp was lying in wait for plunder to subsist upon during his pilgrimage away from our city to some more congenial clime. As the Col. was crossing the culvert a switch engine commenced blowing off steam. This was the time for the assassin to get in his work. The escaping steam prevented his footsteps from being heard, and the first intimation Col. Colley had that danger was near, was the terrible blow on the back of his head, which caused him to stagger forward a few steps and fall on his hands and knees. Although too much stunned to rise up immediately, the Col. managed to turn around and face his would-be murderer, who was coming for him again. The miscreant hesitated in surprise on seeing that his attempt was a

595

failure, and the Col. soon recovered sufficiently to rise up and start for the assailant, calling "police," which caused him to flee. A streak of light from a window falling upon the retreating figure satisfied Col. Colley that it was John Charlton, who had been ejected from the Long Branch a day or two before as a nuisance [Colley then owned one-half of the Long Branch saloon].

Dr. McCarty examined the wound and found that the scull was bare and exposed but not fractured. The weapon used was a stone weighing between eight and ten pounds.

Mr. Charlton was arrested next day on a charge of assault with intent to kill, and last Wednesday was brought before Judge Frost for preliminary examination. He acted as his own lawyer, and managed his case in a cool and sagacious manner which showed he had been there before. But the Judge decided to let the District Court have a whack at him, and bound him over in the sum of $3,000. The prisoner will languish in jail until court sets.

On November 6, 1877, Pat Sughrue was elected constable of the township in the same election that placed Bat Masterson in the sheriff's office.[1] Like Bat, and many other prominent Dodgeites, Sughrue was a member of the volunteer Dodge City Fire Company. On January 7, 1878, he narrowly missed being elected second assistant marshal of the fire fighting unit. Instead Charles S. Hungerford won the position.[2]

One of the Sughrues, possibly Pat, was arrested on March 29, 1878, for fighting at the Long Branch. The *Ford County Globe,* April 2, stated:

A lively rough and tumble fight occurred Friday night at the Long Branch. One Brannon catching it on the head from a six-shooter, and Mr. Sughrue having his eyes somewhat damaged. Squire C[ook]. made it $11.50 for S., and acquitted B.

"Pat Sughrue has discovered a chalk mine of countless value. Some of the chalk is on exhibition at this office," reported the *Times,* April 27, 1878, and "Pat Sughrue and Tom Goodman, blacksmiths, are manufacturing a large number of cattle brands. Some of the brands are ingeniously wrought," it said on September 7, 1878.

As constable, Pat arrested Charles Trask for mule stealing on December 29. The *Times,* January 4, 1879, related:

Sunday last, Constable Pat Sughrue found two of the Government mules which were stolen a few weeks ago on Bluff creek. The mules were in possession of Charles Trask, and were found south of the river. Trask was arrested but the trial was postponed until Monday next. Constable Sughrue received the fifty dollars reward which had been offered for the recovery of the mules.[3]

Pat Sughrue

A few days later Pat testified to one of the more unsavory aspects of frontier life. The *Ford County Globe*, February 17, 1879, reprinted the story from the Leavenworth *Press:*

THE HAYDEN CASE.
A BRIEF RESUME THEREOF, WITH RECENT AFFIDAVITS, RECENTLY FILED FOR DEFENDANT.

On the 6th of December, 1878, the Press published a statement of a rape committed upon a married lady who had arrived in the city [Leavenworth] the night before, from the western part of the State, in search of an erring daughter. The rape alleged had been committed by Isaac Hayden, a colored man who had met her at the depot, found out her mission, and succeeded in decoying her to his house by pretending to assist her in searching for her daughter, where he raped her. Her husband and family, in the western part of the State, were also described as being in very destitute circumstances. The trial of Hayden was had and he was pronounced guilty; but various motions have interposed to prevent his sentence. Among other proceedings had in this interesting case, affidavits were recently filed, the substance of which are as follows:

H. B. BELL
of Dodge City, Ford county, Kansas deposed: That early in the year 1878, he became acquainted with Mrs. Mary Malosh, sometimes known as Mary Castill, whose family consisted of herself, her husband, J. D. Malosh, a fourteen-year old daughter called Bell Castill and two small children. Mrs. Malosh at said time was employed as cook in a dance hall on Locust street, in Dodge City, kept by Henry Heck, and she, with her entire family, lived in the building. The dance house was a long frame building, with a hall and bar in front and sleeping rooms in the rear. The hall was nightly used for dancing, and was frequented by prostitutes, who belonged to the house and for the benefit of it solicited the male visitors to dance. The rooms in the rear were occupied, both during the dancing hours and after, and both day and night by the women for the purpose of prostitution.

Bell Castill, while her mother cooked in the house, to the best of Mr. Bell's belief, carried on prostitution like the other women, and with her mother's knowledge she danced and drank as the rest, and to her friends and acquaintances made no secret of her doings. Furthermore he believed that Bell helped to keep the family with the money she earned by prostitution; and that her mother instructed and encouraged her to do so. And that, after the family left this house Bell was an inmate of other houses; and that he (affiant) believes Mrs. encouraged and consented to the conduct of her daughter.

PATRICK SUGHRUE,
after stating that he had read the affidavit of Mr. Bell, deposed that he believes it to be true to his own knowledge; that he was present at the first dance given after the Malosh family moved into the house, when Mrs. Malosh forced Bell, who was apparently young and inexperienced to dance; that Bell told him it was her first experience in a dance house; that thereafter daily, as he believes,

Bell led the same life of shame and that it was with the advice and encouragement of her mother, and the family used her money so earned for support; that Mrs. Malosh insisted on such a life from her daughter.

Short items in the *Times*, like the flickering and temporary images on a motion picture screen, depicted Pat's life for the next year. August 16, 1879: "Pat Sughrue and J. S. Marcus left for Hays City on Tuesday. Mr. Marcus has a faint hope of finding his lost horses. He has some trace of them." August 30, 1879: "Pat Sughrue and J. S. Marcus returned Tuesday evening, having failed to find the horses lost by Mr. Marcus." September 6, 1879: "Patrick Sughrue has taken the position of farrier at Fort Dodge. He is an excellent workman, and we wish him success." November 8, 1879: "Pat Sughrue, long a resident of these parts, has gone to Colorado, and will take charge of the horse-shoeing of the horses of a mail line into Leadville. Pat's friends wish him success." April 17, 1880: "Patrick Sughrue has taken charge of the blacksmith shop formerly managed by him. Mr. Sughrue was married in Colorado, and with his wife will make a permanent residence in Dodge City."

Pat became a public servant once again with his election to the city council on April 4, 1881. Other councilmen elected were A. H. Boyd, C. M. Beeson, George S. Emerson, and H. T. Drake; A. B. Webster was mayor. This new council and mayor appointed Fred Singer, marshal, and Tom Nixon, assistant marshal.[4]

A year later this same administration was re-elected with the exception that Ham Bell replaced H. T. Drake on the council.[5] Still another year and the old "gang" had suffered a split. Pat Sughrue now supported W. H. Harris for mayor though Webster, Bell, Drake, Emerson, and others chose L. E. Deger.[6] The rift yawned into the almost unspannable chasm of the Dodge City "war." Sughrue and his friends, including T. J. Tate, Nelson Cary, James H. Kelley, W. F. Petillon, etc., were proponents of the Luke Short faction and of course the other side included Webster and Deger. (*See* the section on Luke Short for the story of these troubles.)

One of the adhesives which patched up the battered political arena of Dodge City was a newly formed militia unit, the "Glick Guards." Persons who had been on opposing sides in the recent troubles enlisted side by side. The commander was Capt. Patrick F. Sughrue.[7]

Pat Sughrue

In the fall of 1883 Pat was nominated for sheriff. Apparently a rumor to the effect that, if elected, he would appoint Bat Masterson under sheriff was designed to injure Pat's chances at the polls. In the *Ford County Globe*, October 16, 1883, he discounted the notion:

NOTICE.

Some of the opposition or Singer faction are circulating a report among stockmen that in the event I am elected Sheriff, W. B. Masterson will be my under sheriff, which I positively assert is false; not that Mr. Masterson wouldn't be fully competent and acceptable to a great many people in this county, but he is not a resident of this state and has no intention of becoming such. I am sure, however, that he would reflect as much credit to the office as Mysterious Dave, who will be Mr. Singer's right-hand man.

Respectfully,

P. F. SUGHRUE.

In spite of, or because of, the tactics used on both sides Sughrue won the office with 488 votes to Singer's 343. The election had been held November 6, 1883.[8]

Pat was sworn in January 14, 1884. The *Globe*, January 15, reported:

The new county officers elect took charge of their respective offices yesterday. The county board organized by electing the oldest member of the board, J. D. Shaffer, chairman, a very deserving compliment to that gentleman. Sheriff Sughrue moved into the court house yesterday and has assumed charge of not only presiding officer as sheriff of the county, but as jailor. He will hold the key to the jail. T. J. Tate is his under-sheriff; a good selection, and who will make an excellent officer. . . .[9]

Sughrue's first recorded official act took place three days later. The *Globe*, January 22, 1884, carried this short item:

Sheriff P. F. Sughrue and special deputy sheriff Clark Chipman, took Al. Thurman to Larned on a writ of habeas corpus before Judge Strang, last Thursday, on complaint of an excessive bond. Judge Cook, of this city, bound the defendant over in the sum of $5,000 for his appearance at the next term of our district court on the charge of attempting to take the life of Geo. Miller. Judge Strang reduced the bond to $1,500, and the prisoner was remanded to the jail of the county.

The same day the sheriff "disarmed" some of his incarcerated prisoners. The *Globe*, January 22, 1884, told of it:

Sheriff Sughrue in making the rounds of the jail last Thursday found sundry articles that he did not care to leave in the possession of his prisoners, to-wit: A two-bladed pocket knife, and a case knife which was transformed into a saw. The first article named was supplied by Mrs. Wiggins, who was residing in the

599

jailors rooms, and admitted to have been so supplied by Charles Ellsworth, who is one of the inmates of the jail. Sheriff Sughrue, since he has taken charge of the court house, has laid down some very rigid rules for the government of the temple over which he presides.

"P. F. Sughrue on last Thursday night [January 24] caged a horse thief. We did not learn where he was captured," said the *Globe*, January 29, 1884.

"Sheriff Sughrue and under sheriff Tate started for the state penitentiary Sunday noon [February 10] with Charles Ellsworth and Harry Kennedy, to which place they were sentenced for one year each, on a charge of stealing horses," according to the *Globe*, February 12, 1884.[10]

Leavenworth had been the Sughrues' home. The *Globe*, February 19, 1884, copied from the Leavenworth *Times:*

Pat. Sughrue, formerly of Leavenworth, and now the sheriff of Ford county, Kansas, visited the Times office yesterday, in company with T. J. Tate, Esq., of Dodge City. We are pleased to hear of his prosperity, and also to hear of the good health of his father whom our citizens well remember, and also his brother Michael, who is now the jailor of that county. Mike was a faithful, brave soldier of the old Seventh Kansas, and deserves kindly remembrance for his services in the war for the union.

The sheriff and Deputy Bill Tilghman captured a horse thief on March 16. The Dodge City *Democrat*, March 22, 1884, reported:

Sheriff Sughrue and Deputy Tilghman on last Sunday caught an Edwards county horse thief. Sheriff Billings, of Edwards county, came up on Sunday and found his man safely in jail. Sughrue made Billings a present of him and thereby saved the County of Ford a hundred or two dollars. That's right, Pat, we don't kick; the Colonel told us the fellow was broke, anyhow.

The *Ford County Globe*, April 29, 1884, reported that Sughrue had arrested an accidental murderer:

Sheriff Sughrue returned Saturday from his trip to Hutchinson where he arrested Phil. Leslie, who shot the tramp at Pierceville the day previous. Leslie was placed under a bond for his appearance at next term of court, which he had no trouble giving, and was at once released. This is an unfortunate affair for Leslie, as—if we are correctly informed—he had no intention whatever of killing any of the party that attempted to board the train, but simply fired—as he supposed over their heads—to scare them off. Unfortunately he hit one, who fell dead in his tracks.[11]

Sughrue was one of the sports who organized a Dodge City baseball club in the spring of 1884. Others interested included Bob Wright, Bat Masterson, A. B. Webster, and W. H. Harris.[12]

Pat Sughrue

The enforcement of law kept Sughrue pretty busy, however. When it was reported that former Gov. John P. St. John and A. B. Campbell would come to Dodge to attend a series of temperance meetings it was rumored that liquor loving Dodge Citians would offend them with alcoholic violence. The city and county police co-operated to protect the visitors. The Dodge City *Times*, May 22, 1884, reported their success:

The suggestion that trouble or insult would likely take place should Mr. Campbell and Gov. St. John come to Dodge City, was entirely gratuitous. Whether any insult was apprehended or not we do not know or believe, but we must compliment City Marshal Tilghman and Sheriff Sughrue for their judgement and prudence on the late visit of Mr. Campbell and others. Both of these officers were at the trains during the arrival and departure of Mr. Campbell and both officers were in attendance at the meetings. They would have arrested the first man who would have offered any violence or insult. We highly commend them for this display of official duty, and their conduct will receive the praise from every one who desires peace, good order and good government.

On May 31, 1884, the Dodge City *Democrat* reported that

A brute named Harvey Cox, living with his family in a dugout near the round-house was arrested by Sheriff Sughrue on Monday [May 26] charged with the heinous crime of incest, having defiled the person of his twelve-year-old daughter. He was jailed, and this after-noon Judge Cook held him for trial. The whole family are said to be hard characters.

The *Democrat* of May 31 also asked:

"What has become of 'crazy' Burns?" is what the officers would like to know. When last seen he was crazy as a loon about four miles south of the river, but when Sheriff Sughrue and Marshal Tilghman went out after him he had departed for fields new and pastures green.

A burglar was next, according to the *Globe*, June 3, 1884:

Sheriff Sughrue rounded up another man on Sunday morning [June 1], and placed him behind the bars of our county jail to keep him out of future mischief. This time it was a professional burglar, who broke into the store of Geo. Hall, at Spearville, Saturday night, and carried away a small amount of change, goods etc. Our sheriff was immediately notified of the burglary, and captured him on Sunday morning. On the person of the prisoner were found a full set of keys—blanks and others, a dozen or more of fine saws, picks, cold chisel, a cake of wax, and other implements necessary to the profession of a burglar. He also had in his possession a slip of paper containing the names of Wright, Beverley & Co., and York, Parker Draper, Mercantile company, of this city.

On June 3 Pat took a breather and attended the Republican

national convention in Chicago. The *Globe*, June 3, 1884, told of his departure:

Sheriff Sughrue goes to Chicago to-day and will attend the convention. Pat will meet many of his old comrades in the army. He has a free pass and a ticket for a seat, and he only needs to remind Logan [Gen. John A. Logan who was nominated vice-president] of the forty-seven days fight before Vicksburg to have some one to introduce him.

Perhaps the sheriff returned only to leave Dodge again, or maybe he swung south to Fort Worth before coming home. In any case he appeared in Dodge on June 8 with a prisoner whom he had picked up in Texas. The *Times*, June 12, 1884, said:

Sheriff Sughrue returned Sunday night with Wm. Bird, who is charged with cattle stealing. Bird was arrested in Texas, and will have a trial at the present term of the District Court.

Regarding the arrest the *Globe*, June 10, 1884, said:

Too much credit cannot be given Sheriff Sughrue, who, whenever he has been sent after a criminal, has always brought him back, and has been the means of capturing some very hard citizens. When you want a man send Pat after him.

"Sheriff Sughrue, City Marshal Tilghman and Under Sheriffs Tate and Dave Mather are home again from taking the prisoners to the State penitentiary," reported the Dodge City *Democrat*, June 28, 1884.[13] On his return "Sheriff Sughrue arrested Walter Payne, in this city on last Thursday [July 3], on a charge of horse stealing made by outside parties," according to the *Globe*, July 8, 1884.

Sheriff Sughrue was the arresting officer who apprehended Mysterious Dave Mather after he had killed Tom Nixon on July 21, 1884. For Pat's testimony *see* the section on Mather.

On August 6, 1884, Pat attended a meeting of militia officers in Topeka. The *Democrat*, August 9, reported:

Our sheriff, P. F. Shugrue [*sic*], who is captain of the Glick Guards, attended a meeting of the regimental and company officers of the militia of Kansas, held at Topeka on last Wednesday. While there, Pat. stopped a big row that occurred in one of the hotels, by simply producing his old "45's." The scattering that took place was simply immense.[14]

Upon the sheriff's return he again performed a series of arrests. "Sheriff Shugrue [*sic*], on last Tuesday [August 19], arrested two colored men for stealing saddles out of Wright & Co's store. Both are held for grand larceny," said the *Democrat*, August 23, 1884.[15] On September 6, 1884, the *Democrat* reported:

602

About six weeks ago, H. Longnen had one of his horses stolen, and yesterday Sheriff Sughrue received word that the horse had been found at Newton, and the thief, who gave his name as Alfred D. Partridge, was in custody. The sheriff started after the prisoner to-day.

"Horse thieves are getting numerous around here again, two were brought in last week. Our sheriff don't let them linger around long," the *Democrat* remarked on September 13, 1884. On September 15 Sughrue left for Galveston by way of Topeka where he obtained a requisition for a forger.[16] The *Globe Live Stock Journal*, September 23, 1884, reported Pat's success:

"I told you so," and we did, in our last issue when we said Sheriff P. F. Sughrue had gone to Texas and would return with his man. A telegram from Patrick dated Galveston, Texas, Monday September 22d, says, "I've got my man and start for home this morning." We hope to tell our readers whom he brings next week.

The Dodge City *Kansas Cowboy*, September 27, 1884, said the prisoner was one C. A. Grouthouse:

Sheriff Sughrue returned to Dodge City last Thursday morning, having in charge the man who had a forged draft on the Franklyn Cattle company cashed by R. M. Wright, last July. The forger was arrested at Galveston by John Williamson and Jerry Lordan, special detectives of that place, who held the forger until the arrival there of Mr. Sughrue last week, to whom the criminal was transferred by his captors. Williamson and Lordan accompanied Mr. Sughrue to Dodge City. The amount cashed by Mr. Wright was $3,000, but subsequently $1,000 of it was recovered. The forger claims the cognomen of C. A. Grouthouse. He is now in jail at this place.[17]

A Coolidge man who had killed his wife was next on Sheriff Sughrue's list. The Dodge City *Democrat*, October 4, 1884, reported the facts:

SHOT AND KILLED HIS WIFE.

On Thursday night at Coolidge, Kans., at about 12 o'clock, James Dempsey, shot and killed his wife, while in bed. Mrs. Dempsey had been sick for a few weeks back, and a child was born to them two weeks ago. Dempsey had been on a drunk for a few days, and was drunk on the day previous to the murder, and had repeatedly stated that his wife was a source of expense to him, and that he would kill her. She was shot through the head by a pistol ball, and killed instantly. The pistol was found in the bed.

His version of the story is, that while asleep he was awakened by a pistol shot, and discovered his wife had been shot. He believing that she had shot herself.

He was sent to this city immediately on being arrested, to save him from being lynched. He arrived here on the one o'clock train and was taken back on the 2:40 train accompanied by Sheriff Sughrue, and Deputies Tate and Cary, to be tried. It is generally believed that he is guilty.[18]

A different type of crime resulted in Pat arresting a young Dodge resident. The *Times*, October 23, 1884, reported:

TOTAL DEPRAVITY.

An obscene circular was discovered in this city Monday last. A bundle of these circulars was picked up on the street, having fallen out of the pocket of a young man who lives here. The printing of these circulars was done in the Democrat office in this city, under the direction of the editor of that infamous sheet. The arrest of Edwards was made Monday evening, by Sheriff Sughrue, who swore out the warrant. The arrest of Charley, the young man who ordered the printing, was also made, and these dispensers of villainous trash were admitted to bail, and will have to answer to the charge of printing and circulating obscene literature.

We were shown a copy of the printed slip containing the filthy matter, and we must say that we are utterly surprised to learn that there is a man in Dodge City so low in moral instincts as to give such stuff circulation. The vilest slum on the continent wouldn't tolerate the filthy circular discovered Monday last. A Democratic editor is left to disgrace his office and calling by the printing of such detestible matter.

We are glad to chronicle the fact that the better sentiment of the community is growing sufficiently strong to ferret out the perpetrators of outrages and to give them the benefit of the law. Every one who heard of the obscene matter condemned the authors in unmeasured terms. Sheriff Sughrue and some of our citizens hastily and successfully brought the perpetrators of the outrage to punishment, and deserve the thanks of an injured community. Some of this vile matter had found its way to the school children, and the capture of the vile print and the arrest of the perpetrators was timely.

As sheriff of Ford county Pat Sughrue was interested in the double killing at Ashland November 26, 1884. Pat dispatched his twin brother, Mike, to the scene; the results have been reprinted in the section on Mike Sughrue.

"Last week Sheriff Sughrue arrested three men, charged with burglary and put them in jail. The county officers are on the alert for offenders," said the *Times*, December 18, 1884.

The 1885 Kansas state census for Ford county listed P. F. Sughrue as a 41-year-old sheriff. Also listed was Pat's cousin, Daniel Sughrue, under sheriff, 43 years old.

Sheriff Sughrue arrested Mysterious Dave Mather for murder a second time on May 10, 1885. This crime, the killing of David Barnes, is covered in the section on Mather.

Pat foiled an attempted jail break on the night of May 23, 1885. The *Globe*, May 26, carried the story:

A BOLD ATTEMPT TO BREAK JAIL—
SHERIFF SUGHRUE AS A RECEPTION COMMITTEE.

In one of the large steel cells in our county jail up to Saturday evening were confined ten prisoners. These prisoners are let out from eight in the morning until nine or ten o'clock at night into the room in which their cell is. Last Friday evening Sheriff Sughrue remarked that the boys were in a happy mood as they were singing, and told the jailor to examine the jail carefully; that was all he said, but himself set about to discover why such long and continued hilarity with the prisoners. Saturday he knew all about their little scheme, and appointed himself a committee of one on reception when they should step from the jail.

By some means the prisoners had got hold of a large pocket knife and a razor with which they cut a hole through the ceiling large enough for all but one of the prisoners to get through. The work of enlarging the hole began Saturday evening, and the exact time could be told by the music that arose from that room. The reception committee was also on hand in his stocking feet with a six-shooter in his hand, ready to knock the top of the head off the first man that raised above the floor. From some reason they got suspicious that some one was up stairs and put off further operations for the night, and were soon after locked up in their cells, where they have been kept ever since.

It would have required but a few minutes more work to have enlarged the hole and cut through the floor which was partly cut through when, if the sheriff had not been present, they would have landed in the center of the main hall on the first floor of the court house, about twelve feet from the door. Their plan was to escape a few minutes before nine o'clock when no one was liable to be in the court house, and having the whole night before them and fifteen or twenty minutes time before the jailor would come to lock them in their cells, their chances for escape were pretty good.[19]

In July Sheriff Sughrue was one of those who were asked their opinion of the difficulty in enforcing prohibition. The interrogator was Att. Gen. S. B. Bradford and the interview was mentioned in the Dodge City *Democrat*, July 11, 1885:

The Attorney-General arrived here last Tuesday [July 7] and were met by our mayor, R. M. Wright, sheriff P. Sughrue, A. Gluck and the editor of the DEMOCRAT. In the interview at the hotel with the Attorney-General on the most important subject, (the disturbance caused by the arrival of Griffin and Jetmore in our city,) [see the section on Bat Masterson] the facts were presented to him by the mayor and sheriff, giving him complete outline of the affair. The prohibition faction were invited to present their side of the case but did not appear at that time. During the conversation the Attorney-General asked the sheriff the number of saloons that had been running previous to the passing of the prohibitory law last winter, and was told that there were seventeen. He then asked how many were now running open and was told that there were about ten, and the sheriff also told him that the people here did not feel as though they ought to close, when saloons were running open in such cities as Leavenworth, Atchison, etc. After a little more conversation on the subject, the Attorney-General said it was not his duty to seek this information himself. He stopped in our city two days and visited nearly all the principal business houses. He seemed well pleased with the looks of our city, with its hundreds of new buildings in course of construction.

On August 17 "Sheriff Sughrue arrived in Ashland . . . with McKinney, who committed the murder at Englewood, on July 4th, and will probably arrive here to-day with his prisoner. McKinney will be lodged in our jail until next term of court unless bonds are furnished," reported the *Democrat*, August 22, 1885.

In September Sughrue went to New York where he obtained a prisoner who later escaped on the return trip to Dodge. The *Democrat*, September 12, 1885, said:

Sheriff Sughrue returned last Wednesday morning from his trip to New York. He secured Wiseman at that place after a good deal of trouble, and was bringing him home, but when they reached Godfrey, Ill., Wiseman made his escape through the water closet of the car. The sheriff, however, brought the goods back with him that Wiseman had stolen.

The incident was to give Pat some trouble when he ran for re-election in the fall. The *Globe Live Stock Journal*, October 20, 1885, stated the problem:

Sheriff Sughrue's opponents in the race for sheriff of Ford county, are bringing up the unfortunate escape of Israel Wiseman from said Sughrue, while enroute from New York City to Dodge City, charging him with all kinds of misconduct in this matter. We desire to say to these fellows who still persist in charging sheriff Sughrue with any neglect to duty in this matter, that if they will take as much pains in finding out the truth in this matter as they have in giving credence to the unjust report that he did not do his duty, and will call at this office, we will convince them by official documents that Sughrue is entirely blameless and acted in good faith, and cannot be held responsible for the escape of Mr. Wiseman.

In the same issue the *Globe* reprinted a commendatory letter from Gov. G. W. Glick:

Read what ex-governor G. W. Glick thought of P. F. Sughrue as an officer of the law, and then determine whether he hadn't ought to be re-elected to the office he so honorably filled:

TOPEKA, Sept. 22, 1884.

To P. F. SUGHRUE, SHERIFF, DODGE CITY, KANSAS.

MY DEAR SIR:—I was very much gratified to be reliably informed that under my proclamation and the law your efficiency as an officer in protecting the

606

large stock interests of your county is worthy of the highest commendation. It has been stated to me that you have gone out among incoming herds where Texas fever was feared, and by your promptness and energy, and prudent management (in one instance at least) have turned back herds that would have spread destruction amongst the cattle of Kansas, and would have produced great damage and loss to the stock owners of our state. I understand that the owners, after you stating your authority, and producing the proclamation and notifying them that nothing would save them from the severest prosecution under the law, finally decided to leave the state at once.

I certainly commend your discretion and firmness in this matter. I hope that others will feel the necessity of acting as promptly and discreetly in this matter. I desire, therefore, to thank you in the name of the good people of our state, whom you have protected against that fearful disease—the Texas fever.

I am, sir most respectfully,
Your obedient servant,
G. W. GLICK.[20]

Pat's campaign was successfully managed and when the election was over he had garnered victory with a count of 1,052 votes to R. W. Tarbox's 926, and T. J. Tate's 189.[21]

Though Patrick Sughrue in 1886 was only beginning another term as a major peace officer, research was discontinued at this point because Dodge City was now finished as a trail-end cowtown. Its police officers henceforth would not be unlike similar officers in other settled, progressive communities. What passes for civilization was in the process of taking over.

1. Dodge City *Times,* November 10, 1877. 2. *Ibid.,* January 12, 1878. 3. *See, also, Ford County Globe,* Dodge City, January 1, 1879. 4. Dodge City *Times,* April 7, 1881. 5. *Ibid.,* April 6, 1882. 6. *Ford County Globe,* March 20, 1883. 7. *Ibid.,* June 5, 1883; Dodge City *Times,* August 30, 1883. 8. *Ibid.,* November 22, 1883; *Ford County Globe,* November 20, 1883. 9. *See; also,* Dodge City *Times,* January 17, 1884. 10. *See, also,* Dodge City *Democrat,* February 16, 1884. 11. *See, also,* Dodge City *Democrat,* May 3, 1884. 12. *Ibid.* 13. *See, also, Ford County Globe,* July 1, 1884. 14. *See, also,* Dodge City *Times,* August 14, 1884; Dodge City *Kansas Cowboy,* August 9, 16, 1884. 15. *See, also,* Dodge City *Kansas Cowboy,* August 23, 1884. 16. *Globe Live Stock Journal,* Dodge City, September 16, 1884; Dodge City *Democrat,* September 20, 1884; Dodge City *Kansas Cowboy,* September 20, 1884. 17. Dodge City *Democrat,* September 27, 1884. 18. *See, also, Globe Live Stock Journal,* October 7, 1884. 19. *See, also,* Dodge City *Times,* May 28, 1885; Dodge City *Democrat,* May 30, 1885. 20. *See, also,* "Governors' Correspondence," archives division, Kansas State Historical Society. 21. *Globe Live Stock Journal,* November 10, 1885.

TILGHMAN, WILLIAM MATHEW, JR. (1854-1924)

In the spring of 1877 William Mathew "Bill" Tilghman, Jr., and Henry Garis owned and operated the Crystal Palace saloon in Dodge City. On May 6, 1877, the Dodge City *Times* noted that a

city council meeting of May 1 renewed their license and granted permits to several other dramshop owners whose names are now part of the fact and legend of Dodge City and its riotous past. The list included: McGinty & Deger, Beeson & Harris, Springer & Masterson, A. J. Peacock, Beatty & Kelley, G. M. Hoover, Cox & Boyd, H. J. Fringer, H. B. Bell, Colley & Manion, Henry Sturm, and others. Tilghman and his partner did not have a place in the famed two-block section of Front street. Instead they operated across the tracks, on the sometimes equally popular south side.[1] "Garris and Tilghman's Crystal Palace is receiving a new front and an awning, which will tend to create a new attraction towards the never ceasing fountains of refreshments flowing within," said the Dodge City *Times*, July 21, 1877.

Bill Tilghman

Only 23 years old, Bill Tilghman did not yet enjoy the reputation he later earned as an efficient peace officer. In fact, the first mention of note about him was his arrest on suspicion of being one of the Kinsley train robbers (*see* the section on Bat Masterson). In relating the apprehension of some of the robbers, the Dodge City *Times*, February 9, 1878, reported:

Wm. Tilghman, a citizen of Dodge City, was arrested on the same serious charge of attempt to rob the train. He stated he was ready for trial, but the State asked for ten days delay to procure witnesses, which was granted. Tilghman gave bail. It is generally believed that Wm. Tilghman had no hand in the attempted robbery.

Tilghman was released. The *Times*, February 16, 1878, reprinted the letter he had received from the Edwards county attorney:

608

Bill Tilghman

TILGHMAN DISCHARGED.

The case of Wm. Tilghman, who was arrested on a charge of complicity in the attempted train robbery, has been dismissed on motion of the County Attorney of Edwards county, as will be seen by the following:

Monday, Feb. 12th, 1878.

WM. TILGHMAN, DODGE CITY, KANSAS.

DEAR SIR—Your case was called to-day for examination. There being no evidence against you, I filed a motion for your discharge and the court thereupon ordered your discharge, entering the same on his docket. I congratulate you on your discharge, hoping that you may be so lucky in the future as not to be ever suspected of crime.

Yours very truly,

J. E. McARTHUR,

County Attorney, Edwards county, Kansas.[2]

A couple of months later Bill Tilghman was arrested again, this time for horse thievery and his accuser was the sheriff of Ford county, Bat Masterson. The *Ford County Globe*, April 23, 1878, reported Tilghman's release:

JUSTICES COURT.

On the 16th inst. several parties arrived in town looking for two horses, which had been stolen from M. A. Couch, of Ness county. The horses were found in H. B. Bell's livery stable, in possession of Jack Martin and Wm. H. Tilghman, who claimed to be owners of the property. A warrant was sworn out before Justice R. G. Cook, and the preliminary examination came off at once. Martin was bound over for the District Court, while Tilghman was discharged. Harry E. Gryden defended Tilghman, Martin having no counsel. Martin has since employed Gryden who has sued out a writ of habeas corpus before Judge Peters, which will be heard on the 30th. What the result will be, cannot at present be told, but the chances are decidedly in favor of Martin's discharge.[3]

Tilghman's fortunes with the law began to turn later that year when, with several other since famous peace officers, he assisted in the capture of Dora Hand's supposed murderer, Jim Kennedy. (*See* the section on Bat Masterson.)

A few days after Kennedy had been taken the *Ford County Globe* carried a story which may or may not suggest a reason for part of the earlier suspicion which hung over Tilghman. The newspaper, October 29, 1878, said:

CAPTURE OF MIKE ROURKE.

It appears that Mike Rourke, Dement and Tilman were stopping at a range on Thompson creek, about eleven miles south of Ellsworth, and that it was their intention to burglarize the express office at Ellsworth or to attack the train at Rock Spring, a small water station, on Friday. The sheriff's posse from Brookfield [Brookville] arrived there about daylight that morning and captured Rourke in the stable. A few minutes afterward Dement came out and opened the stable door, but the officers thought at first that he was one of their own men. He fled and was pursued, shot at and wounded, but managed to make his escape to the woods. The gang's outfit was captured, but Tilman and Dement escaped. The officers are making a hot chase and will probably bag the rest of their game in a few days. Rourke is now in jail at Junction City.

Dement was afterward captured and died of his wounds. The Tilman referred to above was not the Wm. Tilghman, of this place, as rumored.

The railroad company were informed of the whereabouts and intentions of the robbers by one of the gang.

In late winter trouble of a sort again dogged Tilghman. The Dodge City *Times,* March 8, 1879, carried a notice that his property would be sold at auction to satisfy a judgment:

SHERIFF'S SALE.

Notice is hereby given that I will offer for sale at Public Auction, at the door of the Court House, in Dodge City, Ford County, Kansas,

On Monday, the 17th day of March, 1879,

At 2 o'clock, P. M. of said day, the following described real estate, to-wit: Lot No. 24, in Block No. 3, on Locust street, in Dodge City, Ford County, Kansas, which said property is appraised at the sum of $500.00, and taken upon execution in favor of G. L. Brinkman, against William Tilghman, issued by the Clerk of the District Court of Barton County and directed to me, as Sheriff of Ford County, Kansas, which said execution has been entered upon docket in Clerk's office in Ford County, Kansas.

Given under my hand this 15th day of February, A. D., 1879.

W. B. MASTERSON,
Sheriff of Ford County.

SUTTON & COLBORN, Atty's for Brinkman.

For the next five years only small and intermittent items concerning Tilghman found their way into the Dodge City papers. They mentioned that he was hunting, that he was a member of the Glick Guards, etc. To add to the confusion in sorting out the scarce material, Tilghman's father, who had the same first and middle names, moved to Dodge in the meantime and one cannot be certain at all times which Tilghman was meant.

It is known that Bill Tilghman, Jr., was appointed deputy sheriff under Pat Sughrue, but apparently little of note has been recorded about him in that office. Only a few mentions of his performance of duties appear. One was in the Dodge City *Democrat,* March 22,

1884. Tilghman, with the sheriff, had captured a horse thief. The short article is included in the section on Pat Sughrue.

In the spring of 1878 Tilghman and his partner Henry Garis disposed of the Crystal Palace [4] but later Tilghman opened another saloon called the Oasis. About the first of April, 1884, the Oasis was rented to Tilghman's younger brother Frank. The *Democrat*, April 5, 1884, predicted refreshments with denominational nomenclatures:

William Tilghman, Esq., proprietor of the "Oasis," has sold out to his brother Frank, who will refit and fix up and make everything smooth and harmonious to the visitor. Methodist cocktails and hard-shell Baptist lemonades a specialty.[5]

Possibly Tilghman was preparing for the office of city marshal which would be offered to him within the next two weeks. Times had changed, and wearing a badge while operating a saloon in prohibition Kansas were no longer compatible occupations. Bill Tilghman's appointment to the police force hinged on the April 8 election of mayor. George M. Hoover (a wholesale liquor dealer) was chosen by the people over George S. Emerson, 270 votes to 60. As the *Times*, April 10, 1884, said: "There was no enthusiasm, but little feeling, and consequently [the election was] a one-sided affair."

The new mayor offered Tilghman's name to the council at the meeting of April 10, 1884, and the appointment was confirmed as was the choice of Thomas C. Nixon for assistant marshal.[6]

Hardly had the new marshal pinned on the badge when he fell ill. The *Democrat*, April 26, 1884, reported he had "St. Anthony's fire":

City Marshal Tilghman is on the sick list, being laid up with the erysipelas, and Assistant Marshal Nixon is in charge. Harry Scott is assisting the officers while the marshal is off duty.

When he recovered he was presented with a $40 gold badge. The *Globe*, May 6, 1884, was one of the papers which recorded the presentation:

City Marshal Tilghman, on Friday evening, was the recipient of a most beautiful badge, presented to him by his host of friends in this city. The shield is solid gold, of a neat and tasty design, and is indeed a valuable and precious gift. On the face of the shield is engraved, "Wm. Tilghman, City Marshal," and on the back, "Presented by your many friends, May 2nd, 1884."

In behalf of Mr. Tilghman we wish to extend to his many friends his most heartfelt thanks, assuring them that this token of friendship has engraved upon his mind a love and kind remembrance never to be obliterated, and hopes to conduct himself in a manner that, when he shall have severed his connection with the position he now holds, the same feeling of friendship may still exist towards him.

In remarking on this presentation we must not overlook Mr. F. J. Durand, of this city, the mechanic who designed and executed this beautiful and very creditable piece of work. We can truly say it is the neatest piece of work of the kind we have yet seen, and speaks volumes for Mr. Durand as a workman of skill.

Bill humbly thanked the group for the two $20 gold pieces hammered "into the shape of an antique bar with a shield pendant," and "there was Mumm's Extra dry all round." [7]

Marshal Tilghman really drew two salaries from the city. He was paid $100 a month for being marshal and another $25 a month as collector of license fees from gamblers, prostitutes, their keepers, etc. Assistant Marshal Nixon earned $100 a month.[8]

In his dual role of city marshal and county deputy sheriff Bill Tilghman was mentioned quite often by the press as accompanying other officers in the performance of their duties. Most of these short items are printed in other sections of this work and are indexed under Tilghman.

During the season of 1884 Dodge pretty well maintained its "reputation," though few of the shootings have become frontier classics. On Monday, May 12, at about eight in the evening, "a cowboy named Bill York shot a woman named Mollie [Mabel] Gorman, at her house [in Dodge City]. The cowboy has been arrested. The woman, it is thought, will recover," reported the Caldwell *Journal*, May 15, 1884.[9]

On July 6 Bing Choate (or H. B. Choate or K. B. Schoat) was shot and killed by gambler Dave St. Clair. One witness gave this description of the shooting:

[I, M. E. Robinson,] was at 1 a. m. Sunday in Webster's saloon. Saw St. Clair and Choate, was present at the time of the tragedy. Choate and the other men were drinking at the bar. Choate was standing with right elbow on the bar with six shooter in hand. As I stepped in the door I heard Choate remark "I am the fastest s-n of a b---h in town." On the west side of the room sat St. Clair. I asked St. Clair what was the matter and he said, "I don't know." After Choate had pounded the revolver three or four times he handed it over the bar.

There were two men with him, whom I did not know and they went out. Presently the man with black whiskers returned, followed by the other two.

Bill Tilghman

The man with the black whiskers called St. Clair about half way down the room. Don't know what was said. They stood there talking when Choate came up. I stepped down close to them on the west side of the building. Choate called St. Clair a cowardly cur or "cowardly s-n of a b---h." Choate had a pistol in his right hand, close to his side. Choate punched St. Clair in his face with a cane and said "I'll teach you a lesson. I'll kill you, you s-n of a b---h," or words to that effect. I heard Choate say he would kill him. St. Clair held his hands folded in arms and stood up and said "Let me explain." Other remarks were made that I did not hear. They then walked down towards the bar. Choate stopped when about 8 feet from the door and faced St. Clair. The man with the black chin whiskers stood with both elbows on the bar. St. Clair then said to Choate, "You have been punching my neck and stomach with that cane, and you have been shaking your gun pretty freely."

As he said that I stepped up from the ice chest to the counter. St. Clair said: "If I had ever a [an even] break with you I would take the pistol from you and shove it ____." That instant Bill Bowles, policeman, stepped inside the door. At the instant, St. Clair said, "I'll take the pistol from you and shove it up ____." Choate put his hand on his pistol and said, "You will, will you." Bill Bowles, I think it was, said, "Look out, Dave." That instant Dave St. Clair drew his pistol and shot Choate—Choate's pistol was sticking in his pants. I saw the pistol before St. Clair fired. St. Clair had not drawn his pistol before. He was facing Choate, with his hand by his side, when St. Clair fired, I supposed there would be promiscuous firing. I did not see St. Clair make any belligerent demonstrations toward Choate until the firing. I was within four feet of St. Clair at the time of the shooting.[10]

Choate, 25 years old, was a cattleman from Goliad, Tex., who was driving 11,000 head of cattle up the trail to Dodge. St. Clair was released and immediately headed west. The *Ford County Globe* on July 8, 1884, blamed the city administration and the police force for permitting such goings on:

We are more than ever inclined to hold to our former opinion as regards the carrying of deadly weapons and particularly the six-shooter. If this law was more rigidly enforced there would be less killing done. Our officers should see to it that this law was enforced and to the very letter. Our mayor should exercise his power and authority in this direction, and see to it that all those not officers of the law (and perhaps some of them), be made to lay aside their shooting irons while in the city. The unfortunate killing of Mr. Schoate might have been prevented had this ordinance been enforced, and both parties disarmed as soon as it was found out that a quarrel was up between them, that might result seriously to either.

Not all the action in Dodge was caused by the big guns. As a matter of fact several who were rounded up for the city calaboose could not even be rated in the light artillery class.

Marshal Tilghman filled the lock-up with tramps, yesterday [July 28, 1884], and proposes to make Dodge a resort that they will not visit so often.[11]

Sex was no denominator either:

MORE BLOOD SPILLING.

ONE OF DODGE CITY'S UNFORTUNATES STABS ANOTHER SEVERELY.

Last Thursday night [August 7, 1884] about ten o'clock a difficulty occurred between two girls in a saloon, in which one of them was severely but it is said not fatally stabbed. The girl wounded is known as Sadie Hudson, and the perpetrator as Bertha Lockwood. They had both just returned from the dance house, and the difficulty was caused by jealousy of a mutual lover. Sadie was stabbed in three different places; one wound pretty near the spinal column under the back bone, one a little forward, and one in the breast. A surgeon was immediately called and dressed the wounds, reporting them not dangerous. They were flesh wounds quite deep, but not necessarily mortal.

The wounded girl was at once taken to her home in the house known as "the Parlor," and at latest accounts was doing well.

The girl who committed the deed was promptly arrested, but is now out on bail.

It appears that the two girls had some words, when Sadie slapped Bertha in the face, and then the cutting commenced.[12]

The Dodge City *Democrat*, August 16, 1884, reported another battle among the distaff portion of humanity:

A FIGHT FOR POSSESSION.

Ollie Hart and Mollie Hart, who both, as we understand it, claim the right of possession to the heart and necessary appendages of their "lover," attempted to settle the mooted question by a free-for-all cat fight, they failed, but Judge [R. G.] Cook gave a clear intimation in open court, by making Ollie's fine $5.00 and costs, and Mollie's $10.00 and costs.

There were other troublemakers besides tramps, prostitutes, and drunken cow hands:

The Chinese laundry on the south side, is a bad hole, generally speaking, and there is no end of trouble with them. Last night [August 18, 1884] they attacked a cowboy who went after his washing, and no doubt would have killed him, but for the timely arrival of the officers. They must reform or a Chinese laundry will go up the spout one of these days.[13]

Marshal Tilghman captured a man in August and the resulting story as published in the *Kansas Cowboy*, August 23, 1884, proved that Dodge had lost little of its earlier "sporting" reputation:

A STALWART RESISTS.

The city marshal brought up a six-footer of monstrous proportions, who got into a dive, and was rattling up the establishment. He was a gentleman of color. He was evidently starting out to paint Dodge City a fiery red, and

614

very appropriately started in the darkest spot in town. His first effort was on a lady of about the color of new sorghum, and she was as hot as that substance comes foaming from the grangers sap boiler when she made her appearance in court. He was from the mountains of Colorado, and his first effort on this lady was to make her as pretty as a spotted horse at a country fair, by adorning her with a flashy dress of more colors than Joseph, though she had none of the qualities which made Joseph famous in the presence of Mrs. Potipher. She was not a beauty unadorned. What she might have been with the spotted dress can only be conjectured. It appears that with a disregard for proprieties she tried to turn the spotted garment into spot cash; and probably into bibulous liquid as red as the dress, and for that purpose left it for sale. This indignantly aroused the gallant gentleman from Colorado, and he attempted to get back his gift. That raised the row. She of the red dress became red with rage, and her eyes shown as fiery as a cat's in a dark garret, and she emitted sparks like those on the feline when rubbed backwards.

Then the row began and the Colorado Sampson took hold of the pillars of that dive, and shook it base to cupola, so to speak. What he would have done if the city marshal had not arrived on the spot will never be known. As it was he struck out from the shoulder, and was about as ugly a customer as need be seen anywhere. The marshal showed himself equal to the emergency and tumbled him into the cooler. The day was hot, but the hero came before the police judge as cool as if he had been in a refrigerator, and plead for mercy, promising future good behavior. His honor fined him twenty-five dollars and costs, remarking very properly that he had personally witnessed his conduct, and that if he ever attempted to run Dodge City again he wouldn't get off with less than a hundred dollars or its equivalent in work on a stone pile. The money was paid, and the Colorado Sampson retired a cooler and wiser man, satisfied that as an artist in red paint he was not a success.

October 16 saw a shootout down by the river between a group of cowboys and Marshal Tilghman. Evidently no one was injured, and the only blood spilled was thought to be that of a wounded horse. The *Globe Live Stock Journal*, October 21, 1884, reported the fracas:

The city marshal and a party of cowboys exchanged twenty-five or thirty shots on or near the bridge about ten o'clock Thursday night. Six-shooters were used for awhile and then Winchesters. It is not known whether any one was hurt or not. The marshal's second shot caused a commotion among the horses, and from spots of blood on the bridge it is thought one of the horses was wounded. When the firing opened the people along Bridge street thought as it was pretty dark and they could not see, that they could hear as well in the nearest house, so they made for shelter, and it was just as well, for the balls came up the street like a young hail-storm striking in the road on the hill.

A man who had stolen two horses from his own father in Wichita apparently was next in the available records on Tilghman. The Dodge City *Democrat* of October 25, 1884, stated:

On last Saturday City Marshal Tilghman arrested Jim Rhodes, who had stolen two horses from his father at Wichita. He had only one of the horses with him, having sold the other at Pratt Centre. The sheriff of Sedgwick county arrived on last Monday and took the prisoner back to Wichita.[14]

The election of November, 1884, came and passed quietly, due largely to the efforts of the police force, reported the *Globe*, November 11, 1884:

We feel proud of the fact that there was no need of a large extra police force in this city on election day. Marshal Tilghman and his usual daily force attended to their duties nobly, and peace and quiet was the order of the day. We feel proud of these facts.

Also in November Marshal Tilghman arrested restaurateur Ed Julian for engaging in a cowboy war of his own. The *Democrat*, November 15, 1884, stated the case:

POLICE COURT DOINGS.

The following cases have come up before Judge Cook since last Monday:
. . .

City of Dodge, vs. E. J. Julian, has attracted considerably attention in the Court during the past week. It seems that several cowboys came into his place with their girls to get supper, and after eating the same they refused to pay up. Mr. Julian said that some one would have to pay, where upon they undertook to clean out the restaurant, and the result was that two of them got knocked down, the third taken to his heels, after getting outside they sent several bullets through the windows and then run. The Marshal arrested Mr. Julian, and after the case was tried, the Judge fined him $10.00 and costs. A bond was immediately given and the case appealed.

Seventeen months later Julian was shot and killed by Ben Daniels, a private citizen, but Marshal Tilghman's assistant when Julian was arrested in November, 1884.[15]

"Marshal Tilghman rounded up a man yesterday morning [January 12] who had the night before broken into a house and stole eighteen dollars in money, a shot gun and some clothing. The thief is now in jail," said the *Globe Live Stock Journal*, January 13, 1885.

In early April Tilghman was unsuccessful in capturing a thief. No one seemed to know much about the robbery including the *Globe Live Stock Journal*, April 7, 1885:

There has been so much said about that robbery a few nights ago, that we are unable to tell anything about it, and aught not to be blamed either, for Judge Cook, before whom the parties who were charged with the crime were taken, said he could make nothing out of it, and all he knows is that some body had some money taken away from them. Marshal Tilghman did everything in his power to ferret out the guilty party.

616

The annual Dodge City election was held April 7, 1885, and Robert M. Wright was chosen mayor. The new officials declared all city positions vacant but immediately reappointed Tilghman marshal and Ben Daniels assistant marshal.[16]

The day after his reappointment Tilghman left Dodge in pursuit of mule thieves. The *Democrat*, April 11, 1885, said:

A man who lives in Meade county lost two mules last October, and two weeks ago gave City Marshal Tilghman the very difficult work of looking them up, and William received word on last Thursday [April 9] that they were in Edwards county, and went after them Thursday afternoon.

A mysterious incident occurred on June 4, 1885, which required the attention of the city marshal, so the *Democrat* of June 6, 1885, reported:

A MYSTERY.

Last Thursday night about 10 o'clock, a colored man by the name of Sanders, who resides on Third Avenue, noticed some one in front of his house, who seemed to be pounding something. He says he thought it was a man killing a dog, and did not pay much attention to it. After the man had gone he concluded he would go and see what it was. He took a light but the wind blew it out. He finally made the object out to be a man. He got another man to go with him in search of an officer. City Marshal Tilghman, immediately proceeded to the spot, but no body was to be found. The only trace was a large pool of blood. This is a mysterious affair, as no one knows who the man was, or whether he is alive or dead. The officers are somewhat suspicious, and somebody will be in limbo before they are aware of it.

The city marshal and his father, of the same name, also shared July 4 as their birthday. On that day in 1885, the father was 65 years old, the son 31. Both lived in Dodge.[17]

"City Marshal Tilghman collected for the month of September, just [an] even six hundred dollars from the saloons and sporting class; being a special tax for the privilege of staying in Dodge City," stated the *Globe Live Stock Journal*, September 29, 1885.

On October 4 Tilghman left for Austin, Tex., to pick up a fugitive; he was back on October 14. The *Globe*, October 20, 1885, said:

Marshal Tilghman returned from Mobeetie, Texas, Wednesday, with his prisoner, George Snyder, who stole a horse from J. C. Briggs about a month ago. Mr. Tilghman was compelled to go to Austin after a requisition, and from there to Mobeetie, making a trip of over two thousand miles. Snyder admits stealing the horse and says he rode out of Dodge and across the bridge after sun up. He will plead guilty to the charge of horse stealing when court convenes.[18]

According to the Dodge City *Democrat* Tilghman called it the "hardest trip ever taken by an officer of Ford county."

In December Marshal Tilghman had the odd experience of arresting his own boss, Mayor R. M. Wright. The Medicine Lodge *Cresset*, December 17, 1885, heard the story from the Wright side:

Bob Wright, mayor of Dodge City, arrested on Monday [December 14], charged with felonious assault on Mike Sutton, formerly of the Lodge, but for several years past a prominent attorney of Dodge City. We have heard the story of the assault from a friend of Bob Wright, which was in substance as follows: After the second fire the rumor was started that the prohibitionists had fired the town and friends of Mr. Sutton feared that an attempt would be made to assassinate him and went to Mayor Wright and asked him to send an extra police to guard the residence of Mr. Sutton. Instead of sending the policeman the mayor said he would go himself, and accordingly armed himself with a revolver and went to Sutton's house. He saw some one moving about in the shadow of the building as he says and ordered him to halt. Instead of that the man started to run around the house and Wright fired at him. All the shots, however, struck the house and Mike, supposing that somebody was trying to shoot him pulled his freight. Even putting the most favorable construction upon this story it seems to us that it is not at all surprising that Mike should suppose that an attempt was being made upon his life and further more if that is the way the Dodge City mayor has of guarding people we don't want him for a body guard of ours.[19]

City Marshal William Tilghman made no more Dodge City news until March 9, 1886, when his resignation was announced just a month before his term expired. The *Globe*, March 9, reported:

William Tilghman tendered his resignation as Marshal of the City of Dodge City, to the Honorable Mayor and Council of the City of Dodge City, Kansas, to take effect March 9th, 1886. The same was duly considered, and on motion moved and carried, accepted.

Tilghman remained in Dodge City as a cattleman though he concurrently carried a county commission as deputy sheriff. He was well thought of as a business man and apparently did his county duty well also. In May, 1886, he took a prisoner before the state supreme court in Topeka [20] and in August he traveled to Ohio. The *Globe Live Stock Journal*, August 17, 1886, described the latter trip:

Under-Sheriff Wm. Tilghman returned home Tuesday from his trip to Greenville, Ohio, where he had gone to recover an escaped prisoner from Ford county, who was charged with horse-stealing, J. W. Graham by name, who about one year ago stole a horse from some person at or near the Mulberry ranch, and who was arrested at the time, waived a preliminary and was bound over for trial at the next term of the district court. Graham jumped

618

his bail, and as soon as his whereabouts were ascertained, was arrested and brought back for trial.

According to Bill's widow, Mrs. Zoe Tilghman, who wrote his biography in 1949, he was called by one of the factions in the Wichita county seat war to guard the polls at one of the several county seat location elections. Possibly this was the election of March, 1888, for Tilghman was absent from Dodge at that time and three months later was holding forth in Farmer City, Wichita county.

This small western Kansas burg was located between Leoti and Coronado, the contestants for the county seat. So close were Leoti and Coronado that Farmer City was barely able to squeeze in between them, and even so was accused of squatting on a portion of the Coronado townsite. Little love was shared among the three towns; in fact, blood had been spilled just the winter prior to Bill's visit. Possibly the intense feelings of the times had something to do with the action which occurred at Farmer City on July 4, 1888.

On that day, Bill Tilghman's 34th birthday, the ex-Dodge City marshal shot and killed Ed Prather. The Leoti *Transcript,* July 5, 1888, told one version of the story:

Farmer City was the scene of a murder yesterday afternoon about seven o'clock. We give the facts below as we learned them. During the night of the 3d. Ed Prather and [County] Commissioner [H. T.] Trovillo were creating considerable disturbance by shooting promiscuously which they kept up the entire night. Soon after breakfast they resumed their shooting and carousing, and at the request of the ladies of Farmer City Wm. M. Tilghman went to Prather and Trovillo and asked them to be more civil and conduct themselves in a more gentlemanly manner. The disturbing parties took offense at this request and came to Leoti to celebrate the Fourth. After spending the morning and part of the evening here in drinking, Prather returned to Farmer City leaving Trovillo lying near the section house too drunk to navigate. While in Leoti Prather made threats on the life of Tilghman, which a friend of Tilghman informed him of.

About seven o'clock Tilghman went into the joint kept by Prather and began drinking, when he came to pay for the beer a quarrel ensued about the change returned. In the course of the conversation Prather told Tilghman he had it in for him and at the same time placed his hand on his gun,   in an instant Tilghman covered him with a pistol and asked him (Prather) to take his hand off his gun, which Prather refused to do.   Tilghman knowing he had a desperate character to deal with shot him in the left breast, the ball coming out his back,   this did not cause Prather to fall,   he remained standing at the bar looking straight at Tilghman and still had his hand on the gun. Tilghman again asked him to take his hand off the pistol but Prather still desisted, then Tilghman shot him through the brain which killed him on the spot. Both parties were bad characters and Prather prided himself as being a "bad man."

Attorney J. Frank Ward went over to-day to investigate the shooting for the state and is convinced from the statement of the citizens of the town, who would be the only witnesses, were he brought to trial, that he did the shooting in self-defense, and any attempt at prosecution would only augment the debt of the county in trying to prosecute her former murderers. Coronado, alias Farmer City, seems intent on sustaining her former reputation as the scene of murderous deeds.

The Farmer City *Western Farmer,* July 5, 1888, offered more details and sympathy for the Tilghmans, junior and senior:

Yesterday, about 7 o'clock p. m., while our people were enjoying themselves in celebrating our national independence, our town was thrown into an intense state of excitement by the report that a man had been shot and killed. As in all communities there are some men who must have some of the vitalizing liquid draught of perdition, and some of the facts in the case are as follows:

On the evening of the 3rd inst. Ed. Prather obtained some beer that had been provided for the celebration and after imbibing freely was ready for the fourth, and early in the morning he started in for a "full" day. Some of the citizens went to him and asked, in a very peaceable and courteous manner, for the sake of the town, the ladies and civil people, to stop drinking and try to have a peaceable day. As is usual in such cases he asserted his right to celebrate as he pleased, and since he could not have his fun in Farmer City he would go somewhere else. He got a team and started for Leoti to help them celebrate. While there his anger became more and more intense, and he resolved to round up this town.

About 5 o'clock p. m. he returned to Farmer City with blood all over his face, hands and clothes. He showed murder in his eye, and often asserted that unless certain retractions be made, that certain parties here would never see the sun rise again. He made frequent threats and insults against Wm. Tilghman, the deputy sheriff, who took all the abuse from the excited man without offering any retaliation. Shortly after his return he began kicking doors in, and demanding with gun in hand, to be waited upon as he should order. Some very dangerous firing was done on the streets by him, and the people became fearful that trouble was nigh. Nobody interfered with him until, in conversation with Mr. Tilghman, he became very abusive and threatened to put an end to him right there, and suiting action to his words, he threw his hand upon his revolver; but Mr. Tilghman was too quick for him and held a revolver in his face. Mr. T. ordered him three times to take his hand off his gun, and would have disarmed him if he had been near enough; but Prather sought a better position, and Tilghman pulled the trigger, and Prather was a dead man.

A coroner's jury consisting of N. Malson, L. L. Stidger, L. D. Hare, Robt. Traver, J. K. Selby and R. S. Bell, was impaneled by coroner [T. J.] McCain,

620

and after a thorough examination of the circumstances, returned a verdict of justifiable killing.

Ed. Prather was about thirty years old, and when sober, was of a kind and accommodating disposition, and was well behaved. He was what was considered a very dangerous man when determined on death, or when drunk and excited. He was an expert with his forty-five Colt's revolver and to pull it on a man meant death. Ed. was not among enemies and was in no danger of hurt. He was killed by a friend who had often stood by him when danger was nigh, and no man would have hesitated longer to pull the trigger than William Tilghman; but death was staring him in the face and he was compelled to shoot.

Mr. William Tilghman was 34 years old yesterday. He has a fine stock farm near Dodge City, and is held in high esteem by all who know him. He has, since he came to Farmer City, shown himself to be a perfect gentleman, and is as highly respected by the citizens of the county as any man can be. He comes from a family whose pure reputation stands at the top of the scale. He has lived seventeen years in Dodge City; and for eight years has been an officer of the peace at that place and to him as much as to any man in the West is due the credit for establishing law and order at that place. Years ago Dodge City was the most noted border ruffian town on the face of the earth. To-day it has the reputation of a first-class moral, civil and religious city. His father is sixty-nine years old, and while he may feel depressed at the news of his son's killing a man, he knows that William is a good man and would not needlessly kill his fellow man. Mr. Tilghman has the entire sympathy of the whole populace, and he must feel that he did no more than right in saving his own life.

Some reports of the killing had it that Bill Tilghman was drinking at the time. On July 12, 1888, the *Western Farmer,* a Prohibition paper, defended Tilghman, saying that he neither drank nor smoked cigars:

Many reports of the killing of Ed Prather here on the fourth have reached us through the papers of this state, and in the main, all are fair accounts of the case. Some few report Mr. Tilghman as being drunk and drinking. Now while Mr. Tilghman is no more to us than any other good citizen, we must say that he was not, in any sense, drinking intoxicants. While we cannot say whether he is a prohibition man or not, we can say that he has neither used cigars nor intoxicating drinks since he has been among us. We have made a careful investigation of this matter, and from all available sources we learn that Mr. Tilghman is a strictly sober man, a kind and accommodating citizen, and as careful of the rights of others as any man can be. At any rate he has the respect of all who know him here.

Six months later Bill Tilghman was involved in another county seat fight, this time in the contest between Ingalls and Cimarron for the seat of Gray county, just west of Ford. Other well-known

Dodge Citians were included in the affair and once again confusion between the Masterson brothers is evident. All contemporary sources checked, however, stated that James Masterson (or merely Masterson) was one of the raiders. Bat Masterson and Wyatt Earp, despite accounts in many latter day publications, were not in the fight. There are many newspaper accounts telling of the "Dodge raid" but only two are published here—two which represent quite opposite views of the battle. The story as printed in the Dodge City *Times*, January 17, 1889, reflected the Ingalls attitude:

THE COUNTY SEAT WAR.

AT CIMARRON OVER THE COUNTY RECORDS.

Of the battle at Cimarron on last Saturday between the deputy sheriffs of Gray county and citizens of Cimarron an eye witness gives the following particulars of the fight:

"On last Saturday morning the Sheriff of Gray county, with Fred Singer, Neal Brown, Jas. Masterson, Edward Brooks, Benj. Daniels and Wm. Tilghman as deputies, went to Cimarron with a wagon to convey the county records to Ingalls, for which they had an order from the Supreme court. On their arrival at the building used for a court house at Cimarron, four of the deputy sheriffs stood guard over the wagon while the sheriff and the balance of his men carried out the books. After they had got all the books loaded and were nearly ready to start, the Cimarron people, who in the meantime had been arming themselves, fired upon the officers. This commenced the battle, and the officers returned the fire. From this out the firing was continuous, fully 1,000 shots being fired. The team was started for Ingalls as soon as the shooting began and was protected on its way out of the city by the four deputies who were left in charge, viz: Ed. Brooks, Benj. Daniels, Wm. Tilghman and Neal Brown, and although lead was flying as thick as hail around them they succeeded in getting away. Fred Singer, Jas. Masterson and Wm. Ainsworth who were in the court house when the firing commenced, were unable to escape on account of the mob surrounding the building and who riddled the windows and floor of the room in which they were with bullets. The deputy sheriffs with the records drove to Ingalls as fast as possible, and then telegraphed to Dodge City for aid in order to release the other officers imprisoned at Cimarron. Upon the receipt of the dispatch a number of the friends of the officers took the afternoon train for Ingalls, but in the evening Sheriff [H. B.] Bell and a number of our influential citizens went on a special train to Cimarron and obtained the release of the Ingalls officers.

"After the battle was over it was found that of the Cimarron people, J. W. English was killed outright; Jack Bliss was wounded in several places with buck shot but will recover; Lee Fairhurst was wounded in the breast but will recover; and a man by the name of Harrington was wounded in the hand.

"Of the Ingalls people, Ed. Brooks fared the worst, being shot in the back just below the shoulder blade and two different places in the legs, it was thought at first that he would die but the doctors now report that he will recover; the teamster who drove the wagon received a wound in the leg; Wm. Tilghman sprained his ankle badly while crossing the irrigating ditch [A. T. Soule's Eureka Irrigating Canal]."

It is very much regretted that the shooting took place, but there is no question but what the Cimarron people were to blame, as they started the fight with the officers from Ingalls, who went there with the proper authority to take the records. It is a wonder to all that any of the officers escaped when fully 75 men were firing upon them, none but brave and determined men would have lived to tell the story of how they were attacked.

Most every daily paper in the east has been filled with news of the fight written by Cimarron people in which they place the Ingalls men in the light of murderers and heap a great deal of abuse on Dodge City, but a true statement of the fight is given above. The citizens of Dodge, although they do not believe in county seat fights, cannot help but sympathize with the officers of Gray county who were fired upon by the Cimarron mob while doing their duty. The Mayor of Cimarron telegraphed for state militia which was at once responded to by Gen. Murray Myers and two companies of militia who arrived at Cimarron Sunday and remained until Tuesday morning. No further trouble is now anticipated.

The Cimarron side was presented by the Cimarron *Jacksonian*, January 18, 1889:

SAD AFFAIR!

THE STORY AS IT IS!

THE FREE SOIL OF GRAY COUNTY IS BAPTIZED WITH BLOOD.

CLOSE SHOTS!

ONE MAN KILLED AND EIGHT WOUNDED.

A FEARFUL CONFLICT!

A FEW FACTS!

A GANG OF TOUGHS REMOVE THE COUNTY CLERK'S RECORDS AND ATTEMPT TO RUN THE TOWN.

Last Saturday morning dawned bright and clear, the sun seemed to shine with unusual brilliancy and splendor and no wind stirred. All nature seemed clothed in a mantle of peace, happiness and contentment. The peaceable citizens of our fair young city arose and resumed their accustomed business, with light hearts and pure minds, all unconscious that danger and death lurked so near, and that in a few short hours there should be a marshaling of the people to defend their town and rights against the most diabolical attack ever perpetrated on a quiet, law-abiding community. No such maligna was dreamed of, but alas! the unwelcomed tidings and task was made known only to soon.

At 11:30 A. M., a wagon with some ten or twelve men concealed in the bottom of it, drove down Main street and halted in front of the court house. Each was armed with a Winchester, shot gun or revolver, and all hailed from the little hamlet of Ingalls, six miles west on the Santa Fe. The object of their visit was soon made apparent when alighting part of them immediately proceeded up stairs to the county clerk's office and began removing the records, while three or four stood guard at the foot of the stairs to see that no one interfered. In a moment, scarcely more than the duration of a flash of lighting, the word was passed from lip to lip and from house to house, and brave men never more promptly responded to a call to arms than did the men of Cimarron.

The mob which had gone up stairs kicked open the door of the clerk's office and entering pulled a Winchester on A. T. Riley and commanded him to throw up his hands. They then began carrying the records down stairs and placing them in the wagon. Mr. Riley allowed them to take the books without any resistance on his part, but asked them to give him a receipt for the same, when he was told to "go to h--l," that "they had no time to receipt for anything," taking particular pains to keep a gun on him all the time. In the mean time that part of the gang which had been stationed down stairs as guards to hold up at the point of their gun all who came near, opened up fire on our citizens. The books and records had all been loaded and the cavalcade from the west was ready to move on its triumphal march homeward, when firing was opened by both sides. During the battle which ensued the wagon was removed and reached Ingalls in safety. The whole affair was a complete surprise to our people and found them unarmed. It is estimated that the firing did not last ten minutes from the time it began until it had ceased and the wagon containing the records had passed out of sight over the hills northwest of the city. But after the battle, which partook of the nature of a guerrilla warfare, it was discovered that in this short space of time our respected citizen

J. W. ENGLISH HAD BEEN MURDERED,

and Jack Bliss and Ed. Fairhurst mortally wounded. When the books and records were all loaded, the driver stepped into the wagon and drove off at a break-neck speed, exchanging shots with his pursuers and stopping to take in those of the gang who had become weak-kneed, and took to their heels. After Mr. English fell and they became aware that our citizens were not to be baffled they scattered like so many birds and run for their lives. They had come prepared for the occasion, however, having several Winchesters and shot guns with them, and would stop at intervals and return fire at some of the citizens, who crazed and enraged over the killing of their comrade were "pumping" lead into them thick and fast.

A GANG OF MURDERERS.

By way of explanation, it might be well to state right here that when we refer to "they" or the "gang" we mean this gang of murderers, cut-throats and fugitives from justice, who came here as deputy sheriffs, (deputized by the sheriff of Gray County, who is a bitter Ingalls man,) without any legal authority whatever to recover the records and shoot down our citizens in cold blood. They are not residents of Gray County, and many of them not residents of the State, they are "killers" and do not claim to be anything else.

624

FOUR OF THEM CORRALED.

During the shooting and excitement which followed, the four men who had taken charge of the clerk's office up stairs were unable to get out without danger of losing their lives and were permitted to remain there until six o'clock in the evening. The Mayor called a meeting of the citizens and after conferring with them decided to telegraph the sheriff at Ingalls to come and take the men under his custody. He arrived here about five o'clock when they were turned over to him with a commitment for each of them to the Ford County jail for murder in the first degree. He took them to Ingalls and allowed them to go scott free, and they are to day roaming about at their own sweet will threatening a repetition of last Saturdays bloody work if an attempt is made to arrest them. Among these prospective candidates for the pentitentiary, was N. F. Watson, the newly elected (by fraudulent votes) county clerk, whose certificate had been mailed him early that morning and at the time the shooting occurred was awaiting him in the Post Office at Ingalls. He had made no demand for the office as his predecessor's time had not yet expired. The other gentlemen with whom he had the pleasure of being caged that day were Billy Allensworth, Fred Singer and Jim Masterson. . . .[21]

A few months later, on April 22, 1889, Oklahoma territory was opened to white settlement and Bill Tilghman was one of the first to settle in newly established Guthrie. He was no longer to play a part in the game of law and disorder in Kansas.

1. *See, also,* Dodge City *Times,* March 31, 1877. 2. *See, also,* Ford County *Globe,* February 12, 1878. 3. *See, also,* the section on W. B. Masterson. 4. Dodge City *Times,* May 11, 1878. 5. *See, also,* Ford County *Globe,* April 1, 1884. 6. *Ibid.,* April 15, 1884; Dodge City *Times,* April 17, 1884. 7. Dodge City *Democrat,* May 10, 1884. 8. *Ibid.,* June 7, July 12, August 9, September 6, October 11, November 8, December 6, 1884; January 10, March 7, April 11, 1885; *Globe Live Stock Journal,* May 12, June 9, July 21, August 11, September 15, October 13, November 10, December 15, 1885; January 12, February 9, March 9, 1886. 9. *See, also,* Ford County *Globe,* May 13; Dodge City *Times,* May 15; Dodge City Kansas Cowboy, May 17, 1884. 10. Dodge City Kansas Cowboy, July 12, 1884; *see, also,* Dodge City *Democrat,* July 5, 1884; Ford County *Globe,* July 8, 1884; *Globe Live Stock Journal,* July 15, 1884. 11. *Ibid.,* July 29, 1884. 12. Dodge City Kansas Cowboy, August 9, 1884. 13. Dodge City *Democrat,* August 16, 1884. 14. *See, also,* Globe Live Stock Journal, October 21, 1884. 15. See the section on Daniels. 16. Dodge City *Democrat,* April 11, 1885; *Globe Live Stock Journal,* April 14, 1885. 17. Dodge City Kansas Cowboy, July 11, 1885. 18. *See, also,* Dodge City *Democrat,* October 10, 17, 1885. 19. *See, also,* Globe Live Stock Journal, December 15, 1885. 20. *Ibid.,* May 11, 1886. 21. *See, also,* Topeka *Capital-Commonwealth,* January 13, 15, 1889; Cimarron New West Echo, January 17, 1889.

WHEELER, BEN F. (1854-1884)

The height of co-operation between Kansas peace officers may be found in the almost identical careers of Caldwell City Marshal Henry N. Brown and his assistant, Ben Wheeler. One finds few newspaper notices in which one and not the other is mentioned in the curtailment of cowboy crime. Continuing their loyalty to the end, they died together—killed by a mob for attempting to rob a bank in Medicine Lodge!

Because of this co-operation between Brown and Wheeler most of the contemporary newspaper items concerning the latter have been included in the section on Henry Brown. However, Wheeler's participation is covered in the index.

When Caldwell Marshal B. P. Carr took a leave of absence in October, 1882, Assistant Marshal Henry Brown temporarily moved up and Ben Wheeler was hired to fill the assistant's spot. The Caldwell *Post*, October 26, 1882, said of him:

Mr. Ben Wheeler is acting as assistant city marshal while Henry Brown is marshal in the absence of Bat Carr. Mr. Wheeler has the sand, so the boys say, to stay with the wild and woolly class as long as they are on the war path.

Marshal Carr returned on November 2, 1882, but in about seven weeks he left the force and Brown was once again promoted, this time permanently. Ben Wheeler was named assistant. "The City Council met last Friday night and appointed Henry Brown marshal in place of Bat. Carr, and Ben Wheeler assistant marshal. The appointments give general satisfaction," said the Caldwell *Commercial*, December 28, 1882.

On January 7, 1883, Wheeler nabbed a petty bedroom thief. The *Commercial*, January 11, reported the crime, arrest, and conviction:

Ben Wheeler, assistant marshal, was walking up the south side of Fifth street about two o'clock last Sunday afternoon, when he discovered a man attempting to hide some plunder under a building in the rear of the Opera House. Ben took in the situation and the man at once. An examination of the fellow's person developed the fact that he had been wandering up and down in a lady's chamber, for he had concealed about him various articles of lady's underware, such as corsets, etc., besides jewelry, neckties, shoes, slippers, stockings, garters and handkerchiefs, in all to the value of nearly $40. Ben locked up the fellow, who gave his name as Smith, and started out to find the owner of the stolen property. Upon inquiry it was learned that some one had entered the rooms occupied by the girls employed in the Leland Hotel, and taken therefrom the articles in question. Smith was brought before Judge Kelly on Tuesday, plead guilty to the charge of larceny and committed for trial at the next term of the District Court. He now enjoys such hospitalities as the county is enabled to furnish through Sheriff Thralls. He seems to be a stranger here, no one knowing who he is or where he came from.

Marshal Brown received a leave in late January, 1883, to be gone

Ben Wheeler

a month. "Ben. Wheeler, during the absence of Henry Brown, will have in charge the peace and good order of our city. Ben is equal to the occasion, being of that class of men who have very little to say but very prompt when action is necessary," explained the *Commercial,* February 1, 1883.

After Henry Brown had returned to his duties Caldwell witnessed a shooting by one of its most respected citizens. Assistant Marshal Ben Wheeler was quickly on hand to disarm the physician who had already wounded his victim twice. The *Commercial,* March 29, 1883, reported the attempted murder:

ANOTHER TRAGEDY.

An unfortunate and tragical affair occurred in this city last Thursday afternoon [March 22], in the shooting of Charles Everhart by Dr. W. A. Noble. Shorn of all details, the facts are that the Doctor had been drinking, and while in McChesney's "Place," took offense at Everhart, who attends the lunch counter in the "Place." Of the cause of the offense—real or supposed—no exact information could be obtained, but it appears that the Doctor suddenly drew a self-cocking pistol and began firing at Everhart. The first shot missed. The second shot struck Everhart in the left breast, an inch or two above the nipple and passed out at his back, just below the shoulder blade. The third shot seems to have been fired as Everhart turned to get out of the way, for the third ball struck him in the back, ranged up and passed out in front a little above the collar bone and about four inches above the place where the first ball entered.

Before the Doctor could fire another shot, the pistol was wrenched from his hand and he was taken in charge by Assistant City Marshal Wheeler. Meantime Everhart had fallen to the floor, and Drs. [Charles R.] Hume and [J. F.] Robertson were called in.

It was at first thought that Everhart could not live, but under the treatment and care which have been given him, he seems in a fair way to recover.

An examination of Dr. Noble before Justice of the Peace T. H. B. Ross, was called on Friday, but the case was continued, and the defendant held in $10,000 [bond] for his appearance on Wednesday, March 28, at 1 p. m. Bail was promptly furnished.

The unhappy affair is a source of regret, not only to the Doctor, but to his numerous friends, by whom he is held in high regard, both as a physician and a man. He is a man of a generous nature, but impulsive, and while strong in his likes and dislikes, we do not believe he bore malice toward any one. He certainly had none for Everhart, and his attack upon the latter can only be accounted for upon the ground of his mental condition previous to and at the time of the occurrence.

Yesterday, at the trial set, Mr. George, deputy county attorney, appeared and requested a continuance. The continuance was granted until April 6th, and a new bond filed.

The shooting prompted the editor of the *Commercial* to moralize on the effects of alcohol, double action revolvers, and democracy:

LAST THURSDAY'S TRAGEDY.

The tragedy which occurred in this city last Thursday, speaks in loud tones for the enactment of two very important laws. The first, prescribing that whisky insanity shall be no excuse for crime, and the second, that where one makes an attempt upon the life of another with a deadly weapon, and it can be proven that the assailant has been in the habit of carrying said weapon concealed, such fact shall be *prima facia* evidence of an intention to commit murder.

This, at first glance, may seem hard. But can adequate reasons be given why a prominent citizen or a so-called "respected member of society" in this or any other well organized community in Kansas should habitually carry double-action revolvers, or for that matter, dangerous weapons of any kind?

With no desire to prejudice the case or add to the misery of the chief participant in last Thursday's affair, it must be honestly confessed that had not Dr. Noble been armed with a weapon upon which he could rely and the merits of which he had undoubtedly tested, no matter to what extent his intoxication, he would have thought twice before making any warlike demonstrations upon anyone, especially upon a man who was in no wise his enemy.

There should be no mawkish sentimentality regarding any man, however high his standing, or whatever his wealth or social position may be, who, habituated to going armed in a civilized community, under a fit of alcoholic insanity makes use of a weapon. The law should be as strictly enforced in this case as in the case of any cowboy who comes off the range, and, unacquainted with the customs and regulations of the town, fails or refuses to lay aside his arms.

Treat all alike, prince or peasant, rich or poor, citizen or stranger, and make no rule in one case that will not be applicable to all other cases under like circumstances.

Dr. Noble was bound over at his examination but since his victim, Everhart, had left the area, it was generally felt by the local populace that the doctor would be released.[1]

"Three innocent cowboys rode out of the city in true cowboy style on Tuesday," reported the Caldwell *Journal*, Thursday, August 9, 1883. "The marshal and his deputy went after them, caught and brought them back. They paid their respects to the Police Judge, after which they rode out of the city in the most gentle manner."

On April 9, 1884, Henry Brown and Ben Wheeler were again reappointed to their respective positions. Brown's salary was fixed at $100 a month and Wheeler's at $75.[2] Exactly three weeks later

C. B. Whitney

they rode into Medicine Lodge to rob a bank and there met death.
(*See* the section on Henry Brown.)

1. Caldwell *Journal*, May 17, 1883. 2. *Ibid.*, April 10, 1884.

WHITNEY, CHAUNCEY BELDEN (1842-1873)

At daylight, September 17, 1868, Chauncey Belden Whitney awoke to find himself and his 50-odd companions surrounded by hundreds of hostile Indians. The group of civilian scouts under the command of Maj. (Bvt. Col.) George A. Forsyth had been pursuing a band of Cheyenne and Sioux which had attacked a freighters' wagon train near the little town of Sheridan (present Logan county) on September 10. Now Whitney and his friends were themselves under severe attack. After the first murderous charge, in which Forsyth, Lt. Fred Beecher, and some eight or ten others were wounded, the men succeeded in digging entrenchments on their little sandy island in the Arickaree (about 20 miles west of present St. Francis) and for the next three days fought off the attackers. On Sunday, September 20, the Indians failed to appear but lack of transportation and the weakened condition of the party prevented the scouts from venturing far from the shelter of their island. Messengers had been dispatched between the attacks, however, seeking relief from Fort Wallace and from other troops in the field.

By September 21 the besieged group was subsisting on horse meat but in only a few more days most of this was gone, with the exception of some putrid remnants which were eaten almost as readily. Coyotes, wolves, and prickly pears supplemented their diet until on September 24 Whitney wrote in his diary, "My God! have you deserted us?"

Whitney's questioning prayer was answered the next morning with the appearance of a strong force of troops, "a day long to be remembered by our little band of heroes," he wrote.

"To-morrow we are to start for Fort Wallace, where I shall bid good-bye to our brave band of scouts to prepare to return east, where I will try to forget in a peaceful home the scenes of the past two years," he wrote on September 26.[1] The place of peace in which he expected to forget the horrors of the Battle of Beecher's Island turned out to be not so tranquil after all, for Chauncey Whitney's "home town" was Ellsworth.

The town had been established in January, 1867, just before the Union Pacific, Eastern Division, built through. In the next few years Ellsworth was to earn a reputation as one of Kansas' wildest and toughest towns.

Whitney was one of its early settlers. At the September 11, 1867, meeting of the Ellsworth county commissioners he was referred to as constable and was directed to ascertain if all persons doing business in the county had obtained licenses. On October 18, 1867, the board ordered that

C. B. Whitney be authorized to purchase lumber and material for repairing the Blake House on Walnut St to be used for Jail and the Clerk is ordered to draw orders on the County Treasure for the amount. Ordered that the
, house of H D Blake be rented at $60.00 per month for six months from date to be used for Jail, payable monthly in advance, rent to commence this Oct. 18th, 1867 and that the county repair said house and put chimney in the same underpin and ceil it in good workman like manner, at its own expense and that at the expiration of six months that the said improvement to belong to the said H. D. Blake, and it is further ordered that C. B. Whitney be authorized to make all necessary repairs and is instructed to draw orders in C. B. Whitney's favor toward paying for lumber &c.

Ellsworth county's second election for sheriff was held November 5, 1867. The field included five hopefuls, among them Whitney, but he was defeated by the county's first sheriff, E. W. Kingsbury. The others in the race were M. R. Lane, a man named Parkes and Wild Bill Hickok who received 155 votes in Ellsworth city, the largest number in that precinct, but only one other vote in the entire county.

In April, 1868, Whitney was re-elected constable [2] and probably was also acting as a deputy sheriff for his name appeared frequently in the commissioners' lists of "bills allowed." Then, on August 28, 1868, Whitney enlisted in Forsyth's scouts and three weeks later participated in the famous Indian battle mentioned earlier. As a scout he was paid $75 per month but had to furnish his own horse and equipment. The battle of the Arickaree was the only major fight in which the little group participated, and on December 31, 1868, they were returned to full civilian status.[3]

Back in Ellsworth, the bonds of Sheriff E. W. Kingsbury were deemed insufficient by the board of county commissioners on Febru-

C. B. Whitney

ary 11, 1869, and, since he had also left the state, the commissioners declared the office vacant.[4] Several letters were sent Gov. James M. Harvey recommending C. B. Whitney for the job. One, from Lorenzo Westover, county superintendent of public instruction, said: "Mr. Whitney whose name is respectfully recommended has served as Under Sheriff & [is] well versed in the business & will discharge the duties the best of any man. . . ."

Probate Judge George Geiger had different feelings about Whitney:

ELLSWORTH KAN Feby 24th 69

GOV HARVEY
   TOPEKA KAN
DR GOV

We are aware that the County Commissioners have recommended C B Whitney to you as a proper person for Sheriff of this County. The only reason they done so was that no one else would accept it, that is better than he. But as you have not sent the commission, we are glad of it, and desire that you will not send a commission to him, until we write you again. He is far from the proper person for sheriff, and we will write you again on this subject and reccommend some suitable person if we can get such a one to take it.

[Ex-Probate] Judge [James] Miller & I have been talking this matter over & I intended this for a joint letter, but he says he wrote you last night & I have read this to him & he approves of it— We are in an almost desperate position here, on a/c of the lawlessness of our people & the disregard of law & justice in some of our officers.

Very Respectfully
GEO GEIGER.

Judge Miller had written:

I am of the opinion it would be well for you to withhold the appointment of C B Whitney as sheriff of our County for a few days waiting developments that will occur soon. He is now acting sheriff and there is no great haste for a few days to have the place filled.

Two weeks after his first letter Mr. Westover had changed his mind. On February 25, 1869, he telegraphed the governor: "Appoint E. A. Kesler sheriff Ellsworth County."[5]

This switch might have helped turn the trick for within a few days the governor issued commission No. 84, dated March 1, 1869, appointing Kesler sheriff of Ellsworth county.[6]

Whitney was not around to run for sheriff at the general election of November 2, 1869. In July he, as a member of Co. A, Second battalion, Kansas State Militia, had been called to active service by the governor to provide frontier protection against hostile Indians.

631

Company A was commanded by Capt. A. J. Pliley, another veteran of the Battle of Beecher's Island. Whitney was the unit's first lieutenant.

Company A spent most of its active duty at a block house on Spillman creek in Lincoln county, just north of Ellsworth. The three officers and 54 men were on constant guard in their area, determined to prevent further depredations against settlers. On November 20, 1869, they were released and returned to their homes.[7]

More than a year later, on January 30, 1871, the board of county commissioners of Ellsworth county again declared the office of sheriff to be vacant. This time the bonds of J. Charles Seiber, who had defeated William Anderson at the general election of 1869, were declared insufficient. Again the name of C. B. Whitney was placed before the governor. Unfortunately a gap in the governor's correspondence prevents the disclosure of his actions but apparently Seiber was advised that he was still sheriff for he remained in office until he resigned July 3, 1871. This time the county commissioners did not recommend a particular person for the job, merely asking instead that the vacancy be filled.[8] No record has been found of the appointee.

The new sheriff was not Chauncey B. Whitney, however, for on July 27, 1871, he was named marshal of the city of Ellsworth, his salary to be $50 per month. His assistant, Tom Clark, earned $40. In addition each officer was paid $2.50 for each conviction resulting from an arrest made by him.[9]

Early records of Ellsworth are so scarce that it is not known how active the marshal and his assistant were during the winter of 1871-1872. It is known that on March 6, 1872, he was ordered by the city fathers to "instruct all 'soiled doves' that they will not be permitted to live in or carry on their business within the limits of the city of Ellsworth." [10] Also, on March 27, 1872, the council ordered that the marshal be paid his back salary. Since an ordinance passed in August, 1871, had raised the pay to $75, Whitney received $450 for the six months he had been without salary.[11]

It may have been that Marshal Whitney had been chosen sheriff at the election of November 7, 1871, for after January, 1872, he was referred to as sheriff in the county commissioners' "bills allowed" sections of their journal.[12] However, no returns

C. B. Whitney

were recorded in the journal as was the usual case in elections. Possibly Whitney was acting as sheriff when he unsuccessfully pursued the murderer mentioned in this Ellsworth *Reporter* article of March 28, 1872:

COLD BLOODED MURDER!

SHOT IN A PLACE OF ILL-FAME!

SLAUGHTERED IN THE HOUSE OF HIS FRIENDS

DIED WITH HIS BOOTS ON!

GONE WHERE THE WOODBINE TWINETH!

LOVE AMONG THE ROSES!

FISK AND STOKES IN LOW LIFE!

TRESPASSING ON ANOTHER MAN'S-FIELD!

THE MURDERER TAKEN WITH A LEAVING!

HYDE PARK BUSTED UP IN BUSINESS!

SOILED DOVES FLAPPING THEIR WINGS EASTWARD. LET 'EM FLAP.

SIC TRANSIT GLORIA MUNDI!

As a reporter, it has become our painful duty to chronicle one of the most scandelous, disgusting and cold blood murders that we have any recollection of.—The facts as brought out by the Coroners Jury are substantially as follows:

George Palmer, well known in this locality, had been for the last seven years living with one Lizzie Adams, a woman of the town. Within the last year they were married clandestinely, and afterward moved on a farm.—But alas, how frail the fair; Lizzie brooded over the solitude of the farm and pined for her numerous love-*yers* and a return to the old political faith, as laid down in the principles of the Victoria C. Woodhull party [which advocated free love].—She left the farm, resumed her occupation as Madam of the "*nauch,*" from which time up to last Friday night one Taylor DuBoise seems to have had full sway over the affections and cash of the frail Lizzie. True love never did run smooth, and did not in this instance. Shortly after her return to town her house and its contents were burned, and Palmer was arrested for starting the fire, but the evidence was not sufficient to hold him.

Not to be outdone, Lizzie fixed up another house, and just one month after the fire moved into her new quarters. The same day she sent the following poetry to Palmer.

TAKE ME BACK HOME AGAIN.

Take me back home again, take me back home,
Hopeless and helpless, in sorrow I roam;
Gone are the roses that gladdened my life,
I must toil on in the wearisome strife.
Once I was happy and friends were my lot,
Now I'm a wand'rer, despised and forgot!
Lonely and weary, in sorrow I roam,
Take me back home again, take me back home,
Take me back home again, take me back home.

633

George, dear George, so gentle and mild,
Look once again on thy pitiful child!
Since we were parted I never have known
Love and affection so pure as thine own!
Days of my childhood, I dream of you now,
While in my sorrow and anguish I bow!
No one to love me 'neath yon starry dome,
Take me back home again, take me back home,
Take me back home again, take me back home.

Oh, could I live but the days that are flown,
Dearest and sweetest that ever were known,
Fondly I weep in my desolate pain,
Longing to be with my George again!
Weary, so weary, my heart yearns for rest,
Poor wounded bird that is robbed of its nest!
Child of affliction! dear George, I come,
Take me back home again, take me back home,
Take me back home again, take me back home.

He went, we presume to take her back home again; stayed for supper; drank whisky and got mellow, in fact was drunk.

A short time after dark Taylor DuBoise entered the kitchen.—George and Lizzie were sitting on a bed talking over the things that were, both drunk and happy and unsuspecting danger.

Three shots were heard, parties were seen leaving the house, report spread that Palmer was killed, a crowd soon assembled and found a horrible, sickening sight. Lying on the floor, weltering in his own blood, was the body, all that was left of George Palmer.

From indications, it is thought that he was knocked down and then shot three times through the head, all the balls entering the forehead.

Palmer leaves considerable property, and, we have heard it stated, a family in Canada, which, if it be true, will be the cause of considerable litigation.

DuBoise, after committing the murder, went to Sanderson & Whites stable, took a pony belonging to Lizzies son and struck over the prarie. Cap. Whitney and others followed, but failed to overtake him. He made an attempt to steal a horse from Charley Bell, six miles from town but was foiled. He has not been heard of since.

The house in which the murder took place has been evacuated. The girls have moved to Kansas City and Madam Lizzie has taken to the farm. So mote it be.

About this same time it was rumored that the sheriff had been killed for trying to steal horses. Of the rumor the *Reporter*, March 28, 1872, said:

Ex-Sheriff Shot.—We notice an item floating around to the effect that the Sheriff of Ellsworth County was shot and killed, at Wichita, while stealing horses. That's hard on Capt. Whitney, but presume he can draw some consolation from the fact that he is getting well, that he was not shot while stealing horses, that he has not been shot since he has been filling the sheriffs office, and that he was not in the wicked burgh mentioned.

We presume the story originated from the shooting of J. C. Sieber, an ex-sheriff of this county, by a deputy U. S. Marshal.

Sieber was charged with stealing horses, the marshal undertook to arrest him, he resisted, got shot, is badly wounded but will hardly die, such men are hard to kill.

On April 3, 1872, Whitney resigned his city position and John L. Councell was appointed marshal.[13]

In December Whitney was after a bond thief. The *Reporter*, December 12, 1872, said he made the arrest at Wallace:

Sheriff Whitney arrested at Wallace a bond thief who was trying to escape with $8,000 he stole in the east. It takes Whitney to find them. The K. P. [formerly the Union Pacific, Eastern Division] is not a safe road for jail birds to fly over.

On August 15, 1873, Sheriff Whitney was shot by Billy Thompson, thus providing material for one of the perennial Western controversies—did Wyatt Earp disarm Ben Thompson, the brother of Whitney's killer? Contemporary records, including the Ellsworth *Reporter*, August 21, 1873, fail to mention the presence of Earp:

COLD BLOODED MURDER.

SHERIFF C. B. WHITNEY SHOT AND KILLED BY A DRUNKEN DESPERADO.

Ellsworth has had a tragedy at last! We had hoped that the season would pass without any sacrifice of citizens or visitors; but it was not to be. In a moment of desperation a reckless, headstrong, half drunken man shot down in cold blood Sheriff C. B. Whitney, who was unarmed, unaided, and was advising in a friendly way the threatening desperado to give up his arms and keep the peace. We will give the particulars of the unfortunate affair as correctly and as briefly as possible. Coroner Duck held an inquest Monday, but we are not at liberty to publish the testimony; the important points will probably agree with the following particulars:

The trouble originated over a game of cards, the players being well filled with whisky. One or two blows were given and the parties rushed for their guns. Ben and Bill Thompson obtained their arms, went into the street and called out: "Bring out your men if you want to fight." At this time Mr. Whitney came over to them and asked them to stop their fussing; then they all started towards [Joe] Brennan's saloon. Ben remained outside, walking up and down in front, with a rifle in his hands. Presently he pointed his rifle up street towards [Jerome] Beebe's store to Happy Jack [Morco], who was standing in the door-way, and fired; the ball hit the door casing, which saved Happy's life. The next moment Bill Thompson came out of the saloon with a double barreled shot gun, which he pointed at Mr. Whitney who made two

635

attempts to get out of the way before he shot and said "don't shoot."—
Thompson fired and Whitney received the charge. He whirled around twice,
screamed out that he was shot and called for his wife. Friends rushed to his
aid and carried him home.

After the shooting Bill Thompson went back into the saloon, and soon afterwards went across the street on horseback, towards the Grand Central [hotel].
Ben met him there, gave him a pistol and said: "For God's sake leave town;
you have shot Whitney, our best friend!" Bill replied that he did not give a
d---! that he would have shot "if it had been Jesus Christ!" He then rode
slowly out of town cursing and inviting a fight. Ben Thompson retained his
arms for a full hour after this, and no attempt was made to disarm him. Mayor
[James] Miller was at his residence during the shooting; he was notified of the
disturbance and he went immediately to Thompson and ordered him to give up
his arms, but his advice was not heeded. During this long hour where were
the police? [City Marshal John W. "Brocky Jack" Norton, Policemen John
"Happy Jack" Morco, and Ed Hogue.]

No arrest had been made, and the street was full of armed men ready to
defend Thompson. The police were arming themselves, and as they claim,
just ready to rally out and take, alive or dead, the violators of the law. They
were loading their muskets just as the Mayor, impatient at the delay in making
arrests, came along and discharged the whole force. It would have been better
to have increased the force, and discharged or retained the old police after
quiet was restored. The Mayor acted promptly and according to his judgment, but we certainly think it was a bad move. A poor police is better than
none, and if, as they claim, they were just ready for work, they should have
had a chance to redeem themselves and the honor of the city. Thus the city
was left without a police, with no one but Deputy Sheriff [Edward O.] Hogue
to make arrests. He received the arms of Ben Thompson on the agreement
of Happy Jack to give up his arms!

The unfortunate Sheriff was, in the meantime, suffering intensely, but there
was a slight hope for his life. Everything was being done to relieve him; Dr.
[William] Finlaw, of Junction City, was sent for, but he could not help him.
The wound was mortal. The gun was loaded with buck shot and the whole
charge was emptied in Whitney's arm, shoulder, and the fatal shot entered
his breast, passed down through the lungs and lodged in the back bone, making
an incurable wound.

Mr. Whitney was a member of the Masonic order, and he was attended
by his brothers in Masonry at his bedside, and buried by them in the Episcopal
church yard. Dr. Sternberg preached the funeral sermon before a very large
audience of mourners and friends. The services at the grave were also impressive. Dust was rendered to dust; safe from the storms, free from cares, in the
bosom of mother earth, rests the body of our late Sheriff C. B. Whitney.

Three and one-half years later Billy Thompson was returned for
trial. In preparation, the defense obtained several statements from
persons who were present at the shooting. One was made by
William Purdy:

C. B. Whitney

My name is William Purdy. I am a resident of the County of Atchison, State of Kansas. I was present at the shooting of C. B. Whitney by William Thompson in Ellsworth on the 15th day of August 1873. I was then acquainted with the said parties, Whitney & Thompson & with Ben Thompson, Happy Jack and John Stirling—Happy Jack was a general rowdy & Stirling was a gambler—each were desperate men and men of desperate characters.

Stirling, Cad Pierce & [Neil] Cain were in a saloon, I think it was, playing cards & when the game ended Ben Thompson having an interest in the game wanted a settlement with Sterling about the game—Stirling was drinking & got mad & struck Ben in the face. Happy Jack then run up & drew his six shooter on Ben. Ben told Jack to take Stirling away & pay attention to his own affairs. Jack & Stirling then went up the street. Shortly after that, Ben having gone into Jo Brennans saloon, Happy Jack & Sterling went to the front door of Brennans saloon, Stirling with a shot gun & Jack with a pair of six shooters. Happy Jack, I think it was, one of the two said so, said "Get your guns you dam Texas sons of bitches & fight." Ben, the next I saw of him, was coming from towards Jake News Saloon going towards the railroad north—After a while Ben & Billy Thompson & Whitney were together near the depot, the three then in an apparently friendly manner went across the railroad towards Brennans saloon and when they had got there, some one cried out "look out, as here they come." Happy Jack and Stirling were the persons refered to & they were then coming down the sidewalk towards Brennans saloon in a fast walk with their weapons (Stirling with a gun & Jack with pistols) drawn.

As this warning was given Ben whirled around towards the direction they were coming from as they advanced upon the Thompsons and the place where they were in a threatening manner Ben fired at them or one of them. Billy at that time I think was in the saloon doorway, Whitney was outside a few paces in advance of Billy Thompson & just to his left; Billy may have been on the walk, he was standing still or trying to do so, being at the time intoxicated. He at the time had his eyes fixed on the two parties advancing on him & Ben, that is, on Stirling & Jack, the shot of Ben did not stop them. They continued to advance the same as before & when within about twenty feet of Billy Thompson, his gun being down below his breast, it went off, one barrel of it only, and the shot took effect in the shoulder or side of Whitney. The parties, Billy Thompson, Whitney & Jack, at least, were in a triangle, Billys gun was cocked & apparently resting in his hands at the time it went off. I thought his right hand was on the hammer of the gun, he took no aim, did not bring the gun up, nor neither was he looking at Whitney, who stood at his left in advance looking towards Jack & Stirling. As the gun was discharged Ben said "My God Billy you have shot your best friend." Billy replied "I am sorry." Whitney said "He did not intend to do it, it was an accident, send for my family." There was no indication at any time, during the time of the shooting, before that time or after the shooting at the place when the shooting occurred, as in going across the street before the shooting that Whitney & the Thompsons were not on the best of terms.

Ben Thompson himself also sent a statement up from Texas. He said:

I will state that [I] was playing cards with John Sterling, Neil Cain and Cad Pierce in the Saloon of Joe Brenan, or rather they were playing and [I] was interested with Sterling. Sterling was drunk, and when the game ended, he had some money part of which was mine, and I asked for a settlement, whereupon he struck me in the face. Happy Jack then ran up and drew his pistol on me, and I told him not to interfere with me but to take this drunken man off, which he did as they started off together up street. I then returned to the Brenan saloon—and I was in conversation with Cad Pierce in the back part of the Saloon when Sterling and Happy Jack came back to the front door of the Saloon, Sterling with a shot-gun and Happy Jack with one or more pistols, then one of them (I do not Know which one it was) cried out get your guns, you Texas Sons of bitches and fight. It created considerable excitement at the time.

I then enquired of several for a pistol or arms, but could not get any, whereupon I ran out the back of the Saloon to Jake News saloon and got my six-shooter and a Winchester rifle & started out in the middle of the street to the railroad, so that if a difficulty should happen we would be in open ground and innocent parties would not get hurt. Just at this time when I left Jake New's Saloon I met my brother Wm. Thompson, who was very drunk and had his double barrel shot gun in his hand with both barrells cocked. I then advised & entreated him to go in the house & put up his gun as he was too drunk to do anything and that he would kill some of his best friends if he was not careful how he handled his gun. I had no sooner told him this, than one barrel of his gun went off accidentally and struck in the lower part of the side-walk in front of New's Saloon very near the feet of two of our friends to wit: Maj. Seth Mabry and Capt. Millett—I then got the gun away from him and tried to remove the catridges but they were brass and so much swollen that I could not get them out.

At this time some one (I do not now Know who it was) came to me & told me I had better look out, that those fellows were after me. I then handed my brother's gun to some party standing by & went out on the railroad in the middle of the street. A moment or so after I got there my brother came out where I was with his gun. I then hallowed back to the crowd that if they, the damn sons of bitches, wanted to fight us here we are. About this time Whitney and John Delong an ex-policeman came out to where we were from the crowd & Whitney said "boys, don't have any row. I will do all I can to protect you. You know that John and I are your friends." I then said I know that Whitney. Whitney then said "Come on let us go over to Brenan's and take a drink." I said all right I will do so and get Billy (meaning my brother) to put up his gun. Whitney said that is right—Billy is drunk and you are sober and he will shoot some one accidentally—we then both requested Billy to let down the hammers of his gun as he had already come very near shooting two of his friends.

We then all walked over to the saloon in a friendly conversation. When

638

C. B. *Whitney*

we asked Billy to let down the hammers of his gun he made no reply & failed
to let them down, but said he would leave the gun when he got to the saloon,
that "he was not going to let those damn Son's of bitches get the best of Ben"
(meaning me). . . .

Whitney, my Brother William Thompson, John Delong, and myself were
going into Brenan's Saloon at the request of Whitney to take a drink, he having invited us, and just as the above named parties were entering the Saloon,
I being behind and just in the act of entering the door, some one from behind, hollowed to me saying "look out Ben" or "look out Thompson" I cannot
now remember which expression was used. I looked around supposing it was
. . . John Sterling & Happy Jack, that were referred to. When I looked
around I saw Happy Jack coming down the street with a Six-shooter in each
hand in a fast run, he came within twenty-five or thirty steps of me and ran
into Bebee's store. Just at time Whitney and William Thompson came out of
the Saloon at the same door they had just entered, Whitney being a step or
two in advance, I being about eight feet from them, my brother at this time
was very drunk, so much so that he staggered a great deal. He had his gun
in his hands at the time both barrells being Cocked, and just as he was coming out of the door the gun went off accidentally and struck Whitney in the
shoulder.

The gun was not pointed at Whitney, but as he staggered out of the door
with the gun in his hands it went off accidentally. A few moments before
both Whitney & myself had cautioned William Thompson to be careful how
he handled his gun or he would shoot one of us—we cautioned him for the
reason that he was very drunk and was carrying the gun in his hands with
both barrells cocked and we were afraid that some such accident might happen—Just as William Thompsons gun fired and shot Whitney, Whitney exclaimed, "My God Billy you have shot me" and at the same time I remarked
"My God you have shot our best friend" or words to that effect. At this time
William Thompson was so drunk that he did not seem to realize what had
occurred. He made some remark but I could not understand what it was.[14]

Billy Thompson was acquitted on September 14, 1877.[15]

1. "Diary of Chauncey B. Whitney," *Kansas Historical Collections*, v. 12, pp. 296-299.
2. "Ellsworth County Commissioners' Records," Journal A (transcribed by the Historical
Records Survey of the Work Projects Administration, in archives division, Kansas State
Historical Society), pp. 14, 19, 21, 37. 3. Copy of undated letter from the War De-
partment, Office of the Quartermaster General, "Forsyth Indian Scouts," *The Beecher Island
Annual* (1930 edition), pp. 59, 60. 4. "Ellsworth County Commissioners' Records,"
loc. cit., Journal A, pp. 55, 56. 5. "Governors' Correspondence," archives division, Kansas
State Historical Society. 6. "Records of the Secretary of State, Commissions, January
12-July 28, 1869," archives division, Kansas State Historical Society. 7. *Report of the
Adjutant General: 1869* (n. p.), pp. 9, 10. 8. "Ellsworth County Commissioners' Rec-
ords," *loc. cit.*, Journal A, pp. 69, 116, 129; "Governors' Correspondence," archives division,
Kansas State Historical Society. 9. "Minutes of the City Council," p. 1; "Ordinance Num-
ber One, Ordinance Book," Records of the City of Ellsworth. 10. "Minutes of the City
Council," Records of the City of Ellsworth, pp. 7, 8. 11. *Ibid.*, p. 12. 12. "Ellsworth
County Commissioners' Records," *loc. cit.*, Journal A, p. 147. 13. "Minutes of the City
Council," Records of the City of Ellsworth, p. 15. 14. "Testimony and Records in the
Case of State of Kansas vs. William Thompson," Records of the Ellsworth County District
Court. 15. Western buffs may be interested in knowing that the shotgun used to kill

Sheriff Whitney is in the possession of Mrs. Merritt Beeson of the Beeson Museum, Dodge City. According to Ben Thompson, in his statement in defense of Billy, "the shot-gun was a present to me from Cad Pierce and was worth about one hundred and fifty dollars. . . ."

For other articles on Ellsworth's early history *see* F. B. Streeter, "Tragedies of a Cow Town," *The Aerend: A Kansas Quarterly*, Hays, v. 5 (Spring, Summer, 1934), pp. 81-96, 145-162; F. B. Streeter, "Ellsworth as a Texas Cattle Market," *The Kansas Historical Quarterly*, Topeka, v. 4 (November, 1935), pp. 388-398; George Jelinek, *Ellsworth, Kansas, 1867-1947* (Salina, n. d.) and *90 Years of Ellsworth and Ellsworth County History* (Ellsworth, n. d.); and Robert Dykstra, "Ellsworth, 1869-1875: The Rise and Fall of a Kansas Cowtown," *The Kansas Historical Quarterly*, Topeka, v. 27 (Summer, 1961), pp. 161-192.

Appendix – The All-Star Cast

Principals and Supporting Players

The names of about 250 peace officers, who served in the seven Kansas cowtowns reviewed in this book, are herewith appended. Although the stories of 57 have been featured individually and at length, there was so little information about the remainder that separate treatment for them was not justified. This list is not to be considered complete, for no effort was made to search out additional names merely for the sake of lengthening the cast of characters.

All the offices fall into two categories: those with a direct succession and those without.

By direct succession is meant offices which have only one occupant at a time, such as U. S. marshal for Kansas, sheriff, city marshal, undersheriff, assistant city marshal and constable. Names of persons occupying these positions may be listed more than once if they served non-consecutive terms.

Appointments of deputy U. S. marshals, deputy sheriffs and policemen were made as needed, and without regard to number. Therefore, names under these titles have been recorded as nearly chronologically as possible beginning with the first mention of their service.

Only year dates have been given. Some persons, though, may have served as little as one day. The years shown are not necessarily terminal, but are merely those within which mention of the officer was found.

FEDERAL OFFICERS

United States Marshals for Kansas (1864 to 1886 Only)

Thomas A. Osborn, 1864-1867
Charles C. Whiting, 1867-1869
Dana W. Houston, 1869-1873
William S. Tough, 1873-1876
Charles H. Miller, 1876-1878
Benjamin F. Simpson, 1878-1886

Deputy United States Marshal at Abilene

James Gainsford, 1871

Deputy United States Marshal at Caldwell

Cassius M. Hollister, 1883-1884

Deputy United States Marshals at Dodge City

Harry T. McCarty, 1878
William B. "Bat" Masterson, 1879
Hamilton B. Bell, 1880-1885
Frederick Singer, 1885

Deputy United States Marshals at Hays

James Butler "Wild Bill" Hickok, 1867-1868
Joe Weiss, 1869
C. J. Cox, 1869
Jack L. Bridges, 1869-1876

Deputy United States Marshal at Newton

Harry Nevill, 1871

Deputy United States Marshals at Wichita

W. N. Walker, 1871
Michael Meagher, 1874
William Smith, 1875
Charles B. Jones, 1879-1881

"Detective"

William Frederick "Buffalo Bill" Cody, 1868

COUNTY, TOWNSHIP, AND CITY OFFICERS

DICKINSON COUNTY

Sheriffs

Thomas Shurn, 1866-1868?
H. H. Hazlett, 1868-1870
Joseph A. Cramer, 1870
T. N. Wiley, 1870-1872?
C. L. Murphy, 1872-1876

Under Sheriffs

Thomas James "Bear River Tom" Smith, 1870
T. N. Wiley, 1870

Deputy Sheriff

Thomas James "Bear River Tom" Smith, 1870

GRANT TOWNSHIP

Constables

William Chapman, 1867-1868
J. Pettit, 1867-1868
C. H. Thompson, 1868-1869
Moses Barber, 1868-1869
M. Benson, 1869-1870
C. Schultree, 1869-1870
T. N. Wiley, 1870-1871
Charles Shane, 1870-1871
James Gainsford, 1871-1872
D. R. Thomas, 1871-1872

ABILENE

Chief of Police or Marshals

Thomas James "Bear River Tom" Smith, 1870 (Chief of Police)
Patrick Hand, 1870-1871 (CofP)
James Butler "Wild Bill" Hickok, 1871
James A. Gauthie, 1871-?

Policemen

James A. Gauthie, 1870
James H. McDonald, 1870-1871
Thomas Carson, 1871
James Gainsford, 1871
John W. "Brocky Jack" Norton, 1871
Mike Williams, 1871

ELLIS COUNTY

Sheriffs

T. Gannon, 1867
James Butler "Wild Bill" Hickok, 1869-1870
Peter Lanihan (or Lanahan), 1870-1872

Deputy Sheriff

Peter Lanihan, 1869-1870

Appendix—The All-Star Cast

BIG CREEK TOWNSHIP

Constables

W. L. Totten, 1867
Peter Carrol, 1867
Frank Shepherd, 1871

ELLSWORTH COUNTY

Sheriffs

E. W. Kingsbury, 1867-1869
E. A. Kesler, 1869
J. Charles Seiber, 1869-1871
Chauncey Belden Whitney, 1871-1873
H. D. Stebbins, 1873-1876

Under Sheriffs

Chauncey Belden Whitney, 1870
———— ———— Stephens, 1874

Deputy Sheriffs

Edward O. Hogue, 1871-1873
Thomas Walker, 1873

ELLSWORTH TOWNSHIP

Constables

Chauncey Belden Whitney, 1867-1873
J. Tobin, 1868-1869
F. Sternberg, 1870-1871
J. J. Kelly, 1871-1872
Thomas O'Laughlin, 1871-1872
A. T. Beebe, 1873-1874
John H. Stevens, 1874-1875
Edward O. Hogue, 1874-1875
William Brown, 1875

ELLSWORTH

Marshals

Chauncey Belden Whitney, 1871-1872
John L. Councell, 1872
Edward O. Hogue, 1872
John W. "Brocky Jack" Norton, 1872-1873
Edward O. Hogue, 1873
Richard Freeborn, 1873
J. Charles Brown, 1873-1875
W. S. Bradshaw, 1875

Assistant Marshals

Tom Clark, 1871
John W. "Brocky Jack" Norton, 1872

Policemen

William "Apache Bill" Semans, 1869 (Ellsworth had no regular force at this time)
Tom Walley (?), 1872
John W. "Brocky Jack" Norton, 1872
J. F. Bugau (Beegan?), 1872
R. V. Welch, 1872
Edward O. Hogue, 1872, 1873
John L. Councell, 1872
B. Searcy, 1872
Casper G. Winfel (?), 1872
W. H. Crowen (?), 1872
J. Samuel Wimsett, 1872
William L. Brooks, 1872
Edwin Doyles (?), 1872
John "Long Jack" DeLong, 1873
W. W. Fletcher, 1873
John "Happy Jack" Morco, 1873
John S. "High Low Jack" Branham, 1873
D. L. Beach, 1873
Ed Crawford, 1873
J. Charles Brown, 1873

FORD COUNTY

Sheriffs

Charles E. Bassett, 1873-1878
William B. "Bat" Masterson, 1878-1880
George T. Hinkle, 1880-1884
Patrick F. Sughrue, 1884-1888

Under Sheriffs

William B. "Bat" Masterson, 1877-1878
Charles E. Bassett, 1878-1880
Frederick Singer, 1880-1884
Ed Cooley, 1880 (acting)
T. J. Tate, 1884
Daniel Sughrue, 1885

643

Deputy Sheriffs

Edward O. Hogue, 1875
Lawrence E. Deger, 1877
Miles Mix, 1877
Joseph W. Mason, 1877, 1878
Simeon Woodruff, 1878
William Duffey, 1878-1880
A. S. Tracy, 1878
John Straughn, 1878-1881
Murray Wear, 1879
L. M. DePuy, 1879-1880
James P. Masterson, 1879
William Morton, 1879
David Boyd, 1879
Thomas Bugg, 1881, 1882
George Baker, 1882
H. P. Myton, 1882-1883
————— ————— Keith, 1882
David "Mysterious Dave" Mather, 1883-1884
William F. Combs, 1883
Nelson Cary, 1883, 1884
Clark E. Chipman, 1884
Michael Sughrue, 1884-1885
William Mathew Tilghman, Jr., 1884-1886
E. G. Barlow, 1884
————— ————— Moreland, 1884
Ben Daniels, 1884
E. E. Davids, 1884
William Thompson, 1884
Frederick Singer, 1885
William B. "Bat" Masterson, 1885, 1886

DODGE TOWNSHIP

Constables

Mick Walch, 1874-1875
Jerome L. Jackett, 1874-1875
David "Prairie Dog Dave" Morrow, 1875, 1883
James Wilson, 1875
James H. McGoodwin, 1877
Patrick F. Sughrue, 1877-1879
Frederick Singer, 1880
Clark E. Chipman, 1882

644

Thomas Bugg, 1882
Nelson Cary, 1884
O. D. Wilson, 1884

DODGE CITY

Marshals

Lawrence E. Deger, 1876-1877
Edward J. Masterson, 1877-1878
Charles E. Bassett, 1878-1879
————— ————— Clark, 1879 (acting)
James P. Masterson, 1879-1881
Frederick Singer, 1881
B. C. Vanderberg (or Vanderburg), 1881
Peter W. Beamer, 1882
Alonzo B. Webster, 1882 (mayor, acting marshal)
Jack L. Bridges, 1882-1884
William Mathew Tilghman, Jr., 1884-1886
T. J. Tate, 1886
Frederick Singer, 1886-1887
Andrew Falkner, 1887

Assistant Marshals

Wyatt Berry Stapp Earp, 1876-1877
Edward J. Masterson, 1877
Charles E. Bassett, 1877-1878
Nat. L. Haywood, 1878
John Brown, 1878
Wyatt Berry Stapp Earp, 1878-1879
Alpha Updegraff, 1879
Neil Brown, 1879-1881
Thomas C. Nixon, 1881-1882
Clark E. Chipman, 1882-1883
David "Mysterious Dave" Mather, 1883-1884
Thomas C. Nixon, 1884
Ben Daniels, 1884-1886

Policemen

Joseph W. Mason, 1877, 1878
David "Prairie Dog Dave" Morrow, 1877
John Brown, 1878
Charles Trask, 1878

Appendix—The All-Star Cast

James P. Masterson, 1878-1879
John Joshua Webb, 1879
Lee Harlan, 1882
Clark E. Chipman, 1883
B. L. Vanderburg, 1883
A. J. Marshall (or Jack A. Marshall), 1884-1886

Special (Extra) Policemen

William B. "Bat" Masterson, 1877
John Joshua Webb, 1877, 1878
William Barkman, 1879
David Boyd, 1880
George Goodell, 1880
Frank Warren, 1880
Louis (or Lewis) C. Hartman, 1883
Grant Wells, 1883
J. J. Clinton, 1883
Frederick Singer, 1883
L. W. Jones, 1883
Nelson Cary, 1883
Clark E. Chipman, 1883
B. C. Vanderberg, 1883
Harry Scott, 1884
William Boles (or Bowles), 1884
Ben Daniels, 1884
W. J. Howard, 1884
F. Sharp, 1884

HARVEY COUNTY

Deputy Sheriff

Carlos B. King, 1871

NEWTON TOWNSHIP

Constable

Tom Carson, 1871

NEWTON

Marshal

William L. Brooks, 1872

SEDGWICK COUNTY

Sheriffs

W. N. Walker, 1870
John Meagher, 1871-1873

William Smith, 1873-1874
Pleasant H. Massey, 1873-1876
H. W. Dunning, 1875

Deputy Sheriffs

J. Charles Seiber, 1871
John Meagher, 1871
John Brennan, 1872
J. C. Morehouse, 1872
George D'Amour, 1871-1873?
William Smith, 1873
Tence Massey, 1874-1876
H. W. Dunning, 1875-1876
Yank Owens, 1875

WICHITA TOWNSHIP

Constables

Simon K. Ohmert, 1872
George D'Amour, 1872
J. W. McCartney, 1873
George W. Prentiss, 1873-1874
William Smith, 1874
J. F. Humphrey, 1875
Charles B. Jones, 1876
D. X. Williams, 1876

WICHITA

Marshals

Ike S. Elder, 1870
Isaac Walker, 1870
John Marshall, 1870-1871
William Smith, 1871
Michael Meagher, 1871-1874
William Smith, 1874-1875
Michael Meagher, 1875-1877

First Assistant Marshals

John Meagher, 1871
Simon K. Ohmert, 1871-1872
Thomas E. Parks, 1872
George D'Amour, 1872-1873
James M. Antrim, 1873
Daniel F. Parks, 1873-1875
John Behrens, 1875-1876

Second Assistant Marshals

Daniel F. Parks, 1871
George D'Amour, 1871
James M. Antrim, 1872

Policemen

Bradford J. (?) Dean, 1871
Adam Roberts, 1871
William E. Reid, 1871
Charles W. Allen, 1871
Simon K. Ohmert, 1871
Charles G. Bratton, 1871-1872
Daniel F. Parks, 1872-1873, 1876
W. E. Harwig, 1872-1873
John Nugent, 1872-1873
James M. Antrim, 1873
William Dibbs, 1873-1874
C. J. Walters, 1873
James Cairns, 1873-1875
Hank Zuber (Henry Luber?), 1873
Joseph T. Hooker, 1874
John Behrens, 1874-1875
Samuel Botts, 1874-1875
John M. Martin, 1875
Wyatt Berry Stapp Earp, 1875-1876
Fred Hannum, 1875-1876
R. C. Richey, 1876

Special (Extra) Policemen

Simon K. Ohmert, 1871, 1872
J. C. Morehouse, 1872, 1873
Caleb Wells, 1872
John S. "High Low Jack" Branham, 1872
Charles G. Bratton, 1872
Thomas E. Parks, 1872
George M. Richards, 1872
George D'Amour, 1872
James Manning, 1872
Ben F. Morris, 1872
George S. Henry, 1872
D. W. Bromwell, 1872
Benjamin Newman, 1873
James W. Ray, 1874
Joseph T. Hooker, 1874
John Nugent, 1874
Myron Baker, 1874

John Crook, 1874
John Doyle, 1874
L. F. Burris, 1874
S. Burris, 1874
John Royal, 1874
C. E. Hall, 1874, 1875
D. X. Williams, 1874, 1875
E. Warren, 1874
J. Emerson, 1875
John Wilson, 1875, 1876
James Cairns, 1875
William Botts, 1875
William Dibbs, 1875
James Gregg, 1875, 1876
James W. Ray, 1875
C. E. Viney, 1875
Phillip Smith, 1875
S. G. Creswell, 1876
Thomas Moore, 1876
Prince Owens, 1876
R. C. Richey, 1876

SUMNER COUNTY

Sheriffs

J. J. Ferguson, 1871
G. A. Hamilton, 1872
John G. Davis, 1872-1875
Joseph M. Thralls, 1875
John K. Hastie, 1875
James E. Reed, 1876
L. K. Myers, 1878
Joseph M. Thralls, 1880-1884
Frank Henderson, 1884

Deputy Sheriffs

Wes E. Thralls, 1882-1883
Hamilton Raynor, 1884
Cassius M. Hollister, 1884

CALDWELL TOWNSHIP

Constables

W. C. Kelly, 1879
W. H. Harrison, 1879
Daniel William Jones, 1880
Willis Metcalf, 1882
——— ——— McCulloch, 1883

Appendix—The All-Star Cast

Deputy Constable
John Wilson, 1879

CALDWELL

Marshals
George W. Flatt, 1879-1880
William N. Horseman, 1880
C. F. Betts, 1880
William N. Horseman, 1880
James W. Johnson, 1880
John W. Phillips, 1881
Michael Meagher, 1881
James Roberts, 1881
John Rowan, 1881
John Wilson, 1881-1882
George S. Brown, 1882
J. A. Neal, 1882
B. P. "Bat" Carr, 1882
Henry Newton Brown, 1882-1884
Cassius M. Hollister, 1884
John W. Phillips, 1884-1885
Bedford B. Wood, 1885

Assistant Marshals
Daniel William Jones, 1879-1880
John Rowan, 1880

Joe Dolan, 1880-1881
Newt Miller, 1881
James Roberts, 1881
Will D. Fossett, 1881
Henry Newton Brown, 1882
Bedford B. Wood, 1882
Ben F. Wheeler, 1882-1884
Cassius M. Hollister, 1883, 1884
Henry Fulton, 1884

Policemen
Samuel H. Rogers, 1880
James W. Johnson, 1880
J. Frank Hunt, 1880
John Wilson, 1880
Newt Miller, 1880-1881
John Rowan, 1881
James Sharpe, 1881
Willis Metcalf, 1882
Henry Fulton, 1884
Bedford B. Wood, 1884-1885

Special (Extra) Policemen
Daniel William Jones, 1880
———— ———— Reed, 1880
Cassius M. Hollister, 1884

GOVERNOR'S PROCLAMATION.

$1700 REWARD!

STATE OF KANSAS,

Executive Department, Topeka, Dec. 9, 1882.

I, JOHN P. ST. JOHN, Governor of the State of Kansas, by virtue of the authority vested in me by law, do hereby offer a reward of **FIVE HUNDRED DOLLARS** for the arrest and conviction of one Jim. Talbott, as principal, and **THREE HUNDRED DOLLARS** each, for the arrest and conviction of Jim. Martin, Bob. Munson, Bob. Bigtree, and Dug. Hill, as accessories, to the murder of **MIKE. MEAGHER,** in Sumner County, Kansas, on or about the 17th day of December, 1881.

In Testimony Whereof, I have hereunto subscribed my name, and affixed the Great Seal of the State, at Topeka, the day and year first above written.

[L. S.]

JOHN P. ST. JOHN.

By the Governor:

JAMES SMITH,

Secretary of State.

Facsimile of reward poster issued by the state of Kansas for the apprehension of the murderers of Mike Meagher at Caldwell, December 17, 1881. (See pp. 498-505.)

Acknowledgments and Credits

We gratefully acknowledge our deep indebtedness to those fine cowtown newspapermen who were responsible for many of these colorful accounts. Since organization of the Kansas State Historical Society in 1875, the editors of Kansas have regularly sent copies of all their issues for permanent preservation at Topeka. Some of these files would not be available anywhere today were it not for the faithfulness of these publishers.

The complete co-operation of the officials of cities and counties represented in this survey should also be made a matter of record. Without their aid, much significant information would not have been accessible.

Deserving of special mention are Waldo E. Koop, Wichita; Robert Dykstra, Iowa City, Iowa; and Joseph G. Rosa, Ruislip, Middlesex, England, for the exchange of information about certain figures and places currently in their fields of study; and to Paul I. Wellman, Los Angeles, Calif., for helpful suggestions.

Our warm thanks are also due the following individuals who helped in various ways to assemble and publish this information: Judge George Allison, McPherson; Frank H. Backstrom, Wichita; Mrs. Lela Barnes, Topeka; Forrest R. Blackburn, Topeka; Mrs. Charles G. C. Blake, Wichita; Albin DeBacker, Topeka; Eugene D. Decker, Topeka; Jess C. Denious, Jr., Dodge City; Mrs. Laura Allyn Ekstrom, Denver, Colo.; Joe Fox, Newton; Mrs. Alys Freeze, Denver, Colo.; Lucile Fry, Boulder, Colo.; Mrs. Caroline Glover, Caldwell; Mrs. Harriet Graham, Wichita; George Hawley, Topeka; Elaine Hayes, St. Louis, Mo.; Daniel D. Holt, Hoyt; Bill Jackson, Wichita; George Jelinek, Ellsworth; Mrs. Mary Lou Jenson, Topeka; Charles E. Jones, Wichita; Harry Kirchmeyer, Topeka; Richard Kerr, Topeka; C. P. Kimble, Los Angeles, Calif.; Roy T. King, St. Louis, Mo.; Stuart N. Lake, San Diego, Calif.; Mrs. Cora Land, Fort Scott; Edgar Langsdorf, Topeka; Raymond McCabe, Topeka; Richard G. Magnuson, Wallace, Idaho; Don Marsh, Topeka; Fred Mazzula, Denver, Colo.; Mary Mewes, St. Louis, Mo.; Bill Nye, Wichita; Harvey Ray, Topeka; Robert W. Richmond, Topeka; Theo. A. Sanborn, Belleville; Agnes Schecher, Topeka; Fred J. Smith, Chanute; Mrs. Lorena Sneller, Topeka; Joe Sughrue, Pueblo, Colo.; Clifford E. Sutton, Wichita; Mrs. Enid T. Thompson, Denver; William Unrau, Lindsborg; and W. J. van Wormer, Wichita.

Special appreciation is extended to Mrs. Merritt L. Beeson, Dodge City, for the many photographs and other items she courteously made available for reproduction here. Several on which she reserves all reproduction rights are so labeled on the pages of publication. In addition to these, the following photographs are credited to her and to the Beeson Museum:

117, Long Branch saloon interior.
118, Ben Daniels.
119, Dodge City, 1878.

233, Dead soldiers at Hays.
238, Delmonico Hotel register.
355, Dodge City peace commission with W. F. Petillon.
356, Nicholas B. Klaine.
476, Pat Sughrue.

Receipt of other photographs is gratefully acknowledged as follows:

114, Ellsworth, 1872; 478, Ben and Bill Thompson: Mrs. Floyd B. Streeter, Hays.

115, Newton, 1872: Waldo E. Koop, Wichita.

118, Clay Allison; 234, Wyatt Earp; 240, Rowdy Joe Lowe: Ed Bartholomew, Toyahvale, Tex.

236, Wichita police committee report: Wichita city clerk's office.

238, Ed and Jim Masterson: Mrs. Cora Land, Fort Scott.

354, Dodge City peace commission with Bill Tilghman: Oklahoma Historical Society.

476, William Smith: Fred J. Smith, Chanute.

476, Mike Sughrue: Herman L. Sughrue, Winslow, Ariz.

477, Bill Tilghman: University of Oklahoma Library.

477, Loading Texas Longhorns, sketch from *Frank Leslie's Illustrated Newspaper*, New York, August 19, 1871.

480, Medicine Lodge bank robbers: C. Q. Chandler, Wichita.

Topeka, Kansas
October 20, 1963

NYLE H. MILLER
JOSEPH W. SNELL

Index

Auling, Henry: 95
Austin, Tex.: 75, 203, 458, 617
Autubees, Mariana: 189
Avery, ――, Fort Scott, Kan.: 285
Avery, C. T.: 167

Baden, B. L.: 272
Bailey, James A.: 367-369, 375-377
Bailey, Lawrence G., Caldwell, Kan.:
    167, 244, 245, 512
Bailey, Nellie C.: 224
Bailey, William: see William Baylor
Baker, ――, Okla.: 57
Baker, George: 644
Baker, H. C.: 471
Baker, J. J.: 106
Baker, Myron: 646
Balderston, J. M., Wichita, Kan.: 283,
    584
Baldwin, Arthur: 365
Baldwin, Lt. Frank D.: 319-321
Baldwin, Fred L.: 406
Baldwin, Nettie: 16
Baldwin, William, Wichita, Kan.:
    146
Bambridge, J.: 213
Banks, Albert: 226
Banks, Gerard: 226
Barber, E., Abilene, Kan.: 107, 171,
    200
Barber, Moses: 413, 415, 642
Barde, Frederick S.: 319
Baris, ――, Dodge City, Kan.: 293
Barkman, William: 342, 645
Barlow, E. G.: 589, 644
Barnard, M. M.: 518
Barnes, David: 604; killed by Dave
    Mather, 467-472
Barnes, John: 468-471
Barrett, Patsey: 458
Barrett's New United Monster Rail-
    road Show: 127
Bass, Sam: 30, 327
Bassett, Charles E., Dodge City, Kan.:
    86, 87, 129, 133, 143, 144, 154,
    210, 211, 220, 275, 279, 294, 297,
    298, 307-310, 323, 324, 327, 328,
    335-339, 345, 350, 363, 376-379,
    381-386, 388, 406, 452, 560, 563,
    643, 644; biographical sketch of,
    28-37; photos of, 354, 355

Bates, R.: 244, 245
Baxter Springs, Kan.: 577
Baylor, William: killed by Mike
    McCluskie, 99, 100, 103
Bayly, Dr. Russell: 451
Beach, D. L.: 643
Beals, E. H., Caldwell, Kan.: 59, 71,
    226
Beamer, Peter W., Dodge City, Kan.:
    108, 109, 644
Bear creek, Clark county, Kan.: 573,
    591
"Bear River Tom": see Thomas
    James Smith
Beard, E. T. "Red": 52, 256, 260,
    268; killed (by Rowdy Joe Lowe?),
    261-267
Beardstown, Ill.: 262, 263
Beatty, P. L., Dodge City, Kan.: 22,
    275, 306, 328, 352
Beatty & Kelley restaurant and saloon,
    Dodge City, Kan.: 14, 17, 34, 323,
    326, 595, 608
Beaver creek, Okla.: 320, 321, 336,
    337, 370
Becker, ――, Wichita, Kan.: 287
Becker, A. A. (alias of Rowdy Joe
    Lowe): 269, 270
Beebe, A. T.: 643
Beebe, Carrie (Mrs. Walter): 266
Beebe, Jerome, Ellsworth, Kan.: 85,
    123, 124, 635
Beebe, Walter, Wichita, Kan.: 263,
    269, 272
Beecher, Lt. Frederick Henry: 629
Beecher Island, battle of: 629, 630,
    632
Beegan, J. F.: see J. F. Bugau
Been, ――, Wise county, Tex.: 63
Been, Ed: 64
Been, Jim: 64
Beer Garden, Abilene, Kan.: 9, 13
Beeson, Chalkley M., Dodge City,
    Kan.: 10, 21, 36, 86, 158, 304, 345,
    395, 410, 427, 519, 520, 539, 551,
    598; photo of, 117
Beeson, Charley: 17
Beeson & Harris saloon, Dodge City,
    Kan.: 323, 519, 608; see, also, Long
    Branch saloon
Behan, Johnny: 159

Index

Brown, John, Caldwell, Kan.: 511
Brown, John, Dodge City, Kan.: 377
Brown, John, Dodge City, Kan.: 307, 308, 644; biographical sketch of, 86, 87
Brown, L. E.: 248
Brown, Maude (Mrs. Henry N.): 80, 81, 83; see, also, Alice Maude Levagood
Brown, Neil (or Neal?), Dodge City, Kan.: 128, 310, 312, 436, 562, 566, 622, 644; biographical sketch of, 87-89; photos of, 354, 355
Brown, W. A.: 494
Brown, W. R.: 376
Brown, William: 643
Brown, William H.: 366-368, 375, 376
Brownsville, Neb.: 576
Brush, G. M.: 592
Brusten, A. J.: 297
Bryson, William: see William Brison
"Buckskin Bill": 576
"Buckskin Joe": 178
Buena Vista, Colo.: 408
"Buffalo Bill": see William Frederick Cody
Buffalo Park, Kan.: 40
Buffalo Springs, Okla.: 56
Buffalo Station, Kan.: 193
Bugau (or Beegan?), J. F.: 643
Bugg, Thomas, Dodge City, Kan.: 413, 414, 567, 570, 644; biographical sketch of, 90, 91
Bullard, —— ——, Dodge City, Kan.: 466
Bullard, S. A., Dodge City, Kan.: 545, 546
Bullwhacker creek, Okla.: 499
Buntline, Ned: 584
Burchett, B. W.: 592
Burk, Jennie: 248
Burlingame, Ward: 30
Burlingame, Kan.: 42
Burns, Lt. N. H.: 174
Burns, Robert E., Dodge City, Kan.: 49, 427, 428, 455, 522, 544, 562, 563
Burris, L. F.: 646
Burris, Samuel: 141, 645, 646
Burroughs, S. A., Abilene, Kan.: 98, 199
Burrus, Cass, Caldwell, Kan.: 502

Burton, Ben F. (alias of Ben Wheeler): 83
Burton, George: 453
Bush, Jim: 257
Buskirk, Frank: 295
Byrd, William: see William Bird

Cahn, Elias: 21, 22
Cain, Neil: 637, 638
Cairns, James, Wichita, Kan.: 139, 145, 148, 491, 492, 585, 646
"Calamity Bill": 330
Caldwell, Kan.: 2, 4, 15, 47, 54-57, 160, 495, 496, 503-505, 554, 556, 571; peace officers at, 57-84, 91-97, 163-170, 221-232, 241-255, 497, 498, 510-519, 625-629, 646, 647; saloon, photo of, 1880's, 116; summary of 1880 arrests, 247, 248
"California Bill": 192
California Hall, Denver, Colo.: 441
Calkins, Judd: 54, 55
Callaham, John F.: 28-30
Callaham, R. C.: 28, 29
Calloway, Thomas: kills Charles Fay, 577
Camp, C. P.: 468
Camp Supply, Okla.: 280, 281, 321, 369, 370
Camp Walker (Mo.? or Ark.?): 175
Campbell, A. B.: 564, 601
Campbell, Dave: 317
Campbell, Thomas: 340
Campbell, W. E.: 498, 499, 502
Campbell, William P.: 164, 263, 282, 287, 289, 582
Canadian river: 315-317, 320, 321, 337
Canby, Gen. Edward R. S.: 554
Canida, C. T.: 169
Canon City, Colo.: 391, 392
Cantonment, Okla.: 68, 500
Caplice and Ryan, Hays, Kan.: 195
Carlyle, James: 317
Carney, Thomas: 11, 12
Carpenter, John, Wichita, Kan.: 287
Carpenter, Samuel, Abilene, Kan.: 98, 199, 200
Carr A. W.: 224, 225
Carr, B. P. "Bat," Caldwell, Kan.: 67, 69, 82, 626, 647; biographical sketch of, 91-97

"Carrie," Dodge City, Kan.: 293
Carrol, Peter: 643
Carson, Christopher "Kit": 103, 201
Carson, Francis M.: 582
Carson, Thomas: 201, 642, 645;
biographical sketch of, 97-108
Carter, — —, Sumner county, Kan.:
62
Carter, J. T.: 341
Carter, J. W.: 40
Cary, Nelson, Dodge City, Kan.: 458,
520, 522, 575, 598, 604, 644, 645
Cary's saloon, Dodge City, Kan.: 127,
522
Cass, John: 571
Cassville, Mo.: 175
Castello, Joseph: killed by Dave
Mather, 450-452
Castill, Bell: 597, 598
Castill, Mary: see Mary Malosh
Castleton, Kate, Opera Company: 441
Cattle trade: preparations for by
cowtowns, 5, 6
Cattle trails: map of, 113
Caylor, Andy: 501
Caypless, John: 73, 224
Cedar Vale, Kan.: 229, 574
Challes, — —, Caldwell, Kan.: 502
Challes, H. C., Caldwell, Kan.: 512
Chamberlain, W. W.: 288
Chambers, Alice: 13
Chambers, Henry: 589
Chambers, Lon: 456, 457
Chambers & Foster saloon, Dodge
City, Kan.: 323
Chambliss, Lutie: 345
Chapman, William, Abilene, Kan.:
642
Chapman, William, Dodge City, Kan.:
212
Chapman creek, Dickinson county,
Kan.: 578
Charlton, John W.: 594-596
Chastain, Albert: 62
Cheyenne and Arapahoe agency,
Okla.: 45, 68, 224
Cheyenne Indians: 32, 188, 189, 396,
397, 629; at Adobe Walls fight,
317-319; Dull Knife raid prisoners,
379-389, photo of, 239
Cheyenne, Wyo.: 83, 209
Chicago, Ill.: 202, 461, 516, 551

Chicago, Rock Island & Pacific
railroad: 583
Chicken creek, Tex.: 321
Chikaskia river: 230
Chillicothe, Mo.: 212
Chipman, Clark E., Dodge City, Kan.:
89, 137, 529, 544, 552, 562, 599,
644, 645; biographical sketch of,
108-111; photo of, 117
Chisholm trail: 4, 472, 495
Choate (or Schoat?), Bing (or H.
B.?): 126; killed by Dave St.
Clair, 612, 613
Chouteau, Dr. A. S., Dodge City,
Kan.: 426, 535
Christy, D. B.: 342
Cimarron, Kan.: 89, 128, 388, 444,
445, 459, 526, 556, 621-624
Cimarron river: 25, 189, 324, 337,
370
Circy, — —, Ellis county(?), Kan.:
190; see, also, — — Surcey
Cisk, Phillip: 316
City hotel, Caldwell, Kan.: 164
Clanton, Billy: 158
Clanton, Ike: 158
Clark, — —, Dodge City, Kan.: 644
Clark, B. F.: 486
Clark, Ben: 68
Clark, John: 317
Clark, T. E.: 52
Clark, Tom: 632, 643
Clark, Kan.: 590, 591
Clark, Treadwell &, ranch: see
Treadwell & Clark ranch
Clarke, John "Red": 324, 335, 337
Clarke, Sidney: 47
Claussen, — —, Newton, Kan.: 127
Clay Center, Kan.: 171
Cleveland, Ohio: 228
Clifton house, Caldwell, Kan.: 502
Clinton, J. J.: 645
Clow, John P.: 436, 437
Clum, John P.: 159
Clute, Brewer: 330, 340
Cockey, Dr. — —, Dodge City, Kan.:
426
"Cockeyed Frank": see Frank Loving
Cockrell, Dr. W. S.: 415
COD ranch, Ford county, Kan.: 551
Cody, Isaac: 111

Cox, — —, Wellington, Kan.: 241
Cox, C. J.: 43, 194, 642
Cox, George B., Dodge City, Kan.: 390, 534, 537
Cox, Harvey: 601
Cox & Boyd saloon, Dodge City, Kan.: 323, 371, 608
Cozad, — —, Sumner county, Kan.: 59
Craig, Joseph: 316
Craiman, — —, Abilene, Kan.: 98
Cramer, Joseph A.: 642
Crane, — —, Dodge City, Kan.: 466
Crane, J. E.: 341
Crawford, — —, Dodge City, Kan.: 466
Crawford, Ed, Ellsworth, Kan.: 220, 507, 643; biographical sketch of, 123-125; kills Cad Pierce, 123, 124; shot and killed (by Putman?), 124, 125
Crawford, Will: 494
Creede, Colo.: 445
Creswell, S. G.: 646
Crider, — —, Topeka, Kan.: 458
Crist, T. L., Caldwell, Kan.: 74, 518
Cronk, A. D.: 368, 437
Crook, John: 646
Crooked creek, Meade county, Kan.: 332, 337, 369, 370, 589
Cross, Robert: kills Cash Hollister, 227-231
Cross, Mrs. Robert: 229, 230
Crow (Cheyenne Indian): photo of, 239
Crow Indians: 383
Crowen, W. H.: 643
Crum, E. P.: 101
Crystal Palace saloon, Dodge City, Kan.: 608, 611
Culbertson, Doc: 55
Culbertson, Nichols &, Dodge City, Kan.: see Nichols & Culbertson
Culver, M. S.: 537
Cunningham, — —, Newton, Kan.: 106
Curly, Mrs. — —, Dodge City, Kan.: 14
Curry, F. H.: 127
Curtiss, Ida E.: 291
Custer, Lt. Col. George Armstrong: 122, 182, 184, 185

Custer, Capt. Thomas W.: 198, 199
Custom House saloon, Wichita, Kan.: 150

Dabertz, — —, Wichita, Kan.: 494
Dagner, — —, Wichita, Kan.: 43
Dallas, Tex.: 97, 423, 452, 453
Dalton, James: 366, 407
D'Amour, George: 483-485, 487, 488, 645, 646; biographical sketch of, 125, 126; killed, 126
Daniels, Ben, Dodge City, Kan.: 89, 436, 616, 617, 622, 644, 645; biographical sketch of, 126-129; kills Ed Julian, 128; photo of, 118
"Dark Alley Jim": 562
Davids, E. E.: 644
Davidson, — —, Abilene, Kan.: 578
Davidson, — —, Wichita, Kan.: 149
Davidson, James: 141
Davis, — —, Dodge City, Kan.: 346
Davis, Charles H.: kills George Wood(s), 512, 513
Davis, George: 229, 230
Davis, John G.: 54, 646
Davis, M. C.: 123
Davis, William: 91
Dawson, Dunham &, saloon, Dodge City, Kan.: see Dunham & Dawson saloon
Dead Scratch mine, Idaho: 162
Deadwood, S. D.: 209
Dean, Bradford J., Wichita, Kan.: 481, 482, 646
Dean, John: 166, 253
Dean, Mack: 456, 457
Deer creek, Okla.: 59, 499
Deerfield, Kan.: 569
Deger, Lawrence E., Dodge City, Kan.: 30, 50, 109, 110, 153, 210, 276, 292, 294, 296, 323-328, 413, 414, 466, 520, 521, 523, 526, 527, 529, 535, 536, 541, 544, 549, 550, 552, 554, 557, 558, 562, 564, 572, 595, 598, 644; biographical sketch of, 129-138; photo of, 118
Deger, McGinty &, saloon, Dodge City, Kan.: see McGinty & Deger saloon
De Grass, James: 455
Delaney, Arthur: see Mike McCluskie
Delano, Wichita, Kan.: 13, 255

Index

Index

Emporia, Kan.: 131, 271, 298, 299, 336, 340, 538, 539
Englewood, Kan.: 606
English, J. W.: killed, 622, 624
English, N. A., Wichita, Kan.: 45
Enola mine, Idaho: 162
Enright, J. E.: 161
Entertainment in cowtowns: 19-23
Esher, J. E.: 361
Eureka, Kan.: 582
Eureka Irrigating Canal: 623
Evans, — —, Quindaro, Kan.: 294
Evans, Frank: 63, 65, 499
Evans, Richard W., Dodge City, Kan.: 11, 17, 339, 537
Evarts, — —, Ann Arbor, Mich.: 294
Evarts, Sgt. Joseph: 403, 404
Everhart, Charles: 627, 628
Exchange saloon, Caldwell, Kan.: 504
Exline, George A.: 591, 592
Eyeston, George W.: 231

Fadel, George: 456, 457
Fairhurst, Lee (or Ed?): 622, 624
Falkner, Andrew: see Andrew Faulkner
Fall creek, Sumner county, Kan.: 73, 226, 232
"Fannie," Dodge City, Kan.: 14
Fardy, Annie: 582
Farmer, — —, Fort Worth, Tex.: 453
Farmer City, Kan.: 619-621
Faulkner (or Falkner?), Andrew, Dodge City, Kan.: 461, 462, 471, 644
Fay, Charles: killed by Thomas Calloway, 577
Fayetteville, Ark.: 181
Febriger (Febiger?), Lt. Lea(?): 415
Ferguson, — —, Dodge City, Kan.: 110
Ferguson, — —, Sheridan, Kan.: 192
Ferguson, — —, Wichita, Kan.: 587
Ferguson, Daniel: 161
Ferguson, J. J.: 646
Fessenden, George: 286
Field, George: 112
Field, Henry: 112
Field, Samuel: 112
Finaty, Harry: 158

Finlaw, Dr. William: 636
Fisher, B. H., Wichita, Kan.: 263
Fisher, Phillip D.: 182
Fitzgerald, — —, Wichita, Kan.: 494
Fitzpatrick, — —, Ellsworth, Kan.: lynched, 18, 19
Flatt, Fanny (Mrs. George): 166, 170
Flatt, George, Caldwell, Kan.: 62, 222, 241, 242, 247, 250, 251, 253, 254, 496, 497, 504, 647; biographical sketch of, 163-170; kills Jack Adams or George Wood, 163, 164; shot and killed, 167-170
Flatt & Horseman saloon, Caldwell, Kan.: 164
Fleming, Harry: 281
Fleming, Patrick H.: 450
Fletcher, A. E.: 56
Fletcher, W. W.: 643
Flick, — —, Kinsley, Kan.: 340
Flint, Mich.: 436
Folks, J. H.: 164, 167
Ford, Bob: 445
Forges, Harry: 570
Forrest, Billy: 350
Forrest, Gen. Nathan B.: 26
Forrest, Nola: 350
Forsyth, Maj. George A.: 629, 630
Fort Clark, Tex.: 153
Fort Dodge, Kan.: 172, 205-207, 294, 300, 301, 306, 314, 318-320, 362, 364, 369, 370, 569, 598
Fort Elliott, Tex.: 280, 281, 368, 403, 404
Fort Griffin, Tex.: 394
Fort Harker, Kan.: 43, 44, 182, 183, 185, 506, 507
Fort Hays, Kan.: 42, 46, 112, 187, 190, 193-195, 198, 199, 260
Fort Huachuca, Ariz.: 159
Fort Laramie, Wyo.: 121, 209
Fort Larned, Kan.: 182, 183
Fort Leavenworth, Kan.: 111, 319, 320, 364, 380, 382, 384, 404
Fort Lyon, Colo.: 189, 346
Fort Philip Kearny, Wyo.: 183
Fort Randall, S. D.: 272
Fort Reno, Okla.: 252
Fort Robinson, Neb.: 381, 386
Fort Scott, Kan.: 285, 306
Fort Sill, Okla.: 38, 57, 149, 150, 490
Fort Wallace, Kan.: 192, 193, 629

661

Fort Worth, Tex.: 154, 423, 452, 453, 458, 563, 564, 602
Fossett, Jack: 514
Fossett, Will D., Caldwell, Kan.: 500-502, 647
Foster, Rev. ——, Caldwell, Kan.: 96
Foster, ——, Nebraska City, Neb.: 576
Foster, George: 345
Foster, Chambers &, saloon, Dodge City, Kan.: see Chambers & Foster saloon
Fowler City, Kan.: 470
Fox, Dr. ——, Ellsworth, Kan.: 218
Fox, ——, Wichita, Kan.: 489
Foy, Eddie: 350
Franklin, Annie: shot, 261, 266
Franklin, Archie: 461, 463, 464
Franklin, Ben: 69
Franklyn Cattle Company: 603
Fredericks, Joshua: 316
Freeborn, Richard: 84, 643
Freeman, ——, Sumner county, Kan.: 499
French, —— "Frenchy," Okla.: 490
French, A. J.: 381, 383, 386
Friedley, George: 78
Friedly, Rev. ——, Medicine Lodge, Kan.: 77
Fringer, Herman J., saloon, Dodge City, Kan.: 323, 608
Frizzle Hair (or Frizzle Head?) (Cheyenne Indian): 386; photo of, 239
Frolic, ——, Dodge City, Kan.: 595
Frost, Daniel M., Dodge City, Kan.: 14, 88, 110, 133, 215, 293, 294, 296, 305, 323, 328, 344, 345, 376, 403-405, 535, 588, 596; photo of, 356
Fry, Ed: 190
Fry, Robert B.: 397, 399-401
Fryer, Dr. B. E.: 364
Fuller, John W.: 330, 339, 340, 342
Fulton, Henry: 647
Furley, Dr. C. C.: 260, 262
Fyan, Col. ——, Springfield, Mo.: 175

Gabel, Milton, Wichita, Kan.: 41, 140, 142
Gage, Frank: 590

Gainsford, James, Abilene, Kan.: 201, 641, 642; biographical sketch of, 171-173
Gainesville, Tex.: 425
Galena, Kan.: 588
Gallagher, Johnson "Cornhole Johnny": 523, 526
Gallagher, Samuel: 588
Galland, Dr. Samuel, Dodge City, Kan.: 88, 214, 275, 296, 433, 434, 529, 545, 547, 562
Gallaway, Martin: 317
Galveston, Tex.: 205, 207, 603
Gambling in cowtowns: 10-12
Gannon, Thomas, Hays, Kan.: 190, 642
Gantz ranch, Meade county(?), Kan.: 369, 370
Garden City, Kan.: 144, 217, 456, 570
Gardiner, Dan: 87
Gardner, ——, Ellsworth, Kan.: killed, 16
Gardner, Lt. ——, Fort Dodge, Kan.: 329, 330
Gardner, ——, Kinsley, Kan.: 329
Garis, Henry, Dodge City, Kan.: 608, 611
Garis & Tilghman saloon, Dodge City, Kan.: 323, 608
Garland, ——, Dodge City, Kan.: 438
Garland, Ed: 21
Garrett, William "Billy": killed, 99, 103, 105
Garrettson, Fannie: 350, 352, 361, 363; photo of, 239
Gauthie, James A., Abilene, Kan.: 98, 204, 642
Gaylor, May: 350
Geary, Thomas: 450
Geiger, George: 631
George, ——, Caldwell, Kan.: 627
George, Thomas: 245
Geppert, George: killed by Ben Wheeler, 77, 78, 80, 81
Germain children: see German children
German (or Germain?), Adelaide: 321
German (or Germain?), Julia: 321

Index

665

Index

Jefferson City, Mo.: 285, 286
Jenkins, E. J.: 494
Jennings, Frank: 367-369, 375, 377
Jennison, — —, Caldwell, Kan.: 92
Jerdon, — —, Dodge City, Kan.: 53
Jersey, — —, Caldwell, Kan.: 253
Jesse Jay mine, Idaho: 162
Jester, — —, Sedgwick county, Kan.: 446, 447
Jetmore, A. B.: 433, 605
Jetmore, Kan.: 467
Jewett, E. B., Wichita, Kan.: 263, 584
John, S. G.: 85
Johnes (or Jones?), Frank: 70
Johns, — —, Dodge City(?), Kan.: 40
Johnson, — —, Wichita, Kan.: 284
Johnson, Andrew, Dodge City, Kan.: 318, 319, 568
Johnson, Bob: see Doug Hill
Johnson, H. B.: 390
Johnson, Ike: 19
Johnson, James W., Caldwell, Kan.: 169, 232, 241-243, 253, 254, 495, 510, 647; biographical sketch of, 246-251; suspected of complicity in Flatt murder, 496, 497
Johnson, L. W. B.: 370
Johnson, Lute: 445
Johnson's ranch, Sumner county, Kan.: 223
Johnston, William A.: 137, 138
Johnston, William H.: 317
Jones, A. C., Caldwell, Kan.: 247
Jones, Bill "Red Bill": 255
Jones, Charles B., Wichita, Kan.: 375, 566, 642, 645
Jones, Daniel William "Red Bill," Caldwell, Kan.: 57, 166, 168-170, 232, 241, 243, 246, 250, 495, 498, 646, 647; biographical sketch of, 251-255; suspected of complicity in Flatt murder, 496, 497
Jones, Frank: see Frank Johnes
Jones, G. F.: 275
Jones, L. W.: 545, 645
Jones, Thomas S., Dodge City, Kan.: 88, 375-377, 399, 400
Jones & Plummer ranch, Okla.(?): 337
Joyce, M. E., Hays, Kan.: 192, 197

Julian, Ed. J.: 616; killed by Ben Daniels, 128
Junction City, Kan.: 60, 171, 181, 184, 342, 578, 610, 636
Junction saloon, Dodge City, Kan.: 468, 470
Jurd, E. B.: 291

Kalbflesch, George: 501
Kalida, Kan.: 491
Kane, Neil: 124
Kansas City, Mo.: 37, 105, 202, 205, 207, 270, 306, 350, 378, 395, 409, 417, 431, 446, 455, 457, 458, 514, 524, 527, 536-540, 544, 554, 634
Kansas Indian Agency, Okla.: 587
Kansas National Guard: 531
Kansas Pacific railroad: 2, 43, 384, 577, 635; longhorns being loaded at Abilene, sketch of, 477; see, also, Union Pacific, Eastern Division
Keach, Archie: 143
Kearnes, Henry: 102, 103, 105
Keefe (or Kief?), Thomas: 317, 318
Keeler, — —, Adobe Walls, Tex.: 318
Keenan, Fannie: see Dora Hand
Keenan, Thomas: 108
Keith, — —, Dodge City, Kan.: 216, 644
Keller, S.: 296
Kelley, James: 262
Kelley, James H. "Dog," Dodge City, Kan.: 17, 21, 31, 37, 130, 154, 276, 291, 292, 297, 311, 312, 323, 345, 362, 413-415, 520, 562, 598; photo of, 474
Kelley, Beatty &, saloon, Dodge City, Kan.: see Beatty & Kelley saloon
Kelley's saloon, Dodge City, Kan.: 413, 414
Kellogg, — —, Wichita, Kan.: 284
Kellogg, George A.: 376, 377
Kelly, J. J.: 643
Kelly, James D., Sr., Caldwell, Kan.: 60, 92-94, 165-167, 231, 244-246, 497, 500, 513, 514, 626
Kelly, John, Caldwell, Kan.: 242
Kelly (or Kile?), Pvt. John, Fort Hays, Kan.: killed by Wild Bill Hickok, 198, 199
Kelly, W. C.: 163, 646
Kelso, Capt. — —, Mo.: 179

667

Index

Lowe, Joseph "Rowdy Joe": 1, 537, 538, 582; biographical sketch of, 255-272; description of, 268; drawing of, 256; kills(?) Red Beard, 261-267; kills A. M. Sweet, 259; photo of, 240; reported killed, 271, 272

Lowe, Kate "Rowdy Kate" (Mrs. Joseph): 13, 255, 258, 259, 268-272

Lowe, Percival G., Leavenworth, Kan.: 383

Lowery, — —, Clark county, Kan.: 591

Lumis, — —, Caldwell, Kan.: 245

Luny (or Looney?), James: 456, 457

LyBrand, W. H., Dodge City, Kan.: 49, 396, 460

Lynchings: 18, 19, 55, 591, 592

Lyon, Charley: 394

Lyon, Jack: 394

Lyon house, Springfield, Mo.: 176, 177, 179

Mabry, Seth: 638

McAdams, Thomas I. (or J.?): 257, 258

McAdams, Lt. W. H.: 174

McArthur, J. E.: 339, 341, 609

McCabe, John: 316, 318

McCain, T. J.: 620

McCall, Jack: kills Wild Bill Hickok, 209

McCandles (or McKandlas or McKandles?), David Colbert: 180-182

McCanse, Robert, Kinsley, Kan.: 325, 330, 467

McCartney, J. W., Wichita, Kan.: 146, 581, 582, 645

McCarty, Harry T., Dodge City, Kan.: 32, 345, 350, 375, 642; biographical sketch of, 273-276; killed by Tom O'Hara(n) (or Roach?), 273-276

McCarty, Henry "Billy the Kid": 78, 82, 343, 504

McCarty, Jack: 542, 543, 549, 550, 572, 573

McCarty, Dr. Thomas L., Dodge City, Kan.: 155, 308, 365, 432, 438, 544, 545, 596

McChesney's "Place," Caldwell, Kan.: 627

McClain, M. F.: see M. F. McLain

McCleod, A.: 471

McCluskie, Mike (or Arthur Delaney?): killed by Hugh Anderson, 99-104

McCollister, J.: 345

McCollum, Charley: 566

McConnell, Andrew: 171; kills John Shea, 578; kills Thomas J. Smith, 578, 579

McCoy, Joseph G.: 13, 199, 200, 472

McCoy's Addition, Abilene, Kan.: 12, 201

McCulloch, — —, Caldwell, Kan.: 73, 646

McCulloch, Gen. Benjamin: 26

McDonald, James H., Abilene, Kan.: 98, 172, 173, 201, 206, 578, 642

McDonald, Joseph: 90; killed by Fred Singer, 567, 568

MacDonald, R. S.: 270, 271

McDonough, James: 270

McDuff, James: 334, 335

McFarland, George W.: 496

McGarry, Harvey: 128

McGee, — —, Okla.(?): 59

McGent, — — (scout): 321

McGinty & Deger saloon, Dodge City, Kan.: 129, 323, 608

McGlue, Luke: 21, 407

McGoodwin, James H.: 21

McGrath, Thomas: 41, 139-142

McGuire, Miss — — (Mrs. Robert Cross): 229-231

McIntire, — —, Arkansas City, Kan.: 222

McIntire, Thomas: 352, 572

Macintosh, Dr. J. V.: 194, 196

McIntosh, William Y.: 17, 18

McIntosh, Mrs. William Y.: 18

McIvor, — —, Wichita, Kan.: 494

McKandlas, David: see David Colbert McCandles

Mackenzie, Col. Ranald S.: 145

McKerlie, C.: 254

McKinley, J. W.: 316

McKinney, — —, Adobe Walls, Tex.: 318

McKinney, — —, Englewood, Kan.: 606

Index

Misner, — —, Wichita, Kan.: 493
Missouri Flats, Kan.: 496
Missouri, Kansas & Texas railroad: 271
Missouri river: 503
Mitchell, D. A., Wichita, Kan.: 495, 582
Mitchell, Joe: kills Adams and Boggs, 590-592; lynched, 591, 592
Mitchell, Lindsay: 291
Mitchell, Col. William G.: 194
Mix, Miles: 31, 278, 334-336, 422, 644
Mobeetie, Tex.: 460, 523, 617
"Moccasin Jim": 318
Modoc Indians: 509, 554
Mohler, J. G.: 390
Monimick (Cheyenne Indian): 319
Monroe, — —: 36
Montgomery, — —, Ellsworth, Kan.: 85
Montgomery, Peyton: 228
Moon, Jesse: 98
Moonlight, Thomas: 545, 549, 550, 555-562; photo of, 353
Moore, Maj. — —: 209
Moore, George: *see* George D'Amour
Moore, John A.: 224
Moore, Rankin: 317
Moore, "Texas Dick": 295
Moore, Thomas: 646
Moores, W.: 518
Moores Brothers saloon, Caldwell, Kan.: 74, 500
Moores & Weller, Caldwell, Kan.: 73
Moran, William N.: 452
Morco, John "Happy Jack": 84, 124, 219, 220, 635-639, 643; biographical sketch of, 506-510; killed by J. Charles Brown, 508-510
Morehead, James: 452
Morehouse, J. C.: 486, 645, 646
Moreland, — —, Dodge City, Kan.: 644
Moreland, James: 163
Moreland house, Caldwell, Kan.: 71
Morgan, Georgia: 453
Morgan, Joseph: 570-572
Morphy, W. N., Dodge City, Kan.: 17, 18, 133, 279, 293, 305, 349
Morris, Ben F.: 646
Morris, William: 59, 226, 230, 513

Morrison, — —, Las Vegas, N. M.: 449
Morrow, Charley: 372, 449
Morrow, Dave "Prairie Dog Dave," Dodge City, Kan.: 332, 333, 413, 415, 644
Morse, — —: 30, 330
Morton, Jennie: 350
Morton, William: 87, 644
Moser, M. R.: 147, 494
Mosier, Burr: 55-57
Mosley, Enos: 324
Moss, Charles: 177
Mt. Savage, Ky.: 592
Mueller, John: 21
Mueller, Otto: 365, 524, 525
Mueller's cattle camp: 343
Mulberry creek: 369
Mulberry ranch, Ford county(?), Kan.: 618
Mule creek: 330
Mullendore, S.: 545
Muller, — —, Dodge City, Kan.: 393
Mulligan, — —, Dodge City, Kan.: 589
Mulrey, Bill(?): 197; killed by Wild Bill Hickok, 191
Munger, D. S.: 494
Munsing, Bob: *see* Bob Munson
Munson (or Munsing?), Bob: 68, 498, 500-502, 504; reward poster for, 648
Murdock, Marshall Marcellus "Marsh": 282, 284
Murphy, C. L.: 107, 642
Murphy, John, Hays, Kan.: 197
Murphy, John, Oro City, Colo.: kills George D'Amour, 126
Murphy, W. W.: 316
Muse, R. W. P.: 105, 108n
Muskekon (Cheyenne Indian): photo of, 239
Myers, Fred: 316
Myers, L. K.: 646
Myers, Murray: 623
Myers, Leonard &, Dodge City, Kan.: *see* Leonard & Myers
Myton, — —, Dodge City, Kan.: 524
Myton, Charles: 572
Myton, H. P.: 215, 375, 377, 572, 644

Nash, Fannie: 127
Nauchville, Ellsworth, Kan.: 13, 125
Neal, J. A.: 91, 647
Nebraska City, Neb.: 576
Needham, Al: 56
Neely, —— —, Fort Worth, Tex.: 453
Neely, —— —, Raton Pass, Colo.: 451
Neil, Doc: 469
Neill, Hyman G. "Hoodoo Brown":
451, 452
Neosho, Mo.: 175
Nessley, —— —, Wichita, Kan.: 284
Nevill, Harry: 103, 642
New Garden, Mo.: 583
New Kiowa, Kan.: 472
New Orleans, La.: 202
New York, N. Y.: 189, 205, 206, 420,
447, 448, 490, 606
Newell, Olney: 426
Newman, —— —, Wichita, Kan.: 140
Newman, Benjamin: 646
News, Jake: 637, 638
News saloon, Ellsworth, Kan.: 637,
638
Newton, John, Dodge City, Kan.: 19,
296, 304
Newton, M.: 86
Newton, Kan.: 2, 3, 8, 51, 53, 127,
203, 224, 225, 258, 259, 265, 342,
481, 531, 603; description of, 1871,
98; peace officers at, 51, 52, 98-107,
645; photo of, 1872, 115
Newton General Massacre: 98-104
Newton, Langton &, saloon, Dodge
City, Kan.: see Langton & Newton
saloon
Newtonia, Mo.: 181
Nichols, George Ward: 178-182
Nichols & Culbertson, Dodge City,
Kan.: 368
Nicholson, Johny: 164
Nickerson, H. R.(?): 570
Niel, Dr. —— —, Dodge City, Kan.:
523
Nipp, Capt. —— —, Arkansas City,
Kan.: 222
Nix, E. D.: 313
Nixon, Thomas C., Dodge City, Kan.:
291, 426, 427, 430, 459, 524, 527,
528, 536, 552, 554, 566, 598, 602,
611, 612, 644; killed by Mysterious

Dave Mather, 459-467; photo of,
240
Nixon, Bond &, saloon, Dodge City,
Kan.: see Bond & Nixon saloon
Noble, E. A.: 330
Noble, P. S.: 383, 386
Noble, Dr. William A., Caldwell,
Kan.: 75, 94, 96, 167, 169, 226,
243-245, 500, 513, 514, 517, 627,
628
Noisy (or Nosey?) Walker (Cheyenne
Indian): 383, 384; photo of, 239
North Platte, Neb.: 122
Norton, —— —: 569, 570
Norton, —— —, Arkansas City, Kan.:
208
Norton, —— —, Fort Elliott, Tex.: 281
Norton, Charles(?): 11, 20, 21
Norton, John W. "Brocky Jack": 107,
123, 217-219, 506, 507, 636, 642,
643
Nugent, John: 268, 646
Nugget, Ben: 178
Nyce, John W.: 80

Oak creek, Ellsworth county, Kan.:
85
Oasis saloon, Dodge City, Kan.: 611
O'Brien, Charles: 317
O'Brien, Mike: 447
O'Brien, Tom: 412
Oburn, —— —, Dodge City, Kan.: 300
Occidental hotel, Wichita, Kan.: 492
Occidental saloon, Caldwell, Kan.:
163
Occidental saloon, Wichita, Kan.: 148
O'Connell, Lum: 246
O'Conner, Barney: 81
O'Connor, Henry: 186, 187
O'Connor, Washington: 382
Odom, B. M.: 244, 245
Offerle, Kan.: 324, 339
Ogallala, Neb.: 409
Ogg(e), William: 316, 318
O'Hara(n), Thomas "Limping Tom"
(alias Tom Roach): 365, 375; kills
H. T. McCarty, 273-276
O'Haran, John: 366, 367
Ohmert, Simon K.: 42, 264, 265, 269,
483, 484, 645, 646
OK corral, Tombstone, Ariz.: 158
Olathe, Kan.: 267

Index

O'Laughlin, Thomas: 643
Old Crow (Cheyenne Indian): 380, 383, 384, 386; photo of, 239
Old House saloon, Dodge City, Kan.: 569
Old Man (Cheyenne Indian): 386; photo of, 239
Olds, George, Adobe Walls, Tex.: killed, 315, 318
Olive, I. P.: 562; shot, 218
Oliver, —— —, Ford county, Kan.: 556
Omaha, Neb.: 206
O'Neill, Jim: 573
Opera house, Caldwell, Kan.: 59, 500-502, 626
Opera house, Dodge City, Kan.: 459, 461-463, 465
Oriental saloon, Tombstone, Ariz.: 159
Oro City, Colo.: 126
Orr, John: kills James Coleman, 177
Orton, —— —, South Dakota: 272
Osage Mission, Kan.: 268
Osborn, Thomas Andrew: 28-30, 582, 641
Osborne, V. B., Ellsworth, Kan.: 219, 506
Ott, E. P.: 588
Ovenshine, Capt. Samuel: 187, 188
Overland Stage Company: 181
Owens, Dr. H., Wichita, Kan.: 262
Owens, Prince: 646
Owens, Yank: 289, 645
Owens, Sanford and, saloon, Eagle, Idaho: see Sanford and Owens saloon

Pagne, Henry: see Andy Payne
Pahaska Teepee, Wyo.: 122
Palmer, Charles: 341
Palmer, George: killed by Taylor DuBoise, 633, 634
Palmer, Thomas: 341
Palmer, William Jackson: 391
Palo Duro creek, Tex.: 320
Pardee, Lt. Julius H.: 382, 383
Paris, Tex.: 79, 83
Parish, E. O.: 349
Parker, George: 406
Parks, —— —: 112

Parks, Daniel F., Wichita, Kan.: 125, 139, 145, 152, 482, 485, 488, 491, 585, 586, 645, 646
Parks, Dr. S. H.: 593
Parks, Thomas E., Wichita, Kan.: 125, 645, 646
Parlor, The, Dodge City, Kan.: 614
Parral, Mexico: 343
Parson, —— —, Bent county, Colo.: 456
Parsons, E. W.: 189
Partridge, Alfred D.: 603
Patrick, William K.: 174
Patten, —— —, Wichita, Kan.: 269
Pawnee City, Neb.: 576
Pawnee creek, Kan.: 298
Payne, Andy (or Henry Pagne?): 346
Payne, E. Wiley, Medicine Lodge, Kan.: killed by Henry N. Brown(?), 77, 78, 81
Payne, W.: 162
Payne, Walter: 602
Peace, Kan.: 291
Peacock, A. J., Dodge City, Kan.: 220, 301, 312, 313, 377, 405, 414, 419, 443; affair with Masterson brothers, 410-413
Peacock, Emma L. (Mrs. A. J.), Dodge City, Kan.: 220, 567
Peacock & Masterson saloon, Dodge City, Kan.: 412
Peacock's saloon, Dodge City, Kan.: 301, 323, 567, 608
Pease, George: 368
Peck, George R.: 548, 549
Peck, Mary (Mrs. William Smith): 581
Pecos City, N. M.: 27
Penrose, Capt. William H.: 189
Percy, —— —, Wichita, Kan.: 586
Peters, Samuel Ritter: 110, 276, 341, 374-377, 609
Peterson, —— —: 456
Petillon, W. F., Dodge City, Kan.: 211, 520, 528, 530, 535, 536, 543-545, 551, 553, 557, 562-564, 598; photo of, 355
Pettibone, W. H.: 329, 330, 339, 341
Pettit, J.: 642
Petty, H. G.: 49, 50
Phelps, —— —, Dodge City, Kan.: 437
Phelps, I. W.: 19

675

St. John, William: 94
St. Joseph, Mo.: 576
St. Louis, Mo.: 36, 100, 105, 202,
361, 429, 452, 494
St. Louis & San Francisco railroad:
451
St. Paul, Kan.: 268
Salem, Mass.: 465
Salina, Kan.: 2, 182, 390, 507-509,
585
Salisbury, — —, Trinidad, Colo.: 371,
374
Saloons: description of, 9, 10
Salt creek, Leavenworth county, Kan.:
111
Samples, William: 324
Samuels, — —, Dodge City, Kan.: 22
San Antonio, Tex.: 272, 452, 453
Sanborn, Gen. John B.: 174, 175
Sand creek, Colo.: 158, 365
Sanders, — —, Dodge City, Kan.: 617
Sanders, Charley: 284; killed by
Ramsey, 585, 586
Sanders & Couch, Okla.: 346
Sanderson, Col. John P.(?): 174
Sanderson & White, Ellsworth, Kan.:
634
Sands, — —, Fort Worth, Tex.: 453
Sanford and Owens saloon, Eagle,
Ida.: 161
Santa Fe, N. M.: 406
Saratoga saloon, Dodge City, Kan.:
10, 20
Sargent, Kan.: 413
Satanta (Kiowa Indian): 380
Saunders, — —, Fort Sill, Okla.: 493
Saunders, — —, Sedgwick county,
Kan.: 587
Saunders, Jim: 317
Saw Log creek, Ford county, Kan.:
28, 40, 324, 343
Sawyer, — —, Dodge City, Kan.:
425
Schaddler, Ike: see Ike Shadler
Schattner, A., Wichita, Kan.: 485
Schmoker, — —, Dodge City, Kan.:
428
Schnover, George: 518
Schoat, K. B.: see Bing Choate
Scholten, Charles: 179
Schultree, C.: 642
Schultz, C. H.: 21

Schurz, Carl: 397
Schuttleman, Ellsworth: 40
Scott, Harry: 611, 645
Scott, John "Scotty": 395
Scragtown, Ellsworth, Kan.: 13
Scully, James: 366
Searcy, B.: 643
Sebastian, M. A.: 375-377
Sedalia, Mo.: 286
Sedgwick City, Kan.: 225
Seffers, Pvt. — —: 122
Seger, — —, Okla.: 68
Segerman, Louis: 168
Seiber, J. Charles: 258, 632, 635, 643,
645
Selby, J. K.: 620
Sell, — —, Dodge City, Kan.: 18
Semans, William "Apache Bill": 643
76 ranch, Clark county, Kan.: 592
Sevier, W. W.: 489, 583
Sexton, — —, Wichita, Kan.: 496
Shadler (or Schaddler?), Ike: killed
in Adobe Walls fight, 315, 318, 320
Shaffer, J. D.: 599
Shane, Charles: 642
Sharp, Dave: 513, 514
Sharp, F.: 645
Sharpe, James: 647
Sharp's creek, Okla.: 317
Shaw, Bob (or Frank?): shoots Ed
Masterson, 294-296
Shea, John: killed by Andrew Mc-
Connell, 578
Shea, Meagher &, saloon, Caldwell,
Kan.: see Meagher & Shea saloon
Shepherd, Frank: 643
Sheppard, Oscar: 316, 318
Sheridan, — —, Dodge City, Kan.:
433, 434
Sheridan, John: 455
Sheridan, Kan.: 19, 189, 190, 192-
195, 629
Sherlock, Kan.: 389
Sherman, James D.: see Jim Talbot
Sherman, Gen. William Tecumseh:
186, 420
Shiner brothers: 273
Shinn, Lloyd, Dodge City, Kan.: 327,
339, 409
Shinn, W. C., Dodge City, Kan.:
88, 89, 312, 327, 409
Shipley, — —, Springfield, Mo.: 180

Index

Wetherill, Lt. Alexander M.(?): 415
Wheeler, Alice M. (Mrs. Ben): 83
Wheeler, Ben F.: 69, 71-75, 95, 223, 515, 647; attempts to rob Medicine Lodge bank, 76-84; biographical sketch of, 625-629; kills Chet Van Meter, 225-227; photo of, 480
Whipple, James E.: 242
Whisner, Clark: 488
White, J. F.: 341
White, Sanderson &, Ellsworth, Kan.: see Sanderson & White
White Antelope (Cheyenne Indian): photo of, 239
White Elephant saloon, Eagle, Idaho: 162
White river: 175
Whiteford, John: 193
Whitelaw, J. T.: 457, 460, 534, 537, 564
Whitfield, Frank P. "Texas Frank": 450
Whiting, Charles C.: 187, 641
Whitman, Nelson: 20, 21
Whitney, Chauncey Belden: 3, 84, 85, 122-124, 145, 219, 220, 507, 643; biographical sketch of, 629-640; killed by Billy Thompson, 635-639; photo of, 478; reward poster for Billy Thompson, 479; sketch of his shooting, 473
Whitson, Nellie: 501
Wichita, Kan.: 2-4, 13, 15, 43-45, 51-53, 55, 158, 166, 224, 225, 227, 228, 232, 241, 255-257, 259-272, 278, 290, 296, 304, 305, 309, 314, 379, 393, 444, 472, 509, 513, 577, 580, 615, 616, 634; peace officers at, 37-39, 40-42, 125, 126, 139-142, 145-153, 282-289, 481-495, 581-588, 645, 646; photo of, 1873, 116; police committee report, 1876, reproduction of, 236; preparations for cattle trade, 5, 6
Wichita & Southwestern railroad: 481, 484
Wichita county, Kan.: county-seat fight, 441-444, 619
Wichita mountains, Okla.: 69
Wickham, Idaho: 247
Wiggins, Mrs. ――, Dodge City, Kan.: 599

Wilcox, Gen. ――, Ariz.: 159
Wilcox, Frank: 212
"Wild Bill": see James Butler Hickok
Wild Hog (Cheyenne Indian): 383-386; photo of, 239
Wilder, D. W.: 8
Wiley, T. N., Abilene, Kan.: 642
Wilkerson, Jim: 102, 103
Wilkes, George: 316
Wilkin, Frank: 582
Wilkinson, Jay: 223
Willett, C. W.(?), Dodge City, Kan.: 370
Willey, John E.(?): 334, 339
Williams, D. X.: 645, 646
Williams, Jack: 317
Williams, Jerry: 56
Williams, Mike: 642; killed by Wild Bill Hickok, 202, 203
Williams, William: 518
Williamson, John: 603
Willingham, Capt. ――, Oldham county, Tex.: 82
Willsie, Charles: 54, 55
Wilson, E. V.: 490
Wilson, G. W.: 341
Wilson, George W.: 31
Wilson, Henry: 179
Wilson, James: 644
Wilson, John, Caldwell, Kan.: 57, 498, 500-502, 647; kills Adams or Wood, 163, 164
Wilson, John, Wichita, Kan.: 646
Wilson, O. D: 458, 570, 644
Wilson, Richard: 501
Wilson, V. P.: 8, 199
Wimsett, J. Samuel: 643
Windsor hotel, Topeka, Kan.: 471, 574
Windthorst, Kan.: 399
Winfel, Casper G.: 643
Winfield, Kan.: 254
Winner, Arthur: 283, 284, 287, 489, 583, 584
Wirtz (or Wert?), Henry: 317, 318
Wiseman, Israel: 606
Witzelben, Albert: 80, 516, 517
Witzelben & Key, Caldwell, Kan.: 516
Wolf, ――, Dodge City, Kan.: 21
Wolf, ――, Ford county, Kan.: 343
Wolf creek, Okla.: 321, 337, 341

Index

685